International and Interarea Comparisons of Income, Output, and Prices

Studies in Income and Wealth
Volume 61

National Bureau of Economic Research
Conference on Research in Income and Wealth

International and Interarea Comparisons of Income, Output, and Prices

Edited by Alan Heston and Robert E. Lipsey

The University of Chicago Press

Chicago and London

ALAN HESTON is professor of economics and South Asia studies at the University of Pennsylvania. ROBERT E. LIPSEY is professor emeritus of economics at Queens College and the Graduate Center, City University of New York, and a research associate of the National Bureau of Economic Research.

The University of Chicago Press, Chicago 60637
The University of Chicago Press, Ltd., London
© 1999 by the National Bureau of Economic Research
All rights reserved. Published 1999
08 07 06 05 04 03 02 01 00 99   1 2 3 4 5
ISBN: 0-226-33110-5 (cloth)

Library of Congress Cataloging-in-Publication Data

International and interarea comparisons of income, output, and prices /
    edited by Alan Heston and Robert E. Lipsey.
        p.   cm. — (Studies in income and wealth ; v. 61)
Rev. papers from the CRIW Conference on International and Interarea
Comparisons of Prices, Income, and Output held in Arlington, Va., Mar.
15–16, 1996.
    Includes bibliographical references and index.
    ISBN 0-226-33110-5 (cloth : alk. paper)
    1. National income Congresses.   2. Prices Congresses.   I. Heston,
Alan W.   II. Lipsey, Robert E.   III. Conference on Research in
Income and Wealth.   IV. CRIW Conference on International and
Interarea Comparisons of Prices, Income, and Output (1996 : Arlington,
Va.)   V. Series
    HC106.3.C714   v. 61
    [HC79.I5]
    330 s—dc21
    [339.3]   99-29819
                                                                   CIP

♾ The paper used in this publication meets the minimum requirements of
the American National Standard for Information Sciences—Permanence
of Paper for Printed Library Materials, ANSI Z39.48-1992.

Contents

Prefatory Note

This volume contains revised versions of most of the papers and discussion presented at the Conference on Research in Income and Wealth entitled "International and Interarea Comparisons of Prices, Income, and Output," held in Arlington, Virginia, on 15–16 March 1996.

Funds for the Conference on Research in Income and Wealth are supplied by the Bureau of Labor Statistics, the Bureau of Economic Analysis, Statistics Canada, the Federal Reserve Board, and the Bureau of the Census; we are indebted to them for their support. This conference was supported by the National Science Foundation under grant SBR-9514990 from the Programs in Economics and Methodology, Measurement, and Statistics; additional funds for international participation were provided by the World Bank.

We also thank Alan Heston and Robert E. Lipsey, who served as conference organizers and editors of the volume, and the planning committee, comprising Peter Hill, Katrina Reut, Michael Ward, and Alwyn Young.

Executive Committee, July 1998

Ernst R. Berndt

Carol S. Carson

Carol A. Corrado

Edwin R. Dean

Robert C. Feenstra

John Greenlees

Zvi Griliches

John C. Haltiwanger

Charles R. Hulten, chair

Lawrence F. Katz

J. Steven Landefeld

Robert H. McGuckin III

Brent R. Moulton

Matthew Shapiro

Robert Summers

Volume Editors' Acknowledgments

The editors acknowledge support for the conference from the National Science Foundation, the World Bank, and the National Bureau of Economic Research. Two anonymous reviewers, for the NBER and the University of Chicago Press, made very helpful comments and suggestions on the volume. We also greatly appreciate the editorial assistance of Helena Fitz-Patrick of the NBER's Publications Department in preparing the volume for publication.

Introduction

Alan Heston and Robert E. Lipsey

Comparisons across countries of prices and of income and output measured in real terms, and comparisons within countries across regions and cities, are an old ambition of economists. The appetite for cross-country comparisons has been attested to by the hundreds of citations of the estimates of real income and prices for many countries constructed by Alan Heston and Robert Summers, now known as the Penn World Tables. Almost the entire recent literature on the determinants of economic growth that covers large numbers of countries is dependent on these data. The Penn World Tables are derived from the UN International Comparison Program (ICP), but few of those who use them know their origin or ever examine the methods underlying the original expenditure and price measures. In organizing this conference, we intended to make the ICP more widely known in the profession; to discuss its problems and new developments, including its extension to the transition economies; to discuss the analogous issues in interarea comparisons; and to illustrate a few of the uses of international and interarea comparisons.

The typical method of making comparisons across countries in real terms before the ICP and the measures derived from it was to translate values from their original currencies into a common currency by the use of exchange rates. That method assumed identical prices everywhere, as do comparisons across areas within countries using nominal values. The absurdity of that assumption for international comparisons, and of the conclusions that result from accepting it, was pointed out by Irving Kravis (1984). His example was that "Japan's per capita GNP was 47 per cent higher than that of the United Kingdom in 1978 and 5 per cent lower than the U.K. level in 1980" when measured by

Alan Heston is professor of economics and South Asia studies at the University of Pennsylvania. Robert E. Lipsey is professor emeritus of economics at Queens College and the Graduate Center, City University of New York, and a research associate of the National Bureau of Economic Research.

1

exchange rates, despite the fact that "the Japanese constant price series for GNP shows an increase of about 8 per cent on a per capita basis while the U.K. constant price series shows an approximate decrease of one per cent" (p. 2). The nonsense result of the exchange rate–based comparison stems from a large devaluation of the yen relative to the pound in these two years.

The ICP has now been running for over thirty years, and the purchasing power parities and real income, consumption, and investment measures derived from it are increasingly used in economic research in place of the distorted values derived from translating by exchange rates. The ICP-based numbers are now a regular feature of the national accounts publications of the European Union and the OECD. Over time, the coverage of the program has increased from the ten countries of the 1970 report to around sixty in 1980 and 1985 and to almost one hundred in 1993. In the last few years, the scope of the program has grown enormously, as it has been joined by China and the formerly planned economies of Central and Eastern Europe, including some of the states of the former Soviet Union. Because prices had been set so arbitrarily in these countries and played such a different role from that in the market economies, the inclusion of these countries presented a variety of new measurement problems.

The Conference on Research in Income and Wealth (CRIW) first took up the problems of international comparisons in one session of a 1945 meeting, the proceedings of which were published in CRIW (1947). Copeland, Jacobson, and Clyman (1947) discussed a report prepared for the Combined Production and Resources Board on the effect of World War II on the civilian economies of the United States, the United Kingdom, and Canada. Among the topics were problems still troublesome today, such as the choice between quantity and price measures, quality differences among products from the three countries, the treatment of differences in consumption baskets, and the increased severity of these problems if the comparisons were to be extended to countries more divergent in economic development than these three. A companion paper, Dominguez (1947), calculated rough purchasing power parities for fourteen countries from data for twelve food items, declaring that "the results will most likely constitute a definite improvement upon foreign exchange rates, the usual base" (p. 239). The average price level for fourteen Latin American countries, relative to the United States as 100, comes to 72. The paper also quotes (p. 236) an earlier estimate by Clark (1940, 52) of a price level of 66 in "the less economically developed part of the world for which records are lacking." Curiously, this session of the conference was the only one for which no comments by other participants were recorded.

The first foundations for the current UN program were laid in the early 1950s, in the OEEC study for five European countries in 1952 by Gilbert and Kravis (1954), which for the first time collected price data for not only personal consumption but also the other elements of national expenditure, such as government consumption and capital formation. That and the subsequent report by Milton Gilbert and Associates (1958) were followed by the beginning of the broader UN project in 1968, which extended the range of the comparisons to some developing countries. The project's progress was documented in a series of reports (Kravis et al. 1975; Kravis, Heston, and Summers 1978, 1982) that covered the growth of the program from ten countries in 1970 to thirty-four in 1975. These reports also contained extensive discussions of methods of price collection, the treatment of particularly difficult measurement problems, and some analyses of economic issues of which the new data permitted much more empirical examination than had been possible before.

The CRIW returned to the issue of international comparisons in volume 20 of the Studies in Income and Wealth series (CRIW 1957), which contained papers on the subject by Brady and Hurwitz (1957) and Kravis (1957). The latter set forth the boundaries of economic activity that were the basis for the OEEC studies and were later carried over to the ICP despite the negative, and mostly impractical, comments by the discussants, Everett E. Hagen (1957) and Jacob Viner (1957).

When the CRIW next returned to this topic at its 1970 meeting (for the proceedings, see Daly [1972a]), the ICP was well under way, and the issue of international comparisons was of particular interest in connection with the desire to judge the relative positions of the United States and the Soviet Union. There were two general papers (Afriat 1972; and Daly 1972b), two papers on specific areas (Bergson 1972; and Grunwald and Salazar-Carrillo 1972), and one on capital goods price comparisons (de Vries 1972).

Since 1970, the CRIW has not held a meeting extensively devoted to interspatial comparisons of prices, incomes, and output, and only a few subsequent conference papers dealt with the issue at all. Jorgenson and Kuroda (1990) in volume 53 did include purchasing power parity calculations and the corresponding adjusted quantity measures for twenty-nine industries in the United States and Japan, based on data in Kravis, Heston, and Summers (1978) adjusted to producer price levels by removing indirect taxes and trade and transportation margins. And a paper by Kravis and Lipsey (1991) in volume 55 reviewed the status of the ICP at that time.

In the meantime, the availability of data, the number of countries covered, and the use of the data by economists have increased enormously, but there have been few opportunities for economists outside the club of practitioners to review the procedures, to learn of innovations, and to hear about the problems involved in extending the studies to the "formerly planned" economies. One purpose of this conference was to go some way to fill these needs and also to acquaint economists with some uses of these data beyond the measurements themselves.

Comparisons of incomes and prices across areas within countries are an even more neglected field than comparisons across countries. With no exchange rates to take into account, it is quite customary for statisticians and policy makers to ignore interarea differences in prices and assume identical price levels across regions, states, and cities of a country, despite wide popular knowledge of differences in living costs. Some consequences of this official neglect for the measurement of poverty and for poverty programs were pointed out in Citro and Michael (1995), but there are many other areas where such information would be valuable. Even though the Bureau of Labor Statistics has had a program of research in this area for a number of years, the results are not widely known; we therefore included several papers in this area.

In addition to the ICP, which measures final expenditures in real terms, using prices for final products, there has been considerable recent research on measurement from the product side, mainly by the International Comparisons of Output and Productivity (ICOP) Program at the University of Groningen Growth and Development Centre. These measures have the virtue of producing comparisons for industries and for intermediate products. The methods have not been as fully presented as those for the final product measurements, and we hoped, with the papers here, to make the methods and the results more accessible.

Some of the recent extensions of the ICP to the transition economies are still in a very tentative state, as is the treatment of certain categories of consumption. Where we thought that full papers could not be prepared, we arranged for brief, informal presentations on some of these since the methods and problems are even less widely known than those of the ICP itself. Four of these presentations are included here, but some had to be omitted because the governments of the countries involved had not accepted the results.

Since these comparison programs and the literature discussing them have developed a specialized language describing the methods used and the economic issues underlying them, we have, as part of the effort to make the literature and the papers here more widely accessible, included a glossary of technical terms and index number formulas at the end of the book. We have also listed in the appendix to this introduction, some sources for the data used in the following papers to encourage further exploration of these topics.

Part I of this volume comprises a pair of papers on the theoretical bases of multilateral interspatial comparisons, asking, essentially, What should we measure, and how should we measure it? The paper by W. Erwin Diewert introduces the conference. It suggests a system of desirable axioms and properties for multilateral comparisons and selects four classes of measurement methods, not including the Geary-Khamis method favored by the ICP, as the best. Diewert's discussant, Irwin Collier, points out some of the assumptions underlying Diewert's tests and takes a more favorable view of Geary-Khamis. The paper by Robert J. Hill proposes a new way to order countries for international comparisons by chaining countries using a spanning tree approach. The spanning tree approach begins with the Paasche-Laspeyres spread in the binary comparison between each pair of countries and builds on the binary chain that minimizes the sum of the spreads.

Part II of the volume is concerned with interarea wage and price comparisons. Two papers, on experimental programs at the Bureau of Labor Statistics (BLS), make both theoretical and empirical contributions. The first of these, by Mary F. Kokoski, Brent R. Moulton, and Kimberly D. Zieschang, illustrates a two-stage process in which the BLS has used its CPI database to estimate entry-level price levels by region and then combined these indexes using weights to estimate city indexes for several commodity groupings. There is a parallel in this approach to what has been done in benchmark ICP comparisons where price parities are first generated at a heading or category level by the use of the country-product-dummy (CPD) method. The authors note that, instead of individual prices, the coefficients in these equations can be made available, a feature that avoids the violation of the confidentiality rules that statistical offices often face. These entry-level parities are then aggregated using a modification of bilateral Törnqvist indexes to produce a transitive multilateral index in a two-step aggregation process, very much like the EKS procedure. The authors suggest that one of the innovative features of their procedure would be applicable to the ICP's international comparisons—that is, the replacement of uniform narrow commodity definitions, prescribed for all respondents, by broader commodity categories, with respondents collecting information on product characteristics that can be used to achieve comparability across areas through hedonic quality adjustments. The discussant, Paul Pieper, expresses some skepticism as to whether this procedure reduces the burden on respondents or only substitutes one type of difficult requirement for another. The paper uses these methods to calculate multilateral place-to-place price indexes for the consumption of food at home for forty-four geographic areas of the United States. The authors find that the price level for the most expensive area, Honolulu, was more than 60 percent above that for the cheapest, Miami. Even within the contiguous states, there was a 25 percent difference between the most and the least expensive areas.

The second of the papers from the BLS, that by W. Brooks Pierce, John W. Ruser, and Kimberly D. Zieschang, provides an application of the same methodology to wage costs and labor compensation across regions of the United States. In a methodological contribution, they formulate the Törnqvist index in a way that incorporates the parameters of a CPD exercise into the index. Place-to-place labor input cost index numbers are constructed for thirty-nine geographic areas at the level of the eighteen thousand or so jobs priced in the BLS employment cost index. The adjustments for the composition of the labor force tend to reduce the measured geographic dispersion in wages. The determinants of wage differences across geographic areas, after industry and occupation are controlled for, are firm size, unionization, and the education and experience of workers. Joel Popkin, the discussant, points out the difficulty of distinguishing, in such measurements, between characteristics of the job and characteristics of the worker.

The other paper on interarea differences, that by Bettina H. Aten, found that, in contrast to the U.S. wage results, adjusting Brazilian income data for regional price differences widened the estimated real income differentials between the poorer northern regions and the wealthier southern ones.

Part III of the volume consists of informal reports on methods and on the geographic expansion of the ICP. In keeping with the aim of displaying some of the measurement issues in "comparison-resistant" sectors and some of the results of the expansion of the ICP to new areas and its accompanying problems, several informal reports were invited, although the work is still in an early stage. These reports included one paper on a comparison-resistant sector by Giuliano Amerini and papers on the expansion of the ICP by Alfred Franz, Seppo Varjonen, and Daniela Elena Ştefănescu and Marilena Chişinevschi.

Also included in this section is a brief statement by Yuri Dikhanov, originally a comment on a paper by Angus Maddison (presented at the conference but not published in this volume; see Maddison 1998). Dikhanov describes the comparative-level calculations carried out by Soviet sources and, as an additional alternative, the linking of the level comparisons within Comecon with the ICP results for Soviet bloc participants in the ICP, such as Hungary. He also reminds the reader of some of the index number issues in these comparisons originally raised by Alexander Gerschenkron.

Three other informal informational reports were presented at the conference but not included in the volume. A paper in progress, "Methodology for Developing Monthly PPPs for the Countries of the CIS," was presented by Anne Harrison in collaboration with Seppo Varjonen. That work has subsequently developed into a full purchasing power comparison for consumption in 1993, 1994, and 1995 for ten of the former Commonwealth of Independent States (CIS) countries, using both Russia and Turkey as the numeraire countries for the comparison. The paper is of particular interest because the inflation rates, national accounts, and even exchange rates for most of these countries have not been readily available. Unfortunately, this paper has not been cleared with all the governments of these countries and therefore could not be included in this volume.

There were also two informal reports involving China: "Comparison of Shanghai with Japan," by Sultan Ahmad, and "China's Regional Disparities," by Albert Keidel III. The preliminary results for 1993 presented in the former paper have not been thought to be robust, but a second part of these 1993 comparisons, between Guangdong and Hong Kong, have now been completed and will be integrated into comparisons by the Economic and Social Commission for Asia and the Pacific (ESCAP). The binary comparisons suggest that the price level in Guangdong is about 48 percent of that in Hong Kong. Of course, one would also wish to know how Guangdong Province compares with the rest of China, and to this end the State Statistical Bureau is currently making comparisons between the coastal and the interior provinces.

Part IV consists of reports from the ICOP Program that extend international comparisons to the product or industry side. These reports also represent extensions of the scope of that project, in terms of both industry and geographic coverage. The paper by Nanno Mulder measures productivity differences in these difficult sectors, adjusting, where possible, for quality differences. Productivity in these sectors in Mexico and Brazil ranges from 15 to over 35 percent of that in the United States, while in France the range is from a third of U.S. levels in communications in the early years to over 90 percent in some years in the transport sector.

The second paper from the ICOP project, by Bart van Ark, Erik Monnikhof, and Marcel Timmer, finds labor productivity in manufacturing in Central and Eastern Europe to have been between 18 and 29 percent of the U.S. level from 1970 through 1987, with a declining relative trend in most cases. Only in East Germany was there a major change after that: more than a doubling relative to the United States between 1987 and 1994 and a more than 50 percent rise relative to West Germany by 1993. Aside from the productivity estimates collected here, the authors examine the nature of price and quantity distortions in the "centrally planned economies" by analyzing the relation between Paasche and Laspeyres price and quantity indexes.

The last part, part V, is on applications of international comparison data, illustrating some uses for price and quantity comparisons. The first paper, by Patricia M. Danzon and Allison Percy, examines the effects of drug price regulation on productivity and productivity growth in five countries. The authors find that estimates of both productivity and productivity growth are sensitive to the choice of price measures used for deflation.

The paper by Edward N. Wolff found that manufacturing industry specializations of fourteen OECD countries remained quite constant from 1970 through 1993 and that changes in relative labor productivity were excellent predictors of changes in country market shares. Rates of capital formation were important for low-tech industries, less so for medium-tech ones, and not at all for high-tech ones, and labor costs were a significant influence on market shares only in low-tech industries and only in the 1970s.

Using both aggregate and disaggregated price-level data from the ICP, Robert E. Lipsey and Birgitta Swedenborg found that higher wage dispersion is associated with lower price levels. The relation exists for both goods and service items but is more frequent and stronger for services. As Andrew Levin points out in his discussion, the equations here imply that the Scandinavian countries, for example, would have substantially lower price levels if their wage structures and agricultural policies were like those of the United States and Canada.

In another application, Robert Summers and Alan Heston examine the material well-being of the world during the period 1960–92. They conclude that differences in average incomes across countries are greater than differences in incomes within countries for nearly all the countries of the world. Alternative measures of well-being are discussed, as are some considerations relating to nonmaterial well-being.

Appendix
Sources of Comparative Data

Benchmark data from the ICP for 1970, 1975, 1980, and 1985 are available on a website at the University of Pennsylvania, pwt.econ.upenn.edu.

The Summers and Heston annual estimates of real GDP, price levels, and other aspects of the ICP, extrapolated to cover countries not participating and periods of nonparticipation for participating countries, are available from the NBER at its website, www.nber.org, under ONLINE DATA, PENN WORLD TABLES.

OECD calculations of purchasing power parities of member countries for fifty expenditure categories, both EKS and GK results, for 1993 are available in three publications listed under PURCHASING POWER PARITIES on the OECD home page, www.oecd.org. The indexes themselves are not on the website.

The results of ICP rounds after 1975 are reported in three publications: UN Statistical Office (1987), UN Statistical Division (1994), and World Bank (1993).

The ICOP Program has been described most recently in van Ark (1996).

References

Afriat, Sidney F. 1972. The theory of international comparisons of real income and prices. In Daly (1972a).

Bergson, Abram. 1972. The comparative national income of the USSR and the United States. In Daly (1972a).

Brady, Dorothy S., and Abner Hurwitz. 1957. Measuring comparative purchasing power. In CRIW (1957).

Citro, Constance, and Robert T. Michael, eds. 1995. *Measuring poverty: A new approach.* Washington, D.C.: National Academy Press.

Clark, Colin. 1940. *The conditions of economic progress.* London: Macmillan.

Conference on Research in Income and Wealth (CRIW). 1947. *Studies in income and wealth, volume ten.* New York: National Bureau of Economic Research.

———. 1957. *Problems in the international comparison of economic accounts.* Studies in Income and Wealth, vol. 20. Princeton, N.J.: Princeton University Press.

Copeland, Morris A., Jerome Jacobson, and Bernard Clyman. 1947. Problems of international comparisons of income and wealth. In CRIW (1947).

Daly, Don J., ed. 1972a. *International comparisons of prices and output.* Studies in Income and Wealth, vol. 37. New York: National Bureau of Economic Research.

———. 1972b. Uses of international price and output data. In Daly (1972a).

de Vries, Barend A. 1972. International price comparisons of selected capital goods industries. In Daly (1972a).

Dominguez, Loreto M. 1947. National income estimates of Latin American countries. In CRIW (1947).

Gilbert, Milton, and Irving B. Kravis. 1954. *An international comparison of national products and the purchasing power of currencies.* Paris: OEEC.

Gilbert, Milton, and Associates. 1958. *Comparative national products and price levels.* Paris: OEEC.

Grunwald, Joseph, and Jorge Salazar-Carillo. 1972. Economic integration, rates of exchange, and value comparisons in Latin America. In Daly (1972a).

Hagen, Everett E. 1957. Comment. In CRIW (1957).

Jorgenson, Dale, and Masahiro Kuroda. 1990. Productivity and international competitiveness in Japan and the United States, 1960–1985. In *Productivity and growth in Japan and the United States* (Studies in Income and Wealth, vol. 53), ed. Charles R. Hulten. Chicago: University of Chicago Press.

Kravis, Irving B. 1957. The scope of economic activity in international income comparisons. In CRIW (1957).

———. 1984. Comparative studies of national incomes and prices. *Journal of Economic Literature* 22, no. 1 (March): 1–39.

Kravis, Irving B., Alan Heston, and Robert Summers. 1978. *International comparisons of real product and purchasing power.* UN International Comparison Project, Phase II. Baltimore: Johns Hopkins University Press.

———. 1982. *World product and income.* UN International Comparison Project, Phase III. Baltimore: Johns Hopkins University Press.

Kravis, Irving B., Zoltan Kenessey, Alan Heston, and Robert Summers. 1975. *A system of international comparisons of gross product and purchasing power.* UN International Comparison Project, Phase I. Baltimore: Johns Hopkins University Press.

Kravis, Irving B., and Robert E. Lipsey. 1991. The International Comparison Program: Current status and problems. In *International economic transactions: Issues in measurement and empirical research* (Studies in Income and Wealth, vol. 55), ed. Peter Hooper and J. David Richardson. Chicago: University of Chicago Press.

Maddison, Angus. 1998. Measuring the performance of a communist command economy: An assessment of the CIA estimates for the U.S.S.R. *Review of Income and Wealth,* ser. 44 (3): 307–23.

UN Statistical Division. 1994. World comparisons of real gross domestic product and purchasing power, 1985. New York: United Nations.

UN Statistical Office. 1987. World comparisons of purchasing power and real product for 1980—Phase IV of the International Comparison Project. New York: United Nations.

van Ark, Bart. 1996. Issues in measurement and international comparison of productivity—an overview. In *Industry productivity: International comparison and measurement issues: Proceedings.* Paris: OECD.

Viner, Jacob. 1957. Comment. In CRIW (1957).

World Bank. 1993. Purchasing power of currencies: Comparing national incomes using ICP data. Washington, D.C.

I Theoretical Bases of Multilateral Interspatial Comparisons

1   Axiomatic and Economic Approaches to International Comparisons

W. Erwin Diewert

For a variety of reasons, it is useful to be able to make accurate comparisons of the relative consumption or real output between countries or between regions within a country; for example, aid flows or interregional transfer payments may depend on these multilateral comparisons. Normal bilateral index number theory cannot be applied in this multilateral context because bilateral comparisons are inherently dependent on the choice of a base country and the resulting rankings of countries are not invariant to the choice of the base country. Moreover, it is usually politically unacceptable to have a single country or region play an asymmetrical role in making multilateral comparisons.

The problem of making bilateral index number comparisons has been intensively studied for about a century. From the viewpoints of both the economic and the test approaches to bilateral index number theory, a consensus has emerged that the Fisher (1922) ideal price and quantity indexes are probably the best functional forms for index number formulas (see Diewert 1992; and Balk 1995a).[1] However, there is no comparable consensus on what is the appropriate method for making symmetric multilateral index number comparisons, that is, comparisons that do not depend on the asymmetrical choice of a base country. Part of the reason for this lack of consensus is that the test or axiomatic approach to multilateral index number theory is not as well devel-

W. Erwin Diewert is professor of economics at the University of British Columbia and a research associate of the National Bureau of Economic Research.

This research was supported by a SSHRC grant. The author thanks Bert Balk, Irwin Collier, and Alice Nakamura for helpful suggestions and Tina Corsi for typing a difficult manuscript.

1. Balk (1995a, 87) argues that the Fisher and the Sato (1976)–Vartia (1974, 1976) price indexes are both the best from the viewpoint of the test or axiomatic approach to index number theory. However, the Sato-Vartia price and quantity indexes are not superlative and hence are not "best" from the perspective of the economic approach. In addition, Reinsdorf and Dorfman (1995) have shown that the Sato-Vartia indexes do not satisfy the monotonicity axioms that the Fisher indexes satisfy.

oped as the bilateral theory. In the last decade, Diewert (1986, 1988), Balk (1989, 1996), and Armstrong (1995) have made a start on developing axiomatic approaches to multilateral comparisons.[2] In section 1.1 below, the present paper draws on this literature by suggesting a list of twelve desirable properties or tests for multilateral methods. In sections 1.3–1.12, I evaluate ten different multilateral methods from the perspective of this test approach to multilateral comparisons. I find that none of these methods satisfies all the suggested tests. Thus, it is necessary to make choices about the relative importance of the various tests.

In section 1.2 below, I suggest a multilateral generalization of the economic approach to making bilateral comparisons. In analogy to the bilateral case (see Diewert 1976), I say that a multilateral system is *superlative* if it is exact for a flexible linearly homogeneous aggregator function. In sections 1.3–1.12, I determine whether the ten multilateral methods studied in this paper are also superlative.

Section 1.13 discusses some of the trade-offs between the various methods, and section 1.14 concludes.

Appendix A contains proofs of various propositions, and appendix B tables numerical results for the ten multilateral methods for a three-country, two-commodity artificial data set.

1.1   Multilateral Axioms or Tests

Suppose that the outputs, inputs, or real consumption expenditures of K countries[3] in a bloc of countries are to be compared. Suppose also that there are N homogeneous commodities consumed (or produced) in the K countries during the time periods under consideration and that the price and quantity of commodity n in country k are $p_n^k > 0$ and $y_n^k \geq 0$, respectively, for $n = 1, \ldots, N$ and $k = 1, \ldots, K$.[4] Denote the country k price and quantity vector by $p^k \equiv [p_1^k, \ldots, p_N^k]^T >> 0_N$ and $y^k \equiv [y_1^k, \ldots, y_N^k]^T > 0_N$, respectively.[5] I assume that

---

2. The study of symmetric multilateral indexes dates back to Walsh (1901, 398–431), Fisher (1922, 297–308), and Gini (1924, 1931). Early research suggesting desirable properties or tests for multilateral indexes includes Drechsler (1973, 18–21), Gerardi (1982, 395–98), Hill (1982, 50), and Hill (1984, 130–32).

3. The "countries" could be different regions or producer establishments. The list of commodities consumed (or produced) by the "countries" must be the same.

4. I interpret y_n^k as the total amount of commodity n consumed (or produced) in country k during the relevant time period and p_n^k as the corresponding average price or unit value. If commodity n is not consumed (or produced) in country k during the period under consideration, then $p_n^k > 0$ is interpreted as the Hicksian (1940, 114) reservation price that would just induce the consumer to purchase zero units of good n (or just induce the producer to supply zero units of good n). This is the convention on the positivity of prices and quantities used by Armstrong (1995).

5. Notation: $y \geq 0_N (y >> 0_N)$ means that each component of the N-dimensional column vector y is nonnegative (strictly positive), $y > 0_N$ means $y \geq 0_N$ but $y \neq 0_N$, and $p^T y = p \cdot y \equiv \sum_{n=1}^N p_n y_n$ denotes the inner product of the vectors p and y. The transpose of the column vector y is y^T.

all prices are positive and are measured in common units and a common numeraire currency. I also assume that the aggregate bloc quantity vector is strictly positive; that is, $\sum_{k=1}^{K} y^k >> 0_N$. Finally, denote the $N \times K$ matrix of country prices by $P \equiv [p^1, \ldots, p^K]$ and the $N \times K$ matrix of country quantities by $Y \equiv [y^1, \ldots, y^K]$.

The share of bloc consumption (or output or input) for country k, S^k, will depend in general on the matrix of prices P and the matrix of quantities Y. Thus, S^k will be a function of the components of P and Y, say, $S^k(P, Y)$ for $k = 1, \ldots, K$. I assume that the domain of definition for these functions is the set of strictly positive country price vectors $p^k >> 0_N$ and nonnegative but nonzero quantity vectors $y^k > 0_N$ for $k = 1, \ldots, K$ with $\sum_{k=1}^{K} y^k >> 0_N$. In the remainder of this paper, I shall call a specific set of functions defined on the above domain of definition, $\{S^1(P, Y), \ldots, S_K(P, Y)\}$, a *multilateral system* of bloc share functions or a *multilateral method* for making international comparisons of aggregate quantities.

If there are only two units being compared, then define

$$Q(p^1, p^2, y^1, y^2) \equiv S^2(p^1, p^2, y^1, y^2)/S^1(p^1, p^2, y^1, y^2)$$

as the ratio of "country" 2's share of "output" to "country" 1's share. The resulting function $Q(p^1, p^2, y^1, y^2)$ can be interpreted as a bilateral quantity index. I view a multilateral system as a generalization of bilateral index number theory to cover the situation where the number of units being compared is greater than two. In the remainder of this paper, I assume that the number of countries in the bloc is $K \geq 3$ (unless I explicitly assume that $K = 2$). If there is only one commodity, then there is no index number problem; that is, we will have $S^k(P, Y) = y_1^k/\sum_{j=1}^{K} y_1^j$ for $k = 1, \ldots, K$. Thus, I also assume that the number of commodities is $N \geq 2$.

In the axiomatic approach to bilateral index number theory (see Walsh 1901, 1921; Fisher 1911, 1922; Eichhorn and Voeller 1976; Diewert 1992, 214–23; Diewert 1993b, 33–34; and Balk 1995a), the function $Q(p^1, p^2, y^1, y^2)$ is hypothesized to satisfy various axioms or tests. I shall follow an analogous approach to multilateral index number theory by placing various tests or axioms on the multilateral system of share functions $S^k(P, Y)$.

Before I list my multilateral axioms, consider the following example of a multilateral system:

(1) $$S^k(P, Y) \equiv p^k \cdot y^k \bigg/ \sum_{j=1}^{K} p^j \cdot y^j, \quad k = 1, \ldots, K.$$

This system of multilateral share functions is the *exchange rate system*, where country k's share of bloc consumption (or output or input) is simply its share of total bloc value and all values are computed using a common numeraire currency.

I now list twelve desirable properties for multilateral systems. I regard the first seven properties as being more essential.

The first multilateral axiom is the following:

T1: SHARE TEST: There exist K continuous, positive functions $S^k(P, Y)$, $k = 1, \ldots, K$, such that $\sum_{k=1}^{K} S^k(P, Y) = 1$ for all P, Y in the domain of definition described above.

It is obvious that share functions must sum to unity. The share test outlined above also added the requirements that each share function be continuous and positive. The test T1 (without the positivity requirement) was proposed in Diewert (1986, 36) and Diewert (1988, 76).

To motivate the second test, suppose that each country's share of bloc output is the same for every commodity, say, β_k for country k. Then it seems reasonable to ask that $S^k(P, Y) = \beta_k$ for each k.

T2: PROPORTIONAL QUANTITIES TEST: Suppose that $y^k = \beta_k y$ for $k = 1, \ldots, K$ with $\beta_k > 0$ and $\sum_{k=1}^{K} \beta_k = 1$. Then $S^k(P, Y) = \beta_k$ for $k = 1, \ldots, K$.

This test is a multilateral counterpart to Leontief's (1936) aggregation theorem.

The next test is a counterpart to Hicks's (1946, 312–13) aggregation theorem: if each country's price vector p^k is proportional to a common positive price vector p, then this p can be used to determine country k's share of bloc output as $p \cdot y^k / \sum_{j=1}^{K} p \cdot y^j$.

T3: PROPORTIONAL PRICES TEST: Suppose that $p^k = \alpha_k p$ for $k = 1, \ldots, K$ with $\alpha_k > 0$ for some $p >> 0_N$. Then $S^k(P, Y) = p \cdot y^k / p \cdot \sum_{j=1}^{K} y^j$ for $k = 1, \ldots, K$.

Thus, if either prices or quantities are proportional across countries, then tests T2 and T3 determine what the country-share functions $S^k(P, Y)$ must be. The tests T2 and T3 can be interpreted as multilateral counterparts to identity tests for bilateral price and quantity indexes.

The next three tests are invariance or symmetry tests.

T4: COMMENSURABILITY TEST (INVARIANCE TO CHANGES IN THE UNITS OF MEASUREMENT): Let $\delta_n > 0$ for $n = 1, \ldots, N$, and let $\hat{\delta}$ denote the $N \times N$ diagonal matrix with the δ_n on the main diagonal. Then $S^k(\hat{\delta}P, \hat{\delta}^{-1}Y) = S^k(P, Y)$ for $k = 1, \ldots, K$.

The test T4 requires that the system of share functions be invariant to changes in the units of measurement for the N commodities. In the multilateral context, this test was proposed in Diewert (1986, 38) and Diewert (1988, 78). In the bilateral context, this test was proposed in Jevons (1884, 23), Pierson (1896, 131), Fisher (1911, 411), and Fisher (1922, 420).

T5: COMMODITY REVERSAL TEST (INVARIANCE TO THE ORDERING OF COMMODITIES): Let Π denote an $N \times N$ permutation matrix. Then $S^k(\Pi P, \Pi Y) = S^k(P, Y)$ for $k = 1, \ldots, K$.

This test implies that a country's share of bloc output remains unchanged if the ordering of the N commodities is unchanged. This test was first proposed in the bilateral context in Fisher (1922, 63) and in the multilateral context in Diewert (1986, 39) and (1988, 79).

T6: MULTILATERAL COUNTRY REVERSAL TEST (SYMMETRICAL TREATMENT OF COUNTRIES): Let $S(P, Y)^T \equiv [S^1(P, Y), \dots, S^K(P, Y)]$ denote the row vector of country-share functions, and let Π^* denote a $K \times K$ permutation matrix. Then $S(P\Pi^*, Y\Pi^*)^T = S(P, Y)^T\Pi^*$.

Thus, if the ordering of the countries is changed or permuted, then the resulting system of share functions is equal to the same permutation of the original share functions. The test T6 means that no country can play an asymmetrical role in the definition of the country-share functions. This property of a multilateral system was termed *base-country invariance* by Kravis et al. (1975). When multilateral indexes are used by multinational agencies such as the European Union, the OECD, or the World Bank, it is considered vital that the multilateral system satisfy T6. This property can be viewed as a fairness test: each country must be treated in an evenhanded, symmetrical manner.

The next test imposes the requirement that scale differences in the price levels of each country (or the use of different monetary units in each country) do not affect the country shares of bloc output.

T7: MONETARY UNITS TEST: Let $\alpha_k > 0$ for $k = 1, \dots, K$. Then $S^k(\alpha_1 p^1, \dots, \alpha_K p^K, Y) = S^k(p^1, \dots, p^K, Y)$ for $k = 1, \dots, K$.

Mathematically, T7 is a homogeneity of degree zero in prices property, a property that is usually imposed on quantity indexes in bilateral index number theory. In the multilateral context, Gerardi (1982, 398), Diewert (1986, 38), and Diewert (1988, 78) proposed this test.

The test T7 is a homogeneity in prices test. The next test is a homogeneity in quantities test.

T8: HOMOGENEITY IN QUANTITIES TEST: For $i = 1, \dots, K, \lambda_j > 0, j \neq i$, $j = 1, \dots, K$, we have $S^i(P, y^1, \dots, y^{i-1}, \lambda_j y^i, y^{i+1}, \dots, y^K)/S^j(P, y^1, \dots, y^{i-1}, \lambda_i y^i, y^{i+1}, \dots, y^K) = \lambda_i S^i(P, Y)/S^j(P, Y)$.

Mathematically, T8 says that the output share of country i relative to country j, S^i/S^j, is linearly homogeneous in the components of the country i quantity vector y^i. This property is usually imposed on bilateral quantity indexes. In the multilateral context, this test was suggested in Gerardi (1982, 397), Diewert (1986, 37), and Diewert (1988, 77).

The next test imposes the following very reasonable property: as any component of country k's quantity vector y^k increases, country k's share of bloc output should also increase.

T9: MONOTONICITY TEST: $S^k(P, y^1, \dots, y^k, \dots, y^K)$ is increasing in the components of the vector y^k for $k = 1, \dots, K$.

Although T9 has not been proposed before in the multilateral context, it has been proposed in the context of bilateral index number theory (see Eichhorn and Voeller 1976, 23; and Vogt 1980, 70).

The next two tests can be viewed as consistency in aggregation tests or country-weighting tests.

T10: COUNTRY-PARTITIONING TEST: Let A be a strict subset of the indexes $\{1, 2, \ldots, K\}$ with at least two members. Suppose that $p^i = \alpha_i p^a$ for $\alpha_i > 0$, $p^a >> 0_N$, and that $y^i = \beta_i y^a$ for $\beta_i > 0$, $y^a >> 0_N$, for $i \in A$ with $\sum_{i \in A} \beta_i = 1$. Denote the subset of $\{1, 2, \ldots, K\}$ that does not belong to A by B, and denote the matrices of country price and quantity vectors that do not belong to A by P^b and Y^b, respectively. Then, (i) for $i \in A, j \in A, S^i(P, Y)/ S^j(P, Y) = \beta_i/\beta_j$, and, (ii) for $i \in B, S^i(P, Y) = S^{i*}(p^a, P^b, y^a, Y^b)$, where $S^{k*}(p^a, P^b, y^a, Y^b)$ is the system of share functions obtained by adding the bloc A aggregate price and quantity vectors p^a and y^a to the bloc B price and quantity matrices P^b and Y^b.

Thus, if the aggregate quantity vector for bloc A, y^a, were distributed proportionally among its bloc members and each bloc A member's price vector were proportional to the price vector p^a, then part i of T10 requires that the bloc A share functions reflect their proportional allocations of outputs, and part ii of T10 requires that the non–bloc A share functions yield the same numerical values if bloc A were aggregated up into a single country (or, conversely, the non–bloc A share functions yield the same values if a single bloc A country is proportionally partitioned into smaller units). Note that T10 requires that $K \geq 3$ and that the system of share functions be defined for varying numbers of countries. Test T10 can be viewed as a generalization of Diewert's (see Diewert 1986, 40; Diewert 1988, 79) *country-partitioning test*. For precursors of this type of test, see Hill (1982, 50) and Kravis, Summers, and Heston (1982, 408). Note that the countries in bloc A satisfy the conditions for *both* Hicks and Leontief aggregation; that is, *both* prices and quantities are proportional for bloc A countries. Under these rather strong conditions, it seems very reasonable to ask that the system of share functions behave in the manner indicated by parts i and ii of T10.

The following test also uses combined Hicks and Leontief aggregation, but it applies these aggregation conditions to countries in blocs A and B:

T11: BILATERAL CONSISTENCY IN AGGREGATION TEST: Let A and B be nonempty disjoint partitions of the country indexes $\{1, 2, \ldots, K\}$. Suppose that $p^i = \alpha_i p^a, y^i = \beta_i y^a, \alpha_i > 0, \beta_i > 0, p^a >> 0_N$, and $y^a >> 0_N$ for $i \in A$ with $\sum_{i \in A} \beta_i = 1$ and that $p^j = \gamma_j p^b, y^j = \delta_j y^b, \gamma_j > 0, \delta_j > 0, p^b >> 0_N$, and $y^b >> 0_N$ for $j \in B$ with $\sum_{j \in B} \delta_j = 1$. Then $\sum_{j \in B} S^j(P, Y)/\sum_{i \in A} S^i(P, Y) = Q_F(p^a, p^b, y^a, y^b)$, where Q_F is the Fisher (1922) ideal quantity index defined by

$$(2) \qquad Q_F(p^a, p^b, y^a, y^b) \equiv [p^a \cdot y^b p^b \cdot y^b / p^a \cdot y^a p^b \cdot y^a]^{1/2}.$$

In this test, the set of countries is split up into two blocs of countries, A and B. Within each bloc, price and quantity vectors are proportional. Hence, if we aggregate country shares over blocs and divide the sum of the bloc B shares by the sum of the bloc A shares, we should get the same answer that the "best" bilateral index number formula $Q(p^a, p^b, y^a, y^b)$ would give, where the bloc A and B aggregate price and quantity vectors p^a, p^b, y^a, y^b are used as arguments in the bilateral index number formula. I chose Q to equal Q_F since the Fisher ideal bilateral quantity index satisfies more "reasonable" bilateral tests than its competitors (see Diewert 1992, 214–23). Of course, it is possible to modify test T11 by replacing the Fisher ideal index Q_F by an alternative "best" bilateral index number formula. However, the basic idea of test T11 seems very reasonable: a good multilateral method should collapse down to a good bilateral method if all price and quantity vectors are proportional within blocs A and B.

The test T11 is related to Diewert's (see Diewert 1986, 41; Diewert 1988, 81) strong dependence on a bilateral formula test. That test required that the limit of $S^i(P, y)/S^i(P, Y)$ equal a bilateral quantity index $Q(p^i, p^j, y^i, y^j)$ as all quantity vectors y^k (except y^i and y^j) tended to 0_N. However, I regard the present bilateral consistency in aggregation test as a more satisfactory test since some multilateral methods will not be well defined as quantity vectors tend to zero.

I regard all the tests presented above as being very reasonable and desirable for a multilateral method. Unfortunately, none of the ten multilateral methods that I study in this paper satisfies all these tests.

Before considering economic approaches to multilateral comparisons, I consider one additional test that practitioners regard as desirable.

I define an *additive multilateral system* of share functions $S^k(P, Y)$, $k = 1$, ..., K, as follows: there exist N once continuously differentiable positive functions of $2NK$ variables, $g_n(P, Y)$, $n = 1, \ldots, N$, such that

$$(3) \quad S^k(P, Y) = \sum_{n=1}^{N} g_n(P, Y)y_n^k \Big/ \sum_{m=1}^{N} g_m(P, Y)\sum_{j=1}^{K} y_m^j, \quad k = 1, \ldots, K,$$

where the functions g_n have the following property:

$$(4) \qquad\qquad g_n(p, p, \ldots, p, Y) = p_n, \quad n = 1, \ldots, N,$$

for all $p \gg 0_N$ and Y in the domain of definition, where $p \equiv [p_1, \ldots, p_N]^T$ is a common price vector across all countries.

Property (3) is the main defining property of an additive system: it says that each country's share is determined by valuing its consumption components (or outputs or inputs) using the common "international" prices $g_1(P, Y), \ldots, g_N(P, Y)$, which in principle can depend on the entire matrices of country prices and quantities, $P \equiv [p^1, \ldots, p^K]$ and $Y \equiv [y^1, \ldots, y^K]$. Property (4) restricts the class of admissible "international" prices in a very sensible way: if all the coun-

20   W. Erwin Diewert

try prices are equal and $p^1 = p^2 = \ldots = p^K = p$, then the "international" prices collapse down to these common national prices.

With the definition given above in mind, I can state the last test:

T12: ADDITIVITY TEST: The multilateral system is additive.

An additive multilateral system has the tremendously attractive feature of being user-friendly: if analysts want to compare the relative performance of countries over subsets of commodities, they can do so using the "international" prices $g_n(P, Y)$ to weight y_n^k for each country k and for n belonging to the subset of commodities to be compared. There is no need to compute a separate set of country parities for each subset of commodities to be compared. Moreover, each commodity component will correctly aggregate up to bloc consumption (or output or input) valued at the international prices $g_n(P, Y)$.

Unfortunately, although additive multilateral methods are very convenient, they are not consistent with the economic approach to multilateral systems, as we shall see.

I now turn to a description of an economic approach to making international comparisons.

1.2 An Economic Approach to Multilateral Index Numbers

The axiomatic approach to multilateral systems of index numbers does not make use of the assumption of optimizing behavior on the part of economic agents. Thus, the country price and quantity vectors, p^k and y^k, were treated as vectors of independent variables in the previous section. In this section, I follow the example of Diewert (1996, 19–25) and assume optimizing behavior on the part of economic agents in each country. Under this assumption, prices and quantities cannot be regarded as independent variables: given prices, quantities are determined (and vice versa).

I shall make the very strong assumption that a common linearly homogeneous aggregator function f exists across countries. This is the assumption that was used by Diewert (1976, 117) in his definition of a superlative bilateral index number formula. Thus, in this section, I am looking for a multilateral counterpart to the bilateral concept of superlativeness. In the consumer context,[6] I assume that each household in each country maximizes the increasing, concave, and linearly homogeneous utility function $f(y)$ subject to its budget constraint. Aggregating over households in country k, we find that the country k quantity vector y^k is a solution to

---

6. In the producer context, I assume *either* (i) that each producer in country k minimizes input cost $p^k \cdot y$ subject to a production function constraint $f(y) = f(y^k)$, where f is increasing, linearly homogeneous, and concave, *or* (ii) that each producer in country k maximizes revenue $p^k \cdot y$ subject to the constraint $f(y) = f(y^k)$, where f is an increasing, linearly homogeneous, and convex factor requirements function. In case ii, $c(p)$ defined by (6) is to be interpreted as a unit revenue function (see Diewert 1974; Diewert 1976, 125).

(5) $\max_y \{ f(y) : p^k \cdot y = p^k \cdot y^k \}, \quad k = 1, \ldots, K.$

Define the increasing, linearly homogeneous, and concave unit cost function that is dual to f by

(6) $c(p) \equiv \min_y \{ p \cdot y : f(y) \geq 1; y \geq 0_N \},$

where $p >> 0_N$ is a positive vector of commodity prices. If all consumers in country k face the same prices p^k and y^k is the total consumption vector for country k, then we have

(7) $p^k \cdot y^k = c(p^k)f(y^k), \quad k = 1, \ldots, K.$

Define the country k aggregate utility level of u_k and the country k unit cost or unit expenditure e_k as follows:

(8) $u_k \equiv f(y^k), \; e_k \equiv c(p^k), \quad k = 1, \ldots, K.$

If the unit cost function c is differentiable, then, by Shephard's (1953, 11) lemma, country k quantities y^k can be defined in terms of country k prices p^k and country k aggregate utility u_k as follows:

(9) $y^k = \nabla c(p^k)u_k, \quad k = 1, \ldots, K,$

where $\nabla c(p^k) \equiv [c_1(p^k), \ldots, c_N(p^k)]^T$ is the vector of first-order partial derivatives of c evaluated at p^k.

On the other hand, if the utility function f is differentiable, then, by Wold's (1944, 69–71) lemma, country k prices p^k can be defined in terms of country k quantities y^k and the country k unit expenditure level e_k as follows (see Diewert 1993a, 117):

(10) $p^k = \nabla f(y^k)e_k, \quad k = 1, \ldots, K,$

where $\nabla f(y^k) \equiv [f_1(y^k), \ldots, f_N(y^k)]^T$ is the vector of first-order partial derivatives of f evaluated at y^k.

Under the assumption outlined above of optimizing behavior on the part of economic agents for a linearly homogeneous aggregator function f, it is natural to ask that my system of multilateral share functions $S^k(P, Y)$ have the following *exactness* property:

(11) $S^i(P, Y)/S^j(P, Y) = f(y^i)/f(y^j), \quad 1 \leq i, j \leq K.$

Thus, under the assumption of homogeneous utility maximization in all countries, it is natural to require that the ratio of the consumption shares for countries i and j, $S^i(P, Y)/S^j(P, Y)$, be equal to the aggregate real consumption ratio for the two countries, $f(y^i)/f(y^j)$, for all countries i and j.

The preliminary definition of exactness (11) does not indicate whether I am regarding prices or quantities as independent variables. Thus, more precisely, I say that the multilateral system $S^k(P, Y), k = 1, \ldots, K$, is *exact* for the *differ-*

entiable homogeneous aggregator function f^7 if for all $y^k > 0_N$ and $e_k > 0$ for $k = 1, \ldots, K$ we have

(12)
$$\frac{S^i[\nabla f(y^1)e_1, \ldots, \nabla f(y^K)e_K, \ y^1, \ldots, y^K]}{S^j[\nabla f(y^1)e_1, \ldots, \nabla f(y^K)e_K, \ y^1, \ldots, y^K]} = f(y^i)/f(y^j), \quad 1 \leq i < j \leq K.$$

In the definition of exactness given above, I assume optimizing behavior, with prices p^k in the share functions $S^k(P, Y)$ being replaced by the inverse demand functions $\nabla f(y^k)e_k$ (see [10] above). Thus, the weakly positive country quantity vectors $y^k > 0_N$ and the positive country unit expenditure levels $e_k > 0$, $k = 1, \ldots, K$, are regarded as the independent variables in the system of functional equations defined by (12).

The definition of exactness given above assumes that each country's system of inverse demand functions (10) exists. Turning now to the dual case where I assume that each country's system of Hicksian demand functions (9) exists, I say that the multilateral system $S^k(P, Y)$, $k = 1, \ldots, K$, is *exact* for the *differentiable* unit cost function c^8 if for all $p^k >> 0_N$ and $u_k > 0$ for $k = 1, \ldots, K$ we have

(13)
$$\frac{S^i[p^1, \ldots, p^K, \nabla c(p^1)u_1, \ldots, \nabla c(p^K)u_K]}{S^j[p^1, \ldots, p^K, \nabla c(p^1)u_1, \ldots, \nabla c(p^K)u_K]} = \frac{u_i}{u_j}, \quad 1 \leq i < j \leq K.$$

In the definition of exactness given above, I am assuming optimizing behavior, with quantities y^k in the share functions $S^k(P, Y)$ being replaced by the Hicksian demand functions $\nabla c(p^k)u_k$ (see [9] above). Thus, the strictly positive country price vectors $p^k >> 0_N$ and the positive country utility levels $u_k > 0$ are regarded as the independent variables in the system of functional equations defined by (13).

In analogy with the economic approach to bilateral index number theory, we would like a given multilateral system of share functions $S^k(P, Y)$ to be *exact* for a *flexible* functional form for either (i) the homogeneous aggregator function f that appears in (12) or (ii) the unit cost function c that appears in (13). This exactness property for a multilateral system is a minimal property (from the viewpoint of economic theory) that the system should possess. If this property is not satisfied, then the multilateral system is consistent only with aggregator functions that substantially restrict substitution possibilities between commodities. If the multilateral system $S^k(P, Y)$ does have the exactness property outlined above for either case i or case ii, I say that the multilateral system is *superlative*. This is a straightforward generalization of the idea of a superlative

7. The aggregator function f is restricted to be linearly homogeneous, strictly increasing ($\nabla f[y] >> 0_N$ for $y > 0_N$), and *concave* in the consumer context and in the cost-minimizing producer context but *convex* in the revenue-maximizing producer context.

8. The unit cost function c is restricted to be linearly homogeneous, weakly increasing ($\nabla c[p] > 0_N$ for $p >> 0_N$), and *concave* in the consumer context and in the cost-minimizing producer context but *convex* in the revenue-maximizing producer context.

bilateral (see Diewert 1976, 117, 134) index number formula to the multilateral context.

In the following ten sections, I shall evaluate many of the commonly used multilateral systems with respect to the twelve tests listed in section 1.1. I shall also determine whether each multilateral system is superlative.

1.3   The Exchange Rate Method

The first multilateral method that I consider is the simplest: all country prices are converted into a common currency (the country price vectors p^k have already incorporated this conversion to a numeraire currency), and the share function for country k, $S^k(P, Y)$, is defined to be its nominal share of bloc output, $p^k \cdot y^k / \sum_{j=1}^{K} p^j \cdot y^j$ (eqq. [1] in sec. 1.1 above).

> PROPOSITION 1: The exchange rate method passes tests T1, T4, T5, T6, T8, and T9 and fails the remaining six tests. The exchange rate method is not exact for any aggregator function or any unit cost function and hence is not a superlative method.
> *Proof:* Proofs of all propositions can be found in appendix A.

Proposition 1 shows that the exchange rate method has very poor axiomatic and economic properties. However, owing to its simplicity and minimal data requirements (it requires only domestic value information plus exchange rate information), it is probably the most commonly used method for making multilateral comparisons.

I turn now to a class of additive methods.

1.4   Symmetric Mean Average Price Methods

Recall the definition of an additive multilateral method defined by (3) and (4) above. In this section, I shall assume that the weighting functions $g_n(P, Y)$ are averages of country prices for commodity n, $p_n^1, \ldots, p_n^K$, for $n = 1, \ldots, N$. Specifically, I assume that

$$(14) \qquad g_n(P, Y) \equiv m(p_n^1, p_n^2, \ldots, p_n^K), \quad n = 1, \ldots, N,$$

where m is a *homogeneous symmetric mean*.[9] Two special cases for m are the arithmetic and geometric means, defined by (15) and (16), respectively:

$$(15) \qquad g_n(P, Y) \equiv \sum_{k=1}^{K} (1/K) p_n^k, \quad n = 1, \ldots, N,$$

$$(16) \qquad g_n(P, Y) \equiv \left[\prod_{k=1}^{K} p_n^k \right]^{1/K}, \quad n = 1, \ldots, N.$$

9. I follow Diewert (1993c, 361) and define a homogeneous symmetric mean $m(x_1, \ldots, x_N)$ to be a continuous, symmetric increasing, and positively linearly homogeneous function that has the mean value property $m(\lambda, \lambda, \ldots, \lambda) = \lambda$.

The geometric average price multilateral system defined by (3) and (16) was originally suggested by Walsh (1901, 381, 398) (his double-weighting method), noted by Gini (1924, 106), and implemented by Gerardi (1982, 387). It turns out that this method satisfies more tests than other symmetric mean average price methods.

PROPOSITION 2: The general symmetric mean average price multilateral method defined by (3) and (14) (but excluding [16]) satisfies all tests except the monetary units test T7 and the two country-weighting tests T10 and T11. The geometric average price method defined by (3) and (16) satisfies all tests except T10 and T11. Symmetric mean average price methods are exact only for the linear aggregator function f defined by (17) below and the linear unit cost function c defined by (18) below. Hence, these methods are not superlative.

A linear aggregator function f is defined as

$$(17) \qquad f(y_1, \ldots, y_N) \equiv \sum_{n=1}^{N} a_n y_n,$$

where the parameters a_n are positive. A linear unit cost function c (dual to a Leontief no substitution aggregator function) is defined as

$$(18) \qquad c(p_1, \ldots, p_N) \equiv \sum_{n=1}^{N} b_n p_n,$$

where the parameters b_n are positive.

From proposition 2, we see that the geometric average price method is quite a good one from the axiomatic perspective: the method fails only the two consistency in aggregation tests T10 and T11. However, from the economic perspective, the Gerardi-Walsh geometric average price method is not satisfactory: it is consistent only with aggregator functions that exhibit perfect substitutability (see [17] above) or complete nonsubstitutability (see [18] above).

Instead of using average prices to define additive quantity indexes, average quantities could be used to define additive price indexes (or *purchasing power parities,* as they are called in the multilateral literature). I turn now to the consideration of this third class of multilateral methods.

1.5 Symmetric Mean Average Quantity Methods

For this class of methods, I first define country k's *price level* P^k as follows:

$$(19) \qquad P^k(P, Y) \equiv \sum_{n=1}^{N} m(y_n^1, \ldots, y_n^K) p_n^k, \quad k = 1, \ldots, K,$$

where m is a homogeneous symmetric mean. If I define $\bar{y}_n \equiv m(y_n^1, \ldots, y_n^K)$ as an average over countries of commodity n, then we see that country k's price level P^k is simply the value of the average basket $[\bar{y}_1, \ldots, \bar{y}_N]^T \equiv \bar{y}$ evaluated using the prices of country $k, [p_1^k, \ldots, p_N^k]^T \equiv p^k$.

Once the price levels P^k have been defined, the corresponding country k *quantity levels*[10] Q^k can be defined residually using the following equations:

$$(20) \qquad\qquad P^k Q^k \ = \ p^k \cdot y^k, \quad k \ = \ 1, \ldots, K;$$

that is, aggregate price times quantity for country k should equal the value of country k consumption (or production or input), $p^k \cdot y^k$. Finally, given the quantity levels Q^k, they can be normalized into shares S^k:

$$(21) \qquad\qquad S^k \ \equiv \ Q^k \Big/ \sum_{i=1}^{K} Q^i$$

$$(22) \qquad\qquad = \ \big[p^k \cdot y^k / p^k \cdot \bar{y} \big] \Big/ \Big[\sum_{k=1}^{K} p^i \cdot y^i / p^i \cdot \bar{y} \Big],$$

where (22) follows by substituting (19) and (20) into (21). Recall that $\bar{y}$ is the average quantity vector that has the nth component equal to $\bar{y}_n \equiv m(y_n^1, \ldots, y_n^K)$.

As in the previous section, two special cases for the homogeneous symmetric mean m that appeared in (19) are of interest: the arithmetic and geometric means defined by (23) and (24):

$$(23) \qquad \bar{y}_n \ = \ m(y_n^1, \ldots, y_n^K) \ \equiv \ \sum_{k=1}^{K} (1/K) y_n^k, \quad n \ = \ 1, \ldots, N,$$

$$(24) \qquad \bar{y}_n \ = \ m(y_n^1, \ldots, y_n^K) \ \equiv \ \Big[\prod_{k=1}^{K} y_n^k \Big]^{1/K}, \quad n \ = \ 1, \ldots, N.$$

Walsh (1901, 431) called the multilateral method defined by (22) and (23) *Scrope's method with arithmetic weights,* while Fisher (1922, 307) called it the *broadened base system,* and Gini (1931, 8) called it the *standard population method.* Walsh (1901, 398) called the multilateral method defined by (22) and (24) *Scrope's further emended method with geometric weights.* This index was later independently advocated by Gerardi (1982, 389).

The following proposition shows that average quantity methods satisfy fewer multilateral tests than average price methods but that they have equivalent exactness properties.

PROPOSITION 3: A symmetric mean average quantity multilateral method defined by (22) and $\bar{y}_n \equiv m(y_n^1, \ldots, y_n^K), n = 1, \ldots, N$, where m is a general homogeneous symmetric mean (excluding the two special cases [23] and [24]), satisfies tests T1–T7 and fails tests T8 and T10–T12. The geometric weights method defined by (22) and (24) passes tests T1–T8 and fails tests T9–T12. The arithmetic weights method defined by (22) and (23) passes tests T1–T7 and T9 and fails tests T8 and T10–T12. Symmetric mean average quantity methods are exact for only the linear aggregator function f defined by (17) and the linear unit cost function c defined by (18). Hence, these methods are not superlative.

10. The terms *price level* and *quantity level* are taken from Eichhorn (1978, 141).

Note that proposition 3 does not determine whether the monotonicity test T9 holds for a general homogeneous symmetric mean: I was able to determine only that the linear mean method defined by (23) satisfies T9 and that the geometric mean method defined by (24) does not satisfy T9.

Comparing propositions 2 and 3, we see that the Gerardi-Walsh geometric average price method defined by (3) and (16) dominates all the methods defined in this section and the previous one, failing only the two country-weighting tests T10 and T11.

I turn now to a more complex average price method.

1.6   The Geary-Khamis Average Price Method

The basic equations defining the Geary-Khamis[11] method can be set out as follows. Define an average price for commodity n by

$$(25) \qquad \pi_n \equiv \sum_{k=1}^{K}\left[y_n^k / \sum_{j=1}^{K} y_n^j \right][p_n^k / P^k], \quad n = 1, \ldots, N,$$

where the country k price level or purchasing power parity P^k is defined as

$$(26) \qquad P^k \equiv p^k \cdot y^k / \pi \cdot y^k, \quad k = 1, \ldots, K,$$

where $\pi \equiv [\pi_1, \ldots, \pi_N]^T$ is the vector of Geary-Khamis bloc average prices. Note that π_n is a weighted average of the purchasing power parity–adjusted country prices p_n^k / P^k for commodity n, where the country k weight is equal to its share of the total quantity of commodity n, $y_n^k / \sum_{j=1}^{K} y_n^j$. Once the π_n and P^k have been determined by (25) and (26), the country k quantity levels Q^k and shares S^k can be determined using equations (20) and (21).

If we substitute equations (26) into (25), the equations that define the Geary-Khamis share functions can be simplified into the following system of equations:

$$(27) \qquad\qquad\qquad [I_N - C]\pi = 0_n,$$

$$(28) \qquad\qquad\qquad y \cdot \pi = 1,$$

$$(29) \qquad\qquad\qquad S^k = \pi \cdot y^k, \quad k = 1, \ldots, K,$$

where I_N is the $N \times N$ identity matrix, $y \equiv \sum_{k=1}^{K} y^k >> 0_N$ is the strictly positive bloc total quantity vector, and the strictly positive $N \times N$ matrix C is defined by

$$(30) \qquad\qquad C \equiv \hat{y}^{-1}\sum_{k=1}^{K} \hat{p}^k y^k y^{kT} / p^k \cdot y^k,$$

where $\hat{p}^k$ is the country k positive price vector $p^k >> 0_N$ diagonalized into a matrix, and $\hat{y}$ is the total quantity vector $y \equiv \sum_{k=1}^{K} y^k$ diagonalized into a matrix.

---

11. Geary (1958) defined the method, and Khamis (1970, 1972) showed that the defining equations have a positive solution.

Using (30), note that $y^T C = y^T$. Thus, the positive vector y is a left eigenvector of the positive matrix C that corresponds to a unit eigenvalue. Hence, by Perron (1907, 46)–Frobenius (1909, 514),[12] $\lambda = 1$ is the maximal eigenvalue of C, and C also has a strictly positive right eigenvector π that corresponds to this maximal eigenvalue; that is, we have the existence of $\pi >> 0_N$ such that $C\pi = \pi$, which is (27). This positive right eigenvector can then be normalized to satisfy (28). From (29), we see that the Geary-Khamis method satisfies the additivity test T12.

The following proposition shows that the Geary-Khamis (GK) multilateral system does rather well from the viewpoint of the axiomatic approach but not so well from the viewpoint of the economic approach.

PROPOSITION 4: The Geary-Khamis multilateral system of share functions defined by (27)–(30) satisfies all the multilateral tests except T8 (homogeneity in quantities), T9 (monotonicity in quantities), and T11 (bilateral consistency in aggregation). However, the Geary-Khamis method does satisfy a reasonable modification of T11. The method is exact only for the linear aggregator function f defined by (17) and the linear unit cost function c defined by (18). Hence, the method is not superlative.

Proponents of the GK system might argue that the method's failure with respect to test T11 is perhaps exaggerated since, instead of ending up with a bilateral Fisher quantity index Q_F under the conditions of test T11, we end up with the bilateral GK quantity index Q_{GK}; that is, under the conditions of test T11, we obtain

$$(31) \qquad \sum_{j \in B} S^j(P, Y) \Big/ \sum_{i \in A} S^i(P, Y) = p^b \cdot y^b / p^a \cdot y^a P_{GK}(p^a, \ p^b, \ y^a, \ y^b),$$

where the GK bilateral price index P_{GK} is defined by[13]

$$(32) \qquad P_{GK}(p^a, \ p^b, \ y^a, \ y^b) \equiv \sum_{n=1}^{N} h(y^a_n, \ y^b_n) p^b_n \Big/ \sum_{m=1}^{N} h(y^a_n, \ y^b_n) p^a_n,$$

and where $h(x, z) \equiv 2xz/[x + z]$ is the harmonic mean of x and z, $[(1/2)x^{-1} + (1/2)z^{-1}]^{-1}$, if both x and z are positive. However, from the viewpoint of the test approach to bilateral index number theory, the Fisher price and quantity indexes pass considerably more tests than the Geary-Khamis price and quantity indexes. The Fisher bilateral price index satisfies all twenty of the tests listed in Diewert (1992, 214–21),[14] while the Geary-Khamis bilateral price index fails six of these tests: PT7 (homogeneity of degree zero in current-period quantities), PT8 (homogeneity of degree zero in base-period quantities), PT13 (price reversal or price weights symmetry), PT16 (the Paasche and Laspeyres bounding test), PT19 (monotonicity in base-period quantities), and PT20

---

12. More accessible references are Debreu and Herstein (1953, 598) and Karlin (1959, 246–56).
13. Geary (1958, 98) first exhibited this formula for the case $K = 2$.
14. For additional tests, see Martini (1992) and Balk (1995a).

(monotonicity in current-period quantities). The failure of bilateral test PT13 is not important, but the failure of the other tests is troubling.

From the viewpoint of the economic approach to index number theory, the Geary-Khamis method is definitely inferior to the multilateral systems that will be discussed in sections 1.9–1.12 below. Note that, even in the two-country case ($K = 2$), the GK method is exact only for the linear aggregator function (17) and the linear unit cost function (18). Thus, the method is consistent only with perfect substitutability or with perfect nonsubstitutability.

1.7   Van Yzeren's Unweighted Average Price Method

In this method, a vector of bloc average prices $p*$ is defined in a manner similar to the definition of the Geary-Khamis average price vector π (recall [25] above) except that the price vector of each country p^k divided by its purchasing power parity or price level P^k is weighted equally. Van Yzeren (1956, 13) originally called this method the *homogeneous group method*. He later called it (Van Ijzeren 1983, 40) a price-combining method or an unweighted international price method. The equations defining this method are (33)–(36) below:

$$(33) \qquad\qquad p* \equiv \alpha \sum_{k=1}^{K} p^k / P^k,$$

$$(34) \qquad\quad P^k \equiv p^k \cdot y^k / p* \cdot y^k, \quad k = 1, \ldots, K,$$

$$(35) \qquad\qquad S^k \equiv p* \cdot y^k, \quad k = 1, \ldots, K,$$

$$(36) \qquad\qquad \sum_{k=1}^{K} S^k = 1,$$

where α is a positive number. If we substitute (34) into (33) and (35) into (36), we find that the vector of bloc average prices $p*$ and the scalar α must satisfy the following two equations:

$$(37) \qquad p* = \alpha \left[\sum_{k=1}^{K} (p^k \cdot y^k)^{-1} p^k y^{kT} \right] p* \equiv \alpha C p*,$$

$$(38) \qquad\qquad 1 = \left[\sum_{k=1}^{K} y^k \right] \cdot p* = y \cdot p*,$$

where $C \equiv [c_{ij}]$ with $c_{ij} \equiv \sum_{k=1}^{K} p_i^k y_j^k / p^k \cdot y^k$, and $y \equiv \sum_{k=1}^{K} y^k$ is the bloc total quantity vector as usual. Since $y^k > 0_N$ and $p^k >> 0_N$ for each k with $\sum_{k=1}^{K} y^k >> 0_N$, C is a matrix with positive elements. Hence, $\alpha = 1/\lambda > 0$, where λ is the largest positive eigenvalue of C, and $p* >> 0_N$ is a normalization of the corresponding strictly positive right eigenvector of C (recall the Perron-Frobenius theorem). Thus, if the number of goods N is equal to two, it is possible to work out an explicit algebraic formula for the S^k.

It is possible to express the defining equations for this method in a different manner, one that will give some additional insight. Substitute (34) into (33), and premultiply the resulting (33) by y^{iT} for $i = 1, \ldots, K$. Using (35), the resulting K equations become

$$(39) \qquad S^i = \alpha \sum_{j=1}^{K} (p^j \cdot y^j)^{-1} p^j \cdot y^i S^j, \quad i = 1, \ldots, K.$$

After defining the vector of shares $s \equiv [S^1, \ldots, S^K]^T$, equations (39) can be rewritten using matrix notation as

$$(40) \qquad s = \alpha D s,$$

where the ijth element of the $K \times K$ matrix D is defined as $d_{ij} \equiv p^j \cdot y^i / p^j \cdot y^j > 0$ for $i, j = 1, \ldots, K$. Since D is positive, take $\alpha = 1/\lambda$, where λ is the maximal positive eigenvalue of D, and s is a normalization of the corresponding strictly positive right eigenvector of D.[15] The definition of s and α using equations (36) and (40) is the way Van Yzeren (1956, 13) originally defined his homogeneous group method. I have used the techniques of Van Ijzeren (1983, 40–41) to show that (36) and (40) are equivalent to (33)–(36).

Before I summarize the properties of Van Yzeren's unweighted homogeneous group method in proposition 5 below, it will be useful to note that the following flexible functional forms are exact[16] for the Fisher ideal quantity index Q_F defined above by (2):

$$(41) \qquad f(y) \equiv (y^T A y)^{1/2}, \quad A = A^T,$$

$$(42) \qquad c(p) \equiv (p^T B p)^{1/2}, \quad B = B^T.$$

The f defined by (41) is the square root quadratic aggregator function, and the cost function defined by (42) is the square root quadratic unit cost function. If either of the matrices A or B has an inverse, then $A = B^{-1}$.

PROPOSITION 5: Van Yzeren's unweighted average price method defined by (36) and (40) satisfies all the multilateral tests except T9 (monotonicity) and the two consistency in aggregation tests T10 and T11. For $K \geq 3$, this method is exact only for the linear aggregator function defined by (17) and the linear unit cost function defined by (18). However, for the two-country case ($K = 2$), this method is exact for the f defined by (41) and the c defined by (42). Finally, in the $K = 2$ case, $S^2/S^1 = Q_F(p^1, p^2, y^1, y^2)$, where Q_F is the Fisher ideal quantity index defined by (2).

Proposition 5 shows that this average price method suffers from the same limitation possessed by the average price methods studied in sections 1.4 and 1.6 above: when $K \geq 2$, these methods are consistent only with perfect substitutability or zero substitutability.

Note that Van Yzeren's unweighted average price method (which fails T9–

---

15. Given $s \equiv [S^1, \ldots, S^K]^T$ and $\alpha \equiv 1/\lambda$, the vector of international prices p^* can be defined as $p^* \equiv \alpha \sum_{k=1}^{K} (p^k \cdot y^k)^{-1} p^k S^k$. It should be noted that the d_{ij} are Afriat's (1967) cross-coefficients.
16. For proofs and references to the literature, see Diewert (1976, 116, 133–34).

T11) is dominated by the Gerardi-Walsh geometric mean average price method (which fails only T10 and T11) discussed in section 1.4 above.

I turn now to an analysis of the average quantity counterpart to the present method.

1.8   Van Yzeren's Unweighted Average Basket Method

In this method, a vector of bloc average quantities $y*$ is defined in a manner that is analogous to the definition of the average prices $p*$ in the previous section, except that the roles of prices and quantities are interchanged. Van Yzeren (1956, 6–14) originally called this method the *heterogeneous group method,* and he later (Van Ijzeren 1983, 40–44) called it an *unweighted basket combining method.*

$$(43) \qquad\qquad y* \;=\; \alpha\sum_{k=1}^{K} y^k/S^k,$$

$$(44) \qquad\qquad P^k \;=\; p^k \cdot y*, \quad k = 1,\dots,K,$$

$$(45) \qquad\qquad P^k S^k \;=\; p^k \cdot y^k, \quad k = 1,\dots,K,$$

$$(46) \qquad\qquad \sum_{k=1}^{K} S^k \;=\; 1.$$

If we substitute (44) and (45) into (43) and (46), we find that the vector of bloc average quantities $y*$ and the scalar α must satisfy the following $N+1$ equations:

$$(47) \qquad y* \;=\; \alpha\left[\sum_{k=1}^{K}(p^k \cdot y^k)^{-1}y^k p^{kT}\right]y* \;=\; \alpha C^T y*,$$

$$(48) \qquad\qquad 1 \;=\; \sum_{k=1}^{K} p^k \cdot y^k/p^k \cdot y*,$$

where $C \equiv [c_{ij}]$ with $c_{ij} \equiv \sum_{k=1}^{K} p_i^k y_j^k/p^k \cdot y^k$ is the same matrix that appeared earlier in (37). We can satisfy (47) by choosing $\alpha = 1/\lambda$, where λ is the maximum positive eigenvalue of the positive matrix C, and by choosing $y*$ to be a normalization of the corresponding positive left eigenvector of C (or positive right eigenvector of C^T). The normalization of the eigenvector is determined by (48). As in the previous section, if the number of commodities N is equal to two, then it is possible to work out an explicit formula for the S^k.

As in the previous section, it is useful to transform the equations given above into a more useful form. For $i = 1, \dots, K$, premultiply both sides of (43) by p^{iT}. Using (44) and (45), the resulting system of equations can be written as

$$(49) \qquad (S^i)^{-1} \;=\; \alpha\sum_{j=1}^{K}[p^i \cdot y^j/p^i \cdot y^i](S^j)^{-1}, \quad i = 1,\dots,K.$$

Define the vector $s^{-1} \equiv [(S^1)^{-1}, (S^2)^{-1}, \dots, (S^K)^{-1}]^T$. Then equations (49) can be written in matrix form as

(50) $$s^{-1} = \alpha D^T s^{-1},$$

where D^T is the transpose of the matrix D defined in the previous section below (40). Thus, as in the previous section, we can take $\alpha = 1/\lambda$, where λ is the maximum positive eigenvalue of the positive matrix D, and, in this section, we let s^{-1} be proportional to the positive left eigenvector of D that corresponds to λ, the factor of proportionality being determined by (46).

Van Yzeren (1956, 25) initially defined his heterogeneous group method using a version of (50), except that the S^k in (50) were replaced by the parities P^k using equations (45). Later, Van Ijzeren (1983, 40) derived the average basket interpretation of this method that was defined by (43)–(46) above.

PROPOSITION 6: Van Yzeren's unweighted average basket method defined by (46) and (50) satisfies all the multilateral tests except the monotonicity test T9, the two consistency in aggregation tests T10 and T11, and the additivity test T12. For $K \geq 3$, the method is exact only for the linear aggregator function defined by (17) and the linear unit cost function defined by (18). However, for the two-country case ($K = 2$), the method is exact for the f defined by (41) and the c defined by (42), and, in this case, $S^2/S^1 = Q_F$ is the Fisher ideal quantity index defined by (2).

Proposition 6 shows that Van Yzeren's average basket method suffers from the same limitation that applied to all the methods studied in sections 1.4–1.7 above: if $K \geq 3$, these methods are consistent only with perfect substitutability or zero substitutability.

The average basket method (which fails T9–T12) is dominated by Van Yzeren's average price method (which fails T9–T11) and the Gerardi-Walsh method (which fails only T10–T11).

The multilateral methods of Van Yzeren presented in this section and the previous one are generalizations of the bilateral Fisher ideal quantity index in the sense that these methods reduce to the Fisher index when there are only two countries. However, these methods are not very satisfactory generalizations in the three-or-more-country case because these methods are not exact for the flexible functional forms defined by (41) and (42). The multilateral methods that will be discussed in the following four sections do not suffer from this inflexibility: the methods that follow are all exact for the f defined by (41) and the c defined by (42) and hence are superlative. Moreover, all the multilateral methods that follow can be viewed as methods that attempt to harmonize the inconsistent comparisons that are generated by using a bilateral quantity index Q in the multilateral context.

1.9   The Gini-EKS System

I turn now to an examination of a multilateral method that uses a bilateral price or quantity index, $P(p^i, p^j, y^i, y^j)$ or $Q(p^i, p^j, y^i, y^j)$, as the basic building block. For the remainder of the paper, I assume that the bilateral price and quantity indexes satisfy[17]

(51) $P(p^i, p^j, y^i, y^j)Q(p^i, p^j, y^i, y^j) = p^j \cdot y^j / p^i \cdot y^i.$

Thus, if P is given, then the corresponding Q can be defined via (51), and vice versa.

Suppose that the bilateral quantity index Q satisfies Fisher's (1922, 413) *circularity test;*[18] that is, for every set of three price and quantity vectors, we have

(52) $Q(p^1, p^2, q^1, q^2)Q(p^2, p^3, q^2, q^3) = Q(p^1, p^3, q^1, q^3).$

I shall show why circularity is a useful property in the context of making multilateral comparisons shortly.

It is obvious that a bilateral quantity index Q can be used to generate a multilateral system of share functions provided that we are willing asymmetrically to single out one country to play the role of base country. For example, suppose that we have a bilateral Q and that we choose country 1 to be the base country. Then the share of country k, S_k say, relative to the share of country 1, S_1 say, can be defined as follows:[19]

(53) $S_k / S_1 \equiv Q(p^1, p^k, y^1, y^k), \quad k = 1, \ldots, K.$

Equations (53) and the normalizing equation

(54) $$\sum_{k=1}^{K} S_k = 1$$

will determine the multilateral shares using country 1 as the base.[20]

The problem with the multilateral star method defined by (53) and (54) is that, in general, the method will not satisfy test T6; that is, the method will not be independent of the choice of base country. However, if the bilateral quantity index Q satisfies the circularity test (52), then the star system would be independent of the base country. I demonstrate this assertion as follows. Consider the multilateral shares S_k^* that are generated by Q using country 2 as the base:

(55) $S_k^* / S_2^* \equiv Q(p^2, p^k, y^2, y^k), \quad k = 1, \ldots, K.$

Now, assume that Q satisfies circularity (52), and premultiply both sides of (55) by the constant $S_2/S_1 \equiv Q(p^1, p^2, y^1, y^2)$:

17. Frisch (1930, 399) called (51) the *product test*. The concept of the test is taken from Fisher (1911, 418).

18. The concept of the test is taken from Westergaard (1890, 218–19).

19. I assume that Q satisfies the identity test $Q(p^i, p^j, y, y) = 1$. In secs. 1.9–1.12, I denote the share and price levels of country k by S_k and P_k, respectively, instead of using the previous notation S^k and P^k. This is done because reciprocals S_k^{-1} and powers S_k^2 of the S_k will appear in the defining equations for these methods.

20. This is what Kravis (1984, 10) calls the *star system* with country 1 as the star.

$$[S^2/S^1][S_k^*/S_2^*] = Q(p^1, p^2, y^1, y^2)Q(p^2, p^k, y^2, y^k)$$
$$= Q(p^1, p^k, y^1, y^k) \quad \text{using (52)}$$
$$= S_k/S_1 \quad \text{using (53)}.$$

Thus, the S_k are proportional to the S_k^*, and hence, after using the normalization (54), they must be identical.

Unfortunately, if the bilateral index Q satisfies the circularity test for all price and quantity vectors, then Eichhorn (1976), Eichhorn (1978, 162–69), and Balk (1995a, 75–77) show that Q does not satisfy many other reasonable bilateral tests. In fact, Eichhorn's methods may be used to prove the following result.

PROPOSITION 7: Suppose that the bilateral quantity index Q satisfies the circularity test (52) and the following bilateral tests: BT1 (positivity), BT3 (identity), BT5 (proportionality in current-period quantities), BT10 (commensurability), and BT12 (monotonicity in current-period quantities). Then $Q(p^1, p^2, y^1, y^2) = \Pi_{n=1}^{N}(y_n^2/y_n^1)^{\alpha_n}$, where the α_n are positive constants summing to unity.

The bilateral tests BT1–BT13 will be defined later in this section. Proposition 7 merely illustrates that Irving Fisher's (1922, 274) intuition was correct: if a bilateral quantity index[21] satisfies the circular test plus a few other reasonable tests, then the index must have constant price weights,[22] which leads to nonsensical results.[23] Thus, as a practical matter, we cannot appeal to circularity to make the star system a symmetrical method.

Returning to the asymmetrical star system defined by (53) and (54), if instead of country 1 we use country i as the base, then the share of country k using i as a base, $S_k^{(i)}$, can be defined using the bilateral quantity index Q as follows:

$$(56) \quad S_k^{(i)} \equiv Q(p^i, p^k, y^i, y^k) \bigg/ \sum_{j=1}^{K} Q(p^i, p^j, y^i, y^j), \quad i, k = 1, \dots, K.$$

Fisher (1922, 305) was perhaps the first to realize that the asymmetrical multilateral methods defined by (56) could be made to satisfy the symmetrical treatment of countries tests T6 by taking the arithmetic mean of the shares defined by (56); that is, the *Fisher blended share*[24] for country k, S_k^F, can be defined by equations (57):

---

21. Fisher (1922, 274–76) was writing about price indexes, but his arguments also apply to quantity indexes.

22. We require only BT1 and BT3 to get the constant price weights representation (A36) in app. A.

23. The Cobb-Douglas price weights bilateral quantity index defined in proposition 7 fails the crucial bilateral test BT4.

24. Fisher (1922, 305) actually averaged price indexes (using each time period as the base) rather than quantity indexes.

(57) $$S_k^F \equiv \sum_{i=1}^{K} (1/K) S_k^{(i)}, \quad k = 1, \ldots, K.$$

Instead of using an arithmetic average of the $S_k^{(i)}$ defined by (56), Gini (see Gini 1924, 110; Gini 1931, 12) proposed using a geometric average. Thus, the Gini share of bloc aggregate quantity for country k turns out to be proportional to $[Q(p^1, p^k, y^1, y^k) \ldots Q(p^K, p^k, y^K, y^k)]^{(1/K)}$; that is,

(58) $$S_k^G \equiv \alpha \left[\prod_{i=1}^{K} Q(p^i, p^k, y^i, y^k) \right]^{(1/K)}, \quad k = 1, \ldots, K,$$

where α is chosen so that the S_k^G sum to one. In general, Gini (1931, 10) required only that his bilateral index number formula[25] satisfy the time reversal test, that is, that $Q(p^2, p^1, y^2, y^1) = 1/Q(p^1, p^2, y^1, y^2)$. In his empirical work, Gini (1931, 13–24) used the Fisher ideal formula. Finally, Gini (1931, 10) called his multilateral method the *circular weight system*. Gini's method, using the Fisher ideal formula, was later independently proposed by Eltetö and Köves (1964) and Szulc (1964) and is known as the *EKS system*.

Eltetö and Köves and Szulc actually derived their multilateral system (58) by a different route, which I shall now explain. Let P_k be the country k price level that corresponds to country k's multilateral share S_k. As usual, I impose the following restriction on the P_k and S_k:

(59) $$P_k S_k = p^k \cdot y^k, \quad k = 1, \ldots, K.$$

Now pick bilateral price and quantity indexes, P and Q, that satisfy the product test (51). The country price levels P_k are determined by solving the following least squares problem:

(60) $$\min_{P_1, \ldots, P_K} \sum_{i=1}^{K} \sum_{j=1}^{K} \{ \ln [(P_i/P_j) P(p^i, p^j, y^i, y^j)] \}^2$$

$$= \min_{P_1, \ldots, P_K} \sum_{i=1}^{K} \sum_{j=1}^{K} \{ \ln [(P_i/P_j) p^j \cdot y^j / p^i \cdot y^i Q(p^i, p^j, y^i, y^j)] \}^2 \quad \text{using (51)}$$

$$= \min_{S_1, \ldots, S_K} \sum_{i=1}^{K} \sum_{j=1}^{K} \{ \ln [(S_j/S_i)/Q(p^i, p^j, y^i, y^j)] \}^2 \quad \text{using (59)}$$

(61) $$= \min_{S_1, \ldots, S_K} \sum_{i=1}^{K} \sum_{j=1}^{K} \{ \ln [(S_j/S_i) Q(p^j, p^i, y^j, y^i)] \}^2,$$

where (61) follows from the line above if Q satisfies the time reversal test. Thus, if the bilateral quantity index Q satisfies the time reversal test, finding the optimal price levels P_k that solve the least squares problem (60) is equivalent to

25. Gini (1924, 1931) was concerned only with making multilateral price comparisons, but his analysis can be adapted to the quantity comparison situation as I have indicated.

finding the optimal country shares S_k that solve the least squares problem (61). Note that the objective function in (60) is homogeneous of degree zero in the P_k and that the objective function in (61) is homogeneous of degree zero in the S_k. Hence, a normalization on the P_k or the S_k is required to determine their absolute levels. As usual, I choose the normalization (54).

Differentiating the objective function in (61) with respect to S_k leads to the following equations for $k = 1, \ldots, K$:

$$\ln S_k - (1/K)\sum_{j=1}^{K} \ln S_j = (1/2K)\sum_{j=1}^{K} \ln Q(p^j,\ p^k,\ y^j,\ y^k)$$
$$(62)$$
$$- (1/2K)\sum_{i=1}^{K} \ln Q(p^k,\ p^i,\ y^k,\ y^i).$$

If Q satisfies the time reversal test,[26] then equations (62) simplify to[27]

$$(63) \quad S_k/[S_1 \ldots S_K]^{1/K} = \left[\prod_{j=1}^{K} Q(p^j,\ p^k,\ y^j,\ y^k)\right]^{1/K}, \quad k = 1,\ldots, K.$$

Using the normalization (54), it can be seen that the shares defined by (63) and (54) are identical to the Gini shares defined by (58) and (54).

Eltetö and Köves (1964) and Szulc (1964) used the least squares problem (60) with P equal to the Fisher ideal bilateral price index P_F to derive the EKS purchasing power parities P_k. Van Ijzeren (1987, 62–65) showed that one also obtained the EKS P_k and S_k if the Fisher, Paasche, or Laspeyres price index was used as the P in (60) or if the Fisher, Paasche, or Laspeyres quantity index was used as the Q in (61).[28] I shall call the system of shares defined by (54) and (58) for a general bilateral Q satisfying the time reversal test the *Gini system*. When Q is set equal to the bilateral Fisher ideal quantity index Q_F, I call the system defined by (54) and (58) the *Gini-EKS system*.

In order to determine the axiomatic properties of the Gini system, I shall assume that the bilateral quantity index satisfies the following thirteen bilateral tests:[29]

26. If Q does not satisfy the time reversal test, then use the Walsh (1921) rectification procedure, and obtain the solution ray to (61) by replacing $Q(p^j, p^k, y^j, y^k)$ in (63) by

$$Q^*(p^j,\ p^k,\ y^j,\ y^k) \equiv [Q(p^j,\ p^k,\ y^j,\ y^k)/Q(p^k,\ p^j,\ y^k,\ y^j)]^{1/2}.$$

27. The solution ray defined by (63) does indeed solve (61) since the objective function is bounded from below by zero and unbounded from above and there is only one ray of critical points.

28. It should be noted that the equality between (60) and (61) is taken from Van Ijzeren (1987, 62–63), except that Van Ijzeren restricted himself to the use of Fisher, Paasche, and Laspeyres price and quantity indexes.

29. For historical references to the originators of the corresponding tests for price indexes, see Diewert (1992, 214–21). For the bilateral tests, I assume that $p^1 \gg 0_N, p^2 \gg 0_N, y^1 \gg 0_N$, and $y^2 \gg 0_N$.

BT1: POSITIVITY: $Q(p^1, p^2, y^1, y^2) > 0$.

BT2: CONTINUITY: Q is a continuous function of its arguments.

BT3: IDENTITY: $Q(p^1, p^2, y, y) = 1$.

BT4: CONSTANT PRICES: $Q(p, p, y^1, y^2) = p \cdot y^2/p \cdot y^1$.

BT5: PROPORTIONALITY IN CURRENT-PERIOD QUANTITIES: $Q(p^1, p^2, y^1, \lambda y^2) = \lambda Q(p^1, p^2, y^1, y^2)$ for all $\lambda > 0$.

BT6: INVERSE PROPORTIONALITY IN BASE-PERIOD QUANTITIES: $Q(p^1, p^2, \lambda y^1, y^2) = \lambda^{-1} Q(p^1, p^2, y^1, y^2)$ for all $\lambda > 0$.

BT7: HOMOGENEITY IN CURRENT-PERIOD PRICES: $Q(p^1, \lambda p^2, y^1, y^2) = Q(p^1, p^2, y^1, y^2)$ for all $\lambda > 0$.

BT8: HOMOGENEITY IN BASE-PERIOD PRICES: $Q(\lambda p^1, p^2, y^1, y^2) = Q(p^1, p^2, y^1, y^2)$ for all $\lambda > 0$.

BT9: COMMODITY REVERSAL: $Q(\Pi p^1, \Pi p^2, \Pi y^1, \Pi y^2) = Q(p^1, p^2, y^1, y^2)$, where Π is an $N \times N$ permutation matrix.

BT10: COMMENSURABILITY: $Q(\delta_1 p_1^1, \ldots, \delta_N p_N^1, \delta_1 p_1^2, \ldots, \delta_N p_N^2, \delta_1^{-1} y_1^1, \ldots, \delta_N^{-1} y_N^1, \delta_1^{-1} y_1^2, \ldots, \delta_N^{-1} y_N^2) = Q(p_1^1, \ldots, p_N^1, p_1^2, \ldots, p_N^2, y_1^1, \ldots, y_N^1, y_1^2, \ldots, y_N^2)$ for all $\delta_1 > 0, \ldots, \delta_N > 0$.

BT11: TIME REVERSAL: $Q(p^2, p^1, y^2, y^1) = 1/Q(p^1, p^2, y^1, y^2)$.

BT12: MONOTONICITY IN CURRENT-PERIOD QUANTITIES: $Q(p^1, p^2, y^1, y^2) < Q(p^1, p^2, y^1, y)$ if $y^2 < y$.

BT13: MONOTONICITY IN BASE-PERIOD QUANTITIES: $Q(p^1, p^2, y^1, y^2) > Q(p^1, p^2, y, y^2)$ if $y^1 < y$.

It should be noted (see Diewert 1992, 221) that the Fisher ideal quantity index Q_F satisfies all thirteen bilateral tests.

PROPOSITION 8: Let the bilateral quantity index Q satisfy tests BT1–BT13. Then the Gini multilateral system defined by (54) and (58) satisfies all the multilateral tests except T10, T11, and T12. However, the Gini system satisfies a modified version of T11, where Q_F is replaced by Q. If Q equals the Fisher ideal quantity index Q_F, then the Gini-EKS system passes all the multilateral tests except the consistency in aggregation test T10 and the additivity test T12. In addition, the Gini-EKS multilateral system is exact for the aggregator function defined by (41) and the unit cost function defined by (42).

Proposition 8 shows that the Gini-EKS system has desirable properties from both the economic point of view (since it is superlative) and the test point of view (since it fails only two tests).

As a useful application of the first part of proposition 8, note that the Walsh (1901, 105) quantity index Q_W defined as

$$(64) \qquad Q_W(p^1, \ p^2, \ y^1, \ y^2) \equiv \sum_{n=1}^{N} (p_n^1 p_n^2)^{1/2} y_n^2 \Big/ \sum_{m=1}^{N} (p_m^1 p_m^2)^{1/2} y_m^1$$

satisfies all the bilateral tests BT1–BT13. Hence, applying proposition 8, the Gini multilateral system defined by (54) and (58), where $Q = Q_W$, satisfies all the multilateral tests except T10, T11, and T12. Moreover, if we modify test T11 by replacing Q_F with Q_W, this modified test T11 will be satisfied by the Gini-Walsh multilateral system. Finally, Diewert (1976, 130–34) showed that the generalized Leontief unit cost function defined by[30]

$$(65) \qquad c(p_1, \ldots, p_N) \equiv \sum_{i=1}^{N} \sum_{j=1}^{N} b_{ij} p_i^{1/2} p_j^{1/2},$$

where $b_{ij} = b_{ji}$, is exact for (64). In a manner analogous to the proof of proposition 8, we can show that the c defined by (65) is exact for the system of functional equations (13) when the country shares are defined by (54) and (58) with $Q \equiv Q_W$. Thus, the Gini multilateral methods that use either the Fisher or the Walsh quantity indexes, Q_F or Q_W, as the bilateral Q in (58) have entirely similar axiomatic and economic properties; both are superlative multilateral methods.

I now turn to another superlative multilateral method with good axiomatic properties.

1.10   The Own Share System

Given a bilateral quantity index Q, if we pick a base country i, we can calculate the quantity aggregate for country k relative to i by $Q(p^i, p^k, y^i, y^k)$. If we sum these numbers over k, we obtain total bloc output or consumption relative to the base country i. Hence, country i's share of bloc output, using country i as the base, is the reciprocal of this sum, S^{i*}, defined as

$$(66) \qquad S^{i*} \equiv \left[\sum_{k=1}^{K} Q(p^i, \ p^k, \ y^i, \ y^k) \right]^{-1} = \left[\sum_{k=1}^{K} Q(p^k, \ p^i, \ y^k, \ y^i)^{-1} \right]^{-1},$$

where the last equality in (66) follows if Q satisfies the time reversal test. Unfortunately, unless Q satisfies the circularity test, the "shares" defined by (66)

---

30. This unit cost function was originally defined in Diewert (1971), where it was shown to be a flexible functional form. It is the special case of the quadratic mean of order r unit cost function that occurs when $r = 1$ (see Diewert 1976, 130).

will not in general sum to unity. Hence, we must normalize the S^{i*} so that they sum to one. Thus, the *own share multilateral system* is defined by (54) and the following K equations:

$$(67) \qquad S^i \equiv \alpha \left[\sum_{k=1}^{K} Q(p^k, \, p^i, \, y^k, \, y^i)^{-1} \right]^{-1}, \quad i = 1, \ldots, K.$$

The own share system was introduced in Diewert (1986) and Diewert (1988, 69). The preliminary "share" S^{i*} defined by (66) defines country i's share of world product (or consumption or input) in the metric of country i. Since, in general, these metrics are not quite compatible, these shares are adjusted to sum to unity using (67) and (54).

It can be shown (see Diewert 1986, 28; and Diewert 1988, 69) that the own shares defined by (67) and (54) will be numerically close to the Gini shares defined by (58) and (54) (if the same Q is used in [58] and [67]) since equations (67) can be replaced by the following equivalent system of equations:

$$(68) \qquad S^i = \alpha \left[\sum_{k=1}^{K} (1/K) Q(p^k, \, p^i, \, y^k, \, y^i)^{-1} \right]^{-1}, \quad i = 1, \ldots, K.$$

In (58), a geometric mean of the numbers $Q(p^1, p^i, y^1, y^i), \ldots, Q(p^K, p^i, y^K, y^i)$ is taken, while, in (68), a harmonic mean is taken. Since a geometric mean will usually closely approximate a harmonic mean, it is evident that the Gini shares will usually be numerically close to the own shares.

The following proposition shows that the axiomatic and economic properties of the own share system are almost identical to the axiomatic and economic properties of the Gini system.

PROPOSITION 9: Let the bilateral quantity index Q satisfy tests BT1–BT13. Then the own share system defined by (54) and (67) fails the multilateral linear homogeneity test T8 and the additivity test T12. Test T11 is satisfied if Q equals Q_F, the Fisher ideal quantity index, and, in general, a modified test T11 is satisfied where the Q_F in the statement of the test is replaced by the bilateral Q. All remaining multilateral tests are satisfied. If Q equals Q_F, then the own share system is exact for the homogeneous quadratic aggregator function f defined by (41) and for the homogeneous quadratic unit cost function c defined by (42).

Proposition 9 shows that the Fisher own share system (where $Q = Q_F$) is superlative and has desirable axiomatic properties. Its properties are identical to the Gini-EKS system studied in the previous section, with the exception of tests T8 and T10: the Fisher own share system satisfies the country-partitioning test T10 and fails the homogeneity in quantities test T8, and vice versa for the Gini-EKS system. Both methods fail the additivity test T12. Thus, if the linear homogeneity property T8 were thought to be more important than the country-weighting property T10, then the Gini-EKS system should be favored over the Fisher own share system, and vice versa.

As a corollary to proposition 9, note that the Walsh index Q_W defined by (64) satisfies the bilateral tests BT1–BT13. Hence, the Walsh own share system (where $Q \equiv Q_W$ in [67]) passes all the multilateral tests except T8, T11, and T12. Moreover, a modified test T11 (where Q_F is replaced by Q_W in the statement of the test) is satisfied. Finally, it can be shown that the generalized Leontief unit cost function defined by (65) is exact for the system of functional equations (13) where the country shares are defined by (54) and (67) with $Q \equiv Q_W$. Hence, the Walsh own share system is also a superlative method.

1.11 Generalizations of Van Yzeren's Unweighted Balanced Method

In this section, I consider generalizations of Van Yzeren's (1956, 25) unweighted balanced multilateral method. In the following section, I consider generalizations of his weighted balanced method.

Let $P(p^j, p^k, y^j, y^k)$ be a bilateral price index, and consider the following minimization problem:

$$(69) \qquad \min_{P_1, \ldots, P_K} \sum_{j=1}^{K} \sum_{k=1}^{K} P(p^j, \ p^k, \ y^j, \ y^k) P_j / P_k.$$

Note the similarity of (69) to the minimization problem (60) that generated the Gini price levels.

Since the multilateral methods defined in this section and in section 1.9 above are both generated by solving minimization problems, both methods are examples of what Diewert (1981, 179) called *neostatistical approaches* to multilateral comparisons.

The first-order necessary conditions for the minimization problem (69) reduce to

$$(70) \qquad \sum_{k=1}^{K} P(p^i, p^k, y^i, y^k) P_i / P_k \ = \ \sum_{j=1}^{K} P(p^j, p^i, y^j, y^i) P_j / P_i, \quad 1, \ldots, K.$$

Note that the objective function in (69) is homogeneous of degree zero in the $P_1, \ldots, P_K$. Thus, a normalization on the P_k can be imposed without changing the minimum. Van Yzeren (1956, 25–26)[31] initially defined the bilateral price index $P(p^j, p^k, y^j, y^k)$ to be the Laspeyres price index[32] and proved that the minimum to (69) exists and is characterized by a unique positive solution ray to the first-order conditions (70).[33] Van Yzeren's proofs of existence and uniqueness go through for the more general model with a general bilateral P provided that the $P(p^j, p^k, y^j, y^k)$ are all positive.

31. See also Van Ijzeren (1983, 44), Van Ijzeren (1987, 60–61), and Balk (1989), who provided an excellent exposition of the balanced method and derived some new properties for it.

32. Gerardi (1974) let $P(p^j, p^k, y^j, y^k) = p^k \cdot y^k/p^j \cdot y^k$, the Paasche price index. Van Ijzeren (1987, 61) later let P be the Laspeyres, Paasche, and Fisher price indexes.

33. Note that, if we sum equations (70) over i, we get an identity; hence, any one of the equations (70) can be dropped. A normalization on the P_k will make a positive solution to (70) unique.

The minimization problem (69) involving the price levels P_k can be converted into a minimization problem involving the S_k if we use equations (59) to eliminate the P_k in (69). If we then eliminate the $P(p^j, p^k, y^j, y^k)$ using the product test (51), the minimization problem (69) becomes

(71)
$$\min_{S_1,\ldots,S_K} \sum_{j=1}^{K} \sum_{k=1}^{K} [1/Q(p^j, \ p^k, \ y^j, \ y^k)][S_k/S_j]$$

$$= \min_{S_1,\ldots,S_K} \sum_{j=1}^{K} \sum_{k=1}^{K} Q(p^k, \ p^j, \ y^k, \ y^j) S_k/S_j,$$

where (71) follows from the line above if Q satisfies the bilateral time reversal test BT11. The first-order conditions for (71) reduce to

(72) $$\sum_{j=1}^{K} Q(p^i, p^j, y^i, y^j) S_i/S_j \ = \ \sum_{k=1}^{K} Q(p^k, p^i, y^k, y^i) S_k/S_i, \quad i = 1,\ldots, K.$$

As was the case with equations (70), equations (72) are dependent, and any one of them can be dropped. Following Van Yzeren's (1956, 25–26) proof again, and assuming that the $Q(p^j, p^k, y^j, y^k)$ are all positive, we obtain a unique positive solution ray to (72). To obtain a unique solution to (72), add the usual normalization

(73) $$\sum_{k=1}^{K} S_k \ = \ 1.$$

Following the example of Van Yzeren (1956, 19), I suggest a practical method for finding the solution to (72) and (73). First, note that equations (72) can be rewritten as follows: for $i = 1, \ldots , K$,

(74) $$S_i \ = \ \left\{ \left[\sum_{k=1}^{K} Q(p^k, \ p^i, \ y^k, \ y^i) S_k \right] \Big/ \left[\sum_{j=1}^{K} Q(p^i, \ p^j, \ y^i, \ y^j) S_j^{-1} \right] \right\}^{1/2} .$$

Temporarily set $S_1 = 1$, and drop the first equation from (74). Insert positive starting values for $S_2, \ldots , S_K$ into the right-hand sides of equations 2–K in (74), and obtain new values for $S_2, \ldots , S_K$. Insert these new values into the right-hand sides of equations (74), and keep iterating until the S_i converge. The final vector $[1, S_2^*, \ldots , S_K^*]$ can then be normalized to sum to unity.[34]

Before we discuss the axiomatic properties of the multilateral method defined by (72) and (73), it is useful to note what happens if the circularity test (52) is satisfied by Q for the observed data set. At the beginning of section 1.9 above, I showed that all the star system shares would coincide in this case. If the common system of shares were denoted by $S_1^*, \ldots , S_K^*$, we would have $Q(p^i, p^j, y^i, y^j) = S_j^*/S_i^*$ for all i and j. Thus, if the bilateral index Q satisfies

---

34. If this procedure does not converge, then use Van Yzeren's (1956, 17) slightly more complicated procedure. Van Yzeren (1956, 27–29) proves convergence of this latter iterative scheme.

circularity for the observed data, then it can be seen that the base-country invariant shares $S_1^*, \ldots, S_K^*$ will satisfy equations (72) and hence that these shares will also be the unweighted balanced method shares.[35]

PROPOSITION 10: Let the once differentiable bilateral quantity index Q satisfy tests BT1–BT13. Then the unweighted Van Yzeren balanced system with this Q defined by (72) and (73) fails the multilateral tests T10 and T12. Test T11 is satisfied if $Q = Q_F$, the Fisher ideal quantity index, and, in general, a modified test T11 is satisfied where the Q_F in the statement of the test is replaced by Q. The remaining multilateral tests are satisfied. If Q equals the Laspeyres, Paasche, or Fisher ideal quantity index, then the corresponding unweighted balanced system is exact for the homogeneous quadratic aggregator function f defined by (41) and for the homogeneous quadratic unit cost function c defined by (42). Moreover, each of these three versions of the unweighted balanced method satisfies all the multilateral tests except the country-partitioning test T10 and the additivity test T12.

Proposition 10 shows that the following multilateral methods are all superlative: (i) Van Yzeren's (1956, 15–20) original unweighted balanced method that set $Q = Q_L$, where Q_L is the Laspeyres quantity index (which corresponds via [51] to the Paasche price index); (ii) Gerardi's (1974) modified unweighted balanced method that set $Q = Q_P$, where Q_P is the Paasche quantity index (which corresponds to the Laspeyres price index); and (iii) Van Ijzeren's (1987, 61) Fisher ideal balanced method that set $Q = Q_F$, where Q_F is the Fisher ideal quantity index (which corresponds via [51] to the Fisher ideal price index). Moreover, these three methods all have the same axiomatic properties, failing only tests T10 and T12.

Since the Walsh bilateral quantity index Q_W satisfies tests BT1–BT13, proposition 10 shows that the unweighted balanced method that sets $Q = Q_W$ in (72) also satisfies all the multilateral tests except T10, T11, and T12. However, the modified version of T11 where Q_F is replaced by Q_W is satisfied. Moreover, it is straightforward to show that this Walsh unweighted balanced method is exact for the flexible unit cost function defined by (65) and hence that this multilateral method is also superlative.

It is possible to follow the example of Balk (1989, 310–11) and show that the shares generated by the unweighted balanced method with an arbitrary bilateral Q (recall [72] above) will be numerically close to the shares generated by the Gini system (recall [58] above). First, note that, if we multiply both sides of (72) by $1/K$, we obtain arithmetic means of K numbers on each side of (72). These arithmetic means can usually be closely approximated by geometric means. Hence, the equations (72) are approximately equivalent to

---

35. If Q empirically satisfies circularity, then the base invariant shares $S_1^*, \ldots, S_K^*$ will also satisfy eqq. (58) and (67); i.e., the Gini system, the own share system, the unweighted balanced system, and the weighted balanced system (to be studied in the next section) all collapse to the same system of shares.

(75) $\displaystyle\prod_{j=1}^{K}[Q(p^i,p^j,y^i,y^j)S_i/S_j]^{1/K} = \prod_{k=1}^{K}[Q(p^k,p^i,y^k,y^i)S_k/S_i]^{1/K}, \quad 1,\ldots,K.$

These equations simplify to

(76) $\displaystyle S_i^2 = \alpha^2\left[\prod_{k=1}^{K}Q(p^k,p^i,y^k,y^i)\Big/\prod_{j=1}^{K}Q(p^i,p^j,y^i,y^j)\right]^{1/K}, \quad i = 1,\ldots,K,$

where $\alpha \equiv [\Pi_{k=1}^{K}S_k]^{1/K}$. If Q satisfies the time reversal test BT11, then equations (76) further simplify to equations (58), the defining equations for the Gini shares with a general Q. Finally, note that, if the bilateral Q in (76) is either the Laspeyres index Q_L or the Paasche index Q_P, then the resulting equations (76) are equivalent to equations (58) with the bilateral Q in (58) set equal to the Fisher ideal quantity index Q_F. This last observation helps explain Van Ijzeren's (1987, 63) observation that the unweighted balanced method shares are numerically close no matter whether Q_L, Q_P, or Q_F is used as the bilateral Q in equations (72) and (76).[36]

The argument in the previous paragraph showed that the Fisher unweighted balanced method, where $Q = Q_F$ in (72), will generate shares that are numerically close to the Gini-EKS shares, where $Q = Q_F$ in (58). Propositions 8 and 10 above also show that these two multilateral methods *have identical axiomatic properties* (they both fail the country-partitioning test T10 and the additivity test T12) and that *they have identical economic properties* (they are both exact for the homogeneous quadratic functional forms defined by [41] and [42] above).

In the following section, I shall study another class of multilateral methods derived originally by Van Ijzeren (1983, 45). The method studied in section 1.12 below turns out to have axiomatic and economic properties identical to those of the own share system studied in section 1.10 above.

1.12 Generalizations of Van Yzeren's Weighted Balanced Method

Following Van Yzeren (1956, 25) (who chose the bilateral Q to be Q_L, the Laspeyres quantity index), I introduce the following weighted version of the minimization problem (71):

$$\min_{S_1,\ldots,S_K}\sum_{j=1}^{K}\sum_{k=1}^{K}w_j w_k Q(p^k, p^j, y^k, y^j)S_k/S_j,$$

where the positive weights w_j are given numbers that somehow reflect the relative size or importance of the countries. The first-order necessary conditions for this minimization problem reduce to (77) for $i = 1, \ldots, K$:

---

36. Van Ijzeren (1987, 63–64) made a different theoretical argument showing why the three variants of the unweighted balanced method will be numerically close.

(77) $$\sum_{j=1}^{K} w_j Q(p^i,\ p^j,\ y^i,\ y^j) S_i / S_j\ =\ \sum_{k=1}^{K} w_k Q(p^k,\ p^i,\ y^k,\ y^i) S_k / S_i.$$

If the bilateral Q satisfies BT1 and we add the normalization (73) to (77), then the arguments of Van Yzeren (1956, 25–26) can be adapted to show that there is a unique positive set of shares $S_1(P,\ Y,\ w),\ \ldots,\ S_K(P,\ Y,\ w)$ that solve (73) and (77). Note that the solution shares now depend on the vector of country weights $w \equiv (w_1,\ \ldots,\ w_K)^T$ as well as the matrix of country prices P and the matrix of country quantities Y. At this point, note that Balk's (1989, 1996) axiomatic treatment of multilateral index numbers works with this weighted system of share functions, $S_1(P,\ Y,\ w),\ \ldots,\ S_K(P,\ Y,\ w)$, rather than the unweighted shares, $S_1(P,\ Y),\ \ldots,\ S_K(P,\ Y)$, that have been studied in the present paper. I will not pursue Balk's axiomatic treatment since it adds an extra layer of complication in determining exactly what weights w should be used. Moreover, my axiomatic treatment of the multilateral case seems to be the simplest extension of the bilateral axiomatic approach.

I now follow Van Ijzeren (see Van Ijzeren 1983, 45; and Van Ijzeren 1987, 65) and set $w_j = S_j$ for $j = 1,\ \ldots,\ K$ in (77).[37] This leads to the following system of equations:

(78) $$\sum_{j=1}^{K} Q(p^i,\ p^j,\ y^i,\ y^j) S_i^2\ =\ \sum_{k=1}^{K} Q(p^k,\ p^i,\ y^k,\ y^i) S_k^2,\quad i\ =\ 1,\ldots,K.$$

Equations (78) and the normalizing equation (73) define the Van Ijzeren weighted balanced shares with a general bilateral Q. Summing equations (78) over all i leads to an identity, so only $K - 1$ of the K equations in (78) are independent.

In order to establish the existence of a positive unique solution to equations (73) and (78),[38] define the ikth element of the matrix A by

(79) $$a_{ik}\ \equiv\ Q(p^k,\ p^i,\ y^k,\ y^i)\Big/ \sum_{j=1}^{K} Q(p^i,\ p^j,\ y^i,\ y^j),\quad 1\ \le\ i,\ k\ \le\ K.$$

It can be seen that equations (78) are equivalent to the following system of equations, where $x^T \equiv [x_1,\ \ldots,\ x_K] \equiv [S_1^2,\ \ldots,\ S_K^2]$:

(80) $$Ax\ =\ x.$$

I assume that Q satisfies BT1 and hence that A has positive elements. Define the vector $v \equiv [v_1,\ \ldots,\ v_K]^T$, where $v_i \equiv \sum_{j=1}^{K} Q(p^i, p^j, y^i, y^j)$ for $i = 1,\ \ldots,\ K$. Using this definition for v and (79), we have

---

37. Van Ijzeren (1983, 45–46) chose the bilateral quantity index Q to be either the Laspeyres quantity index Q_L, the Paasche quantity index Q_P, or the Fisher ideal quantity index Q_F.
38. The method of proof is an adaptation of Van Ijzeren's (1987, 65) and Balk's (1996, 204) method of proof.

(81) $$v^T = v^T A.$$

Equation (81) shows that the positive vector v is a *left* eigenvector of the positive matrix A that corresponds to a unit eigenvalue. Hence, by the Perron (1907)–Frobenius (1909) theorem, the maximal positive eigenvalue of A is one, and there exists a corresponding strictly positive *right* eigenvector x that satisfies (80). Once x is determined, the corresponding S_i satisfying (73) and (78) can be defined by

(82) $$S_i = x_i^{1/2} \Big/ \sum_{j=1}^{K} x_j^{1/2}, \quad i = 1,\ldots,K.$$

The numerical calculation of the weighted balanced shares can readily be accomplished if we make use of the theory of positive matrices. Let us drop the last equation in equations (80) and set the last component of the x vector equal to one. Define the top-left $K - 1 \times K - 1$ block of the $K \times K$ matrix A as the positive matrix $\tilde{A}$, define the first $K - 1$ components of the K-dimensional column vector x as $\tilde{x}$, and define the top-right $K - 1 \times 1$ block of A as the positive vector $\tilde{a}$. Setting $x_K = 1$, the first $K - 1$ equations in (80) may be rewritten as

(83) $$\tilde{x} = [I_{K-1} - \tilde{A}]^{-1}\tilde{a},$$

where I_{K-1} is a $K - 1 \times K - 1$ identity matrix. Using a result taken from Frobenius (1908, 473), the maximal positive eigenvalue of $\tilde{A}$ is strictly less than the maximal positive eigenvalue of A, which is one. Thus, the inverse of $I_{K-1} - \tilde{A}$ has the following convergent matrix power series representation:

(84) $$[I_{K-1} - \tilde{A}]^{-1} = I_{K-1} + \tilde{A} + \tilde{A}^2 + \ldots,$$

and, hence, using the positivity of $\tilde{A}$, $[I_{K-1} - \tilde{A}]^{-1}$ is a matrix with strictly positive elements. Thus, using the positivity of $\tilde{a}$, the $\tilde{x}$ defined by (83) has positive components. Equations (83), $x_N = 1$, and equations (82) can be used to define numerically the weighted balanced shares S_i using a general bilateral Q satisfying BT1.[39]

The following proposition lists the axiomatic and economic properties of the multilateral method defined by (73) and (78).

PROPOSITION 11: Let the once differentiable bilateral quantity index Q satisfy tests BT1–BT13. Then the weighted balanced method with the general bilateral Q defined by (73) and (78) fails the multilateral homogeneity in quantities test T8 and the additivity test T12. Test T11 is satisfied if $Q = Q_F$, the Fisher ideal quantity index, and, in general, a modified test T11 is satisfied where the Q_F in the statement of the test is replaced by the Q sat-

39. Note that it is much easier to calculate the weighted balanced shares with a general Q than it is to calculate the unweighted balanced shares where a closed-form solution does not seem to exist.

isfying the bilateral tests BT1–BT13. The remaining multilateral tests are satisfied. If the bilateral quantity index Q in (78) equals the Laspeyres, Paasche, or Fisher ideal quantity index, then the resulting Van Ijzeren (1983, 45) weighted balanced systems are exact for the homogeneous quadratic functions f and c defined by (41) and (42), and, hence, each of these systems is superlative. Moreover, each of these three versions of the weighted balanced method satisfies all the multilateral tests except T8 and T12.

Proposition 11 shows that the Van Ijzeren (1983, 45–46) weighted balanced methods that used the Laspeyres, Paasche, and Fisher quantity indexes as the bilateral quantity index are all superlative multilateral systems; that is, they are exact for the flexible functional forms defined by (41) and (42). Moreover, these three weighted balanced methods all have excellent axiomatic properties, failing only tests T8 and T12.

Since the Walsh bilateral quantity index satisfies tests BT1–BT13, proposition 11 implies that the weighted balanced method that uses Q_W in (78) will satisfy all the multilateral tests except T8, T11, and T12. Moreover, this Walsh weighted balanced method will satisfy the modified version of test T11 where Q_F is replaced by Q_W. It can be shown that this method is exact for the flexible unit cost function defined by (65) and hence that the Walsh weighted balanced method is also superlative.

Adapting the method used by Balk (1989, 310–11), it is possible to show that the shares generated by the weighted balanced method using the bilateral quantity index Q (see eqq. [78] above) will usually be numerically close to the shares generated by the Gini system using the same bilateral Q (see eqq. [58] above). Multiply both sides of equations (78) by $1/K$, and note that we have an arithmetic mean of K numbers on each side of each equation in (78). Approximating these arithmetic means by geometric means leads to the following system of equations:

$$(85) \quad \prod_{j=1}^{K}[Q(p^i, p^j, y^i, y^j)S_i^2]^{1/K} = \prod_{k=1}^{K}[Q(p^k, p^i, y^k, y^i)S_k^2]^{1/K}, \quad i = 1, \dots, K.$$

Equations (85) simplify to equations (76), and, if Q satisfies the time reversal test, equations (76) further simplify to equations (58), the defining equations for the Gini system shares. Thus, if the arithmetic means are close to the corresponding geometric means in (85), the Gini shares using a bilateral Q that satisfies BT11 will be close to the corresponding weighted balanced shares using the same bilateral Q.

Recall that, if the geometric means in (75) are close to the corresponding arithmetic means, then the Gini shares using a Q that satisfies BT11 will be close to the corresponding unweighted balanced shares using the same bilateral Q. Finally, recall that, if the harmonic means in (68) are close to the corresponding geometric means, then the own shares using Q will be close to the corresponding Gini shares using the same Q. Under normal conditions, these arithmetic, geometric, and harmonic means will closely approximate each other, so the Gini shares, own shares, unweighted balanced shares, and weighted balanced shares using the same bilateral Q should closely approximate each other.

In sections 1.9 and 1.11 above, I showed that the Gini-EKS system and the unweighted balanced method with $Q = Q_F$ had identical axiomatic properties (both failed tests T10 and T12) and economic properties (both were exact for the same flexible functional forms defined by [41] and [42] above). Propositions 9 and 11 show that the own share system with $Q = Q_F$ and the weighted balanced system with $Q = Q_F$ have identical axiomatic properties (both fail tests T8 and T12) and economic properties (both are exact for the flexible functional forms defined by [41] and [42] above).

1.13   What Are the Trade-Offs?

We have considered in some detail the axiomatic and economic properties of ten methods for making multilateral comparisons.[40] From the axiomatic perspective, we find that the methods described in sections 1.3, 1.5, 1.7, and 1.8 are dominated by other methods. The undominated methods are (i) the Gerardi-Walsh geometric average price method defined in section 1.4 by equations (3) and (16), which fails only T10 and T11; (ii) the Geary-Khamis method defined in section 1.6, which fails only T8, T9, and T11 (but satisfies a modified version of T11); (iii) the Gini system defined in section 1.9, which fails only T10 and T12; (iv) the unweighted balanced system defined in section 1.11, which also fails only T10 and T12; (v) the own share system defined in section 1.10, which fails only T8 and T12; and (vi) the weighted balanced system defined in section 1.12, which also fails only T8 and T12.

From the economic perspective, we found that the four methods described in sections 1.9–1.12 were superior to the remaining six methods: the Gini-EKS system, the weighted and unweighted balanced systems with the bilateral quantity index Q chosen to be the Fisher ideal index Q_F, and the own share system with $Q = Q_F$ were all superlative methods; that is, they were exact for the flexible functional forms defined by (41) and (42). The other six methods were either not exact for any aggregator function or consistent only for preference functions or production functions that exhibited either perfect substitutability (a linear aggregator function) or zero substitutability (a Leontief aggregator function or a linear unit cost function).

Examining the four superlative methods defined in sections 1.9–1.12, we found that, if various harmonic and arithmetic means are close to the corresponding geometric means, the shares for these four methods will be numerically close to each other if the same bilateral Q is used in each method. Assum-

40. Other notable multilateral methods that I have not studied (owing to limitations of space and time) include methods developed by Iklé (1972) (see also Dikhanov 1994), Van Ijzeren (1983, 45), Van Ijzeren (1987, 64–67), Diewert (1986, 1988), Kurabayashi and Sakuma (1990), Hill (1995), and Balk (1996).

ing that the bilateral quantity index used in each of these four methods is the Fisher ideal quantity index, propositions 8–11 showed that it was not possible for any of these superlative methods to satisfy test T8 (linear homogeneity in quantities) and test T10 (country partitioning) simultaneously: the Gini-EKS system and the unweighted balanced method satisfied T8 but not T10, while the own share and the weighted balanced methods satisfied T10 but not T8.[41]

How should we resolve the conflict between T8 and T10? There is no completely scientific answer to this question, but consider the following opinions. First, Peter Hill (1982, 50) noted that a major advantage of the Geary-Khamis method, which satisfies T10, over the Walsh-Gerardi method, which does not, is that the former method would not change very much if a large country were split up into several small countries: "Thus, the contribution of the United States to the determination of the average international price would tend to be the same whether or not the United States were treated as a single country or fifty or more separate states." In a similar vein, Kravis, Summers, and Heston (1982, 408) make the following comment on the Walsh-Gerardi method: "The Gerardi method would assign the same weight to Luxembourg and Belgium prices as to German and Netherlands prices in a comparison involving the four countries. However, if Belgium and Luxembourg become one country their average prices would have a combined weight of one. The comparison between Germany and Netherlands would differ according to whether Luxembourg and Belgium were treated as two countries or one." Finally, Van Ijzeren (1987, 67) summarizes his discussion of whether a weighted method (which satisfies test T10) should be used as follows: "Hence, theory rejects non-weighting. Surely, common sense does too!"

I tend to agree with these authors on the importance of weighting: it seems reasonable that the chosen multilateral method should reflect the fact that, if big countries are broken up into a bunch of smaller countries, comparisons between the unpartitioned countries should remain the same. This is the essence of the country-partitioning test T10. Thus, it seems to me to be more important to satisfy T10 rather than T8.

Propositions 9 and 11 show that the Fisher own share system and the Fisher weighted balanced method have identical axiomatic and economic properties: both are superlative, and both fail the linear homogeneity test T8 and the additivity test T12 but pass the other tests, including T10. Moreover, I have provided theoretical arguments to show that they will normally closely approximate each other numerically.[42] Which of these two methods should be used in practice? Balk (1989, 310) provides a theoretical argument (which I find unconvincing) for preferring the weighted balanced method over the own share method. However, a major advantage of the own share method is its relative

41. This equivalent performance of the own share and the weighted balanced methods was also obtained by Balk (1989, 310) for his set of axioms.

42. This close numerical approximation property is verified for the numerical example described in app. B.

simplicity. Statistical agencies can readily explain the essence of the method to the public as follows: each country's preliminary share of "world" output or consumption is determined by making bilateral index number comparisons (using the best available index number formula) with all other countries. These preliminary shares are then scaled (if necessary) to sum to one. It is very difficult to explain the mechanics of the weighted balanced method in an equally simple fashion.

In some situations, it may not be important for the multilateral method to satisfy the country-partitioning test T10. For example, the multilateral method might be required to determine the relative price levels (or purchasing power parities) in a number of cities where an international organization or multinational firm has employees so that salaries can be set in an equitable manner. In this case, it will probably be more important to satisfy the linear homogeneity test T8 rather than test T10. In this situation, it will be important to use a superlative method, which will recognize the realities of consumer substitution. In this situation, I would recommend the use of the Gini-EKS system or the unweighted balanced method with $Q = Q_F$ since these methods are superlative and fail only tests T10 and T12. In section 1.11, I indicated that these two methods will normally numerically approximate each other quite closely.[43] Which of these two methods should be used in empirical applications? On grounds of simplicity, I would favor the Gini-EKS system over the unweighted balanced system. In the former case, there is at least a closed-form formula for the country shares, while, in the latter case, iterative methods must be used in order to determine the country shares. Thus, it will be more difficult for international agencies or multinational firms to explain the mechanics of the unweighted balanced method to their employees.

Having discussed the trade-offs between test T8 and test T10 in the context of the four superlative multilateral methods analyzed in this paper, I now turn to a discussion of the trade-offs between superlativeness and additivity. For the ten multilateral methods studied in this paper, it is impossible to satisfy both properties simultaneously if the number of countries K exceeds two.[44] I will now indicate why the quest for an additive superlative method will be futile in general in the many-country case (i.e., when $K \geq 3$).

Consider the two-good, three-country case. Suppose that we are in the consumer context, that the preferences of each country over combinations of the two goods can be represented by the same utility function, and that the observed consumption vector (y_1^k, y_2^k) for each country k is on the same indifference curve. Suppose further that relative prices p_2^k/p_1^k differ dramatically

43. This theoretical approximation result is verified for the numerical example described in app. B.

44. If $K = 2$, proposition 5 shows that Van Yzeren's unweighted average price method is a superlative additive system. Another example of a superlative additive method when $K = 2$ is the Walsh-Gerardi system defined by (3) and (16). In this case, $S^2/S^1 = Qw(p^1, p^2, y^1, y^2)$, where Qw is the Walsh (1901, 552) quantity index defined by (64) above.

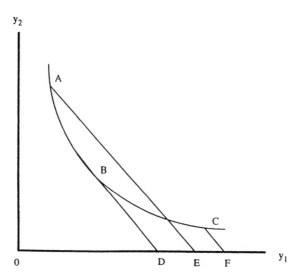

Fig. 1.1   Additive multilateral methods and substitution effects

across the three countries. The situation is depicted in figure 1.1. The points A, B, and C represent the consumption vectors (y_1^1, y_2^1), (y_1^2, y_2^2), and (y_1^3, y_2^3) for countries 1, 2, and 3, respectively. Since the consumption vectors are all on the same indifference curve, a multilateral method based on the economic approach should make the country shares of world consumption equal; that is, an economic-based multilateral method should yield $S^1 = S^2 = S^3$. Depending on how well the flexible functional form associated with a superlative multilateral method approximates the indifference curve in figure 1.1, a superlative multilateral method should lead to approximately equal shares for the three countries. The set of consumption vectors that an additive method will regard as being equal can be represented as a straight line with a negative slope in figure 1.1. If we take the prices of country 2 as the world average prices associated with an additive multilateral method, it can be seen that the share of country 1 will be proportional to the distance OE, that the share of country 2 will be proportional to OD (too small), and that the share of country 3 will be proportional to OF (too big). As the reader can see, there is no choice of price weights that will generate a straight line that will pass through each of the points A, B, and C simultaneously. Thus, additive methods, which implicitly assume that indifference curves are linear, are inherently biased if indifference curves are nonlinear.

Figure 1.1 can also be used to demonstrate the general impossibility of finding an additive superlative multilateral method if the number of countries $K \geq$ 3 and the number of commodities $N \geq 2$: if $N > 2$ and $K \geq 3$, then let the last $N - 2$ components of the country consumption vectors $y^1, y^2, \ldots, y^K$ be identical, and let the first two components of y^1, y^2, and y^3 be the points A, B, and C

in figure 1.1, so that the utility of y^1, y^2, and y^3 is identical. Since there is still no straight line that will pass through the points A, B, and C, the general impossibility result follows.

Figure 1.1 also illustrates the Gerschenkron effect: in the consumer theory context, countries whose price vectors are far from the "international" or world average prices used in an additive method will have quantity shares that are biased upward.[45] Marris (1984, 52) has a diagram similar to my figure 1.1 to illustrate the bias associated with additive methods in the consumer theory context. It can be seen that these biases are simply quantity index counterparts to the usual substitution biases encountered in the theory of the consumer price index.[46] However, the biases will usually be much larger in the multilateral context than in the intertemporal context since relative prices and quantities will be much more variable in the former context.

As an aside, R. J. Hill (1995, 73) noted that the average basket methods studied in section 1.5 above will suffer from a reverse Gerschenkron bias: in the consumer theory context, countries whose quantity vectors are far from the average basket quantities will have quantity shares S^k that are biased downward, and this bias is reversed in the producer theory context.

The bottom line on the discussion presented above is that the quest for an additive multilateral method with good economic properties (i.e., a lack of substitution bias) is a doomed venture: nonlinear preferences and production functions cannot be adequately approximated by linear functions. Put another way, if technology and preference functions were always linear, there would be no index number problem, and hundreds of papers and monographs on the subject would be superfluous! Thus, from the viewpoint of the economic approach to index number theory (which assumes optimizing behavior on the part of economic agents), it is not reasonable to ask that the multilateral method satisfy the additivity test, T12.

I conclude this section by reinterpreting the quest for additivity. Suppose that we want an additive method, not to provide accurate economic relative shares for K countries in a bloc, but simply to value the country quantity vectors $y^1, \ldots, y^K$ at a common set of "representative" prices $\pi \equiv [\pi_1, \pi_2, \ldots, \pi_N]^T$. The question is, How should we choose these "representative" or "reasonable" international prices? There appear to be two main alternatives: one proposed by Balk (1989, 299), and one proposed by Hill (1982, 59).

Suppose that, in defining the international price vector π, we are allowed to use the country shares S^k and country purchasing power parities or price levels P^k, $k = 1, \ldots, K$, that are generated by the investigator's "best" multilateral

---

45. For statements of this effect, see Gini (1931, 14), Drechsler (1973, 26), Gerardi (1982, 383), Hill (1982, 54), Hill (1984, 128), Kravis (1984, 8–9), Marris (1984, 52), and Hill (1995, chap. 4). In the producer theory context, the indifference curve through A, B, and C is replaced with a production possibilities curve that has the opposite curvature. Hence, the biases are reversed in the producer theory context.

46. Gini (1931, 14) had a clear understanding of substitution bias in the context of consumer price indexes.

method. Balk (1989, 299), drawing on the work of Van Ijzeren (1983, 1987), defined his vector of international prices π as the following country-share-weighted average of the country price vectors p^k deflated by their purchasing power parities:

$$(86) \qquad\qquad \pi \equiv \sum_{k=1}^{K} S^k (p^k / P^k).$$

On the other hand, the generalized Hill (1982, 59) international prices π_n, $n = 1, \ldots, N$, can be defined by equations (25) above, except that the Geary-Khamis price levels P^k that appeared in those equations should be replaced by the analyst's "best" multilateral price levels. Hill (see Hill 1982, 50; and Hill 1984, 129) explained why the π_n's defined by (25) are natural ones to use to define international average prices: these prices are the natural extension to the multilateral context of the prices used in the national accounts of a single country. In a single country, the average price used for a commodity is its *unit value*, that is, its total value divided by its total quantity.[47] It can be seen that the π_n defined by (25) are precisely of this character, except that the country prices p_n^k are replaced by the purchasing power parity–adjusted prices p_n^k / P^k. However, Hill did not emphasize the fact that it is not necessary to use the Geary-Khamis P^k in (25): the P^k generated by any multilateral method could be used.

To summarize the discussion presented above, I followed the example of Balk (1989, 310) and suggested that it is not necessary that the multilateral method satisfy the additivity test: the country shares S^k and the country price levels P^k generated by the "best" multilateral method can be used in equations (25) or (86) to generate "representative" international prices or unit values π_n that can be used by analysts in applications where it is important that commodity flows across countries in the bloc be valued at constant prices.[48]

1.14 Conclusion

In section 1.1, I developed a "new"[49] system of axioms or desirable properties for multilateral index numbers. Tests T1–T9 are adaptations of bilateral index number tests to the multilateral context. Tests T10 and T11 are genuine multilateral properties that do not have bilateral counterparts. I have included the additivity test T12 in my list of axioms because so many analysts find this property very useful in empirical applications. However, in the previous section, I concluded that the additivity test was not at all desirable from the viewpoint of the economic approach to index number theory since additive methods cannot deal adequately with nonlinear preference and technology functions.

47. For further references to the use of unit values to aggregate commodities over time and place, see Diewert (1995, 28) and Balk (1995b).

48. Of course, the resulting constant international "dollar" country aggregate values $\pi \cdot y^k$ will not generally be proportional to the country shares S^k generated by the "best" multilateral method.

49. Actually, only tests T2, T3, T9, T10, and T11 are new, and some of these tests are straightforward modifications of existing tests.

Thus, axioms T1–T11 are a very reasonable set of properties that can be used to assess the usefulness of a multilateral system of index numbers.

In section 1.2, I pursued the economic approach to index number comparisons. In particular, I adapted the exact and superlative index number methodology developed for bilateral index numbers to the multilateral context. If a multilateral system is superlative, then it is consistent with optimizing behavior on the part of economic agents where the common preference or technology function can provide a second-order approximation to an arbitrary differentiable linearly homogeneous function. Thus, a superlative method will tend to minimize various substitution biases that nonsuperlative methods will possess. Superlativeness is a minimal property from the viewpoint of the economic approach to index numbers that a multilateral system should possess.

In sections 1.3–1.12, I evaluated ten leading multilateral methods from the economic and axiomatic perspectives. From the axiomatic perspective, six methods satisfied more axioms than the remaining methods. These best methods were the Gerardi-Walsh geometric average price method, defined in section 1.4 (which fails T10 and T11); the Geary-Khamis method, defined in section 1.6 (which fails T8, T9, and T11); the Gini system and the unweighted balanced system, defined in sections 1.9 and 1.10 (which fail T10 and T12); and the own share and weighted balanced systems, defined in sections 1.10 and 1.12 (which fail T8 and T12). From the economic perspective, the four methods defined in sections 1.9–1.12 were the best.

To see that the ten multilateral methods studied in this paper can generate a very wide range of outcomes, the reader should view the results of a three-country, two-commodity artificial empirical example in appendix B.

If the multilateral method is required to determine purchasing power parities in the K locations so that satisfaction of the country-partitioning test T10 is not important in this context, then, in section 1.13, I concluded that either the Gini-EKS system or the unweighted balanced method (using the bilateral Fisher ideal quantity index) was probably best for this purpose. Between these two methods, I have a slight preference for the Gini-EKS method owing to its relative simplicity.

On the other hand, if the multilateral method is required to rank the relative outputs or real consumption expenditures between the K countries (or provinces or states), then, since satisfaction of test T10 is important in this context, I concluded (in sec. 1.13) that the own share or the weighted balanced method (using the bilateral Fisher ideal quantity index) was probably best for this purpose. Between these two methods, I have a slight preference for the own share system owing to its relative simplicity.[50]

Finally, it is appropriate to end this paper by noting the pioneering contributions of Van Yzeren (1956) (also Van Ijzeren 1983; 1987): of the ten methods studied in this paper, he was the originator of four of them.

---

50. However, since I introduced this method, the reader should be aware of a potential bias problem in this recommendation.

Appendix A
Proofs of Propositions

In most cases, verifying whether a multilateral method satisfies a given test is a straightforward calculation. Hence, many proofs will be omitted.

Proof of Proposition 1

T9: To verify monotonicity, differentiate S^k with respect to the components of y^k,

$$\nabla_{y^k} S^k(P, Y) = \left[\sum_{i=1}^{K} p^i \cdot y^i \right]^{-1} [1 - S^k(P, Y)] p^k \gg 0_N ,$$

since $p^k \gg 0_N$ and $0 < S^k(P, Y) < 1$.

T11: Under the conditions of T11, we find that

$$\sum_{j \in B} S^j(P, Y) \Big/ \sum_{i \in A} S^i(P, Y) = \sum_{j \in B} \gamma_j \delta_j p^b \cdot y^b \Big/ \sum_{i \in A} \alpha_i \beta_i p^a \cdot y^a$$

$$\neq Q_F(p^a, p^b, y^a, y^b).$$

Exactness Properties

The system of functional equations (12) becomes

$$e_i \nabla f(y^i) \cdot y^i / e_j \nabla f(y^j) \cdot y^j = f(y^i) / f(y^j),$$

or

$$e_i f(y^i) / e_j f(y^j) = f(y^i) / f(y^j) \quad \text{since } \nabla f(y^i) \cdot y^i = f(y^i),$$

or

$$e_i / e_j = 1.$$

Hence, there is no differentiable linearly homogeneous f that satisfies (12).
    The system of functional equations (13) becomes

$$p^i \cdot \nabla c(p^i) u_i / p^j \cdot \nabla c(p^j) u_j = u_i / u_j,$$

or

$$c(p^i) u_i / c(p^j) u_j = u_i / u_j \quad \text{since } p^i \cdot \nabla c(p^i) = c(p^i),$$

or

$$e_i / e_j = 1 \quad \text{since } c(p^i) = e_i.$$

Hence, there is no differentiable unit cost function c that satisfies (13).

Proof of Proposition 2

T3: Let $p \gg 0_N$, $\alpha_k > 0$, and $p^k = \alpha_k p$ for $k = 1, \ldots, K$. Then for $k = 1, \ldots, K$:

$$S^k(P, Y) = \sum_{n=1}^{N} m(\alpha_1 p_n, \ldots, \alpha_K p_n) y_n^k \Big/ \sum_{j=1}^{N} m(\alpha_1 p_j, \ldots, \alpha_K p_j) \sum_{i=1}^{K} y_j^i$$

$$= \sum_{n=1}^{N} m(\alpha_1, \ldots, \alpha_K) p_n y_n^k \Big/ \sum_{j=1}^{N} m(\alpha_1, \ldots, \alpha_K) p_j \sum_{i=1}^{K} y_j^i$$

using the linear homogeneity of m

$$= p \cdot y^k \Big/ \sum_{i=1}^{K} p \cdot y^i.$$

T7: Let $\alpha_k > 0$ for $k = 1, \ldots, K$. Then

$$S^k(\alpha_1 p^1, \ldots, \alpha_K p^K, Y)$$

$$= \sum_{n=1}^{N} m(\alpha_1 p_n^1, \ldots, \alpha_K p_n^K) y_n^k \Big/ \sum_{j=1}^{N} m(\alpha_1 p_j^1, \ldots, \alpha_K p_j^K) \sum_{i=1}^{K} y_j^i$$

$$\neq \sum_{n=1}^{N} m(p_n^1, \ldots, p_n^K) y_n^k \Big/ \sum_{j=1}^{N} m(p_j^1, \ldots, p_j^K) \sum_{i=1}^{K} y_j^i$$

unless

(A1) $\quad m(\alpha_1 p_n^1, \ldots, \alpha_K p_n^K) = \phi(\alpha_1, \ldots, \alpha_K) m(p_n^1, \ldots, p_n^K)$

for some function ϕ. Using the properties of m, we can deduce that ϕ must be continuous, strictly increasing, positive for positive α_k with $\phi(1, \ldots, 1) = 1$. Equation (A1) is one of Pexider's functional equations and, by a result in Eichhorn (1978, 67), there exist positive constants C, $\beta_1, \ldots, \beta_k$ such that

$$m(x_1, \ldots, x_K) = C x_1^{\beta_1} \ldots x_K^{\beta_K}, \quad \phi(\alpha_1, \ldots, \alpha_K) = \alpha_1^{\beta_1} \ldots \alpha_K^{\beta_K}.$$

Since m is symmetric all the β_k must be equal to a positive constant. Since m is positively linearly homogeneous, each β_k must equal $1/K$. Finally, the mean property for m implies $C = 1$. Thus,

(A2) $$m(x_1, \ldots, x_K) \equiv \left[\prod_{k=1}^{K} x_k \right]^{1/K}.$$

Hence, the symmetric mean multilateral system will satisfy T7 only if m is defined by (A2), which is the geometric average price method defined by (3) and (16).

T9: $\nabla_{y^k} S^k(P, Y) = [\bar{p} \cdot y]^{-1}[1 - S^k(P, Y)]\bar{p} \gg 0_N$, where $y \equiv \sum_{k=1}^{K} y^k$ and $\bar{p} \equiv [m(p_1^1, \ldots, p_1^K), \ldots, m(p_N^1, \ldots, p_N^K)]^T$.

T10: Part i is satisfied but not part ii.

T11: $\sum_{j \in B} S^j(P, Y)/\sum_{i \in A} S^i(P, Y)$ is not independent of the α_i and γ_j and hence is not a function of only p^a, p^b, y^a, and y^b.

Exactness Properties

Assuming (3) and (14), Diewert (1996, 255–56) showed that the only differentiable linearly homogeneous solution to (12) is the f defined by (17) and that the only differentiable solution to (13) is the unit cost function c defined by (18).

Proof of Proposition 3

To ensure that the S^k defined by (22) are well defined, I assume that all quantity vectors are strictly positive; that is, I assume that $y^k >> 0_N$ for $k = 1$, $2, \ldots, K$.

T8: Substituting (22) and (23) into the equations defining the test leads to the following system of equations that m must satisfy: for $\lambda_i > 0$, $p^i >> 0_N$, $p^j >> 0_N$, $y^k >> 0_N$ for $k = 1, \ldots, K$ and $1 \leq i \neq j \leq K$:

$$(A3) \quad \frac{\sum_{n=1}^N p_n^j m(y_n^1, \ldots, \lambda_i y_n^i, \ldots, y_n^K)}{\sum_{r=1}^N p_r^i m(y_r^1, \ldots, \lambda_i y_r^i, \ldots, y_r^K)} = \frac{\sum_{n=1}^N p_n^j m(y_n^1, \ldots, y_n^K)}{\sum_{r=1}^N p_r^i m(y_r^1, \ldots, y_r^K)}.$$

Cross-multiplying terms in (A3), collecting terms in $p_n^j p_r^i$, and choosing a grid of p^i and p^j vectors imply that equations (A3) will hold only if the following system of equations holds for all $\lambda_i > 0$, $i = 1, \ldots, K$ and $n, r = 1, \ldots, N$:

$$(A4) \quad \frac{m(y_n^1, \ldots, \lambda_i y_n^i, \ldots, y_n^K)}{m(y_r^1, \ldots, \lambda_i y_r^i, \ldots, y_r^K)} = \frac{m(y_n^1, \ldots, y_n^K)}{m(y_r^1, \ldots, y_r^K)}.$$

Repeated use of (A4) for $i = 1, \ldots, K$ implies that the following equation must hold:

$$(A5) \quad \frac{m(\lambda_1 y_n^1, \lambda_2 y_n^2, \ldots, \lambda_K y_n^K)}{m(\lambda_1 y_r^1, \lambda_2 y_r^2, \ldots, \lambda_K y_r^K)} = \frac{m(y_n^1, y_n^2, \ldots, y_n^K)}{m(y_r^1, y_r^2, \ldots, y_r^K)}.$$

Let $(y_n^1, \ldots, y_n^K) \equiv (y_1, \ldots, y_K)$, $(y_r^1, \ldots, y_r^K) \equiv (z_1, \ldots, z_K) >> 0_K$, and $(\lambda_1, \ldots, \lambda_K) \equiv (z_1^{-1}, \ldots, z_K^{-1})$. Making these substitutions into (A5) and using $m(1_K) = 1$ transform (A5) into:

$$(A6) \quad m(z_1^{-1} y_1, z_2^{-1} y_2, \ldots, z_K^{-1} y_K) = m(y_1, y_2, \ldots, y_K)/m(z_1, z_2, \ldots, z_K).$$

Define $g(x_1, x_2, \ldots, x_K) \equiv 1/m(x_1^{-1}, x_2^{-1}, \ldots, x_K^{-1})$. Letting $x_k = z_k^{-1}$ for $k = 1$, $\ldots, K$, and using the definition of g, (A6) becomes the following functional equation:

(A7) $\quad m(x_1 y_1, \ x_2 y_2, \ldots, x_K y_K) \ = \ m(y_1, \ y_2, \ldots, y_K) g(x_1, \ x_2, \ldots, x_K),$

which must hold for all $x >> 0_K$ and $y >> 0_K$. Now apply a result taken from Eichhorn (1978, 67) to (A7), use the assumption that m is a homogeneous mean, and conclude that m must be defined by (24) in order that (A7) hold. It is straightforward to show that, if m is defined by (24), then test T8 holds. Hence, a symmetric mean average quantity method will satisfy T8 if and only if the homogeneous symmetric mean m is the geometric mean defined by (24).

T9: Consider first the arithmetic mean case where S^k is defined by (22) and (23). A straightforward calculation shows that, for $j = 2, \ldots, K$ and $z > 0_N$, we have

(A8) $\quad S^1(P, \ y^1 + \ z, \ y^2, \ldots, y^K)/S^j(P, \ y^1 + \ z, \ y^2, \ldots, y^K)$

$$> \ S^1(P, \ Y)/ \ S^j(P, \ Y).$$

The inequalities (A8) imply that $S_1(P, y^1, y^2, \ldots, y^K)$ is increasing in the components of y^1. We can similarly show that $S^k(P, Y)$ is increasing in the components of y^k for any k.

Now consider the geometric mean case where S^k is defined by (22) and (24). Let $K = 2$ and $N = 2$, and calculate the derivative of $S^1(P, Y)/S^2(P, Y)$ with respect to y_1^1. It is possible to find positive vectors p^1, p^2, y^1, y^2 that make this derivative negative. Hence, the geometric weights method fails the monotonicity test T9.

T10: Part i holds, but part ii does not.

T11: $\sum_{j \in B} S^j(P, Y)/\sum_{i \in A} S^i(P, Y)$ is not independent of the β_i and δ_j and hence is not a function of only $p^a, p^b, y^a,$ and y^b.

Exactness Properties

Diewert (1996, 257) showed that, for this method, the only differentiable linearly homogeneous solution to (12) is the f defined by (17) and that the only differentiable solution to (13) is the unit cost function defined by (18).

Proof of Proposition 4

T1: The Perron-Frobenius theorem implies that the maximal eigenvalue eigenvector of the positive matrix C, subject to the normalization (28), is unique and thus that the components of π will be continuous functions of the elements of C and hence of the elements of P and Y.

T3: Let $p >> 0_N$, $\alpha_k > 0$, and $p^k = \alpha_k p$ for $k = 1, \ldots, K$. Define $y \equiv \sum_{k=1}^K y^k$. We need to show that $S^k = p \cdot y^k/p \cdot y$ for $k = 1, \ldots, K$. Hence, we need show only that $\pi \equiv p/p \cdot y$ satisfies (27) or, equivalently, that $Cp = p$. We have

$$Cp \;=\; \hat{y}^{-1}\sum_{k=1}^{K} \alpha_k \hat{p}\, y^k y^{kT} p/\alpha_k p^T y^k$$

$$=\; \hat{y}^{-1}\hat{p}\sum_{k=1}^{K} y^k$$

$$=\; \hat{y}^{-1}\hat{y}p$$

$$=\; p.$$

T7: The matrix C defined by (30) remains invariant if p^k is replaced by $\alpha_k p^k$ for $k = 1, \ldots, K$.

T8: For this test to pass when $K = 2$, we require P_{GK} defined by (32) to be homogeneous of degree zero in the components of y^a, which is not true.

T9: When $K = 2$, we require that S^2/S^1 be increasing in the components of y^2. In this case, we obtain an explicit function of p^1, p^2, y^1, y^2 for S^2/S^1 (see the right-hand side of [31] with $a = 1$ and $b = 2$), and, by differentiating this function with respect to a component of y^2, we can verify that monotonicity fails.

T10i: Let $p^a \gg 0_N$, $p^i = \alpha_i p^a$, $\alpha_i > 0$, $y^a > 0_N$, $y^i = \beta_i y^a$, $\beta_i > 0$ for $i \in A$ with $\sum_{i \in A} \beta_i = 1$. For $i \in A$ and $j \in A$, we have

$$S^i(P,\ Y)/S^j(P,\ Y) \;=\; \pi \cdot y^i/\pi \cdot y^j \;=\; \pi \cdot \beta_i y^a/\pi \cdot \beta_j y^a \;=\; \beta_i/\beta_j.$$

T10ii: If we premultiply (27) by the diagonal matrix $\hat{y}$, the resulting system of equations becomes:

(A9)
$$\left[\sum_{i \in A}\hat{y}^i + \sum_{j \in B}\hat{y}^j - \sum_{i \in A}(p^i \cdot y^i)^{-1}\hat{p}^i y^i y^{iT} \right.$$
$$\left. - \sum_{j \in B}(p^j \cdot y^j)^{-1}\hat{p}^j y^j y^{jT}\right]\pi \;=\; 0_N,$$

or

$$\left[\sum_{i \in A}\beta_i\hat{y}^a + \sum_{j \in B}\hat{y}^j - \sum_{i \in A}(\alpha_i\beta_i p^a \cdot y^a)^{-1}\alpha_i\hat{p}^a\beta_i y^a\beta_i y^{aT}\right.$$
$$\left. - \sum_{j \in B}(p^j \cdot y^j)^{-1}\hat{p}^j y^j y^{jT}\right]\pi \;=\; 0_N,$$

or

(A10)
$$\left[y^a + \sum_{j \in B}\hat{y}^j - (p^a \cdot y^a)^{-1}\hat{p}^a y^a y^{aT}\right.$$
$$\left. - \sum_{j \in B}(p^j \cdot y^j)^{-1}\hat{p}^j y^j y^{jT}\right]\pi \;=\; 0_N.$$

If we premultiply (A10) by $\hat{y}^{-1}$, we obtain $[I_N - C^*]\pi = 0_N$, where C^* is the matrix that corresponds to the aggregated (over countries in the subbloc A) model. Hence, if π satisfies (A9) and (28), it will also satisfy (A10) and (28).

T11: Under the restrictions for this test, the system (27) or, equivalently, the system (A9) reduces to

$$[\hat{y}^a + \hat{y}^b - (p^a \cdot y^a)^{-1}\hat{p}^a y^a y^{aT} - (p^b \cdot y^b)^{-1}\hat{p}^b y^b y^{bT}]\pi = 0_N,$$

or

(A11) $$[\hat{y}^a + \hat{y}^b]^{-1}[(p^a \cdot y^a)^{-1}\hat{p}^a y^a y^{aT} + (p^b \cdot y^b)^{-1}\hat{p}^b y^b y^{bT}]\pi = \pi.$$

Define the vectors of expenditure shares for subblocs A and B by $s^a \equiv \hat{p}^a y^a / p^a \cdot y^a$ and $s^b \equiv \hat{p}^b y^b / p^b \cdot y^b$, respectively, and the quantity shares of "world" output for the two blocs A and B by $q^a \equiv [\hat{y}^a + \hat{y}^b]^{-1} y^a$ and $q^b \equiv [\hat{y}^a + \hat{y}^b]^{-1} y^b$, respectively. Note that $q^a + q^b = 1_N$, a vector of ones. Now premultiply both sides of (A11) by y^{aT}. Rearranging terms in the resulting equation, we find that

$$\pi \cdot y^b / \pi \cdot y^a = [1 - s^a \cdot q^a]/s^b \cdot q^b$$

$$= [s^a \cdot 1_N - s^2 \cdot q^a]/s^b \cdot q^b \quad \text{since } s^a \cdot 1_N = 1$$

(A12) $$= s^a \cdot q^b/s^b \cdot q^a \quad \text{since } 1_N - q^a = q^b$$

$$= \{p^{aT}\hat{y}^a[\hat{y}^a + \hat{y}^b]^{-1}y^b / p^{bT}\hat{y}^b[\hat{y}^a + \hat{y}^b]^{-1}y^a\}$$

$$\times \{p^b \cdot y^b/p^a \cdot y^a\}$$

$$= p^b \cdot y^b/p^a \cdot y^a P_{GK}(p^a, p^b, y^a, y^b),$$

where P_{GK} is the bilateral Geary-Khamis price index defined by (32). Since the left-hand side of (A12) is $\sum_{j \in B} S^j / \sum_{i \in A} S^i$, we see that test T11 fails: we do not obtain the bilateral Fisher ideal quantity index on the right-hand side of (A12).

Exactness Properties

We first consider the two-country case, $K = 2$. In this case, when we have differentiable demand functions, using (A12), equations (13) reduce to the following single equation:

$$p^2 \cdot y^2/p^1 \cdot y^1 P_{GK}(p^1, p^2, y^1, y^2) = u_2/u_1,$$

or

$$c(p^2)u_2/c(p^1)u_1 P_{GK}[p^1, p^2, \nabla c(p^1)u_1, \nabla c(p^2)u_2] = u_2/u_1,$$

or

$$P_{GK}[p^1, p^2, \nabla c(p^1)u_1, \nabla c(p^2)u_2] = c(p^2)/c(p^1),$$

or

$$(A13) \quad \frac{\sum\limits_{n=1}^{N} p_n^2 c_n(p^1) c_n(p^2) u_1 u_2 / [c_n(p^1) u_1 + c_n(p^2) u_2]}{\sum\limits_{m=1}^{N} p_m^1 c_m(p^1) c_m(p^2) u_1 u_2 / [c_m(p^1) u_1 + c_m(p^2) u_2]} = \frac{c(p^2)}{c(p^1)}.$$

The left-hand side of (A13) is independent of u_1 and u_2 only if $c_n(p^1) = c_n(p^2)$ for $n = 1, 2, \ldots, N$ for all price vectors p^1 and p^2; that is, the first-order partial derivatives of the unit cost function $c(p)$ must be constant in order for (13) to hold. Hence, in the case of differentiable demand functions and only two countries, the unit cost function must be linear.

Now consider the two-country case with differentiable inverse demand functions. In this case, equations (12) reduce to the following single equation:

$$f(y^2) e_2 / f(y^1) e_1 P_{GK}[\nabla f(y^1) e_1, \ \nabla f(y^2) e_2, \ y^1, \ y^2] = f(y^2)/f(y^1),$$

or

$$y^{2T}[\hat{y}^1 + \hat{y}^2]^{-1} \hat{y}^1 \nabla f(y^2) e_2 / y^{2T}[\hat{y}^1 + \hat{y}^2]^{-1} \hat{y}^1 \nabla f(y^1) e_1 = e_2/e_1,$$

or

$$(A14) \quad y^{2T}[\hat{y}^1 + \hat{y}^2]^{-1} \hat{y}^1 [\nabla f(y^2) - \nabla f(y^1)] = 0.$$

For $n = 1, 2, \ldots, N$, set $y^1 = i_n$, the nth unit vector, and substitute into (A14). We find that we must have $f_n(y^2) = f_n(i_n)$ for all y^2 for $n = 1, \ldots, N$. Hence, the first-order partial derivatives of f are constant, and the only solution to (12) is the linear f defined by (17) in the two-country case.

Now consider the case where $K \geq 3$. In the case of differentiable demand functions, using (8) and (29), equations (13) reduce to

$$(A15) \quad \pi \cdot \nabla c(p^i) u_i / \pi \cdot \nabla c(p^j) u_j = u_i / u_j,$$

or

$$\pi \cdot [\nabla c(p^i) - \nabla c(p^j)] = 0 \quad \text{for } 1 \leq i, \ j \leq K.$$

Recall that the equations that define π are (27) and (28). Using (8), and letting $\hat{}$ denote the operation of diagonalizing a vector into a matrix, (27) is equivalent to

$$(A16) \quad \left\{ \sum_{m=1}^{K} \nabla \hat{c}(p^m) u_m - \sum_{m=1}^{K} [c(p^m)]^{-1} \hat{p}^m \nabla c(p^m) \nabla^T c(p^m) u_m \right\} \pi = 0_N.$$

To show that (A16) implies that $\nabla c(p^i) = \nabla c(p^j)$ for all p^i and p^j (and hence that c must be defined by [18]), we need show only that, by varying p^k (where k is not equal to i or j), we can find N linearly independent π^k that satisfy (A15). By examining (A16), we see that this can be done. If we let all the u_m in (A16) be close to zero except for u_k, then (A16) is approximately equivalent to the following system of equations:

$$\pi_n c_n(p^k)u_k - p_n^k c_n(p^k)\nabla c(p^k) \cdot \pi/c(p)u_k = 0, \quad n = 1,\ldots,N,$$

or

$$\pi_n = p_n^k \pi \cdot \nabla c(p^k)/c(p^k), \quad n = 1,\ldots,N.$$

Hence, π is proportional to p^k, and, by choosing N linearly independent p^k vectors, we can obtain N linearly independent π^k vectors.

For the case of differentiable inverse demand functions when $K \geq 3$, a proof of exactness in Diewert (1996, 257) can be adapted to the present situation to show that the differentiable linearly homogeneous aggregator function f must be the linear one defined by (17).

Proof of Proposition 5

T1: By the Perron-Frobenius theorem, the maximum eigenvalue right eigenvector s of the positive matrix D, subject to the normalization (36), is strictly positive and unique. Thus, s will be a continuous function of the elements of D and hence of the components of P and Y.

T2: Under the assumptions for this test, equations (39) become

$$S^i = \alpha\sum_{j=1}^{J} (\beta_i/\beta_j)S^j \quad \text{for } i = 1,\ldots,K.$$

Thus, $\alpha = 1/K$, $S^k = \beta_k$ for $k = 1,\ldots,K$, satisfy (36) and (39).

T3: Let $p >> 0_N$, $\alpha_k > 0$, $p^k = \alpha_k p$ for $k = 1,\ldots,K$. Equations (39) become

$$S^i = \alpha\sum_{j=1}^{K} (\alpha_j p \cdot y^i/\alpha_j p \cdot y^j)S^j \quad \text{for } i = 1,\ldots,K$$

or

$$S^i/p \cdot y^i = \alpha\sum_{j=1}^{k} S^j/p \cdot y^j \quad \text{for } i = 1,\ldots,K.$$

Hence, $\alpha \equiv 1/K$ and $S^k \equiv p \cdot y^k/p \cdot y$ will satisfy (36) and (39).

T4: From equations (36) and (39), s and α are determined by the elements of the matrix D. Since these elements are invariant to changes in the units of measurement, so are the elements of s.

T5: Since the elements of D remain unchanged if we change the ordering of the commodities, the elements of s will also remain unchanged.

T6: By examining equations (39), we see that changing the ordering of the countries simply changes the ordering of the elements of s and that the maximum positive eigenvalue of D remains unchanged by a simultaneous permutation of its rows and columns.

T9: For $K = 2$, equations (39) can be rewritten as follows:

$$1 = \alpha[1 + (p^2 \cdot y^1/p^2 \cdot y^2)(S^2/S^1)],$$

$$S^2/S^1 = \alpha[(p^1 \cdot p^2/p^1 \cdot y^1) + (S^2/S^1)].$$

Eliminating α from these two equations leads to the following single equation:

$$S^2/S^1 = [p^1 \cdot y^2 p^2 \cdot y^2/p^1 \cdot y^1 p^2 \cdot y^1]^{1/2} \equiv Q_F(p^1, \; p^2, \; y^1, \; y^2).$$

Note that $S^2/S^1 = Q_F(p^1, p^2, y^1, y^2)$ is increasing in the components of y^2 and decreasing in the components of y^1. Thus, for $K = 2$, monotonicity is satisfied.

However, for $K \geq 3$, monotonicity is not satisfied in general. The $K + 1$ equations that define the K-dimensional vector of shares s and the maximum positive eigenvalue λ of D are (recall [36] and [40] with $\lambda \equiv 1/\alpha$)

(A17) $$[D - \lambda I_K]s = 0_K, \quad 1_K \cdot s = 1,$$

where $d_{ij} \equiv p^j \cdot y^i/p^j \cdot y^j$ for $i, j = 1, \ldots, K$. Note that $d_{ii} = 1$ for all i. When $K = 3$, λ is the maximal root of the determinantal equation $|D - \lambda I_3| = 0$. Define $x \equiv 1 - \lambda$, and this determinantal equation becomes

$$x^3 - [d_{12}d_{21} + d_{31}d_{13} + d_{32}d_{23}]x + [d_{12}d_{23}d_{31} + d_{13}d_{21}d_{32}] = 0.$$

We need to find the smallest real root of this equation. In order to find an explicit solution, consider the case where $d_{13} = d_{23} = 0$. In this case, we find that $\lambda = 1 + [d_{12}d_{21}]^{1/2}$. Substitute this value for λ into (A17) when $K = 3$ to determine the components of $s \equiv [S^1, S^2, S^3]^T$:

(A18)
$$S^1 = (d_{21})^{1/2}d_{12}/D, \quad S^2 \equiv (d_{12})^{1/2}d_{21}/D,$$
$$S^3 \equiv [(d_{12})^{1/2}d_{31} + (d_{21})^{1/2}d_{32}]/D,$$

with $D \equiv (d_{21})^{1/2}d_{12} + (d_{12})^{1/2}d_{21} + (d_{12})^{1/2}d_{31} + (d_{21})^{1/2}d_{32} > 0$. By substituting $d_{ij} \equiv p^j \cdot y^i/p^j \cdot y^j$ into (A18) and differentiating S_1 with respect to the components of y^1, it can be verified that S^1 is not always increasing in the components of y^1.

T10: Part i is satisfied, but part ii is not.

T11: Substitute the assumptions of the test into equations (39). Then, for $i \in A$, (39) reduces to (A19), and, for $j \in B$, (39) reduces to (A20):

(A19)
$$S^i = \alpha\sum_{k \in A}(\alpha_k p^a \cdot \beta_k y^a)^{-1}\alpha_k p^a \cdot \beta_i y^a S^k$$
$$+ \; \alpha\sum_{j \in B}(\gamma_j p^b \cdot \delta_j y^b)^{-1}\gamma_j p^b \cdot \beta_i y^a S^j,$$

(A20)
$$S^j = \alpha\sum_{i \in A}(\alpha_i p^a \cdot \beta_i y^a)^{-1}\alpha_i p^a \cdot \gamma_j y^b S^i$$
$$+ \; \alpha\sum_{k \in B}(\gamma_k p^b \cdot \delta_k y^b)^{-1}\gamma_k p^b \cdot \delta_j y^b S^k.$$

Now let $S^i = \beta_i S^a$ for $i \in A$ and $S^j = \gamma_j S^b$ for $j \in B$. Substituting these equations into (A19) and (A20), we find that each equation in (A19) reduces to (A21) and that each equation in (A20) reduces to the single equation (A22):

(A21) $\quad S^a = \alpha(\#A)(p^a \cdot y^a/p^a \cdot y^a)S^a + \alpha(\#B)(p^b \cdot y^a/p^b \cdot y^b)S^b,$

(A22) $\quad S^b = \alpha(\#A)(p^a \cdot y^b/p^a \cdot y^a)S^a + \alpha(\#B)(p^b \cdot y^b/p^b \cdot y^b)S^b,$

where #A is the number of countries in A, and #B is the number of countries in B. Eliminating α from (A21) and (A22), we obtain the following single equation in S^b/S^a:

(A23) $\quad \beta(p^b \cdot y^a/p^b \cdot y^b)Q^2 + (1 - \beta)Q - (p^a \cdot y^b/p^a \cdot y^a) = 0,$

where $\beta \equiv \#B/\#A$ and $Q \equiv S^b/S^a$. If #A = #B and hence $\beta = 1$, the Q solution to (A23) reduces to $Q = Q_F(p^a, p^b, y^a, y^b) = S^b/S^a$. However, in general, the number of countries in each subbloc A and B is not restricted to be the same, so, in general, test T11 fails.

Exactness Properties

When $K = 2$, in the proof of T9, we established a result taken from Van Yzeren (1956, 15); namely, $S^2/S^1 = Q_F(p^1, p^2, y^1, y^2)$, the Fisher quantity index. Thus, (41) and (42) are exact for this method when $K = 2$.

For $K \geq 3$, replace S^j/S^i with $f(y^j)/f(y^i)$ and p^j with $\nabla f(y^j)e_j$ in equations (39). Letting $\lambda = 1/\alpha$, the transformed equations (39) become, using $y^k \cdot \nabla f(y^k) = f(y^k)$,

(A24) $\quad \sum_{k=1}^{K} [y^i \cdot \nabla f(y^k)e_k/f(y^k)e_k][f(y^k)/f(y^i)] = \lambda, \quad i = 1, \ldots, K,$

or

$$\sum_{K=1}^{k} y^i \cdot \nabla f(y^k)/f(y^i) = \lambda, \quad i = 1, \ldots, K.$$

Let $j \neq i$, and subtract equation j in (A24) from equation i. We obtain the following system of equations for $i \neq j$:

(A25) $\quad \sum_{k=1}^{K} \nabla f(y^k) \cdot \{[y^i/f(y^i)] - [y^j/f(y^j)]\} = 0.$

If f is the linear aggregator function defined by (17), it is easy to verify that this f satisfies (A25) (and [A24] with $\lambda = K$). For $K \geq 3$, I now show that this is the only solution to (A25).

Let f be linearly homogeneous, increasing, and once continuously differentiable, and let f satisfy (A25). *Suppose* that the first-order partial derivatives of f are not all constant. Then we can find two strictly positive vectors $y^{(1)}$ and $y^{(2)}$ such that $\nabla f_r(y^{(1)})$ and $\nabla f_r(y^{(2)})$ are linearly independent, nonnegative, and nonzero vectors. Pick commodities r and s such that the vectors $[f_r(y^{(1)}), f_s(y^{(1)})]$ and $[f_r(y^{(2)}), f_s(y^{(2)})]$ are linearly independent. Fix i and j with $i \neq j$, and choose $y_n^i = y_n^j$ for all n except when $n = r$ or $n = s$. For the r and s components of y^i and y^j, choose $y_r^i, y_s^i, y_r^j, y_s^j$ such that $f(y^i) = f(y^j)$ and

(A26)
$$\{y_r^j/f(y^j)\} - \{y_r^i/f(y_i)\} \equiv z_r > 0,$$
$$\{y_s^j/f(y^j)\} - \{y_s^i/f(y^i)\} \equiv z_s \leq 0.$$

Substitute these choices for y^i and y^j into (A25) to obtain

(A27)
$$\left[\sum_{k=1}^{K} f_r(y^k)\right]z_r + \left[\sum_{k=1}^{K} f_s(y^k)\right]z_s = 0.$$

Since $K \geq 3$, there exists a country k not equal to i or j. For such a k, replace y^k in (A27) by $y^{(1)}$ and then $y^{(2)}$. Rewrite the resulting two equations as

(A28) $x_{11}z_r + x_{12}z_s = 0, \quad x_{21}z_r + x_{22}z_s = 0.$

Note that the vectors $[x_{11}, x_{12}]$ and $[x_{21}, x_{22}]$ are equal to the linearly independent vectors $[f_r(y^{(1)}), f_s(y^{(1)})]$ and $[f_r(y^{(2)}), f_s(y^{(2)})]$ plus a common vector. Since the first-order partial derivatives are continuous, we can perturb $y^{(1)}$ and $y^{(2)}$ slightly if necessary to ensure the linear independence of $[x_{11}, x_{12}]$ and $[x_{21}, x_{22}]$. The linear independence of these two vectors and (A28) implies that $z_r = 0$ and $z_s = 0$, which contradicts (A26). Thus, the *supposition* that the first-order partial derivatives of f are not all constant leads to a contradiction.

I now determine what unit cost functions c are consistent with equations (39). Substituting (9) and (13) into (39) and letting $\lambda = 1/\alpha$ leads to the following system of functional equations:

$$\sum_{k=1}^{K} [p^k \cdot \nabla c(p^i)u_i/c(p^k)u_k][u_k/u_i] = \lambda \quad \text{for } i = 1,\dots, K,$$

or

(A29)
$$\sum_{k=1}^{K} p^k \cdot \nabla c(p^i)/c(p^k) = \lambda \quad \text{for } i = 1,\dots, K.$$

Let $j \neq i$, and subtract equation j in (A29) from equation i. We obtain the following system of equations for $1 \leq i \neq j \neq K$:

(A30)
$$\sum_{k=1}^{K} [p^{kT}/c(p^k)][\nabla c(p^i) - \nabla c(p^j)] = 0.$$

Since $K \geq 3$, there exists an m not equal to i or j. Choose $N p^m$ vectors, say p^{mn}, $n = 1, \dots, N$, such that the vectors $p^{mn}/c(p^{mn}) + \sum_{k=1,k\neq m}^{K}[p^k/c(p^k)]$, $n = 1$, $\dots, N$, are linearly independent. Substitute these p^{mn} into (A30), and we deduce that $\nabla c(p^i) = \nabla c(p^j)$ for all p^i and p^j. Hence, the first-order partial derivatives of c must be constants. Using the fact that c must be linearly homogeneous, we further deduce that c must be the linear unit cost function defined by (18).

Proof of Proposition 6

T1: By the Perron-Frobenius theorem, the maximum eigenvalue left eigen-vector, $[(S^1)^{-1}, \ldots ,(S^K)^{-1}]^T$, of the positive matrix D, subject to the normalization (46), is strictly positive and unique. Thus, $[(S^1)^{-1}, \ldots ,(S^K)^{-1}]$ and hence $[S^1, \ldots , S^K]$ will be continuous functions of the elements of D and hence of the components of P and Y.

T2: Let $y^k = \beta_k y$, $y >> 0_N$, $\beta_k > 0$ for $k = 1, \ldots , K$ with $\sum_{k=1}^K \beta_k = 1$. Equations (49) become

$$(S^i)^{-1} = \alpha \sum_{k=1}^K [\beta_k/\beta_i](S^k)^{-1}, \quad i = 1,\ldots, K.$$

Thus, $\alpha = 1/K$, $S^k = \beta_k$ satisfy (46) and (49).

T3: Let $p >> 0_n$, $\alpha_k > 0$, $p^k = \alpha_k p$ for $k = 1, \ldots , K$. Equations (49) become

$$(S^i)^{-1} = \alpha \sum_{k=1}^K [\alpha_i p \cdot y^k/\alpha_i p \cdot y^i](S^k)^{-1}, \quad i = 1,\ldots, K,$$

or

$$p \cdot y^i/S^i = \alpha \sum_{k=1}^K p \cdot y^k/S^k, \quad i = 1,\ldots, K.$$

Hence, $\alpha = 1/K$ and $S^k = p \cdot y^k/p \cdot \sum_{j=1}^K y^j$ will satisfy (46) and (49).

T4–T6: Similar to the proofs of T4–T6 in proposition 5.

T9: For $K = 2$, equations (49) can be written as follows:

$$1 = \alpha[1 + (p^1 \cdot y^2/p^1 \cdot y^1)(S^1/S^2)],$$

$$S^1/S^2 = \alpha[(p^2 \cdot y^1/p^2 \cdot y^2) + (S^1/S^2)].$$

Eliminating α from these two equations leads to $S^2/S^1 = Q_F(p^1, p^2, y^1, y^2)$. Thus, in the two-country case, Van Yzeren's unweighted average basket method leads to the Fisher ideal quantity index, which satisfies monotonicity in quantities. However, for $K \geq 3$, we can proceed as in the proof of T9 for proposition 5 and demonstrate that monotonicity does not always hold.

T10: Part i is satisfied, but part ii is not.

T11: The proof is analogous to the proof of T11 in proposition 5. If the number of countries in the subbloc A is equal to the number of countries in the subbloc B, then $\sum_{j \in B} S^j/\sum_{i \in A} S^i = Q_F(p^a, p^b, y^a, y^b)$, but, in general, this equality does not hold.

Exactness Properties

For $K = 2$, the exactness properties are the usual ones for the Fisher ideal quantity index (see the proof of proposition 5 above).

For $K \geq 3$, replace S^i/S^j by $f(y^i)/f(y^j)$ and p^j by $\nabla f(y^j)e_j$. Letting $\lambda = 1/\alpha$, the transformed equations (49) become

$$\sum_{k=1}^{K} [y^k \cdot \nabla f(y^i)e_i / f(y^i)e_i][f(y^i)/f(y^k)] = \lambda, \quad i = 1, \dots, K,$$

or

(A31) $$\sum_{k=1}^{K} y^k \cdot \nabla f(y^i)/f(y^k) = \lambda, \quad i = 1, \dots, K.$$

Let $j \neq i$, and subtract equation j in (A31) from equation i. We obtain the following system of functional equations for $i \neq j$:

(A32) $$\sum_{k=1}^{K} [y^{kT}/f(y^k)][\nabla f(y^i) - \nabla f(y^j)] = 0, \quad 1 \le i \neq j \le K.$$

This is the same system of functional equations as (A30) except that f replaces c and y^k replaces p^k. Thus, the only differentiable linearly homogeneous solution to (A31) is the linear aggregator function defined by (17).

Similarly, substituting (9) and (13) into (49) and letting $\lambda = 1/\alpha$ leads to the following system of functional equations:

$$\sum_{k=1}^{K} [p^i \cdot \nabla c(p^k)u_k / c(p^i)u_i][u_i/u_k] = \lambda, \quad i = 1, \dots, K,$$

or

(A33) $$\sum_{k=1}^{K} p^i \cdot \nabla c(p^k)/c(p^i) = \lambda, \quad i = 1, \dots, K.$$

Let $j \neq i$, and subtract equation j in (A33) from equation i. We obtain

(A34) $$\sum_{k=1}^{K} \nabla c(p^k) \cdot \{[p^i/c(p^i)] - [p^j/c(p^j)]\} = 0, \quad i \le i \neq j \le K.$$

The system (A34) is identical to (A25) except that c replaces f and p^k replaces y^k. Thus, as usual, we deduce that the only linearly homogeneous solution to (A34) is the Leontief unit cost function defined by (18).

Proof of Proposition 7

I restrict the domain of definition to strictly positive quantity vectors. Using the positivity test BT1 and the circularity test (52), we have, following Eichhorn (1978, 67),

(A35)
$$Q(p^1, p^2, y^1, y^2) = Q(p^0, p^2, y^0, y^2)/Q(p^0, p^1, y^0, y^1)$$
$$= h(p^2, y^2)/h(p^1, y^1),$$

where I fixed p^0 and y^0 and defined $h(p, y) \equiv Q(p^0, p, y^0, y)$. Now let $y^1 = y^2 = y$ in (A35), and, applying the identity test BT3, we find that $h(p^1, y) = h(p^2, y)$ for all $p^1 \gg 0$ and $p^2 \gg 0$, which means that $h(p, y)$ is independent of p. Defining $m(y) \equiv h(1_N, y)$, (A35) becomes

(A36) $Q(p^1, \ p^2, \ y^1, \ y^2) \ = \ m(y^2)/m(y^1).$

Now apply commensurability test BT10 to (A36) with $\delta_n \equiv y_n^1$ for $n = 1, \ldots,$ N. We obtain

(A37) $m(y^2)/m(y^1) \ = \ m[(y_1^1)^{-1}y_1^2, \ldots, (y_N^1)^{-1}y_N^2]/m(1_N).$

Define $g(x_1, \ldots, x_N) \equiv m(1_N)/m(x_1^{-1}, \ldots, x_N^{-1})$, and (A37) becomes the functional equation (A7), with N replacing K. Note that the monotonicity in quantities test BT12 implies that m and g are strictly increasing functions. Hence, we may apply Eichhorn's (1978, 66–68) theorem (noting that $g[1_N] = 1$) and conclude that

(A38) $m(y_1, \ldots, y_N) \ = \ \beta y_1^{\alpha_1} \ldots y_N^{\alpha_N}.$

Setting $y^1 = y^2 = 1_N$ in (A37) and using BT3 implies that $[m(1_N)]^2 = 1$. Using BT1, $m(1_N) = 1$, and, hence, the β in (A38) must equal one. The monotonicity test BT12 implies that each α_n is positive, and the linear homogeneity test BT5 implies that the α_n sum to one.

Proof of Proposition 8

T1: Using (58), BT1, and BT2, it is evident that T1 is satisfied.
T2: Let $y \gg 0_N$, $\beta_k > 0$, $y^k = \beta_k y$ for $k = 1, \ldots, K$ with $\sum_{k=1}^{K}\beta_k = 1$. Then

$$Q(p^i, \ p^k, \ y^i, \ y^k) \ = \ Q(p^i, \ p^k, \ \beta_i y, \ \beta_k y)$$

$$= \ (\beta_k/\beta_i)Q(p^i, \ p^k, \ y, \ y) \quad \text{using BT5 and BT6}$$

$$= \ \beta_k/\beta_i \quad \text{using BT3.}$$

Substituting the above into (58), we obtain $S_k^G = \beta_k \alpha/[\beta_1 \ldots \beta_K]^{1/K}$ for $k = 1, \ldots, K$. Thus, $\alpha \equiv [\beta_1 \ldots \beta_K]^{1/K}$, and $S_k^G = \beta_k$, as required.
T3: Let $p \gg 0_N$, $\alpha_k > 0$, $p^k = \alpha_k p$ for $k = 1, \ldots, K$. Then

$$Q(p^i, \ p^k, \ y^i, \ y^k) \ = \ Q(\alpha_i p, \ \alpha_k p, \ y^i, \ y^k)$$

$$= \ Q(p, \ p, \ y^i, \ y^k) \quad \text{using BT7 and BT8}$$

$$= \ p \cdot y^k/p \cdot y^i \quad \text{using BT4.}$$

Substituting the above into (58), we obtain

$$S_k^G \ = \ \alpha\left[\prod_{i=1}^{K} p \cdot y_k/p \cdot y^i\right]^{1/K}$$

$$= \ \alpha p \cdot y^k/[p \cdot y^1 \ldots p \cdot y^K]^{1/K} \quad \text{for } k = 1, \ldots, K.$$

Thus, S_k^G is proportional to $p \cdot y^k$, and T3 is satisfied.
T4: This test follows using (58) and BT10.

T5: This test follows using (58) and BT9.

T6: This test follows from the symmetrical nature of (58).

T7: Let $\alpha_k > 0$ for $k = 1, \ldots, K$. Consider equations (58) when p^k is replaced by $\alpha_k p^k$ for $k = 1, \ldots, K$:

$$S_k^G(\alpha_1 p^1, \ldots, \alpha_K p^K, Y) = \alpha \left[\prod_{i=1}^{K} Q(\alpha_i p^i, \alpha_k p^k, y^i, y^k) \right]^{1/K}$$

$$= \alpha \left[\prod_{i=1}^{K} Q(p^i, p^k, y^i, y^k) \right]^{1/K} \quad \text{using BT7 and BT8}$$

$$= S_k^G(p^1, \ldots, p^K, Y).$$

T8: Let $\lambda > 0$, and use (58) to obtain a formula for the following share ratio:

$$S_1^G(P, \lambda y^1, y^2, \ldots, y^K) / S_2^G(P, \lambda y^1, y^2, \ldots, y^K)$$

$$= \frac{\left[Q(p^1, p^1, \lambda y^1, \lambda y^1) \prod_{i=2}^{K} Q(p^i, p^1, y^i, \lambda y^1) \right]^{1/K}}{\left[Q(p^1, p^2, \lambda y^1, y^2) \prod_{j=2}^{K} Q(p^j, p^2, y^j, y^2) \right]^{1/K}}$$

$$= \left[\lambda^{K-1} \prod_{i=1}^{K} Q(p^i, p^1, y^i, y^1) / \lambda^{-1} \prod_{j=1}^{K} Q(p^j, p^2, y^j, y^2) \right]^{1/K} \quad \text{using BT5 and BT6}$$

$$= \lambda S_1^G(P, y^1, y^2, \ldots, y^K) / S_2^G(P, y^1, y^2, \ldots, y^K).$$

The proof for the other share ratios follows in an analogous manner.

T9: Using (58), BT3, BT12, and BT13, we see that, if any component of y^k increases, S_k^G/α increases, and the other S_j^G/α decrease. Hence, using (54), S_k^G will increase as any component of y^k increases.

T10i: Under the hypotheses of the test, for $k \in A$, we have, using (58),

$$S_k^G = \alpha \left[\prod_{i=1}^{K} Q(p^i, p^k, y^i, y^k) \right]^{1/K}$$

$$= \alpha \left[\prod_{i \in A} Q(\alpha_i p^a, \alpha_k p^a, \beta_i y^a, \beta_k y^a) \prod_{j \in B} Q(p^j, \alpha_k p^a, y^j, \beta_k y^a) \right]^{1/K}$$

$$= \alpha \left[\prod_{i \in A} (\beta_k/\beta_i) Q(p^a, p^a, y^a, y^a) \prod_{j \in B} Q(p^j, p^a, y^j, y^a) \right]^{1/K} \quad \text{using BT5–BT8}$$

$$= \beta_k \alpha \left[\prod_{j \in B} Q(p^j, p^a, y^j, y^a) \Big/ \prod_{i \in A} \beta_i \right]^{1/K} \quad \text{using BT3.}$$

Therefore, for $i \in A, j \in A$, we have $S_i^G/S_j^G = \beta_i/\beta_j$. Hence, part i of T10 passes. However, part ii fails.

T11: Under the conditions of the test, for $i \in A$, using (58), we have

$$S_i^G = \alpha \left[\prod_{k=1}^{K} Q(p^k, p^i, y^k, y^i) \right]^{1/K}$$

$$= \alpha \left[\prod_{k \in A} Q(\alpha_k p, \alpha_i p, \beta_k y^a, \beta_i y^a) \prod_{m \in B} Q(\gamma_m p^b, \alpha_i p^a, \delta_m y^b, \beta_i y^a) \right]^{1/K}$$

(A39)

$$= \alpha \beta_i \left[\prod_{k \in A} \beta_k^{-1} \prod_{m \in B} \delta_m^{-1} Q(p^b, p^a, y^b, y^a) \right]^{1/K} \quad \text{using BT3 and BT5–BT8}$$

$$= \beta_i \alpha \left[\prod_{k \in A} \beta_k^{-1} \right] \left[\prod_{m \in B} \delta_m^{-1} \right] Q(p^b, p^a, y^b, y^a)^{\#B/K},$$

where $\#B$ is the number of countries in the set of countries B. For $j \in B$, we have

$$S_j^G = \alpha \left[\prod_{k=1}^{K} Q(p^k, p^j, y^k, y^j) \right]^{1/K}$$

$$= \alpha \left[\prod_{k \in A} Q(\alpha_k p^a, \gamma_j p^b, \beta_k y^a, \delta_j y^b) \prod_{m \in B} Q(\gamma_m p^b, \gamma_j p^b, \gamma_m y^b, \delta_j y^b) \right]^{1/K}$$

(A40)

$$= \alpha \delta_j \left[\prod_{i \in A} \beta_k^{-1} Q(p^a, p^b, y^a, y^b) \prod_{m \in B} \delta_m^{-1} \right]^{1/K} \quad \text{using BT3 and BT5–BT8}$$

$$= \delta_j \alpha \left[\prod_{k \in A} \beta_k^{-1} \right] \left[\prod_{m \in B} \delta_m^{-1} \right] Q(p^a, p^b, y^a, y^b)^{\#A/K}.$$

Using $\sum_{i \in A} \beta_i = 1$, $\sum_{j \in B} \delta_j = 1$, (A39), and (A40), we find

$$\sum_{j \in B} S_j^G \Big/ \sum_{i \in A} S_i^G = Q(p^a, p^b, y^a, y^b)^{\#A/K} / Q(p^b, p^a, y^b, y^a)^{\#B/K}$$

$$= Q(p^a, p^b, y^a, y^b)^{[(\#A)+(\#B)]/K} \quad \text{using BT12}$$

$$= Q(p^a, p^b, y^a, y^b) \quad \text{since } (\#A) + (\#B) = K.$$

Exactness Properties of the Gini-EKS System

Using (58) with $Q = Q_F$, the system of functional equations (12) becomes, for $1 \le i \ne j \le K$,

$$\prod_{k=1}^{K} Q_F[\nabla f(y^K) e_k, \nabla f(y^i) e_i, y^k, y^i] \Big/ \prod_{m=1}^{K} Q_F[\nabla f(y^m) e_m, \nabla f(y^j) e_j, y^m, y^j]$$

(A41)
$$= [f(y^i)/f(y^j)]^K.$$

If f is the homogeneous quadratic defined by (41), then it is known (for references to the literature, see Diewert [1976, 116]) that

(A42) $Q_F[\nabla f(y^k) e_k, \nabla f(y^i) e_i, y^k, y^i] = f(y^i)/f(y^k)$ for all i and k.

Substituting (A42) into (A41) leads to the identity

$$[f(y^i)/f(y^j)]^K = [f(y^i)/f(y^j)]^K.$$

Hence, the Gini-EKS system is exact for the f defined by (41) and hence is a superlative system.

A similar proof shows that the unit cost function $c(p) \equiv (p^T B p)^{1/2}$ defined by (42) satisfies the system of functional equations (13) when the country shares are defined by (58) and $Q = Q_F$. The counterpart to (A42) that we require is

(A43) $Q_F[p^k, \ p^i, \ \nabla c(p^k) u_k, \ \nabla c(p^i) u_i] \ = \ u_i / u_k$ for all i and k.

To establish (A43), use a result in Diewert (1976, 133–34) with $r = 2$.

Proof of Proposition 9

T1: Using (67), BT1, and BT2, it is evident that T1 is satisfied.

T2: Using BT3, BT5, and BT6, and substituting into (67), we obtain

$$S^i \ = \ \alpha \left[\sum_{k=1}^{K} (\beta_k / \beta_i) \right]^{-1} \ = \ \alpha \beta_i, \quad i \ = \ 1, \ldots, K.$$

Thus, $\alpha = 1$, and $S^i = \beta_i$, as required.

T3: Using BT4, BT7, and BT8, and substituting into (67), we obtain

$$S^i \ = \ \alpha \left[\sum_{k=1}^{K} p \cdot y^k / p \cdot y^i \right]^{-1} \ = \ p \cdot y^i \alpha \left/ \left[\sum_{k=1}^{K} p \cdot y^k \right] \right., \quad i \ = \ 1, \ldots, K.$$

Thus, S^i is proportional to $p \cdot y^i$, and T3 is satisfied.

T4: This follows from (67) and BT10.

T5: This follows from (67) and BT9.

T6: This is obvious from the symmetry of (67).

T7: Use BT7 and BT8 to establish this property.

T9: Using (67), BT3, BT12, and BT13, we see that, if any component of y^i increases, S^i / α increases, and the other S^j / α decrease. Hence, S^i will increase as any component of y^i increases.

T10i: Using (67), for $i \in A$, we have

$$S^i = \alpha \left[\sum_{k=1}^{K} Q(p^k, \ p^i, \ y^k, \ y^i)^{-1} \right]^{-1}$$

$$= \alpha \left[\sum_{k \in A} Q(\alpha_k p^a, \ \alpha_i p^a, \ \beta_k y^a, \ \beta_i y^a)^{-1} + \sum_{k \in B} Q(p^k, \ \alpha_i p^a, \ y^k, \ \beta_i y^a)^{-1} \right]^{-1}$$

$$= \alpha \left[\sum_{k \in A} (\beta_k / \beta_i) Q(p^a, \ p^a, \ y^a, \ y^a)^{-1} + \sum_{k \in B} \beta_i^{-1} Q(p^k, \ p^a, \ y^k, \ y^a)^{-1} \right]^{-1}$$

$$\text{using BT5–BT8}$$

$$= \beta_i \alpha \left[1 + \sum_{k \in B} Q(p^k, \ p^a, \ y^k, \ y^a)^{-1} \right]^{-1} \quad \text{using BT3 and } \sum_{k \in A} \beta_k \ = \ 1.$$

Therefore, for i and j belonging to A, we have $S^i/S^j = \beta_i/\beta_j$, which establishes part i.

T10ii: To establish part ii, let $i \in B$. Using (67),

$$S^i = \alpha \left[\sum_{k=1}^{K} Q(p^k,\ p^i,\ y^k,\ y^i)^{-1} \right]^{-1}$$

$$= \alpha \left[\sum_{k \in A} Q(\alpha_k p^a,\ p^i,\ \beta_k y^a,\ y^i)^{-1} + \sum_{k \in B} Q(p^k,\ p^i,\ y^k,\ y^i)^{-1} \right]^{-1}$$

$$= \alpha \left[\sum_{k \in A} \beta_k Q(p^a,\ p^i,\ y^a,\ y^i)^{-1} + \sum_{k \in B} Q(p^k,\ p^i,\ y^k,\ y^i)^{-1} \right]^{-1}$$

using BT6 and BT8

$$= \alpha \left[Q(p^a,\ p^i,\ y^a,\ y^i)^{-1} + \sum_{k \in B} Q(p^k,\ p^i,\ y^k,\ y^i)^{-1} \right]^{-1}$$

using $\sum_{k \in A} \beta_k = 1$

$$= \alpha S^{i*}.$$

T11: Making the assumptions for T11, and using (67), for $i \in A$ we have

$$S^i = \alpha \left[\sum_{k=1}^{K} Q(p^k,\ p^i,\ y^k,\ y^i)^{-1} \right]^{-1}$$

(A44)
$$= \alpha \left[\sum_{k \in A} Q(\alpha_k p^a,\ \alpha_i p^a,\ \beta_k y^a,\ \beta_i y^a)^{-1} + \sum_{k \in B} Q(\gamma_k p^b,\ \alpha_i p^a,\ \delta_k y^b,\ \beta_i y^a)^{-1} \right]^{-1}$$

$$= \alpha \left[\sum_{k \in A} (\beta_k/\beta_i) Q(p^a,\ p^a,\ y^a,\ y^a)^{-1} + \sum_{k \in B} (\delta_k/\beta_i) Q(p^b,\ p^a,\ y^b,\ y^a)^{-1} \right]^{-1}$$

using BT5–BT8

$$= \beta_i \alpha [1 + Q(p^b,\ p^a,\ y^b,\ y^a)^{-1}]^{-1} \quad \text{using BT3, } \sum_{k \in A} \beta_k = 1, \text{ and } \sum_{k \in B} \delta_k = 1.$$

Similarly, for $j \in B$ we have

$$S^j = \alpha \left[\sum_{k=1}^{K} Q(p^k,\ p^j,\ y^k,\ y^j)^{-1} \right]^{-1}$$

(A45)
$$= \alpha \left[\sum_{k \in A} Q(\alpha_k p^a,\ \gamma_j p^b,\ \beta_k y^a,\ \delta_j y^b)^{-1} + \sum_{k \in B} Q(\gamma_k p^b,\ \gamma_j p^b,\ \delta_k y^b,\ \delta_j y^b)^{-1} \right]^{-1}$$

$$= \alpha \left[\sum_{k \in A} (\beta_k/\delta_j) Q(p^a,\ p^b,\ y^a,\ y^b)^{-1} + \sum_{k \in B} (\delta_k/\delta_j) Q(p^b,\ p^b,\ y^b,\ y^b)^{-1} \right]^{-1}$$

$$= \delta_j \alpha [Q(p^a,\ p^b,\ y^a,\ y^b)^{-1} + 1]^{-1}.$$

Using (A44), (A45), $\sum_{i \in A} \beta_i = 1$, and $\sum_{j \in B} \delta_j = 1$, we have

$$\sum_{j \in B} S^j(P, Y) \Big/ \sum_{i \in A} S^i(P, Y)$$

$$= [1 + Q(p^b, p^a, y^b, y^a)^{-1}]/[1 + Q(p^a, p^b, y^a, y^b)^{-1}]$$

$$= [1 + Q(p^a, p^b, y^a, y^b)]/[1 + Q(p^a, p^b, y^a, y^b)^{-1}] \quad \text{using BT11}$$

$$= Q(p^a, p^b, y^a, y^b)$$

since $(1 + \beta)/(1 + \beta^{-1}) = \beta$, where $\beta \equiv Q(p^a, p^b, y^a, y^b)$.

Exactness Properties of the Fisher Own Share System

Using (67) with $Q = Q_F$, the system of functional equations (12) becomes for $1 \le i \ne j \le K$

$$\frac{\left\{ \sum_{k=1}^{K} Q_F[\nabla f(y^k)e_k, \nabla f(y^i)e_i, y^k, y^i]^{-1} \right\}^{-1}}{\left\{ \sum_{m=1}^{K} Q_F[\nabla f(y^m)e_m, \nabla f(y^j)e_j, y^m, y^j]^{-1} \right\}^{-1}} = f(y^i)/f(y^j).$$

Substituting (A42) into the equations given above leads to the following system of equations for $1 \le i \ne j \le K$:

$$\left[\sum_{k=1}^{K} f(y^k)/f(y^i) \right]^{-1} \Big/ \left[\sum_{m=1}^{K} f(y^m)/f(y^j) \right]^{-1} = f(y^i)/f(y^j).$$

which is a system of identities. Hence, the f defined by (41) is exact for the Gini-EKS system.

Turning now to the system of functional equations (13), substituting (67) into these equations with $Q \equiv Q_F$ leads to the following system of equations for $1 \le i \ne j \le K$:

$$\frac{\left\{ \sum_{k=1}^{K} Q_F[p^k, p^i, \nabla c(p^i)u_k, \nabla c(p^i)u_i]^{-1} \right\}^{-1}}{\left\{ \sum_{m=1}^{K} Q_F[p^m, p^j, \nabla c(p^m)u_m, \nabla c(p^j)u_j]^{-1} \right\}^{-1}} = u_i u_j.$$

Substituting (A43) into the equations given above leads to the system of identities

$$\left[\sum_{k=1}^{K} u_k/u_i \right]^{-1} \Big/ \left[\sum_{m=1}^{K} u_m/u_j \right]^{-1} = u_i/u_j.$$

Hence, the c defined by (42) is exact for the Gini-EKS system.

Proof of Proposition 10

T1: The proof of existence and continuity of the share functions is somewhat involved. Consider the minimization problem (71). If we set $S_K = 1$ and solve the resulting minimization problem in $S_1, \ldots, S_{K-1}$, we can normalize the solution to satisfy (73). Denote the objective function in (71) with $S_K = 1$ by $f(S_1, \ldots, S_{K-1})$. Denote $Q(p^j, p^k, y^j, y^k)$ by Q_{jk} for $1 \leq j, k \leq K$. Note that BT1 implies that $Q_{jk} > 0$. The first-order necessary conditions for my $S_K = 1$ modification of (71) are

$$(A46) \quad \sum_{j=1}^{K-1} [Q_{ij}/S_j^*] - \sum_{k=1}^{K-1} [Q_{ki}S_k^*/S_i^{*2}] - Q_{Ki}/S_i^{*2} = -Q_{iK}, \quad i = 1, \ldots, K-1.$$

The arguments of Van Yzeren (1956, 25–26) can be adapted to show that a unique positive $S_1^*, \ldots, S_{K-1}^*$ solution to (A46) exists. I now show that the matrix of second-order partial derivatives of f evaluated at the solution, $\nabla^2 f$ $(S_1^*, \ldots, S_{K-1}^*) \equiv [f_{ij}(S_1^*, \ldots, S_{K-1}^*)]$, is positive definite. Differentiating the left-hand side of (A46) with respect to S_j, we obtain the following expressions for the second-order partial derivatives of f:

$$(A47) \quad f_{ii}(S_1, \ldots, S_{K-1}) = 2 \sum_{k=1, k \neq i}^{K-1} [Q_{ki}S_k/S_i^3] + 2Q_{Ki}/S_i^3, \quad i = 1, \ldots, K-1.$$

$$(A48) \quad f_{ij}(S_1, \ldots, S_{K-1}) = -[Q_{ij}/S_j^2] - [Q_{ji}/S_i^2], \quad 1 \leq i \neq j \leq K-1.$$

Use the ith equation in (A46) to solve for $\sum_{k=1, k \neq i}^{K-1} Q_{ki}S_k^*/S_i^{*2}$, and substitute the resulting expression into the right-hand side of (A47). Using the resulting equation and equations (A48) evaluated at $S_1^*, \ldots, S_{K-1}^*$, we find that

$$(A49) \quad \sum_{j=1}^{K-1} f_{ij}(S_1^*, \ldots, S_K^*)S_j^* = Q_{iK} + Q_{Ki}/S_i^{*2} > 0, \quad i = 1, \ldots, K-1,$$

where the inequalities in (A49) follow from the positivity of the Q_{ij}. The positivity of the Q_{ij} also implies via (A47) that $f_{ii}(S_1^*, \ldots, S_{K-1}^*) > 0$ for $i = 1, \ldots, K-1$ and that $f_{ij}(S_1^*, \ldots, S_{K-1}^*) < 0$ for $1 \leq i \neq j \leq K-1$. Since the S_i^* are all positive, the inequalities (A49) imply that the matrix $\nabla^2 f(S_1^*, \ldots, S_{K-1}^*)$ is *dominant diagonal* (for a definition, see Gale and Nikaido [1965, 84]). Note also that $\nabla^2 f(S_1^*, \ldots, S_{K-1}^*)$ has positive main diagonal elements and negative off-diagonal elements and hence is what Gale and Nikaido (1965, 86) call a *Leontief-type matrix*. Thus, the matrix $\nabla^2 f(S_1^*, \ldots, S_{K-1}^*)$ is a dominant diagonal Leontief-type matrix, and, by the result noted by Gale and Nikaido (1965, 86), this matrix is a *P*-matrix; that is, all its principle submatrices have positive determinants. In particular, the determinant of $\nabla^2 f(S_1^*, \ldots, S_{K-1}^*)$ is positive, and hence the inverse matrix $[\nabla^2 f(S_1^*, \ldots, S_{K-1}^*)]^{-1}$ exists. (For later reference, by another result in Gale and Nikaido [1965, 86], all the elements in this inverse matrix are positive.) Since the $Q_{ij} \equiv Q(p^i, p^j, y^i, y^j)$ are once continuously differentiable functions of their arguments by assumption, and using the fact that $[\nabla^2 f(S_1^*, \ldots, S_{K-1}^*)]^{-1}$ exists, we can apply the implicit function theorem (see Rudin 1953, 177–82) to the system of equations (A46) to obtain the continuity (and once continuous differentiability) of the solution functions $S_i^*(P, Y)$ with respect to the elements of the matrices P and Y.

T2: Substituting the assumptions of the test into (72) and using BT3, BT5, and BT6 yields the following system of equations:

$$\sum_{j=1}^{K} (\beta_j/\beta_i)(S_i/S_j) = \sum_{k=1}^{K} (\beta_i/\beta_k)(S_k/S_i), \quad i = 1, \ldots, K.$$

Obviously, the unique solution to this system of equations that also satisfies the normalization (73) is $S_k = \beta_k$ for $k = 1, \ldots, K$.

T3: Substituting the assumptions of the test into (72) and using BT4, BT7, and BT8 yields the following system of equations:

$$\sum_{j=1}^{K} (p \cdot y^j/p \cdot y^i)(S_i/S_j) = \sum_{k=1}^{K} (p \cdot y^i/p \cdot y^k)(S_k/S_i), \quad i = 1, \ldots, K.$$

Obviously, the solution ray to this system of equations is $S_k = \alpha p \cdot y^k, k = 1, \ldots, K, \alpha > 0$. Using the normalization (73) picks a unique point on this solution ray and demonstrates that test T3 is satisfied.

T4: This test follows from (72) and BT10.

T5: This test follows from (72) and BT9.

T6: This test follows from the symmetrical nature of equations (72) and (73).

T7: This test follows using BT7 and BT8.

T8: Let $S_1^*, \ldots, S_K^*$ be the solution to (72) and (73) when we have price vectors p^k and quantity vectors y^k for $k = 1, \ldots, K$. For $\lambda > 0$, change y^1 into λy^1. Using BT5 and BT6, it is easy to show that $\lambda S_1^*, S_2^*, \ldots, S_K^*$ will satisfy equations (72) with y^1 replaced everywhere by λy^1 (the λ factors cancel out, leaving the original system of equations). An analogous property holds if y^2 is replaced by λy^2 etc.

T9: Consider the minimization problem (71) when we set $S_K = 1$. Denote the remaining shares as $S_1^*(P, Y), \ldots, S_{K-1}^*(P, Y)$. Using the results established in the proof of T1, and differentiating equations (A46) with respect to the components of y^K, we obtain the following formula for the derivatives of the S_i^* with respect to the components of y^K for $i = 1, 2, \ldots, K - 1$:

$$\nabla_{y^K} S_i^*(P, Y) = \sum_{j=1}^{K-1} e_i^T[\nabla^2 f(S_1^*, \ldots, S_{K-1}^*)]^{-1} e_j[-\nabla_{y^K} Q(p^j, p^K, y^j, y^K)$$

$$+ (S_j^*)^{-2} \nabla_{y^K} Q(p^K, p^j, y^K, y^j)],$$

where e_i is the *i*th unit vector of dimension $K - 1$. From the proof of T1, the $K - 1 \times K - 1$ matrix $[\nabla^2 f(S_1^*, \ldots, S_{K-1}^*)]^{-1}$ has all elements positive. Using BT12, the vector of derivatives $\nabla_{y^K} Q(p^i, p^K, y^i, y^K)$ is nonnegative and positive almost everywhere. Using BT13, the vector of derivatives $\nabla_{y^K} Q(p^K, p^i, y^K, y^i)$ is nonpositive and negative almost everywhere. Hence, the vector of derivatives $\nabla_{y^K} S_i^*(P, Y)$ is nonpositive and negative almost everywhere. Thus, S_i^* (P, Y) is decreasing in the components of y^K for $i = 1, 2, \ldots, K - 1$. Switching now to the model that uses the normalization (73), we see that the results presented above imply that $S_K(P, Y)$ is increasing in the components of y^K. Using

74 **W. Erwin Diewert**

the symmetry of equations (72) and (73), this suffices to establish that each $S_k(P, Y)$ is increasing in the components of y^k for $k = 1, \ldots, K$.

T10i: Under the assumptions for the test, for $i \in A$ equations (72) become

$$\sum_{k \in A} (\beta_k/\beta_i)(S_i/S_k) + \sum_{k \in B} \beta_i^{-1} Q(p^a, \ p^k, \ y^a, \ y^k) S_i/S_k$$

$$= \sum_{k \in A} (\beta_k/\beta_k) S_k/S_i + \sum_{k \in B} \beta_i Q(p^k, \ p^a, \ y^k, \ y^a) S_k/S_i,$$

where I have used BT3 and BT5–BT8. For $k \in A$, set $S_k = \beta_k S_a$. Then the equations given above become for $i \in A$

$$(A50) \quad \begin{aligned} (\# A) + \sum_{k \in B} Q(p^a, \ p^k, \ y^a, \ y^k) S_a/S_k \\ = (\# A) + \sum_{k \in B} Q(p^k, \ p^a, \ y^k, \ y^a) S_k/S_a. \end{aligned}$$

Note that equations (A50) do not depend on i. Thus, there is only one independent equation in (A50). For $j \in B$, equations (72) become (assuming that $S_k = \beta_k S_a$ for $k \in A$)

$$(A51) \quad \begin{aligned} (\# A) Q(p^j, \ p^a, \ y^j, \ y^a) S_j/S_a + \sum_{k \in B} Q(p^j, \ p^k, \ y^j, \ y^k) S_j/S_k \\ = (\# A) Q(p^a, \ p^j, \ y^a, \ y^j) S_a/S_j + \sum_{k \in B} Q(p^k, \ p^j, \ y^k, \ y^j) S_k/S_j. \end{aligned}$$

Equation (A50) and equations (A51) for $j \in B$ along with the normalizing equation $S_a + \sum_{k \in B} S_k = 1$ can be solved for S_a and S_j for $j \in B$. Once S_a has been determined, we have $S_i \equiv \beta_i S_a$ for $i \in A$, and part i of T10 holds.

T10ii: However, equations (A51) show that part ii of T10 does not hold; note that the factor $\#A \equiv$ the number of countries in the subbloc A.

T11: Substitute the assumptions of test T11 into equations (72). For $i \in A$, let $S_i = \beta_i S_a$, and, for $j \in B$, let $S_j = \delta_j S_b$. For $i \in A$, each of these equations in (72) reduces to

$$(A52) \quad \begin{aligned} (\# A) + (\# B) Q(p^a, \ p^b, \ y^a, \ y^b) S_a/S_b \\ = (\# A) + (\# B) Q(p^b, \ p^a, \ y^b, \ y^a) S_b/S_a, \end{aligned}$$

where we have used BT3 and BT5–BT8. For $j \in B$, each of these equations in (72) reduces to

$$(A53) \quad \begin{aligned} (\# A) Q(p^b, \ p^a, \ y^b, \ y^a) S_b/S_a + (\# B) \\ = (\# A) Q(p^a, \ p^b, \ y^a, \ y^b) S_a/S_b + (\# B). \end{aligned}$$

Both of the equations (A52) and (A53) simplify to

$$(A54) \quad \begin{aligned} \sum_{j \in B} S_j \Big/ \sum_{i \in A} S_i = S_b/S_a = [Q(p^a, \ p^b, \ y^a, \ y^b)/Q(p^b, \ p^a, \ y^b, \ y^a)]^{1/2} \\ = Q(p^a, \ p^b, \ y^a, \ y^b), \end{aligned}$$

where (A54) follows from the line above if Q satisfies the bilateral time reversal test BT11. Note that this is the only part of the proof where test BT11 is used. If Q is equal to either the Paasche Q_P or the Laspeyres Q_L quantity index, then it can be verified that these two indexes satisfy all the bilateral tests except BT11. However, if either $Q = Q_L$ or $Q = Q_P$ is inserted into (A54), we find that $S_b/S_a = Q_F(p^a, p^b, y^a, y^b)$, the Fisher ideal index. Thus, if $Q = Q_L$ or Q_P, all multilateral tests except T10 and T12 are satisfied.

Exactness Properties of the Unweighted Balanced Method

For $Q = Q_F$, substituting (10), (12), and (A42) into (72) leads to the following equations for $i = 1, \ldots, K$:

$$\sum_{j=1}^{K}[f(y^j)/f(y^i)][f(y^i)/f(y^j)] = \sum_{k=1}^{K}[f(y^i)/f(y^k)][f(y^k)/f(y^i)],$$

which is a system of identities. Hence, the homogeneous quadratic f defined by (41) is exact for this method. Similarly, for $Q = Q_F$, substituting (9), (13), and (A42) into (72) leads to the following equations for $i = 1, \ldots, K$:

$$\sum_{j=1}^{K}[u_j/u_i][u_i/u_j] = \sum_{k=1}^{K}[u_i/u_k][u_k/u_i],$$

which is a system of identities. Hence, the homogeneous quadratic unit cost function defined by (42) is also exact for the unweighted balanced method when $Q = Q_F$.

For $Q = Q_L(p^i, p^j, y^i, y^j) \equiv p^i \cdot y^j/p^i \cdot y^i$, the Laspeyres quantity index, equations (72) become

$$\sum_{j=1}^{K}(p^i \cdot y^j/p^i \cdot y^i)(S_i/S_j) = \sum_{k=1}^{K}(p^k \cdot y^i/p^k \cdot y^k)(S_k/S_i),$$

(A55)
$$i = 1, \ldots, K.$$

Substituting (10) and (12) into (A55) and letting f be defined by (41) lead to the following system of equations:

(A56) $$\sum_{j=1}^{K}[y^{iT}Ay^j/f(y^i)f(y^j)] = \sum_{k=1}^{K}[y^{kT}Ay^i/f(y^i)f(y^k)], \quad i = 1, \ldots, K,$$

where I have used $\nabla f(y^i) = Ay^i/f(y^i)$. Since $A = A^T$, it can be verified that (A56) is a system of identities.

Substituting (9) and (13) into (A55), letting c be defined by (42), and using $\nabla c(p^i) = Bp^i/c(p^i)$ lead to

(A57) $$\sum_{j=1}^{K}[p^{iT}Bp^j/c(p^i)c(p^j)] = \sum_{k=1}^{K}[p^{kT}Bp^i/c(p^i)/c(p^k)], \quad i = 1, \ldots, K.$$

Using $B = B^T$, it can be verified that (A57) is a system of identities.

The use of $Q = Q_P$ in (72) where $Q_P(p^i, p^j, y^i, y^j) \equiv p^j \cdot y^j/p^j \cdot y^i)$ corresponds to Gerardi's (1974) version of the unweighted balanced method (see also Van Ijzeren 1983, 45–46). Hence, the identities (A56) and (A57) show that this version of the unweighted balanced method is exact for the homogeneous quadratic aggregator function defined by (41) and is also exact for the homogeneous quadratic unit cost function defined by (42). Hence, when $Q = Q_P$, the unweighted balanced method is superlative.

Suppose now that $Q = Q_L$ where $Q_L(p^i, p^j, y^i, y^j) \equiv p^i \cdot y^j / p^i \cdot y^i$ is the Laspeyres bilateral quantity index. This corresponds to Van Yzeren's (1956, 15–20) original unweighted balanced method (see also Van Ijzeren 1983, 44–45; Van Ijzeren 1987, 59–61). In a manner similar to the derivation of equations (A55)–(A57) above, I can show that the homogeneous quadratic f and c defined by (41) and (42) are also exact for this $Q = Q_L$ version of the unweighted balanced method. Hence, Van Yzeren's original unweighted balanced method is also superlative.

Proof of Proposition 11

T1: I have already established the existence and positivity of the S_i using only BT1. It remains to establish the continuity of the $S_i(P, Y)$. Using (79), BT1, and BT2, the elements in the matrix A will be continuous functions of the elements in the matrices P and Y. Using a theorem of Frobenius's (1908, 473), the determinant $| I_{K-1} - \tilde{A} | > 0$ and therefore the $\tilde{x}$ defined by (83) will be continuous in the elements of A. Thus, using $x_N = 1$ and (82), the continuity of the $S_i(P, Y)$ in the elements of P and Y follows.

T2: Substituting the conditions of the test into (78) and using BT3, BT5, and BT6 yield the following system of equations:

$$\sum_{j=1}^{K} (\beta_j / \beta_i) S_i^2 = \sum_{k=1}^{K} (\beta_i / \beta_k) S_k^2, \quad i = 1, \ldots, K.$$

Substituting $S_i = \beta_i$ into these equations yields a system of identities.

T3: Substituting the conditions of the test into (78) and using BT4, BT7, and BT8 yield

$$\sum_{j=1}^{K} (p \cdot y^j / p \cdot y^i) S_i^2 = \sum_{k=1}^{K} (p \cdot y^i / p \cdot y^k) S_k^2, \quad i = 1, \ldots, K.$$

Setting $S_i = \alpha p \cdot y^i$ for $i = 1, \ldots, K$ solves these equations.

T4: This test follows using equations (78) and BT10.

T5: This test follows using (78) and BT9.

T6: This test follows from the symmetrical nature of equations (73) and (78).

T7: This test follows using BT7 and BT8.

T8: This test fails in general unless the bilateral quantity index Q satisfies circularity. But proposition 7 shows that circularity is not consistent with the satisfaction of tests BT1–BT13. Thus, under my hypotheses on Q, test T8 fails.

T9: By the symmetry of the method, we need only set $x_N = 1$ and show that the $x_1, \ldots, x_{N-1}$ that satisfy (83) are decreasing functions of the components of the country K quantity vector y^K. Define the jth column of the A matrix with row K deleted by $\tilde{A}_{\bullet j}$ for $j = 1, 2, \ldots, K$. Note that $\tilde{A}_{\bullet K} = \tilde{a}$ where $\tilde{a}$ appears in (83). Differentiating equations (83) with respect to the elements of y^K yields the following formula for the $K - 1 \times N$ matrix of derivatives of the elements of $\tilde{x}$ with respect to the elements of y^K:

$$(A58) \qquad \nabla_{y^K}\tilde{x} = \left[I_{K-1} - \tilde{A}\right]^{-1}\left\{\nabla_{y^K}\tilde{A}_{\bullet K} + \sum_{j=1}^{K-1}\left(\nabla_{y^K}\tilde{A}_{\bullet j}\right)x_j\right\}.$$

From (84), the elements of $[I_{K-1} - \tilde{A}]^{-1}$ are all positive. Differentiating the elements of the A matrix using definitions (79) and the monotonicity properties of Q, BT12, and BT13, the matrices of derivatives $\nabla_{y^K}\tilde{A}_{\bullet j}$ are nonpositive and negative almost everywhere for $j = 1, \ldots, K$. Using these facts plus the positivity of the x_j, (A58) implies that $\nabla_{y^K}\tilde{x}$ is nonpositive and negative almost everywhere. Thus, the $x_i(P, Y)$ for $i = 1, \ldots, K - 1$ are decreasing in the components of y^K.

T10: Let $p^a \gg 0_N$, $y^a \gg 0_N$, $\alpha_i > 0$, $\beta_i > 0$, $p^i = \alpha_i p^a$, $y^i = \beta_i y^a$ for $i \in A$ with $\sum_{i \in A}\beta_i = 1$. For $i \in A$, equations (78) become, using BT3 and BT5–BT8,

$$\sum_{j \in A}(\beta_j/\beta_i)S_i^2 + \sum_{j \in B}\beta_i^{-1}Q(p^a, p^j, y^a, y^j)S_i^2$$

$$= \sum_{k \in A}(\beta_i/\beta_k)S_k^2 + \sum_{k \in B}\beta_i Q(p^k, p^a, y^k, y^a)S_k^2.$$

For $k \in A$, let $S_k = \beta_k S_a$. Using $\sum_{j \in A}\beta_j = 1$ and BT3, these equations become for $i \in A$

$$(A59) \qquad Q(p^a, p^a, y^a, y^a)S_a^2 + \sum_{j \in B}Q(p^a, p^j, y^a, y^j)S_a^2$$

$$= Q(p^a, p^a, y^a, y^a)S_a^2 + \sum_{k \in B}Q(p^k, p^a, y^k, y^a)S_k^2.$$

Note that equations (A59) do not depend on i, so there is only one independent equation in (A59). For $i \in B$, equations (78) become, using BT5–BT8 and $S_k = \beta_k S_a$ for $k \in A$,

$$(A60) \qquad Q(p^i, p^a, y^i, y^a)S_i^2 + \sum_{j \in B}Q(p^i, p^j, y^i, y^j)S_i^2$$

$$= Q(p^a, p^i, y^a, y^i)S_a^2 + \sum_{k \in B}Q(p^k, p^i, y^k, y^i)S_k^2.$$

Equations (A59) and (A60) along with the equation $S_a + \sum_{k \in B}S_k = 1$ can be solved for positive S_a and S_k for $k \in B$. Once S_a has been determined, we set $S_i = \beta_i S_a$ for $i \in A$, and part i of T10 holds. Examination of (A59) and (A60) shows that part ii also holds.

T11: Substitute the assumptions of T11 into equations (78). For $i \in A$, let

$S_i = \beta_i S_a$, and, for $j \in B$, let $S_j = \delta_j S_b$. For $i \in A$, using BT3 and BT5–BT8, each of these equations in (78) reduces to

(A61) $S_a^2 + Q(p^a,\ p^b,\ y^a,\ y^b)S_a^2 = S_a^a + Q(p^b,\ p^a,\ y^b,\ y^a)S_b^2$.

For $i \in B$, each of these equations in (78) reduces to

(A62) $Q(p^b,\ p^a,\ y^b,\ y^a)S_b^2 + S_b^2 = Q(p^a,\ p^b,\ y^a,\ y^b)S_a^2 + S_b^2$.

Each of the equations (A61) and (A62) simplifies to

(A63) $$\sum_{j \in B} S_j \Big/ \sum_{i \in A} S_i = S_b / S_a$$

$$= [Q(p^a,p^b,\ y^a,\ y^b)/Q(p^b,\ p^a,y^b,\ y^a)]^{1/2}$$

(A64) $$= Q(p^a,\ p^b,\ y^a,\ y^b),$$

where (A64) follows from (A63) if Q satisfies the time reversal test BT11. This is the only place in the proof of proposition 11 where I use property BT11. Using (A63), if $Q = Q_L$ or $Q = Q_P$, we find that $S_b/S_a = Q_F(p^a, p^b, y^a, y^b)$. As in the proof of proposition 10, note that Q_L and Q_P satisfy all the bilateral tests except BT11. Hence, if $Q = Q_L$ or $Q = Q_P$, then the resulting weighted balanced methods satisfy all the multilateral tests except T8 and T12.

Exactness Properties of the Weighted Balanced Method

For $Q = Q_F$, substituting (10), (12), and (A42) into (78) leads to the following system of equations for $i = 1, \dots, K$:

$$\sum_{j=1}^{K}[f(y^j)/f(y^i)] = \sum_{k=1}^{K}[f(y^i)/f(y^k)][f(y^k)/f(y^i)]^2$$

$$= \sum_{k=1}^{K}[f(y^k)/f(y^i)],$$

which is a system of identities. Hence, the homogeneous quadratic f defined by (41) is exact for this method. Similarly, for $Q = Q_F$, substituting (9), (13), and (A43) into (78) leads to the following system of equations for $i = 1, \dots, K$:

$$\sum_{j=1}^{K}[u_j/u_i] = \sum_{k=1}^{K}[u_i/u_k][u_k/u_i]^2 = \sum_{k=1}^{K}[u_k/u_i],$$

which is a system of identities. Hence, the homogeneous quadratic unit cost function c defined by (42) is also exact for this method.

For $Q = Q_L$, the Laspeyres quantity index, equations (78) become

(A65) $$\sum_{j=1}^{K}[p^i \cdot y^j/p^i \cdot y^i] = \sum_{k=1}^{K}[p^k \cdot y^i/p^k \cdot y^k][S_k/S_i]^2, \quad i = 1,\dots,K.$$

Substituting (10) and (12) into (A65) and letting f be defined by (41) lead to the following system:

(A66) $\sum_{j=1}^{K}[y^{iT}Ay^j/f(y^i)^2] = \sum_{k=1}^{K}[y^{kT}Ay^i/f(y^i)^2], \quad i = 1, \dots, K,$

which is a system of identities using $A = A^T$. Hence, the homogeneous quadratic f defined by (41) is exact for the weighted balanced method with $Q = Q_L$. In a similar fashion, we can show that the c defined by (42) is exact for the weighted balanced method with $Q = Q_L$.

Finally, in an analogous fashion, it can be shown that the f defined by (41) and the c defined by (42) are exact for the weighted balanced method with $Q = Q_P$.

Appendix B
A Simple Numerical Example

Consider the simplest possible example of a multilateral method where there are three countries ($K = 3$) and two commodities ($N = 2$). As usual, let p^k and y^k denote the price and quantity vectors for country k. These six vectors are defined below:

$p^1 \equiv (p_1^1, p_2^1) \equiv (1, 1);\ p^2 \equiv (p_1^2, p_2^2) \equiv (10, .1);\ p^3 \equiv (p_1^3, p_2^3) \equiv (.1, 10);$

$y^1 \equiv (y_1^1, y_2^1) \equiv (1, 2);\ y^2 \equiv (y_1^2, y_2^2) \equiv (1, 100);\ y^3 \equiv (y_1^3, y_2^3) \equiv (1,000, 10).$

Note that the geometric mean of the two prices in each country is unity across all countries; however, the structure of relative prices (and relative quantities) differs vastly across the three countries.

Nominal expenditures (expressed in a common currency) in the three countries are $p^1 \cdot y^1 \equiv \sum_{n=1}^{2} p_n^1 y_n^1 = 3, p^2 \cdot y^2 = 20,$ and $p^3 \cdot y^3 = 200$. Thus, country 1 is tiny, country 2 is medium sized, and country 3 is large. Note that the expenditure shares on each commodity are equal for countries 2 and 3.

To get a preliminary idea of the variation in multilateral shares that the example given above generates, first table S^2/S^1 and S^3/S^1 for the Paasche and Laspeyres star systems where the price vector for each country is used to value outputs. Thus, in table 1B.1, methods 1–3 correspond to the indexes $p^1 \cdot y^i/ p^1 \cdot y^1, p^2 \cdot y^i/p^2 \cdot y^1, p^3 \cdot y^i/p^3 \cdot y^1$ for $i = 2, 3$.

Examining table 1B.1, we see that using the prices of each country to value every country's quantity vector (methods 1–3) causes the share of country 2 relative to 1, S^2/S^1, to range from about 2 to 50 while S^3/S^1 ranges from about 10 to 980. I also calculated the Fisher star relative shares in table 1B.1 (methods 4–6); see equations (56) with $Q = Q_F$. We find that, using the Fisher star systems, the relative share variation is dramatically reduced but still is quite big: S^2/S^1 ranges from about 5.8 to 8.1, while S^3/S^1 ranges from about 58 to 81. One would expect that a satisfactory multilateral method should generate relative shares S^2/S^1 and S^3/S^1 that fall in the ranges spanned by the Fisher stars—namely, 5.8–8.1 and 58–81, respectively. The Fisher blended shares defined by (57) are listed as method 7 in table 1B.1.

In table 1B.2, I listed the exchange rate and average price and average quantity methods that were defined in sections 1.3–1.8 of the main text of this paper. Method 8 is the exchange rate method (see eqq. [1]). This method does rather well in this artificial model, probably because the geometric mean of prices in each country is identical. Hence, there are no grossly overvalued or undervalued country exchange rates. One would not expect this good performance to carry over to examples where some countries had grossly overvalued exchange rates.

Turning now to the average price methods defined in section 1.4, we find that the arithmetic and geometric mean price methods defined by (15) and (16) generate equal average prices. Hence, both these methods are equivalent to method 1 in table 1B.1, where the equal prices of country 1 were used to value quantities in each country.

Method 9 is the Walsh (1901, 431)–Fisher (1922, 307) arithmetic mean average quantity method defined by (22) and (23), while method 10 the Walsh (1901, 398)–Gerardi (1982, 398) geometric mean average quantity method defined by (22) and (24). The arithmetic mean quantity vector turns out to be [334, 37.3], while the geometric mean quantity vector is [10, 12.6]. Thus, methods 9 and 10 generate quite different relative shares in table 1B.2.

The Geary (1958)–Khamis (1970) average prices method defined in section 1.6 is method 11. The vector of international prices (times 1,000) turns out to be [.4974, 4.4783], which is closest to the structure of relative prices in the large country, country 3. This method seems to lead to a tremendous overevaluation of the share of country 2; S^2/S^3 for the GK method is $47.42/57.35 = .83$, which seems too large.

Van Yzeren's (1956, 13) unweighted average price method defined in section 1.7 is the next method we consider. The international price vector $[p_1^*, p_2^*]$ defined by (33) turns out to be [1, 1], so, again, this method reduces to method 1. Van Yzeren's (1956, 6–14) unweighted average quantity method defined in section 1.8 is method 12. The vector of average quantities defined by (43) for this method turns out to be $[y_1^*, y_2^*] \equiv [.99342, 1]$. This method leads to a share for country 1 that is too large.

Table 1B.3 lists the superlative methods discussed in sections 1.9–1.12 with the bilateral Q equal to Q_F, the Fisher ideal quantity index.

The effects of weighting are evident in table 1B.3. The two superlative methods that satisfy the country-partitioning test T10 (methods 15 and 16) have shares that are relatively close to the big country's Fisher star shares (method 6), while the two superlative methods that do not satisfy T10 (methods 13 and 14) have shares that are very close to the arithmetic average of the Fisher star shares (method 7, a democratically weighted method).

The numerical example given above shows that the choice of a multilateral method is very important from an empirical point of view—more important

Table 1B.1   Paasche and Laspeyres Star and Fisher Star Systems

	Method 1 (country 1 prices)	Method 2 (country 2 prices)	Method 3 (country 3 prices)	Method 4 (Fisher star 1)	Method 5 (Fisher star 2)	Method 6 (Fisher star 3)	Method 7 (blended Fisher)
S^2/S^1	33.67	1.96	49.76	8.12	8.12	5.79	7.25
S^3/S^1	336.67	980.49	9.95	57.88	81.25	57.88	64.12

Table 1B.2   Exchange Rate and Average Price and Quantity Methods

	Method 8 (exchange rate)	Method 9 (arithmetic mean average quantities)	Method 10 (geometric mean average quantities)	Method 11 (Geary-Khamis)	Method 12 (Van Yzeren average quantities)
S^2/S^1	6.67	.74	1.49	47.42	1.32
S^3/S^1	66.67	60.86	11.86	57.35	13.16

Table 1B.3   **Superlative Methods Using the Fisher Bilateral Index**

	Method 13 (Gini-EKS)	Method 14 (unweighted balanced)	Method 15 (own share)	Method 16 (weighted balanced)
S^2/S^1	7.2563	7.2563	6.024	6.001
S^3/S^1	64.8062	64.8062	59.970	59.697

than the choice of a bilateral index number formula in the time-series context because the variation in relative prices and quantities will usually be much greater in the multilateral context. Even when choosing between superlative multilateral methods, we see that there can be substantial differences between methods 13 and 14 (which pass the linear homogeneity test T8) and methods 15 and 16 (which pass the country-partitioning test T10).

If the quantity vector for country 1 is changed to $y_1 \equiv (y_1^1, y_2^1) \equiv (1, 1)$, then the expenditure shares on each commodity will equal 1/2 in each country. Hence, for this new data set, the data are consistent with economic agents maximizing the utility function $f(y_1, y_2) \equiv y_1^{1/2} y_2^{1/2}$ subject to country budget constraints. This functional form is a special case of (41) and (65) (with $a_{11} \equiv a_{22} \equiv 0$ and $a_{12} \equiv 1/2$), and, hence, the Fisher and Walsh bilateral quantity indexes defined by (2) and (64) will empirically pass the circularity test (52). (The direct and indirect Persons [1928, 21–22]–Törnqvist [1936] quantity indexes Q_0 and $\tilde{Q}_0$ defined in Diewert [1976, 120–21] will also pass the circularity test for this data set since Cobb-Douglas utility functions are exact for these functional forms as well.) For this modified data set, the entries in table 1B.1 for the Fisher star methods, methods 4–6, all reduce to $S^2/S^1 = 10$ and $S^3/S^1 = 100$. In this case, all the superlative methods listed in table 1B.3 also have $S^2/S^1 = 10$ and $S^3/S^1 = 100$. Thus, it is deviations from circularity of the bilateral index number formula that cause the superlative methods to yield different numerical results. As an aside, for this circular data set, it should be noted that the Geary-Khamis relative shares are $S^2/S^1 = 90.13$ and $S^3/S^1 = 108.73$. Thus, the share of country 2 still seems to be too large in this case. To further illustrate that Geary-Khamis indexes can be quite different from Fisher ideal indexes, consider table 1B.4, where the Geary-Khamis bilateral index number formula (31) was used to form star system shares. The results using countries 1–3, respectively, as the base country are tabled in columns 1–3 and are compared with the common Fisher star shares in column 4.

I now return to the original noncircular data set and calculate the four superlative indexes when I use the bilateral Walsh quantity index Q_W defined by (64) in place of the bilateral Fisher quantity index Q_F defined by (2).

In table 1B.5, I list the Walsh star shares S^2/S^1 and S^3/S^1 using countries 1–3 as the base (see eqq. [56], which define the star shares), which are methods 17–19. I also list the corresponding Fisher-Walsh blended shares defined by (57), where $Q = Q_W$ (method 20).

Table 1B.4   **Geary-Khamis Star Shares versus Fisher Shares Using the**
                     Circular Data

	Geary-Khamis 1	Geary-Khamis 2	Geary-Khamis 3	Fisher
S^2/S^1	2.92	2.92	17.34	10
S^3/S^1	20.76	3.50	20.76	100

Table 1B.5   **Walsh Star Shares and Walsh Blended Shares**

	Method 17 (Walsh star 1)	Method 18 (Walsh star 2)	Method 19 (Walsh star 3)	Method 20 (blended shares)
S^2/S^1	9.167	9.167	5.238	7.603
S^3/S^1	52.381	91.667	52.381	61.381

Table 1B.6   **Superlative Methods Using the Walsh Bilateral Index**

	Method 21 (Gini-Walsh)	Method 22 (unweighted balanced)	Method 23 (own share)	Method 24 (weighted balanced)
S^2/S^1	7.6067	7.6067	5.630	5.572
S^3/S^1	63.1227	63.1228	55.892	55.195

Comparing table 1B.5 with table 1B.1, it can be seen that the Walsh star shares are less variable than the country price star shares (methods 1–3) but that the Walsh star shares (methods 17–19) are more variable than the Fisher star shares (methods 4–6). Thus, the Walsh star relative shares, S^2/S^1, range from about 5.2 to 9.2 (while the corresponding Fisher variation was from 5.8 to 8.1), and the Walsh relative shares, S^3/S^1, range from about 52 to 92 (while the corresponding Fisher variation was from 58 to 81). Since the Fisher indexes satisfy circularity better than the Walsh indexes, one would expect that the variation in the four Walsh superlative indexes will be greater than the variation in the four Fisher superlative indexes. This expectation is verified by the results of table 1B.6.

Comparing table 1B.6 with table 1B.3, we see some similarities: the democratically weighted Gini-Walsh and Walsh unweighted balanced methods (methods 21 and 22) closely approximate each other, while the plutocratically weighted Walsh own share and Walsh weighted balanced methods (methods 23 and 24) also approximate each other reasonably closely. However, the spread between the methods that satisfy the linear homogeneity test T8 (methods 21 and 22) and the methods that satisfy the country-partitioning test T10 (methods 23 and 24) is much wider in table 1B.6 than it was in table 1B.3, where the more nearly circular Fisher bilateral indexes were used as the basic building blocks. In table 1B.6, note that the shares corresponding to the plutocratic meth-

Table 1B.7   **International Prices Using Own Share Price Levels and GK Prices**

	Balk's Method	Hill's Method	Geary-Khamis
π_2/π_1	8.895	9.028	9.003

ods 23 and 24 are closer to the shares of the big country star shares (method 19), whereas the shares corresponding to the equally weighted methods 21 and 22 are very close to the arithmetic average of the Walsh star shares (method 20).

The fact that, empirically, the Fisher bilateral indexes satisfy the circularity test more closely than the Walsh indexes reinforces the case for preferring the Fisher index over its bilateral competitors. In addition to being superlative and satisfying more reasonable tests than its competitors, the Fisher ideal quantity index is the only superlative index that is consistent with (bilateral) revealed preference theory (see Diewert 1976, 137). Thus, I prefer the Fisher superlative methods listed in table 1B.3 over the Walsh superlative methods listed in table 1B.6.

I conclude this appendix by calculating the international prices that were suggested at the end of section 1.13 for the noncircular data set.

Balk's suggested vector of international prices $\pi \equiv (\pi_1, \pi_2)$ was defined by (86), and the generalized Hill prices were defined by (25), where the price levels (or purchasing power parities) P^k and the country shares S^k that appear in these equations were defined by the analyst's "best" multilateral method. In table 1B.7, I used the Fisher own share P^k and S^k (see method 15 in table 1B.3) in equations (86) and (25) to calculate the Balk and Hill international prices. Both these international price relatives π_2/π_1 are close to the Geary-Khamis international price relative, $\pi_2/\pi_1 = 9.004$. Recall that the structure of relative prices in the three countries is $p_2^1/p_1^1 = 1$, $p_2^2/p_1^2 = .01$, and $p_2^3/p_1^3 = 100$ for countries 1–3, respectively. Thus, the international price ratios in table 1B.7 all tend to lean toward the structure of relative prices in the big country, country 3. Note that, if I used the Balk or Hill international prices to value the quantity vectors in each country, the resulting country shares of world consumption at these constant prices would be very close to the Geary-Khamis shares (see method 11 in table 1B.2), and these shares are very different from the shares generated by the suggested best methods listed in table 1B.3.

The numerical example suggests that additive multilateral methods should not be used if the structure of relative prices is very different across countries. In this case, no single international price vector can adequately represent the prices faced by producers or consumers in each country. In order to model adequately the very large substitution effects that are likely to be present in this situation, an economic approach based on the use of superlative indexes should be used.

References

Afriat, S. N. 1967. The construction of utility functions from expenditure data. *International Economic Review* 8:67–77.

Armstrong, K. G. 1995. Multilateral approaches to the theory of international comparisons. Ph.D. diss., University of British Columbia.

Balk, B. M. 1989. On Van Ijzeren's approach to international comparisons and its properties. *Statistische Hefte* 30:295–315.

———. 1995a. Axiomatic price index theory: A survey. *International Statistical Review* 63:69–93.

———. 1995b. On the use of unit value indices as consumer price subindices. Voorburg: Statistics Netherlands, Division of Research and Development, 14 March.

———. 1996. A comparison of ten methods for multilateral international price and volume comparisons. *Journal of Official Statistics* 12:199–222.

Debreu, G., and I. N. Herstein. 1953. Nonnegative square matrices. *Econometrica* 21:597–607.

Diewert, W. E. 1971. An application of the Shephard duality theorem: A generalized Leontief production function. *Journal of Political Economy* 79:481–507.

———. 1974. Functional forms for revenue and factor requirements functions. *International Economic Review* 15:119–30.

———. 1976. Exact and superlative index numbers. *Journal of Econometrics* 4: 115–45.

———. 1981. The economic theory of index numbers: A survey. In *Essays in the theory and measurement of consumer behavior in honour of Sir Richard Stone,* ed. A. Deaton. London: Cambridge University Press.

———. 1986. Microeconomic approaches to the theory of international comparisons. Technical Working Paper no. 53. Cambridge, Mass.: National Bureau of Economic Research.

———. 1988. Test approaches to international comparisons. In *Measurement in economics,* ed. W. Eichhorn. Heidelberg: Physica.

———. 1992. Fisher ideal output, input and productivity indexes revisited. *Journal of Productivity Analysis* 3:211–48.

———. 1993a. Duality approaches to microeconomic theory. In *Essays in index number theory,* vol. 1, ed. W. E. Diewert and A. O. Nakamura. Amsterdam: North-Holland.

———. 1993b. The early history of price index research. In *Essays in index number theory,* vol. 1, ed. W. E. Diewert and A. O. Nakamura. Amsterdam: North-Holland.

———. 1993c. Symmetric means and choice under uncertainty. In *Essays in index number theory,* vol. 1, ed. W. E. Diewert and A. O. Nakamura. Amsterdam: North-Holland.

———. 1995. Axiomatic and economic approaches to elementary price indexes. Discussion Paper no. 95-01. University of British Columbia, Department of Economics.

———. 1996. Price and volume measures in the system of national accounts. In *The new system of national accounts,* ed. J. W. Kendrick. Boston: Kluwer Academic.

Dikhanov, Y. 1994. Sensitivity of PPP-based income estimates to choice of aggregation procedures. Paper presented at the conference of the International Association for Research in Income and Wealth, St. Andrews, New Brunswick, August.

Drechsler, L. 1973. Weighting of index numbers in multilateral international comparisons. *Review of Income and Wealth,* ser. 19 (March): 17–47.

Eichhorn, W. 1976. Fisher's tests revisited. *Econometrica* 44:247–56.

———. 1978. *Functional equations in economics.* London: Addison-Wesley.

Eichhorn, W., and J. Voeller. 1976. *Theory of the price index.* Berlin: Springer.

Eltetö, O., and P. Köves. 1964. On a problem of index number computation relating to international comparisons. *Statisztikai Szemle* 42:507–18.

Fisher, I. 1911. *The purchasing power of money.* London: Macmillan.

———. 1922. *The making of index numbers.* Boston: Houghton Mifflin.

Frisch, R. 1930. Necessary and sufficient conditions regarding the form of an index number which shall meet certain of Fisher's tests. *American Statistical Association Journal* 25:397–406.

Frobenius, G. 1908. Über Matrizen aus positiven Elementen. *Sitzungsberichte der königlich preussischen Akademie der Wissenschaften,* pt. 1:471–76. Berlin: Royal Prussian Academy of Sciences.

———. 1909. Über Matrizen aus positiven Elementen II. *Sitzungsberichte der königlich preussischen Akademie der Wissenschaften,* pt. 1:514–18. Berlin: Royal Prussian Academy of Sciences.

Gale, D., and H. Nikaido. 1965. The Jacobian matrix and the global univalence of mappings. *Mathematische Annalen* 159:81–93.

Geary, R. G. 1958. A note on comparisons of exchange rates and purchasing power between countries. *Journal of the Royal Statistical Society* A121:97–99.

Gerardi, D. 1974. Sul problema della comparazione dei poteri d'acquisto delle valute. Serie papers. Instituto di Statistica dell'Universita di Padova, August.

———. 1982. Selected problems of inter-country comparisons on the basis of the experience of the EEC. *Review of Income and Wealth,* ser. 28:381–405.

Gini, C. 1924. Quelques considérations au sujet de la construction des nombres indices des prix et des questions analogues. *Metron* 4, no. 1:3–162.

———. 1931. On the circular test of index numbers. *Metron* 9, no. 9:3–24.

Hicks, J. R. 1940. The valuation of the social income. *Economica* 7:105–40.

———. 1946. *Value and capital.* 2d ed. Oxford: Clarendon.

Hill, R. J. 1995. Purchasing power parity methods of making international comparisons. Ph.D. diss., University of British Columbia.

Hill, T. P. 1982. *Multilateral measurements of purchasing power and real GDP.* Luxembourg: Eurostat.

———. 1984. Introduction: The Special Conference on Purchasing Power Parities. *Review of Income and Wealth,* ser. 30:125–33.

Iklé, D. M. 1972. A new approach to the index number problem. *Quarterly Journal of Economics* 86:188–211.

Jevons, W. S. 1884. *Investigations in currency and finance.* London: Macmillan.

Karlin, S. 1959. *Mathematical methods and theory in games, programming and economics.* Vol. 1. Reading, Mass.: Addison-Wesley.

Khamis, S. H. 1970. Properties and conditions for the existence of a new type of index number. *Sankhya* B32:81–98.

———. 1972. A new system of index numbers for national and international purposes. *Journal of the Royal Statistical Society* A135:96–121.

Kravis, I. B. 1984. Comparative studies of national incomes and prices. *Journal of Economic Literature* 22:1–39.

Kravis, I. B., Z. Kenessey, A. Heston, and R. Summers. 1975. *A system of international comparisons of gross product and purchasing power.* Baltimore: Johns Hopkins University Press.

Kravis, I. B., R. Summers, and A. Heston. 1982. Comments on "Selected problems of intercountry comparisons on the basis of the experience of the EEC." *Review of Income and Wealth,* ser. 28:407–10.

Kurabayashi, Y., and I. Sakuma. 1990. *Studies in international comparisons of real products and prices.* Hitotsubashi University, Institute of Economic Research, Economic Research Series no. 28. Tokyo: Kinokuniya.

Leontief, W. 1936. Composite commodities and the problem of index numbers. *Econometrica* 4:39–59.

Marris, R. 1984. Comparing the incomes of nations: A critique of the international comparison project. *Journal of Economic Literature* 22, no. 1:40–57.

Martini, M. 1992. A general function of axiomatic index numbers. *Journal of the Italian Statistical Society* 3:359–76.

Perron, O. 1907. Grundlagen für eine Theorie des Jacobischen Kettenbruchalgorithmus. *Mathematische Annalen* 64:1–76.

Persons, W. M. 1928. *The construction of index numbers.* Cambridge, Mass.: Riverside.

Pierson, N. G. 1896. Further considerations on index-numbers. *Economic Journal* 6: 127–31.

Reinsdorf, M. B., and A. H. Dorfman. 1995. The Sato-Vartia index and the monotonicity axiom. Washington, D.C.: U.S. Bureau of Labor Statistics.

Rudin, W. 1953. *Principles of mathematical analysis.* New York: McGraw-Hill.

Sato, K. 1976. The ideal log-change index number. *Review of Economics and Statistics* 58:223–28.

Shephard, R. W. 1953. *Cost and production functions.* Princeton, N.J.: Princeton University Press.

Szulc, B. 1964. Indices for multiregional comparisons. *Przeglad Statystyczny* 3:239–54.

Törnqvist, L. 1936. The Bank of Finland's consumption price index. *Bank of Finland Monthly Bulletin* 10:1–8.

Van Yzeren, J. 1956. *Three methods of comparing the purchasing power of currencies.* Statistical Studies no. 7. The Hague: Netherlands Central Bureau of Statistics.

Van Ijzeren, J. 1983. *Index numbers for binary and multilateral comparison.* Statistical Studies no. 34. The Hague: Netherlands Central Bureau of Statistics.

Van Ijzeren, J. 1987. *Bias in international index numbers: A mathematical elucidation.* Eindhoven: Dissertatiedrukkerij Wibro.

Vartia, Y. O. 1974. Relative changes and economic indices. Licenciate thesis, Department of Statistics, University of Helsinki.

———. 1976. Ideal log-change index numbers. *Scandinavian Journal of Statistics* 3: 121–26.

Vogt, A. 1980. Der Zeit und der Faktorumkehrtests als "Finders of Tests." *Statistiche Hefte* 21:66–71.

Walsh, C. M. 1901. *The measurement of general exchange value.* New York: Macmillan.

———. 1921. Discussion of the best form of index number. *Journal of the American Statistical Association* 17:537–44.

Westergaard, H. 1890. *Die Grundzüge der Theorie der Statistik.* Jena: Fischer.

Wold, H. 1944. A synthesis of pure demand analysis, part III. *Skandinavisk Aktuarietidskrift* 27:69–120.

Comment   Irwin L. Collier Jr.

Erwin Diewert has produced another magnificent paper. One could say that this work is genuinely Fisheresque, both in its comprehensiveness and in its dogged pursuit of relevant detail. All that is missing is a sprinkling of the homely touches that distinguish Irving Fisher's work on index numbers and economics in general, for example, a comparison of the precision of quantify-

Irwin L. Collier Jr. is professor of economics at the Freie Universität Berlin.

ing the purchasing power of money with the precision of measuring the height of the Washington Monument. Instead, Diewert packs his results modestly in the streamlined style of present-day economic theory. He takes us farther faster so that we may have more time to do what we have to do once we get there, assuming that we knew where we wanted to go in the first place. It is the discussant's job to help the hurried traveler distinguish a few landmarks in the blur of Diewert's forward motion.[1]

Ten classes of multilateral index number methods are rigorously examined, and four of the methods actually succeed in winning the Diewert seal of approval on a combination of axiomatic merits and economic flexibility. This is the immediate contribution of this paper to the debate on multilateral index number methods. Since there will be undoubtedly future contenders for the title of best multilateral method, the lasting value of Diewert's paper will be found in the testing procedures implemented as well as their careful documentation by Diewert in his appendix A. These proofs will help future index formula inventors and users judge for themselves.

The axiomatic method is similar to the Ten Commandments approach to virtue. Good people honor their fathers and mothers and do not covet their neighbors' goods, and good index numbers do not change their values simply because we change our units of measurement from pounds to ounces (T4) or our price measurements from dollars to cents (T7). Diewert's tablets in fact list eleven tests, but most of his followers will probably regard them as ten commandments plus a normalization condition (thou shalt have output shares that add up to unity, T1).

There are several reasons why composing lists of index number axioms is both a satisfying and a worthwhile task in economic measurement.

One important reason is that we are practical only once we become specific in these matters. An axiom that "the index number should not be misleading" is as worthless as a commandment that "thou shalt not be evil." "Nobody is special" (T6) and "no commodity is special" (T5) are the sort of axioms that should indeed receive immediate and unanimous agreement and ones where a violation is immediately demonstrated whenever the simple act of swapping i, j country superscripts or commodity subscripts leads to a change in a country's relative performance. Of course, a potential danger in getting specific is that our list of tests can begin to grow and approach the length of a checklist for a space shuttle liftoff.

This leads to another reason why this approach is both satisfying and worthwhile. The act of whittling down a list of axioms involves distinguishing those axioms that are in some sense fundamental from those that can be derived from subsets of the fundamental axioms. Here, the point is not checking whether a

1. Actually, Diewert himself provides his passengers an excellent aid for orientation with his simple numerical example that works through an artificial three-country, two-good case. The impatient reader who has jumped this far forward should mark those pages to consult during a detailed reading of Diewert's paper.

particular formula complies with the tests but instead analyzing the interaction of the tests among themselves. This aspect of the axiomatic approach to international comparisons is not touched on in this particular paper.[2]

Index number formulas and tests are like people and commandments; one need not look very far to find seemingly simple rules in conflict with each other. Since it is natural for economists to think in terms of choice between competing goods, this is hardly the stuff of tragedy. In section 1.13, Diewert proves that he is a wise judge, much as appendix A reveals him to be a strict judge.

The choice of an index number formula for a multilateral comparison is analogous to the problems of designing a voting procedure for multicandidate/issue elections, a system to rank competing athletic teams in a league, or a method to aggregate the opinions of independent experts.[3] There is an essential difference in that most of these other problems seek nothing more than an ordinal ranking (A gets the gold medal, B the silver, and C the bronze), whereas the business of multilateral comparisons of real income and product loses most, if not all, of its charm should it fail to deliver an answer to the question just how much closer B is to A than C. It is hardly coincidental that the axiomatic method plays a prominent role in all these areas.

Useful in thinking about such problems is the presumed existence of some underlying latent variable of real consumption or production (the concern of this volume) or of performance/ability/political strength (such as when a university department votes to rank job candidates). Here is where the economic approach to international comparisons enters the picture. Working backward from the actual latent index of real consumption, one easily calculates a consistent matrix of bilateral comparisons. We adopt the convention of assigning the column country in each binary comparison the role of base country (the denominator of the ratio). To illustrate, suppose that the true shares of world output are those given in the lean-truth vector in table 1C.1. One can immediately verify that each column of the fat-truth matrix is the lean-truth vector divided by one of the country values. Some of the values are completely uninformative; the diagonal of ones will be found for all fat-truth matrices. Furthermore, there is a redundancy between elements located above and below the diagonal. Obviously, the lean-truth vector can be calculated from any single row or column of the fat-truth matrix.

One very good reason for thinking about the truth in terms of a matrix of binary comparisons is that the analyst is often given something related to the true matrix of binary comparisons. Many (although not all!) of the methods of multilateral comparison attempt to find the lean-truth vector hiding inside a fat matrix of *actual* binary comparisons. Returning to the related problems just

2. For an example of this sort of work, see Eichhorn and Voeller (1990).
3. For an entry point into this literature, one can consult David (1988) as well as the papers in Fligner and Verducci (1993)—in particular the paper by Stern (1993)—that give a statistical twist. Young (1995) offers a very readable survey of voting mechanisms.

Table 1C.1   **A True Multilateral Vector Generates a Single True Matrix of Bilateral Comparisons**

	Lean-Truth Vector		Fat-Truth Matrix[a]		
			Country 1	Country 2	Country 3
Country 1	.10	Country 1	1.00	.33	.17
Country 2	.30	Country 2	3.00	1.00	.50
Country 3	.60	Country 3	6.00	2.00	1.00

[a]Row country compared to column country.

Table 1C.2   **Empirical Bilateral Comparisons Generate Multiple Multilateral Vectors**

	Fisher Quantity Index				Three Versions of the Truth		
	Country 1	Country 2	Country 3		First "Truth"	Second "Truth"	Third "Truth"
Country 1	1.000	.121	.017	Country 1	1.000	1.000	1.000
Country 2	8.125	1.000	.100	Country 2	8.125	8.125	5.788
Country 3	57.879	10.000	1.000	Country 3	57.879	81.248	57.879

mentioned, in the public choice literature, such matrix entries could be the actual outcomes of head-to-head elections, or, in the problem of ranking individual chess players, these could be the outcomes of games between pairs of players at a tournament. As we see from the matrix of Fisher quantity indexes taken from Diewert's example (see table 1C.2), each of the Fisher columns is consistent only with a different lean-truth vector. This is precisely the sort of discrepancy that led Irving Fisher to reach for his statistical blender (Diewert's method 7).

There are plenty of bilateral index formulas that one might have chosen, and one is not necessarily limited to any one matrix of binary comparisons. Thus, it was entirely appropriate for Diewert to think about the appropriate choice of binary indexes for many of the multilateral methods. One should also note that one might choose to work with *less* information than a complete bilateral comparison matrix or that one might work with the entire set of underlying price and quantity data. An interesting structural characteristic of the differing multilateral methods is the degree of disaggregation in the underlying data that is required for their calculation. The four methods favored in the end by Diewert are all generated directly from a matrix of binary comparisons. In contrast, the well-known Geary-Khamis system, a method that did not make it into Diewert's final four, requires a finer disaggregation of the expenditure and quantity data.

With an eye to the aggregation requirements in a computational sense, I now look at the ten classes of multilateral methods examined by Diewert. This will involve traveling a slightly different route, one that takes us from the minimum to the maximum disaggregation of the underlying price and quantity data. The minimum disaggregation method is also the method that Diewert chose to evaluate first.

The data requirements for the exchange rate method are so minimal that one need not actually compare anything to set up shop—a list of nominal expenditures, along with a list of exchange rates, is enough to become a comparisons consultant. Sure, one must divide nominal expenditures in one country by nominal expenditures in another to obtain a kind of binary comparison. No pain, no gain. But the reason that Laspeyres and Paasche started us all worrying about index numbers is the fact that ratios of nominal values confound price with quantity changes. Diewert is able to keep a straight face testing "probably the most commonly used method for making multilateral comparisons." The man is a professional. It is appropriate to include under this method all attempts to unlock nominal expenditures with a single price, such as the *Economist*'s tongue-in-cheek (maybe) Big-Mac-Index.

The next set of indexes constitutes the so-called star systems, which are simply single columns (normalized to sum to unity) plucked from the Laspeyres, Fisher, Geary-Khamis (bilaterals), or Walsh quantity index matrices. One column from any of these matrices represents a considerable information advance compared to the exchange rate method since a revaluation of market baskets actually takes place. On the other hand, it is quite obvious that other columns need never be calculated once the role of the star country has been cast. In table 1C.2, the three columns on the right correspond to Fisher star 1–3 in Diewert's numerical example. Any one column is distinguished from the other columns by the asymmetrical treatment given the country chosen as the base country in the binary comparisons. In the first column, all countries are compared to country 1, in the second column to country 2, and in the third column to country 3. One significant reason for the Eastern European origins of the EKS method in multilateral international comparisons was a political desire to have a reason for knocking the Soviet Union out of its key role as base country in all CMEA (Council for Mutual Economic Assistance) comparisons, making things a little more mutual, at least in a statistical sense.

The three columns on the right of table 1C.2 represent three different points on the unit simplex, the geometric representation of the normalization of world output equal to 100 percent. In figure 1C.1, three such points are plotted (that have been drawn to correspond to different underlying data in the interests of visual clarity). Since there is no objective reason to favor one base country over another, one can see why Irving Fisher would have thought of (implicitly) finding that point on the unit simplex that was closest to the three points of the Fisher star system. An unweighted arithmetic averaging of the coordinates of the original three points is what Diewert has listed as method 7 in his appendix B. The first thing to note is that the blended Fisher index requires knowledge

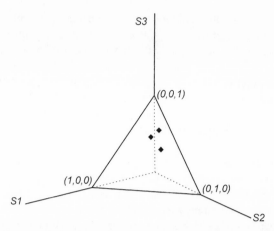

Fig. 1C.1   Points on the unit simplex are normalized Fisher quantity indexes for different base countries

of the entire Fisher quantity index matrix, making it really the first of the multi-lateral methods we meet that exploits all the information from a bilateral comparisons matrix. Hence, while it is logical in one sense to place the blended Fisher in a table next to the stars that generated it, it turns out (as Diewert indeed notes) to be numerically a next-door neighbor to the unweighted superlative indexes (Gini-EKS and unweighted balanced) in his table 1B.3. This proximity, along with the fact that the blended Fisher index is the outcome of an explicit minimization problem (i.e., minimizing the sum of squared distances from the three stars on the simplex), would have made it an outstanding candidate for an axiomatic and economic testing by Diewert. Instead, it is left as an interesting exercise for the reader.

However, before moving on to consider other formulas that blend an entire matrix of binary comparisons into a single multilateral index, there are two relatively primitive methods discussed by Diewert that start by blending the price *or* quantity data before any comparisons are attempted. This is a relatively unimaginative way to eliminate the inconsistency between individual binary comparisons calculated with only one or two of the K different columns from the $N \times K$ matrices of prices and quantities. In table 1C.3, one can directly compare the i, jth elements of the bilateral quantity comparisons from the multilateral symmetric means methods with their respective Laspeyres bilateral comparisons. In the first row, the average price method is compared to the corresponding Laspeyres quantity index, and, in the second row, the average quantity method index is compared with the Laspeyres quantity index obtained by deflating nominal expenditures with a Paasche price index.

In the first row of table 1C.3, one can see that the prices used in the Laspeyres matrix (which differ for each column j) have been replaced by an aver-

Table 1C.3   **Average Price and Average Quantity Methods Compared to Laspeyres Bilateral Indexes and the Geary-Khamis Multilateral Index**

Bilateral Laspeyres Quantity Index		Symmetric Means Methods	Geary-Khamis Method
$\displaystyle\frac{\sum_{n=1}^{N} p_n^j y_n^i}{\sum_{n=1}^{N} p_n^j y_n^j}$	Using average prices	$\displaystyle\frac{\sum_{n=1}^{N} m(p_n)y_n^i}{\sum_{n=1}^{N} m(p_n)y_n^j}$	$\displaystyle\frac{\sum_{n=1}^{N} \pi(p,\,y)y_n^i}{\sum_{n=1}^{N} \pi(p,\,y)y_n^j}$
$\displaystyle\frac{p^i \cdot y^i}{p^j \cdot y^j} \times \frac{\sum_{n=1}^{N} y_n^j p_n^j}{\sum_{n=1}^{N} y_n^j p_n^i}$	Using average quantities	$\displaystyle\frac{p^i \cdot y^i}{p^j \cdot y^j} \times \frac{\sum_{n=1}^{N} m(y_n)p_n^j}{\sum_{n=1}^{N} m(y_n)p_n^i}$	

age of K country prices. Similarly, the quantities used in the (inverse of the) Paasche price index in the second row have been replaced by an average of K country quantities.[4] Diewert rightly remarks that the Geary-Khamis method is a "more complex average price method," and his discussion of the Geary-Khamis method immediately follows his own discussion of the symmetric means methods. In my opinion, the far greater complexity of the Geary-Khamis international prices puts the GK method into an entirely different class. The so-called international prices used to value the country quantities (in the first row of table 1C.3) are functions, not just of p_n (a single column of the p matrix), but of the entire p and y matrices together.

Returning to our lean-truth vector from a fat-truth matrix extraction problem, the first two methods based on a complete matrix of binary comparisons that Diewert analyzes are Van Yzeren's unweighted average price (UAP) and unweighted average basket (UAB) methods. Diewert notes a certain similarity between the UAP and the Geary-Khamis definition of average bloc prices. However, from the standpoint of price and quantity disaggregation, the difference is really what counts. The fact that the UAP method does not employ quantity weights in averaging the (purchasing power parity–deflated) individual country prices is the reason that one is able to work at the level of the matrix of binary comparisons. This can be seen immediately in Diewert's useful reformulation of the UAP (eqq. [39], [40]) and UAB (eqq. [49], [50]) systems. Although not explicitly identified as such, the D matrix in Diewert's reformulation is nothing other than the matrix of Laspeyres quantity indexes:

$$D \equiv \{(p^j \cdot y^j)^{-1}(p^j \cdot y^i)\}.$$

4. It will be recalled that the exchange rate method required the N-vector of nominal expenditures and the N-vector of exchange rates. The average price method requires the original $N \times K$ matrix of quantities, y, and an N-vector of average prices. The average quantity method requires the original $N \times K$ matrix of prices, p, an N-vector of average quantities, and the N-vector of nominal expenditures.

An appropriately normalized eigenvector from D is shown by Diewert to be the UAP multilateral quantity index. He also proves that an eigenvector from the matrix transpose of D can be used to calculate the multilateral quantity index for the UAB method. Thus, two of the Van Yzeren methods appear to offer an alternative to the statistical approach of a Fisher blending of the columns of a matrix of binary comparisons. However, it is hardly obvious to this Perron-Frobenius-challenged reader which economic or even statistical truth the positive eigenvector pulled from a Laspeyres matrix of bilateral comparisons (or its transpose) is actually trying to tell us. Diewert shows that it is not an exact truth for the flexible functional forms defined by his equations (41) and (42).

One of the puzzles in Diewert's appendix B are the identical values in table 1B.3 calculated using the Gini-EKS formula (eq. [63]) and Van Yzeren's unweighted balanced method (UBM) (eq. [74]). Since Gini's priority is indisputable, one should abbreviate this to GEKS. Anyone who goes to the trouble of checking these calculations will find that the agreement continues for many more digits than shown in the table. This is not simply an artifact of the particular numbers chosen for the example. Diewert attributes this "similarity" to an approximation of arithmetic means by geometric means. There is in fact a better argument for treating GEKS and UBM as a single method, at least for economic data from this world. One should not be too surprised that they have identical axiomatic and "economic" properties—they are "approximately" identical twins.

The source of the near identity of the methods can be seen once we write the minimization problems behind the respective formulas in such a way as to reveal the particular loss functions that turn out not to be so very different at all. First, restate the minimization problems as found in Diewert's paper:

(UBM[71]) $\min_{S^1,\ldots,S^K} \sum_{j=1}^{K}\sum_{k=1}^{K} Q(p^k,\ p^j,\ y^k,\ y^j)S^k/S^j,$

(GEKS[61]) $\min_{S^1,\ldots,S^K} \sum_{j=1}^{K}\sum_{k=1}^{K} \{\ln[Q(p^k,\ p^j,\ y^k,\ y^j)S^k/S^j]\}^2.$

The UBM minimization problem can be easily rewritten to highlight a distinct family resemblance to the GEKS:

(71′) $\min_{S^1,\ldots,S^K} \sum_{j=1}^{K}\sum_{k=1}^{K} \exp\{\ln[Q(p^k,\ p^j,\ y^k,\ y^j)S^k/S^j]\}.$

Instead of the conventional quadratic loss function used in (61), Van Yzeren's UBM uses an asymmetric loss function, the exponential. However, the asymmetry is apparent only as long as the underlying bilateral index numbers satisfy the country reversal test, as do the Fisher bilateral indexes. If we rewrite (71′) by grouping the (k, j) terms with their (j, k) partner terms and exploit the country reversal test, we obtain

$$\min_{S^1,\ldots,S^K} \sum_{j>k}^{K} \sum_{k=1}^{K} (\exp\{\ln[Q(p^k,\ p^j,\ y^k,\ y^j)S^k/S^j]\}$$

$$+\ \exp\{\ln[Q(p^j,\ p^k,\ y^j,\ y^k)S^j/S^k]\}),$$

(UBM-1)

$$\min_{S^1,\ldots,S^K} \sum_{j>k}^{K} \sum_{k=1}^{K} (\exp\{\ln[Q(p^k,\ p^j,\ y^k,\ y^j)S^k/S^j]\}$$

$$+\ \exp\{-\ln[Q(p^k,\ p^j,\ y^k,\ y^j)S^k/S^j]\}).$$

Next, perform the same regrouping of the terms in the GEKS sum of squared deviations:

$$\min_{S^1,\ldots,S^K} \sum_{j>k}^{K} \sum_{k=1}^{K} (\{\ln[Q(p^k,\ p^j,\ y^k,\ y^j)S^k/S^j]\}^2$$

$$+\ \{\ln[Q(p^j,\ p^k,\ y^j,\ y^k)S^j/S^k]\}^2),$$

(GEKS-1) $$\min_{S^1,\ldots,S^K} \sum_{j>k}^{K} \sum_{k=1}^{K} (\{\ln[Q(p^k,\ p^j,\ y^k,\ y^j)S^k/S^j]\}^2$$

$$+\ \{-\ln[Q(p^k,\ p^j,\ y^k,\ y^j)S^k/S^j]\}^2),$$

$$\min_{S^1,\ldots,S^K} 2\sum_{j>k}^{K} \sum_{k=1}^{K} \{\ln[Q(p^k,\ p^j,\ y^k,\ y^j)S^k/S^j]\}^2.$$

Finally, define the logarithmic deviation for an arbitrary bilateral comparison (j, k):

$$u^{k,j} \equiv \ln Q(p^k,\ p^j,\ y^k,\ y^j) - (\ln S^j - \ln S^k).$$

Each of the (k, j) terms in the GEKS and UBM sums can be written (dropping the k, j superscripts), respectively, as

$$2u^2 \text{ (GEKS)} \quad \text{vs.} \quad e^u + e^{-u} \text{ (UBM)}.$$

It is obvious that the GEKS term is nonnegative and increasing, which is precisely why the squared deviation has been the classic specification of the loss function. The convexity of the exponential function guarantees the non-negativity of the GEKS term. It, too, increases with the size of the deviation u (see fig. 1C.2). For our purposes, nothing speaks against using this unconventional specification of the loss function.

Without changing the solution of the respective minimization problems, we can divide all the GEKS terms by two and subtract two from each of the UBM terms. The resulting functions are plotted in figure 1C.3, where we can see that these two modified functions of u are not identical. On the other hand, the approximation around the point of zero deviation looks good enough to be, well, superlative. A Taylor series expansion of the UBM loss function at $u = 0$ shows us that the two functions begin to go their separate ways only after the third derivative:

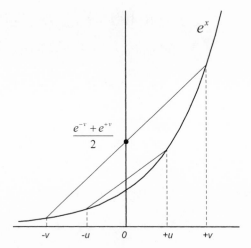

Fig. 1C.2   The loss function for country pairs implicit in Van Yzeren's unweighted balanced method

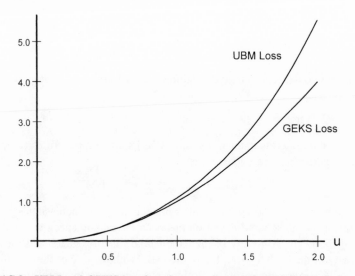

Fig. 1C.3   UBM and GEKS loss functions are "approximately" identical

$$e^u + e^{-u} - 2 \approx u^2 + \frac{u^4}{12} + \frac{u^6}{360}.$$

Charles Kindleberger used to warn his students that the second derivative is the refuge of a scoundrel. Fortunately, Diewert was not one of his students, and, anyway, Kindleberger never warned against consorting with higher derivatives. From the point of view of computation, GEKS is so much simpler to calculate than UBM that Diewert's discussion will likely be one of the very last sightings of this Rube Goldberg model index number, a nice example of overengineering (of course nondeliberate) in empirical economics.

Having just reunited one pair of twins found in Diewert's paper, one will perhaps be less surprised that there happens to be a pair of half siblings living separate lives in this paper as well. It turns out that Diewert's own share method (DOS) and the weighted balanced method (WBM) of Van Yzeren are linked by a common loss function, although one must challenge the legitimacy of the latter's claim in mathematical court. The two methods can be motivated by considering the problem of minimizing the weighted sum of the expression that we have just encountered in the UBM method:

$$(71) \qquad \min_{S_1,\dots,S_K} \sum_{j=1}^{K} \sum_{k=1}^{K} w_j w_k Q(p^k, \; p^j, \; y^k, \; y^j) S_k / S_j.$$

Suppose that one believes that it would be appropriate to use the yet-to-be-estimated shares as the weights in the minimization problem, $w_i = S_i$.[5] Diewert tells us that Van Yzeren makes this substitution, but only *after* deriving the first-order conditions that are used to define his WBM. The reason for WBM's illegitimacy (in a mathematical sense) is that one may not derive the first-order conditions for (71) with respect to the S parameters as though the weights were constant and then ex post substitute the S's into the first-order conditions for the weights to calculate the index. The easy way to demonstrate that (71) was not minimized this way is to take the figures from Diewert's example for WBM in his table 1B.3 and plug them directly into (71). The numerical value is 1.2356. The S parameters obtained from the DOS method in Diewert's table 1B.3 give a lower value, 0.9999. As seen in Diewert's tables 1B.3 and 1B.6, the WBM numbers are nonetheless quite close to those from the DOS method.

Now suppose that we decide instead to try to be right for the right reasons and substitute the weights into (71) from the start. This simplifies the minimization problem enormously:

$$(71') \quad \min_{S_1,\dots,S_K} \sum_{j=1}^{K} \sum_{k=1}^{K} Q(p^k, \; p^j, \; y^k, \; y^j) S_k^2 \; = \; \sum_{k=1}^{K} S_k^2 \sum_{j=1}^{K} Q(p^k, \; p^j, \; y^k, \; y^j),$$

where the last summation is the column sum of the underlying binary index matrix, and things are beginning to look suspiciously like the DOS method.

To enforce the normalization, rewrite the problem as the minimization of the Langrangian expression:

$$\min_{S_1,\dots,S_K} \sum_{k=1}^{K} S_k^2 \sum_{j=1}^{K} Q(p^k, \; p^j, \; y^k, \; y^j) - \lambda\left(\sum_{k=1}^{K} S_k - 1\right).$$

After deriving the ith first-order condition, solve for the quantity index:

---

5. The appropriateness of these weights is by no means obvious.

$$S_i = \lambda \cdot \frac{1}{2\sum_{j=1}^{K} Q(p^i, p^j, y^i, y^j)}.$$

Sum over i, and use the normalization of the shares to obtain an expression for the Langrangian multiplier in terms of the observable column sums:

$$\sum_{i=1}^{K} S_i = 1 = \lambda \cdot \sum_{i=1}^{K} \frac{1}{2\sum_{j=1}^{K} Q(p^i, p^j, y^i, y^j)},$$

$$\lambda = \left(\sum_{i=1}^{K} \left\{ \left[2\sum_{j=1}^{K} Q(p^i, p^j, y^i, y^j) \right]^{-1} \right\} \right)^{-1}.$$

This last result is now plugged back into the original first-order conditions for the problem to obtain the DOS formula:

$$S_i = \frac{\left[\sum_{j=1}^{K} Q(p^i, p^j, y^i, y^j) \right]^{-1}}{\left\{ \sum_{k=1}^{K} \left[\sum_{j=1}^{K} Q(p^k, p^j, y^k, y^j) \right]^{-1} \right\}}.$$

The utter simplicity of the DOS method can be appreciated by turning this last expression into words. Given a matrix of, say, Fisher quantity indexes, first calculate the column sums, which are then inverted. The share of the ith country is the inverted ith-column sum divided by the sum of all the inverted column sums.

Thus, we have found that the final four methods surveyed in Diewert's paper actually boil down to only two distinct methods. These two surviving methods, GEKS and DOS (the latter being the youngest of the class), are exceedingly simple to calculate in practice—that is, of course, after someone else has gone to all the trouble of calculating the underlying matrix of bilateral comparisons.

Still, one might wonder whether there was really no useful information contained in the underlying $N \times K$ price and quantity matrices that could have been destroyed in compressing the data into a $K \times K$ matrix of bilateral comparisons. In multiple-candidate voting procedures, one is faced with a similar question: Is it enough for us to know the proportions of voters who preferred candidate i over candidate j for all pairwise comparisons, or should we also consider how the individual voters completely ranked all the candidates? This is one of two reasons why it would be premature to disregard the Geary-Khamis method entirely in favor of GEKS and DOS.

To see the informational requirements of the Geary-Khamis method, it proves to be convenient to derive a closed-form solution for the GK quantity indexes. Instead of writing the problem in terms of finding a set of international

prices and purchasing power parities (PPPs), modify the method so that international expenditures and country quantity indexes become the variables that
are determined by the system of Geary-Khamis equations.

Start with the familiar N Geary-Khamis international price equations:

$$(25) \qquad \pi_n = \sum_{k=1}^{K} \left(\frac{y_n^k}{y_n} \right) \left(\frac{p_n^k}{P^k} \right).$$

The trained eye immediately spots the weighted averages of PPP–adjusted
country prices, where the weight of the kth term is equal to the kth country's
share of the aggregate quantity of good n. Summations of goods across countries are designated by dropping the country superscript:

$$y_n \equiv \sum_{k=1}^{K} y_n^k.$$

However, instead of proceeding to define K PPP equations for the unknown
P^k terms in equation (25), as is usually done, we may easily transform these
international *price* equations into international *expenditure* equations. Multiply each side of the N equations in (25) with the corresponding total quantities
of the countries in the comparison, thereby eliminating that term from the denominator of the right-hand side of (25). Next, divide and multiply each of the
k terms of the sum by total expenditure in the kth country, and rearrange to
obtain a new weighted average:

$$(25') \qquad \pi_n y_n = \sum_{k=1}^{K} \left(\frac{p^k \cdot y^k}{P^k} \right) \left(\frac{p_n^k y_n^k}{p^k \cdot y^k} \right) = \sum_{k=1}^{K} S^k w_n^k,$$

where the quantity index for country k is defined by deflating nominal expenditures with the PPP index (cf. Diewert's eq. [20]). International expenditures on
the nth good in the Geary-Khamis system are defined to be the weighted average of the budget shares (the weights have become the weighted!) of the N
goods in the K countries, w_n^k, where country quantity indexes, S^k, have been
used as weights. It is important to note that we treat the *product* $\pi_n y_n$ as an
unknown variable in this system of equations. To calculate international prices
later, one only need divide the derived international expenditures by the appropriate y_n.

The second modification of the traditional Geary-Khamis system is to rearrange equation (26) to obtain K equations for the country quantity indexes,
S^k, expressed as weighted averages of each country's respective shares of world
quantities, v_n^k:

$$(26') \quad S^k \equiv \frac{p^k \cdot y^k}{P^k} = \pi \cdot y^k = \sum_{n=1}^{N} \pi_n y_n^k = \sum_{n=1}^{N} \left(\frac{y_n^k}{y_n} \right) (\pi_n y_n) = \sum_{n=1}^{N} v_n^k (\pi_n y_n).$$

Writing (25') and (26') in matrix notation, one can see the raw material out of which Geary-Khamis indexes are manufactured: an $N \times K$ matrix of country budget shares (columns sum to unity) and a $K \times N$ matrix of the structure of world consumption by countries (columns likewise sum to unity):

$$
\begin{bmatrix} \pi_1 y_1 \\ \vdots \\ \pi_n y_n \\ \vdots \\ \pi_N y_N \end{bmatrix} = \begin{bmatrix} w_1^1 & \cdots & w_1^k & \cdots & w_1^K \\ \vdots & \ddots & \vdots & & \vdots \\ w_n^1 & & w_n^k & & w_n^K \\ \vdots & & \vdots & \ddots & \vdots \\ w_N^1 & \cdots & w_N^k & \cdots & w_N^K \end{bmatrix} \begin{bmatrix} S^1 \\ \vdots \\ S^k \\ \vdots \\ S^K \end{bmatrix},
$$

$$
\begin{bmatrix} S^1 \\ \vdots \\ S^k \\ \vdots \\ S^K \end{bmatrix} = \begin{bmatrix} v_1^1 & \cdots & v_n^1 & \cdots & v_N^1 \\ \vdots & \ddots & \vdots & & \vdots \\ v_1^k & & v_n^k & & v_N^k \\ \vdots & & \vdots & \ddots & \vdots \\ v_1^K & \cdots & v_n^K & \cdots & v_N^K \end{bmatrix} \begin{bmatrix} \pi_1 y_1 \\ \vdots \\ \pi_n y_n \\ \vdots \\ \pi_N y_N \end{bmatrix}.
$$

Defining the matrices $W \equiv [w_n^k]$, $V \equiv [v_n^k]$, $z \equiv [\pi_n y_n]$, $s \equiv [S^k]$, the alternate Geary-Khamis multilateral system can be compactly written as

(GK-1)
$$
z = Ws,
$$
$$
s = V^T z.
$$

Substituting the country real consumption (output) equations (s) into the international expenditure equations (z), we obtain

$$
z = WV^T z,
$$

which can be written

(GK-2)
$$
0_N = [I_N - WV^T]z.
$$

One might stop at the first of the last two equations and think of z as an eigenvector of the matrix WV^T, or one might look at the second equation and wish that there were something other than a zero vector on the left-hand side so that the matrix expression in brackets could be inverted and solved for z.

However, the matrix expression in brackets is not invertible since the matrix difference $I_N - WV^T$ can easily be seen to be singular, which is definitely for the good since, otherwise, the international expenditure vector z would really have to stand for the zero vector.

To demonstrate the singularity of $I_N - WV^T$, consider an element i, j of WV^T,

$$
w_i = [w_i^1, \ldots, w_i^K], \quad \text{the } i\text{th row of } W,
$$

$$
v_j^T \equiv [v_j^1, \ldots, v_j^K]^T, \quad \text{the } j\text{th column of } V^T,
$$

$$
[WV^T]_{i,j} = w_i v_j^T = \sum_{k=1}^K w_i^k v_j^k.
$$

Summing over i, we obtain the sum of the elements of the jth column:

$$\sum_{i=1}^{N}\sum_{k=1}^{K}w_i^k v_j^k = \sum_{k=1}^{K}v_j^k\sum_{i=1}^{N}w_i^k = \sum_{k=1}^{K}v_j^k = 1.$$

The sum of each column of the identity matrix is likewise equal to unity. Thus, the sum of each of the columns of $I_N - WV^T$ is zero (i.e., $1 - 1 = 0$), and therefore the sum of any $K - 1$ rows is equal to the negative of the remaining row. Therefore, the matrix $I_N - WV^T$ is singular.

Fortunately, the singularity of a matrix is a rather special circumstance, much as the zero point on the number line is pretty special. This means that fairly minor changes to the matrix WV^T can destroy its singularity, and that would allow us to invert the new matrix in the process of solving the matrix equation for z. The trick here is to add a normalization condition on the s vector that will also help us eliminate the problem of having a zero vector on the left-hand side of (GK-2).

A convenient normalization is to set the value of world quantities equal to some constant. Like Diewert, I normalize the value of world output to be equal to unity:

$$(28) \qquad\qquad 1 = \sum_{n=1}^{N}\pi_n y_n,$$

a constraint that can be written in matrix form,

$$c = R\begin{bmatrix} \pi_1 y_1 \\ \vdots \\ \pi_N y_N \end{bmatrix},$$

where $c = [1\ 0\ \cdots\ 0]^T$ is an $N \times 1$ vector, and

$$R = \begin{bmatrix} 1 & 1 & \cdots & 1 \\ 0 & \cdots & \cdots & 0 \\ \vdots & & & \vdots \\ 0 & \cdots & \cdots & 0 \end{bmatrix} \text{ is an } N \times N \text{ matrix.}$$

Now we add the constraint matrix equation to the original matrix equation,

$$(\text{GK-3}) \qquad\qquad c = [I_N - WV^T + R]z.$$

By adding a one to each element of the first row of the original singular matrix, the sum of any column of $I_N - WV^T + R$ is now unity, thus eliminating the original dependency among the rows. This will be enough to get nonsingularity into the bracketed expression in (GK-3), and we can solve (GK-3) for the international expenditure vector z:

$$(\text{GK-4}) \qquad\qquad z = [I_N - WV^T + R]^{-1}c.$$

This result can now be substituted back into the second equation of (GK-1) for the Geary-Khamis multilateral country quantity indexes:

(GK-5) $s = V^T[I_N - WV^T + R]^{-1}c$.

To calculate the GK international prices, construct the $K \times K$ diagonal matrix

$$\hat{y}^{-1} \equiv \begin{bmatrix} (1/y_1) & 0 & \cdots & \cdots & 0 \\ 0 & \ddots & \ddots & 0 & \vdots \\ \vdots & \ddots & (1/y_n) & \ddots & \vdots \\ \vdots & 0 & \ddots & \ddots & \vdots \\ 0 & \cdots & \cdots & 0 & (1/y_N) \end{bmatrix}.$$

Now, premultiplying the world expenditure vector, we obtain a closed-form solution for GK international prices as well:

(GK-6) $\pi = \hat{y}^{-1}z = \hat{y}^{-1}[I_N - WV^T + R]^{-1}c$.

Up to this point, we have seen so many expressions for multilateral index numbers computed directly from a matrix of bilateral comparisons that it might go unnoticed that the GK method indeed requires a fully disaggregated data set, in the form of an $N \times K$ matrix of budget shares by good and by country (W) and a $K \times N$ matrix of quantity shares by country and good (V). This is not just a multilateral method resting on a foundation of aggregate bilateral comparisons but rather a genuinely multilateral method from the ground up.

While there can be no fundamental mathematical claim for preferring (GK-4) and (GK-5) over Diewert's modifications of GK in his equations (27)–(30), or the reverse for that matter, it is a safe bet that more people could *correctly* program (GK-5) in a *shorter* period of time than could program a solution to the GK equations by any other method, including that used by Diewert in his paper. Diewert rightly points out that a strength of GEKS and DOS methods is their relative ease of computation. The closed-form expression (GK-5) demonstrates that a GK quantity index can be a simple one-liner itself, computationally speaking.

Besides the disaggregated nature of the price and quantity data required for implementing the GK method in international comparisons, there is a second distinguishing characteristic for this method that has the potential to enrich the discussion of multilateral methods. I learned of this second characteristic of the GK method only during a conversation with D. S. Prasada Rao:[6]

RAO'S OBSERVATION: Suppose that we assume that each country has simple Cobb-Douglas preferences but that tastes differ between countries; that is, different budget shares are observed. The international prices generated by the GK method are Walrasian exchange equilibrium prices.

6. He was referring to his working paper (Rao 1985).

Before demonstrating this proposition and considering further implications, it is important to provide an answer to the "so what?" question. There is an ambiguity in Diewert's paper about whether he is dealing with *an* economic theory of index numbers or *the* economic theory of index numbers. He is not alone. It is surely an interesting question whether the bilateral comparisons from a computed quantity index are exact for a particular specification of an underlying aggregator function. Indeed, it is a fascinating question of the quality of the approximation that a particular specification might offer to an arbitrary aggregator function. But do these questions really exhaust the economic interpretation of our index numbers? I believe that Rao's observation points us in yet another promising direction. For international and historical comparisons we are pushing the methodological envelope when we insist on playing the game solely under the assumption of identical preferences. Perhaps it is better to structure our comparisons to generate a set of mutually agreed-on prices (this happens all the time in markets where fundamental differences in tastes help compel the search for mutually agreeable valuations). The point is, one hopes, established: because of the enormous economic content in methods that rely on "virtual markets" to provide valuations for comparisons, *the* economic theory of multilateral index numbers could be profitably expanded beyond the exact-and-flexible core of *the current* economic theory of index numbers.[7]

I turn now to a demonstration of Rao's observation.

Budget shares will remain constant in all countries even after virtual trading has been completed since all countries were assumed to have simple Cobb-Douglas preferences. Once the international (Walrasian exchange) prices are determined, we have

$$w_n^k = \frac{\pi_n \tilde{y}_n^k}{\sum_{j=1}^{N} \pi_j \tilde{y}_j^k},$$

$$w_n^k \sum_{j=1}^{N} \pi_j \tilde{y}_j^k = \pi_n \tilde{y}_n^k,$$

where the budget shares on the left-hand side are the initial, observed NK budget shares. Summing over the K countries for each of the N goods, we obtain N international expenditure equations:

$$\sum_{k=1}^{K} w_n^k \sum_{j=1}^{N} \pi_j \tilde{y}_j^k = \pi_n y_n.$$

The new budget constraint in each of the K countries is equal to the old budget constraint plus an adjustment term for the change in the value of the original endowment:

7. The concept *virtual prices,* which was introduced by Erwin Rothbarth (1941), is quite different from the GK international prices. The former are shadow prices, reflecting subjective trade-offs, rather than valuations determined in a market process.

$$\sum_{k=1}^{K} w_n^k \left[\sum_{j=1}^{N} p_j^k y_j^k + \sum_{j=1}^{N} (\pi_j - p_j^k) y_j^k \right] = \pi_n y_n,$$

(GK-6)
$$\sum_{k=1}^{K} w_n^k \left(\sum_{j=1}^{N} \pi_j y_j^k \right) = \pi_n y_n,$$

$$\sum_{k=1}^{K} \frac{p_n^k y_n^k}{\left(\sum_{j=1}^{N} p_j^k y_j^k \right) \Big/ \left(\sum_{j=1}^{N} \pi_j y_j^k \right)} = \pi_n y_n.$$

The denominator of this last expression is the Geary-Khamis purchasing power parity index for the kth country (cf. Diewert's eq. [26]). Now, writing the Geary-Khamis PPP index as P^k and rearranging, we immediately see that the Walrasian exchange equilibrium prices indeed correspond to the Geary-Khamis international prices (cf. Diewert's eq. [25]):

$$\sum_{k=1}^{K} \frac{p_n^k}{P^k} \frac{y_n^k}{y_n} = \pi_n.$$

With this particular economic interpretation embodied in the GK quantity index, it now becomes understandable why small countries have been found generally to look "better" in GK multilateral comparisons. Big countries would dominate the determination of international prices in such a Walrasian exchange world, and one of the principles of international trade is that small countries stand to gain most since they are typically in a position to exploit relatively larger differences between the structure of their domestic prices and that of international prices. Thus, we may conclude that the fundamental weakness of the Geary-Khamis quantity index is that the revaluation of each country's market basket implicitly adds in gains from trade that have never taken place! In his example, Diewert comments that country 2 seems too large (his table 1B.2, method 11). This now comes as no surprise since country 2's relative price structure is indeed the farthest from the GK international price structure (one hundred to one as opposed to the international price relation of one to nine).

The discussion presented above points to an obvious remedy for this particular shortcoming of the GK method. One could save the GK international prices and use geometric mean price indexes (exact for the underlying Cobb-Douglas preferences) to deflate nominal expenditures (cf. Rao and Salazar-Carrillo 1990).

Begin with a Cobb-Douglas indirect utility function and the relevant data from the kth country:

$$U[p^k/(p^k \cdot y^k)] = \sum_{n=1}^{N} w_n^k [\ln(p^k \cdot y^k) - \ln p_n^k] = \ln(p^k \cdot y^k) - \sum_{n=1}^{N} w_n^k \ln p_n^k.$$

This is the level of utility that we wish to hold constant and equal to the indirect utility function at $U(\pi/S^k)$. Thus, we need to solve the following equation:

$$\ln(S^k) - \sum_{n=1}^{N} w_n^k \ln \pi_n = \ln(p^k \cdot y^k) - \sum_{n=1}^{N} w_n^k \ln p_n^k.$$

Exponentiating each side of the equation, and solving for S^k, we obtain

$$S^k = (p^k \cdot y^k)\left[\prod_{n=1}^{N}(p_n^k)^{-(w_n^k)}\right]\prod_{n=1}^{N}(\pi_n)^{(w_n^k)}$$

$$= (p^k \cdot y^k)\prod_{n=1}^{N}\left(\frac{\pi_n}{p_n^k}\right)^{(w_n^k)} = \frac{p^k \cdot y^k}{\prod_{n=1}^{N}\left(\frac{p_n^k}{\pi_n}\right)^{(w_n^k)}}.$$

When GK international prices are used to calculate geometric mean PPPs in Diewert's appendix B example, we obtain $S^2/S^1 = 4.62$ and $S^3/S^1 = 46.22$, bringing the relative shares of countries 2 and 3 with respect to each other into complete agreement with those calculated by the DOS method and WBM. The results for country 1 are clearly distinct from Diewert's preferred four as reported in his table 1B.3, but it is not nearly the discrepancy we observed between the classic GK results reported in his table 1B.2 (47.42 and 57.35) and those of the "superlative" methods.

The cost to our analysis of acknowledging different preferences between countries is that we have lost our common money metric. However, people from different countries have little problem thinking about other countries' incomes, just as most of us find the salaries of our colleagues interesting economic information, even knowing the enormous differences in tastes and efficiency as utility producers that make it impossible to say how much less happy our colleagues would be living on our salaries than on their own. Most of us talk as though we have a very good idea of what living on our colleague's salary would mean to us. The point here is not to argue for the wholesale abandonment of one of the assumptions that helps distinguish *Homo economist* from other social scientists but to recognize that *the* economic theory of index numbers is not necessarily pinned to the identical preferences assumption.

Having provided the reader with a field manual to help distinguish the different multilateral methods tested by Diewert according to the degree of informational disaggregation, and, I hope, having broadened at least in a few readers' minds the notion of what belongs in *the* economic theory of index numbers, I close my comment with one important empirical reminder.

There are really only two empirical results in economics that have passed the tests of both time and cross-national comparisons: Engel's law and the Gerschenkron-Gilbert-Kravis effect.[8] The assumption of linearly homogeneous utility functions is an extremely polite way of ignoring Engel's law, understood here in a general sense to mean that significant differences exist in

8. The second relation is the subject of van Ark, Monnikhof, and Timmer (chap. 12 in this volume).

income elasticities between certain expenditure groups, for example, basic foodstuffs and foreign holidays. In the interest of sufficiently flexible specifications to capture all possible substitution effects, Diewert has assumed that all income elasticities are equal to unity in judging the "economic" quality of ten classes of multilateral methods. One recalls that Erwin Diewert did tease an important theorem out of the nonhomothetic case in his classic 1976 paper on exact and superlative index numbers, showing that, in one sense, a Törnqvist price index is exact for a nonhomothetic translog utility function. This is the sort of result in a multilateral context that readers of this paper might still hope to see in their lifetimes. But, until then, users must beware: when GEKS and DOS are good, they are simply superlative, but, when they are bad, they break Engel's law.

Appendix
Obtaining a Closed-Form Solution for WBM

The system of i equations for WBM is

$$(78) \qquad \left[\sum_{j=1}^{K} Q(p^i,\ p^j,\ y^i,\ y^j)\right] S_i^2 = \sum_{k=1}^{K} [Q(p^k,\ p^i,\ y^k,\ y^i) S_k^2],$$

where the left-hand side is the sum of the elements in the ith column of the matrix of binary indexes Q times the square of the ith country's quantity index, and the right-hand side is the sum of the products of the elements of the ith row of the matrix Q with the corresponding squares of the country quantity indexes.

$$S_i^2 = \sum_{k=1}^{K} \left[\frac{Q(p^k,\ p^i,\ y^k,\ y^i)}{\sum_{j=1}^{K} Q(p^i,\ p^j,\ y^i,\ y^j)} S_k^2\right]$$

$$= \sum_{k=1}^{K} a_{ik} S_k^2,$$

where the elements of the newly defined matrix A are the elements of the matrix of binary indexes Q divided by the respective column sums; that is, the columns of A have been normalized to add up to unity. Now, writing the vector of squares of the country quantity indexes as x, we can write Diewert's equation (80) in slightly modified form:

$$(80') \qquad\qquad (A - I_K)x = 0_K.$$

But now the matrix premultiplying the x vector is singular (its columns sum to zero, just as was the case for the Geary-Khamis method). Using the normalization matrix R and normalization vector c defined as

$$c = [1 \quad 0 \quad \cdots \quad 0]^T, \quad \text{a } K \times 1 \text{ vector,}$$

and

$$R = \begin{bmatrix} 1 & 1 & \cdots & 1 \\ 0 & \cdots & \cdots & 0 \\ \vdots & & & \vdots \\ 0 & \cdots & \cdots & 0 \end{bmatrix}, \quad \text{a } K \times K \text{ matrix,}$$

we can directly compute the vector of squared WBM quantity indexes with the formula

$$x = (A - I_K + R)^{-1} c .^9$$

To get a closed-form solution of this, first normalize the unknown x vector to sum to unity; then, after taking the square roots of the x vector, normalize the resulting raw WBM quantity indexes to sum to unity.

References

David, H. A. 1988. *The method of paired comparisons.* 2d ed. London: Charles Griffin.

Diewert, W. Erwin. 1976. Exact and superlative index numbers. *Journal of Econometrics* 4:115–45.

Eichhorn, Wolfgang, and Joachim Voeller. 1990. Axiomatic foundation of price indexes and purchasing power parities. In *Price level measurement,* ed. W. E. Diewert. Amsterdam: North-Holland.

Fligner, Michael A., and Joseph S. Verducci, eds. 1993. *Probability models and statistical analyses for ranking data.* New York: Springer.

Rao, D. S. Prasada. 1985. A Walrasian exchange equilibrium interpretation of the Geary-Khamis international prices. Working Paper in Econometrics and Applied Statistics no. 20. University of New England, Department of Econometrics.

Rao, D. S. Prasada, and Jorge Salazar-Carrillo. 1990. A generalized Konus system of index numbers for multilateral comparisons. In *Comparisons of prices and real products in Latin America,* ed. J. Salazar-Carrillo and D. S. Prasada Rao. Amsterdam: North-Holland.

Rothbarth, Erwin. 1941. The measurement of changes in real income under conditions of rationing. *Review of Economic Studies* 8 (February): 100–107.

Stern, H. 1993. Probability models on rankings and the electoral process. In Fligner and Verducci (1993).

Young, H. P. 1995. Optimal voting rules. *Journal of Economic Perspectives* 9, no. 1: 51–64.

9. The mathematical intuition of this step can be found in the analogous step used to derive the closed form of the Geary-Khamis index (see eq. GK-3 above).

2 International Comparisons Using Spanning Trees

Robert J. Hill

A large number of index number methods have been proposed for making multilateral comparisons across countries. A distinction can be drawn between methods that compare all countries in a comparison simultaneously and those that compare countries by simply linking together bilateral comparisons. Methods of the former type are surveyed in Hill (1997). Here, I focus on methods of the latter type. This procedure of linking bilateral comparisons is often referred to as *chaining*. Chaining has a long history. In fact, it dates all the way back to Marshall (1887). However, historically, interest in chaining has focused primarily on time-series comparisons. This is because of the natural chronological ordering of time-series data. In particular, chronological chaining (i.e., linking together bilateral comparisons between adjacent time periods) has been widely advocated for measuring inflation.

Nevertheless, some work has been done on chaining across countries. Two notable references are Kravis, Heston, and Summers (1982) and Szulc (1996). Kravis, Heston, and Summers focus on chaining in the context of multilateral comparisons, while Szulc focuses on bilateral comparisons. More specifically, Szulc argues that, under certain conditions, a chained bilateral comparison is preferable to a direct bilateral comparison.

The analysis in this paper is framed using spanning trees. This is because spanning trees provide the underlying structure for any method of chaining. In fact, in a comparison between K countries, K^{K-2} different spanning trees are defined, each of which generates different results. This paper argues that the preferred method of linking should be the one that minimizes the sensitivity of the results to the choice of index number formula. Two methods are then proposed on the basis of this criterion. The minimum spanning tree (MST) method

Robert J. Hill is a senior lecturer in economics at the University of New South Wales in Sydney, Australia.

selects the spanning tree that is least sensitive to the choice of index number formula, while the shortest path (SP) method selects the path between two countries that is least sensitive to the choice of index number formula. The MST method develops the work of Kravis, Heston, and Summers, while the SP method builds on Szulc. These methods are illustrated using OECD data.

2.1 Spanning Trees

A spanning tree links vertices (in this case countries) in such a way that there is exactly one path between any pair of vertices. An edge connecting two vertices in a spanning tree denotes a bilateral index number comparison between those two countries. The comparison could be made using any bilateral formula, such as Paasche, Laspeyres, Fisher, or Törnqvist. Multilateral indexes are obtained by linking the bilateral indexes as specified by the spanning tree. However, it matters whether the bilateral formula satisfies the country reversal test. A purchasing power parity (PPP) index P_{jk} between countries j and k with j as the base satisfies the country reversal test if $P_{jk} = 1/P_{kj}$. Fisher and Törnqvist satisfy this test, while Paasche and Laspeyres do not. If the bilateral index that is used violates the country reversal test, then the edges in the spanning tree must have directional arrows to indicate the base country in each bilateral comparison. Directional arrows are not necessary if the bilateral formula satisfies the country reversal test.

Three examples of spanning trees defined on the set of five vertices are depicted in figure 2.1. In general, K^{K-2} different spanning trees are defined on the set of K vertices. The *star* spanning tree depicted in figure 2.1a and the *string* spanning tree in figure 2.1b have both been widely used to measure inflation. An important issue in the inflation-measurement literature has been the debate over the relative merits of a fixed-base-price index as opposed to a chronologically chained price index. Ultimately, this is just a debate over two alternative spanning trees. By a *fixed-base-price index* is meant a price index constructed using the star spanning tree with the base time period placed at the center of the star. Conversely, by a *chronologically chained price index* is meant a price index constructed using the string spanning tree with the time periods linked chronologically.[1]

In the international comparison literature, Kravis, Heston, and Summers (1982) suggest using a variant on the star spanning tree. Using cluster analysis techniques, the set of countries can be divided into more homogeneous subsets. Various criteria are considered for measuring similarity across countries to enable cluster formation. These criteria range from geographic propinquity and price correlation coefficients to Paasche-Laspeyres spreads. Then star spanning trees defined over these clusters are linked to form a spanning tree defined

---

1. The measurement of inflation using spanning trees is discussed in greater detail in Hill (1999a).

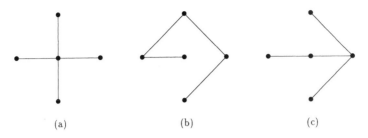

Fig. 2.1   **Examples of spanning trees**

over the whole set. However, the problem with this approach is that it imposes arbitrary constraints on the spanning tree. In particular, the center country for each cluster and the link countries between clusters are both chosen arbitrarily.

The minimum spanning tree (MST) method developed in this paper extends the pioneering work of Kravis, Heston, and Summers. However, rather than using Paasche-Laspeyres spreads to form clusters of countries along the lines of Kravis, Heston, and Summers and then constructing a spanning tree indirectly by linking together star spanning trees defined over these clusters, the MST method obtains a spanning tree directly by feeding the Paasche-Laspeyres spreads into Kruskal's minimum spanning tree algorithm without imposing any arbitrary restrictions. It is argued later that this spanning tree minimizes the sensitivity of the results of a multilateral comparison to the choice of bilateral index number formula.

Szulc instead focuses on bilateral comparisons and establishes conditions under which a chained comparison is preferable to a direct comparison. His criterion selects the path between two countries that most closely resembles successive linear combinations of their expenditure vectors. Sometimes the selected path is a direct comparison, while at other times it links the two countries indirectly via one or more other countries in the set. The shortest path (SP) method proposed here approaches the same problem from a different perspective. My criterion uses the shortest path algorithm to find the path between two countries with the smallest chained Paasche-Laspeyres spread. Again, it is argued later that such a path minimizes the sensitivity of the results of a bilateral comparison to the choice of bilateral index number formula. If the shortest path is calculated between one specific country and all other countries in the set, then the union of these shortest paths constitutes a spanning tree. Each country has its own shortest path spanning tree.

2.2   Notation and Definitions

The set of countries is indexed by $k = 1, \ldots, K$. It is assumed that each country supplies price and quantity data (p_{ki}, q_{ki}), defined over the same set of goods and services, indexed by $i = 1, \ldots, N$. Let P_{jk} and Q_{jk} denote, respectively, a bilateral purchasing power parity (PPP) and quantity index between countries j and k. Three important bilateral formulas are Paasche, Laspeyres, and Fisher. These indexes are defined as follows:

(1) $\qquad$ Paasche: $\quad P^P_{jk} = \dfrac{\displaystyle\sum_{i=1}^{N} p_{ki} q_{ki}}{\displaystyle\sum_{i=1}^{N} p_{ji} q_{ki}}, \quad Q^P_{jk} = \dfrac{\displaystyle\sum_{i=1}^{N} p_{ki} q_{ki}}{\displaystyle\sum_{i=1}^{N} p_{ki} q_{ji}},$

(2) $\qquad$ Laspeyres: $\quad P^L_{jk} = \dfrac{\displaystyle\sum_{i=1}^{N} p_{ki} q_{ji}}{\displaystyle\sum_{i=1}^{N} p_{ji} q_{ji}}, \quad Q^L_{jk} = \dfrac{\displaystyle\sum_{i=1}^{N} p_{ji} q_{ki}}{\displaystyle\sum_{i=1}^{N} p_{ji} q_{ji}},$

(3) $\qquad$ Fisher: $\quad P^F_{jk} = (P^P_{jk} P^L_{jk})^{1/2}, \quad Q^F_{jk} = (Q^P_{jk} Q^L_{jk})^{1/2}.$

The Paasche-Laspeyres spread (PLS) index between countries j and k is defined as follows:

(4) $\qquad$ $\text{PLS}_{jk} = \log\left[\dfrac{\max(P^P_{jk}, P^L_{jk})}{\min(P^P_{jk}, P^L_{jk})}\right] = \log\left[\dfrac{\max(Q^P_{jk}, Q^L_{jk})}{\min(Q^P_{jk}, Q^L_{jk})}\right].$

The PLS index has the following properties:

PROPERTY 1: $\text{PLS}_{jj} = 0.$

PROPERTY 2: $\text{PLS}_{jk} = \text{PLS}_{kj}.$

PROPERTY 3: $\text{PLS}_{jk} \geq 0.$

In a bilateral context, the spread between corresponding Paasche and Laspeyres indexes may be interpreted as a measure of the sensitivity of the results to the choice of index number formula. This is because, as Paasche and Laspeyres converge, so do all other bilateral index number formulas.[2] In the limit, if the price data satisfy the conditions for Hicks's (1946) composite commodity theorem, then all price index formulas give the same answer.[3] Similarly, in the limit, if the quantity data satisfy the conditions for Leontief's (1936) aggregation theorem, then all quantity index formulas give the same answer.[4] Under both scenarios, $\text{PLS}_{jk} = 0.$ This paper develops a framework for generalizing this idea to both chained bilateral and multilateral comparisons.

2. In fact, if preferences are homothetic, then Paasche and Laspeyres provide lower and upper bounds on the true underlying cost-of-living index.
3. The price data of countries j and k satisfy the conditions for Hicks's composite commodity theorem if $p_{ji} = \lambda p_{ki}$, $\forall\, i = 1, \ldots, N$, where λ denotes an arbitrary positive scalar.
4. The quantity data of countries j and k satisfy the conditions for Leontief's aggregation theorem if $q_{ji} = \lambda q_{ki}$, $\forall\, i = 1, \ldots, N$, where λ denotes an arbitrary positive scalar.

2.3   The Shortest Path (SP) Method

The SP method selects the path between two countries with the smallest summed PLS index. For example, suppose that there are three countries, A, B, and C, and that we wish to find the shortest path between A and B. If $PLS_{AB} \leq PLS_{AC} + PLS_{CB}$, then the shortest path is a direct comparison between A and B. Otherwise, the shortest path is via country C. The shortest path is the path between two countries with the smallest chained Paasche-Laspeyres spread. Hence, it minimizes the sensitivity of the results to the choice of bilateral index number formula.

The shortest path can be calculated between one specific country and all other countries in the set. The union of these $K - 1$ shortest paths is a spanning tree. This spanning tree for each country is easily calculated using the shortest path spanning tree algorithm run on Mathematica (see Skiena 1990). Figures 2.2 and 2.3 depict the shortest path spanning trees, respectively, of the United States and Turkey calculated over the set of twenty-four OECD countries for 198 goods and services headings in 1990. In figure 2.2, for only seven of twenty-three countries is a direct comparison the shortest path to the United States. For example, the shortest path between the United States and Sweden

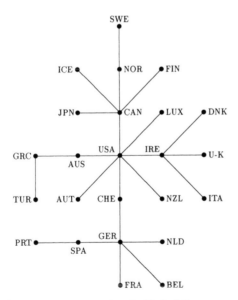

Fig. 2.2   Shortest path spanning tree for the United States

Note: The country codes are as follows: GER = Germany, FRA = France, ITA = Italy, NLD = Netherlands, BEL = Belgium, LUX = Luxembourg, U-K = United Kingdom, IRE = Ireland, DNK = Denmark, GRC = Greece, SPA = Spain, PRT = Portugal, AUT = Austria, CHE = Switzerland, FIN = Finland, ICE = Iceland, NOR = Norway, SWE = Sweden, TUR = Turkey, AUS = Australia, NZL = New Zealand, JPN = Japan, CAN = Canada, USA = United States.

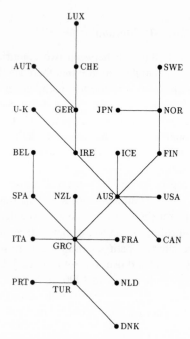

Fig. 2.3   Shortest path spanning tree for Turkey
Note: See note to fig. 2.2.

is via Canada and Norway. Similarly, in figure 2.3, for only three countries is a direct comparison the shortest path to Turkey. Hence, the results obtained here support the conclusion of Szulc (1996) that chaining is often desirable even in bilateral comparisons.

Table 2.1 compares the direct Paasche-Laspeyres spreads with the shortest path chained Paasche-Laspeyres spreads obtained from figures 2.2 and 2.3 for the United States and Turkey. Chaining along the shortest path reduces the ratio of Laspeyres to Paasche by up to 10 percent. The biggest reduction in this ratio is obtained in a comparison between Turkey and Luxembourg. Table 2.2 compares the direct Fisher PPPs with the shortest path chained Fisher PPPs for the United States and Turkey. Again, the biggest change is obtained in a comparison between Turkey and Luxembourg. This time the change is about 11 percent. It is worth noting that Turkey appears relatively poorer compared with most other OECD countries if it is compared directly using Fisher indexes as opposed to along the shortest path. By contrast, no systematic pattern emerges for the United States. For eight countries, it appears relatively richer when compared by chaining Fisher indexes along the shortest path, but, conversely, for eight other countries, it appears relatively richer when compared directly. For the other seven countries, it makes no difference since the shortest path is a direct comparison.

Table 2.1   Laspeyres PPPs Divided by Paasche PPPs

	Direct (D), United States	Chained (C), United States	D/C, United States	Direct, Turkey	Chained, Turkey	D/C, Turkey
Germany	1.055	1.050	1.005	1.270	1.167	1.088
France	1.092	1.075	1.016	1.192	1.157	1.030
Italy	1.098	1.084	1.014	1.163	1.152	1.010
Netherlands	1.081	1.066	1.014	1.225	1.169	1.049
Belgium	1.081	1.070	1.010	1.247	1.169	1.067
Luxembourg	1.051	1.051	1	1.312	1.189	1.104
United Kingdom	1.079	1.058	1.021	1.180	1.171	1.008
Ireland	1.047	1.047	1	1.177	1.159	1.016
Denmark	1.128	1.078	1.046	1.162	1.162	1
Greece	1.142	1.118	1.022	1.079	1.079	1
Spain	1.098	1.095	1.003	1.129	1.121	1.007
Portugal	1.189	1.143	1.040	1.094	1.094	1
Austria	1.051	1.051	1	1.216	1.179	1.031
Switzerland	1.049	1.049	1	1.237	1.168	1.059
Finland	1.074	1.065	1.009	1.168	1.166	1.002
Iceland	1.079	1.078	1.001	1.189	1.182	1.005
Norway	1.090	1.061	1.027	1.281	1.173	1.092
Sweden	1.097	1.079	1.017	1.215	1.192	1.020
Turkey	1.317	1.207	1.091	1	1	1
Australia	1.056	1.056	1	1.192	1.143	1.044
New Zealand	1.068	1.068	1	1.180	1.160	1.018
Japan	1.101	1.079	1.021	1.298	1.203	1.079
Canada	1.034	1.034	1	1.263	1.169	1.080
United States	1	1	1	1.317	1.207	1.091

Table 2.2   **Direct and Chained Fisher PPPs**

	Direct, United States = 1	Chained, United States = 1	Max(Direct, Chained)/ Min(Direct, Chained), United States	Direct, Turkey = 1,000	Chained, Turkey = 1,000	Max(Direct, Chained)/ Min(Direct, Chained), Turkey
Germany	2.050	2.107	1.028	1.373	1.430	1.042
France	6.585	6.605	1.003	4.490	4.662	1.038
Italy	1,438	1,475	1.026	923.0	1,002	1.086
Netherlands	2.126	2.176	1.024	1.490	1.501	1.007
Belgium	38.91	39.91	1.026	26.52	27.33	1.031
Luxembourg	40.02	40.02	1	25.00	27.87	1.115
United Kingdom	.6074	.6180	1.017	.4060	.4152	1.023
Ireland	.7100	.7100	1	.4340	.4769	1.099
Denmark	9.208	9.656	1.049	6.364	6.364	1
Greece	141.0	142.4	1.010	98.51	98.51	1
Spain	112.2	111.0	1.011	75.14	76.20	1.014
Portugal	104.0	103.5	1.005	70.88	70.88	1
Austria	14.28	14.28	1	9.126	9.667	1.059
Switzerland	2.190	2.190	1	1.478	1.486	1.005
Finland	6.489	6.213	1.044	4.343	4.407	1.015
Iceland	82.58	80.12	1.031	54.01	56.16	1.040
Norway	9.795	9.464	1.035	6.268	6.675	1.065
Sweden	9.246	9.020	1.025	6.199	6.361	1.026
Turkey	1,481	1,446	1.024	1,000	1,000	1
Australia	1.381	1.381	1	.9590	.956	1.003
New Zealand	1.587	1.587	1	1.122	1.118	1.004
Japan	197.2	190.2	1.037	136.0	131.5	1.034
Canada	1.274	1.274	1	.8850	.8944	1.011
United States	1	1	1	.6750	.6918	1.025

2.4   The Minimum Spanning Tree (MST) Method

The observation that the PLS index between two countries provides a measure of the sensitivity of the results of a bilateral comparison to the choice of index number formula can be generalized to spanning trees. A comparison between K countries has a $K \times K$ matrix of PLS indexes. The matrix is symmetrical (property 2) with zeros on the lead diagonal (property 1). Hence, the matrix has $K(K - 1)/2$ distinct PLS indexes. However, a spanning tree defined on K vertices has only $K - 1$ edges. Each edge has a corresponding PLS index. Therefore, each spanning tree uses only $K - 1$ of the possible $K(K - 1)/2$ PLS indexes. An overall measure of sensitivity to the choice of index number formula for each spanning tree can be obtained from the $K - 1$ PLS indexes of the bilateral comparisons contained within the spanning tree.

The minimum spanning tree is the spanning tree defined on a set of vertices with the smallest sum of weights. In our context, the weight on each edge is its corresponding PLS index. Hence, the minimum spanning tree is the spanning tree with the smallest sum of PLS indexes. The minimum spanning tree is a natural extension of the shortest path to multilateral comparisons.

A number of equivalent algorithms exist in the graph theory literature for computing the minimum spanning tree of a graph. The minimum spanning tree for the OECD countries in figure 2.4 was computed using Kruskal's algorithm run on Mathematica (again, see Skiena 1990). It should be noted that the algorithm is very efficient. In a comparison of over 24^{22} spanning trees, it finds the optimal spanning tree almost instantly.

Kruskal's algorithm proceeds as follows. The algorithm begins by ranking the edges according to the size of their weights (PLS indexes).[5] Then the edge with the smallest weight is selected, subject to the constraint that it does not create a cycle. If selecting this edge creates a cycle, then the algorithm skips it and moves on to the edge with the next smallest weight. This procedure for selecting edges is repeated until it is no longer possible to select any more edges without creating a cycle, at which point the algorithm terminates. In practice, this implies that the algorithm always selects exactly $K - 1$ edges. The set of vertices and selected edges constitutes the minimum spanning tree. Hence, the minimum spanning tree is constructed from edges connecting pairs of countries with the smallest Paasche-Laspeyres spreads. A proof that Kruskal's algorithm finds the spanning tree with the smallest sum of weights can be found in Wilson (1985, 55).

The minimum spanning tree in figure 2.4 is compared to the star spanning trees with the United States and Turkey at the center, respectively, in table 2.3. The PPPs in table 2.3 are calculated by chaining Fisher PPPs across the respective spanning tree. Each set of PPPs is normalized so that the PPP for

---

5. The probability of encountering ties becomes negligible if the PLS indexes are calculated to a sufficiently large number of decimal places.

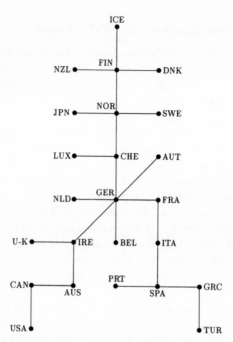

Fig. 2.4   Minimum spanning tree for the OECD
Note: See note to fig. 2.2.

the United States equals one. A clear pattern emerges from table 2.3. For eight of twenty-three countries, the MST PPP lies between the two star PPPs. However, for the remaining fifteen countries, the MST PPP is less than both star PPPs. This implies that the United States will tend to appear richer relative to the other OECD countries in 1990 if a comparison is made by chaining Fisher PPPs across either star spanning tree as opposed to the minimum spanning tree. (It is not clear whether this result generalizes to other years.)

Once selected, the minimum spanning tree can be used for subsequent multilateral comparisons.[6] This greatly simplifies international comparisons by dramatically reducing the number of countries that must be compared directly. By chaining across the minimum spanning tree, each country is compared only with its neighbors in the tree. Hence, these comparisons can be made over a more representative set of goods and services, especially since by construction the neighbors have relatively similar price and expenditure patterns. In contrast, most other multilateral PPP methods require all countries in a compari-

6. Admittedly, the minimum spanning tree is unlikely to be very robust. However, the minimum spanning tree at one point in time is likely to be only slightly suboptimal at a later date. Hence, it is not necessarily unreasonable to use the same spanning tree for a number of years. A sensitivity analysis of the MST method is provided in Hill (1999b).

Table 2.3   **Star and Minimum Spanning Tree Chained Fisher PPPs**

	Star with United States at Center	Star with Turkey at Center	Minimum Spanning Tree
Germany	2.050	2.034	2.037
France	6.585	6.652	6.384
Italy	1,438	1,367	1,372
Netherlands	2.126	2.207	2.104
Belgium	38.91	39.28	38.58
Luxembourg	40.02	37.03	39.70
United Kingdom	.607	.601	.591
Ireland	.710	.643	.679
Denmark	9.208	9.428	9.208
Greece	141.0	145.9	137.2
Spain	112.2	111.3	106.1
Portugal	104.0	105.0	99.03
Austria	14.28	13.52	13.77
Switzerland	2.190	2.190	2.117
Finland	6.489	6.434	6.244
Iceland	82.58	80.01	79.43
Norway	9.795	9.286	9.457
Sweden	9.246	9.184	9.013
Turkey	1,481	1,481	1,393
Australia	1.381	1.421	1.361
New Zealand	1.587	1.662	1.577
Japan	197.2	201.5	186.3
Canada	1.274	1.311	1.274
United States	1	1	1

son to supply price and expenditure data over the same basket of goods and services. This requirement creates difficulties since a staple good in one country may be rare or even unobtainable in another country. This is particularly a problem in comparisons between rich and poor countries.

2.5   Conclusion

Any method of chaining index numbers has an underlying spanning tree. However, a comparison between K countries has K^{K-2} possible spanning trees, each of which generates different results. This paper uses this insight to develop two new methods of making international comparisons. Both methods discriminate between spanning trees on the basis of the sensitivity of their resulting indexes to the choice of index number formula. The shortest path (SP) method minimizes sensitivity in bilateral comparisons, while the minimum spanning tree (MST) method minimizes sensitivity in multilateral comparisons. Both methods are illustrated using OECD data.

References

Hicks, J. R. 1946. *Value and capital.* 2d ed. Oxford: Clarendon.

Hill, R. J. 1997. A taxonomy of multilateral methods for making international comparisons of prices and quantities. *Review of Income and Wealth,* ser. 43, no. 1:49–69.

———. 1999a. Measuring inflation and growth using spanning trees. *International Economic Review,* forthcoming.

———. 1999b. Comparing price levels across countries using minimum-spanning trees. *Review of Economics and Statistics* 81, no. 1:135–42.

Kravis, I. K., A. Heston, and R. Summers. 1982. *World product and income: International comparisons of real gross product.* Baltimore: Johns Hopkins University Press.

Leontief, W. 1936. Composite commodities and the problem of index numbers. *Econometrica* 4:39–59.

Marshall, A. 1887. Remedies for fluctuations of general prices. *Contemporary Review* 51:355–75.

Skiena, S. 1990. *Implementing discrete mathematics: Combinatorics and graph theory with mathematica.* Redwood City, Calif.: Addison-Wesley.

Szulc, B. 1996. Criterion for adequate linking paths in chain indices. In *Improving the quality of price indices,* ed. L. Biggeri. Luxembourg: Eurostat.

Wilson, R. J. 1985. *Introduction to graph theory.* 3d ed. New York: Longman.

II Interarea Price and Wage Comparisons

3 Interarea Price Comparisons for Heterogeneous Goods and Several Levels of Commodity Aggregation

Mary F. Kokoski, Brent R. Moulton, and Kimberly D. Zieschang

There has been steady interest for many years among academic, business, and policy users of economic data for "purchasing power parities" permitting conversions of the gross domestic product of two or more countries, which information is compiled in national currency, into common units so that the real size of one economy can be measured relative to another. In the available literature on international comparisons, the microeconomic foundations for such conversion measures have been most definitively considered by Diewert (1986). In this paper, we focus on a part of the consumption component of GDP and consider comparing the price of consumption among areas within a given country rather than between countries. Judging from periodic contacts from data users with Bureau of Labor Statistics (BLS) staff, such place-to-price comparisons for areas within the United States are very much in demand. In our approach to this problem, we contribute to the resolution of several technical issues in compiling both interarea and international price indexes, including imposing transitivity (the so-called aggregation problem of international comparisons) and the problem of adjusting for interarea differences in the composition and quality of consumption, among others. Although not specifically designed for producing interarea comparisons, the database from

Mary F. Kokoski is an economist in the division of price and index number research at the Bureau of Labor Statistics, U.S. Department of Labor. Brent R. Moulton is associate director for national income, expenditure, and wealth accounts at the Bureau of Economic Analysis, U.S. Department of Commerce. This paper was completed while he was chief of the division of price and index number research at the Bureau of Labor Statistics, U.S. Department of Labor. Kimberly D. Zieschang is a senior economist with the International Monetary Fund. This paper was completed while he was associate commissioner for compensation and working conditions at the Bureau of Labor Statistics, U.S. Department of Labor.

The opinions expressed in this paper are those of the authors and do not represent the policies of the Bureau of Labor Statistics (BLS) or the views of other BLS staff members.

which the U.S. consumer price index (CPI) is calculated is nevertheless a rich source of geographic price information, one that we exploit in this study.

We adopt a Törnqvist measurement framework and derive a very general form for a transitive, multilateral system of parities within that framework. The Caves, Christensen, and Diewert (CCD) (1982b) implementation of the Eltetö, Köves, and Szulc (EKS) methodology (described in English in Dreschler [1973]) for multilateral price measurement uses a special case of this general multilateral form, one involving the estimation of $2N - 1$ parameters when there are N items in the index aggregate. The unknown parameters represent a reference set of value shares and prices against which the shares and prices of all areas are compared. We show that, if Törnqvist aggregates are to be formed from lower-level aggregates on a single, that is, commodity, aggregation tree, the adjustment can be applied successively from the lowest to the highest levels of aggregation to produce a set of reference prices that, while fixed across areas, have components corresponding to each level of item aggregation.

We adapt earlier index number results from Zieschang (1985, 1988) and Fixler and Zieschang (1992) to incorporate information on the characteristics of the products that are systematically randomly sampled for the CPI using country-product-dummy regression at "entry-level item" product detail. In this index number framework, coefficients from these regressions are used in constructing quality-adjustment factors for the place-to-place price comparisons.

We show how the parameters of the transitive Törnqvist system can be estimated with a particular regression model to impose transitivity with minimal adjustment of the data. We believe that the model represents, if not a completely new approach, a substantive refinement of the regression-based multilateral adjustment that underlies the versions of EKS expounded by, for example, Cuthbert and Cuthbert (1988) and Selvanathan and Rao (1992).

Kokoski, Cardiff, and Moulton (1994) estimate country-product-dummy regressions on micro data from the U.S. consumer price index for the thirteen-month period June 1988–July 1989. The models are fitted at the index item level to produce quality-adjusted price indexes for the lowest, item level of aggregation. The regression methodology developed in this paper for imposing transitivity is demonstrated on data for a small, three-aggregation-level example problem for fruits and vegetables from an extract of 1993 data based on the Kokoski, Cardiff, and Moulton (1994) study, presaging the computation of price indexes for successively higher commodity aggregates for the forty-four major urban centers and region-city size groups covered by the CPI.

We close by summarizing the methodological and empirical results, by describing an application of the methodology enforcing consistency between comparisons across areas within a given time period and comparisons across time within a given area. Finally, we point out a notable advantage of this framework for compiling international parities over the narrow specification approach now used in the International Comparisons Project (ICP). Provided that a standard list of item characteristics and item groups is promulgated, item strata can be broadened, increasing the likelihood of finding a useful specification from country to country. Further, this advantage is not bought at the cost of operational feasibility since calculation can be decentralized, obviating the need for central, transnational access to closely guarded national micro data.

3.1   Economic Index Number Concepts Incorporating Information on the Characteristics of Heterogeneous Goods

Let p_i^a be the price in area a, of which there are A areas in total, of commodity i. Let q_i^a be the corresponding quantity purchased, and let x_i^a be the vector of characteristics of the ith item specification transacted in area a. Let e_h^a represent the total expenditures of consumer unit h in area a. We will use interchangeably the terms *economic household* and *consumer unit* for the economic unit of analysis, following BLS terminology. A consumer unit is a group of individuals whose consumption decisions for significant components of expenditure are joint or shared. Let q_h^a denote the vector of goods consumed by household h in area a with vector of characteristics x_h^a and prices p_h^a.

We suppose that each consumer unit in area a minimizes the cost of achieving a given level of welfare at expenditure level e_h^a so that the consumer unit cost of consumption of a given quality of goods as determined by the vector x_h^a would be

$$e_h^a = E_h^a(u_h^a, \ x_h^a, \ p_h^a) = \min_{q_h^a} \{p_h^a q_h^a : F_h^a(x_h^a, \ q_h^a) \geq u_h^a\},$$

where $F_h^a(x_h^a, q_h^a)$ is the utility function of consumer unit h, and u_h^a is the unit's welfare index.

We suppose further that the consumer unit in area a faces a hedonic locus of market equilibrium prices across the quality spectrum given by $p_h^a = H^a(x_h^a)$ and that the unit minimizes the cost of achieving welfare level u_h^a over the characteristics of goods, with the result that

(1) $$\nabla_{x_h^a} E_h^a(u_h^a, \ x_h^a, \ p_h^a) + \nabla_{x_h^a} p_h^{a\prime} \nabla_{p_h^a} E_h^a(u_h^a, \ x_h^a, \ p_h^a) = 0.$$

Since $\nabla_{x_h^a} p_h^a = \nabla_{x_h^a} H^a$ and $\nabla_{p_h^a} E_h^a(u_h^a, x_h^a, p_h^a) = q_h^a$, the latter by the Shephard/ Hotelling lemma, we have

(2) $$\nabla_{x_h^a} E_h^a(u_h^a, \ x_h^a, \ p_h^a) = -\nabla_{x_h^a} H^{a\prime} q_h^a.$$

If H^a is semilog, as generally assumed in hedonic studies, so that

(3) $$\ln H_i^a = \alpha_i^a + \beta_i^{a\prime} x_i^a,$$

then the characteristics gradient expression can be rewritten

(4) $$\nabla_{x_h^a} E_h^a(u_h^a, \; x_h^a, \; p_h^a) \; = \; -\beta^{a'} w_h^a e_h^a,$$

where

$$w_{i,h}^a \; = \; \frac{p_{i,h}^a q_{i,h}^a}{\sum_i p_{i,h}^a q_{i,h}^a},$$

$$w_h^a \; = \; \begin{bmatrix} w_{1,h}^a \\ \vdots \\ w_{N_q,h}^a \end{bmatrix}, \quad N_q \; = \; \text{number of commodities},$$

$$\beta^{a'} \; = \; \begin{bmatrix} \beta_1^{a'} \\ \vdots \\ \beta_{N_x}^{a'} \end{bmatrix}, \quad N_x \; = \; \text{number of product characteristics}.$$

Turning now to aggregate expenditure over consumer units in an area, Diewert (1987) has considered this problem as a weighted average of individual household index numbers comparing the prices in two areas in the "democratic-weighting" case. In this paper, we follow his characterization of the "plutocratic" expenditure-weighted case with some modifications for the heterogeneity of goods within and between areas. The area aggregate expenditure function is

$$E^a(\vec{u}^a, \; \vec{x}^a, \; \vec{p}^a) \; = \; \sum_h E_h^a(u_h^a, \; x_h^a, \; p_h^a),$$

where the arrow over an argument indicates the concatenation of vectors across households. We then consider the expenditure function in terms of log transformed price arguments as

$$Q^a(\vec{u}^a, \; \vec{x}^a, \; \ln \vec{p}^a) \; = \; E^a(\vec{u}^a, \; \vec{x}^a, \; \vec{p}^a) \; = \; \sum_h E_h^a(u_h^a, \; x_h^a, \; p_h^a)$$

$$= \; \sum_h Q_h^a(u_h^a, \; x_h^a, \; \ln p_h^a).$$

We "plutocratically" aggregate across households in area a such that the expenditure-weighted averages for characteristics and log prices represent the indicators determining area demand behavior, where area item demand is the sum of the economic household item demands for the area.[1] We do not require strong aggregation conditions but effectively hold the distribution of product characteristics and prices fixed across economic households within area a as in

(5) $\tilde{Q}^a(\vec{u}^a, \; \overline{x}^a, \; \overline{\ln p}^a) = Q^a(\vec{u}^a, \iota \otimes \; \overline{x}^a + \; v_x^a, \; \iota \otimes \; \overline{\ln p}^a + \; v_{\ln p}^a),$

---

1. Actually, the results to follow do not depend on the particular form of area aggregation for product characteristics and prices. Although this discussion is couched in terms of an arithmetic area mean for characteristics and a geometric mean for prices, others will work as well.

where $v_x^a = \vec{x}^a - \iota \otimes \bar{x}^a$, $v_{\ln p}^a = \overrightarrow{\ln p}^a - \iota \otimes \overline{\ln p}^a$, $\iota =$ a vector of ones of dimension equal to the number of households, and $\otimes =$ Kronecker product, all giving the deviations of the area means from the individual household values for commodity characteristics and prices paid.

Using the derivatives of the expenditure function with respect to log prices expressed in terms of observable expenditure shares, Diewert (1976) and Caves, Christensen, and Diewert (1982a) have shown that the Törnqvist index number is exact for the translog flexible functional form. The translog aggregator function differentially approximates any price aggregator function (i.e., cost of utility, input cost, revenue function) to the second order at a point, and it is exact for the Törnqvist index number even when some of the parameters (those on the first-order terms) of the underlying aggregator function are different in the two periods or localities compared. We take the derivative of the area expenditure function with respect to interarea average household characteristics and price arguments to obtain

$$
(6) \quad \frac{\partial}{\partial \bar{x}_{iz}^a} \ln \tilde{E}^a\left(\bar{u}^a,\ \bar{x}^a,\ \exp\left(\overline{\ln p}^a\right)\right) = \frac{\partial}{\partial \bar{x}_{iz}^a} \ln \tilde{Q}^a\left(\bar{u}^a,\ \bar{x}^a,\ \overline{\ln p}^a\right)
$$

$$
= \sum_h \frac{\partial}{\partial x_{izh}^a} Q_h^a\left(u_h^a,\ x_h^a,\ \ln p_h^a\right) / \tilde{Q}^a = \beta_{iz}^a \sum_h w_{ih}^a s_h^a = -\beta_{iz}^a \bar{w}_i^a,
$$

$$
(7) \quad \frac{\partial}{\partial \ln p_i^a} \ln \tilde{E}\left(\bar{u}^a,\ \bar{x}^a,\ \exp\left(\overline{\ln p}^a\right)\right) = \frac{\partial}{\partial \ln p_i^a} \ln \tilde{Q}\left(\bar{u}^a,\ \bar{x}^a,\ \overline{\ln p}^a\right)
$$

$$
= \sum_h \frac{\partial}{\partial \ln p_{ih}^a} Q_h^a\left(u_h^a,\ x_h^a,\ \ln p_h^a\right) / \tilde{Q}^a = \sum_h w_{ih}^a s_h^a = \bar{w}_i^a,
$$

where

$$
w_{ih}^a = \frac{p_{ih}^a q_{ih}^a}{\sum_i p_{ih}^a q_{ih}^a} = \frac{p_{ih}^a q_{ih}^a}{e_h^a},
$$

$$
s_h^a = \frac{e_h^a}{\sum_h e_h^a},
$$

are, respectively, the within-household expenditure shares of commodities and the between-household total expenditure shares of consumer unit h in area a.

Finally, we assume that the area aggregate expenditure function $\ln \tilde{Q}^a(e^a, \bar{x}^a, \ln p^a)$ has a quadratic, "semi-translog" functional form in its arguments with coefficients of second-order terms independent of location but with possibly location-specific coefficients on linear terms. Following Caves, Christensen, and Diewert (1982a), then, we can derive the following (logarithmic) index number result:

$$\ln I^{ab} = \frac{1}{2}\left[\ln \tilde{Q}^a\left(\bar{u}^a, \bar{x}^b, \overline{\ln p^b}\right) - \ln \tilde{Q}^a\left(\bar{u}^a, \bar{x}^a, \overline{\ln p^a}\right)\right.$$

$$+ \ln \tilde{Q}^b\left(\bar{u}^b, \bar{x}^b, \overline{\ln p^b}\right) - \ln \tilde{Q}^b\left(\bar{u}^b, \bar{x}^a, \overline{\ln p^a}\right)\Bigg]$$

(8)

$$= \frac{1}{2}\left[\nabla_{\ln p}\ln \tilde{Q}^a\left(\bar{u}^a, \bar{x}^a, \overline{\ln p^a}\right) + \nabla_{\ln p}\ln \tilde{Q}^b\left(\bar{u}^b, \bar{x}^b, \overline{\ln p^b}\right)\right]\left(\overline{\ln p^b} - \overline{\ln p^a}\right)$$

$$+ \frac{1}{2}\left[\nabla_x\ln \tilde{Q}^a\left(\bar{u}^a, \bar{x}^a, \overline{\ln p^a}\right) + \nabla_x\ln \tilde{Q}^b\left(\bar{u}^b, \bar{x}^b, \overline{\ln p^b}\right)\right]\left(\bar{x}^b - \bar{x}^a\right).$$

Substituting (6) and (7) into (8), following Caves, Christensen, and Diewert (1982a) again, and with reference to Fixler and Zieschang (1992), we have

$$\ln I^{ab} = \ln T^{ab}$$

(9)

$$\equiv \frac{1}{2}\sum_i\left[\left(\bar{w}_i^a + \bar{w}_i^b\right)\left(\overline{\ln p_i^b} - \overline{\ln p_i^a}\right) - \sum_z(\beta_{iz}^a\bar{w}_i^a + \beta_{iz}^b\bar{w}_i^b)(\bar{x}_{iz}^b - \bar{x}_{iz}^a)\right].$$

This formula for the bilateral index between areas is an extremely flexible result that permits all parameters of the semilog "hedonic" price equations to differ by area, fully reflecting household optimization over measured product quantities and characteristics.

3.2 Törnqvist Multilateral (Transitive) Systems of Bilateral Index Numbers

In another paper, Caves, Christensen, and Diewert (1982b) noted that the system of bilateral Törnqvist interarea indexes is not transitive but developed a simply calculated multilateral variant satisfying the transitivity property. Returning to lowercase notation for the index arguments for areas, we derive the following general implication of transitivity for this class of index number:

PROPOSITION 1: For the bilateral Törnqvist item index to be transitive, it is necessary and sufficient that, for all a, b, there exist constant vectors w^0 and $\ln p^0$ such that

(10)
$$\sum_i w_i^a \ln p_i^b - \sum_i w_i^b \ln p_i^a = \sum_i w_i^0(\ln p_i^b - \ln p_i^a)$$
$$- \sum_i \ln p_i^0(w_i^b - w_i^a),$$

where w_i^0 = a reference share for index item i for the entire region, with $\sum_i w_i^0 = 1$, and p_i^0 = a reference price for index item i across the entire region. Furthermore, if this condition holds, the multilateral Törnqvist index has the form

$$\ln T^{ab} \equiv \sum_i \left[\frac{1}{2}(w_i^0 + w_i^b)(\ln p_i^b - \ln p_i^0) \right.$$

(11)

$$\left. - \frac{1}{2}(w_i^0 + w_i^a)(\ln p_i^a - \ln p_i^0) \right].$$

The proof is given in appendix A. Caves, Christensen, and Diewert (1982b) showed that application of the EKS principle to a system of bilateral Törnqvist indexes yields the formula given above with the reference shares and log prices set at their simple arithmetic averages across areas. Clearly, these simple averages could also be replaced with total expenditure-weighted averages. We consider still another way of estimating the reference shares and prices in the next section.

The overall system can be adjusted to be transitive in both prices and item characteristics by applying the principle underlying proposition 1. This is stated in proposition 2:

PROPOSITION 2: If the area-specific country-product-dummy (CPD) coefficients are known, for the bilateral quality-adjusted Törnqvist item index to be transitive it is necessary and sufficient that, for all a, b,

$$\sum_n w_i^a \left(\ln p_i^b - \left(\sum_z \beta_{iz}^a x_{iz}^b \right) \right) - \left[\sum_i w_i^a \left(\ln p_i^a - \left(\sum_z \beta_{iz}^a x_{iz}^a \right) \right) \right]$$

(12)

$$= \sum_i \sum_{z^b} [-\beta_{iz}^0 w_i^0](x_{iz}^b - x_{iz}^a) + \sum_i \sum_z x_{iz}^0 (\beta_{iz}^b w_i^b - \beta_{iz}^a w_i^a)$$

$$+ \sum_i w_i^0 (\ln p_i^b - \ln p_i^a) + \sum_i [-\ln p_i^0](w_i^b - w_i^a),$$

where x_{iz}^0 = a reference characteristic z for index item i across the entire region, β_{iz}^0 = a reference coefficient for the characteristic z of item i in a semilog hedonic equation explaining specification price across the entire region, p_i^0 = a reference price for item i across the entire region, and w_i^0 = a reference share for item i for the entire region. Furthermore, if this condition holds, the bilateral Törnqvist index for item group i has the form

$$\ln T^{ab} =$$

(13)

$$-\sum_i \sum_z \frac{1}{2}(\beta_{iz}^0 w_i^0 + \beta_{iz}^b w_i^b)(x_{iz}^b - x_{iz}^0) + \sum_i \frac{1}{2}(w_i^0 + w_i^b)(\ln p_i^b - \ln p_i^0)$$

$$- \left[-\sum_i \sum_z \frac{1}{2}(\beta_{iz}^0 w_i^0 + \beta_{iz}^a w_i^a)(x_{iz}^a - x_{iz}^0) + \sum_i \frac{1}{2}(w_i^0 + w_i^a)(\ln p_i^a - \ln p_i^0) \right].$$

3.3 Multilateral Price Measurement with Subaggregates of Items

Let p_{ijklmn}^a be the price in area a, of which there are A areas in total, of specification n in item group m in stratum class l in basic heading class k in group j

in major group or division i. Let q_{ijklmn}^a be the corresponding quantity purchased. The bilateral Törnqvist index comparing the prices in areas a and b for item aggregate $ijklm$ is

$$\ln T_{ijklm}^{ab} \equiv \sum_n \frac{1}{2}(w_{ijklmn}^a + w_{ijklmn}^a)(\ln p_{ijklmn}^b - \ln p_{ijklmn}^a),$$

where w_{ijklmn}^a = the value share in area a of specification $ijklmn$ within the next-higher group $ijklm$, with $w_{ijklmn}^a \equiv (p_{ijklmn}^a q_{ijklmn}^a)/(\sum_n p_{ijklmn}^a q_{ijklmn}^a)$ and with q_{ijklmn}^a the quantity of the specification transacted, so that $\sum_n w_{ijklmn}^a = 1$.

3.3.1 Analysis of the Contribution of Subaggregates to Levels of Place-to-Place Indexes

In practice, index numbers are produced for hierarchical classification trees of products, industries, occupations, etc. Because Törnqvist indexes are linear in the log differences of detailed specification prices, the contribution of each subaggregate, say, women's apparel, to the all-items-level ratio between two areas can be readily calculated by exponentiating the appropriate weighted sums of log price differences. These sums would be calculated from the transitive expression for the index given in equation (11), where it is expressed in terms of locality weights averaged with reference weights and price differentials from reference prices. In this case, *all-items* bilateral indexes are constructed as the direct aggregation of the specification prices as

$$\ln T^{ab} \equiv \sum_i \sum_j \sum_k \sum_l \sum_m \sum_n \left[\frac{1}{2}(w_{ijklmn}^0 + w_{ijklmn}^b)(\ln p_{ijklmn}^b - \ln p_{ijklmn}^0)\right.$$

$$\left. -\frac{1}{2}(w_{ijklmn}^0 + w_{ijklmn}^a)(\ln p_{ijklmn}^a - \ln p_{ijklmn}^0)\right].$$

The contribution to the level of $\ln T^{ab}$ of major commodity group i would simply be the subordinate sum

$$\ln C_i^{ab} \equiv \sum_j \sum_k \sum_l \sum_m \sum_n \left[\frac{1}{2}(w_{ijklmn}^a + w_{ijklmn}^0)(\ln p_{ijklmn}^b - \ln p_{ijklmn}^0)\right.$$

$$\left. -\frac{1}{2}(w_{ijklmn}^a + w_{ijklmn}^0)(\ln p_{ijklmn}^a - \ln p_{ijklmn}^0)\right].$$

The simplicity of this approach to analysis of the place-to-place price differentials of subaggregates, and its focus on subaggregate change within the larger all-items context, has a great deal of appeal. The extension of this discussion to quality-adjusted price indexes, including characteristics, is straightforward and left to the reader.

3.3.2 Transitivity Simultaneously across Several Aggregation Levels

Nevertheless, when place-to-place subaggregate indexes are to be published in addition to the all-items index, it may not be seen as sufficient to adjust only the all-items index to be transitive. The subaggregates would then be required not only to satisfy transitivity but also to aggregate according to an index number rule to successively higher levels. This is a property distinct from consistency in aggregation, whereby an index formula for an aggregate calculated directly is the same as that calculated with the same formula successively applied to intermediate subaggregates. Rather, assuming that the same index formula is repeatedly applied at each level, as in the latter case, we would like all levels of aggregation to satisfy transitivity while preserving the aggregation rule so that users might also combine low-level aggregates following the same formula and weighting and be assured of obtaining the higher-level aggregates. We show that it is possible to construct such aggregation-consistent place-to-place indexes under a multilevel Törnqvist aggregation rule.

Having dealt with the first level of aggregation in section 3.1 above, we now consider aggregation of the item indexes $ijklm$ to the stratum level $ijkl$. We first observe from proposition 2 that the transitivity of the item aggregate $ijklm$ permits us to identify average price levels for the aggregate for each area in the region as

$$\ln \bar{p}^{a}_{ijklmn} = \sum_{n} \frac{1}{2}(w^{0}_{ijklmn} + w^{a}_{ijklmn})(\ln p^{a}_{ijklmn} - \ln p^{0}_{ijklmn}),$$

allowing us to rewrite the expression for the bilateral item index as

$$\ln T^{ab}_{ijklm} = \ln \bar{p}^{b}_{ijklm} - \ln \bar{p}^{a}_{ijklm}.$$

The bilateral index between areas a and b of the stratum aggregate $ijkl$ over item groups $ijklm$ is

$$\ln T^{ab}_{ijkl} = \sum_{m} \frac{1}{2}(w^{a}_{ijklm} + w^{b}_{ijklm})\ln T^{ab}_{ijklm}$$

$$= \sum_{m} \frac{1}{2}(w^{a}_{ijklm} + w^{ab}_{ijklm})(\ln \bar{p}^{b}_{ijklm} - \ln \bar{p}^{a}_{ijklm}).$$

Applying the proposition to the stratum level, the transitive bilateral index between areas a and b of the stratum aggregate $ijkl$ over item groups $ijklm$ is, therefore,

$$\ln T^{ab}_{ijkl} \equiv \sum_{m} \left[\frac{1}{2}(w^{0}_{ijklm} + w^{b}_{ijklm})(\ln \bar{p}^{b}_{ijklm} - \ln p^{0}_{ijklm}) \right.$$

$$\left. - \frac{1}{2}(w^{0}_{ijklm} + w^{a}_{ijklm})(\ln \bar{p}^{a}_{ijklm} - \ln p^{0}_{ijklm}) \right].$$

We note that the expression for the transitive Törnqvist *item* index given above would have been obtained if the reference *specification* prices had been $\ln p_{ijklmn}^{0(m)} = \ln p_{ijklmn}^{0} + \ln p_{ijklm}^{0}$. Further, if the specification reference prices were so adjusted, the transitivity of the lower-level item indexes would continue to hold. Further still, because each level's log index is the difference between weighted log price relatives, those components constant within group cancel, leaving only those elements varying with members of the group. To confirm,

$$\ln T_{ijklm}^{ab}$$

$$\equiv \sum_n \left[\frac{1}{2}(w_{ijklmn}^0 + w_{ijklmn}^b)(\ln \bar{p}_{ijklmn}^b - \ln p_{ijklmn}^0 - \ln p_{ijklm}^0) \right.$$

$$\left. - \frac{1}{2}(w_{ijklmn}^0 + w_{ijklmn}^a)(\ln \bar{p}_{ijklmn}^a - \ln p_{ijklmn}^0 - \ln p_{ijklm}^0) \right]$$

$$= \sum_n \left[\frac{1}{2}(w_{ijklmn}^0 + w_{ijklmn}^b)(\ln \bar{p}_{ijklmn}^b - \ln p_{ijklmn}^0) \right.$$

$$\left. - \frac{1}{2}(w_{ijklmn}^0 + w_{ijklmn}^a)(\ln \bar{p}_{ijklmn}^a - \ln p_{ijklmn}^0) \right]$$

$$- \sum_n \left[\frac{1}{2}(w_{ijklmn}^0 + w_{ijklmn}^b)\ln p_{ijklm}^0 - \frac{1}{2}(w_{ijklmn}^0 + w_{ijklmn}^a)\ln p_{ijklm}^0 \right]$$

$$= \sum_n \left[\frac{1}{2}(w_{ijklmn}^0 + w_{ijklmn}^b)(\ln \bar{p}_{ijklmn}^b - \ln p_{ijklmn}^0) \right.$$

$$\left. - \frac{1}{2}(w_{ijklmn}^0 + w_{ijklmn}^a)(\ln \bar{p}_{ijklmn}^a - \ln p_{ijklmn}^0) \right].$$

In effect, then, each level of aggregation adds a component to the reference price vector, and a system transitive at all levels of aggregation would therefore require specification reference prices of the form

$$\ln p_{ijklmn}^{0(ijklm)} = \ln p_{ijklmn}^{0} + \ln p_{ijklm}^{0} + \ln p_{ijkl}^{0} + \ln p_{ijk}^{0} + \ln p_{ij}^{0} + \ln p_{i}^{0}.$$

Finally, only the components of the reference price vector relevant to (within) a given aggregation level enter into that level's transitivity-adjustment equation. This permits a decomposition of the estimation procedure allowing the lowest aggregate reference shares and reference price components to be estimated first (using the regression equation presented in the proposition), followed by successively higher levels in turn. Again, the extension to quality-adjusted price indexes accounting for the differences in product characteristics across areas is straightforward.

3.3.3 More Than One Aggregation Tree

Statistical price series are often published on more than one aggregation scheme. For example, establishment data are often published on commodities and industries (producer price indexes) and occupations and industries (employment cost indexes). Multiple trees can be incorporated into the structure just elucidated by merging the trees and defining cells by crossing the classification strata in the two (or more) structures. There is a new consistency issue introduced, namely, that comparable aggregates formed from differing subaggregates in the distinct classification structures should be the same. Most obviously, the all-items price index on establishment data should be the same whether the subaggregates are industries or occupations/commodities. Similarly, the Industry Division 1 labor compensation index should be the same number, whether calculated as an aggregate of the two-digit industries or of major occupation groups within Division 1. Constraints of this type bring us much closer to imposing a de facto requirement of traditional consistency in aggregation on the data but are not equivalent to imposing the property unless each elementary price is contained in a distinct cross-cell of the two or more structures. In this paper, we consider only a one-commodity aggregation tree.

3.4 Estimation of the Reference Values for Shares, Prices, and Determinants of Quality

3.4.1 Adjusting for Quality from Place to Place

Data permitting, it is standard practice in constructing place-to-place price indexes to adjust for known price-determining specification characteristics using a regression of specification prices on measured characteristics and a set of dummy variables for locality. This country-product-dummy (CPD) approach is relatively simple and easily implemented. The most obvious way of controlling for quality in constructing a place-to-place index is to use the intercept plus coefficients on the area dummy variables as quality-adjusted price levels in the bilateral price index for the item group. In this section, we show that the use of the CPD model in this way is a special case of an exact Törnqvist index number that incorporates quality characteristics when there is a known hedonic function. The special case is that the hedonic function is the same from area to area, other than the intercept.

Suppose that the characteristics of specification n in area a are given by the vector x^a_{ijklmn} and that we define the set of dummy variables

$$L^a = \left[\text{For } b = 2, 3, \cdots, A, \quad \Delta^{ab} = \begin{cases} 1 \text{ if } b = a \\ 0 \text{ otherwise} \end{cases} \right].$$

A CPD regression would be run by fitting the following model:

$$\ln p^a_{ijklmn} = \alpha^0_{ijklm} + \alpha'_{ijklm} L^a + \beta'_{ijklm} x^a_{ijklmn} + \varepsilon^a_{ijklmn}.$$

As described above, the conventional technique is to use the estimates of the area dummy parameters $\hat{\alpha}_{ijklmn}$ as the item log prices to be used in further aggregation. Alternatively, from equation (13), the exact bilateral Törnqvist item index between areas a and b is

$$\ln T^{ab}_{ijklm} = -\sum_n \sum_z \frac{1}{2}(\beta^a_{ijklmnz} w^a_{ijklmn} + \beta^b_{ijklmnz} w^b_{ijklmn})(x^b_{ijklmnz} - x^a_{ijklmnz})$$

$$+ \sum_n \frac{1}{2}(w^a_{ijklmn} + w^b_{ijklmn})(\ln p^b_{ijklmn} - \ln p^a_{ijklmn}),$$

where the first term is a quality adjustment and the second is the familiar price index.

If the slopes are the same across areas, as in country-product-dummy models, the bilateral index reduces to

$$\ln T^{ab}_{ijklm} = \sum_n \frac{1}{2}(w^a_{ijklmn} + w^b_{ijklmn})\left(\ln p^b_{ijklmn} - \sum_z \beta_{ijklmnz} x^b_{ijklmnz}\right.$$

$$\left. - \left(\ln p^a_{ijklmn} - \sum_z \beta_{ijklmnz} x^a_{ijklmnz}\right)\right),$$

which is an index number of quality-adjusted specification prices. This is equivalent to the conventional practice of using the intercept estimates for each area as the quality-corrected area price level for the specifications within the item group since, from the CPD model, the area intercept coefficient for the item group can be expressed in terms of quality-corrected prices as

$$\alpha^0_{ijklm} + \alpha'_{ijklm} L^a = \ln p^a_{ijklmn} - \beta'_{ijklm} x^a_{ijklmn} - \varepsilon^a_{ijklmn}.$$

Although individual hedonic models by area are desirable, there may be insufficient data to obtain tight estimates of the coefficients or to identify the coefficients at all. In the first case, noisy coefficients can be estimated more accurately by blending them with a pooled regional regression. An example of this approach is set out in Randolph and Zieschang (1987) with application to a rent model for the CPI shelter component.

3.4.2 The EKS/CCD Approach

Caves, Christensen, and Diewert (1982a) show that application of the unweighted Elteto, Köves, and Szulc approach to making a system of bilateral parities transitive is equivalent to choosing the reference shares and prices as

$$w^0_{ijklmn} = \frac{1}{A}\sum_a w^a_{ijklmn},$$

$$\ln p^0_{ijklmn} = \frac{1}{A}\sum_a \ln p^a_{ijklmn}.$$

A (preferable) version of the CCD formula would select the reference values as the weighted average across the area share in the next-higher-level aggregate, as in the following for aggregation of items to strata:

$$w^0_{ijklmn} = \sum_a s^a_{ijklm} w^a_{ijklmn},$$

$$\ln p^0_{ijklmn} = \sum_a s^a_{ijklm} \ln p^a_{ijklmn},$$

where

$$s^a_{ijklm} \equiv \frac{\sum_n p^a_{ijklmn} q^a_{ijklmn}}{\sum_a \sum_n p^a_{ijklmn} q^a_{ijklmn}}.$$

When quality-adjustment information is available, the reference hedonic prices (or coefficients) and item characteristics are determined (in weighted form) by

$$\beta^0_{ijklmnq} w^0_{ijklmn} = \sum_a s^a_{ijklm} \beta^a_{ijklmnq} w^a_{ijklmn},$$

$$x^0_{ijklmnq} = \sum_a s^a_{ijklm} x^a_{ijklmnq}.$$

3.4.3 A Regression Approach for Minimal Adjustment of the Data

An alternative to (or, as noted below, a likely superclass of) the EKS/CCD approach is to apply the proposition 1 transitivity condition directly. When this condition on the cross-weighted differences of log regional prices is not met, the data may be minimally adjusted to satisfy transitivity by fitting the following equation using least squares to obtain estimates $[\hat{w}^0_{ijklmn}, \hat{p}^0_{ijklmn}]$ for each specification n in item group $ijklm$:

$$w^a_{ijklmn} \ln p^b_{ijklmn} - w^b_{ijklmn} \ln p^a_{ijklmn} = w^0_{ijklmn}(\ln p^b_{ijklmn} - \ln p^a_{ijklmn})$$

$$- \ln p^0_{ijklmn}(w^b_{ijklmn} - w^a_{ijklmn}) + \varepsilon^{ab}_{ijklmn},$$

with the parameter restriction[2]

$$\sum_n w^0_{ijklmn} = 1.$$

Recalling that A is the number of areas in the region, there will be at most $A(A - 1)/2$ independent observations to estimate this equation for each specification $ijklmn$, and the model would be run as a stacked regression of specifications n within the item group $ijklm$.

---

2. This restriction is not required for transitivity, but it is required for aggregation consistency at the next level up and embodies an inherent property of the solution to the variant of the transitivity functional equation leading to the reference shares and prices form for the transitive system of bilateral Törnqvist index numbers.

In considering possible schemes for performing weighted estimation of the reference share and price parameters, each record could be weighted by the average importance of areas a and b at the next-higher-level (item) aggregate, that is, by

$$\sqrt{\frac{1}{2}(s^a_{ijklm} + s^b_{ijklm})}.$$

In this scheme, areas with higher overall shares for the item across the region would carry more weight in determining the estimated within-item specification reference shares and prices. This is reminiscent of, if distinct from, the weighting approach suggested by Selvanathan and Rao (1992) and is more transparent as to how a weighting methodology would actually work in a system of transitive Törnqvist parities—it affects the estimates of the reference shares and prices.[3]

When quality-adjustment information is available, the reference variables would be estimated in a way analogous to that for imposing transitivity in prices only as follows.

Estimate hedonic equations for each area as

$$\ln p^a_{ijklmn} = \alpha^a_{ijklm} + \beta^{a'}_{ijklm} x^a_{ijklmn} + \varepsilon^a_{ijklmn},$$

obtaining the estimates

$$\begin{bmatrix} \hat{\alpha}^a_{ijklm} \\ \hat{\beta}^a_{ijklm} \end{bmatrix}$$

for each area. Then, using least squares, estimate the vector

$$\begin{bmatrix} x^0_{ijklmnq} \\ -\beta^0_{ijklmnq} w^0_{ijklmn} \\ -\ln p^0_{ijklmn} \\ w^0_{ijklmn} \end{bmatrix}$$

by fitting the equation

$$w^a_{ijklm}\left(\ln p^b_{ijklmn} - \left(\sum_q \hat{\beta}^a_{ijklmnq} x^b_{ijklmn}\right)\right) - w^a_{ijklm}\left(\ln p^a_{ijklmn} - \left(\sum_q \hat{\beta}^b_{ijklmnq} x^a_{ijklmn}\right)\right)$$

$$= \sum_q [-\beta^0_{ijklmnq} w^0_{ijklmn}](x^b_{ijklmnq} - x^a_{ijklmnq}) + \sum_q x^0_{ijklmnq}(\hat{\beta}^b_{ijklmnq} w^b_{ijklm} - \hat{\beta}^a_{ijklmnq} w^a_{ijklm})$$

$$+ w^0_{ijklmn}(\ln p^b_{ijklmn} - \ln p^a_{ijklmn}) + [-\ln p^0_{ijklmn}](w^b_{ijklmn} - w^a_{ijklmn}) + \varepsilon^{ab}_{ijklmn}$$

3. Actually, there is probably a weighting scheme for the transitivity fitting equation that generates the EKS/CCD versions of the transitive Törnqvist system of parities, but it does not seem obvious how these weights would be determined.

with the parameter restriction

$$\sum_n w^0_{ijklmn} = 1.$$

There will be at most $A(A - 1)/2$ independent observations to estimate this equation for each specification $ijklmn$, and the model would be run as a stacked regression of specifications n within the item group $ijklm$. The observation weighting would follow the same scheme as in the simple case without specification characteristics and quality adjustment.

Notice that, if the hedonic slope coefficients are the same across areas for each specification characteristic, with the result that $\beta^a_{ijklmnq} = \beta^b_{ijklmnq} = \beta^0_{ijklmnq}$, then the estimating equation collapses to

$$w^a_{ijklm}\left(\ln p^b_{ijklmn} - \left(\sum_q \hat{\beta}^0_{ijklmnq} x^b_{ijklmn}\right)\right) - w^a_{ijklm}\left(\ln p^a_{ijklmn} - \left(\sum_q \hat{\beta}^0_{ijklmnq} x^a_{ijklmn}\right)\right)$$

$$= [w^0_{ijklmn}]\left(\ln p^b_{ijklmn} - \sum_q \hat{\beta}^0_{ijklmnq} x^b_{ijklmnq} - \left(\ln p^a_{ijklmn} - \sum_q \hat{\beta}^0_{ijklmnq} x^a_{ijklmnq}\right)\right)$$

$$+ \left[-\left(\ln p^0_{ijklmn} + \sum_q \hat{\beta}^0_{ijklmnq} x^0_{ijklmnq}\right)\right](w^b_{ijklmn} - w^a_{ijklmn}) + \varepsilon^{ab}_{ijklmn}.$$

In this case, the coefficient on the difference between the share vectors of the two areas is a *quality-adjusted reference price vector,* and no reference characteristics vector can be separately identified. It can, if desired, be independently determined as the EKS/CCD weighted average.

3.5   An Application to U.S. CPI Data

An empirical example of the methodology is provided by interarea prices for U.S. urban areas derived from hedonic regressions on data from the consumer price index. The CPI collects prices on a large sample of individual products, that is, on a probability sample of those specific products consumers are most likely to purchase in specific outlets in specific urban areas (see U.S. Department of Labor 1992). This approach results in a sample that is representative of household consumption choices but heterogeneous in nature. For example, the category for instant coffee consists of observations on instant coffee products of different sizes, brands, caffeine content, and other characteristics. In order to compare the prices of instant coffee across cities, these differences in characteristics must be explicitly accounted for, circumstances ideal for applying a hedonic regression approach. A recent major effort at the BLS has produced such interarea price indexes for most of the major categories of goods and services for forty-four U.S. urban areas; this effort is described in detail in Kokoski, Cardiff, and Moulton (1994). A more recent application of this approach to 1991 CPI data provided the data input for this example.

The CPI categories are organized in a hierarchical classification scheme as follows. The lowest level of aggregation, that at which individual prices are collected, is the entry-level item (ELI), designated by a five-digit code. The next highest level is the item stratum, designated by a four-digit code. Each stratum comprises one or more ELIs. The item strata are then aggregated into expenditure classes (ECs), designated by a two-digit code. These ECs may be organized into higher-level definitions, such as major groups, and then into the all-items CPI. For example, rice is ELI 01031, which is a member of the item stratum rice, pasta, and cornmeal (0103), which, in turn, is a member of EC 01, cereal and cereal products. Aggregating EC 01 and EC 02 provides the major group cereal and bakery products, which is part of the category food-at-home. The detailed classification structure for the entire CPI is provided in U.S. Department of Labor (1992).

For this example, we demonstrate the aggregation methodology on the food-at-home portion of the CPI. This group comprises eighty-eight ELIs, which are organized into eighteen ECs, and five major groups, providing the most detailed set of items in the CPI classification. For purposes of exposition, we will let the lowest level of aggregation, subscripted *ijklmn*, be represented by the ELIs (which, in many cases for food-at-home, map uniquely into item strata). The next highest level, subscripted *ijklm*, is represented by the expenditure class, and the ECs will be aggregated to a higher level, *ijkl*, the major groups. These major groups are then aggregated into an index for all food-at-home. This aggregation structure is presented in appendix B, table 3B.1. Table 3B.2 provides the expenditure shares for each major group as a component of all food-at-home and for each area as a proportion of all areas' total food-at-home.

The initial step is a log-linear hedonic regression, which was performed on each of these ELIs separately, as in equation (3) above:

$$\ln p^a_{ijklmn} = \alpha^0_{ijklm} + \alpha'_{ijklm} L^a + \beta'_{ijklm} x^a_{ijklmn} + \varepsilon^a_{ijklmn},$$

where $\ln p^a_{ijklmn}$ represents the log of the price of each item specification n in the mth ELI for the ath area, $x^a_{ijklmnz}$ are the variables defining the characteristics of each item specification, including the type of outlet where priced, and L^a is the dummy variable vector for area a. It has been shown (Summers 1973) that the exponentiated coefficients a_{ijklm} are bilateral price indexes for area a relative to the reference area (arbitrarily chosen as area $a = 1$). Space does not permit presentation of the results of the regressions for all eighty-eight ELIs, so the eight ELIs that compose fresh fruits and vegetables are provided as a representative example of the information available in the CPI data; these are presented in appendix C.

For exposition of the mechanics of the aggregation procedure, a simplified example for six ELIs and three areas is provided in appendix D. The six ELIs are apples, bananas, oranges, potatoes, lettuce, and tomatoes, which are aggregated into simplified hypothetical expenditure classes for fresh fruits and fresh vegetables. In table 3D.1 are presented the bilateral interarea indexes implied by the hedonic regression coefficients for each ELI. Table 3D.2 presents the expenditure shares that are used in the aggregation regression equation, and table 3D.3 provides the multilateral interarea index values that result from the aggregation. In this table, TORNxy is the index value comparing city y to city x. The ELIs are aggregated into ECs, and these ECs are then aggregated into a composite of the two (EC11 + EC12). The coefficient values from the aggregation regression equation are provided in tables 3D.4 and 3D.5, along with the adjusted R^2 values of the regression.

For comparison with the multilateral Törnqvist indexes in table 3D.3, a set of bilateral, and thus not necessarily transitive, parities was produced. These are provided in table 3D.6. This comparison shows, for this simplified example, the degree of empirical adjustment required to achieve the transitivity property. Recognizing that transitivity must be achieved at the cost of characteristicity, it is useful to assess this trade-off (see Dreschler 1973). In this case, the magnitude of the difference between the multilateral Törnqvist and its bilateral counterpart is less than 2 percent of the index value.

Appendix E contains results for the entire food-at-home group for all urban areas in the CPI. As in the example, the aggregation procedure is based on subsequent regressions at each level of aggregation. The adjusted R^2 values, given in table 3E.1, indicate that the equations fit well. (The value of 1.00 for EC08 occurs because there is only one ELI in that expenditure class.) Although the index values generated by the aggregation methodology are transitive, it is unwieldy to present the complete matrix of forty-four by forty-four area comparisons for each EC and major group. Thus, Philadelphia was arbitrarily chosen as the reference area for exposition of the results. The first set of index values, calculated by aggregating the ELIs into the expenditure classes, is presented in table 3E.2. The aggregation of these indexes into their respective major groups provides the index values in table 3E.3. The last column of this table provides the result of aggregating the five major groups into an all-food-at-home index. As expected, the indexes for Honolulu and Anchorage are well above the others, and, in general, the index values for the smaller urban areas are below that of the Philadelphia reference area, reflecting a priori expectations. As a result of the geometric averaging process, the variability of the index values is reduced at each higher level of aggregation.

3.6   Conclusion and an Extension

In this paper, we have considered the case of a single cross section of areas within which transitive bilateral quality-adjusted price comparisons are to be made between areas. We have also considered commodity aggregation within this framework, whereby transitivity is imposed while preserving a staged Törnqvist index aggregation rule. We have applied the technique to a small subset of the commodities priced in the U.S. consumer price index.

Our approach to transitivity has been a "minimum-data-adjustment" criterion with weighting specific to bilateral comparisons and therefore differs from other methods of imposing transitivity in a system of bilateral place-to-place Törnqvist index numbers. Although our method has some appeal because we can claim minimally to perturb the data in order to impose the transitive property with weighting sensitive to specific bilateral comparisons, the area expenditure-weighted sum of the log locality price levels will not necessarily be equal to zero, in contrast with the EKS/CCD approach, which satisfies this property by construction. The need for this property, as well as operational considerations such as ease of computation and calculation of measures of precision, would need to be weighed in deciding on an estimator for production of a regular statistical series of interarea price indexes. Before closing, we would like briefly to describe a promising avenue of research using this framework in a time-series context.

3.6.1 The Single Chain Link Case

It has been a problem in the interpretation of data from the International Comparisons Project that the change in the levels of real GDP implied by the international purchasing power parities from time to time has not been the same as the growth in national GDPs measured by direct deflation using a(n implicit) time-series GDP deflator. We consider here a remedy within the Törnqvist system of interarea and time-series index numbers by considering a system of area indexes that are transitive both among areas within the same time period and between areas from differing time periods. A direct implication of this is that the index change between two periods for a given area, say, a, can be expressed as the product of the relative level between two areas, say, a and b, in the first period, times the relative change in b between the two periods for any two areas a and b.

The Törnqvist item index $\ln T_{ijklm}^{ab,uv}$ between area a in time period u and area b in time period v, where $u, v \in \{t - 1, t\}$, is

$$\ln T_{ijklm}^{ab,uv} = \sum_n \frac{1}{2}(w_{ijklmn}^{au} + w_{ijklmn}^{bv})(\ln p_{ijklmn}^{bv} - \ln p_{ijklmn}^{au}).$$

It is straightforward to see that, for the system of between-area, between-period parities to be transitive, proposition 1 applies directly in this case, with reference share and price vectors determined for the union of the two time periods and collections of areas. If quality adjustments are possible using hedonic regressions, then proposition 2 can be applied to show the transitive form of the quality-adjusted system of parities as a function of a reference share, price and hedonic coefficients vectors across areas and time periods. We note below that, under international decentralization of compilation, the country hedonic regression coefficients would generally not be the same as in the CPD approach.

An additional comparison generally computed in this case is the change over time of the regional aggregate of areas. Examples of such indexes would be national consumer price and producer price and labor compensation indexes as composites of the subnational areas sampled to obtain the data. This index can be written as

$$\ln T^{R,uv}_{ijklm} = \sum_a \frac{1}{2}(s^{au}_{ijklm} + s^{av}_{ijklm})\ln T^{aa,uv}_{ijklm}$$

$$= \sum_a \frac{1}{2}(s^{au}_{ijklm} + s^{av}_{ijklm})\sum_n \frac{1}{2}(w^{au}_{ijklmn} + w^{av}_{ijklmn})(\ln p^{av}_{ijklmn} - \ln p^{au}_{ijklmn}).$$

By period-to-period and interarea transitivity

$$\ln T^{R,uv}_{ijklm} = \sum_a \frac{1}{2}(s^{au}_{ijklm} + s^{av}_{ijklm})(\ln \bar{p}^{av}_{ijklmn} - \ln \bar{p}^{au}_{ijklmn}),$$

where

$$\ln \bar{p}^{au}_{ijklm} = \sum_n \frac{1}{2}(w^{00}_{ijklmn} + w^{au}_{ijklmn})(\ln p^{au}_{ijklmn} - \ln p^{00}_{ijklmn}).$$

The aggregate time-series index under period/area transitivity between the two periods is, therefore, a weighted average of the relative change in a set of area price levels, ensuring consistency between the levels within period across area and rates of change between periods within area.

3.6.2 Time-Series/Cross-Sectional Transitivity over Multiple Periods

Clearly, the single chain link, two-period case can be extended to the multiple-period case by pooling the data for multiple periods. A distinct advantage of the application of this procedure is that the problem of chain drift is eliminated over the multiple-period epoch being adjusted while maintaining much of the period specificity of the weight and price components of the Törnqvist index formula. The reason is that transitivity eliminates drift, which is usually defined as the persistent deviation of a direct index between nonadjacent periods as compared with the product of adjacent period chain links covering the multiple period interval. An issue to be resolved in applying this technique is that it refers to a moving window of a fixed time duration. Data passing outside the window would not exactly satisfy the transitive property. Choosing the window as a long-enough period could be expected to result in very slow change in the reference prices and shares, however, so that the effect could be minimized, at the cost of providing less of Drechsler's (1973) "characteristicity" for relatively recent time periods.

3.6.3 Decentralized Computing of International Parities While Controlling for the Quality of Goods Available in Different Countries

The methodology outlined here, which uses a hedonic, characteristics-based quality-adjustment procedure, permits decentralized, within-country estimation of the hedonic equation coefficients. This is especially attractive in view of the great and generally justified reluctance with which most statistical offices grant access to the micro-data sources of their price indexes. The prerequisite for this would be that a standard product classification would have to be adopted by all countries and also that, with each product class, a standard list of product characteristics or specification measures would have to be adopted. One such set of standards might be derived by merging the U.S. CPI specification file, listing the characteristics measures for some 365 product categories, with a standard international commodity classification, such as the central product classification or CPC of the United Nations, itself a superset of the now standard harmonized classification for internationally traded commodities.

A compilation strategy such as this for the ICP would have a distinct advantage over the current approach of pricing a long, detailed list of narrowly specified items. The number of product strata required would be smaller, and the countries could use the estimates for their own, internal quality-adjustment needs for time-series and within-country geographic comparisons.

Appendix A
Proofs of Propositions

Proof of Proposition 1

The proof of this proposition follows methods used in, for example, Aczel (1966) and Eichhorn (1978). First, we establish the following solution of the *transitivity (functional) equation* for all single-valued functions g of two vectors of identical dimension in an argument set D that satisfy an identity condition $g(x, x) = 0$:

$$g(x, y) + g(y, z) = g(x, z) \quad \text{and} \quad g(x, x) = 0, \quad \forall (x, y, z) \in D,$$

if and only if

$$g(x, y) = h(y) - h(x).$$

Let $y = y^0$. Then, for all x and z in the domain of g,

$$g(x, y^0) + g(y^0, z) = r(x) + h(z) = g(x, z).$$

Substituting this back into the transitivity equation,

$$r(x) + h(y) + r(y) + h(z) = g(x, z).$$

By identity

$$g(y, \ y) \ = \ r(y) + \ h(y) \ = \ 0,$$

and, hence,

$$r(y) \ = \ -h(y).$$

We can now express $g(x, z)$ in terms of h as

$$g(x, \ z) \ = \ h(z) - \ h(y),$$

yielding the desired result.

From this, transitivity of the Törnqvist bilateral relative requires that, for all a, b,

$$\ln T^{ab} \ = \ h(\vec{w}^b, \ \vec{p}^b) - \ h(\vec{w}^a, \ \vec{p}^a).$$

Expanding the bilateral relative expression, we have

$$\ln T^{ab} \ \equiv \ \sum_i \frac{1}{2}(w_i^a + \ w_i^b)(\ln p_i^b - \ \ln p_i^a)$$

$$= \ \frac{1}{2}\sum_i (w_i^b \ln p_i^b - \ w_i^b \ln p_i^b + \ w_i^a \ln p_i^b - \ w_i^b \ln p_i^a)$$

$$= \ h(\vec{w}^b, \ \vec{p}^b) - \ h(\vec{w}^a, \ \vec{p}^a).$$

We set $b = 0$ and solve for $h(\vec{w}^a, \vec{p}^a)$ in terms of reference area 0 as

$$h(\vec{w}^a, \ \vec{p}^a) \ = \ \left[h(\vec{w}^0, \ \vec{p}^0) - \ \frac{1}{2}\sum_i w_i^0 p_i^0 \right] + \ \frac{1}{2}\sum_i w_i^0 \ln p_i^a - \ \frac{1}{2}\sum_i \ln p_i^0 w_i^a$$

$$+ \ \frac{1}{2}\sum_i w_i^a p_i^a.$$

Substituting this into the expanded equation for the transitive bilateral log parity, multiplying through by two, and subtracting $w_i^b \ln p_i^b - w_i^a \ln p_i^a$ inside the summations from both sides, we have

$$\sum_i (w_i^a \ln p_i^b - \ w_i^b \ln p_i^a) \ = \ \sum_i w_i^0(\ln p_i^b - \ \ln p_i^a) - \ \sum_i \ln p_i^0(w_i^b - \ w_i^a).$$

The expression for the transitive Törnqvist bilateral parity obtains by substituting this expression for the cross-product between the area weights and the prices into the expanded expression for the parity, adding and subtracting the term $\sum_i w_i^0 \ln p_i^0$, and collecting terms.
Q.E.D.

Proof of Proposition 2

The proof of proposition 2 follows very closely that of proposition 1. It is easy to see from this that the price level for each area now has a price- and quality-adjustment component.

Appendix B
Structure and Expenditure Shares of Division "Food-at-Home"

Table 3B.1   CPI Classification Structure for Food-at-Home as Aggregated for Interarea Indexes

Group 1: Cereal and bakery products

ECO1 Cereal and cereal products

1011 Flour
1012 Prepared flour mixes
1021 Cereal
1031 Rice
1032 Macaroni, similar products, and cornmeal

EC02 Bakery products

2011 White bread
2021 Bread other than white
2022 Rolls, biscuits, and muffins (excluding frozen)
2041 Cakes and cupcakes (except frozen)
2042 Cookies
2061 Crackers
2062 Bread and cracker products
2063 Sweetrolls, coffee cake, and doughnuts (excluding frozen)
2064 Frozen bakery products and frozen/ refrigerated doughs and batters
2065 Pies, tarts, turnovers (excluding frozen)

Group 2: Meat, poultry, fish, and eggs

EC03 Beef and veal

3011 Ground beef
3021 Chuck roast
3031 Round roast
3041 Other roasts (excluding chuck and round)
3042 Other steak (excluding round and sirloin)
3043 Other beef
3051 Round steak
3061 Sirloin steak

EC04 Pork

4011 Bacon
4021 Pork chops
4031 Ham (excluding canned)
4032 Canned ham
4041 Pork roast, picnics, other pork
4042 Pork sausage

EC05 Other meats

5011 Frankfurters
5012 Bologna, liverwurst, salami
5013 Other lunchmeats (excluding bologna, liverwurst, salami)
5014 Lamb, organ meats, and game

EC06 Poultry

6011 Fresh whole chicken
6021 Fresh and frozen chicken parts
6031 Other poultry

Table 3B.1   (continued)

EC07 Fish and seafood	7011 Canned fish or seafood
	7021 Shellfish (excluding canned)
	7022 Fish (excluding canned)
EC08 Eggs	8011 Eggs
Group 3: Dairy products	
EC09 Fresh milk and cream	9011 Fresh whole milk
	9021 Other fresh milk and cream
EC10 Processed dairy products	10011 Butter
	10012 Other dairy products
	10021 Cheese
	10041 Ice cream and related products
Group 4: Fruits and vegetables	
EC11 Fresh fruits[a]	11011 Apples
	11021 Bananas
	11031 Oranges
	11041 Other fresh fruits
EC12 Fresh vegetables[a]	12011 Potatoes
	12021 Lettuce
	12031 Tomatoes
	12041 Other fresh vegetables
EC13 Fruit juices and frozen fruit	13011 Frozen orange juice
	13012 Other frozen fruits and fruit juices
	13013 Fresh, canned, or bottled fruit juices
	13031 Canned and dried fruits
EC14 Processed vegetables	14011 Frozen vegetables
	14021 Canned beans other than lima beans
	14022 Canned cut corn
	14023 Other processed vegetables
Group 5: Other foods-at-home	
EC15 Sugar and sweets	15011 Candy and chewing gum
	15012 Other sweets (excluding candy and chewing gum)
	15021 Sugar and artificial sweeteners
EC16 Fats and oils	16011 Margarine
	16012 Other fats and oils
	16013 Nondairy cream substitutes
	16014 Peanut butter
EC17 Nonalcoholic beverages	17011 Cola drinks
	17012 Carbonated drinks other than cola
	17031 Roasted coffee
	17032 Instant and freeze-dried coffee
	17051 Noncarbonated fruit-flavored drinks
	17052 Tea
	17053 Other noncarbonated drinks

(continued)

Table 3B.1   (continued)

EC18 Other prepared food	18011 Canned and packaged soup
	18021 Frozen prepared meals
	18022 Frozen prepared food other than meals
	18031 Potato chips and other snacks
	18032 Nuts
	18041 Salt and other seasonings and spices
	18042 Olives, pickles, relishes
	18043 Sauces and gravies
	18044 Other condiments (excluding olives, pickles, relishes)
	18061 Canned or packaged salads and desserts
	18062 Baby food
	18063 Other canned or packaged prepared foods

[a]Items for which detailed calculations are shown in apps. C and D.

Table 3B.2   **Expenditure Shares for Food-at-Home, 1991**

A. Shares of major groups in food-at-home	
Cereal and bakery products	.13876
Meat, poultry, fish, and eggs	.27262
Dairy products	.13245
Fruits and vegetables	.18144
Other food-at-home	.27473
B. Food-at-home shares of each area in national food-at-home	
Northeast region	.211814
Philadelphia	.025485
Boston	.016779
Pittsburgh	.011474
Buffalo	.008681
New York City	.027687
New York–Connecticut suburbs	.021090
New Jersey suburbs	.029169
Northeast, B PSUs	.033929
Northeast, C PSUs	.027482
Northeast, D PSUs	.010038
North Central region	.224254
Chicago	.040356
Detroit	.020599
St. Louis	.011198
Cleveland	.013992
Minneapolis	.010670
Milwaukee	.014031
Cincinnati	.009500
Kansas City	.008020
North Central, B PSUs	.028207
North Central, C PSUs	.038570
North Central, D PSUs	.029111

South region	.283384
Washington, D.C.	.017232
Dallas	.019052
Baltimore	.013888
Houston	.018058
Atlanta	.010608
Miami	.013914
Tampa	.013365
New Orleans	.005904
South, B PSUs	.076899
South, C PSUs	.061897
South, D PSUs	.032567
West region	.280549
Los Angeles County	.061876
Greater Los Angeles	.061876
San Francisco	.035026
Seattle	.014656
San Diego	.012288
Portland, Oreg.	.013951
Honolulu	.002924
Anchorage	.001103
Denver	.008912
West, B PSUs	.026148
West, C PSUs	.025536
West, D PSUs	.016253

Note: PSU = primary sampling unit.

Appendix C
Hedonic Regression Results for Fresh Fruits and Vegetables

Table 3C.1   Hedonic Regression Results for Fresh Fruit

	Coefficient			
Variable	11011 Apples	11021 Bananas	11031 Oranges	11041 Other Fresh Fruit
Mean of dependent variable: log price	-2.8886	-3.5118	-2.8848	-2.7285
Adjusted R^2	.3329	.3314	.3403	.5932
Sample size	9,423	6,791	12,610	26,069
Area				
Philadelphia-Wilmington-Trenton, PA-DE-NJ-MD	REF	REF	REF	REF
Boston-Lawrence-Salem, MA-NH	-.11302*	-.01941	.06634	-.03617
Pittsburgh–Beaver Valley, PA	-.07054	-.18766*	.03833	-.10519*
Buffalo–Niagara Falls, NY	-.20282*	-.01421	-.00287	-.20930*
New York City	.06071*	.01522	.13458*	-.01446
New York–Connecticut suburbs	-.05384*	-.02748	-.02681	-.02877
New Jersey suburbs	-.02993	-.00491	-.12221*	-.05622*
Northeast region, B size PSUs	-.04942	-.05294	.01369	-.03246
Northeast region, C size PSUs	-.09681*	-.13774*	-.03222	-.13600*
Northeast region, D size PSUs	-.08744*	.06198	.18581*	.06941*
Chicago–Gary–Lake County, IL-IN-WI	.06099*	-.02261	.23166*	-.00033
Detroit–Ann Arbor, MI	-.04564	-.22780*	.01161	-.16026*
St. Louis–East St. Louis, MO-IL	-.02697	.04932	.06972	-.02078
Cleveland-Akron-Lorain, OH	-.16546*	-.14305*	.02411	-.01462
Minneapolis–St. Paul, MN-WI	-.00094	-.23664*	.07582	-.09512*

Milwaukee, WI	.01006	−.11808*	.01591	−.04899
Cincinnati–Hamilton, OH–KY–IN	−.08656	−.18154*	.01295	−.00455
Kansas City, MO–Kansas City, KS	−.01494	−.10477*	.44553*	−.05681
North Central region, B size PSUs	.01421	−.18972*	.19250*	−.03791
North Central region, C size PSUs	−.05190	−.23027*	.09794*	−.09401*
North Central region, D size PSUs	−.15361*	−.08938*	−.11770*	−.20600*
Washington, DC–MD–VA	−.01403	.01819	−.00686	.08002*
Dallas–Fort Worth, TX	−.05908*	−.25484*	−.14995*	−.03552
Baltimore, MD	−.04353	−.05988	−.02344	.03504
Houston-Galveston-Brazoria, TX	−.11871*	−.12477*	−.22791*	−.18318*
Atlanta, GA	−.00259	−.30016*	.11588*	.01898
Miami–Fort Lauderdale, FL	−.03459	−.50646*	−.3650*	−.31861*
Tampa–St. Petersburg–Clearwater, FL	.05230	−.31348*	−.65656*	−.07724*
New Orleans, LA	−.02976	−.00361	−.02918	−.00581
South region, B size PSUs	−.01420	−.20297*	.01788	−.07499*
South region, C size PSUs	−.10217*	−.22290*	−.08665*	−.10318*
South region, D size PSUs	−.04820*	−.04390	−.06157*	−.08453*
Los Angeles County, CA	−.17093*	−.02534	−.08845*	−.12754*
Greater Los Angeles, CA	−.20649*	−.10411*	−.07800*	−.07642*
San Francisco–Oakland–San Jose, CA	−.19800*	−.08328*	.06305	−.02541
Seattle-Tacoma, WA	.19215*	.12307*	.05389	.15074*
San Diego, CA	−.17869*	−.17004*	−.04144*	−.12074*
Portland-Vancouver, OR–WA	−.17181*	−.12146*	.10993	.01383
Honolulu, HI	.00481	.55898*	.22252*	.11750*
Anchorage, AK	−.10670	.43803*	.35183*	.12539*
Denver-Boulder, CO	−.03535	.08929	.21348*	.02031
West region, B size PSUs	−.11932*	−.05745	.06924	.02278
West region, C size PSUs	−.12937*	−.09631*	.04585	−.05945
West region, D size PSUs	−.07509*	−.27655*	−.02118	−.08199*

(continued)

Table 3C.1 (continued)

	Coefficient			
Variable	11011 Apples	11021 Bananas	11031 Oranges	11041 Other Fresh Fruit
Rotation group				
Same sample as previous month	REF	REF	REF	REF
New sample	−.03224*	−.01012	−.04340*	.04082*
Month of collection (11 months of data)				
January	REF	REF	REF	REF
February	.03022*	.09711*	.08286*	−.04646*
March	.04515*	.27093*	.12605*	−.06279*
April	.05623*	.22156*	.14488*	−.01630
May	.10186*	.23920*	.14072*	−.01466*
June	.15730*	.15363*	.25007*	−.05689*
July	.19332*	.12148*	.29341*	−.14868*
August	.20836*	−.08925*	.34215*	−.26625*
September	.17460*	−.04995*	.39708*	−.23102*
October	.01422	−.14127*	.23935*	−.18405*
November	.03296*	−.05280*	−.04562*	−.13335*
Outlet type				
Chain grocery	REF	REF	REF	REF
Independent grocery stores	−.07482*	−.04932*	−.10642*	−.04624*
Full service department stores	−.11568	−.23667	−.00639	.24117*
Produce market	−.18148*	−.13124*	−.15877*	−.14419*
Convenience stores	.05972	.39717*	.01025	−.00807
Commodity oriented outlet not elsewhere classified	−.41615*	−.23223*	−.61553*	−.00207
Outlet not elsewhere classified	−.41217*	−.60950*	−.95862*	−.72177*

(continued)

Package type				
Packaging: loose	-.07769			
Packaging multi-pack	-.33425*		-.19648*	.00157
Packaging: single item, individually wrapped	-.43312*		-.06804	.04563*
Other	REF		REF	REF
Package size				
0–10 pounds	REF			
Above 10 pounds	.01042			
Size represents: weighed one multipack	-.09754*		-.11644*	-.39775*
Size represents: weight labeled	-.03956		-.10879*	-.33027*
Size represents: weighed one bunch	[a]	-.03506*		
Size: weigh 2 items	-.05256	REF	-.22778*	-.31620*
Size: other			REF	REF
Grade				
Store seconds or other than first quality		.06409		
First quality or class		.01581		
U.S. fancy	.01337		.01961*	.04234*
U.S. extra fancy	REF	REF	REF	REF
Other grade/grade not available		REF		
Variety				
Delicious	.00968			
Golden delicious	-.03918			
Red delicious	-.04676			
Other delicious	[a]			
Granny Smith	.03385*			
Gravenstein	-.17583*			
Jonathan	-.17352*			
McIntosh	-.05280*			
Rome Beauty (Red Rome)	-.03041			

Table 3C.1 (continued)

| | Coefficient | | | |
Variable	11011 Apples	11021 Bananas	11031 Oranges	11041 Other Fresh Fruit
Stayman	-.11321*			
Winesap	-.06369*			
York (York Imperial)	.74756*			
Navel			.29912*	
Temple			-.11816*	
Valencia			.14359*	
Tangelo			.28032*	
Tangerine			.44601*	
Avocados				.19300*
Berries				.28592*
Blueberries				.25617*
Cranberries				-.02272
Raspberries				.99209*
Strawberries				-.30166*
Cherries (sweet/tart)				.28835*
Grapefruit				-.90631*
Pink grapefruit				-.03686
Red (ruby) grapefruit				-.06126
White (yellow) grapefruit				-.12095

Grapes			−.18645*
Red (flame) seedless grapes			−.00638
Emperor or tokay grapes			−.05662
Rebier grapes			.04156
Concord grapes			−.00026
Thompson seedless			.05003
Lemons			−.26529*
Limes			−.28323*
Melons			−.82440*
Watermelon			−.71551*
Cantaloupe melons			−.19234*
Honeydew melons			−.01389
Casaba melons			−.07582
Crenshaw melons			.29155*
Persian melons			.26967*
Santa Claus melons			−.08431
Peaches			−.44508*
Pears			−.19322*
Anjou pears			−.46646*
Bartlett pears			−.45497*
Bosc pears			−.34758*
Seckel pears			.01742
Pineapples			−1.02458*
Plums			−.21393*
Other	REF	REF	REF

Note: REF = reference.

[a]There were insufficient records with this characteristic to include it in the model.

*Statistically significant at the 5 percent level.

Table 3C.2 Hedonic Regression Results for Fresh Vegetables

	Coefficient			
Variable	12011 Potatoes	12021 Lettuce	12031 Tomatoes	12041 Other Fresh Vegetables
Mean of dependent variable: log price	-3.7367	-3.1222	-2.7011	-3.0502
Adjusted R^2	.6228	.5385	.1991	.4872
Sample size	6,770	6,764	6,769	14,241
Area				
Boston-Lawrence-Salem, MA-NH	-.06387	-.29268*	.01678	-.18035*
Pittsburgh–Beaver Valley, PA	-.23146*	-.25850*	-.05929	-.19013*
Buffalo–Niagara Falls, NY	-.07529	-.23543*	-.13822*	.16605*
New York City	-.11552*	-.04737	-.02569	.08782*
New York–Connecticut suburbs	-.08816*	-.14394*	-.13951*	-.11219*
New Jersey suburbs	-.07603*	-.12854*	-.00121	-.07710*
Northeast region, B size PSUs	-.02074	-.15127*	-.06827*	-.09467*
Northeast region, C size PSUs	-.08409*	-.13739*	-.13375*	-.23278*
Northeast region, D size PSUs	-.00174	-.05323	.19425*	-.12643*
Chicago–Gary–Lake County, IL-IN-WI	.15525*	-.08079*	-.05506	.07671*
Detroit–Ann Arbor, MI	-.20893*	-.25233*	-.12991*	-.23765*
St. Louis–East St. Louis, MO-IL	.17335*	-.10762	-.24150*	.04041
Cleveland-Akron-Lorain, OH	-.15117	-.36251*	-.33654*	-.25811*
Minneapolis–St. Paul, MN-WI	-.44411*	-.37324*	-.19602*	-.06638*
Milwaukee, WI	-.18660	-.28823*	-.30839*	-.10271*
Cincinnati–Hamilton, OH-KY-IN	-.10455	.04950	-.04369	-.04813
Kansas City, MO–Kansas City, KS	-.12530*	-.19183*	-.15001	-.01079
North Central region, B size PSUs	-.16171*	-.25840*	-.12224*	-.18928*

North Central region, C size PSUs	−.18821*	−.27277*	−.22069*	−.10230*
North Central region, D size PSUs	−.35833*	−.31699*	−.24259*	−.33089*
Washington, DC–MD–VA	.03654	−.05585	.00536	.05914
Dallas–Fort Worth, TX	−.18926*	−.10340*	−.27754*	−.03080
Baltimore, MD	−.14338*	−.15619	−.09699	−.13070*
Houston-Galveston-Brazoria, TX	.04671	−.04106	−.1059*	−.21465*
Atlanta, GA	−.05600	−.22134*	−.05248	−.16305*
Miami–Fort Lauderdale, FL	−.15124*	−.27921*	−.50285*	−.15624*
Tampa–St. Petersburg–Clearwater, FL	−.04608*	−.33078*	−.16919*	−.16947*
New Orleans, LA	−.31242*	−.37557*	−.14505*	−.12714*
South region, B size PSUs	−.16423*	−.15786*	−.20441*	−.11132*
South region, C size PSUs	−.11572*	−.16706*	−.28840*	−.15629*
South region, D size PSUs	−.16923*	−.05474	−.21121*	−.06746*
Los Angeles County, CA	−.06874	−.42383*	−.32307*	−.30328*
Greater Los Angeles, CA	−.02597	−.46923*	−.39316*	−.30388*
San Francisco–Oakland–San Jose, CA	−.03646*	−.42209*	−.25084*	−.25710*
Seattle-Tacoma, WA	−.21794*	−.31179*	−.29454*	.28713*
San Diego, CA	−.26552*	−.63145*	−.52545*	−.41637*
Portland-Vancouver, OR-WA	−.19012*	−.36026*	−.17875*	−.41273*
Honolulu, HI	.57928*	.11241*	.04541	.52045*
Anchorage, AK	.31145*	.24406	.13065	.34271*
Denver-Boulder, CO	.07387	−.01414	−.11228*	.04067
West region, B size PSUs	−.27332*	−.39816*	−.31270*	−.38406*
West region, C size PSUs	−.15643*	−.30573*	−.28317*	−.13431*
West region, D size PSUs	−.28844*	−.43150*	−.46059*	−.21889*
Rotation group				
Same sample as previous month	REF	REF	REF	REF
New sample	−.02658	−.00552	−.02653	−.07898

(continued)

Table 3C.2   (continued)

	Coefficient			
	12011 Potatoes	12021 Lettuce	12031 Tomatoes	12041 Other Fresh Vegetables
Month of collection (11 months of data)				
January	REF	REF	REF	REF
February	.01009	−.17981*	−.06562*	−.04138*
March	−.00178	−.27424*	.03005	−.06361*
April	.02363	−.19154*	.24313*	.04834*
May	.06245*	−.10586	.38750*	−.03054
June	.16776*	−.02842*	.54470*	.01922
July	.17522*	−.29127*	.20950*	−.07667*
August	.11864*	−.32081*	−.19194*	−.14672*
September	.01893	−.29942*	−.18685*	−.17824*
October	−.07231*	−.28473*	−.25130*	−.18042*
November	−.09234	.02991	−.12365*	−.10289*
Outlet type				
Chain grocery	REF	REF	REF	REF
Full service department stores	−.61027*	.12446	−.19366	.02692
Independent grocery stores	−.02169	−.02528	−.05455*	−.03887
Produce market	−.12607*	−.08024*	−.25519*	−.12645*
Convenience stores	.27450*	.30320*	.57844*	.21838*
Commodity oriented outlet not elsewhere classified	−.39201*	−.49838*	−.73586*	−.35484*
Outlet not elsewhere classified	−.31633*	−.66851*	−.69563*	−.55401*

Package type				
Packaging: loose	−.78494*			
Trimmed				−.02206
Packaging: single item, individually wrapped			.48149*	.36462*
Packaging: multipack		−.12828	.16951*	
Packaging: multipack, weight: 0–9.999 lb.	.35237*			
Packaging: multipack, weight: greater than or equal to 1 lb.	−.51911*			
Other	REF	REF	REF	REF
Package size				
Size represents: weighed one multipack		.17900*		−.44977*
Weighed 2 potatoes	−.32016*		−.14385*	
Weight labeled	−.10378			
Other	REF	REF	REF	REF
Variety				
White potato	−.11197			
Round or long russet	−.12073*			
Round or long white	−.08151*			
Round red	.13440*			
Baking potato	.07752*			
Yam	−.25983*			
Sweet potato/yam	.28265			
Sweet potato	−.45422*			
Unable to determine variety	−.40993*			

(*continued*)

Table 3C.2 (continued)

	Coefficient			
	12011 Potatoes	12021 Lettuce	12031 Tomatoes	12041 Other Fresh Vegetables
Bibb		.59326*		
Boston		.13274*		
Butterhead		.91953*		
Cos/Romaine		.36190*		
Green leaf		.60410*		
Red leaf		.64647*		
Unspecified variety			−.05647*	
Field grown/vine-ripened			−.30496*	
Hot house or greenhouse			−.26962*	
Unable to determine type			−.26013*	
Radishes with tops				−.01645
Radishes without tops				−.76580*
Yellow corn				−.50855*
White corn				−.13763*
Artichokes				.56677*
Asparagus				.58202*
Bean sprouts				.04937
Miniature carrots				.11278
Green snap beans				−.01606

Pole beans			−.05602
Yellow wax beans			.42235*
Lima beans			.60288*
Domestic (green) cabbage			−1.01275*
Savoy (crinkled leaf) cabbage			−.68162*
Chinese (celery) cabbage			−.12622
Hearts of celery			−.02623
Yellow onions			−.95681
White onions			−.38899*
Pickling cucumbers			−.04579
Spaghetti squash			−.49575*
Yellow straightneck squash			−.08479
Yellow crookneck squash			.06090
Butternut squash			−.31871*
Acorn squash			−.29270*
Zucchini (Italian) squash			−.11483
Green peppers			.20108*
Regular mushrooms			−.27425*
Spanish onion			−.52453*
Red onion			−.11692*
Other	REF	REF	REF	REF

Note: REF = reference.

*Statistically significant at the 5 percent level.

Appendix D
Sample Index Calculation for Fruits and Vegetables and Three Areas

Table 3D.1   CPD Results for Bilateral Relatives for Fruits and Vegetables Entry-Level Items (ELIs)

ELI	Description	AREA1 (PHILA)	AREA2 (BOSTON)	AREA3 (PITTSBG)
11011	Apples	1.0000	.89618	.96884
11021	Bananas	1.0000	.98656	.83609
11031	Oranges	1.0000	1.04715	1.05667
12011	Potatoes	1.0000	.95105	.81712
12021	Lettuce	1.0000	.78312	.75877
12031	Tomatoes	1.0000	1.03136	.95217

Table 3D.2   Expenditures Shares within and across Areas

Share Type	AREA1 (PHILA)	AREA2 (BOSTON)	AREA3 (PITTSBG)
	ELI Shares by Area		
W11011	.39638	.40456	.52877
W11021	.33412	.27270	.31936
W11031	.26950	.32273	.15187
W12011	.41063	.36953	.35684
W12021	.29234	.34244	.37069
W12031	.29704	.28803	.27247
	Expenditure Class Shares by Area		
S(EC11)	.46262	.33328	.20410
S(EC12)	.42243	.38425	.19331

Note: ELI = entry-level items.

Table 3D.3   Multilateral Törnqvist Indexes

Item	TORN12	TORN13	TORN21	TORN23	TORN31	TORN32
EC11	.9614	.9455	1.0402	.9835	1.0576	1.0167
EC12	.9140	.8345	1.0941	.9131	1.1983	1.0952
EC11+EC12	.9382	.8897	1.0659	.9483	1.1240	1.0545

Note: EC = expenditure class.

Table 3D.4   **Estimated Reference Shares and Prices at the ELI Level**

EC/ELI	Variable	Coefficient Estimate
Fruits[a]		
Apples	W0 (11011)	.4391
Bananas	W0 (11021)	.3094
Oranges	W0 (11031)	.2515
Apples	P0 (11011)	−.0458
Bananas	P0 (11021)	−.0585
Oranges	P0 (11031)	.0318
Vegetables[b]		
Potatoes	W0 (12011)	.3803
Lettuce	W0 (12021)	.3331
Tomatoes	W0 (12031)	.2866
Potatoes	P0 (12011)	−.0780
Lettuce	P0 (12021)	−.1671
Tomatoes	P0 (12031)	−.0041

Note: EC = expenditure class. ELI = entry-level item.
[a]Adjusted R^2 = 0.9708.
[b]Adjusted R^2 = 0.9980.

Table 3D.5   **Estimated Reference Expenditure Shares and Prices at the Expenditure Class**

EC	Variable	Coefficient Estimate
Fruits[a]	W0 (EC11)	.5041
	P0 (EC11)	−.0005
Vegetables[a]	W0 (EC12)	.4959
	P0 (EC12)	−.0006

Note: EC = expenditure class.
[a]Adjusted R^2 = 0.9947.

Table 3D.6   **Unadjusted Bilateral Törnqvist Indexes**

EC	TORN12	TORN13	TORN21	TORN23	TORN31	TORN32
EC11	.96622	.94033	1.03496	.98959	1.06346	1.01052
EC12	.91564	.83279	1.09213	.91505	1.20078	1.09284

Note: EC = expenditure class.

Appendix E

Results for Division Food-at-Home and 44 CPI Areas

Table 3E.1   Adjusted R^2 of Transitivity Regressions at Each Aggregation Level

Group	Adjusted R^2	Definition	Number of Subaggregate Items
		Expenditure Class (subaggregate item = entry-level item [ELI])	
EC1	.8333	Cereals and cereal products	5
EC2	.9266	Bakery products	10
EC3	.9494	Beef and veal	8
EC4	.9395	Pork	6
EC5	.9717	Other meats	4
EC6	.9737	Poultry	3
EC7	.8940	Fish and seafood	3
EC8	1.0000	Eggs	1
EC9	.9673	Fresh milk and cream	2
EC10	.9819	Processed dairy products	4
EC11	.9832	Fresh fruits	4
EC12	.9918	Fresh vegetables	4
EC13	.9567	Processed fruits	4
EC14	.9682	Processed vegetables	4
EC15	.9791	Sugar and sweets	3
EC16	.9722	Fats and oils	4
EC17	.9443	Nonalcoholic beverages	7
EC18	.9444	Other prepared foods	12
		Major Group (subaggregate item = expenditure class [EC])	
CERBAK	.9936	Cereal and bakery products (EC01–EC02)	2
MPFE	.9839	Meat, poultry, fish, and eggs (EC03–EC08)	6
DAIRY	.9952	Dairy products (EC09–EC10)	2
FRTVEG	.9902	Fruits and vegetables (EC11–EC14)	4
OTHER	.9721	Other food at home (EC15–EC18)	4
		Division (subaggregate item = major group)	
FOOD	.9934	All food at home	5

Table 3E.2   Index Values Aggregated by Expenditure Class, Reference Area Philadelphia

Area	EC1	EC2	EC3	EC4	EC5	EC6	EC7	EC8	EC9	EC10	EC11	EC12	EC13	EC14	EC15	EC16	EC17	EC18
Philadelphia	1.000	1.000	1.000	1.000	1.000	1.000	1.000	1.000	1.000	1.000	1.000	1.000	1.000	1.000	1.000	1.000	1.000	1.000
Boston	.957	.974	1.012	.889	.899	1.137	.977	.904	.939	.852	.983	.840	.854	.927	.798	.966	.950	.759
Pittsburgh	.864	.889	.897	.923	.924	.865	.942	.740	.976	.800	.924	.823	.816	.849	.978	.946	.891	.877
Buffalo	.852	.957	.987	.964	.975	.929	.829	.789	.791	.759	.877	1.034	.715	.886	.914	1.010	1.089	.793
New York City	.956	.969	1.006	1.050	1.105	.985	1.061	1.063	1.074	1.001	1.022	1.021	1.036	.931	1.150	1.127	1.081	.987
New York-Connecticut suburbs	.908	1.032	1.075	1.020	1.040	1.025	.820	1.051	1.090	1.006	.968	.885	.861	.856	1.015	.924	.976	.966
New Jersey suburbs	.894	1.105	1.096	.992	1.056	.995	.900	1.063	1.134	.982	.950	.909	.834	.933	1.308	.957	.905	.866
Northeast, B PSUs	.811	1.017	1.017	.991	.967	.946	1.020	.930	.998	.897	.981	.924	.828	.893	1.033	.920	.960	.824
Northeast, C PSUs	.928	1.025	1.013	1.034	.952	.785	.990	.787	.897	.867	.907	.821	.780	.819	1.201	.962	1.088	.852
Northeast, D PSUs	.817	1.052	.976	.997	.850	1.000	.956	.863	.916	.789	1.056	.965	.847	.784	1.142	.959	.993	.944
Chicago	.847	.984	1.017	.968	1.011	.923	.905	.822	1.010	.958	1.043	1.059	.871	.874	1.035	.979	.948	.876
Detroit	.883	.852	.996	.995	.947	1.041	.965	.809	1.039	.881	.888	.806	.823	.843	.992	.959	1.045	.870
St. Louis	1.031	.988	.992	1.005	1.047	.894	.949	.845	1.143	.806	.999	1.009	.877	.798	.870	.981	1.026	.981
Cleveland	.742	.899	1.001	1.005	.918	.887	.859	.760	1.058	.904	.977	.797	.903	.857	.784	.971	1.051	.900
Minneapolis	1.045	.734	.987	1.063	.987	.914	1.056	.712	.975	.655	.923	.829	.810	.825	1.006	.964	.952	.880
Milwaukee	.834	.714	1.061	1.123	.872	.863	.815	.690	.993	.919	.979	.855	.770	.740	.610	.920	.899	.831
Cincinnati	.810	1.148	1.022	1.076	.926	1.137	1.060	.786	.983	.996	.965	.960	1.026	.964	1.298	.907	.887	.797
Kansas City	1.054	1.024	.967	.906	1.050	1.424	.838	.762	.983	.697	1.016	.911	.818	.990	1.167	1.050	.829	.868
North Central, B PSUs	.844	.841	.940	.966	.980	.889	.796	.742	.934	.869	.979	.842	.891	.794	1.093	1.006	1.002	.814
North Central, C PSUs	.827	1.000	.946	.940	.951	.852	.990	.805	1.030	.808	.930	.861	.836	.866	1.133	.938	.877	.815
North Central, D PSUs	.798	.896	.923	.878	.886	.775	.991	.755	.961	.782	.860	.750	.846	.858	1.009	.894	.989	.880
Washington, D.C.	.935	1.047	1.062	1.027	1.062	.922	1.138	.870	1.043	.994	1.055	1.033	.940	.934	1.033	1.093	.876	.976
Dallas	.890	.776	.942	.956	.954	.834	.977	.756	.995	.948	.916	.886	.888	.845	1.135	.955	.933	.927
Baltimore	.847	1.005	1.000	.964	.971	.849	1.030	.876	1.064	.986	.991	.861	.952	1.054	.930	.990	.890	.989

(continued)

Table 3E.2 (continued)

Area	EC1	EC2	EC3	EC4	EC5	EC6	EC7	EC8	EC9	EC10	EC11	EC12	EC13	EC14	EC15	EC16	EC17	EC18
Houston	.906	.906	1.018	1.078	1.101	1.140	.801	.867	1.354	.970	.830	.859	.840	.865	1.012	1.027	.943	.977
Atlanta	.983	1.017	.996	1.171	1.109	.855	.823	.729	1.011	1.007	.969	.853	.888	1.033	1.280	1.117	1.045	.822
Miami	.947	.735	1.000	.882	.924	.710	.940	.862	1.255	.957	.745	.798	.807	.665	1.571	.875	.941	.928
Tampa	.913	1.002	.970	.882	.918	.782	.927	.767	1.075	.707	.858	.859	.790	.861	.881	.831	.830	.802
New Orleans	1.039	1.175	.973	.995	1.004	.859	.875	.750	1.263	.822	.989	.824	.924	.886	.729	1.014	.883	.945
South, B PSUs	.845	.844	1.035	1.020	.973	.851	.845	.789	1.125	.850	.933	.872	.815	.832	.861	.886	.875	.855
South, C PSUs	.898	.810	.970	.988	.913	.863	.789	.775	1.148	.836	.884	.845	.854	.830	.985	.909	.913	.855
South, D PSUs	.965	.887	1.029	1.009	.960	.832	.815	.850	1.089	.848	.930	.907	.897	.886	.879	.971	.952	.916
Los Angeles County	.931	.847	1.031	.995	.962	1.065	1.073	1.506	1.036	.939	.911	.755	.898	.878	1.049	1.050	.998	.936
Greater Los Angeles	.938	1.041	.966	.965	.964	.948	.845	1.384	1.003	.930	.899	.738	.886	.882	1.243	.999	.939	.877
San Francisco	.995	1.052	1.071	1.097	1.092	1.086	1.036	1.281	.930	1.027	.939	.774	.904	1.075	1.290	1.015	1.068	.916
Seattle	1.065	.984	.927	.904	1.000	.905	1.075	.885	1.054	.956	1.169	1.064	.940	.930	.804	1.079	1.343	1.034
San Diego	.826	1.137	1.052	1.058	.954	1.368	.802	1.814	1.092	.979	.865	.643	1.144	.844	1.619	.915	.772	.859
Portland, Oreg.	.945	.761	1.011	.960	1.016	1.012	.904	.845	.852	.969	.964	.691	.881	.899	1.363	.995	1.144	.992
Honolulu	1.333	1.795	1.342	1.172	1.305	1.410	1.349	1.398	1.763	1.179	1.197	1.390	1.218	1.219	1.020	1.454	1.054	1.360
Anchorage	1.091	1.042	1.031	1.114	1.172	1.586	.833	1.374	1.439	1.007	1.178	1.322	1.008	1.003	1.374	1.087	1.201	.947
Denver	.922	.987	1.099	.976	.702	.918	.986	.759	1.056	.880	1.048	1.016	.929	.879	1.330	.940	.821	1.031
West, B PSUs	.853	1.104	.916	.944	.904	.925	.888	1.052	.939	.878	.975	.713	1.023	.945	.755	.950	.843	.862
West, C PSUs	.973	.815	.962	.963	.932	.977	.853	.914	.995	.897	.951	.823	.935	.820	.978	.984	.976	.894
West, D PSUs	1.076	.931	.961	.991	.987	.855	1.011	.846	1.121	.943	.893	.729	.878	.990	.772	1.004	.863	.860

Table 3E.3　　　**Index Values by Major Group and All Food-at-Home, Reference Area Philadelphia**

Area	CERBAK	MPFE	DAIRY	FRTVEG	OTHER	FOOD
Philadelphia	1.000	1.000	1.000	1.000	1.000	1.000
Boston	.969	1.007	.888	.901	.789	.888
Pittsburgh	.881	.890	.877	.856	.897	.872
Buffalo	.924	.947	.770	.874	.842	.863
New York City	.965	1.018	1.032	1.010	1.025	1.007
New York-Connecticut suburbs	.997	1.022	1.043	.901	.970	.941
New Jersey suburbs	1.044	1.024	1.049	.907	.917	.946
Northeast, B PSUs	.955	.983	.939	.913	.863	.915
Northeast, C PSUs	.994	.921	.879	.843	.892	.877
Northeast, D PSUs	.976	.975	.844	.931	.970	.933
Chicago	.941	.965	.977	.978	.907	.962
Detroit	.860	1.001	.950	.841	.901	.865
St. Louis	1.000	.960	.954	.931	.973	.951
Cleveland	.849	.944	.971	.885	.902	.891
Minneapolis	.798	.970	.788	.853	.907	.845
Milwaukee	.747	.963	.951	.855	.809	.843
Cincinnati	1.040	1.053	.993	.977	.858	.966
Kansas City	1.032	1.068	.819	.934	.912	.927
North Central, B PSUs	.842	.919	.896	.886	.865	.878
North Central, C PSUs	.943	.910	.904	.878	.860	.889
North Central, D PSUs	.864	.858	.860	.823	.902	.846
Washington, D.C.	1.011	1.011	1.018	1.002	.991	1.004
Dallas	.805	.904	.966	.890	.954	.897
Baltimore	.952	.940	1.022	.954	.983	.964
Houston	.904	1.051	1.138	.848	.987	.907
Atlanta	1.006	.959	1.002	.924	.896	.941
Miami	.790	.861	1.088	.762	.975	.830
Tampa	.973	.874	.868	.846	.816	.862
New Orleans	1.137	.929	1.010	.909	.927	.957
South, B PSUs	.844	.952	.970	.871	.862	.878
South, C PSUs	.834	.918	.973	.858	.878	.871
South, D PSUs	.910	.938	.952	.910	.923	.918
Los Angeles County	.871	1.045	.981	.855	.964	.888
Greater Los Angeles	1.009	.960	.962	.844	.926	.894
San Francisco	1.034	1.086	.973	.898	.966	.934
Seattle	1.012	.929	.999	1.042	1.020	1.036
San Diego	1.027	1.135	1.027	.832	.920	.891
Portland, Oreg.	.816	.991	.907	.848	1.036	.874
Honolulu	1.668	1.334	1.416	1.264	1.321	1.344
Anchorage	1.055	1.207	1.192	1.144	1.008	1.112
Denver	.967	.964	.957	.982	1.048	.990
West, B PSUs	.957	.925	.903	.910	.859	.909
West, C PSUs	.863	.954	.939	.885	.917	.894
West, D PSUs	.978	.927	1.021	.856	.863	.894

References

Aczel, J. 1966. *Lectures on functional equations and their applications.* New York: Academic.
Caves, W., L. Christensen, and W. Diewert. 1982a. The economic theory of index numbers and the measurement of input, output, and productivity. *Econometrica* 50:1393–1414.
———. 1982b. Multilateral comparisons of output, input, and productivity using superlative index numbers. *Economic Journal* 92:73–86.
Cuthbert, J., and M. Cuthbert. 1988. On aggregation methods of purchasing power parities. Working Paper no. 56. Organization for Economic Cooperation and Development, Department of Economics and Statistics.
Diewert, W. 1976. Exact and superlative index numbers. *Journal of Econometrics* 4: 114–45.
———. 1986. Micro economic approaches to the theory of international comparisons. Technical Paper no. 53. Cambridge, Mass.: National Bureau of Economic Research.
———. 1987. Index numbers. In *The new Palgrave dictionary of economics,* ed. J. Eatwell, M. Milgate, and P. Newman. New York: Stockton.
Drechsler, L. 1973. Weighting of index numbers in multilateral international comparisons. *Review of Income and Wealth,* ser. 19, no. 1:17–34.
Eichhorn, W. 1978. *Functional equations in economics.* Reading, Mass.: Addison-Wesley.
Fixler, D., and K. Zieschang. 1992. Incorporating ancillary measures of process and quality change into a superlative productivity index. *Journal of Productivity Analysis* 2, no. 2:245–67.
Kokoski, Mary, Pat Cardiff, and Brent Moulton. 1994. Interarea price indices for consumer goods and services: An hedonic approach using CPI data. Working Paper no. 256. Washington, D.C.: Bureau of Labor Statistics, July.
Moulton, B. R. 1995. Interarea indexes of the cost of shelter using hedonic quality adjustment techniques. *Journal of Econometrics* 68, no. 1:181–204.
Randolph, W., and K. Zieschang. 1987. Aggregation consistent restriction based improvement of local area estimators. In *American Statistical Association: Proceedings of the Section on Business and Economic Statistics.* Alexandria, Va.: American Statistical Association.
Selvanathan, E., and D. Prasada Rao. 1992. An econometric approach to the construction of generalized Theil-Törnqvist indices for multilateral comparisons. *Journal of Econometrics* 54:335–46.
Summers, R. 1973. International comparisons with incomplete data. *Review of Income and Wealth,* ser. 19, no. 1 (March): 1–16.
U.S. Department of Labor. Bureau of Labor Statistics. 1992. *BLS Handbook of Methods.* Bulletin 2414. Washington, D.C., September.
Zieschang, K. 1985. Output price measurement when output characteristics are endogenous. Working Paper no. 150. Washington, D.C.: Bureau of Labor Statistics. Revised, 1987.
———. 1988. The characteristics approach to the problem of new and disappearing goods in price indexes. Working Paper no. 183. Washington, D.C.: Bureau of Labor Statistics.

Comment   Paul Pieper

A major gap in the U.S. system of economic statistics is the absence of any regional or area price indexes. While the Bureau of Labor Statistics publishes consumer price indexes for major U.S. cities, these indexes do not permit comparisons between cities, only comparisons over time at the same city. Area price indexes are likely to be in great demand by both academics and the general public. This paper makes several contributions, including incorporating hedonic quality adjustments into Törnqvist bilateral indexes, developing a multilateral Törnqvist index that minimally adjusts the Törnqvist system of bilateral index comparisons and aggregating the multilateral Törnqvist index so that it is transitive in both the index subcomponents and the index total.

I agree with the authors' focus on a multilateral index. A system of bilateral Törnqvist indexes will be unwieldy if there are more than a handful of areas. For example, if there are forty-four different areas, as in the authors' empirical work, there will be 946 (44 × 43/2) possible bilateral price comparisons. This would entail significantly more reporting expenses than a single index with forty-four entries. In addition, bilateral Törnqvist indexes are not necessarily transitive. Finally, while a bilateral price index is appropriate for some purposes, such as comparing the real wage of job offers in two different cities, in many cases it is necessary to make multilateral comparisons. This is especially true in academic work, where regional or area price indexes are most likely to be used to deflate cross-sectional data.

Given that a multilateral index is preferable to a bilateral index, how should it be constructed? The authors propose a multilateral Törnqvist index constructed using reference price and share vectors estimated from a regression of the cross-weighted differences of log area prices against the area differences of log prices and the area share differences. The authors argue that this index will minimally perturb the system of bilateral Törnqvist index comparisons, but, unfortunately, it is difficult to see from the paper why this is the case. Their point can be more easily seen if one starts by minimizing the squared deviations (weighted if desired) between the bilateral Törnqvist index (eq. [9]) and the multilateral Törnqvist index (eq. [11]). Expanding the two equations and simplifying yields the regression used in the paper.

Minimizing the squared deviations from the bilateral Törnqvist index comparisons is on the surface a reasonable objective for a multilateral index, but at what cost is it achieved? The paper is largely silent on this issue except for a passing reference in the concluding section. An evaluation of the merits of the authors' proposed index requires a discussion of the advantages and disadvantages of their index in relation to the Caves, Christensen, and Diewert (CCD) method or some other competing alternative. The authors' index has the disadvantage of significantly greater computational cost relative to the CCD index

Paul Pieper is associate professor of economics at the University of Illinois at Chicago.

since a regression is necessary for each category in each level of aggregation to determine reference shares and prices. Their index by construction has the advantage of minimizing squared deviations from the bilateral Törnqvist index, but the importance of this effect is unclear. Tables 3D.3 and 3D.6 of the paper provide a comparison of the multilateral Törnqvist index with the bilateral Törnqvist index, but, for this to be put in perspective, a similar comparison needs to be made with other indexes.

Table 3F.1 amends the authors' bilateral price comparisons to include two other index types: an unweighted CCD index and a CCD index where reference shares are weighted by area shares.[1] The three areas are Philadelphia (Phi), Boston (Bos), and Pittsburgh (Pit). The differences between the authors' index (KMZ) and the CCD indexes are trivial. The largest difference between the authors' index and the unweighted CCD index in the six comparisons is only 0.00057. The unweighted CCD index and the KMZ index are identical when rounded to three decimal places, which is the likely number of decimal places to be reported by the BLS. This example is not conclusive since it includes only three areas and two product categories, but it raises doubts as to whether the reduction in deviations from the bilateral Törnqvist index is worth the additional computational cost of the authors' proposed index.

A major part of both the theoretical and the empirical sections of the paper concerns the use of hedonic price indexes to adjust for quality differences in products across areas. However, with the major exception of housing, most products in the United States are homogeneous across areas. Hedonic quality adjustments are necessary in the authors' data set not because the goods themselves differ across regions but because the product definitions are imprecise. Thus, it would be possible to control for quality differences directly, without the use of hedonic regressions, by narrowly defining the good, for example, Red Delicious apples, unpackaged and sold at a chain grocery store, versus just apples. The advantages of a narrow definition are a better control for quality differences and lower computational costs, whereas the hedonic method has the advantage of allowing a greater coverage of products. It is probably not possible to construct area price indexes using narrow product definitions with the authors' data set because there are likely to be only a few observations in a given area at the narrowest level of product definition. However, it is unclear whether the authors' preference for hedonic quality adjustments is based on principle or is necessitated by their data. Some discussion of this issue in the paper would be useful.

Area price indexes must also deal with thorny issues of area differences in nonmarket consumption owing to weather or other factors. Do the extra expenses for warm clothing and heating in Northern cities represent an increase in consumption or simply an increase in costs? One could argue that these

---

1. The weights should be based on the area's share in the next-higher-level aggregate, i.e., fruits or vegetables. In the absence of this information, I used the food-at-home shares of each area (table 3B.2) as weights.

Table 3F.1   Comparison of Törnqvist Indexes

	Bilateral Törnqvist (1)	KMZ (2)	Unweighted CCD (3)	Weighted CCD (4)
Index level:				
Fruits				
Phi-Bos	.96622	.96136	.96086	.96275
Phi-Pit	.94033	.94553	.94558	.94525
Bos-Pit	.98959	.98353	.98410	.98179
Vegetables				
Phi-Bos	.91564	.91397	.91379	.91445
Phi-Pit	.83279	.83453	.83448	.83437
Bos-Pit	.91505	.91308	.91321	.91242
Deviation from bilateral				
Törnqvist index:				
Fruits				
Phi-Bos	.0	−.00486	−.00536	−.00347
Phi-Pit	.0	.00520	.00525	.00492
Bos-Pit	.0	−.00606	−.00549	−.00780
Mean absolute deviation	.0	.00537	.00537	.00540
Vegetables				
Phi-Bos	.0	−.00167	−.00185	−.00119
Phi-Pit	.0	−.00174	.00169	.00158
Bos-Pit	.0	−.00197	−.00184	−.00263
Mean absolute deviation	.0	.00179	.00179	.00180

Note: Abbreviations are defined in the text.

same heating services are provided Southern residents for free by nature and that their price vector should show a zero price. A similar argument could be made for the extra expenses incurred for security in a crime-ridden city as opposed to a crime-free city. These issues are unlikely to be confronted directly by a government-produced index. The practice of using only market consumption and prices implicitly means that any "necessary" consumption purchases for heating, security, or the like will be measured as an increase in quantity rather than an increase in price. However, it is possible that differences in weather-related consumption items may in practice account for the bulk of actual area price differences.

While the authors' work on improving the construction of an area price index is laudable, I hope that the search for index perfection does not delay the introduction of area price indexes by the statistical agencies. Since the U.S. government does not presently produce any area price indexes, academics must use either undeflated data or crude proxies such as median housing prices or average wages. Seen in this light, virtually any well-defined method of indexation, whether based on the authors' minimum-adjustment criteria, the CCD method, or even a fixed basket of goods, would be a major improvement.

4 Constructing Interarea Compensation Cost Indexes with Data from Multiple Surveys

W. Brooks Pierce, John W. Ruser,
and Kimberly D. Zieschang

Place-to-place compensation cost comparisons for areas within the United States are very much in demand to inform facility location decisions and locality salary administration policy in both the private and the public sectors. The Bureau of Labor Statistics (BLS) has operated geographically comprehensive surveys measuring locality wage levels since 1991, primarily to support the Federal Employee Pay Comparability Act (FEPCA). This law was enacted to align the locality compensation for federal employees with that of the comparable nonfederal workforce. Similar studies oriented more toward place-to-place comparisons of compensation are undertaken in the private sector by several companies, often with specialties in certain industry and/or occupation groups.

Labor services differ in type and quality from area to area. The central problem this paper considers is how indexes comparing employee compensation costs across geographic areas that account for the heterogeneity of jobs and workers may be formulated and calculated. A long-standing approach to the heterogeneity problem, taken, for example, by the BLS in the Occupational Compensation Survey program, is to make interarea comparisons only between the same narrowly defined jobs that exist in every area for which comparisons are to be made. The limitation of this approach is that the comparisons apply only to the population of jobs that are found in all areas, while jobs that are specific to only certain areas are excluded from the comparisons.

W. Brooks Pierce is a senior economist and John W. Ruser the chief economist in the Compensation Research and Program Development Group of the Bureau of Labor Statistics' Office of Compensation and Working Conditions. Kimberly D. Zieschang is a senior economist with the International Monetary Fund. This paper was completed while he was associate commissioner for compensation and working conditions at the Bureau of Labor Statistics, U.S. Department of Labor.

The views expressed are those of the authors and do not necessarily reflect the views or policies of the Bureau of Labor Statistics or the International Monetary Fund.

Another approach, which we follow in this paper, is to define jobs more broadly by industry and occupation and to utilize data for all jobs to make interarea comparisons. Within these broader groups, the compensation rates received by specific jobs are then related to specific quantitative information on the characteristics of the jobs using a statistical model known in the economics and economic statistics literature as a *hedonic* model. Heterogeneity is controlled for by employing the parameters estimated in these hedonic models, fitted using regression analysis, to adjust for observable characteristics of workers and jobs. This approach has the advantage of covering all jobs in each labor market. However, it requires additional information about jobs or workers that can be used as covariates in the hedonic regressions.

To provide a context and rigorous interpretation for our indexes, we begin with a standard microeconomic framework for input price indexes developed in a long economic index number literature, positing a model of producer input cost minimization conditioning on output and exogenously determined input prices. A good statement of this basic economic input price index framework applied to labor input cost measurement is given in Triplett (1983). Triplett also discusses the application of hedonic regression methods to adjust for labor quality.

We take these index number concepts and hedonic labor quality measurement methods and incorporate them into an integrated, computable index number system. To construct place-to-place compensation comparisons, we use a Törnqvist index formula. We adopt the Törnqvist formula, rather than alternatives also used in geographic price comparisons such as the Geary (1958)–Khamis (1970) "international prices" system or an adjusted Fisher ideal approach, because the Törnqvist framework simultaneously displays five important features:

First, the Törnqvist formulas that we use for bilateral comparisons have been shown by Diewert (1976) to be exact for the translog flexible functional form. By implication, they accurately accommodate producers' substitution decisions among types of labor services as their relative prices differ from place to place.

Second, Caves, Christensen, and Diewert (1982a) have shown that the Törnqvist index number is exact even when there are significant differences in the underlying technology between situations compared. These indexes therefore accommodate variations in the technology that producers select as they consider various site locations.

Third, Kokoski, Moulton, and Zieschang (chap. 3 in this volume) provide a closed form for the class of all-systems Törnqvist bilateral index numbers that are transitive, generalizing a result along these lines introduced by Caves, Christensen, and Diewert (1982b), and provide a feasible algorithm for computing such systems of index numbers. Clearly, use of our compensation indexes to inform a salary administration policy for geographically dispersed organizations would require the transitivity property to eliminate the possibility of gains and losses accruing to reassigned staff as a sole result of a series of relocations.

Fourth, Kokoski, Moulton, and Zieschang (chap. 3 in this volume) demonstrate that the Törnqvist multilateral system of parities will aggregate in a natural way with respect to a given classification hierarchy for types of labor. This facilitates explaining variations in aggregate compensation in terms of variations in the component occupations making up the aggregate, an important property for a system of public compensation statistics.

Fifth, Kokoski, Moulton, and Zieschang (chap. 3 in this volume) have adapted earlier exact index number results from Zieschang (1985, 1988) and Fixler and Zieschang (1992a, 1992b) to incorporate information on variation in the characteristics of detailed items when making Törnqvist index number comparisons. In this index number framework, coefficients from hedonic compensation regressions are used in constructing labor quality–adjustment factors for place-to-place indexes of compensation rates. Because of the heterogeneity in the measured characteristics of labor employed within industry/occupation groups across areas, these exact quality adjustments are important for making accurate compensation comparisons from place to place.

In section 4.1, we briefly state the microeconomic foundations of our approach using standard production theory and show how the aggregate conceptual bilateral area indexes of this framework can be operationalized using Törnqvist exact and superlative index numbers. We then show how the differing measured labor services characteristics that are encountered in various areas can be accounted for in the index framework. In section 4.2, we establish the implications of transitivity in our Törnqvist interarea index system, and, in section 4.3, we show how transitivity can be imposed with minimal adjustment of the data. In section 4.4, we apply this methodology to both establishment micro data on jobs from the U.S. Employment Cost Index (ECI) and area/occupation/industry data on workers from the Current Population Survey (CPS) and present labor services characteristics–adjusted interarea wage and compensation indexes for thirty-nine major urban centers and rest-of-regional-division geographic areas. We conclude in section 4.5.

4.1 Economic Index Number Concepts Incorporating Information on the Characteristics of Heterogeneous Labor Services

Let p_i^a be the price or compensation rate in area a, of which there are A areas in total, of labor services of occupation i. Let q_i^a be the corresponding quantity purchased, and let x_i^a be the vector of characteristics of the ith job specification for labor services transacted in area a. Let e_h^a represent the total labor services expense of establishment h in area a, and let q_h^a denote the vector of labor services consumed by establishment h in area a with vector of characteristics x_h^a and prices p_h^a.

We suppose that each establishment in area a minimizes the cost of achieving a given level of output u_h^a at expenditure level e_h^a so that the establishment expense incurred for a given quality of labor services as determined by the vector x_h^a would be

$$e_h^a = E_h^a(u_h^a, x_h^a, p_h^a) = \min_{q_h^a}\{p_h^{a\prime}q_h^a : d_h^a(u_h^a, x_h^a, q_h^a) \geq 1\},$$

where $d_h^a(u_h^a, x_h^a, q_h^a)$ is the joint production function of establishment h.[1] To reduce clutter, we condition on and suppress the nonlabor inputs used by establishment h.

We suppose further that an establishment in area a faces a hedonic locus of market equilibrium prices across the labor services quality spectrum given by $p_h^a = H^a(x_h^a)$ and that the establishment minimizes the cost of achieving outputs u_h^a over the characteristics of labor services, with the result that

$$(1) \qquad \nabla_{x_h^a}E_h^a(u_h^a, x_h^a, p_h^a) + \nabla_{x_h^a}p_h^{a\prime}\nabla_{p_h^a}E_h^a(u_h^a, x_h^a, p_h^a) = 0.$$

Since $\nabla_{x_h^a}p_h^a = \nabla_{x_h^a}H^a$ and $\nabla_{p_h^a}E_h^a(u_h^a, x_h^a, p_h^a) = q_h^a$, the latter by the Shephard/ Hotelling lemma, we have

$$(2) \qquad \nabla_{x_h^a}E_h^a(u_h^a, x_h^a, p_h^a) = -\nabla_{x_h^a}H^{a\prime}q_h^a.$$

If H^a is semilog, as generally assumed in hedonic studies, so that

$$(3) \qquad \ln H_i^a = \alpha_i^a + \beta_i^{a\prime}x_i^a,$$

then the characteristics gradient expression can be rewritten

$$(4) \qquad \nabla_{x_h^a}E_h^a(u_h^a, x_h^a, p_h^a) = -\beta^{a\prime}w_h^a e_h^a,$$

where

$$w_{i,h}^a = \frac{p_{i,h}^a q_{i,h}^a}{\sum_i p_{i,h}^a q_{i,h}^a},$$

$$w_h^a = \begin{bmatrix} w_{1,h}^a \\ \vdots \\ w_{N_q,h}^a \end{bmatrix}; \quad N_q = \text{number of types (occupations) of labor, and}$$

$$\beta^{a\prime} = \begin{bmatrix} \beta_1^{a\prime} \\ \vdots \\ \beta_{N_x}^{a\prime} \end{bmatrix}; \quad N_x = \text{number of labor services characteristics.}$$

---

1. This particular joint production function is the *input distance function,* given by

$$d_h^a(u_h^a, x_h^a, q_h^a) = \sup_\theta\left\{\theta : \left(u_h^a, x_h^a, \frac{1}{\theta}q_h^a\right) \text{ is feasible}\right\}.$$

Diewert (1987) considers the area aggregation of individual establishments in the context of an area production function. We follow this general notion but will require some modifications to handle the heterogeneity of labor service types and their prices within and between areas. Turning now to aggregate labor input expense over establishments in an area, we have

$$E^a(\vec{u}^a,\ \vec{x}^a,\ \vec{p}^a)\ =\ \sum_h E_h^a(u_h^a,\ x_h^a,\ p_h^a),$$

where the arrow over an argument indicates the concatenation of vectors across establishments. We then consider the labor services expenditure or cost function in terms of log transformed price arguments as

$$Q^a(\vec{u}^a,\ \vec{x}^a,\ \ln \vec{p}^a)\ =\ E^a(\vec{u}^a,\ \vec{x}^a,\ \vec{p}^a)$$

$$=\ \sum_h E_h^a(u_h^a,\ x_h^a,\ p_h^a)\ =\ \sum_h Q_h^a(u_h^a,\ x_h^a,\ \ln p_h^a).$$

We aggregate across establishments in area a such that the expenditure-weighted average for characteristics and log-labor services prices represents the indicators determining area demand behavior, where area item demand for labor services is the sum of the establishment item demands for the area. We do not require strong aggregation conditions but effectively hold the distribution of labor services characteristics and compensation rates fixed across establishments within area a as in

$$(5)\quad \tilde{Q}^a\!\left(\vec{u}^a,\ \overline{x}^a,\ \overline{\ln p}^a\right)\ =\ Q^a\!\left(\vec{u}^a,\ \iota \otimes \overline{x}^a + v_x^a,\ \iota \otimes \overline{\ln p}^a + v_{\ln p}^a\right),$$

where $v_x^a = \vec{x}^a - \iota \otimes \overline{x}^a$, $v_{\ln p}^a = \ln \vec{p}^a - \iota \otimes \overline{\ln p}^a$, $\iota = $ a vector of ones equal in dimension to the number of establishments in area a, and $\otimes = $ Kronecker product, which give the deviations of the area means from the individual establishment values for labor services characteristics and log compensation rates paid.

Using the derivatives of the expenditure function with respect to log prices expressed in terms of observable expenditure shares, Diewert (1976) and Caves, Christensen, and Diewert (1982a) have shown that the Törnqvist index number is exact for the translog flexible functional form, which differentially approximates any price aggregator function (i.e., cost of utility, input cost, revenue function) to the second order at a point, and it is exact even when some of the parameters (those on the first-order terms) of the underlying aggregator function are different in the two periods or localities compared. We take the derivative of the area expenditure function with respect to establishment labor cost–weighted aggregate arguments to obtain

$$(6)\quad \frac{\partial}{\partial \overline{x}_{iz}^a}\ln \tilde{E}^a\!\left(\vec{u}^a,\ \overline{x}^a,\ \exp(\overline{\ln p}^a)\right)\ =\ \frac{\partial}{\partial \overline{x}_{iz}^a}\ln \tilde{Q}^a\!\left(\vec{u}^a,\ \overline{x}^a,\ \overline{\ln p}^a\right)$$

$$=\ \sum_h \frac{\partial}{\partial x_{izh}^a}Q_h^a\!\left(u_h^a,\ x_h^a,\ \ln p_h^a\right)\!/\tilde{Q}^a\ =\ -\beta_{izx}^a\sum_H w_{ih}^a s_h^a\ =\ \beta_{izx}^a\,\overline{w}_i^a,$$

$$\text{(7)}\quad \frac{\partial}{\partial \ln p_i^a} \ln \tilde{E}\big(\vec{u}^a,\ \vec{x}^a,\ \exp(\overline{\ln p^a})\big) = \frac{\partial}{\partial \ln p_i^a} \ln \tilde{Q}\big(\vec{u}^a,\ \vec{x}^a,\ \overline{\ln p^a}\big)$$

$$= \sum_h \frac{\partial}{\partial \ln p_{izh}^a} Q_h^a\big(u_h^a,\ x_h^a,\ \ln p_h^a\big)/\tilde{Q}^a = \sum_h w_{ih}^a s_h^q = \overline{w}_i^a,$$

where

$$w_{ih}^a = \frac{p_{ih}^a q_{ih}^a}{\sum_i p_{ih}^a q_{ih}^a} = \frac{p_{ih}^a q_{ih}^a}{e_h^a},$$

$$s_h^a = \frac{e_h^a}{\sum_h e_h^a},$$

are, respectively, the within-firm labor cost shares of occupations and the between-firm labor cost shares of establishments in area a.

Finally, we assume that the area aggregate labor services cost function $\ln \tilde{Q}^a$ $(u^a, \vec{x}^a, \overline{\ln p^a})$ has a quadratic, "semi-translog" functional form in its arguments with coefficients of second-order terms independent of location but with possibly location-specific coefficients on linear terms. Following Caves, Christensen, and Diewert (1982a), then, we can derive the following (logarithmic) index number result:

$$\ln I^{ab}$$

$$= \frac{1}{2}\big[\ln \tilde{Q}^a\big(\vec{u}^a, \vec{x}^b, \overline{\ln p^b}\big) - \ln \tilde{Q}^a\big(\vec{u}^a, \vec{x}^a, \overline{\ln p^a}\big)$$

$$\text{(8)}\quad + \ln \tilde{Q}^b\big(\vec{u}^b, \vec{x}^b, \overline{\ln p^b}\big) - \ln \tilde{Q}^b\big(\vec{u}^b, \vec{x}^a, \overline{\ln p^a}\big)\big]$$

$$= \frac{1}{2}\big[\nabla_{\ln p} \ln \tilde{Q}^a\big(\vec{u}^a, \vec{x}^a, \overline{\ln p^a}\big) + \nabla_{\ln p} \ln \tilde{Q}^b\big(\vec{u}^b, \vec{x}^b, \overline{\ln p^b}\big)\big]\big(\overline{\ln p^b} - \overline{\ln p^a}\big)$$

$$+ \frac{1}{2}\big[\nabla_x \ln \tilde{Q}^a\big(\vec{u}^a, \vec{x}^a, \overline{\ln p^a}\big) + \nabla_x \ln \tilde{Q}^b\big(\vec{u}^b, \vec{x}^b, \overline{\ln p^b}\big)\big]\big(\vec{x}^b - \vec{x}^a\big).$$

Substituting (6) and (7) into (8), we have

$$\text{(9)}\quad \ln I^{ab} = \ln T^{ab} \equiv \frac{1}{2}\sum_i \Big[\big(\overline{w}_i^a + \overline{w}_i^b\big)\big(\overline{\ln p_i^b} - \overline{\ln p_i^a}\big)$$

$$- \sum_z \big(\beta_{iz}^a \overline{w}_i^a + \beta_{iz}^b \overline{w}_i^b\big)\big(\overline{x}_{iz}^b - \overline{x}_{iz}^a\big)\Big].$$

This is an extremely flexible result that permits all parameters of the semilog "hedonic" labor services compensation equations to differ by area and reflects establishments' optimizing behavior in considering location and the available characteristics of labor services.

4.2   Törnqvist Multilateral (Transitive) Systems of Bilateral Compensation Index Numbers

In another paper, Caves, Christensen, and Diewert (1982b) noted that the system of bilateral Törnqvist interarea indexes is not transitive but developed a simply calculated multilateral variant satisfying the transitivity property. Following Kokoski, Moulton, and Zieschang (chap. 3 in this volume), we apply the following general implication of transitivity for this class of index number:

$$\sum_n w_i^a \left(\ln p_i^b - \left(\sum_z \beta_{iz}^a x_{iz}^b \right) \right) - \left[\sum_i w_i^a \left(\ln p_i^a - \left(\sum_z \beta_{iz}^a x_{iz}^a \right) \right) \right]$$

$$(10) \quad = \sum_i \sum_z [-\beta_{iz}^0 w_i^0](x_{iz}^b - x_{iz}^a) + \sum_i \sum_z x_{iz}^0 (\beta_{iz}^b w_i^b - \beta_{iz}^a w_i^a)$$

$$+ \sum_i w_i^0 (\ln p_i^b - \ln p_i^a) + \sum_i [-\ln p_i^0](w_i^b - w_i^a),$$

where $x_{iz}^0 = $ a reference characteristic z for index item i across the entire region, $\beta_{iz}^0 = $ a reference coefficient for the characteristic z of item i in a semilog hedonic equation explaining specification price across the entire region, $p_i^0 = $ a reference price for item i across the entire region, and $w_i^0 = $ a reference share for item i for the entire region, where $\sum_i w_i^0 = 1$. If this condition holds, the multilateral Törnqvist index has the form

$$\ln T^{ab} = -\sum_i \sum_z \frac{1}{2} (\beta_{iz}^0 w_i^0 + \beta_{iz}^b w_i^b)(x_{iz}^b - x_{iz}^0) + \sum_i \frac{1}{2}(w_i^0 + w_i^b)(\ln p_i^b - \ln p_i^0)$$

$$(11) \quad -\left[-\sum_i \sum_z \frac{1}{2}(\beta_{iz}^0 w_i^0 + \beta_{iz}^a w_i^a)(x_{iz}^a - x_{iz}^0) + \sum_i \frac{1}{2}(w_i^0 + w_i^a)(\ln p_i^a - \ln p_i^0) \right].$$

The proof is given in Kokoski, Moulton, and Zieschang (chap. 3 in this volume). Caves, Christensen, and Diewert (1982b) showed that application of the EKS principle to a system of bilateral Törnqvist indexes yields the price component of the above formula with the reference shares and log prices set at their simple arithmetic averages across areas. Clearly, these simple averages could also be calculated as total compensation expenditure–weighted averages. Extension for the EKS/Caves, Christensen, and Diewert (CCD) approach to our labor quality–adjusted index given by equation (11) would simply require that the zero-superscripted terms constituting the product of the reference hedonic coefficients of each characteristic with the reference share weight of the index items be set to the regional averages for these terms. In this paper, however, we use the Kokoski, Moulton, and Zieschang regression method for determining the reference parameters, as detailed in section 4.3 below.

4.2.1   Analysis of the Contribution of Labor Quality Indicators to Levels of Place-to-Place Indexes

Because Törnqvist indexes are linear in the log differences of detailed, quality-adjusted specification prices, the contribution of each quality indicator, say, full-time status, to the quality-level ratio between two areas can be readily calculated by exponentiating the appropriate weighted sums of log price differences. These sums would be calculated from the transitive expression for the index given above, where it is expressed in terms of locality weights averaged with reference weights and price differentials from reference prices. The contribution to the level of $\ln T^{ab}$ of labor characteristic z would simply be the subordinate sum

$$\ln C_z^{ab} = -\sum_i \frac{1}{2}(\beta_{iz}^0 w_i^0 + \beta_{iz}^b w_i^b)(x_{iz}^b - x_{iz}^0)$$

$$-\left[-\sum_i \frac{1}{2}(\beta_{iz}^0 w_i^0 + \beta_{iz}^a w_i^a)(x_{iz}^a - x_{iz}^0)\right].$$

4.3   Estimation of the Reference Values for Shares, Prices, and Determinants of Quality

4.3.1   Adjusting for Labor Quality from Place to Place

In the present study, we utilize wage and compensation cost data from the employment cost index (ECI) survey. This survey contains a limited amount of information about each surveyed job. We augment the observed characteristics of jobs with additional data on worker characteristics from the Current Population Survey (CPS).

We follow the method of Kokoski, Cardiff, and Moulton (1994), who construct interarea price indexes for consumer goods using country-product-dummy (CPD) regression (Summers 1973). We first estimate wage and compensation costs regressions for each broadly defined job, where the covariates include worker and job attributes and local area dummies. Let p_{ij}^a represent the wage in the jth quote for job i in location a, where a job is defined to be in an industry/occupation group. The wage can be described by the following regression equation:

(12) $$\ln p_{ij}^a = X_{ij}^a \beta_i + L_i^a + \varepsilon_{ij}^a,$$

where X_{ij}^a represents data on the characteristics of the job and the worker and where L_i^a represents a local area effect for job i in area a. This regression equation allows the coefficients on X_{ij}^a and the local area effects to vary across jobs. Equation (12) is estimated by weighted least squares, where the weights are the sample weights from the ECI.

A standard practice is to utilize the estimation results from equation (12) to make interarea wage comparisons. The regression defines a decomposition of interarea wage differences into components due to interarea differences in attributes X_{ij}^a and residual terms L_i^a. Let $\hat{\beta}_{iz}$ be the zth element of the vector of weighted least squares estimates of β_i from equation (12), and let x_{ijz}^a be the zth element of the vector X_{ij}^a. Also let $\overline{\ln p_i^a}$ and $\overline{x}_{iz}^a$ be weighted (by ECI sample weights) averages over j of $\ln p_{ij}^a$ and x_{ijz}^a, respectively. Then, by the properties of the weighted least squares estimators,

$$\overline{\ln p_i^a} = \sum_z \hat{\beta}_{iz} \overline{x}_{iz}^a + \hat{L}_i^a.$$

A Törnqvist index comparing wages in local area b to those in area a is defined (in logs) as

(13) $$\ln T^{ab} = \frac{1}{2}\sum_i \left(w_i^a + w_i^b\right)\left(\overline{\ln p_i^b} - \overline{\ln p_i^a}\right),$$

where w_i^a is cell i's share of the labor expenditure in locality a. This differential can in effect be decomposed into contributions of the various covariates in X and contributions of the local area dummies. The contribution of the local area dummies takes the same form as (13),

$$\ln T_L^{ab} = \frac{1}{2}\sum_i (w_i^a + w_i^b)(\hat{L}_i^b - \hat{L}_i^a).$$

Further, the contribution of the zth characteristic of the job or worker to the index in (13) is

$$-\frac{1}{2}\sum_i (w_i^a + w_i^b)\hat{\beta}_{iz}(\overline{x}_{iz}^b - \overline{x}_{iz}^a).$$

This contribution depends on interarea differences in average characteristics (the difference in the mean X's) in conjunction with the importance of the zth characteristic in determining the wages in each job i (the $\hat{\beta}_{iz}$). The sum of these z contributions, plus $\ln T_L^b$, equals the Törnqvist index in (13). In the following sections, we present this decomposition for a (transitive, multilateral) set of Törnqvist bilateral index numbers.

4.3.2 Multilateral Compensation Indexes: A Regression Approach for Imposing Transitivity with Minimal Adjustment of the Data

In this paper, we employ an alternative to (or a likely superclass of) the EKS/CCD approach from Kokoski, Moulton, and Zieschang (chap. 3 in this volume) for making the system of bilateral indexes transitive. When this condition on the cross-weighted differences of labor characteristics–adjusted log regional prices is not met, the data may be minimally adjusted to satisfy transitivity by fitting the equation

$$w_i^a \left(\ln p_i^b - \left(\sum_z \beta_{iz} x_{iz}^b \right) \right) - w_i^a \left(\ln p_i^a - \left(\sum_z \hat\beta_{iz} x_{iz}^a \right) \right)$$

$$= [w_i^0] \left(\ln p_i^b - \sum_z \hat\beta_{iz} x_{iz}^b - \left(\ln p_i^a - \sum_z \hat\beta_{iz} x_{iz}^a \right) \right)$$

$$+ [-\ln p_i^0](w_i^b - w_i^a) + \varepsilon_i^{ab}$$

using least squares to obtain the estimates

$$\begin{bmatrix} -\ln \hat p_i^0 \\ \hat w_i^0 \end{bmatrix}.$$

This is a simplification of equation (10) since, if, as our CPD model assumes, the hedonic slope coefficients are the same across areas for each specification characteristic so that $\beta_{iz}^a = \beta_{iz}^b = \beta_{iz}^0$, the coefficient on the difference between the share vectors of the two areas is a *characteristics-adjusted reference price vector* and no reference characteristics vector can be separately identified.

4.4   An Application to U.S. Labor Compensation Data

4.4.1   Data

The micro data used to construct the interarea indexes come from two sources: the employment cost index (ECI) and the Current Population Survey (CPS). The ECI data program produces quarterly indexes that measure changes over time in wages and salaries and in the cost of total compensation. These indexes are calculated from micro data collected for sampled jobs in sampled establishments. All jobs in nonfarm private industry and in state and local governments are within the scope of the survey, meaning that the occupation coverage of the survey is nearly complete. The micro data available include the mean hourly wage and mean hourly compensation costs for all incumbents in the sampled jobs. Other data elements describe job or establishment characteristics: the establishment's number of employees; whether the employment is full-time or part-time; and whether the job is covered by a collective-bargaining agreement. This study utilized the data for 18,486 sampled jobs for the fourth quarter of 1993 in nonagricultural private industry. Details of variable definitions, sample exclusion restrictions, and summary statistics for all data are in appendix A.

A shortcoming of the ECI is that it does not collect key variables that are widely believed to measure human capital: education and labor market experience. To obtain these variables, data from the CPS were merged with the ECI micro data. The CPS is a monthly survey of households that contains information about the demographic characteristics and employment outcomes of individuals. For current purposes, we used the three monthly surveys for the fourth quarter of 1993 and restricted our sample to employed individuals in nonagricultural private industry. We collected information on schooling, age, industry, occupation, and area of residence for a sample of almost 140,000 workers.

Merging the data from the CPS with the ECI presents a challenge because the ECI micro data contain the means for jobs while the CPS contains data for individuals and, of course, the individuals covered in the two surveys are not necessarily the same. The strategy we followed was to calculate weighted mean values for CPS variables for cells defined by local area, occupation, and industry. The industry and occupation cell classification used for this purpose was determined by the availability of data; we chose to create cells defined by local area, major occupation group, and six industry groups.

After matching the CPS cell-level data to the ECI micro data for individual jobs, we had to determine an appropriate locality/industry/occupation classification for the purposes of computing the interarea indexes. The methodology in the previous section, specifically equation (12), calls for estimating separate regressions for cells defined by industry and occupation in order to recover estimates of local area dummies for each cell. There is a trade-off between the size of the smallest local area for which we can calculate interarea indexes and how finely the industry/occupation cells can be disaggregated. We selected a set of cities that included both those that are the largest and those that are of interest in the federal pay-setting process. The remainder of the data were aggregated into census geographic divisions (as "rest of division"). We then determined that indexes could be calculated for these local areas using eighteen industry/occupation cells, defined by major occupation group and whether the job is in a goods- or service-producing industry.

To give the reader a feel for the underlying data, we present some summary data in tables 4.1 and 4.2. Table 4.1 gives wage and compensation shares and levels by our job classification scheme; major occupation groups are presented within the two broad industrial groupings. The first column, labeled *wage share,* reports the fraction of total wages that falls in the given category. These statistics are useful for showing where the bulk of the data reside. The second column simply reports the average hourly wage in the given cell (all figures are in nominal dollars). Roughly speaking, the professional, technical, and executive occupations have the highest hourly wages, production workers and operatives have average wages, and laborers and service workers have below-average wages. There is a noticeable difference between the broad industry aggregates, with average wages in any particular occupation group being higher in the goods-producing industries. The third column gives shares of total compensation. Goods-producing industries have higher shares of total compensation than of total wages, reflecting the fact that a higher fraction of compensation comes in the form of benefits for workers in those industries. This fact is apparent in comparing average wages, in the second column, to average hourly compensation costs, in the final column. Finally, one other obvious inference that can be drawn from this table is that, given the wide variation in wages and compensation costs across jobs, index numbers might be

Table 4.1   **Industry/Occupation Shares, Wages, and Compensation**

	Wage Share	Average Wage	Compensation Share	Average Compensation
Goods-producing industries:				
Professional/technical	.047	22.60	.047	31.98
Executive/administrative	.054	26.03	.054	36.84
Sales	.007	17.09	.007	22.92
Administrative support	.042	11.60	.044	17.08
Precision production	.094	15.80	.102	24.12
Machine operatives	.066	10.74	.075	17.04
Transport operatives	.029	12.76	.032	19.73
Laborers	.030	9.70	.033	14.78
Service workers	.008	14.08	.008	20.30
Service industries:				
Professional/technical	.145	19.33	.140	26.17
Executive/administrative	.101	20.95	.098	28.47
Sales	.095	10.12	.087	13.14
Administrative support	.120	9.93	.118	13.75
Precision production	.029	11.93	.028	16.28
Machine operatives	.009	8.18	.009	11.55
Transport operatives	.014	9.28	.014	13.18
Laborers	.027	7.03	.026	9.54
Service workers	.084	6.00	.079	7.89

Source: Winter 1993 employment cost index.

Note: Wage share and compensation share are wage and compensation shares in the nonhousehold, nonfederal, nonagricultural economy. Average wage and average compensation refer to average hourly wages and compensation in nominal dollars, where averages within industry/occupation class are weighted by ECI sample weights.

expected to yield very different results than simple interarea differences in average compensation rates whenever there are interarea differences in the distribution of jobs.

Table 4.2 gives employment shares and average compensation by local area. The compensation shares, showing each local area's compensation as a fraction of total U.S. compensation, give some idea as to which metropolitan statistical areas have relatively few ECI job quotes. Because of their small sizes, localities such as Charlotte and Columbus might be expected to have fairly noisy compensation index estimates. The "rest-of-division" localities, on the other hand, tend to be rather large. Comparing column 2 with column 1 shows that larger metropolitan areas tend to have the highest average compensation costs, the "rest-of-division" localities the lowest. The final column (*compensation relative*) gives average compensation in the local area relative to the overall average compensation level in the data. The range in these area relatives is quite large. At one extreme, compensation in the Detroit, New York, and San Francisco areas is approximately 134 percent of average compensation in the United States; at the other extreme lies the East South Central locality, with 73 percent

Table 4.2   **Compensation by Local Area**

Local Area and Rest of Regional Division	Compensation Share	Average Hourly Compensation ($)	Compensation Relative
		Northeast Region	
Boston	.029	19.75	116.4
Hartford	.009	20.60	121.4
New England	.016	14.04	82.8
New York	.116	22.73	134.0
Philadelphia	.027	19.93	117.5
Pittsburgh	.011	20.22	119.2
Middle Atlantic	.070	17.18	101.3
		North Central Region	
Chicago	.039	19.19	113.1
Detroit	.024	22.70	133.8
Cleveland	.010	17.33	102.2
Milwaukee	.008	16.34	96.3
Dayton	.007	17.46	102.9
Cincinnati	.006	15.89	93.7
Columbus	.006	15.99	94.3
Indianapolis	.005	18.59	109.6
East North Central	.062	14.23	83.8
Minneapolis	.011	17.35	102.2
Kansas City	.006	20.94	123.4
St. Louis	.006	18.27	107.7
West North Central	.052	14.74	86.9
		South Region	
Washington, D.C.	.026	21.84	128.7
Atlanta	.014	17.81	105.0
Miami	.009	14.45	85.2
Tampa	.008	13.89	81.9
Charlotte	.005	14.32	84.4
South Atlantic	.077	13.82	81.5
East South Central	.042	12.35	72.8
Houston	.020	19.21	113.2
Dallas	.018	17.17	101.2
West South Central	.056	14.00	82.5
		West Region	
Denver	.008	15.08	88.9
Phoenix	.007	16.24	95.7
Mountain	.028	13.26	78.2
Los Angeles	.060	20.02	118.0
San Francisco	.032	22.74	134.0
Seattle	.012	21.61	127.4
San Diego	.010	20.86	123.0
Portland	.008	18.66	110.0
Pacific	.039	15.42	90.9

Source: Winter 1993 employment cost index.

Note: Compensation share is the area share of compensation in the nonhousehold, nonfederal, nonagricultural economy. *Average compensation* is average hourly compensation in nominal dollars, weighted by ECI sample weights. *Compensation relative* is the ratio of the local area average compensation to the U.S. average compensation.

of overall average compensation. A comparison of these figures with the index numbers presented below will give some idea as to the importance of interarea differences in job characteristics for compensation cost comparisons.

4.4.2 Regressions

The first step in the construction of the interarea indexes was the estimation of log wage and log compensation cost regressions (eq. [12]). In addition to local area dummies, five sets of covariates were included as explanatory variables in the regressions to capture factors that affect worker productivity. Following a long tradition in the labor economics literature dating back to Mincer (1962) and Becker (1964), years of schooling, years of potential labor market experience (age minus education minus six), and potential experience squared were included. These measure the average amount of human capital possessed by incumbents in the job.

The labor literature has shown that wages are positively associated with establishment size. Brown and Medoff (1989) argue that part of this wage-size relation arises because large firms attract higher-quality workers (even after controlling for observable characteristics). In order to control for this in the present study, we include a set of eight establishment-size class dummies.

In the literature, unionization is claimed both to increase and to decrease worker productivity. The traditional view holds that unions lower productivity by imposing staffing requirements and other restrictive work practices that prevent firms from efficiently utilizing capital and labor (Lewis 1986; Rees 1989). A more recent literature argues that unions enhance worker productivity (Freeman and Medoff 1984). First, unions provide a collective voice that communicates workers' preferences. This lowers worker discontent and turnover, increasing firms' incentives to invest in job-specific human capital. Second, unions typically establish seniority rules that may promote an environment where more senior workers are willing to provide less senior workers with informal on-the-job training. Finally, unions may enhance worker morale, motivation, and effort. While the literature is ambiguous about the effect of unions on productivity, most studies show that unions increase wages. To capture the effects of unions on productivity in our regressions, we include a dummy indicating whether a job is covered by a collective-bargaining agreement.

The literature generally shows that, after accounting for observed differences in human capital, part-time workers earn less than full-time workers (see Lettau [1997] and the citations therein). For at least two reasons, this differential may arise because part-time workers are on average less productive than their full-time counterparts. First, it is argued that innately less productive workers are more likely to select part-time jobs. For example, more productive workers may find it advantageous to work more intensively if their wages reflect their productivity. Second, average productivity might be lower for part-time workers owing to fixed daily setup costs that are spread over more working hours for full-time workers. We include a part-time dummy in our regressions to capture these productivity effects.

It is important to note that, while the education and potential experience variables are widely viewed as measuring human capital, the other three variables—establishment size, unionization, and part-time status—may have effects on wages that are not strongly associated with labor productivity. All three represent or proxy to some extent characteristics of the labor services transaction in an industry and locality as much as the characteristics of the service itself. Although the nature of the transaction may have productivity effects, this is not a foregone conclusion. Large nonunion firms, for example, may pay higher wages simply to forestall unionization. Union wages may be higher simply because of union monopoly power. If the purpose of including explanatory variables in the regressions is to control for factors that affect productivity, then it is possible that our index factors overcontrol for some of these transaction and other effects. In the analysis that follows, we include all the explanatory variables in the regressions, but we provide a set of adjustment factors associated with the explanatory variables. These factors measure the contribution of each variable (or variable group) to the unadjusted interarea differential. One advantage of our methodology is that analysts can add back the differential associated with a variable if they judge that it is not appropriate to control for that variable. In tables 4.3 and 4.4 below, *adjusted* refers to interarea measures adjusted for differences in all our conditioning variables explaining wage and compensation variation. Future formats for interarea compensation data could reasonably include multiple summary columns of adjusted data corresponding to multiple subsets of conditioning factors to satisfy the interests of various users.

Eighteen regressions were estimated separately for wages and compensation costs. There is a regression for each of nine major occupation groups in either the goods- or the service-producing industries. The regressions for wages appear in appendix table 4B.1, while those for compensation costs appear in table 4B.2.

The adjusted R^2's for the regressions are comparable to or higher than those found for wage regressions estimated on individual micro data. The regressions typically explain between 20 and 50 percent of the variation of wages, while the corresponding range for compensation costs is 30–60 percent.

As expected by theory and found in most data, wages and compensation costs tend to rise with education. The returns to education are perhaps on average slightly smaller than would be obtained from person-level micro data. However, there are a few instances in our regressions where the education coefficient is anomalously negative (although not large relative to the standard error). This may arise in part owing to small sample sizes for some of the regressions. Further, it is important to stress that we have an imperfect measure of education that is measured as a cell mean from CPS data. Within a regression, education varies across areas and across some industry groups but does not vary for a given industry and area. It is likely that the education variable would perform better if it were collected for the same unit of observation as the wage and compensation data.

Previous empirical work has shown that wages display an increasing, concave profile with experience. This is often observed in our regressions as well, although there are a number of instances where the profile is convex and downward sloping at relevant experience levels. As with the education variable, problems with the experience variable might arise because its values are cell means whose source of variation for any regression is across areas and to a lesser extent across broad industry groups. The sample statistics indicate that the standard deviation of experience is much lower in our data than it is in micro data. This low variance is not unexpected but could indicate that the variable cannot discriminate well in explaining wage variation.

As expected, jobs that are covered by union contracts command higher wages than uncovered jobs, while part-time jobs tend to receive lower wages. The return to union contract coverage is on average higher in these regressions than estimates derived from older data (Lewis 1986). Finally, also as expected, larger establishments tend to pay higher wages, with especially notable premiums for establishments with five hundred or more employees. Comparisons of the establishment-size coefficients across industry/occupation groups are difficult because of substantial variability across those cells in the average compensation of workers in the omitted category (one to nine workers). However, the establishment-size coefficient point estimates typically rise with establishment size.

4.4.3 Interarea Indexes of Wages and Compensation for the United States

Table 4.3 gives our main results for interarea wage rate differentials. The second column of the table presents Törnqvist wage indexes that control for the composition of employment across nine major occupation groups and two industry groups but where there are no other adjustments for observed differences in worker or job characteristics. The index numbers are relative to the reference wage generated by our method (described in sec. 4.3 above) of making the bilateral comparisons transitive; one may loosely interpret 100.0 as average for the United States.[2] As an example, the first entry in the second column indicates that wages, adjusted for broad differences in employment but unadjusted for observed differences in worker and job characteristics, are 10.1

---

2. Actually, neither the area share-weighted arithmetic nor geometric average of these locality levels is generally equal to 100.0 because of the way the reference shares and prices are determined using the "minimum bilateral relative adjustment" criterion implicit in our regression approach, in concert with our observation weighting, which gives greater importance to records representing relatively large bilateral average expense shares. Bilateral ratios of the index numbers in tables 4.3 and 4.4 produce a transitive system of parities as provided by the objective of our algorithm but do not provide a particular-level normalization. Interpretation of these data as levels requires a normalization to, e.g., the national average level, much as a time series of price index numbers would be normalized to be 100.0 in a particular time period to align it with other data series so normalized for a given analytic purpose. The data in tables 4.3 and 4.4 are, therefore, valid for ranking localities in terms of labor services input price levels. As we note elsewhere in the paper, the weighted EKS/CCD method of determining the reference shares and prices of the transitive parities implicitly does normalize the regional geometric average level to 100.0.

Table 4.3   **Wage Indexes**

Local Area and Rest of Regional Division	Average Wage Relative	Wage Index	Education	Experience	Establishment Size	Full-Time/Part-Time	Union	Adjusted Wage Index
Northeast Region								
Boston	118.8	110.1	102.5	99.5	100.2	99.6	99.2	109.1
Hartford	120.9	111.9	99.6	102.6	102.1	96.0	101.1	110.6
New England	84.6	88.8	98.4	98.6	97.2	98.1	98.3	97.7
New York	132.7	128.0	100.6	100.7	100.0	101.1	100.6	124.2
Philadephia	116.2	111.2	101.4	99.7	99.5	100.0	101.0	109.4
Pittsburgh	118.1	108.8	102.4	103.6	101.7	100.9	102.2	97.8
Middle Atlantic	99.0	101.6	99.2	98.8	101.5	99.1	100.6	102.4
North Central Region								
Chicago	111.9	108.8	101.3	100.3	99.1	100.6	101.7	105.6
Detroit	115.7	114.4	101.6	98.9	105.8	99.4	103.2	104.9
Cleveland	94.9	98.6	97.9	100.1	102.0	98.0	102.4	98.2
Milwaukee	96.8	101.2	97.7	99.5	100.3	100.9	100.8	102.0
Dayton	103.8	91.2	98.5	99.1	99.0	99.2	100.2	94.9
Cincinnati	95.2	100.9	100.3	99.4	100.3	100.5	99.4	101.2
Columbus	98.2	96.4	102.5	99.3	99.8	101.6	99.6	93.7
Indianapolis	106.8	101.0	98.1	106.9	98.9	102.9	101.1	93.5
East North Central	83.4	88.9	98.9	98.9	99.4	99.9	100.6	91.0
Minneapolis	100.6	107.0	102.2	97.9	100.0	99.5	102.1	105.1
Kansas City	120.7	110.9	103.6	99.2	99.0	102.3	101.6	104.9
St. Louis	101.3	95.1	104.5	99.8	98.4	101.6	101.2	90.2
West North Central	85.6	85.7	98.9	98.2	100.9	99.6	99.9	87.9

(continued)

Table 4.3 (continued)

Local Area and Rest of Regional Division	Average Wage Relative	Wage Index	Education	Experience	Establishment Size	Full-Time/Part-Time	Union	Adjusted Wage Index
				South Region				
Washington, D.C.	127.5	112.9	100.9	100.7	102.0	100.9	100.4	107.5
Atlanta	104.2	105.1	100.7	101.2	101.6	102.2	100.6	98.7
Miami	89.2	92.4	97.7	100.5	98.8	100.0	98.5	96.6
Tampa	84.7	87.4	99.7	99.7	100.3	99.3	97.8	90.3
Charlotte	86.4	87.3	100.7	96.4	101.7	99.3	97.2	91.6
South Atlantic	83.4	86.6	98.6	99.3	99.3	99.9	97.8	91.2
East South Central	74.2	78.1	99.2	99.3	98.2	99.8	100.0	80.9
Houston	116.4	111.1	100.0	101.2	99.2	98.8	98.3	113.9
Dallas	102.4	97.0	98.2	99.4	102.1	102.4	100.1	95.0
West South Central	84.2	81.4	97.8	98.8	99.3	99.7	98.2	86.7
				West Region				
Denver	94.3	96.2	100.6	98.7	97.9	99.9	99.6	99.4
Phoenix	98.0	98.6	98.8	101.4	105.2	100.1	98.4	95.0
Mountain	80.4	87.6	100.7	100.5	98.8	98.8	98.2	90.4
Los Angeles	119.4	114.0	100.3	100.6	101.0	99.6	99.9	112.3
San Francisco	136.7	128.6	103.8	101.4	100.9	99.7	100.9	120.5
Seattle	127.9	118.2	102.4	101.5	102.0	102.1	102.3	106.8
San Diego	119.7	115.3	102.7	98.9	98.4	99.1	99.5	117.1
Portland	108.7	109.6	102.1	98.6	97.9	101.0	99.9	110.1
Pacific	91.7	101.5	100.2	98.9	99.2	100.1	100.8	102.2

Source: Winter 1993 employment cost index.

Note: The adjusted wage index in the last column is the wage index in col. 2 divided by the product of the characteristics indexes in cols. 3–7, normalized to base 100.

percent higher in Boston than in the United States as a whole. The amount of interarea variation in employment-adjusted wage indexes is striking, with numbers ranging from 128.6 for San Francisco to 78.1 for the East South Central rest-of-division locality. Generally, one tends to find that wages are higher than average in the larger CMSAs (consolidated metropolitan statistical areas) and along the West Coast; wage indexes are much smaller than average in the rest-of-division localities. Controlling for the composition of employment across industry and occupation by using a wage index tends to reduce interarea differentials as compared to the unadjusted wage relatives that appear in the first column of table 4.3. This is most clearly seen in figure 4.1, which plots the wage indexes against the average wage relatives. The figure contains a regression line through the data points (estimated with unweighted OLS) and a forty-five-degree line. If controlling for the composition of industry and occupation employment had no effect on interarea wages, then the regression line would have a forty-five-degree slope. Instead, the regression line is flatter than the forty-five-degree line, indicating that, in part, wages are low in low-wage areas because employment is more heavily concentrated in low-wage industries and occupations.

The rightmost column of table 4.3 gives adjusted wage differentials corresponding to the Törnqvist indexes calculated using the local area dummies ($\hat{L}_i^a$). Comparing the wage index column with the adjusted wage index column of table 4.3, the interarea variation in characteristics-adjusted wages is generally smaller than the interarea variation in wages alone. The standard deviation of the wage index is 12.2, as opposed to a standard deviation of 9.8 for the adjusted wage index. This can be seen graphically in figure 4.2, which plots one index against the other. The regression line through the plot is again less steep than the forty-five-degree line, indicating that controlling for worker and job attributes raises the wage index for low-wage areas and lowers it for high-wage areas. That is to say, some of the interarea variation about U.S. mean

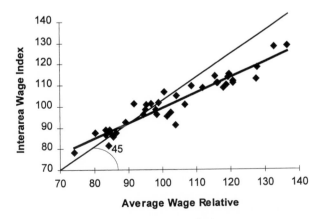

Fig. 4.1   Relation of interarea wage index to relative average wages

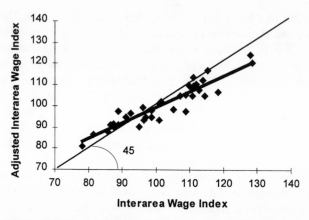

Fig. 4.2   Relation of characteristics-adjusted interarea wage index to interarea wage index

wages can be attributed to interarea differences in the observable characteristics X, even after accounting for interarea differences in industry/occupation employment distributions. One of the larger adjustments is in Detroit, where the observed differences in characteristics would imply an approximately 9 percent (114.4/104.9 = 1.09) premium to hire labor. The seven localities with the lowest employment-adjusted wage indexes (five of which are rest-of-division localities) have on average a 4.2 percent increase in wage indexes through our labor characteristics adjustments. In contrast, the seven localities with the highest employment-adjusted wage indexes have on average a 4.9 percent decrease through characteristics adjustments.

Whether the characteristics adjustment for a particular locality reflects a premium mainly attributable to larger establishment size, greater unionization rates, a more educated workforce, or some other reason is not clear from comparing the wage indexes. To address that question, table 4.3 contains a set of columns that report the contributions of the observable characteristics to unadjusted wage differentials. Recalling the discussion following equation (13), variations in the area relatives for a characteristic will be larger the larger is the coefficient for that characteristic in the wage regressions and the larger is the variation in the characteristic across areas. Our decomposition methodology implies that, for any given local area, the quality-adjusted index and the covariate contributions (appropriately scaled by one hundred) must multiply up to equal the employment-adjusted wage index. Whenever a number in one of the covariate columns exceeds 100 for a given area, the observed characteristic tends to raise wages in that area. For example, the covariate contribution for education in Boston, 102.5, indicates that Boston's workers are more highly educated than average, so their unadjusted pay is 2.5 percent higher than the average area owing to this characteristic. Although there is substantial noisiness in the results, especially among the smaller local areas, what one not surprisingly sees is that most of the adjustment factors for worker and job characteristics tend to exceed 100 for the highest-wage areas (e.g., San Francisco) and to fall short of 100 for the lowest-wage areas (including most of the "rest of regions"). Finally, as stated earlier, note that these adjustment factors can be used to add back to the characteristics-adjusted indexes the influence of variables that an analyst does not wish to remove in making interarea comparisons.

To get some sense of the relative contributions of the worker and job characteristics to wage differentials, figure 4.3 graphs the data from table 4.3 on area relatives for these characteristics against the interarea wage indexes. Each figure also plots the (unweighted) regression line through the points, and the scales of each figure are made the same to facilitate comparison. Each figure shows a positive correlation between the particular area relative and the wage index, indicating that, on average, all the characteristics contribute to interarea wage differentials. More significantly, the steepest regression line is for education, indicating that this characteristic is most important in explaining observed interarea differentials in the wage index. The union variable has the second steepest slope, while the part-time dummy variable has the flattest regression line. Since our wage regressions indicated that wages tend to be significantly lower for part-time jobs, the fact that this variable accounts for little variation in wages across areas stems from the fact that the proportion of part-time jobs varies little across areas.

Table 4.4 gives analogous calculations for hourly compensation, as opposed to wages. Given that wages constitute approximately 70 percent of compensation costs, it is not surprising to find that the gross patterns apparent in table 4.3 hold here as well. Controlling for industry/occupation and worker and job characteristics reduces interarea compensation differentials, implying that high-compensation areas receive high compensation partly for observable reasons. One difference between table 4.3 and table 4.4 is that the interarea differences in compensation indexes are slightly larger than those for wage indexes. One extreme example is Detroit, whose characteristics-adjusted compensation index (113.0) is much larger than its characteristics-adjusted wage index (104.9).

The greater interarea dispersion when computing compensation indexes holds for both the employment-adjusted and the characteristics-adjusted series. The compensation share–weighted standard deviations for these series are 17.2 and 13.3, respectively. Controlling for job and worker characteristics, therefore, reduces the interarea variation in compensation by about 23 percent. The greater interarea variation in compensation, as opposed to wages, no doubt reflects some combination of income effects (workers have income-elastic demands for health care, pensions, and other benefits) and tax effects (benefits are generally lightly taxed or not taxed at all, and the occupation composition of the labor force and income tax rates vary by locality). As employers making location decisions presumably care about compensation costs broadly defined, it is useful to know that interarea wage comparisons are likely to understate the interarea compensation differentials.

A. Education

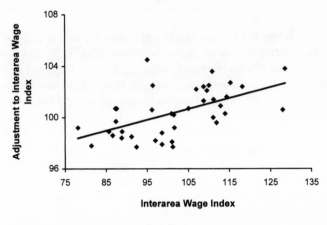

B. Experience

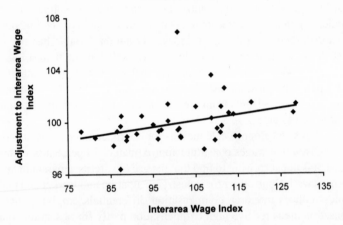

C. Establishment Size

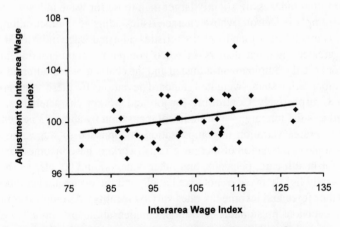

Fig. 4.3 **Relation of labor services characteristics adjustment factors to interarea wage index:** *a*, education; *b*, experience; *c*, establishment size; *d*, full-time status; *e*, union status

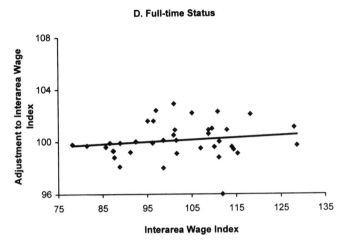

D. Full-time Status

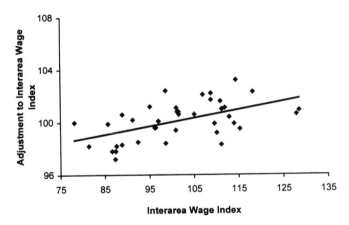

E. Union Status

Fig. 4.3   (cont.)

4.5   Conclusion

We have applied a promising methodology for place-to-place price measurement to the problem of constructing interarea characteristics-adjusted compensation indexes, a methodology that blends hedonic regression and economic index number techniques. We have used a combination of establishment data from the BLS employment cost index program and household data on individual workers from the BLS Current Population Survey to provide a more complete picture of labor quality than has been available to analysts working with only household data. As would be expected, incorporation of the labor quality information generally reduced the variability of labor costs from place to place and provided insights into the contribution of various factors, such as educa-

Table 4.4 Compensation Indexes

Local Area and Rest of Regional Division	Average Compensation Relative	Compensation Index	Education	Experience	Establishment Size	Full-Time/Part-Time	Union	Adjusted Compensation Index
Northeast Region								
Boston	116.4	111.2	102.7	99.5	100.0	99.2	98.8	110.9
Hartford	121.4	115.5	99.9	102.7	102.4	95.1	101.6	113.9
New England	82.8	87.0	98.4	98.8	96.1	97.6	97.5	97.8
New York	134.0	130.3	100.7	100.9	99.8	101.4	101.1	125.2
Philadelphia	117.5	113.1	101.1	99.9	99.2	99.6	101.8	111.3
Pittsburgh	119.2	109.3	102.1	103.0	101.4	100.3	102.3	99.8
Middle Atlantic	101.3	103.2	99.2	99.0	102.1	99.0	100.9	103.0
North Central Region								
Chicago	113.1	110.6	101.3	100.3	98.8	100.2	102.5	107.3
Detroit	133.8	129.5	101.3	99.1	109.1	99.6	105.1	113.0
Cleveland	102.2	104.4	98.5	100.5	103.1	98.3	103.7	100.3
Milwaukee	96.3	102.2	98.1	99.6	100.7	101.5	101.1	101.2
Dayton	102.9	92.3	98.0	98.9	99.1	99.5	100.2	96.3
Cincinnati	93.7	101.0	100.2	99.4	100.4	100.5	99.2	101.2
Columbus	94.3	93.6	102.0	98.7	100.1	102.1	99.5	91.5
Indianapolis	109.6	101.0	98.4	106.8	99.1	102.8	101.5	93.0
East North Central	83.8	88.9	98.7	98.8	99.4	99.8	100.9	91.0
Minneapolis	102.2	107.5	102.3	97.8	100.7	99.3	103.1	104.2
Kansas City	123.4	112.6	103.2	99.7	99.3	102.9	102.1	104.9
St. Louis	107.7	99.1	104.8	99.3	98.3	101.9	101.6	93.7
West North Central	86.9	85.8	98.8	98.1	101.0	99.6	99.7	88.3

	South Region						
Washington, D.C.	128.7	114.3	101.0	100.8	103.1	101.2	100.7	106.9
Atlanta	105.0	105.0	101.1	100.5	101.8	102.6	100.8	98.2
Miami	85.2	88.9	97.5	100.1	98.6	100.2	97.8	94.1
Tampa	81.9	85.5	99.9	99.9	100.1	99.6	96.8	88.8
Charlotte	84.4	84.7	100.7	96.7	101.6	99.8	96.0	89.4
South Atlantic	81.5	84.2	98.5	99.3	99.0	100.0	96.8	89.7
East South Central	72.8	76.4	99.2	99.3	97.9	99.8	99.8	79.6
Houston	113.2	109.3	100.0	101.6	99.3	98.2	97.4	113.1
Dallas	101.2	96.3	98.5	99.3	102.3	102.7	100.0	93.7
West South Central	82.5	79.1	97.7	98.7	98.9	99.8	97.4	85.3
	West Region						
Denver	88.9	91.2	101.3	98.4	97.5	99.3	99.5	95.0
Phoenix	95.7	97.1	98.8	100.7	107.1	100.2	97.6	93.2
Mountain	78.2	85.2	100.6	100.2	98.1	98.5	97.3	89.8
Los Angeles	118.0	112.8	100.3	100.5	101.3	99.6	99.8	111.2
San Francisco	134.0	127.8	103.7	101.4	101.1	99.6	101.6	118.9
Seattle	127.4	118.0	101.9	102.0	101.5	102.7	103.2	105.6
San Diego	123.0	119.9	102.2	99.1	98.8	99.0	99.5	121.7
Portland	110.0	111.6	101.8	98.3	97.0	101.0	100.1	113.7
Pacific	90.9	100.6	99.8	99.0	98.9	99.9	101.0	102.1

Source: Data from winter 1993 employment cost index; October, November, and December 1993 Current Population Survey.

Note: The adjusted compensation index in the last column is the compensation index in col. 2 divided by the product of the characteristics indexes in cols. 3–7, normalized to base 100.

tion, experience, establishment size, union status, and full-time work status, to the level of labor compensation in major urban centers of the United States.

Enhancements to the data are needed. Fortunately, there are prospective developments on this score. The BLS Office of Compensation and Working Conditions is currently undertaking a major redesign and integration of its three major compensation surveys, the employment cost index, the Employee Benefit Survey, and the Occupational Compensation Survey. One salutary result of this for the ECI is a substantial increase in sample size from the current five thousand establishments to at least twice that number. Of particular interest for interarea comparisons is the adoption of an area-and-industry-based rather than a solely industry-based rotational scheme for the samples in the new integrated survey, whose total size will be approximately thirty thousand establishments. Comprehensive data on job content is included in the list of data elements to be collected from all establishments in the survey, greatly expanding the number and explanatory power of the covariates that can be used for characteristics adjustment.

Appendix A
Data

The Employment Cost Index (ECI)

The ECI is a quarterly survey of randomly sampled establishments designed to produce estimates of wage and compensation cost changes. Within establishment, jobs are randomly sampled at the establishment initiation into the sample (sampling is carried out with probability proportional to establishment employment in the occupation). For each job, the ECI collects average wages and average compensation costs for the workers in the job. Nonwage compensation includes leave (sick leave, vacations, and holidays), supplemental pay (overtime, nonproduction bonuses), employer contributions to pensions and retirement savings accounts, health benefits, life and accident insurance, legally required labor expenses (state and federal unemployment insurance, workers' compensation, social security), and some other miscellaneous fringes. The ECI converts all data collected to a cost-per-hour-worked basis. The ECI micro data also attach various establishment or job characteristics to each job quote, including more detailed industry and occupation codes, establishment size, the job's work schedule, and whether the job is covered by a union contract. The ECI collects quarterly updates on the wages and compensation costs and uses these updates to compute quarter-over-quarter and year-over-year indexes of change. Establishments are replaced in the sample using an industry rotation; the entire sample is replaced over the course of four to five years.

For this study, we gathered a data extract from the ECI for the last quarter of 1993. We kept all private-sector job quotes for which we had valid wage and compensation data, meaning that the job quote was used in computing the ECI. Data can be invalid for two main reasons. The first is that the data represent the establishment's responses at initiation, which of course are not used in computing the most recent ECI change. We exclude these data mainly so our sampling weights remain approximately correct; including these observations would improperly overweight the industries that are the focus of initiation. The second is that establishments may be unable to, or may refuse to, report some benefits or wages for a particular job. In this case, the BLS attempts to impute wages or benefits on the basis of the nonmissing data available; cases where these attempts fail are essentially dropped from the ECI calculations. Finally, we note that, in some instances, the job's work schedule cannot be calculated and hourly compensation must be imputed even though the ECI has valid compensation data. Once exclusion restrictions are made, we have a sample of 18,468 job quotes.

Because sample replacement is made on an industry rotation pattern and sample weights are not adjusted through the life of the industry panel, normal sample attrition results in cross-sectional samples that overweight more recently initiated industries. Accordingly, we adjust the ECI sampling weights to bring them current by adjusting two-digit SIC employments to equal those published in the BLS *Employment and Earnings* series. References to the ECI sampling weights in the text and tables reflect this weighting adjustment.

The Current Population Survey (CPS)

While the ECI attempts to sample establishments randomly, the CPS is designed to sample addresses randomly and collect information on the households at each sampled address. The main function of these surveys is to generate official employment and unemployment statistics; however, they are utilized by researchers in a number of other ways as well. The survey is conducted monthly, with a given household surveyed for four months, not surveyed for eight months, and then surveyed for four final months, at which point the household leaves the sample. The survey collects demographics and current employment outcomes, among other items, for each person in a sampled household.

We pooled the October, November, and December 1993 CPS surveys to gather worker characteristics by industry, occupation, and local area at approximately the same time frame as our ECI data. The sampling design guarantees some overlap in the month-to-month samples, but that overlap does not imply redundant information in all cases because of changing employment rates, industry and occupation distributions, etc. Our sample exclusions were made primarily to maintain comparability with the ECI sample: we included only individuals employed by nonagricultural, private-sector employers. Our final sample contains 138,902 observations.

The covariates from the CPS data are mainly measures to proxy for human capital or other factors typically thought to affect wages. We have data on educational attainment, which we have converted into a measure of the years of schooling acquired by the individual. We derive "years of potential labor market experience," or approximate years out of school, as a proxy measure for the amount of general human capital acquired by the individual through work; it is defined as age − years of schooling − 6 (if less than zero, it is recoded to zero). Experience is entered as a quadratic to capture depreciation and decreasing investment rates through time (see Mincer 1974).

In order to match these data to our ECI sample, we averaged these covariates up to cell levels, where cells are defined by the area locations, six industry groups, and the nine major occupation groups. Averages are weighted averages, with weights being CPS sample weights. In matching the CPS to the ECI data, a small number of localities had missing values for some of the industry/occupation cells. These were allocated values from a donor cell of similar attributes within the local area. As these imputations account for a very small portion of the data, our results do not depend on the particular allocation method used.

Appendix table 4A.1 contains summary statistics, weighted by sample weights, for hourly wages, hourly compensation, and various job characteristics from the ECI.

Table 4A.1   Sample Statistics

Variable	Mean	SD	Minimum	Maximum
		ECI Variables		
Average hourly wage	12.07	9.31	2.13	277.38
Average hourly compensation	16.97	12.96	2.13	470.34
ln(hourly wage)	2.30	.59	.76	5.63
ln(hourly compensation)	2.62	.64	.76	6.15
Establishment size 10–19	.10	.29	0	1
Establishment size 20–49	.15	.36	0	1
Establishment size 50–99	.13	.34	0	1
Establishment size 100–249	.18	.38	0	1
Establishment size 250–499	.09	.28	0	1
Establishment size 500–999	.08	.26	0	1
Establishment size 1,000–2,499	.08	.28	0	1
Establishment size 2,500+	.09	.28	0	1
Works < 35 hours/week	.21	.41	0	1
Covered by union contract	.14	.35	0	1
		CPS Variables		
Years of schooling	12.95	1.25	4	17
Years of potential experience	17.39	3.87	0	48
Experience squared	466.54	149.31	0	2,304
Number of observations	18,468			

Source: Winter 1993 employment cost index; October, November, and December 1993 Current Population Survey.

Note: Data are weighted by employment cost index sampling weights.

Appendix B
Hedonic, Country-Product-Dummy Regressions

The regressions in equation (12),

(12) $$\ln p_{ij}^a = X_{ij}^a \beta_i + L_i^a + \varepsilon_{ij}^a,$$

where p_{ij}^a represents the average hourly wage or compensation for the jth quote for job i in location a, X_{ij}^a represents data on the characteristics of the job and the worker, and L_i^a represents a local area effect for job i in area a, are essentially analogs to the country-product-dummy model in international product price comparisons. These regressions allow the coefficients on X_{ij}^a and the local area effects to vary across jobs. Tables 4B.1 and 4B.2 give weighted least squares estimates for (12), where the weights are the sample weights from the ECI.

It is worth discussing a few obvious points of interpretation. The coefficients give the estimated marginal effect on wages within the industry/occupation cell. One would expect these marginal effects to depend on how broadly or narrowly the cells are defined and to differ from the marginal effect from a regression over all industry/occupation cells. Furthermore, the CPS covariates are averages; a given CPS covariate value is not ECI quote specific as multiple ECI quotes have the same values attached. In that case, the proper interpretations to place on the marginal effects are less clear. For example, one tends to find higher wages in the ECI sample in locations and jobs where the population workforce (not the ECI sample workforce, as this aspect is unknown) is more highly educated. Does the schooling variable proxy for the ECI sample workforce's schooling, its cognitive abilities more generally, or some other factors that are also related to wages? This leads to another issue, namely, the question of which variables to use as regressors. Presumably the "proper" selection of covariates depends on what they proxy for as well as on the end purpose of the generated statistics. If the end purpose of the statistics is to inform business location decisions, then one would want to control for those factors that are productivity related or that capture labor cost premiums that do not reflect productivity differences but that can be avoided by prospective new firms. Although sensible readers might disagree with details of our specification, we feel that the covariates with the largest effects on the interarea wage indexes would fall primarily into these categories. Finally, the standard errors in tables 4B.1 and 4B.2 are likely to be biased downward for the CPS variables since the regression equation disturbances are correlated within groups (Moulton 1986, 1990). At this point, we are mainly interested in generating consistent estimates of the local area effects and are less interested in confidence intervals. Presumably, generating correct standard errors would be more straightforward if estimating the hedonic regressions and interarea indexes simultaneously were practicable.

Table 4B.1   Hedonic Wage Regressions

	Professional/ Technical	Executive/ Administrative	Sales	Administrative Support	Precision Production	Machine Operatives	Transport Operatives	Laborers	Service Workers
					A. Goods-Producing Industries				
Establishment size 10–19	1.02	−.03	.04	.12	.09	.25	−.24	.02	.41
	(.24)	(.11)	(.21)	(.05)	(.03)	(.07)	(.08)	(.07)	(.32)
Establishment size 20–49	1.13	0.24	.20	.06	.08	.08	−.14	.05	.65
	(.20)	(.09)	(.22)	(.05)	(.03)	(.07)	(.07)	(.06)	(.44)
Establishment size 50–99	1.11	.29	.61	.21	.17	.09	−.09	−.01	.48
	(.20)	(.09)	(.20)	(.05)	(.03)	(.07)	(.07)	(.07)	(.26)
Establishment size 100–249	1.14	.40	.29	.06	.15	.08	−.08	.02	.84
	(.20)	(.09)	(.19)	(.05)	(.03)	(.06)	(.07)	(.06)	(.27)
Establishment size 250–499	1.16	.28	.72	.20	.16	.08	.03	.07	.80
	(.20)	(.09)	(.22)	(.05)	(.04)	(.07)	(.08)	(.06)	(.28)
Establishment size 500–999	1.30	.43	.73	.19	.31	.21	−.16	.22	.85
	(.20)	(.09)	(.31)	(.05)	(.04)	(.07)	(.09)	(.07)	(.30)
Establishment size 1,000–2,499	1.32	.46	.47	.24	.30	.37	.09	.17	.98
	(.20)	(.09)	(.31)	(.05)	(.04)	(.07)	(.08)	(.07)	(.27)
Establishment size 2,500+	1.50	.47	.18	.30	.29	.50	.02	.27	1.10
	(.20)	(.08)	(.30)	(.05)	(.04)	(.07)	(.09)	(.08)	(.28)
Works < 35 hours/week	.14	−.40	−.80	−.27	−.12	−.19	−.08	−.17	.43
	(.08)	(.18)	(.17)	(.03)	(.06)	(.12)	(.07)	(.05)	(.11)
Covered by union contract	.23	.07	.16	.15	.20	.22	.23	.46	.31
	(.05)	(.10)	(.30)	(.02)	(.02)	(.02)	(.03)	(.03)	(.09)
Years of schooling	−.03	.02	.11	.02	.06	.00	.13	.06	.06
	(.04)	(.04)	(.07)	(.03)	(.02)	(.04)	(.03)	(.02)	(.05)
Years of potential labor market experience	.01	−.05	−.04	.03	−.01	.04	−.05	.01	.07
	(.03)	(.03)	(.04)	(.01)	(.02)	(.03)	(.02)	(.02)	(.02)
Experience squared/100	−.05	.08	.09	−.07	−.03	−.04	.13	−.06	−.13
	(.06)	(.06)	(.12)	(.03)	(.04)	(.07)	(.04)	(.05)	(.05)
Observations	829	675	97	1,128	1,649	1,208	339	500	124
Adjusted R^2	.32	.25	.58	.34	.37	.47	.43	.55	.75

B. Service Industries

	(1)	(2)	(3)	(4)	(5)	(6)	(7)	(8)	(9)
Establishment size 10–19	−.24 (.05)	.14 (.05)	.19 (.04)	−.05 (.02)	.18 (.06)	.01 (.18)	.01 (.07)	.24 (.05)	−.10 (.03)
Establishment size 20–49	−.14 (.05)	.13 (.05)	.18 (.04)	−.04 (.02)	.25 (.05)	−.11 (.13)	.18 (.06)	.06 (.04)	−.10 (.03)
Establishment size 50–99	−.04 (.04)	.21 (.05)	.27 (.04)	−.07 (.02)	.38 (.06)	.02 (.13)	.22 (.07)	.05 (.04)	−.14 (.03)
Establishment size 100–249	.01 (.04)	.05 (.05)	.09 (.03)	−.04 (.02)	.36 (.07)	−.20 (.10)	.24 (.08)	.11 (.04)	−.02 (.03)
Establishment size 250–499	.04 (.05)	.22 (.06)	.05 (.05)	−.02 (.02)	.32 (.10)	−.04 (.13)	.12 (.09)	.13 (.05)	−.03 (.03)
Establishment size 500–999	.09 (.05)	.39 (.06)	.08 (.07)	−.03 (.02)	.45 (.10)	−.16 (.13)	.35 (.13)	.13 (.07)	.03 (.04)
Establishment size 1,000–2,499	.08 (.04)	.32 (.06)	.14 (.09)	.01 (.02)	.31 (.11)	−.13 (.23)	.22 (.19)	.38 (.06)	−.02 (.04)
Establishment size 2,500+	.05 (.04)	.29 (.06)	.04 (.06)	.00 (.03)	.42 (.10)	.11 (.20)	.20 (.30)	.17 (.08)	.15 (.05)
Works < 35 hours/week	−.17 (.02)	−.46 (.08)	−.62 (.02)	−.23 (.01)	−.34 (.08)	−.40 (.10)	−.35 (.06)	−.28 (.02)	−.22 (.02)
Covered by union contract	.06 (.04)	−.26 (.13)	.09 (.05)	.12 (.03)	.21 (.07)	.25 (.10)	.24 (.06)	.29 (.03)	.07 (.03)
Years of schooling	−.01 (.03)	.09 (.03)	.29 (.03)	.09 (.02)	.01 (.06)	−.07 (.06)	.06 (.05)	−.01 (.02)	.01 (.03)
Years of potential labor market experience	−.01 (.02)	−.01 (.02)	.07 (.02)	−.01 (.01)	−.05 (.02)	.02 (.03)	.04 (.02)	.01 (.01)	.06 (.01)
Experience squared/100	−.01 (.06)	.00 (.05)	−.12 (.05)	.03 (.02)	.12 (.05)	−.09 (.03)	−.09 (.03)	.00 (.03)	−.11 (.03)
Observations	2,058	1,482	1,692	3,259	425	165	246	659	1,933
Adjusted R^2	.21	.25	.48	.28	.32	.38	.45	.43	.41

Source: Winter 1993 employment cost index.

Table 4B.2   Hedonic Compensation Regressions

	Professional/ Technical	Executive/ Administrative	Sales	Administrative Support	Precision Production	Machine Operatives	Transport Operatives	Laborers	Service Workers
					A. Goods-Producing Industries				
Establishment size 10–19	1.11	−.01	.04	.17	.14	.30	−.15	.07	.32
	(.22)	(.11)	(.21)	(.06)	(.04)	(.08)	(.08)	(.07)	(.30)
Establishment size 20–49	1.21	.31	.28	.17	.14	.14	−.04	.16	.84
	(.19)	(.09)	(.21)	(.05)	(.03)	(.08)	(.07)	(.07)	(.42)
Establishment size 50–99	1.22	.33	.69	.30	.24	.13	.01	.03	.63
	(.19)	(.09)	(.20)	(.05)	(.03)	(.08)	(.07)	(.07)	(.25)
Establishment size 100–249	1.26	.42	.36	.18	.20	.15	−.02	.09	.93
	(.19)	(.09)	(.18)	(.05)	(.03)	(.07)	(.07)	(.07)	(.25)
Establishment size 250–499	1.28	.34	.82	.35	.23	.20	.14	.18	.93
	(.19)	(.09)	(.21)	(.05)	(.04)	(.07)	(.08)	(.07)	(.26)
Establishment size 500–999	1.48	.52	.81	.37	.40	.32	−.04	.30	1.01
	(.19)	(.09)	(.30)	(.06)	(.04)	(.08)	(.09)	(.07)	(.28)
Establishment size 1,000–2,499	1.48	.55	.53	.39	.41	.53	.22	.33	1.19
	(.19)	(.09)	(.30)	(.05)	(.04)	(.08)	(.08)	(.08)	(.26)
Establishment size 2,500+	1.66	.59	.20	.49	.43	.74	.33	.44	1.33
	(.18)	(.08)	(.30)	(.05)	(.04)	(.08)	(.09)	(.09)	(.27)
Works < 35 hours/week	.06	−.47	−.91	−.37	−.16	−.22	−.24	−.20	.31
	(.08)	(.18)	(.17)	(.04)	(.06)	(.14)	(.08)	(.05)	(.10)
Covered by union contract	.24	.19	.15	.21	.29	.29	.32	.56	.32
	(.05)	(.10)	(.29)	(.03)	(.02)	(.02)	(.04)	(.04)	(.09)
Years of schooling	−.04	.04	.11	−.01	.03	.00	.11	.06	.06
	(.04)	(.04)	(.07)	(.03)	(.02)	(.04)	(.03)	(.03)	(.05)
Years of potential labor market experience	.02	−.04	−.05	.04	.00	.03	−.05	.02	.06
	(.02)	(.03)	(.04)	(.01)	(.02)	(.03)	(.02)	(.02)	(.02)
Experience squared/100	−.07	.08	.14	−.08	−.02	−.01	.12	−.09	−.13
	(.06)	(.06)	(.12)	(.03)	(.04)	(.08)	(.04)	(.05)	(.05)
Observations	829	675	97	1,128	1,649	1,208	339	500	124
Adjusted R^2	.37	.32	.64	.41	.48	.56	.55	.62	.80

B. Service Industries

	(1)	(2)	(3)	(4)	(5)	(6)	(7)	(8)	(9)
Establishment size 10–19	-.22	.15	.21	-.04	.23	.08	.04	.27	-.11
	(.05)	(.05)	(.04)	(.02)	(.06)	(.20)	(.07)	(.05)	(.03)
Establishment size 20–49	-.11	.15	.17	-.01	.30	-.11	.22	.09	-.08
	(.05)	(.05)	(.04)	(.02)	(.05)	(.14)	(.07)	(.04)	(.03)
Establishment size 50–99	-.01	.25	.28	-.05	.43	.10	.28	.09	-.09
	(.04)	(.05)	(.04)	(.02)	(.06)	(.11)	(.08)	(.05)	(.03)
Establishment size 100–249	.03	.07	.10	-.02	.37	-.13	.29	.16	.02
	(.04)	(.05)	(.03)	(.02)	(.07)	(.11)	(.08)	(.04)	(.03)
Establishment size 250–499	.07	.27	.06	.02	.41	.02	.17	.16	-.02
	(.05)	(.06)	(.05)	(.03)	(.10)	(.14)	(.09)	(.06)	(.03)
Establishment size 500–999	.16	.46	.13	.01	.52	-.06	.51	.17	.09
	(.05)	(.06)	(.07)	(.03)	(.10)	(.14)	(.14)	(.07)	(.04)
Establishment size 1,000–2,499	.16	.36	.22	.07	.41	-.18	.32	.42	.05
	(.04)	(.06)	(.09)	(.03)	(.11)	(.25)	(.20)	(.07)	(.04)
Establishment size 2,500+	.10	.34	.09	.05	.46	0.25	.15	.18	.21
	(.04)	(.05)	(.06)	(.03)	(.10)	(.22)	(.31)	(.08)	(.05)
Works < 35 hours/week	-.26	-.53	-.70	-.35	-.42	-.55	-.47	-.34	-.27
	(.02)	(.08)	(.02)	(.02)	(.08)	(.11)	(.07)	(.03)	(.02)
Covered by union contract	.12	-.14	.19	.19	.30	.31	.37	.42	.16
	(.04)	(.13)	(.05)	(.03)	(.07)	(.11)	(.07)	(.04)	(.03)
Years of schooling	.00	.12	.29	.10	-.01	-.05	.03	-.02	.03
	(.03)	(.03)	(.03)	(.03)	(.06)	(.06)	(.05)	(.02)	(.03)
Years of potential labor market experience	-.02	-.01	.07	.00	-.05	.02	.05	.01	.08
	(.02)	(.02)	(.02)	(.01)	(.02)	(.03)	(.02)	(.01)	(.01)
Experience squared/100	.01	.00	-.12	.00	.09	-.13	-.10	-.01	-.14
	(.05)	(.04)	(.05)	(.02)	(.05)	(.08)	(.04)	(.03)	(.03)
Observations	2,058	1,482	1,692	3,259	425	165	246	659	1,933
Adjusted R^2	.26	.30	.53	.33	.38	.43	.56	.49	.50

Source: Winter 1993 employment cost index.

References

Becker, Gary S. 1964. *Human capital.* New York: Columbia University Press.
Brown, Charles, and James Medoff. 1989. The employer size–wage effect. *Journal of Political Economy* 97, no. 2:1027–59.
Caves, W., L. Christensen, and W. Diewert. 1982a. The economic theory of index numbers and the measurement of input, output, and productivity. *Econometrica* 50:1393–1414.
————. 1982b. Multilateral comparisons of output, input, and productivity using superlative index numbers. *Economic Journal* 92:73–86.
Diewert, W. 1976. Exact and superlative index numbers. *Journal of Econometrics* 4:115–45.
————. 1987. Index numbers. In *The new Palgrave dictionary of economics,* ed. J. Eatwell, M. Milgate, and P. Newman. New York: Stockton.
Fixler, D., and K. Zieschang. 1992a. Erratum. *Journal of Productivity Analysis* 2, no. 3:302.
————. 1992b. Incorporating ancillary product and process characteristics information into a superlative productivity index. *Journal of Productivity Analysis* 2, no. 2:245–67.
Freeman, Richard B., and James L. Medoff. 1984. *What do unions do?* New York: Basic.
Geary, R. G. 1958. A note on comparisons of exchange rates and purchasing power between countries. *Journal of the Royal Statistical Society* A121:97–99.
Khamis, S. H. 1970. Properties and conditions for the existence of a new type of index number. *Sankya* B32:81–98.
Kokoski, M., P. Cardiff, and B. Moulton. 1994. Interarea price indices for consumer goods and services: An hedonic approach using CPI data. Working Paper no. 256. Washington, D.C.: Bureau of Labor Statistics.
Lettau, Michael K. 1997. Compensation in part-time jobs versus full-time jobs: What if the job is the same? *Economics Letters* 56, no. 1:101–6.
Lewis, H. Gregg. 1986. *Union relative wage effects: A survey.* Chicago: University of Chicago Press.
Mincer, Jacob. 1962. On-the-job training: Cost, returns, and some implications. *Journal of Political Economy* 70, no. 5, pt. 2:50–79.
————. 1974. *Schooling, experience, and earnings.* New York: National Bureau of Economic Research.
Moulton, Brent R. 1986. Random group effects and the precision of regression estimates. *Journal of Econometrics* 32, no. 3:385–97.
————. 1990. An illustration of a pitfall in estimating the effects of aggregate variables in micro units. *Review of Economics and Statistics* 72, no. 2:334–38.
Rees, Albert. 1989. *The economics of trade unions.* Chicago: University of Chicago Press.
Summers, R. 1973. International comparisons with incomplete data. *Review of Income and Wealth,* ser. 19, no. 1 (March): 1–16.
Triplett, J. E. 1983. An essay on labor cost. In *The measurement of labor cost* (Studies in Income and Wealth, vol. 48), ed. J. E. Triplett. Chicago: University of Chicago Press.
Zieschang, K. 1985. Output price measurement when output characteristics are endogenous. Working Paper no. 150. Washington, D.C.: Bureau of Labor Statistics. Revised, 1987.
————. 1988. The characteristics approach to the problem of new and disappearing goods in price indexes. Working Paper no. 183. Washington, D.C.: Bureau of Labor Statistics.

Comment   Joel Popkin

Summary of Paper

Broadly speaking, Pierce, Ruser, and Zieschang construct a spatial version of the employment cost index (ECI) for wages and for compensation with two differences in method from the time-series ECI. One is their use of transitive (or multilateral) Törnqvist place-to-place index number techniques. The ECI, by contrast, is neither superlative nor transitive. The Törnqvist method used by Pierce, Ruser, and Zieschang is derived from previous work by Caves, Christensen, and Diewert and by Kokoski, Moulton, and Zieschang. The second difference in method is that Pierce, Ruser, and Zieschang adjust the Törnqvist by using a hedonic regression incorporating both ECI and household survey data to control for labor composition effects. The ECI maintains looser controls in this regard by estimating separate indexes by industry, occupation, bargaining status of workers, etc. The two improvements have the effect of narrowing the spread in wages and compensation across the United States. For wages, just using the Törnqvist accounts for a major portion of the narrowing. For compensation, each of the two improvements narrows most measures of the spread by about equal amounts. For one measure, however, the regression accounts for more of the narrowing.

In their paper, Pierce, Ruser, and Zieschang present the two spatial indexes of the ECI that they have constructed, that is, the unadjusted and the regression-adjusted Törnqvist index. The unadjusted Törnqvist index that they present controls for nine major occupations and two major industry groupings (goods and services) in thirty-nine areas of the United States. In Pierce, Ruser, and Zieschang's parlance, that index is a composition-unadjusted index. The adjusted Törnqvist is adjusted for labor composition effects. For purposes of comparison, they also present a third index, which is a simple spatial index of wages and compensation relatives based on ECI sample weights for the same thirty-nine areas.

The method used for constructing the Törnqvist index adjusted for labor composition effects is based on micro data on jobs from the ECI and on the household survey from the Current Population Survey (CPS). ECI data are combined with CPS data to estimate hedonic regressions similar in specification to the country-product-dummy approach. The regression coefficients, that is, estimates of labor characteristic prices and local area effects, form the inputs to a multilateral Törnqvist index number construct. The unit of observation for the regression is a job. This is the unit priced in the establishment-based survey that underlies the ECI. The labor composition variables in the regression include ECI data on establishment size and the union and part-time status of the job priced.

Joel Popkin is president of Joel Popkin and Company, an economic consulting company, and was director of the former Washington office of the National Bureau of Economic Research.

Table 4C.1   A Comparison of the Three Interarea Indexes in the Pierce, Ruser, and Zieschang Paper

	Wages			Compensation		
	R	T	T^A	R	T	T^A
High values	136.7	128.6	124.2	134.0	130.3	125.2
Low values	74.2	78.1	80.9	72.8	76.4	79.6
Spread	62.5	50.5	43.3	61.2	53.9	45.6
Ratio to R	. . .	.81	.69	. . .	.88	.75
High/low	1.84	1.65	1.54	1.84	1.71	1.57
SD	19.49	15.61	12.58	20.44	17.18	13.28

The list of independent variables is enhanced by the use of CPS data to add the following additional variables to the regression: schooling, experience, part-time status, and union coverage status. Since the unit of observation in the CPS is the individual worker, the CPS variables in the hedonic regression represent group means computed over workers falling within specified area, occupation, and industry cells. These group means are mapped onto the corresponding observations on jobs from the ECI. It appears that 2,106 cell means from the CPS were mapped to 18,486 ECI job-price quotes. Thus, the mapping is not one to one; each CPS cell mean was, on average, matched to nine ECI job-price quotes.

Table 4C.1 shows the effect of using the unadjusted and adjusted Törnqvists. The table compares the three indexes in Pierce, Ruser, and Zieschang's paper. The column labeled R is the simple spatial relative, the column labeled T is the unadjusted Törnqvist, while the column labeled T^A is the adjusted Törnqvist. The high and low values presented in the table for each of the indexes are the highest and lowest values of the indexes. The highest values, however, do not always represent the same area. For example, the highest value for wages for R and T is for San Francisco, while the highest value for T^A is for New York.

From the estimates in Pierce, Ruser, and Zieschang's paper and supplemental data supplied by them, there are four ways of looking at how T and T^A improve spatial comparisons relative to R. One is by looking at the difference between the high and the low values of each index. That difference is labeled *spread* in the table. Another way is by looking at the ratio of the spread of T and of T^A, respectively, to the spread of R. It is labeled *ratio* in the table. A third way of looking at the improvement is from the ratio of the high to the low values of each of the indexes; it is labeled *high/low*. The final and most meaningful way of looking at the improvements is from the standard deviation of each of the indexes. That is labeled *SD* in the table.

From table 4C.1, it is apparent that all three of the indexes that the authors construct separately for wages and compensation show a wide dispersion across the United States. What the table demonstrates, however, is that the dispersion is narrowed by the use of T^A in comparison to T and R. One conclusion that can be drawn from the smaller dispersion of T^A relative to T and R is that labor composition has a sizable influence on estimates of wage costs and compensation cost relatives across areas in the United States.

For wages, a comparison of R to T shows that just moving from the simple spatial ECI to the unadjusted Törnqvist reduces the spread of high and low values by twelve index points (from 62.5 to 50.5). The adjustment to the Törnqvist narrows the spread by an additional 7.2 index points (from 50.5 to 43.3). Overall, when moving from the simple spatial ECI to the adjusted Törnqvist, the spread in wage costs is reduced by somewhat less than one-third ($1 - 0.69 = 0.31$ [from the line labeled *ratio*]). Another way of looking at the narrowing of the spread is to observe the relative costs of the highest wage area to the lowest one (the *high/low* line in the table). Before any adjustment for composition effects, the highest-cost area is 84 percent more expensive than the lowest-cost area. After application of the Törnqvist and the adjustment to it, the highest-cost area is only 54 percent more expensive in terms of wages, with most of the narrowing accounted for by moving to the Törnqvist alone. A comparable effect is observed for the standard deviation. Moving from the simple spatial ECI to the Törnqvist reduces the standard deviation by about 20 percent, while moving to the adjusted Törnqvist reduces it by an additional 15 percentage points.

To sum up the effects of the adjustments made by Pierce, Ruser, and Zieschang in measuring wages spatially, the use of T in place of R narrows considerably the dispersion of wages in the United States; the use of T^A in place of T narrows the dispersion further but by somewhat less.

For compensation, a similar narrowing is observed in the dispersion. Specifically, the measure labeled *spread* in the table shows that moving from the spatial ECI to the Törnqvist narrows the spread by 7.3 index points (from 61.2 to 53.9), and that is comparable to the narrowing of 8.3 points (from 53.9 to 45.6) when moving to the adjusted Törnqvist. The measures labeled *ratio* and *high/low* also show about equal narrowings between R and T and between T and T^A. For the standard deviation, the result is somewhat different. The standard deviation shows a greater narrowing between T and T^A than between R and T (19 vs. 16 percent). For compensation, then, the improvements made by the authors to the spatial indexes are by some measures split about evenly between just using the Törnqvist and using the adjusted Törnqvist. When, however, the standard deviation is used to assess the improvements made by the authors, the adjusted Törnqvist shows a larger improvement over the unadjusted Törnqvist than the latter does over the simple spatial measure.

The differences observed between wages and compensation in the extent to which the unadjusted Törnqvist and the adjusted Törnqvist account for the narrowing of the spatial indexes seem to suggest the following: that labor composition effects account for more of the difference in benefits than they do of differences in wages.

A more micro analysis of the labor composition effects shows that the key variables that Pierce, Ruser, and Zieschang used to explain wage cost differences across areas are establishment size, union coverage, schooling, and experience. However, a particular labor composition effect found to be important in one area is not found to be important in other areas. For example, establishment size and union status effects are key factors explaining the results for Detroit but not for New York, where full- versus part-time status appears more important.

For wages, an interesting result in the paper is that, the higher the level of R in an area, the higher is T^A *in percentage terms* for that area. For example, New York's R is 132.7, while the ratio of T^A/R in New York is 1.068 (a 6.8 percent adjustment). By contrast, in East South Central, R is 74.2, while its ratio of T^A/R is 0.917 (a -8.3 percent adjustment). This result points to an interesting asymmetry in the data: above-average wage costs are symptomatic of superior labor quality, while below-average wage costs are symptomatic of factors not related to labor quality. This asymmetry is worth further investigation. Is it, for example, an artifact of the methodology? Would this finding be affected if the regression methodology allowed labor characteristic prices to vary across areas? Is the finding consistent with what is known about local area labor market demand and supply conditions?

Comment 1: Work versus Worker

The paper needs to be mindful of the distinction between work (or the job) and the worker in the job. Is it the intent of the paper to estimate how compensation varies across areas in the United States for work having similar characteristics? Or does the paper intend to measure relative compensation across areas for workers having similar characteristics? In the former case, the hedonic regression should include only characteristics that are job descriptive, whereas, in the latter case, the regression should be limited to characteristics that are worker descriptive.

If the intent is to explain *all* interarea wage dispersion and then decompose it into job characteristic and work characteristic effects, it becomes even more important to be mindful of the distinction between the two. One distinction between the two is that worker characteristics are portable; that is, they move with the worker. Some variables appear to be both worker and job descriptive, but it is important to note that their interpretation changes depending on their use. For example, union coverage should be used as a job descriptive variable only if one believes that workers sort themselves randomly into union and nonunion jobs. But, if there are systematic differences in skills required for union and nonunion jobs, then union coverage should be used as a worker characteristic.

The existing literature should be referenced more fully to sort through these choices. For example, the seminal work by Brown and Medoff (1989) considered both worker- and job-descriptive aspects of employer size and their effect on wages. Brown and Medoff found support for the view that the employer size–wage effect is a consequence of differences in worker quality but little support for the view that the wage effect is a consequence of differences in job-related characteristics across employers of different size.

There is also a growing literature within labor economics that attempts to sort through the relative effects of job and worker characteristics on wages. Unfortunately, the variables typically used as job descriptive[1] in this literature are not currently available in either the ECI or the CPS. However, this literature can be fruitfully consulted if Pierce, Ruser, and Zieschang wish to decompose interarea wage dispersion into work and worker components. Their present method of distinguishing between ECI and CPS covariates is inadequate in this regard.

Comment 2: The ECI versus the CPS

The authors have given primacy to the ECI data, retaining the job as a unit of observation and molding the CPS data to fit this requirement. The reasons for this appear to be a desire to produce a spatial analog to the current ECI and the availability of data on benefits in the ECI. However, this approach is not as inexpensive as it is presented to be.

The authors extract three explanatory variables from the ECI—establishment size, union coverage, and part-time status. As discussed above, none of these variables is uniquely interpretable as job descriptive. In fact, there is considerable evidence pointing to their status as worker-descriptive variables. If data are available only on characteristics of workers, the appropriate choice of a unit of observation is a worker, not a job. And the proper data to use are household survey data, not establishment data.

The ECI variables used by Pierce, Ruser, and Zieschang are all recorded in the CPS on an annual basis. The ECI data could be used as a supplemental source of information. Data on nonwage compensation could be aggregated within cells defined by detailed occupation, establishment size, union status, region, etc. and merged with the CPS. Also, the merger of the two data sets in this manner is likely to be less costly from the point of view of the regression analysis than the gross aggregation of the CPS data presently adopted by the authors.

The main problem with the CPS data would be that establishment size is available only on an annual basis. Thus, quarterly indexes could not be computed. There may also be a loss in timeliness. Nonetheless, the advantages of the CPS data are sufficient to argue that, at least at this stage of the development of the index, the authors should also estimate a CPS-based interarea wage-cost index.

---

1. These are mostly *Dictionary of Occupational Titles*–type variables attempting to measure job objectives and complexity.

Comment 3: The Ultimate Uses of the Index

The paper alludes to two possible uses of the index. First, it suggests that the index could be used to inform employers' plant location decisions. From that point of view, the index would probably be more useful if disaggregated by industry and employer size rather than by industry and occupation. Second, the paper suggests that the index could be used to compare wage levels to implement the Federal Employee Pay Comparability Act (FEPCA). From this point of view, the index would be better served by relying more on CPS data and using more worker-descriptive variables. A worker-descriptive variable that immediately comes to mind in the context of FEPCA is gender.

Whether gender should be used as a variable in a hedonic wage regression has been previously debated in the literature. It is sufficient to note here that some of the most significant contributions to the field of measuring labor composition/quality have opted to use gender as an explanatory variable. These include the seminal work by Gollop and Jorgenson (1983) and U.S. Department of Labor (1993), the BLS's own index of labor composition (produced by its Office of Productivity and Technology). Note that the use of a gender variable would probably rule out the use of a job as the unit of observation.

Comment 4: Regression Results

The merger of the ECI and CPS data produces a variety of oddities in the regression results. One oddity is that the CPS variables are cell means; hence, the coefficients attached to them cannot be interpreted as characteristics prices (on the margin). Do these coefficients belong in the hedonic index? Another oddity is that, among the eighteen regressions estimated, about one-third have the wrong sign on the schooling variable. Yet another oddity can be seen in the coefficient of the experience variable. It appears to be significant in only seven regressions and has the wrong sign in two of these cases. A final oddity is in two of the ECI covariates. Specifically, wages appear to decline with establishment size in some regressions. These anomalies and the interpretation of CPS-variable coefficients as characteristic prices are issues that need to be analyzed in greater detail by the authors.

References

Brown, Charles, and James Medoff. 1989. The employer size–wage effect. *Journal of Political Economy* 97, no. 2:1027–59.
Gollop, F., and D. Jorgenson. 1983. Sectoral measures of labor cost for the United States, 1948–78. In *The measurement of labor cost* (Studies in Income and Wealth, vol. 48), ed. J. E. Triplett. Chicago: University of Chicago Press.
U.S. Department of Labor. Bureau of Labor Statistics. 1993. *Labor composition and U.S. productivity growth*. Bulletin 2429. Washington, D.C.: U.S. Government Printing Office.

5   Cities in Brazil: An Interarea Price Comparison

Bettina H. Aten

The geographic diversity and physical size of countries such as Brazil have generated much interest in regional and interarea comparisons. However, regional comparisons of state product, gross incomes, and salaries, for example, often do not take into account differences in the cost of living, which are likely to be substantial in large countries. Aside from differential costs incurred in transporting goods to physically remote areas, the relative prices of goods will tend to vary from region to region, as they do from country to country. This is even more likely in countries with historically different regional patterns of development, such as the United States, India, China, and Brazil. A recent study of regional incomes in the United Kingdom suggests that this is also true for a relatively small country. In terms of levels, nominal incomes in Southeast England were 25 percent above the national average in 1988 but, when put in real terms, were only 2 percent above the average. Further, the changes over time were not consistent: between 1988 and 1993, the Southeast declined in nominal terms from 25 to 17 percent above the national average and rose from 2 to 6 percent above the average in real terms (Kern 1995).

Unfortunately, Brazilian price statistics have been politicized because of inflation rates that have reached 30 percent a month in recent years.[1] As a consequence, regional price statistics are not widely available, and there have been few studies of interarea prices in Brazil. How different are relative prices

Bettina H. Aten is assistant professor of earth sciences and geography at Bridgewater State College and an associate of the Center for Interarea and International Comparisons at the University of Pennsylvania.

The author thanks Nanno Mulder for providing the detailed price and expenditure data, Mary Kokoski and Prasada Rao for discussions on applying multilateral methods to interarea indexes, and Robert Lipsey and conference participants for their comments and suggestions.

1. In 1989, the annual inflation rate reached 1,783 percent a year, topped only by Argentina's rate of 3,079 percent for the same period.

among Brazil's cities and regions, and how much effect do the differences have on comparisons of regional income levels? This paper examines three issues related to price differences of food products within Brazil: (1) whether there are substantial differences in price levels between the more prosperous South and Southeastern regions and the poorer areas in the North and Northeast;[2] (2) whether differentials are more pronounced during periods of very rapid price increase; and (3) which methods for estimating regional parities are more robust given the character of price collection in a large country like Brazil. In order to illustrate the price differences, I compare the changes in nominal and in real income levels between cities during the period and test the sensitivity of the food price–level estimates to consumer budget levels and to the inclusion of nonservice headings as well as to the choice of estimating method.

5.1 Background to Price Collection Practices in Brazil: Consumer Price Indexes and Inflation Rates, 1984–87

Until 1985, Brazil's inflation rate was estimated by the Fundação Getulio Vargas using a weighted average of wholesale price indexes, consumer prices in Rio de Janeiro, and a national construction cost index. In November 1985, the official index was changed to the Broad National Consumer Price Index (IPCA), estimated by the IBGE (Instituto Brasileiro de Geografia e Estatística). The main difference lay in the scope of price collection and in the weighting system, which had previously been based on urban populations rather than household expenditures.[3] Also, the expenditures surveys sampled households earning between one and thirty times the minimum salary. However, in November 1986, the government once more decreed a change in the indexing system: the new official inflation measure (INPC) would use the consumer price index as before, but the weights would be restricted to expenditure surveys of households earning only one to five times the minimum salary.

Despite the multiplicity of methodologies, the IBGE publishes time series for the various indexes at the national level from 1979 to February 1986 and from March 1986 to 1988. A break in the series occurs on 28 February 1986, when the Cruzado Plan took effect and a new vector of prices was created.[4] The levels relative to base periods for the end-of-the-year broad consumer price indexes (IPCA) are shown in table 5.1. December 1979 is the base period

---

2. The per capita GDP in the Northeast was 44.5 percent of Brazil's per capita GDP in nominal terms, rising to about 53 percent in 1985. Total product was 13 percent of Brazil's total nominal GDP in 1970 and 15 percent in 1985 (SUDENE 1987).

3. Population estimates up to May 1983 are based on 1975 data, where later estimates use the 1980 census results. Also, with the exception of São Paulo, which uses more current results from a 1981–82 survey, expenditure weights for this period are based on a 1975 survey.

4. Instead of 15 February–15 March variation, the first indexes computed subsequent to the plan refer to a fifteen-day period from 1 March to 15 March.

Table 5.1   Consumer Price Index (December 1979 = 100, March 1986 = 100)

1983	2,017	1986	133
1984	6,324	1987	617
1985	20,795		

Source: IBGE (1990a).

Table 5.2   Annual Inflation Rates: IPCA (%)

1984	213	1986	33
1985	229	1987	363

Table 5.3   Metropolitan Areas and 1987 Economically Active Population

North		South	
Belem	446,000	Brasilia	767,000
Fortaleza	806,000	Curitiba	873,500
Salvador	854,000	Porto Alegre	1,249,000
Recife	1,005,000	Belo Horizonte	1,391,000
		Rio de Janeiro	4,553,000
		São Paulo	7,082,000

Source: IBGE (1988b).

until 1986, and March 1986 is the base for 1986 and 1987. The annual inflation rates are shown in table 5.2.[5]

The IPCA is the benchmark for estimating the differences in rates among ten metropolitan areas since this survey is more inclusive of consumers at all income levels. These areas are Belem, Fortaleza, Recife, and Salvador in the North and Northeast, Rio de Janeiro, São Paulo, Belo Horizonte, Curitiba, and Porto Alegre in the Southeast and South, and Brasilia in the geographic center of Brazil. Table 5.3 shows the regional classification of these areas and their approximate 1987 economically active populations.

The North and Northeast are geographically distant from the main industrial centers of the Southeast. Belem is located at the mouth of the Amazon River, approximately sixteen hundred miles north of São Paulo. The distance between the northernmost city, Belem, and the southernmost, Porto Alegre, is about two thousand miles, while the most easterly city, Recife, is about one thousand miles from Belem. Brasilia is in the Central West region, but, when a North-South dichotomy is used, it is considered part of the South. In this paper, the same convention is followed, although, if the effect of its regional classification

5. These rates are slightly lower than the official rates since the official index uses the restricted consumer price index (INPC) for households earning between one and five times the minimum salary.

is large enough to change the results of an analysis significantly, both results are discussed.

5.2 Interarea Price Levels

5.2.1 Estimating Method

The IPCA measures consumer price changes relative to a base period, without accounting for differences in relative prices across areas. In this section, I look at whether these differences are substantial and whether one can observe any regional pattern with respect to the inflation rates and the changes in income levels. The published price sample (IBGE 1986, 1988a) used in this paper is neither comprehensive nor representative of all consumption goods, but its primary goal is to provide a rough estimate of the magnitude of differences in the relative price levels in each metropolitan area.

A second important caveat with respect to the results, other than sample size, is the existence of control mechanisms. During the years 1984–87, not only was there a major currency reform, but two smaller shocks followed within the next twenty-four months: the Cruzado Plan II and the Bresser Plan. The period was one of severe instability,[6] and, although consumption rose and inflation rates were low for a brief period in 1986, by the end of the year inflation had begun soaring to pre–Cruzado Plan levels, and minimum wage increases were well below inflation (dos Santos 1990).

5.2.2 Data and Method

The original sample consists of thirty-five item prices within detailed headings for food products, household utility rates, and transport goods and services. The appendix lists the mean expenditure weights for each of them. Item prices are themselves derived from approximately 460 subitems and products,[7] but expenditure weights by area are available only for items, so area price levels are calculated only at this or at higher aggregation levels. The expenditure weights for the priced items correspond to approximately 20 percent of average household expenditures. These proportions are normalized so that ex-

6. In his five years in office (1985–89), President Sarney appointed four different finance ministers, who issued five different economic programs. In addition, businesses used various strategies to protect themselves from price controls, including withholding products, reducing the contents of packages, and charging black market prices (Payne 1995, 22).

7. At the lowest level, the IBGE calculates product prices (e.g., butter brand A, two hundred grams in Recife) as the arithmetic average of all the butters of that brand and size surveyed in Recife. At the item level (butter), brand and packaging differences are averaged out using, again, a simple arithmetic mean of all the products. It is only at the heading level that weights are introduced. For example, some seasonal headings, such as vegetables, use current-period weights and item prices, while others, such as butter, milk, and eggs, use previous-period weights. One of the indexes, the cost of living index for São Paulo (Indice de Preços ao Consumidor/Fundação Instituto de Pesquisas Economicas), uses a weighted geometric average at the heading level (IBGE 1990b, 173).

penditures in all cities total 100 percent. The weights reflect households earning one to forty times the minimum wage. In a later section, the price levels
are reestimated using a set of expenditures that reflect only lower-income-
household consumption patterns.

The prices are retail prices and, in many cases, linked to previously subsidized agricultural products such as wheat, whose internal demand has historically exceeded local supply. However, subsidies are generally implemented at
a national level, and the variation in metropolitan retail prices will reflect how
local prices adjust to federal policies. The effects of such policies on some of
the major staples, such as rice and wheat, are discussed in more detail below.

Beginning in 1980, the government began reducing the wheat subsidies as
part of an IMF agreement,[8] and, consequently, the prices of wheat-based products such as flour, bread, and pastas increased. Rice, on the other hand, remained subsidized, and the government paid higher-than-market prices in
1985, resulting in a large surplus and below-market prices at the retail level.
This, in turn, led to scarcity by the end of the year, fostering another round of
government purchases of rice, this time imported from Thailand (IBGE 1986).
Other staples such as beans and coffee were also heavily controlled by government mechanisms. For example, a ceiling for retail profit margins was instituted in 1985 for a number of products, including meats and meat products, and
imports were authorized for corn and soybean oil when prices began escalating
owing to expected shortages (IBGE 1986). In addition, droughts in many
Southern agricultural regions, such as São Paulo, Paraná, and Mato Grosso do
Sul, led to losses in the coffee, bean, sugarcane, and orange harvests and further fueled increasing inflation rates (IBGE 1986). The government reacted by
importing many of these goods in large quantities. But, because it was impossible to measure the actual extent of harvest loss or predict the resulting increase in demand, there were even larger distortions in market prices. For example, in 1987, the increase in the price of many of the agricultural products
was due to an increase in distribution costs rather than scarcity (IBGE 1987).

Some service headings, such as urban bus fares and taxi fares, were also
under regulatory price controls at various periods, most notably in 1986. This
was also true of other years, such as the 1984 removal of a tax on automobiles
purchased for public transport services, which in turn led to an oversupply and
to a fall in taxi fares. In 1987, a fixed tariff on all cars was removed in an effort
to boost demand in what had become an overheated economy following the
Cruzado Plan, but this did not increase demand, and most of the automobile
manufacturers suffered losses during the period (IBGE 1987). Other service
headings in the sample (e.g., electricity, water, and sewer taxes) were also subject to some form of regulation but generally at the state or municipal level, so

8. Demand for wheat was approximately 7 million tons per year. The government bought national production and imported the remainder. The suppliers were paid an average of the internal
market prices and those in effect for the imports. The wheat was then sold to the grain mills at a
fifth of this price (IBGE 1988a, 35).

area differences were likely to remain. For the purposes of this study, the price levels are estimated first without the service headings; that is, only food products enter the sample. In the latter part of the study, the differences arising out of the price levels owing to the inclusion of the service headings are discussed in more detail.

As a first estimate of the general price level in each metropolitan area, I use a model based on the work of Summers (1973) and Kravis et al. (1975) for international comparisons: the country-product-dummy method, or CPD. The CPD consists of weighted least squares parameter estimates that calculate the countries' departure from the mean product prices; in this study, regions and areas are substituted for countries. Alternative estimators to the CPD are discussed in a later section.

The prices, in natural logarithms, for each item and each of the ten metropolitan areas are regressed on a set of dummy variables corresponding to the item headings and to one region:

$$(1) \qquad \ln P_{ij} = \sum_{i=1}^{m} \beta_i X_i + \gamma_{\text{South}} Y_j + \varepsilon_{ij},$$

where i (items) = 1, 2, . . . , 31 and j (areas) = 1, 2, . . . , 10. P_{ij} are the prices of each item at each location, and X_i are dummy variables such that $X_i = 1$ for observations on prices of items i and $X_i = 0$ for observations on prices of items other than i. The regional dummy Y_j is equal to one for observations on cities in the South ($j \in$ South) and zero for observations on cities in the base region, the North. For any one observation P_{ij}, only one X_i, and only one Y_j, is different from zero.

The observations are weighted by the expenditures on that item for a typical consumer in the area. These expenditure weights are derived from area weights published at the detailed level for approximately four hundred item headings (IBGE 1994).[9] The β's capture the expected average log price of the items for the base region, while γ reflects the regional effect. Thus, a negative coefficient on Y indicates that, on average, prices in the South are lower than those in the North. The antilog of the estimated coefficients gives us the expected item prices in cruzeiros (prior to 1986) and in cruzados (after 1986). For example, in 1986, the dummy coefficients for rice are $\beta_1 = 2.017$ and $\gamma = -0.087$, so the expected price of rice in the North is Cz$7.52, and prices in cities in the South are on average lower, by a factor of 0.92, or 8 percent.

Table 5.4 shows the ordinary least squares parameter estimate for the regional dummy variable for each year, with the corresponding t-value. The number of observations, n, is 230 (10 cities times 26 items minus missing values, which vary in number across cities).

The regional effect was negative in all years, indicating lower price levels in

---

9. The item's share of expenditures for each area is standardized so that the sample share totals 100.

Table 5.4   Parameter Estimates Equation (1), 1984–87

	1984	1985	1986	1987
γ_{South}	−.009	−.043	−.087**	−.043*
t-values	−.52	−1.91	−4.18	−2.32

*Significant at the 5 percent level.
**Significant at the 1 percent level.

the South. Also, the largest estimated difference between regions is in 1986, with price levels in the North exceeding those in the South by 8 percent on average. These results are somewhat surprising in that price levels in international studies tend to rise with increasing incomes, whereas, here, the higher price levels are associated with the poorer Northern region and the largest difference in price levels is 1986, the year of the price freeze. One factor that may contribute to the estimates of high price levels in poorer areas such as Belem and Salvador is that there are no service items included in the sample. Heston and Summers (1992) have shown that the price level of services at the country level tends to increase with higher real incomes. If this is true within Brazil, the inclusion of service headings should lower these differentials, and this is examined in the final section of the paper.

Another possibility is that the methodology of price collection and reporting may be such that the results reflect institutional bias or differences in data quality among the regional reporting agencies. But, if that is the case, one might expect the results to be conservative, that is, to show smaller differences in price levels between rich and poor regions and smaller variations immediately following the Cruzado Plan. On the other hand, given that wage adjustments are based on changes in the price indexes, it is hard to second-guess the possible direction of any bias. One obvious step toward a better sense of the overall interarea consumption price levels would be to obtain more detailed price data since the more detailed expenditure surveys are already available.

What is the pattern at the level of individual cities? Metropolitan area dummies are substituted for the regional dummy variable. The omitted area, São Paulo, is the base, and the coefficients indicate the approximate percentage difference in prices for each city from prices in São Paulo. These coefficients reflect the average difference in prices regardless of item. The estimating equation is rewritten as

$$(2) \qquad \ln P_{ij} = \sum_{i=1}^{m} \beta_i X_i + \sum_{j=1}^{n} \gamma_j Y_j + \varepsilon_{ij},$$

where j refers to areas or locations, as in equation (1), but $Y_i = 0$ for j equal to São Paulo and $Y_i = 1$ for all other areas. São Paulo was chosen as the base because it is the largest and most industrialized city in Brazil, located in the South. Recalling that the regional dummy coefficient previously estimated was negative for the Southern region, one would expect positive coefficients for the

Table 5.5   Parameter Estimates, Equation (2), 1987

	γ_j (t-values)	Price Level		γ_j (t-values)	Price Level
Brasilia (S)	.086* (2.30)	109	Rio de Janeiro (S)	.014 (.38)	101
Salvador (N)	.076* (2.00)	108	São Paulo (S)	0	100
Fortaleza (N)	.077* (2.07)	108	Belem (N)	.0002 (.00)	100
Recife (N)	.071 (1.87)	107	Belo Horizonte (S)	−.010 (−.26)	99
Porto Alegre (S)	.034 (.91)	103	Curitiba (S)	−.047 (−1.26)	95
			Range (high-low) (%)	14	

Note: S = South. N = North.
*Significant at the 5 percent level.
**Significant at the 1 percent level.

Northern cities in equation (2)—that is, unless São Paulo has relatively high prices compared to the average prices in the other Southern regions.

Table 5.5 shows the estimated γ_j parameters and their t-statistics as well as the corresponding antilogs (multiplied by 100) for 1987, the latest year available. Note that the β_i's are not given since they are simply the expected item prices in the base city. The cities are listed in decreasing-price-level order.

Brasilia's level is high, as expected, and three of the four cities in the North also have high levels. Conversely, the cities with the two lowest price levels are in the South: Belo Horizonte and Curitiba have an average level of 95, or 5 percent below that of São Paulo. The range of levels is 14 percent. Although the t-values are low for many of the cities, the estimated parameters are consistent with the regional results: high in the North, lower in the South.

The estimates for other years are shown in table 5.6, converted so that Brazil is the base with a price level of 100. The cities are listed by decreasing 1987 price levels.

Some of the causes of the fluctuating price levels were alluded to earlier, varying from federal control of the retail profit margins for meat products to IMF-related wheat subsidies. Broadly speaking, the only patterns that are constant for the four years are lower-than-average price levels for Belo Horizonte and Curitiba in the South and higher-than-average levels for Salvador and Recife in the North. This is consistent with the negative coefficients for the Southern regional dummy shown in table 5.4 above. Belem, also in the North, has the highest levels during 1985 and 1986, while Brasilia is highest in 1984 and 1987. The geographic isolation of both Brasilia and Belem may partially account for their higher food price levels. The largest increases over the period are also in the Northern cities: Fortaleza with 6 percent, followed by Salvador and Recife, each with 3 percent, and then Brasilia with 2 percent. These results suggest that the poorer areas are relatively more expensive, at least for basic

Table 5.6   **Area Food Price Levels (Brazil = 100)**

	Plan Year				
	1984	1985	1986	1987	1984–87
Brasilia (S)	104	99	101	106	+2
Fortaleza (N)	99	97	100	105	+6
Salvador (N)	101	103	109	104	+3
Recife (N)	101	102	101	104	+3
Porto Alegre (S)	101	95	93	100	−1
Rio de Janeiro (S)	102	99	96	98	−4
Belem (N)	101	109	111	97	−4
São Paulo (S)	98	100	103	97	−1
Belo Horizonte (S)	96	97	95	96	0
Curitiba (S)	96	99	91	92	−4
Brazil	100	100	100	100	
Range (%)	8	14	20	14	

Note: N = North. S = South.

Table 5.7   **1987 Nominal and Real Incomes**

	Nominal Income (Cz$)	Real Income (Cz$)	Real Rank
São Paulo (S)	14,509	14,968	1
Brasilia (S)	13,633	12,907	2
Curitiba (S)	11,881	12,849	3
Porto Alegre (S)	10,990	10,948	4
Rio de Janeiro (S)	10,227	10,402	5
Salvador (N)	10,880	10,401	6
Belo Horizonte (S)	9,878	10,290	7
Belem (N)	8,971	9,253	8
Recife (N)	7,996	7,682	9
Fortaleza (N)	7,170	6,846	10
Range	7,339	8,122	

Note: N = North. S = South.

food products, and that the Cruzado Plan did little to alleviate the differences in price levels between regions: for three of four cities (Fortaleza, Salvador, and Recife) it appears to have exacerbated the differential.

5.2.3   Interarea Income Differences

Do the higher food price levels imply that income differentials between regions are even greater than one would expect from examining the nominal income levels? That is, do the price levels lead to a greater range in real incomes than the range in nominal terms? Table 5.7 shows the 1987 mean monthly incomes in nominal and in real terms (adjusted by the food price levels).

The real income range increases by 10.7 percent, from Cz\$7,339 to Cz\$8,122, but, with the exception of Salvador and Rio de Janeiro, the relative rankings of the cities do not change. The differences are slightly more dramatic in 1985 and 1986: Belem's high price level in 1985 (109) results in a drop from a rank of sixth in nominal terms to a rank of eighth in real income terms. A similar drop occurs for Salvador in 1986, when its price level is also nearly 10 percent higher than the national average. Note that three of the four highest price levels were in the North and that the richest five cities are in the South.

5.3 Alternative Price-Level Calculations

5.3.1 Multilateral Methods

The CPD method essentially estimates the weighted mean difference between each area's weighted prices and those of a base area. Three alternative index number methods, the Geary method, the EKS method, and the Fisher averages,[10] are discussed below. The Geary method is the one used by the International Comparison Program at levels above the basic item heading, that is, for all aggregation levels, including total GDP. It consists of the solution for a set of $m + n$ equations as follows:

$$
\pi_i = \frac{\sum\limits_{j=1}^{n} \dfrac{p_{ij}}{\mathrm{PPP}_j} q_{ij}}{\sum\limits_{j=1}^{n} q_{ij}}, \quad
\mathrm{PPP}_j = \frac{\sum\limits_{i=1}^{m} p_{ij} q_{ij}}{\sum\limits_{i=1}^{m} \pi_i q_{ij}},
$$

where m is the number of items and n the number of cities. The quantities q for each city are the value shares of expenditure—that is, the expenditure shares $(pq)_{ij}$ divided by the corresponding prices, p_{ij}. The resulting π_i's correspond to the price parameters β_i in the CPD method and the PPP_j's to the area dummy variables γ_j.

The second set of indexes are the Fisher indexes, constructed for each pair of cities as follows:

$$
F_{jk} = \sqrt{\left(\frac{\sum\limits_{i=1}^{m} p_{ij} q_{ik}}{\sum\limits_{i=1}^{m} p_{ik} q_{ik}}\right) \times \left(\frac{\sum\limits_{i=1}^{m} p_{ij} q_{ij}}{\sum\limits_{i=1}^{m} p_{ik} q_{ij}}\right)},
$$

where the summation is over the m items for which there are both price and expenditure data in both cities, and j, k denote cities. This results in an $n \times n$ matrix of binary price ratios between all possible pairs of cities. The elements of this matrix are used in the EKS comparison:

---

10. For a discussion of the CPD and the EKS, see Kravis, Heston, and Summers (1982, 88–89).

Table 5.8   **1987 Price Levels—CPD, Geary, Fisher, and EKS**

	CPD	Geary	Fisher	EKS	Range (%)
Brasilia (S)	106	105	106	106	1
Fortaleza (N)	105	105	107	105	2
Salvador (N)	104	105	102	103	3
Recife (N)	104	104	101	103	4
Porto Alegre (S)	100	100	100	100	0
Rio de Janeiro (S)	98	99	98	98	1
Belem (N)	97	97	101	101	4
São Paulo (S)	97	97	97	97	0
Belo Horizonte (S)	96	96	96	95	1
Curitiba (S)	92	92	92	93	1
Brazil	100	100	100	100	
Range (%)	14	13	15	13	

Note: N = North. S = South.

$$\text{EKS}_{jk} = \left(\prod_{l=1}^{n} F_{jl} \times F_{lk} \right)^{1/n}.$$

The EKS comparison of city j relative to city k is the geometric average of all the possible binary indexes between j and k, with greater weight given to the direct j/k binary. Table 5.8 shows the 1987 indexes for all cities. They are normalized so that Brazil is one and are listed by decreasing CPD price-level estimates.

The estimates are fairly consistent for all cities, and the largest difference is 4 percent in Belem. In general, the larger differences are between the Fisher and the EKS methods and between the CPD and the Geary methods. This is because the Fisher and the EKS methods are based on binary price ratios, and, if there is a missing value in at least one city for one of the elements, the ratio is not computed. Thus, cities with more missing values are apt to have greater differences in their estimates.

5.3.2   Alternative Samples

The price levels discussed above were for food products in the sample. If services are included, will they affect the price levels in any systematic manner? For example, will they raise the levels in the higher-income cities and lower the price levels in the poorer regions? Data on prices and expenditures in the ten cities are available for four service headings, and they are added to the food item list. The headings are urban bus fares and taxi fares, water and sewage taxes, and electricity charges.

An additional three headings—bottled gas, gasoline, and cigarettes—were added to the food and service categories. Their prices were federally controlled and remained uniform across all cities. However, local expenditures on these items were not necessarily uniform, and, by including these weights in the estimated price levels, we can see if their effect varies across the cities' consumption levels.

A final set of price-level estimates was obtained by applying a different expenditure survey to the initial food prices samples. This budget survey is based on households earning only one to five times the minimum salary, in contrast to the previous estimates, which were based on households earning one to thirty times the minimum salary. One reason for looking at this survey is to see how sensitive price levels are to the expenditure weights and also to see whether differences in prices are reflected in the consumption levels of a specific income group. Since price levels appear to be high in the poorer areas, do we expect them to be even higher for poorer households in poor areas, or will price-level differences be more marked in the larger and more wealthy cities? The estimates are shown in table 5.9 for 1987.

The two wealthiest cities, São Paulo and Brasilia, show a marked increase in price levels with the inclusion of the service headings (col. 1) and with the uniformly priced headings (col. 2). The two poorest areas, Fortaleza and Recife, have a corresponding decrease in price levels from about 5 percent above average to 3 percent below the national average. The only change that is not in the expected direction is for Curitiba, a city that is relatively wealthy but whose price level drops when services are included. The range in levels rises from 14 percent for food to 26 percent with services and to 33 percent with the additional controlled prices, but, if the two outliers in the South—Brasilia and Curitiba—are removed, the range does not vary so dramatically. Curitiba has a world-renowned public bus transport system, one that is both cheap and efficient (World Resources Institute 1996, 120). Brasilia, on the other hand, was planned on a scale that is not conducive to pedestrians or to transport modes other than the private automobile. In addition, the large influx of rural migrants in the 1980s led to inadequate and costly provision of public utilities such as water, sewage facilities, and electric power. For the other cities, the results

Table 5.9   1987 Expanded Samples and Low-Income Budget

	Food Plus Services	Food Plus Uniform Prices	Low-Income Budget Weights	Food Price Levels
Brasilia (S)	120	115	106	106
Salvador (N)	100	100	105	105
Fortaleza (N)	96	97	104	105
Recife (N)	97	97	105	104
Porto Alegre (S)	102	102	100	100
Rio de Janeiro (S)	101	101	99	98
Belem (N)	98	99	96	97
São Paulo (S)	104	104	97	97
Belo Horizonte (S)	95	96	96	96
Curitiba (S)	87	89	93	92
Range (%)	33	26	13	14

Note: N = North. S = South.

suggest that disparities between the North and the South remain but that the higher service prices in the wealthier cities and the lower service prices in poorer cities lead to smaller overall price-level differences, a result that is consistent with international price-level studies.

With respect to the low-income budget survey, the largest differences in expenditures are in the following headings: rice, potatoes, *chã-de-dentro* (a choice cut of meat), dried meat, chicken, and pasteurized milk. The lower-income households showed an increase in rice, dried meat, and chicken consumption for most of the cities and an across-the-board decrease in the proportion spent on prime beef such as *chã-de-dentro* and on pasteurized milk. The maximum difference was almost 4 percent less on choice cuts, especially in the North, and increases between 2 and 3 percent in the consumption of chicken. The total proportion of the household budget spent on food averaged about 20 percent.

Although the differences in consumption levels between the two samples are not trivial, differentials between the two price levels are much smaller, not exceeding 1 percent. The direction of change is positive, that is, higher, for one of the poorer cities, Recife, but lower for another poor city, Fortaleza. In other words, in Recife, expenditures of low-income groups on staples such as chicken and rice outweighed those on products such as prime beef. But the reverse was true of another relatively poor area, Fortaleza. There is no apparent change in Brasilia or São Paulo and only a slight increase in levels for Curitiba.

5.4 Conclusion

The first part of this paper discussed the motivation for examining price levels in a country such as Brazil and some of the reasons why price-level changes might be particularly interesting to study during the period 1984–87. It also raised the issue of North-South differentials and whether regional income differences might be understated if price levels are not taken into account. However, since the data are predominantly for food prices and the sample is not very large, the price levels were estimated using alternative aggregation methods and an expanded set of headings and expenditure weights.

Brazil is a geographically large and diverse country, and its economic history has included a widening gap between Northern and Southern regions. The changeover from a military dictatorship to a civil regime in the early 1980s led to changes in federal policies and subsidies, many of them in the agricultural sector. Since prices were highly politicized, there have been few studies of the internal price structure of large cities within Brazil. The period was also one in which inflation rates rose and some drastic measures were instituted in an effort to contain prices. The first major one was the 1986 Cruzado Plan. The effects of the plan varied. For example, lower financing costs and interest rates and a decrease in risk with respect to agricultural loans positively affected many rural production areas. But the price freeze led to lower margins between the prices received by producers and those charged to consumers, resulting in conflicts between different sectors of the market. The price freeze also increased the demand for food products, and the inelasticity of the short-run supply caused tremendous pressure on the prices, culminating in the hyperinflation of the late 1980s (IBGE 1987).

One of the interesting findings of this paper was that poorer cities did tend to have higher food price levels, on average, than the cities in the wealthier Southern regions. Thus, real income differentials were greater and the North-South income gap wider when adjusted for relative food prices. This finding was true of all the years, but the differential was higher in the period of escalating inflation rates. In addition, the highest overall change between 1984 and 1987 occurred in the Northern cities of Fortaleza, Salvador, and Recife, all of which saw increases of at least 3 percent in the overall food price level. In contrast, most of the wealthy Southern cities experienced a decrease in their food prices.

Although the small sample size and missing values possibly affected the results, different aggregation methods did not produce substantively different results, with a generally higher range among the Northern cities. The price levels for food were then compared to a set of price levels from an expanded set of items and to price levels based on the consumption patterns of a low-income population group. The first set of expanded items included nonfood items and service headings, such as utilities and public transport, and it raised the price level significantly in the high-income areas, most notably in São Paulo and Brasilia. The second set added items that were uniformly priced (but consumed at different quantities), such as bottled gas and cigarettes. The effect of these uniform prices varied, increasing price levels in the poorer cities and lowering them marginally in the wealthier areas. Finally, a set of estimates based on a lower-income-household survey showed that, although expenditures varied by about 4 percent for some items, this did not translate into a visible pattern with respect to average incomes and the price levels. There was no a priori expectation, but a higher low-income food price level for poorer areas would indicate greater disparities in income levels within a city. However, there was both an increase in food price levels in some of the wealthier areas, Curitiba and Rio de Janeiro (suggesting that the poor are worse off than the average population), and a decrease in some of the poorer cities, such as Fortaleza.

International price-level studies have also found a correlation between service price levels and incomes, one that may lead to a convergence of overall price levels in the long run. In some cities in the United States, low-income consumers faced higher food costs than middle-income shoppers, 9 percent in New York City and up to 28 percent in Los Angeles (Alwitt and Donley 1996, 127), in part due to the existence of fewer large retail outlets in poorer neighborhoods. With respect to low-income expenditures, the results for Brazil are not sensitive to within-area differences in consumption patterns, but they do suggest that, in the very poor cities, the cost of purchasing basic food products may be even higher than expected. Another reason for these differences may be due to higher distribution and transportation costs in the Northeast and Northern regions. Given these preliminary findings, it would be interesting to examine price differentials further using a more comprehensive list of items as well as explicitly modeling some of the locational effects, for example, to see whether distance or transport costs directly affect the price-level estimates.

Appendix

Table 5A.1   Expenditure Weights

Item	Weight (average)
1 Cereals	6.52
2 Sugars	1.49
3 Vegetables	2.05
4 Fruits	1.45
5 Fish	2.23
6 Meats	7.62
7 Poultry	2.95
8 Milk products	2.22
9 Breads	1.68
10 Oils	.65
11 Beverages	1.92
12 Canned goods	.97
13 Meals	8.16
14 Rents	4.01
15 Household supplies	1.71
16 Gas & electricity	1.17
17 Furniture	1.81
18 Household furnishings	2.41
19 Household appliances	1.94
20 Electronic equipment	1.17
21 Clothing	9.12
22 Shoes & miscellaneous	3.35
23 Accessories	1.28
24 Public transport	3.39
25 Private transport	6.19
26 Fuel	2.13
27 Postage	.63
28 Pharmaceutical products	2.16
29 Medical: doctors & labs	1.65
30 Hospitals	1.47
31 Personal hygiene	1.85
32 Personal services	3.97
33 Recreation	3.95
34 Cigarettes	1.21
35 Educational materials	3.49
Total	100.00

References

Alwitt, Linda, and Thomas Donley. 1996. *The low-income consumer.* Newbury Park, Calif.: Sage.

dos Santos, W. G., V. Monteiro, and A. M. Caillaux. 1990. *Que Brasil é este?* Rio de Janeiro: Instituto Universitário de Pesquisas do Estado do Rio de Janeiro.

Heston, Alan, and Robert Summers. 1992. Measuring final product services for international comparisons. In *Output measurement in the service sectors* (Studies in Income and Wealth, vol. 56), ed. Z. Grilliches. Chicago: University of Chicago Press.

Instituto Brasileiro de Geografia e Estatística (IBGE). 1986. Analise de inflacão—medida pelo IPCA 1985. Rio de Janeiro: Equipe Tecnica da Divisao de Índices de Preços ao Consumidor/Departamento de Estatísticas e Índices de Preços, March. Mimeo.

———. 1988a. Analise da inflação—medida pelo INPC 1987. Rio de Janeiro: Equipe Tecnica do Sistema Nacional de Índices de Preços ao Consumidor/Departamento de Estatísticas e Índices de Preços, August. Mimeo.

———. 1988b. *Indicadores sociais para regiões metropolitanas, aglomerações urbanas e municipios com mais de 100,000 habitantes.* Rio de Janeiro.

———. 1990a. *Estatísticas historicas do Brasil, 2a.edição, series economicas, demograficas e sociais, 1550–1988.* Rio de Janeiro.

———. 1990b. *PNAD, sintese de indicadores basicos, 1981–89.* Vol. 14. Rio de Janeiro.

———. 1994. *Sistema nacional de preços ao consumidor, estrutura de ponderações.* Rio de Janeiro.

Kern, David. 1995. *Economic and financial outlook.* London: National Westminster Bank, Market Intelligence Department.

Kravis, I., A. Heston, and R. Summers. 1982. *World product and income—international comparisons of real gross product.* Baltimore: Johns Hopkins University Press.

Kravis, I., Z. Kenessey, A. Heston, and R. Summers. 1975. *A system of international comparisons of gross product and purchasing power.* Baltimore: Johns Hopkins University Press.

Payne, Leigh. 1995. Brazilian business and the democratic transition: New attitudes and influence. In *Business and democracy in Latin America,* ed. E. Bartell and L. Payne. Pittsburgh: University of Pittsburgh Press.

Summers, R. 1973. International comparisons with incomplete data. *Review of Income and Wealth,* ser. 19, no. 1 (March): 1–16.

Superintendencia de Desenvolvimento do Nordeste (SUDENE). 1987. *Boletim socioeconomico do nordeste* (Departamento de Planejamento Socio-Economico), vol. 1, nos. 1 and 2.

World Resources Institute. 1996. *World resources, 1996–97.* Oxford: Oxford University Press.

Comment   Jorge Salazar-Carrillo

It has been unfortunate that, over the years, very little attention has been given to price differences among different areas of the same country. This is even

Jorge Salazar-Carrillo is director of the Center of Economic Research and professor of economics at Florida International University.

more so if developing countries are considered. This is why price comparisons for various regional concepts in one of the major developing nations, namely, Brazil, are a welcome addition to the literature, particularly when a paper of the general quality of that commented on here comes along.

Notwithstanding the above, major limitations still affect this research subject. The first and foremost limitation is data availability and quality. No empirical study can rise above the quality of the basic statistics collected. When the information concerns developing countries and is of a weaker quality, it is incumbent on the researcher to explain fully the sources used. Aten does not do so adequately in her succinct contribution. The figures are manipulated to obtain many kinds of results based on small baskets of commodities, for subsets of goods and services and various index number formulas. This is a heavy burden to place on statistics that are not considered reliable by Brazilian regional economists and are gathered for time-series price index calculations, not interregional comparisons.

The first of the detailed results presented by the author is that the prices for food products are higher in the poorer regions of Brazil, the North and Northeast, than in the South. This goes against the grain of international and interregional research (see Food and Agriculture Organization 1988). This finding is predicated on the specification of more or less similar-quality goods across space. From the information provided, it is not possible to determine whether incomparability in specifications is the source of the incongruence, but this is likely since the objective of the price collection is to trail the trending of prices over time. Another explanation of this *contrario sensu* behavior of the interarea food comparisons in Brazil is the paucity of information provided for twenty-six items with practically no identification except quantities and weights. The small number of products comes with a practically unexplained weighting system (see the appendix). The weighting patterns are depicted sometimes as covering families earning from one to thirty (or forty) times the minimum wage, but it is unclear whether the same weights apply to those with incomes ranging between one and five times the minimum wage.

In addition, it is found that there are significant differences in the results over the four-year period considered. The intercept-dummy variables used to measure average price differences have a range that is a multiple of ten (see table 5.4). How can such discrepancies in regional differentials exist without exchange rate distortions during a three-year time span? If comparisons are made with strictly designed interspatial price indexes,[1] it is found that there is substantial stability in the results.

The parameter estimates on which the interregion and city price differences are based (the intercept dummies) are seldom significant at the 5 percent level (see table 5.5). Moreover, they show a remarkable variability over the four years. And why are we not given the four-year information for the estimates at

1. Consult comparisons reported for Florida in Simmons (1988).

the city level, rather than only the one year shown in table 5.5? This was done for the North-South differentials shown in table 5.4.

It would have been useful to carry out both analyses jointly by combining the city and the region differences into a measurement of both intercept and slope dummies. In this fashion, the interactions between urban and geographic areas could have been more clearly spelled out. It may have been possible to determine which cities contributed to the regional differentials the most and how the two variables interacted with one another. Perhaps there were not enough degrees of freedom for this type of flexible pooling, but, again, no information is given by the author on this matter. On this point, as on many others, no details are available about the different procedures presented in the chapter and about the estimates obtained[2] in it. This makes it practically impossible to validate or replicate the study.

One of the major results that the research emphasizes is that the price levels widen the income discrepancies across cities.[3] But how can a set of price-adjustment factors for food reflecting less than 20 percent of family expenditures be used to express interspatial income differences in real terms? Such interarea price deflators should be applied only to food expenses in the various cities and regions. Thus, the conclusion is flawed *ab initio,* and this would calm the fears of the reader that evidence has been found, contrary to what is usually reported in the literature, with respect to international and interregional comparisons.

Perhaps the most enlightening table of the nine presented is table 5.9. It uses weights from low-income families in contrast to previous results (i.e., families earning just up to five times the minimum salary rather than thirty or forty times). As expected, with the inclusion of services, the rich Southern cities become the more expensive ones. If the weights had encompassed the richer families, at least similar results would have been expected because they consume as many or more services than the lower classes in both quantities and expenditures, according to national surveys (see Salazar-Carrillo 1990). (It is unclear from table 5.9 and the accompanying text which weights are used; conflicting relative intercity price ranges are also reported.) But it is important that services consist of only four items, and those tend to be regulated because they constitute public services. With the major changes obtained with just a slight expansion of the basket, it could be expected that very different results would be forthcoming if other goods and services were to be included.

A result that the author should have stressed more is that, at least between the years 1984 and 1987 inclusive (however special these years were because of the Cruzado Plan and its descendants and the existing political instability in Brazil), there is no convergence of income and price levels among the cities

2. Most egregious, is the Brazil base in table 5.8 a simple or a weighted mean?
3. Presumably, this would also happen for the two regions distinguished since the cities are classified as belonging to either the North or the South. This assures that the two results must be consistent and thus cannot be used to validate one another, as is alleged.

Table 5C.1   **Items Originating in the South**

1. Rice	7. Lettuce	13. Chicken
2. Pastas	8. Refined sugar	14. French rolls
3. Corn meal	9. Pork (boneless)	15. Butter, margarine
4. Potatoes	10. Meat (*pa*)	16. Ground coffee
5. Tomatoes	11. Sardines	17. Gasoline
6. Onions	12. Salted meat	18. Cigarettes

examined. But, again, this may just be a reflection of the fact that the data at hand were designed, not to measure this phenomena, but rather to track intertemporal movements of prices. This is particularly evident if the source of the food items is considered: a great majority are Southern Brazilian products transported to the Northern cities (this is also true of about half the remaining services and nondurable goods). In table 5C.1, these products are identified. Therefore, what the differentials across cities in the North and South are probably measuring is transportation cost, very partially compensated for by the opposite effect with respect to services.

In a country like Brazil, one that does not have regional product and income accounts, little could have been expected to result from an interarea price comparisons exercise. As Aten admits, the data are predominantly for food prices, and the sample is not very large. However, this paper represents a good beginning, and it may prompt the national statistical institute (IBGE) to improve its collection efforts in this regard. However, the paper falls far short of what could have been expected in the description and explanation of the information utilized for the reader of this volume—and even more so if validation and replication are considered. Sophisticated estimation cannot rise above the weakness of the figures used.

References

Food and Agriculture Organization. Statistics Division. 1988. International comparison of agricultural output. In *World comparison of incomes, prices and product*, ed. J. Salazar-Carrillo and D. S. Prasada Rao. Amsterdam: North-Holland.

Salazar-Carrillo, J. 1990. Comparisons of purchasing power and real income in Latin America: A review of methods. In *Comparisons of prices and real products in Latin America*, ed. J. Salazar-Carrillo and D. S. Prasada Rao. Amsterdam: North-Holland.

Simmons, James C. 1988. The development of spatial price level comparison in the state of Florida. In *World comparison of incomes, prices and product*, ed. J. Salazar-Carrillo and D. S. Prasada Rao. Amsterdam: North-Holland.

III Informal Reports on Methods and the Geographic Expansion of the International Comparison Program

6   Purchasing Power Parities for Medical Care and Health Expenses: An Informal Report

Giuliano Amerini

This paper describes the methods and the classification that were used by Eurostat in March 1996 for calculating purchasing power parities (PPPs) in the framework of the Eurostat-OECP PPP Programme. It also presents the possible developments in methods and classification that could be foreseen at that time.

6.1   The Present PPP (Purchasing Power Parity) Classification for Goods and Services for Medical and Health Care

The present PPP classification for medical and health care goods and services used by Eurostat (see the appendix) has been developed following the same principles that govern the development of the PPP classification in the other sectors of the economy. This involves the definition of classes of products (PPP basic headings) (*a*) that are relatively homogeneous in terms of spatial price ratios so that the principle of representativity can be used (a sample of products is selected the price ratios of which represent the price ratios for all the products of that class) and (*b*) for which national accounts expenditure data can be supplied by all the participating countries. Because of the first principle (representativity), one could say that the PPP classification is a *homogeneous price ratio–oriented classification*. The development of such a classification is based on the fact that prices are economically linked to each other inside a certain economic area (e.g., a country), and this is the more true the more homogeneous the products are.

As a consequence, the variability of spatial price ratios is in general relatively small within a homogeneous class of products, enabling the use of the

Giuliano Amerini is a staff member of Eurostat (the Statistical Office of the European Communities).

The views expressed are those of the author and do not necessarily reflect those of Eurostat.

aforementioned principle of representativity. However, the state is heavily involved in the health care sector of the economy, at different levels and in different ways in different countries. Because of this intervention, "market prices" could be "disturbed" or may not exist at all for certain services (nonmarket services). This could endanger the basic principles on which the classification is built (the homogeneous price ratio–oriented classification).

Another problem is that, because of institutional differences between the countries and because of a lack of harmonization between countries concerning the national rules for recording this expenditure, expenditure for the same goods and services is classified under *household final consumption expenditure* in some countries, under *government final consumption expenditure* in other countries, and under both in yet other countries.[1] This is a major problem because the detailed levels of the two sectors of the classification (household and government expenditure), for which all the countries can supply data on values, are very different. In fact, there are *twenty* basic headings on the household consumption side and just *one* basic heading on the government consumption side used in the calculations. These basic headings are indicated by an asterisk in the appendix.

Since all these goods and services are actually consumed by individuals, in order to compare the total volume of *household actual individual final consumption,* government final consumption expenditure must be added to household final consumption expenditure. To sum household and government expenditure appropriately, one should have the same level of detail for the government part of the classification as for the household part (twenty basic headings). In this situation, after having summed the twenty values of household expenditure with the twenty corresponding values of government expenditure, one could use twenty specific parities (already available—see sec. 6.2) to deflate the twenty "sum values." But, as we saw above, a breakdown of government expenditure for medical and health care goods and services is not available for all countries. As a consequence, this operation can be carried out only *at the global level* (i.e., group 133 in the appendix is added to group 115).

This means that the government expenditure values (group 133) are deflated using the global PPP for medical care and health expenses calculated for the household consumption sector (group 115) as if the internal structures of household consumption and government consumption were similar (in fact they are not). This is probably an important source of error in the results, one that could be corrected if all the countries provided the necessary information. This is why Eurostat started trying to collect from all countries government expenditure data for the four major aggregates plus a residual class (see the basic headings carrying a dagger in the appendix), in order to reduce the imbalance between the two sectors of the classification.

---

1. For the sake of simplicity, I do not consider in this paper the final consumption expenditure of nonprofit institutions serving households.

Finally, because of the differences between the countries in the definition of the national health service and of the social security system, the expenditure for certain services may be classified under *medical care and health expenses* (group 133) in some countries and under *social security and welfare expenses* (group 134) in others.

6.2   The Present System for Calculating PPP

6.2.1   Household Final Consumption Expenditure

For *group 1151* (medical and pharmaceutical products), market prices (global prices) are collected. *Global price* is defined as the price that the consumer would have paid in the case of the absence of any social security subsidy. In other words, the prices to be collected are the sum of the consumer contribution and the social security system contribution.[2]

For *subgroup 11511* (pharmaceutical products), the number of products in the survey list is large (more than seven hundred). There are two main reasons for this: (1) The national markets are very different (products popular in certain countries are not available in other countries), and all the countries should have their own characteristic products on the list in order to respect the principle of the equicharacteristicity of the basket.[3] (2) The market prices are disturbed by the intervention of state subsidies. As a consequence, price ratios are less homogeneous than in other sectors of the economy. The result is that one needs a bigger sample of products to obtain sound PPP estimates (i.e., it is more difficult to apply the principle of representativity). In fact, Eurostat could introduce up to fourteen basic headings (therapeutic classes) if the corresponding values were available for all countries. Three classes (analgesics, anticoagulants, and products for ophthalmology) in particular seem to exhibit "price-level behavior" in the various countries that is very different from that of the rest of the group.

For *subgroup 11512* (other medical products), and for *group 1152* (therapeutic appliances and equipment), market prices (global prices) are collected. The situation is similar to that described for group 11511. However, since the size (and weight) of these groups is smaller, the number of products in the survey list is also smaller (about twenty and fifty, respectively).

For *group 1153* (services of physicians, nurses, and related practitioners outside hospitals), market prices (global prices) are collected. It may be very difficult to estimate global prices, especially when the direct payment is zero (i.e., when the whole cost is sustained by the social security system). Another prob-

---

2. Accordingly, the values should be classified partially under household final consumption expenditure and partially under government final consumption expenditure; the same parity (based on global prices) should be used to deflate both values.

3. Compliance with the equicharacteristicity of the basket is essential to avoid distortions in the results, distortions that are due to the Gerschenkron effect.

lem for this group is the quality difference between the same kind of service in different countries.

For *group 1154* (hospital care and the like), the market prices approach has not given convincing results, first, because it is very difficult to estimate the global cost of a specific service in public hospitals and, second, because private clinics are of such limited significance that they may not yield representative figures. Furthermore, the national accounts values for hospitals are calculated using the "input costs" approach. For these reasons, the "input prices" approach is used to calculate PPP in this field.

The input costs approach is based on the assumption that services not sold at market prices have a value equal to the value of production, estimated on the basis of the costs incurred (a national accounts convention). These costs are mainly (1) intermediate consumption, (2) consumption of fixed capital (depreciation), and (3) compensation of employees. For intermediate consumption, specific surveys are not carried out, but the PPPs calculated for the corresponding household consumption items are used. For the consumption of fixed capital, specific surveys are not carried out, but the PPP calculated for gross fixed capital formation is used. For the compensation of employees (the most important in terms of weight), the remuneration costs for twelve types of job are collected and compared.

This method fails to take into consideration differences in productivity in nonmarket service production in the countries compared. Methods to estimate differences in productivity are currently being studied.

6.2.2   Government Final Consumption Expenditure

As already mentioned, the values of group 133 are deflated using the PPPs of group 115.

6.3   The Direct Approach?

It has been suggested that an alternative approach for medical and health care services (groups 1153 and 1154) would be to use "output indicators" (physical indicators) to arrive directly at a volume comparison (without calculating PPPs). There are, however, many practical problems with this approach.

Whereas it is possible to create a homogeneous price ratio–oriented classification, it is not feasible to create a homogeneous *quantity* ratio–oriented classification. This is because the quantities consumed of a given set of products vary considerably in time and in space and their behavior does not have the same economic rationale as does that of prices (quantities depend on national consumers' habits). This implies that the representativity principle used to select a sample of products cannot be applied in this case. So it can be argued that the only way to use this approach would be to create a very detailed classification of all the different services provided and collect both values (expenditure) and quantities for each of them.

Therefore, if the direct approach is to be used, two major problems must be solved: (1) the problem of creating a common and very detailed classification (at "product level") in a sector where many problems of product comparability between the countries exist; and (2) the practical problem of collecting both quantities and expenditure for all the services offered in the different countries. Is this possible?

6.4 A Summary of Actions for Possible Future Improvements

Regarding problems with classification and expenditure, a possible goal would be to reduce the imbalance between the detailed levels of the two sectors of the classification (household and government expenditure) and to agree on the boundaries between "medical care and health expenses" and "social security and welfare services." Regarding problems with the services of physicians, nurses, and related practitioners outside hospitals, a possible goal would be to improve the definitions of the services for which prices are collected in order to reduce the distorting effects on results that are due to the quality differences between different countries for the same kind of service. Regarding the compensation of employees providing hospital and similar care, a possible goal would be to improve the definitions of the standard types of jobs for which remuneration costs are collected and compared and to continue to study new methods of estimating differences in productivity between countries. Finally, regarding the direct approach, a possible goal would be to investigate whether such an approach is in fact feasible.

Appendix
Eurostat PPP Classification for Medical Care and Health Expenses

Table 6A.1   **Codes and Descriptions**

Code	Description
1	Gross domestic product
11	Household final consumption expenditure
115	Medical care and health expenses
1151	Medical and pharmaceutical products
11511	Pharmaceutical products
115111.1	Pharmaceutical products*
11512	Other medical products
115121.1	Other medical products*

(continued)

Code	Description
1152	Therapeutic appliances and equipment
11521	Eyeglasses
115211.1	Eyeglasses*
11522	Orthopedic appliances and other therapeutic appliances and equipment
115221.1	Orthopedic appliances and other therapeutic appliances and equipment*
1153	Services of physicians, nurses, and related practitioners
115311.1	Services of general practitioners*
115321.1	Services of specialists*
115331.1	Services of dentists*
115341.1	Services of nurses*
115351.1	Services of other medical practitioners outside hospitals*
115361.1	Medical analyses*
1154	Hospital care and the like
11541	Compensation of employees
115411.1	Physicians*
115411.2	Nurses and other medical staff*
115412.1	Nonmedical staff*
11542	Intermediate consumption
115421.1	Food and beverages*
115422.1	Pharmaceutical products*
115423.1	Therapeutic equipment*
115424.1	Other equipment*
115425.1	Water, energy products*
115426.1	Other goods and services*
11543	Depreciation
115431.1	Depreciation*
13	Government final consumption expenditure
133	Medical care and health expenses*
133111.1	Medical and pharmaceutical products[†]
133211.1	Therapeutic appliances and equipment[†]
133311.1	Services of physicians, nurses, and related practitioners[†]
133411.1	Hospital care and the like[†]
133511.1	Other public health services[†]
134	Other individual services
134111.1	Social security and welfare services

*Basic headings used for calculating PPP.

[†]Basic headings for which Eurostat is trying to collect expenditure data from all the countries.

7   Comparisons for Countries of Central and Eastern Europe: An Informal Report

Alfred Franz

The subsequent summary deals with a group of countries that have a relatively long history of participation within the ICP (International Comparison Programme) framework, some of them being among the real pioneers of this exercise.[1] Since those early days, major political, economic, and social changes have taken place. All those well-known changes have affected the structures and arrangements of the ICP work in that area. While, in the past, the basic socioeconomic differences between the then centrally planned economies and the market economies were immediately reflected in their ECP (European Comparison Programme) patterns, these divergences have now somewhat receded. However, it would be only naive misunderstanding to ignore the still substantial differences on all levels affecting all features of the comparison. This is true for the weighting structures and the particular circumstances of sector delimitation as well as for the availability and the properties of the individual items, the outlets and other concomitant elements of supply, and so forth.

To understand these particular peculiarities of Group II, a brief review of the surprisingly varied ECP *history* may be most useful first. Then, and on that basis, a few most significant features may be added, throwing light on *peculiarities,* such as the scope of the information basis and the classification structures actually used or the use of quality-adjustment techniques. A major change toward the establishment of a general *multilateral* framework over all

Alfred Franz is presently head of the Social Statistics Department of the Austrian Central Statistical Office and also teaches at the University of Vienna.

1. In the course of the European ICP work, the term *Group II* has been established for this group of countries. The actual comparison work going on under the auspices of the ECE (Economic Commission for Europe) is termed the European Comparison Programme (ECP), encompassing OECD countries also (Group I). For a listing of the countries in each group, see the notes to fig. 7.2 below.

Europe is the most recent achievement in this context. The paper is organized accordingly, drawing on diagrammatic and/or tabular presentation for easier explanation.[2]

7.1   The History of Group II in Brief

Group II dates back to 1980. Since its beginning, the basic structure was a "star" of bilateral comparison relations, with Austria serving as the "base" or "reference country" in the center of this star. The actual star shape changed from round to round, owing to changing (mostly increasing) participation (see fig. 7.1). Most spectacular, the participation rate doubled from 1990 to 1993. For 1993, the "Moldova appendix" might be mentioned, compared indirectly (via Romania). The Baltic group (three Baltic countries and Austria), which was also a part of ECP'93/II (see fig. 7.2), has been compared multilaterally.

The jump from the 1993 shape to the 1996 shape is decisive in two respects: (*a*) In terms of membership, Hungary, Poland, the Czech Republic, and the Slovak Republic are no longer in Group II since it was felt that they would be better suited to Group I now; the Baltic group (Estonia, Latvia, Lithuania), compared in a separate subgroup related to Finland in 1993, joined Group II directly; and Albania and Macedonia joined Group II as newcomers. (*b*) In terms of methodology, the *multilateral approach* of price observation and further data processing, always used in Group I, has been extended to Group II, too.

By 1996, membership remained similar in size but changed in composition so that more requirements for taking care of less-experienced countries must be expected. On the whole, there is almost no experience with multilateral methodologies to be used in an area like Group II, so expectations of their suitability/applicability are mixed at best (see Rittenau 1995).

The transition to multilateral methods is tantamount to a major change of the role of Austria in that it acts no longer as the center of a star but as an *equal partner* among others. However, in the "joint venture"[3] represented by Group II, it is likely that not much will change in terms of practical work; the main responsibility to look for comparable prices will continue to fall on Austria. In perspective, the transition to the multilateral approach is a clear progress toward achieving greater uniformity of the whole procedure, of comparison philosophies as well as of horizontal integration; it may also gradually result in decreasing resource requirements, depending on the convergence of markets.

To get a better idea of the overall complexity of the ECP framework, see figure 7.2, which reflects the overall group structure in 1993. Country participation in 1996 is represented in figure 7.3.

---

2. This part has largely benefited from preparatory work done by S. Sergeev, presently working as ECP consultant in the ACSO (Austrian Central Statistical Office).

3. This term is used to indicate the close cooperation of the ECE, Eurostat, the OECD, the World Bank, and the ACSO in this group, in terms of common conceptual work, shared data processing, and financial resources.

7.2   Some Peculiarities of Group II

7.2.1   Magnitude of Price Observations

Owing to the obvious (although decreasing) market limitations, the number of observations may be expected to be generally lower than in Group I. For example, since the beginning, a clear tendency of increasing numbers can be seen in both private household final consumption expenditures (PHFCE) and in gross fixed capital formation (GFCF). However, these were consistently lower than in Group I, mostly reaching not more than half (see table 7.1).

However, a smaller number of price observations does not necessarily mean lesser representativity, which depends only on the homogeneity (variation) of market structures. Indeed, the problems rest not so much with representation as with comparability.

7.2.2   The Quality-Adjustment Issue

Quality-adjustment techniques have always been used in Group II and with increasing intensity (see table 7.2).[4] Most striking are the relatively evenly spread cases of quality adjustment across countries and the relative preponderance in producer items. Admittedly, the methods used are still far from being "scientific." However, given recent developments to establish more advanced methods to render CPI more comparable, a "renaissance" of quality adjustment on that level may be diagnosed, which throws interesting light on this continuing practice.

7.2.3   Classification Structures

As regards classification, the general standards have always been used without significant change. In the past, however, this meant that the MPS (material product system) design had to be transposed into system of national accounts (SNA)–type structures, not always an easy task. The problems of redoing still largely existing statistical anomalies as regards market/nonmarket distinctions (health, education, social services, dwellings) are far from being resolved. However, control of these problems is more quickly achieved than on the part of representative commodities thanks to the progress in establishing official SNA-type accounts. Another, less promising area is the "hidden economy," where, according to recent reports, the size and the extent of actual observations are still extremely varied.[5]

---

4. In this table, no further distinction is made between different subcategories of quality adjustment. These are extensively documented elsewhere (see Auer 1995, 5; and Franz 1995). A distinction between more "quantitative" and more "qualitative" or "mixed situations" is of importance in practice.

5. Particular information on this will be given in United Nations (in press). More thoroughgoing description of the Group II peculiarities is regularly found in the respective ECE documents (see United Nations 1994, in press). A most useful and up-to-date description of the numerous peculiarities of and requirements for Group II has been given in OECD (1995).

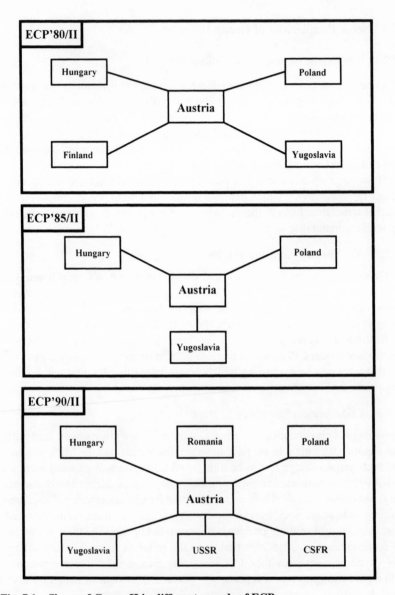

Fig. 7.1   Shape of Group II in different rounds of ECP

Note: The arrows in the shape for "ECP'96/II" indicate the multilateral potential, here exemplarily shown for two countries (Austria and Albania). CSFR = Czechoslovak Federal Republic.

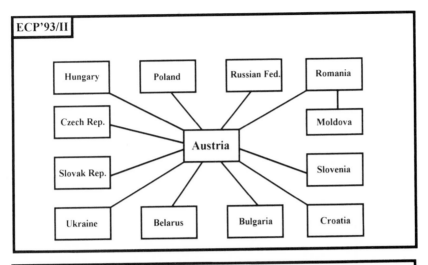

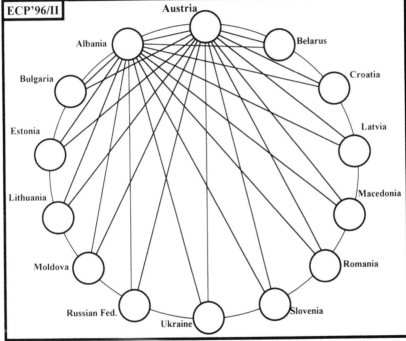

Fig. 7.1   (cont.)

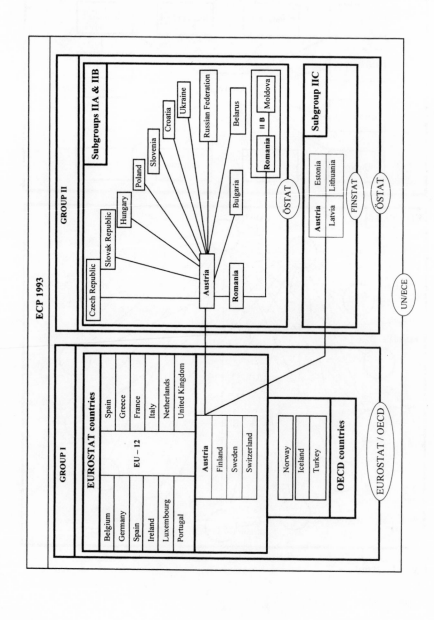

ECP 1993

GROUP I

EUROSTAT countries

Belgium	Spain
Germany	Greece
Spain	France
Ireland	Italy
Luxembourg	Netherlands
Portugal	United Kingdom

EU – 12

Austria
Finland
Sweden
Switzerland

Norway
Iceland
Turkey

OECD countries

EUROSTAT / OECD

GROUP II

Subgroups IIA & IIB

Czech Republic
Slovak Republic
Hungary
Poland
Slovenia
Croatia
Ukraine
Russian Federation
Belarus
Bulgaria

Austria

Romania

Romania	II B	Moldova

ÖSTAT

Subgroup IIC

Austria	Estonia
	Lithuania
	Latvia

FINSTAT

ÖSTAT

UN/ECE

Fig. 7.2 Shape of the European Comparison Programme (reference year 1993)

Note: *Rectangles* indicate a country or group of countries. *Ovals* indicate the office or organization responsible.

The thirty-four countries have been involved with the ECP since reference year 1993. They were divided in two groups.

Group I was organized by Eurostat and the OECD within the framework of the Eurostat-OECD PPP Programme, including nineteen European countries. Eurostat coordinated the data collection in twelve EU (European Union) countries and also in Austria, Finland, Sweden, and Switzerland. These sixteen countries are referred to as *Eurostat countries.* (Poland also joined the Eurostat comparison on an experimental basis; however, its data were incorporated into the overall ECP through its participation in the Group II comparison, i.e., bilateral comparison with Austria.) The OECD coordinated the data collection in the remaining three Group I countries—Iceland, Norway, and Turkey (i.e., OECD countries)—and ensured that the two sets of data could be combined so that results could be calculated for all nineteen Group I countries. In Group I, a multilateral approach involving the collection and processing of basic data was used.

Group II consists of three subgroups: Group II A: Austria, Poland, the Czech Republic, the Slovak Republic, Hungary, Slovenia, Croatia, Romania, Bulgaria, Belarus, the Russian Federation, and Ukraine; Group II B: Romania and Moldova; Group II C: Finland (as country coordinator only), Austria, Latvia, Lithuania, and Estonia. The ACSO coordinated the general work within Group II and assisted in all subgroups. Group II A has been organized in a "star" shape with Austria as the center of the star and direct bilateral comparisons with each of the eleven countries. Moldova was bilaterally compared with Romania (Group II B) and in this way was indirectly linked with Austria. Coordinated by Statistics Finland, the Baltic group (Group II C) has been compared multilaterally (Baltic countries and Austria).

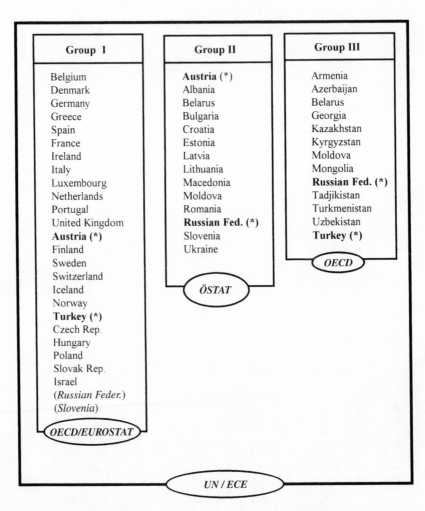

Group I	Group II	Group III
Belgium	Austria (*)	Armenia
Denmark	Albania	Azerbaijan
Germany	Belarus	Belarus
Greece	Bulgaria	Georgia
Spain	Croatia	Kazakhstan
France	Estonia	Kyrgyzstan
Ireland	Latvia	Moldova
Italy	Lithuania	Mongolia
Luxembourg	Macedonia	**Russian Fed. (*)**
Netherlands	Moldova	Tadjikistan
Portugal	Romania	Turkmenistan
United Kingdom	**Russian Fed. (*)**	Uzbekistan
Austria (*)	Slovenia	**Turkey (*)**
Finland	Ukraine	
Sweden		*OECD*
Switzerland		
Iceland	*ÖSTAT*	
Norway		
Turkey (*)		
Czech Rep.		
Hungary		
Poland		
Slovak Rep.		
Israel		
(Russian Feder.)		
(Slovenia)		
OECD/EUROSTAT		

UN / ECE

Fig. 7.3   Shape of the European Comparison Programme, 1996
Note: Rectangles indicate groups of countries. *Ovals* indicate the leading office or organization responsible. An asterisk indicates expected linking countries. The Russian Federation and Slovenia participate in Group I on an experimental basis only. ÖSTAT = ACSO.

Table 7.1 ECP Group II: Number of Items Used in Bilateral Comparisons, 1980–93

| | ECP 1980 | | | ECP 1985 | | | ECP 1990 | | | ECP 1993 | | |
| | | Of Which: | | | Of Which: | | | Of Which: | | | Of Which: | |
Country	Total	PHFC	GFCF	Total	PHFC	GFCF	Total	PHFC	GFCF	Total	PHFC	GFCF
Austria	1,353	1,005	348	1,425	1,049	376	2,862	1,714	1,148	2,965	1,419	1,546
Hungary	764	638	126	864	714	150	910	690	220	899	699	200
Poland	691	554	137	776	580	196	847	634	213	992	706	286
Romania	⋮	⋮	⋮	⋮	⋮	⋮	524	414	110	752	590	162
Belarus	⋮	⋮	⋮	⋮	⋮	⋮	⋮	⋮	⋮	849	630	219
Bulgaria	⋮	⋮	⋮	⋮	⋮	⋮	⋮	⋮	⋮	852	709	143
Croatia	⋮	⋮	⋮	⋮	⋮	⋮	⋮	⋮	⋮	784	611	173
Czech Republic	⋮	⋮	⋮	⋮	⋮	⋮	⋮	⋮	⋮	937	746	191
Russian Federation	⋮	⋮	⋮	⋮	⋮	⋮	⋮	⋮	⋮	1,061	774	287
Slovak Republic	⋮	⋮	⋮	⋮	⋮	⋮	⋮	⋮	⋮	1,043	771	272
Slovenia	⋮	⋮	⋮	⋮	⋮	⋮	⋮	⋮	⋮	932	744	188
Ukraine	⋮	⋮	⋮	⋮	⋮	⋮	⋮	⋮	⋮	714	625	89
Finland	436	275	161	⋮	⋮	⋮	⋮	⋮	⋮	⋮	⋮	⋮
Former CSFR	⋮	⋮	⋮	⋮	⋮	⋮	878	661	217	⋮	⋮	⋮
Former Soviet Union	⋮	⋮	⋮	⋮	⋮	⋮	842	623	219	⋮	⋮	⋮
Former Yugoslavia	601	436	165	824	683	141	931	726	205	⋮	⋮	⋮
Average (excluding Austria)	623	476	146	821	659	162	822	625	197	892	691	201
Group I (for comparison)	1,275	1,000	275	3,101	2,751	350	2,500	2,150	350	3,436	3,200	236

Note: CSFR = Czechoslovak Federal Republic.

PHFC = private household final consumption.

GFCF = gross fixed capital formation (producer durables only).

Table 7.2   ECP Group II: Number of Items with "Quality Adjustments" Used in Bilateral Comparisons, 1980–93

| | Items Used | | | | | | | | | | | |
| | ECP 1980 | Of Which: | | ECP 1985 | Of Which: | | ECP 1990 | Of Which: | | ECP 1993 | Of Which: | |
Country	Total	PHFC	GFCF	Total	PHFC	GFCF	Total	PHFC	GFCF	Total	PHFC	GFCF
Hungary	92	79	13	267	218	49	453	381	72	285	256	29
Poland	125	110	15	328	210	118	529	368	161	477	223	254
Romania	:	:	:	:	:	:	345	228	117	382	223	159
Belarus	:	:	:	:	:	:	:	:	:	599	381	218
Bulgaria	:	:	:	:	:	:	:	:	:	339	207	132
Croatia	:	:	:	:	:	:	:	:	:	300	141	159
Czech Republic	:	:	:	:	:	:	:	:	:	420	244	176
Russian Federation	:	:	:	:	:	:	:	:	:	673	392	281
Slovak Republic	:	:	:	:	:	:	:	:	:	506	245	261
Slovenia	:	:	:	:	:	:	:	:	:	353	177	176
Ukraine	:	:	:	:	:	:	:	:	:	462	376	86
Finland	0	0	0	:	:	:	:	:	:	:	:	:
Former CSFR	:	:	:	:	:	:	519	337	182	:	:	:
Former Soviet Union	:	:	:	:	:	:	601	374	227	:	:	:
Former Yugoslavia	131	126	5	212	204	8	231	219	12	:	:	:
Average per country	116	105	11	269	211	58	447	318	129	436	260	176

Note: CSFR = Czechoslovak Federal Republic.
PHFC = private household final consumption.
GFCF = gross fixed capital formation (producer durables only).

7.3   Conclusions

In spite of clear and generally welcomed tendencies of adaptation and convergence toward Western standards, Group II still represents a specific identity in the overall comparison framework. This is true with regard to both price observations and weighting. It is, therefore, legitimate to keep this group separate within the overall framework.

Recent developments may even suggest the use of Group II structures as a sort of "training camp" leading to equal participation in the ICP.

References

Auer, J. 1995. Report on the Central and Eastern European comparison. Paper presented to the Conference of European Statisticians (Economic Commission for Europe [ECE]) Consultation on the European Comparison Programme (ECP) within Group II, Vienna, 25–28 September.

Franz, A. 1995. ECP and "QA" ["quality-adjustment"] issues. Paper presented to the joint ECE/International Labor Organization Meeting on Consumer Price Indices, Geneva, 20–24 November.

Organization for Economic Cooperation and Development. 1995. *Purchasing power parities for countries in transition: Methodological papers.* Paris: OECD and the Center for Cooperation with the Economies in Transition.

Rittenau, R. 1995. Future ECP work in Group II: The multilateral challenge. Paper presented to the CES (ECE) Consultation on the ECP within Group II, Vienna, 25–28 September.

United Nations. 1994. *International comparison of gross domestic product in Europe, 1990.* New York.

———. 1997. *International comparison of gross domestic product in Europe, 1993.* New York.

8   Multilateral Comparison of the Baltic Countries, 1993: An Informal Report

Seppo Varjonen

The Baltic countries—Estonia, Latvia, and Lithuania—formed Subgroup C within the Group II comparisons for 1993. The comparisons were based on the Group II A product lists, and they were linked to Group II A and to Group I through Austria.

Statistics Finland acted as the coordinating agency for the Baltic comparison, checking and coordinating price collection and making all the necessary calculations. Finland, however, did not participate in the comparisons.

The main difference between the Baltic comparison and the Group II A comparison was that the Baltic comparison was not a star system of bilateral comparisons but a multilateral EKS comparison comprising four countries, namely, Austria and the three Baltic countries. The multilateral method was applied at each stage of work, including the calculation of reference parities and the productivity adjustment for nonmarket services.

The other basic difference between the Baltic comparison and the Group II A comparison was that the parities for consumer goods and services were calculated by identifying representative and nonrepresentative products (i.e., asterisked and nonasterisked products) and using this information in the calculation in the same way as in the Group I comparison.

The work was carried out in close cooperation with the Austrian Central Statistical Office (ACSO) in order to guarantee comparability with the Group II A comparison.

In what follows, the comparison work is not thoroughly described. Instead, attention is focused on the methodological differences between the Group II A comparison and the Baltic comparison and what can be learned from the experience gained.

Seppo Varjonen was responsible for the Baltic PPP comparison while working in Statistics Finland. He is now working in the Transition Economies Division of the OECD.

8.1   Organization of the Baltic Comparison

Five workshops were held during the project. These workshops replaced the bilateral meetings held by Austria with each of its partner countries. The group meetings provided an opportunity to discuss ways to improve the comparability of data supplied by the countries.

Before starting the price collection, a Finnish expert visited each Baltic country in order to prepare the item selection and practical price collection work.

The fourth workshop dealt mainly with the results of price surveys. The price data supplied were checked in the light of the first approximations of the price-level indexes. A first check had been made in Finland, and the countries had replied to written questions. After clarifications as to which discrepancies could be neglected, and after removing errors, the countries agreed to find comparable prices to be included in the comparison.

The way the Baltic countries would be compared with other countries was also discussed. One possibility was to use price data from Poland and Belarus to strengthen the link to Group II A. Especially the Polish prices for consumer goods and durables seemed in many cases to be comparable with those of the Baltic countries. Prices from Poland and Belarus were used as background material when prices were analyzed.

8.2   Price Surveys and Quality of Price Data

The price surveys were based on Group II A, but some items were added to the lists and specified tightly in order to strengthen the comparability of prices.

As usual, price data for consumer goods and services are partly based on price surveys conducted by countries and partly on national CPIs. In Estonia, as much as 40 percent of prices are taken from CPI data files. In other Baltic countries, the share was around 20 percent.

For consumer goods and services, the overlap between the countries was relatively high (see tables 8.1 and 8.2).

In some cases, a country could not find any prices for a basic heading. The EKS methodology was then applied to prices at the next highest level and the result taken as a reference parity.

At the final stage of work, all consumer prices were checked, and quality corrections were made when necessary. The quality adjustments were made in accordance with the principles governing the bilateral comparisons with the other Group II countries and Austria. Data on adjustments made for prices in Poland were used as background material in the evaluation of adjustments needed.

Prices for machinery and equipment were the main problem areas in the comparison. Price data had to be gathered by special surveys in each country.

Table 8.1   Total Number of Consumer Prices and, of Them, the Prices of
           Asterisked Products

	Estonia		Latvia		Lithuania	
	Total	Aster.	Total	Aster.	Total	Aster.
111 Food, beverages, and tobacco	153	139	144	138	152	113
112 Clothing and footwear	108	96	75	66	93	62
113 Gross rents, fuel and power	32	26	17	16	23	20
114 Furniture, fixtures, household operation	126	103	101	68	124	74
115 Medical care and health	29	27	14	11	28	25
116 Transport and communication	45	37	33	28	53	34
117 Recreation, entertainment, education	58	40	62	41	65	50
118 Miscellaneous goods and services	51	49	47	36	51	44
Total	602	517	493	404	589	422

Table 8.2   Total Number of Consumer Prices and, of Them, Adjusted Prices

	Estonia		Latvia		Lithuania	
	Total	Adj.	Total	Adj.	Total	Adj.
111 Food, beverages, and tobacco	153	15	144	13	152	7
112 Clothing and footwear	108	10	75	14	93	11
113 Gross rents, fuel and power	32	0	17	0	23	1
114 Furniture, fixtures, household operation	126	10	101	12	124	8
115 Medical care and health	29	0	14	0	28	0
116 Transport and communication	45	17	33	14	53	18
117 Recreation, entertainment, education	58	0	62	5	65	0
118 Miscellaneous goods and services	51	2	47	1	51	2
Total	602	54	493	59	589	47

This information was not easily obtained because 1993 was a transition period in the Baltic countries.

There were large discrepancies in terms of quality of data available, and only a small number of price quotations were submitted by the countries owing to the exceptional circumstances prevailing in 1993. In 1993, investments were cut to the minimum, and the equipment that entered the countries was often secondhand or obtained as a result of humanitarian aid.

As in Group II A, there was little overlap among equipment prices, and the inventory in the Austrian database showed that only a few products priced by the Baltic countries were priced by some Group II A countries. The Austrian database also showed that the dispersion of price ratios within the same basic heading was very wide. To avoid the risk of basing the comparison on too few prices, it was necessary to break the comparison rules and use exchange rates as price parities.

Price parities for construction could be calculated without any major problems.

Inflation was slowing down in the Baltic countries in 1993 but was still quite high. The yearly inflation figures in the latter part of 1993 were around 50 percent in Estonia and Latvia and higher in Lithuania. That 1993 was a year of transition and the statistical standards prevailing in these countries during that year influenced the comparability of results to some extent.

8.3   Results and the Influence of Differences in Methods on the Comparability with Group II A Countries

As explained above, the main differences between the methods applied in the Baltic subgroup and those applied in Group II A were the use of the asterisked products in the calculation of parities and the multilateral processing of the data. In the following, it is shown by a set of tables how much the volume results differ from the results that would have been obtained had the Baltic countries been treated in the same way as any other country in Group II A.

Table 8.3 describes the results when the same methodology is applied to the Baltic group as is applied to the Group II A countries. Table 8.4 describes the actual treatment of the Baltic countries in the comparison. Tables 8.5 and 8.6 show how much the different methodology has influenced the volume results.

The tables show that the different approach applied by the Baltic group has only a minor influence on the results. When the asterisked characteristics of products are taken into account, there is a tendency to get slightly higher volumes for the Baltic countries. It should be noted that the tendency is strongest for Lithuania, which submitted more prices than the other Baltic countries.

When interpreting the test results of the importance of representativity, it should be also noted that the Austrian list was quite strictly followed in the Baltic comparison. The results could be different if more prices outside the Austrian list would have been used.

The multilateral processing of Baltic countries has even less influence on overall results. This is not surprising since the EKS method changes the bilateral parities as little as possible. The advantage of the use of multilateral data processing has been indirect—the countries have had the opportunity to compare prices directly at each stage of work and at each level of detail of data.

8.4   Comparison of Nonmarket Services and the Productivity Adjustment

In Group II A, methods applied for measuring purchasing power parities (PPPs) and volumes for nonmarket services differ somewhat country by country depending on the availability of base data. Mostly, volumes for the compensation of employees are based on the number of employees (or, for some countries, PPPs are calculated on the basis of wage comparisons), which are then

Table 8.3   Indexes of Real Value per Capita of Final Expenditure on GDP for the Baltic Group by Group II A Methodology

		Austria	Estonia	Latvia	Lithuania
1	Final consumption of population (national)	100	25.0	19.5	29.1
2	Food, beverages, tobacco	100	43.4	36.3	50.7
3	Food	100	44.1	37.3	63.6
4	Bread and cereals	100	41.9	49.3	117.1
5	Meat	100	46.3	34.6	77.1
6	Fish	100	67.4	70.4	64.5
7	Milk, cheese, and eggs	100	67.8	61.7	88.2
8	Oils and fats	100	36.4	32.0	67.6
9	Fruits, vegetables, potatoes	100	41.6	32.4	26.6
10	Other food	100	30.3	20.0	37.7
11	Beverages	100	30.0	36.8	12.7
12	Nonalcoholic beverages	100	5.4	3.9	4.4
13	Alcoholic beverages	100	38.6	47.4	15.2
14	Tobacco	100	84.4	20.4	19.3
15	Clothing and footwear	100	14.2	10.2	24.2
16	Clothing	100	13.1	9.0	25.3
17	Footwear	100	18.6	14.0	21.9
18	Gross rents, fuel and power	100	33.4	25.8	49.3
19	Gross rents	100	20.7	17.1	35.9
20	Fuel and power	100	71.0	49.1	85.3
21	Household equipment and operation	100	6.0	3.7	6.0
22	Furniture	100	3.0	1.8	4.1
23	Household textiles	100	4.7	5.7	9.2
24	Appliances	100	6.7	1.7	3.9
25	Other household goods and services	100	12.4	10.3	12.6
26	Medical care	100	17.5	13.9	19.6
27	Transport and communication	100	9.7	6.9	.0
28	Transport equipment	100	3.0	.6	2.2
29	Operation of equipment	100	9.9	4.2	4.8
30	Purchased transport services	100	24.4	40.0	36.1
31	Communication	100	23.8	13.0	40.5
32	Recreation, education	100	37.3	25.6	35.3
33	Equipment for recreation	100	8.3	4.2	4.1
34	Recreational, cultural services	100	21.5	7.5	6.5
35	Books, newspapers, magazines	100	86.7	17.0	43.1
36	Education	100	64.0	58.9	77.8
37	Miscellaneous goods & services	100	9.1	5.1	8.7
38	Restaurants, cafés, hotels	100	7.7	3.9	3.6
39	Other goods and services (including nonprofit institutions)	100	12.8	7.5	16.2
40	Net purchases abroad	−100	−1.8	.6	.4
41	Collective consumption of government	100	30.3	25.6	20.0
42	Gross fixed capital formation	100	9.2	5.1	8.6
43	Construction	100	12.2	7.5	17.7
44	Residential buildings	100	3.1	10.0	20.1
45	Nonresidential buildings	100	25.1	9.5	19.5
46	Other construction etc.	100	5.7	3.7	12.6
47	Machinery and equipment	100	6.5	3.2	3.2
48	Transport equipment	100	1.3	7.1	4.8
49	Nonelectrical machinery	100	7.0	2.5	3.4
50	Electrical machinery	100	10.9	1.1	.8
51	Changes in stocks	100	72.0	−112.0	−42.9
52	Balance of imports and exports	100	−13.8	52.8	−23.5
53	Gross domestic product	100	19.4	16.1	18.8

Note: Each country has been compared bilaterally with Austria without taking the representativity of products into account. The results are based on EKS processing for all sixteen Group II countries. Austria = 100.

Table 8.4   **Indexes of Real Value per Capita of Final Expenditure on GDP for the Baltic Group by Methodology Used in the Comparison**

		Austria	Estonia	Latvia	Lithuania
1	Final consumption of population (national)	100	25.7	19.7	29.8
2	Food, beverages, tobacco	100	45.6	36.4	52.3
3	Food	100	46.2	36.7	62.6
4	Bread and cereals	100	53.5	46.5	115.4
5	Meat	100	45.5	34.7	72.2
6	Fish	100	72.8	67.7	64.3
7	Milk, cheese and eggs	100	67.8	61.6	88.3
8	Oils and fats	100	36.4	32.0	67.6
9	Fruits, vegetables, potatoes	100	42.1	32.2	28.5
10	Other food	100	31.9	19.5	37.1
11	Beverages	100	32.4	40.8	17.6
12	Nonalcoholic beverages	100	6.1	3.5	4.3
13	Alcoholic beverages	100	41.7	55.2	22.0
14	Tobacco	100	84.3	20.4	19.3
15	Clothing and footwear	100	15.3	10.1	24.5
16	Clothing	100	14.3	9.4	26.1
17	Footwear	100	18.9	13.0	21.2
18	Gross rents, fuel and power	100	33.5	27.0	50.4
19	Gross rents	100	21.3	18.5	37.7
20	Fuel and power	100	69.1	47.6	86.1
21	Household equipment and operation	100	6.9	3.8	6.6
22	Furniture	100	3.5	1.6	3.9
23	Household textiles	100	5.1	5.8	10.4
24	Appliances	100	7.7	2.2	4.6
25	Other household goods and services	100	14.8	10.9	15.3
26	Medical care	100	17.0	15.7	18.6
27	Transport and communication	100	9.8	6.4	6.9
28	Transport equipment	100	3.1	.7	2.1
29	Operation of equipment	100	10.2	4.0	4.5
30	Purchased transport services	100	26.8	37.3	35.2
31	Communication	100	21.9	13.2	40.8
32	Recreation, education	100	36.8	24.9	36.2
33	Equipment for recreation	100	8.0	4.4	4.4
34	Recreational, cultural services	100	22.3	6.7	6.3
35	Books, newspapers, magazines	100	71.5	12.7	28.8
36	Education	100	63.6	58.1	80.0
37	Miscellaneous goods & services	100	9.3	5.2	9.1
38	Restaurants, cafés, hotels	100	8.0	3.9	3.7
39	Other goods and services (including nonprofit institutions)	100	12.8	7.8	16.8
40	Net purchases abroad	−100	−1.8	.6	.4
41	Collective consumption of government	100	29.3	25.9	20.9
42	Gross fixed capital formation	100	8.9	5.3	8.6
43	Construction	100	11.2	8.1	17.7
44	Residential buildings	100	3.1	10.0	20.1
45	Nonresidential buildings	100	24.7	9.9	18.8
46	Other construction etc.	100	4.3	4.5	13.4
47	Machinery and equipment	100	6.6	3.2	3.2
48	Transport equipment	100	1.3	7.3	4.8
49	Nonelectrical machinery	100	7.0	2.5	3.4
50	Electrical machinery	100	10.9	1.1	.8
51	Changes in stocks	100	76.5	−110.9	−42.3
52	Balance of imports and exports	100	−13.8	52.8	−23.5
53	Gross domestic product	100	19.5	16.3	19.1

Note: PPSs are calculated multilaterally within the Baltic group taking the representativity of products into account. The results are based on the EKS processing of all sixteen Group II countries. (Table is the sum of tables 8.3, 8.5, and 8.6.) Austria = 100.

		Austria	Estonia	Latvia	Lithuania
	Table 8.5 Influence on Results Incorporating Representativity of Products				
1	Final consumption of population (national)	0	.4	.6	.7
2	Food, beverages, tobacco	0	1.1	1.3	1.5
3	Food	0	1.0	.2	−.8
4	Bread and cereals	0	3.7	1.6	5.2
5	Meat	0	−.3	−.1	−5.3
6	Fish	0	4.6	−.1	−2.9
7	Milk, cheese, and eggs	0	.0	−.1	.0
8	Oils and fats	0	.0	.0	.0
9	Fruits, vegetables, potatoes	0	.3	.0	1.6
10	Other food	0	1.5	.3	−1.4
11	Beverages	0	1.8	9.4	4.2
12	Nonalcoholic beverages	0	.0	.0	.0
13	Alcoholic beverages	0	3.1	14.9	5.9
14	Tobacco	0	.0	.0	.0
15	Clothing and footwear	0	.7	.1	.1
16	Clothing	0	.7	.4	.1
17	Footwear	0	.5	−1.0	−.9
18	Gross rents, fuel and power	0	−.1	.6	3.8
19	Gross rents	0	.0	.7	5.1
20	Fuel and power	0	−.8	.0	.0
21	Household equipment and operation	0	.9	.2	.6
22	Furniture	0	.3	−.3	−.2
23	Household textiles	0	.4	.2	.8
24	Appliances	0	.9	.4	1.1
25	Other household goods and services	0	2.6	1.2	1.8
26	Medical care	0	.0	.8	.0
27	Transport and communication	0	−.5	−.1	7.5
28	Transport equipment	0	.0	.0	.0
29	Operation of equipment	0	−1.0	−.1	.2
30	Purchased transport services	0	.0	.0	1.1
31	Communication	0	−1.4	.0	.2
32	Recreation, education	0	.9	.6	−.4
33	Equipment for recreation	0	−.3	.5	.2
34	Recreational, cultural services	0	−.2	−.3	−.6
35	Books, newspapers, magazines	0	6.6	−.1	−16.4
36	Education	0	.1	.1	.1
37	Miscellaneous goods & services	0	.1	.2	.4
38	Restaurants, cafés, hotels	0	.0	.3	.0
39	Other goods and services (including nonprofit institutions)	0	.2	.2	1.1
40	Net purchases abroad	0	.0	.0	.0
41	Collective consumption of government	0	.2	.3	.3
42	Gross fixed capital formation	0	.0	.0	.0
43	Construction	0	.0	.0	.0
44	Residential buildings	0	.0	.0	.0
45	Nonresidential buildings	0	.0	.0	.0
46	Other construction etc.	0	.0	.0	.0
47	Machinery and equipment	0	.0	.0	.0
48	Transport equipment	0	.0	.1	.0
49	Nonelectrical machinery	0	.0	.0	.0
50	Electrical machinery	0	.0	.0	.0
51	Changes in stocks	0	1.0	−2.9	−.5
52	Balance of imports and exports	0	.0	.0	.0
53	Gross domestic product	0	.2	.3	.4

Table 8.6   Influence on Results When Price Parities of the Baltic Countries Are Estimated Multilaterally

		Austria	Estonia	Latvia	Lithuania
1	Final consumption of population (national)	0	.3	−.3	−.2
2	Food, beverages, tobacco	0	1	−1.1	0
3	Food	0	1.1	−.7	−.3
4	Bread and cereals	0	7.8	−4.3	−6.3
5	Meat	0	−.5	.2	.5
6	Fish	0	.9	−2.3	2.7
7	Milk, cheese and eggs	0	0	0	.1
8	Oils and fats	0	0	0	0
9	Fruits, vegetables, potatoes	0	.2	−.3	.3
10	Other food	0	.2	−.7	.8
11	Beverages	0	.7	−3.3	.7
12	Nonalcoholic beverages	0	.7	−.3	−.1
13	Alcoholic beverages	0	.4	−4.2	1
14	Tobacco	0	−.1	0	0
15	Clothing and footwear	0	.4	0	.4
16	Clothing	0	.5	−.1	.6
17	Footwear	0	−.2	.1	.2
18	Gross rents, fuel and power	0	.3	.6	−1.7
19	Gross rents	0	.9	1.6	−3.5
20	Fuel and power	0	−2.1	−1.3	.6
21	Household equipment and operation	0	.1	0	0
22	Furniture	0	.1	.1	0
23	Household textiles	0	0	−.1	.3
24	Appliances	0	.2	.1	−.4
25	Other household goods and services	0	−.1	−.6	.5
26	Medical care	0	−.6	.9	−.9
27	Transport and communication	0	.7	−.4	−.4
28	Transport equipment	0	0	−.3	−.2
29	Operation of equipment	0	1.4	−.2	−.5
30	Purchased transport services	0	.8	−1.8	−.6
31	Communication	0	−.6	.2	.1
32	Recreation, education	0	−1	−1.1	.9
33	Equipment for recreation	0	0	−.3	.1
34	Recreational, cultural services	0	−.1	−.3	.2
35	Books, newspapers, magazines	0	−21.1	−4.5	1.9
36	Education	0	−.5	−1.3	2
37	Miscellaneous goods & services	0	.1	−.1	−.1
38	Restaurants, cafés, hotels	0	.3	−.2	0
39	Other goods and services (including nonprofit institutions)	0	−.1	.1	−.2
40	Net purchases abroad	0	0	0	0
41	Collective consumption of government	0	−1.3	0	.6
42	Gross fixed capital formation	0	−.4	.2	0
43	Construction	0	−.9	.6	0
44	Residential buildings	0	0	0	0
45	Nonresidential buildings	0	−.3	.5	−.7
46	Other construction, etc.	0	−1.3	.8	.9
47	Machinery and equipment	0	0	0	0
48	Transport equipment	0	0	.1	−.1
49	Nonelectrical machinery	0	0	0	0
50	Electrical machinery	0	0	0	0
51	Changes in stocks	0	3.5	4	1.1
52	Balance of imports and exports	0	0	0	0
53	Gross domestic product	0	−.1	−.1	−.1

corrected by taking into account the differences in general productivity levels between countries. The general productivity level of a country is measured by comparing the ratio of value added in real values to the number of employees in market industries (excluding agriculture). General productivity adjustment was used in all other nonmarket services except education, where special adjustments were developed.

Methods used in the Baltic comparison of nonmarket services do not essentially differ from those used generally in Group II A. Number of employees was used as a volume indicator, which was then corrected by the productivity adjustment. Measurement on the basis of wage data was not possible in any Baltic country.

The Baltic comparison differed in method from Group II A only when dealing with education. In the Baltic comparison, the volume indicator for the compensation of teaching staff was simply the number of teachers. In Group II A, the volume at the university level of education was the number of teachers corrected by the student/teacher ratio (leading to the outcome that the volume equals the number of students) and at other levels of education the number of teachers corrected by the teacher/pupil ratio.

The productivity-level index compared to Austria was 0.22 for Estonia, 0.18 for Latvia, and 0.16 for Lithuania. Use of the indexes for adjusting the volumes of nonmarket services (excluding education) decreased the GDP volumes by about three units (where Austria = 100), or by about 15 percent of the GDP of the Baltic countries.

The productivity level is certainly lower in Group II countries than in Group I on average, and it can be concluded that, in order to obtain more realistic results, productivity adjustments are necessary. But what is the right amount of adjustment, and is it possible to improve the estimation?

One possibility is to improve the measurement of adjustment coefficients by eliminating the influence of different production structures on the result. Preliminary tests done for OECD countries show that estimating value added/ number of employees ratios by industry and using these instead of the ratio obtained from the total of market industries may result in the lower dispersion of adjustments. However, it is obvious that the use of any reference productivity-level index is not suitable for all countries and cannot replace a direct estimation of productivity levels.

9   Report on the Romania–Republic of Moldova Bilateral Comparison, Benchmark Year 1993: An Informal Report

Daniela Elena Ştefănescu and Maria Chişinevschi

Romania participated in two rounds of the European Comparison Programme (ECP), a part of the International Comparison Program (ICP) focusing on GDP. This took the form of a Romania-Austria bilateral comparison with 1990 and 1993 as the benchmark years, Austria being the bridge country between the Group II countries (in transition) and other European countries.

After the end of the 1990 ECP round, preparations for the next round coincided with the political changes in Central and Eastern Europe and the breakup of the Soviet Union.

As a result, twenty-three countries applied for inclusion in the Group II comparisons for 1993. Although the increase in the number of countries did not mean greater geographic coverage (which is more or less the same as in 1990), it proved to be beyond the power of the Austrian Central Statistical Office (ACSO). Thus, the organizers of the European comparison concluded that the work efforts must be shared.

In this context, at the beginning of February 1993, the OECD asked the National Commission for Statistics (NCS) of Romania to assume the burden of carrying out a bilateral comparison within the next round. In this way, Romania had as a major task in this comparison organizing and carrying out everything required of a "bridge country." The reference pattern was Austria, the center of the star-shaped organization of bilateral comparisons within the Group II A countries.

The main objective of this report is to illustrate the procedure for the bilateral comparison between Romania (the National Commission for Statistics)

Daniela Elena Ştefănescu has been director of Co-operation and European Integration Direction of the National Commission for Statistics of Romania since 1996. She is a Ph.D. candidate in statistics at the Academy of Economic Studies in Bucharest. Maria Chişinevschi is head of the International Comparison Division, Direction of Co-operation and European Integration within the National Commission for Statistics of Romania.

and the Republic of Moldova (the Statistical State Department) as well as giving the results of this comparison.
The Republic of Moldova has been included in the Group II D subgroup.

9.1   Organization of the Comparison

With a view to establishing the organizational and conceptual framework as well as the working schedule, in May 1993, in Bucharest, a meeting of representatives of the OECD, the ACSO, the NCS, and the State Department of Statistics of the Republic of Moldova took place. As it was the first time the Republic of Moldova joined the comparison, it was necessary to explain the comparison's aims, the methods and techniques used, and the informational burden of each participating country.

The Moldavian experts were informed that joining the comparison assumes ensuring that the following necessary data are available: (*a*) gross domestic product, broken down into homogeneous basic headings; (*b*) the list of typical items with significant shares in each GDP expenditure basic heading, together with the detailed technical characteristics for each item; (*c*) the average annual and national prices for selected goods and services; and (*d*) other additional information needed to compare nonmarket services and other GDP expenditure.

A few meetings took place in order to clear up methodological issues, especially those referring to GDP computation in accordance with ESA methodology, moving from the material product system to the European system of accounts, and observing the rules of the ECP methodology, very important elements in ensuring the indicators' comparability.

As national practices always differ to a certain extent, the differences in the international recommendations have been noticed, discussed, and corrected; likewise, issues connected to data collection and computing the annual average and national prices for the selected products have been tackled.

Besides the working meeting, it was deemed that, with a view to gathering evidence, the Moldavian representatives would benefit from the translation into Romanian (which is also spoken in the Republic of Moldova) of papers describing the basic methodology used to obtain the purchasing power parities (PPPs).

On the basis of the list of representative products established by the ACSO for the Group II countries, the Romanians settled on the representative products typical of both economies, pointing out the characteristics of each product.

At the bilateral meetings organized during 1993–95 in Bucharest and Kishinev, all the representative products selected by the Republic of Moldova from the list proposed by Romania were investigated; the characteristics of products were matched, and time was allocated for Romanian experts to visit Moldavian shops. When necessary, the method of quality adjustment was tackled.

Prices have been further analyzed, and the GDP breakdown by basic headings has been surveyed (with a view to obtaining a more representative composition), as has the coverage of all groups with representative products. Finally, the preliminary results of the bilateral comparison have been examined in detail.

9.2   GDP Disaggregation by Expenditure Categories

The GDP breakdown for the bilateral comparisons of Group II involved 295 basic headings. Data were collected in accordance with a detailed questionnaire (common for all Group II countries). Because the Moldavian statistics did not use the expenditures method to estimate GDP at that time, the Romanian experts worked together with the Moldavians to determine the indicators specific to this method.

To establish population final consumption in keeping with the methodology of the ECP, issues related to the differences between the content of this aggregate with a significant share in GDP and of the population final consumption concept computed on the basis of ESA methodology were clarified. Final consumption of public administration was carefully broken down into individual consumption and government consumption using specific data sources for each of the fields education, health, and social welfare.

The disaggregation of GDP expenditure by basic heading was examined in detail, taking into account that the available data sources did not fully meet the requirements. Therefore, these were analyzed with a view to determining the GDP expenditure groups, and different data sources were compared in order to estimate more accurately each basic heading of expenditure, those concerning both population final consumption and governmental consumption.

In terms of the correct disaggregation of expenditure into basic headings, greater accuracy was achieved for three reasons: the coverage for all expenditure aggregates was ensured; the dispersion of individual price ratios was lower within the basic heading than between the commodity groups within aggregations at a high level; and the weighted averages parities could be computed at a relatively detailed level.

9.3   Item Selection

On the basis of the items selected by Romania within the bilateral comparison with Austria, the Romanian experts worked out the item list to be as representative of and as comparable between both countries as possible.

For countries belonging to a homogeneous group, the variance of individual price ratios tends to be lower if the compared items are described through trademark and model number instead of functional specification. In this way, equivalent pricing for items of the same content and quality could be assured. Nevertheless, in the bilateral comparison between Romania and Moldova, this procedure could be followed only in a few cases.

Under these circumstances, we used the technical characteristics of items, without specifying the brand and the model. Therefore, the item specifications were mostly generic, and, consequently, differences in the quality of priced items required price adjustments to compensate for the quality differences.

This was the case for consumer goods and services, specifying in detail the characteristics of items to be priced. Because of the general lack of products on the Moldavian market and an extremely low volume of imported goods, it was necessary that the initial list of population final consumption items match the features specific to the Moldavian market. At the beginning, the Romanian experts put together a list of 609 goods and services. After discussion with their Moldavian colleagues, a final list of 479 items was agreed to, for which the Moldavians were supposed to provide the price data (table 9.1 shows the number of items by categories initially proposed by the NCS and finally priced by the Statistical Department of Moldova).

In the process of selecting consumer goods and services, for most cases the Moldavian experts picked out items priced for the consumer price index computation rather than collect additional prices. For very few items, a special investigation was undertaken (e.g., medicines).

For population final consumption, the list was drawn up so that it met, well enough, the two fundamental comparison principles: comparability and equirepresentativity.

However, for certain basic headings, it was impossible for experts to select representative products, and the expenditure for these commodity groups was computed again by means of the price ratios from other similar analytic aggregates, in keeping with ECP methodology (e.g., sea fruit, 11110331; or products made of potatoes, 11110721; or other varieties of bread, 11110134).

For machinery and equipment to be assigned to gross fixed capital formation, the Romanian experts drew up a representative list containing 233 items. After the proposals had been reviewed, the Moldavian experts selected only 42 items.

The pricing of these items required a special (survey) investigation. Specifications for selected machinery and equipment referred to brand and model to be priced. More than 80 percent of these items were imported, especially from the countries of the former Soviet Union, built in accordance with standards incompatible with Romanian ones. Thus, the Romanian experts also needed to identify other items compatible to those proposed by the Moldavians.

For construction, the bills of quantities proposed by the Austrians were used (detailed descriptions of the seven standard but fictive construction objectives). The bills of quantities were priced by experts working within a specialized institute.

This ECP segment was complex because such pricing requires information not usually available to statistical offices. This was the reason why exact harmonizing with the structure and the content of bills of quantity was required for each objective.

Table 9.1   **Consumer Goods and Services**

	Number of Items Initially Proposed by NCS Romania	Number of Items Priced by SSD Moldova	Number of P-type Quality Adjustments	Number of Items Finally Used
111 Food, beverages, and tobacco	180	137	10	122
112 Clothing and footwear	113	101	1	86
113 Gross rent, fuel and power	15	13	. . .	13
114 Household equipment and operation	120	93	6	78
115 Health	25	13	. . .	9
116 Transport and communication	38	30	3	25
117 Education, recreation, and culture	64	44	4	37
118 Miscellaneous goods and services	54	48	. . .	38
Total	609	479	24	408

9.4   Nonmarket Services and Rent Comparison

In the case of nonmarket services, there are no market prices for the so-called comparison-resistant services; the standard method could not be used because these services are provided either free of charge or at prices that do not fully cover the cost. The following services belong to this area: health, education, and welfare services and collective government consumption. As is well known, for these service comparisons two approaches can be used: the input method in monetary terms (based on annual compensation of selected and specified occupations) and in quantitative terms (based on number of employees) and the output method (based on data in physical terms representing the output of the services concerned, e.g., number of pupils, number of births in hospitals, number of hospital bed days, etc.). Both approaches require a detailed database, collected by means of a questionnaire.

In table 9.2, the methods used in the bilateral comparison for the detailed categories of nonmarket services are illustrated. The PPP computation for the intermediate consumption and the consumption of fixed capital in these services was imputed with the benchmark parities of other similar categories of household consumption or gross fixed capital formation, as appropriate.

The use of the input approach could raise serious problems for the comparison results when data are not adjusted because of the productivity differences caused by the different organizational conditions, educational standards, or endowments with technical equipment. Consequently, two types of adjustment were needed.

First was an adjustment based on a general relative productivity level (GRPL) assuming that the differences in productivity prevailing in the nonmar-

Table 9.2   **Nonmarket Services**

	Method Used
1153 Medical services outside hospitals	IMPI (GRPL)
1154 Hospital care and the like (compensation of employees):	
Physicians	OMPI (GRPL)
Other medical staff	OMPI (GRPL)
Nonmedical staff	OMPI (GRPL)
1174 Education (compensation of employees):	
First and second school level	IMMI (SRPL)
Third school level	IMPI (SRPL)
Universities	IMMI (SRPL)
Other personnel	IMPI (GRPL)
1184 Welfare services (compensation of employees)	IMMI (GRPL)
1300 Final consumption of general government:	
Employees with university level of education	IMMI (GRPL)
Other employees (nonacademic)	IMMI (GRPL)

Note: IMPI = input method physical indicators. IMMI = input method monetary indicators. SRPL = specific relative productivity level. OMPI = output method physical indicators. GRPL = general relative productivity level.

ket sector roughly equal the productivity differences in the market sector (excluding agriculture). Information necessary to compute GRPL was obtained from an additional questionnaire (value added and number employed in the sectors concerned). The experts from Statistical Department of Moldova could not supply the information requested, so data on the Republic of Moldova were estimated on the basis of Romanian data, namely, of the value-added structure from the nonagricultural market.

Second was an adjustment based on the specific relative productivity level (SRPL). For instance, for preuniversity education, the use of the SRPL assumes that the time allocated by a teacher to a pupil is a decisive factor in the quality of education, meaning that the productivity coefficient is inversely related to the number of pupils per teacher. For higher education, the situation seems to be the opposite, the productivity coefficient being directly related to the number of students per professor since this kind of education is based on a great deal of individual study.

In the housing rents comparison in the Group II countries, certain difficulties were faced. For most of the countries, these difficulties were solved by means of quantitative indicators, in accordance with a special questionnaire drawn up for this purpose, with a view to substituting for information on housing rents. If this information had been available, it would not have been reliable or comparable because rents actually paid were lower than the cost of the housing supply.

In the bilateral comparison between Romania and Moldova, as a first variant the same method as for most of the Group II countries was first attempted, but the Moldavian experts could not provide all the information needed for imputation. Consequently, taking into account that the policy adopted in the establishment of housing rents did not differ between the two countries, data on housing rents (in both the state and the private sectors) were deemed to be comparable, and, therefore, expenditure on rents was deflated by means of the PPP computed on the basis of rents per square meter. However, the data obtained were considered unreliable. An explanation could be the tendency to underestimate the rent levels of the private sector. Finally, the PPP of the heading "household repairs maintenance" was used.

9.5 Quality Adjustments

As it cannot be asserted that the situation in the Romanian and the Moldavian markets is identical (although much alike from the consumer preferences point of view), the possibility of comparing physically identical or economically equivalent items was constrained, to some extent, although the second comparability principle, namely, representativity, was not neglected. Thus, the quality adjustments, a typical feature of comparisons within Group II, could not be avoided in the case of the bilateral comparison between Romania and Moldova (they were, however, few in number).

Experience with this practical tool had already been gained in comparison rounds in which Romania participated and in several discussions between the two countries' experts, examining the issues in detail in order to distinguish the discrepancies to be adjusted/removed. In short, it is well known that the theoretical background to support such quality adjustment does not yet exist, so we "learned by doing."

As concerns the C-type quality adjustments, the bulk of them were made by the State Statistical Department. Either the differences on the selling or packing units were adjusted, or the prices were adjusted in the case of a priced item that was noncomparable because of a single parameter in direct relation with price.

In any event, the adjustment as such did not raise serious challenges.

In some cases, the Romanians changed the items proposed at the beginning in order that they be comparable to the Moldavian items.

The P-type quality adjustments solving the quality differences that are noticed but that cannot be directly measured were subject to uncertainty. To remove these differences, which could have affected the Romania-Moldova comparison results, we utilized the experience of the Romania-Austria comparison, employing, for instance, the "analogy method."

Following the bilateral debates, the adjustment factors were agreed on, and, even if they remain subjective, arbitrary, and nonscientific, they obviously improved the comparison results. Thus, for the items belonging to population final consumption, there were twenty-four P-type quality adjustments (their breakdown by commodity groups is illustrated in table 9.1). For machinery and equipment, there were six P-type quality adjustments.

After the preliminary computation of individual price ratios and of the basic headings, unweighted geometric averages were calculated and the relations between the price ratios within the groups analyzed: some initial prices were revised or some items removed when the dispersion of the individual price ratios was high relative to the group average or when there were significant differences between the Moldavian prices for different items.

It must be pointed out that, for much of 1993, Moldavian product prices were in rubles, the national currency being at the time the Soviet ruble and the so called Moldavian coupon. On 30 November 1993, the ruble was replaced with the *leu moldovenesc,* the current national currency. Consequently, even if the Moldavian product prices had been computed in rubles, they were converted in Moldavian lei on the basis of the Moldavian lei/ruble ratio holding as of 30 November 1993.

Finally, 408 consumer goods and services, 36 equipment goods, and 6 construction objectives remained in the comparison.

At the Kishinev meeting in January 1995, the last meeting before the preliminary computations, which an ACSO expert also attended, the benchmark PPP was agreed on to recompute the expenditure on those commodity groups for which representative goods and services were not selected (especially for equipment).

9.6   Results of the Romania–Republic of Moldova Comparison

The detailed data obtained from the Romania–Republic of Moldova bilateral comparison were analyzed by Austrian experts on the occasion of the bilateral Austria-Romania meeting at the beginning of May 1995. All the proposals and results were debated with the Moldavian experts at the last bilateral Romania-Moldova meeting at the end of May 1995. On that occasion, it was agreed that the Moldavian experts would reexamine some data from the content point of view (in accordance with the ECP methodology) and transmit corrections and explanations.

According to bilateral Romania-Moldova results (see tables 9.3 and 9.4), Moldavian GDP per capita was 590,897.66 Romanian leu, representing 63.7

Table 9.3   **Bilateral Results: Main Indicators**

	Romania	Moldova
GDP in national currency (billions)	19,738	2,210.514
PPP (Romanian leu)	1	.0009199
GDP converted to Romanian leu using PPP (billions)	19,738	2,403
Overall volume index	100.0	12.17
Volume index for household consumption	100.0	10.8
Volume index for gross fixed capital formation	100.0	6.5
PPP for household consumption	1	.0009091
PPP for gross fixed capital formation	1	.0013660
Relative price-level index for gross fixed capital formation	100.0	148.5
Relative price-level index for household consumption	100.0	98.8

Table 9.4   **Share of Main Components in GDP per Capita, Volume Indexes, and Purchasing Power Parities**

	GDP/Inhabitant			
	Structure (%) Computed in Romanian Leu		Moldova as against Romania (%)	PPP (Moldavian leu/ Romanian leu)
	Romania	Moldova		
Total GDP	100.0	100.0	63.7	.0009199
Population final consumption	68.1	57.8	56.2	.0009091
Collective consumption of government	6.9	8.3	90.7	.0009401
Gross fixed capital formation	15.8	9.5	34.1	.0013660
Changes in inventories	14.2	31.5	150.3	.0009873
Net exports of goods and services	−5.0	−7.1	95.9	.0021900

percent of that of Romania. The total volume of goods and services purchased in Romania was 8.21 times that in Moldova.

Unlike the exchange rate, which takes into account the short-term economic and financial situation, expressed through relations in the field of commercial and financial transactions, PPP expresses the ratio between prices employed in the internal markets of both countries. The overall ratio is the result of a comparison of ratios determined for 295 basic headings, on the basis of individual indexes of representative product prices within each commodity group, taking into account the quality adjustment and the differences between the technical parameters of products. PPP for the overall GDP, computed on the basis of Fisher indexes, eliminating the structural differences, is of 0.0009199 Moldavian leu/1 Romanian leu as against 0.00219 Moldavian leu/1 Romanian leu, which is the average official commercial exchange rate for 1993; therefore, the ratio between the exchange rate and parity is about 2.4:1. This result reflects the tendency of the less-developed countries to underestimate real purchasing power by using the exchange rate. The discrepancy is a result of the differences between the prices employed on national market, especially for goods and services that are not subject to external trade. Dividing the PPP by the exchange rate, the comparative price-level index is obtained, statistical information well understood and often used by those traveling abroad. Thus, to buy the same volume of GDP in Romania and Moldova, one would pay one hundred Romanian leu and forty-two Romanian leu, respectively. One can conclude that Romanian tourists find the Republic of Moldova a cheap tourist destination.

Vis-à-vis the GDP price level, equipment goods prices are 48.5 percent higher and consumer goods and services prices 1.2 percent lower in Moldova than in Romania.

The results of the bilateral comparison were transmitted to the ACSO, to ensure the linkage computation with Austria, and in this way they could be linked in a European comparison.

10 A Critique of CIA Estimates of Soviet Performance from the Gerschenkron Perspective

Yuri Dikhanov

In this paper, I briefly discuss some information on comparisons from sources other than the CIA or ICP that can be brought to bear in calculating the Soviet Union/United States GDP ratio (for a discussion of CIA estimates, see Maddison 1998). The Soviet Union took part in the Comecon comparisons. These were conducted every five years (the last was done in 1988) and covered not only national income but also industrial and agricultural production and investments in considerable detail. Of these countries, several (Poland, Yugoslavia, Romania, and Hungary) had also taken part in the ICP exercises in various years. Thus, they can serve as a bridge between the Soviet Union and, for example, the United States. Also, I should like to mention the special Soviet Union–Hungary (1985) and Soviet Union–Germany (1988) GDP binary comparisons that were made according to the full ICP methodology, which an inquisitive observer can apply as links in the Soviet Union–United States comparison. The last two comparisons were broadly consistent with the later 1990 ICP exercise in which the Soviet Union took part for the first time.

It seems to me, however, that a part of the problem encountered in the Soviet Union–United States comparisons is of a broader methodological nature and is, in fact, inherent to any comparison or growth rate calculation. Moreover, this issue may influence the outcome of a comparison considerably more than deficiencies in basic numbers that arise from suspected under- or overreporting, hidden military expenditures, etc. or even quality differentials (let us call them *real* differences due to basic data). I refer here to the index number prob-

Yuri Dikhanov is employed with the Development Economics Department of the World Bank, Washington, D.C. He has worked in the areas of index number theory and international comparisons as well as macro modeling.
This paper was originally a comment on a paper presented at the conference but not published in this volume, "Measuring the Performance of a Communist Command Economy: An Assessment of the CIA Estimates for the U.S.S.R." by Angus Maddison.

lem. This problem has become so acute in recent years that the Bureau of Economic Analysis (BEA) has recently abandoned fixed-based indexes in the national accounts of the United States altogether. I will illustrate this assertion that a more fundamental core problem lurks concealed in the series by reference to mostly U.S. numbers that may be deemed more reliable. As an additional consideration in using U.S. numbers, it is only fair to look closely at the other side of the Soviet Union–United States comparisons instead of assuming the U.S. numbers as given.

10.1   Index Number Problem

The issue goes back to the classic index number problem. Alexander Gerschenkron was really the first to pay close attention to this question in comparisons—across countries and time (growth rates). In his now classic *Dollar Index of Soviet Machinery Output* (1951), he investigated not only Soviet machinery output but also American machinery output in similar detail. His estimate, which gave rise to the term *Gerschenkron effect*, was based on calculations for the American machinery industry.[1] Specifically, he estimated the growth of American machinery production during 1899–39 at both 1899 and 1939 prices. His results are quoted in panel A of table 10.1.

Gerschenkron (1951, 55) went on to state, "Clearly, in the case of formidable differentials of this sort no adjustment of the index will do. Naturally, there would be nothing meaningful, let alone 'ideal', about taking the square root of the product of 1542 and 198 [he refers here to the Fisher index, which is sometimes called *ideal*]. The difference of regimens must be accepted and taken into account rather than disguised by some mode of averaging it, even though the result may meet certain technical tests." Similar effects can still be

---

1. The Gerschenkron effect is intrinsically related to the Paasche-Laspeyres spread (PLS). Let us define Q_L as the *quantity Laspeyres index* and Q_P as the *quantity Paasche index*. Then we can express the PLS as

$$PLS = \frac{Q_P}{Q_L} = 1 + r_{p.q}\sigma_{\frac{p}{r_L}}\sigma_{\frac{q}{Q_L}},$$

where $\sigma_{p/P}, \sigma_{q/Q}$ = weighted variances in relative prices and quantities, and $r_{p.q}$ = weighted coefficient of correlation between price and quantity relatives.

The expression given above simply states that the Laspeyres index exceeds the Paasche index if the correlation between relative price and quantity changes is negative, i.e., if the direction of movements in price ratios en masse is opposite to those in quantity ratios (or most of the product mix are normal goods). This intuitively looks right: if technical change (or something else) makes products cheaper, then their consumption increases; or, when some goods experience a price shock, their consumption decreases. Moreover, it can be observed that the hypothesis of normality of goods is validated by the whole experience of the ICP: examining a table of the PLS compiled from the ICP results for different years, one can find that the PLS is *always* less than unity for any pair of countries.

The Paasche-Laspeyres spread has a deep economic sense: all indexes allowing an economic interpretation are bounded by these two indexes, including those corresponding to nonhomothetic utility functions.

Table 10.1   **Effect of Base Year on Some U.S. Manufacturing Volume Indexes**

A. Indexes and growth rates of machinery output in the United States
    during 1899–1939 (1899 = 100):[a]
    At 1899 prices   1,542 (7.1% per year)
    At 1939 prices   198 (1.7% per year)
B. Annual growth rates (%) of expenditures on producers' durable
    equipment in the United States during 1959–87:[b]
    At 1959 prices   26.1
    At 1987 prices   4.7
C. Annual growth rates (%) of manufacturing output in the United
    States during 1977–1987:[c]
    At 1977 prices   4.7
    At 1987 prices   1.6

[a]From Gerschenkron (1951, 52).
[b]From Young (1992, tables B and D). Young does not show the 1959-based index explicitly, but
he does provide the corresponding 1987-based price index (−13.6 percent, table D); the two
together when multiplied over produce the index of nominal change (+9.0 percent). From there,
we can find the 1959-based quantity index as (100 + 9.0)/(100 − 13.6) = 126.1.
[c]From Young (1992, 34).

observed in the United States (only on a larger scale): discrepancies in indexes
for the producers' durable equipment category of the GDP are even more mani-
fest during 1959–87. The difference between the two indexes (the Paasche-
Laspeyres spread) amounts to 20 percent a year in this case (see panel B of
table 10.1).

The examples given above probably tell us that the Gerschenkron effect has
become even more pronounced since World War II. One can notice, however,
that the time differential between the base years is forty and twenty-eight years,
respectively. During that time, one can expect immense changes in the product
mix and relative prices. But what would happen if the time span were smaller?
Another example from the same source, this time concerned with manufacturing output, is even more dramatic because the two base years are separated by
only ten years (see panel C of table 10.1).

The above conveys the difficulties of making adequate comparisons (both
cross-time and cross-country) in such a fast-moving world. We can now describe this effect in more detail:

The Gerschenkron effect can be defined as follows: For any pair of countries
(or years), a quantity index (GDP, industrial production, consumption, etc.)
for a given country (year) at another country's (year's) prices will be higher
than the index at that country's (year's) own prices.

Thus, the Soviet Union/United States GDP ratio as measured at U.S. prices
will always be higher than that measured at Soviet prices, just as the United
States/Soviet Union GDP ratio computed at Soviet prices will come out higher
than the same ratio at U.S. prices. For growth rates (both positive and negative), the effect would result in the following: the growth rates would always

be higher when computed at the beginning year's prices, and lower if estimated at the concluding year's prices.

Given the above examples, it is in no way surprising that the CIA results are different from the official growth rates (7.2 vs. 3.7 percent for 1913–50 for Soviet industry). But it *is* surprising that they differ so little given the fact that the official industrial growth rates were computed at 1926/27 prices.

Against this background, it does not seem unreasonable for the indexes calculated on the basis of different methodologies to differ that much.[2] In such comparisons involving time series, the main emphasis should be on making the time series for two countries completely compatible from a methodological perspective, that is, using a set of common prices and identical index numbers. The common price vector would enforce compatibility between growth rates and levels at different time points. One cannot calculate growth rates of Soviet manufacturing at 1987 Soviet prices and U.S. manufacturing at 1987 U.S. prices and expect both growth rates to be compatible. The 1987 Soviet prices may be even further from the 1987 U.S. prices than are the 1967 U.S. own prices. However, from panel C of table 10.1, we know what just a ten-year difference in base years can do to the growth rates.

10.2   Contrasting CIA and Goskomstat Estimates of GDP Levels

It is known that the CIA estimates portrayed the Soviet Union more favorably than Goskomstat itself: the CIA had 49 percent for the GNP ratio for 1990 (Fisher index), with a corresponding GNP per capita number of 42.5 percent. For 1987, Goskomstat estimated the GNP ratio at 58 percent (64 percent for net material product [NMP]). However, that estimate was based on U.S. prices. For the Fisher index, the GNP ratio would amount to approximately 45.5 percent,[3] which in turn would render the GNP per capita ratio for 1987 at around 39 percent. Again, extrapolated to 1990, this ratio would become 36 percent. Actually, one can observe that the corresponding Goskomstat GNP per capita number was rather close to the 1990 ICP results:[4] 31.6 percent. On the other

2. That an index employs a certain index number formula does not automatically make it right or wrong. That index just cannot be considered in conjunction with another index utilizing some other aggregation procedure. Only the differences between indexes that are irreducible to the index number problem (i.e., distortion in basic physical units, misrepresentation of prices) can be regarded as "real" differences.

3. The ratio of ruble- and schilling-based GDP estimates for the Soviet Union (the Paasche-Laspeyres spread) in the 1990 Soviet Union–Austria comparison was around 0.617 (ECE 1994). That makes the ratio of the Fisher to the Schilling-based numbers $0.785 = (0.617)^{1/2}$. I use the same ratio in a shortcut to render the Goskomstat U.S. dollar–based results into the Fisher index. In reality, the PLS could be even more dramatic in a Soviet Union–United States direct comparison because usually, the more countries are different in GDP per capita terms, the further the Paasche index stands from the Laspeyres.

4. Linked through the 1985 Hungary–Soviet Union comparison to the Austria–United States pair, the Soviet Union/United States GDP per capita ratio stood at 38 percent in that year. Extrapolated to 1990, this ratio would have decreased to 35 percent. A part of the difference between this

Table 10.2   CIA Soviet Union/United States Ratios Contrasted to Official Goskomstat Estimates (%)

	1960	1987
CIA (GNP, Fisher)	48	53
Goskomstat (NMP, U.S. dollars)	58	64

Source: CIA estimates from Becker (1994), Goskomstat estimates from statistical yearbooks from various years.

hand, it is not improbable that, being naturally focused on Soviet military expenditures, the CIA could have been exaggerating their value. In this case, in fact, apart from an understandable disagreement over Soviet military expenditures, the CIA and Goskomstat numbers come out surprisingly similar. Moreover, the changes in Soviet Union/United States GDP ratios over time according to official Soviet estimates correlate very closely with those from the CIA sources (see table 10.2): both stipulate a 10 percent increase during 1960–87.

10.3 Conclusions

It would be very useful indeed to make the CIA archives containing documentation on the estimates of Soviet performance available to the public. That would enable further finessing of Soviet historical time series. However, it would be no less important for the United States to continue full participation in the ICP to remain an anchor in the future long-term economic comparisons (in a broader sense and not only with the Soviet Union/Russia). The ICOP (International Comparisons of Output and Productivity) project begot by Maddison can serve as an extremely valuable tool to cross-check the ICP results from various benchmarks and national growth rates. Finally, as can be seen, the methodological index number issues are of paramount importance and need to be thoroughly addressed in any such comparison to make the results compatible across countries.

References

Becker, Abraham. 1994. Intelligence fiasco or reasoned accounting? CIA estimates of Soviet GNP. *Post-Soviet Affairs* 10, no. 4:291–329.

number and the 1990 ECP result (31.6 percent) can be attributed to productivity adjustments in services made in the 1990 ECP comparison but not in the 1985 exercise. The other part can be attributed to lack of consistency between national growth rates and changes in ICP benchmark results for the United States and Austria (bridge country). This inconsistency amounted to 12 percent during 1985–90 (it is within the ICP error range, however).

Economic Commission for Europe (ECE). 1994. *International comparison of gross domestic product in Europe, 1990.* New York and Geneva: United Nations.

Gerschenkron, Alexander. 1951. *A dollar index of Soviet machinery output, 1927–28 to 1937.* Santa Monica, Calif.: Rand.

Maddison, Angus. 1998. Measuring the performance of a communist command economy: An assessment of the CIA estimates for the U.S.S.R. *Review of Income and Wealth,* ser. 44 (3): 307–23.

Young, Allan. 1992. Alternative measures of change in real output and prices. *Survey of Current Business* 72, no. 4:32–48.

IV

Reports from the International Comparisons of Output and Productivity Program

11   The Measurement of Performance in Distribution, Transport, and Communications: The ICOP Approach Applied to Brazil, Mexico, France, and the United States

Nanno Mulder

This paper presents new methods for comparing output and productivity in transport, communications, and wholesale and retail trade[1] among countries. Although the importance of these services combined surpasses that of manufacturing in terms of employment in most countries, they receive little attention in research on international productivity comparisons. The main reasons for this are the nontradability of these services and the difficulty of measuring physical output, which is a central part of productivity analysis. However, their large share in total employment makes them an important determinant of overall productivity, and, therefore, they merit more study.

Productivity is measured by value added per employee. In order to compare value added among countries, a converter is needed to express value added in a common currency. For this purpose, I use purchasing power parity (PPP), which is the price of a service in one country relative to that in another. The paper presents new methods for estimating the relative price of these services. For transport, I made separate estimates for the loading and unloading of freight and passengers and included these in the total output measure, in contrast to traditional approaches, which consider only the movement of freight and passengers. Differences in the quality of the transport service rendered among countries are also taken into account. For wholesale and retail trade, PPPs were derived by traditional single deflation and by a new double deflation procedure, using expenditure PPPs for sales and industry-of-origin PPPs for purchases of distributive establishments.

Nanno Mulder is an economist at the Centre d'Etudes Prospectives et d'Informations Internationales.

This research was conducted at the Groningen Growth and Development Centre of the University of Groningen. The author is grateful to Angus Maddison for comments on a draft of this paper. This research was supported by the Dutch Foundation for Scientific Research (NWO).

1. These services combined are referred to in the text as *distributive services*.

These methods were tested in binary comparisons between Brazil, Mexico, and France, on the one hand, and the United States, the international productivity leader, on the other. Table 11.1 presents the main results for the benchmark years: 1975 for the Brazil/United States and Mexico/United States comparisons and 1987 for the France/United States comparison. Time series of GDP at constant prices, population, and employment were used to extrapolate the results for the period 1970–93 (for a description of sources, see app. B). Brazilian productivity and per capita income levels in transport and communications improved relative to the U.S. levels until 1982, after which its performance worsened. The wholesale and retail trade performance in Mexico showed a slow catch-up process relative to the United States until 1982. Between 1982 and 1993, relative productivity and income per capita fell by more than 15 percentage points in these services. Wholesale trade in France was characterized by falling relative per capita and productivity levels from 1970 to 1993. The retail per capita income level fell, whereas productivity improved relative to the United States. The French transport performance improved until 1982, whereas that of communications continued to rise until 1990.

11.1 Value Added and Employment

Table 11.2 shows value added and employment in distributive services. The contribution of a sector to overall GDP is best measured by value added,[2] assuming that the degree of competition is similar across industries and countries.[3] To utilize the advantage of census information over national accounts,[4] I focus on census data where possible. Although the coverage of economic activity of the national accounts is superior, census data are often more reliable in countries such as Brazil and Mexico. Census data constitute the basic source for wholesale and retail trade and transport, except for the United States. The national accounts were used when exploring transport in the United States and communications in all countries.

Wholesale trade accounted for a larger share of value added and a lower share of employment than retail trade in all countries, except for Mexico, where it represented only 24 percent of the total value added in distribution. Therefore, productivity was much higher in wholesale than in retail trade. The share of nondurables in wholesale trade seemed negatively correlated with in-

---

2. The gross value of output as a "contribution measure" would involve double-counting the production of other industries because of the inclusion of inputs.

3. If this assumption is not fulfilled, then higher value added may represent monopoly power rather than production. The degree of competition was similar in the services studied here, except in railways, airlines, postal services, and telecommunications in Brazil, Mexico, and France. The overstatement of production in these countries by the value-added measure is probably similar. Therefore, the productivity results of Brazil and Mexico vis-à-vis those of the United States remain comparable.

4. Census information is preferred over the national accounts because of its greater detail and the internal consistency of output and employment data.

Table 11.1   Value Added per Capita and Value Added per Person Engaged in Distributive Services, 1970–93

	Value Added per Head of Population (United States = 100)						Value Added per Person Engaged (United States = 100)					
	1970	1975	1982	1987	1990	1993	1970	1975	1982	1987	1990	1993
Brazil/United States												
Distribution	9.9	12.9	11.4	9.6	8.0	7.3	35.7	35.2	30.1	23.9	18.2	15.8
Transport & communications	3.4	5.2	6.2	5.6	5.0	4.7	20.7	27.5	33.9	29.8	22.1	25.6
Mexico/United States												
Distribution	25.2	27.6	32.8	21.8	21.4	17.6	27.9	29.0	31.3	22.8	20.8	18.8
Transport & communications	15.5	21.3	25.5	18.6	18.5	18.8	25.9	28.8	24.1	20.6	22.4	20.9
France/United States												
Distribution:	65.2	66.7	62.4	54.2	56.0	51.1	62.3	65.2	68.5	68.6	71.7	68.8
Wholesale trade	66.5	66.5	56.2	50.3	52.8	N.A.	61.6	61.1	54.8	53.3	56.8	N.A.
Retail trade	65.7	67.8	67.8	57.2	58.2	N.A.	63.3	67.6	78.3	77.6	80.4	N.A.
Transport	88.9	108.3	118.1	100.4	89.3	81.2	74.3	84.6	92.2	84.2	91.9	77.9
Communications	57.9	60.4	79.5	91.8	111.7	116.5	33.4	33.6	43.8	43.4	54.5	52.7

Sources: GDP per capita for benchmark years was converted by the Fisher PPPs (see tables 11.5 and 11.10 below) and extrapolated using GDP at constant prices series as described in app. B. Population series are from Maddison (1995). Labor productivity estimates for benchmark estimates are from tables 11.6 and 11.11 below and extrapolated using a series of GDP at constant prices and employment as described in app. B.

Table 11.2   Value Added and Employment in Distributive Services: Brazil (1975), Mexico (1975), France (1987), and the United States (1975/77, 1987)

	Nominal Value Added (millions national currency)					Persons Engaged (thousands)				
	Brazil, 1975	Mexico, 1975	France, 1987	United States 1975/77	United States 1987	Brazil, 1975	Mexico, 1975	France, 1987	United States 1975/77	United States 1987
Wholesale trade										
Durables	26,901	7,696	124,461	99,693	136,092	127	47	508	2,458	3,182
Nondurables	55,123	11,188	97,936	79,373	99,353	248	80	428	1,817	2,295
Food	11,701	3,769	36,240	23,630	28,132	102	29	175	613	771
Total (all branches)	82,024	18,185	222,397	179,065	235,445	375	127	937	4,276	5,477
Retail trade										
Durables	40,239	31,457	106,077	66,991	121,517	521	246	697	4,815	4,014
Nondurables	36,890	27,646	195,610	58,556	186,061	1,425	696	1,392	4,652	8,415
Food	17,886	15,264	111,559	26,265	61,268	852	475	817	2,042	3,047
Total (all branches)	77,128	59,103	301,686	125,547	307,578	1,946	942	2,089	9,467	12,429
Distribution	159,152	77,988	524,084	304,612	543,023	2,321	1,069	3,026	13,743	17,906

tant in Brazil, Mexico, and France was road passenger transport, but the proportion was much smaller (6.1 percent) in the United States, where private car ownership is so widespread. Private passenger transport is not regarded here as a market activity. It does not enter the national accounts and is therefore excluded from the sectoral totals.[7] U.S. railways and air transport accounted for a much larger share of transport GDP than their Brazilian, Mexican, and French counterparts. Telecommunications is the major part of the communications sector in all countries. Most employees were engaged in road goods transport in Mexico, France, and the United States, whereas in Brazil road passenger transport was the primary employment source. The second most important branch of transport in Brazil, Mexico, France, and the United States was trucking, road passenger transport, transport services, and railways, respectively. No breakdown existed of GDP and employment in communications. Working hours were available only for France and the United States: in 1987, road passenger transport was the branch with the most and rail and air transport those with the least hours worked per person. Persons engaged in transport and communications in France worked on average 1,725 and 1,556 hours, respectively, compared to 1,899 and 1,780 hours, respectively, in the United States (Mulder 1994c).

11.2   The Assessment of Sectoral Output, PPPs, and Productivity

The exchange rate is a poor indicator of the relative price of a service[8] and is therefore not used here. Instead, I estimated PPPs, representing the price of a good or service in relation to the price of that same item in another country. A major part of Mulder (1999) deals with the estimation of PPPs for services on a detailed level. This was difficult because, for this part of the economy, little price information was available. In cases where no prices were available, they were derived implicitly with the use of quantity indicators representing the output of a service. For some services produced, the measurement of quantity is relatively straightforward, for example, liters of water distributed. However, for many services, such as wholesale and retail trade and health care, it is unclear what production is. Mulder (1999) developed several techniques to estimate the output of these comparison-resistant services.

7. Per capita expenditure on (public and private) passenger transport in 1975 was Cr\$690 in Brazil, \$1,027 in Mexico, and U.S.\$600 in the United States. Private (mainly car) transport expenditure accounted for 74.9 percent of the total in Brazil, 66.5 percent in Mexico, and 93.3 percent in the United States. The imputed value of private passenger transport was Cr\$55,562 million in Brazil, \$41,081 million in Mexico, and U.S.\$120,901 in the United States (see Kravis, Heston, and Summers 1982, 272). Transport GDP was Cr\$36,759 million, \$55,158 million, and U.S.\$57,095, respectively.
Note: Throughout this paper, the symbol "\$" will indicate the Mexican peso and "U.S.\$" the U.S. dollar.
8. The exchange rate is at best an indicator of the relative price of tradables. However, most distributive services are not traded between countries. Relative prices may also deviate from the exchange rate because the latter is targeted by monetary policy or affected by capital flows.

As many as possible services within each branch were matched. For each service, a PPP is calculated by dividing its producer price in country X (Brazil, Mexico, or France) by its price in the base country U (the United States). Producer prices are not available for the services treated here. However, price relatives were derived implicitly using the indirect method shown below: quantity ratios of the service industry j (Q_{ij}^X/Q_{ij}^U) were weighted by their corresponding values of output in national currencies of either country X or country U (see eqq. [1] and [2]). Using the values of output of country X ($GVO_{ij}^{X(X)}$) as weights equals a Paasche price index:

$$(1) \qquad PPP_j^{XU(X)} = \frac{\sum_{i=1}^{r}\left[GVO_{ij}^{X(X)} \Big/ \dfrac{Q_{ij}^X}{Q_{ij}^U}\right]}{GVO_j^{U(U)}}.$$

Using the base country's values of output ($GVO_{ij}^{U(U)}$) yields a Laspeyres price index:

$$(2) \qquad PPP_j^{XU(U)} = \frac{GVO_j^{X(X)}}{\sum_{i=1}^{r}\left[\dfrac{Q_{ij}^X}{Q_{ij}^U} \times GVO_{ij}^{U(U)}\right]},$$

where $i = 1, \ldots, r$ is the sample of matched items within the matched industry j. The United States is the denominator in both formulas as it is the base country.

The second stage of aggregation from the industry to the branch level was made by weighting the PPPs for gross output as derived above by value added (VA) in national currencies of either U.S. or the own country's industry. Value added is a superior measure of the contribution to GDP than the gross value of output because it excludes intermediate inputs that are the output of other industries. When country X's industry value added in national currency is used, a Paasche PPP for branch k is obtained:

$$(3) \qquad PPP_k^{XU(X)} = \frac{VA_k^X}{\sum_{j=1}^{r}[VA_j^X/PPP_{j(go)}^{XU(X)}]}.$$

where the subscript go stands for gross output. Or, when U.S. industry value added in U.S. dollars is used as a weight, a Laspeyres PPP for branch k is obtained:

$$(4) \qquad PPP_k^{XU(U)} = \frac{\sum_{j=1}^{r}[PPP_{j(go)}^{XU(U)} \times VA_j^U]}{VA_k^U},$$

where $j = 1, \ldots, r$ are the industries j in branch k, and VA is value added in national currency. Branch PPPs were aggregated to the total sector level using value-added weights as well. The geometric average of the Paasche and Laspeyres PPPs is the Fisher PPP.

The benchmark year for the Brazil/United States and Mexico/United States comparisons was 1975 because this year was in the middle of the period 1950–93 and because my benchmark results could be compared with those of the International Comparison Project (ICP) of Kravis, Heston, and Summers (1982). The France/United States comparison was for 1987, which was, at the time the comparison was carried out, the most recent year for which census results were available in the United States.

11.2.1   Transport and Communications

The methods of measuring physical output in transport and communications have varied. Researchers most often used the ton kilometer and the passenger kilometer,[9] tons transported, passengers handled at airports or subways, the vehicle kilometer, or pieces of mail sent. Several studies included aggregated physical output of branches by weighting each branch by "unit values" (cost or revenue per kilometer).

Various authors (see Hariton and Roy 1979; Meyer and Gómez-Ibáñez 1980; and Scheppach and Woehlcke 1975) have criticized the ton kilometer and the passenger kilometer yardstick because it fails to take into account the "terminal" cost of loading and unloading. A zero growth of the number of ton kilometers of goods transported in a certain period does not necessarily mean a zero growth of output. One should also consider the average distance over which these goods were transported, which gives an indication of the volume of terminal work. If the average distance falls over time, the proportionate amount of terminal work will increase, as will overall transport output. Meyer and Gómez-Ibáñez (1980) found that Kendrick (1973), who used the ton kilometer as the output measure, overstated U.S. intercity trucking output (and productivity) growth in 1948–70 because the average distance increased over time and the relative importance of terminal work declined. Deakin and Seward (1969) weighted passenger and freight kilometers by the price per kilometer in 1962 in order to adjust for terminal work; for example, a higher price per kilometer was assumed to indicate a larger amount of terminal work. This overlooks the fact that price differences may also reflect differences in the type of commodity transported or quality of the service.

The freight (or passenger) kilometer measure also fails to adjust for the type and quality of transport. Bulk transport is very different from transport of meat or jewelry. Meyer and Morton (1975) made this point, criticizing conventional measures of trends in U.S. railways in 1947–70 because they failed to account

---

9. The transport of one ton of goods or one passenger over a distance of one kilometer generates a ton kilometer or passenger kilometer (see Barger 1951; Deakin and Seward 1969; Kendrick 1973; Pilat 1994; and Sandoval 1987).

for shifts in the composition of goods transported. The share of passenger traffic, which is more expensive than goods transport, also declined over time. Most authors neglect this point (except for Meyer and Gómez-Ibáñez 1980),[10] probably because of empirical difficulties of measurement.

Some who have written on international comparisons use only physical measures of output, for example, freight and passenger kilometer (Girard 1958; Gadrey, Noyelle, and Stanback 1990) or number of calls and access lines (Rostas 1948; Paige and Bombach 1959). Other studies weight physical output by relative prices (e.g., revenue per passenger kilometer or freight kilometer), deriving Laspeyres and Paasche PPPs, which they then use to convert output into a common currency. When countries with very different average freight hauls or passenger trip lengths are compared, the output measure should take separate account of loading and unloading costs and services that will be more important proportionately in a country with shorter hauls. A number of studies neglect terminal work (Rostas 1948; Girard 1958; Mulder 1991; Pilat 1994); others explicitly include it in the total output measure (Paige and Bombach 1959; Smith, Hitchens, and Davies 1982).

Physical output produced in transport consists essentially of two parts: (a) moving freight or passengers over a certain distance ("movement services") and (b) loading and unloading ("terminal") services. Appendix tables 11A.1–11A.3 present the movement and terminal services for my three binary comparisons. The estimation of physical output is explained below for each mode of transport, using the Mexico/United States example.

Rail Transport

Freight transport is the predominant rail activity in Mexico and the United States: gross revenues from freight accounted for 98 percent of railway revenue in the United States in 1975 and 97 percent in 1987, 94 percent in Mexico, 89 percent in Brazil, and 34 percent in France (see tables 11A.1–11A.3).

To get an impression of the amount of terminal work in Mexico and the United States, the average distances are compared in table 11.3. The average freight haul was 870 kilometers in the United States and 532 kilometers in Mexico. The average passenger journey was 59 kilometers in the United States and 168 kilometers in Mexico in 1975. While terminal work in freight transport had relatively more importance in Mexico compared to the United States, data for passenger transport show the opposite. Local train transport was regrouped from railways to bus transport in 1987 to match French transport activity, explaining the longer passenger trip relative to 1975. Output estimates that make no allowance for terminal services would underestimate Mexican

10. They analyzed long-term trends in the quality of U.S. mass transit. On the one hand, quality improved over time because of the introduction of air-conditioning, the increase in the speed of the vehicle, and the decrease in the crowded conditions (measured by passenger per vehicle kilometer). Offsetting declines in quality took also place, especially in terms of the frequency of service.

Table 11.3 Length of Average Passenger Trip and Average Freight Haul in Kilometers: Brazil/United States, 1975; France/United States, 1987; and Mexico/United States, 1975

	Brazil, 1975	France, 1987	Mexico, 1975	United States 1975	United States 1987	Share of Terminal Services Brazil/ United States	Share of Terminal Services France/ United States	Share of Terminal Services Mexico/ United States
Passenger transport								
Rail	36	76	168	59	417	.39	.82	.65
Bus		121			106		.12	
Air								
Domestic	831			1,121		.26		
International	3,914			3,127		.20		
Total	1,385	1,588	999	1,334	1,452		.09	.25
Freight transport								
Rail	469	349	532	870	1,107	.46	.68	.39
Road	343		323	523		.34		.38
Domestic water		146		614			.76	

Sources: Average distances estimated by ratio of passenger kilometers to passsenger or by ratio of ton kilometers to tons (see appendix tables 11A.1–11A.3).

Note: The share of terminal services is estimated as explained in the text.

freight transport and overstate passenger transport. At least six ways to impute the varying proportionate importance of loading and unloading services exist:

a. When similar hauls prevail among countries, the proportionate amount of terminal work should be equal for each country, implying that freight kilometers and passenger kilometers are good proxies for transport output.

b. Separate costs, output, and employment of a branch for movement and terminal services (e.g., a split of air transport into flight and ground services), with estimation of PPPs and productivity for each service separately.

c. Split costs into movement and terminal components (Smith, Hitchens, and Davies 1982), and estimate PPPs for each separately. Subsequently, estimate a PPP for total transport by weighting the individual PPPs.

d. Estimate PPPs on the basis of prices in each country that reflect the proportionally higher costs of transporting goods over shorter distances.[11]

e. Correct the physical output measure by the relative cost of operating short- and long-distance haulage.

f. Adjust the physical output measure to take account of terminal work. Two indicators may be used: the ton kilometer for movement and the ton for the terminal work (Paige and Bombach 1959). A total output index can be constructed weighting each component by the shares of transport and terminal cost in total cost.

Data limitations did not permit the use of methods *b–e*. Therefore, method *f* was used to account for terminal work. Data on the share of terminal services in total costs were lacking, so I developed an indirect method to estimate the component shares of total output, as explained below.

I estimated U.S. relative output (Q^{USA}) by a composite index in which Mexican output (Q^{MX}) equaled one hundred. This composite index was derived from the weighted average of (i) the relative amount of U.S. freight or passenger movement compared to Mexico and (ii) the relative amount of U.S. terminal services compared to Mexico (see eq. [5]). M^{USA} and M^{MX} represent the movement of freight or passengers in the United States and Mexico, respectively, and are measured by the number of ton kilometers or passenger kilometers. T^{USA} and T^{MX} represent terminal services in the United States and in Mexico, respectively, and are measured by the amount of tons of freight or number of passengers loaded or unloaded. The weights are $(1 - S)$ for movement services (i.e., M^{USA}/M^{MX}) and S for the terminal services (i.e., T^{USA}/T^{MX}). The weight S lies between zero and one.

---

11. Smith, Hitchens, and Davies (1982) cite data from British sample surveys of road goods transport in the mid-1960s to estimate transport charges broken down between a terminal charge and a charge per kilometer of haul: $Y = a + b \times X$, in which Y = transport charge per ton, X the length of haul, a is the intercept representing the terminal charge for a specific commodity, and b is the increment in cost for each kilometer of haul. Coefficients for different commodity groups were used with data on tons carried and lengths of haul in order to derive a price ratio for the United States/United Kingdom. This price ratio was used to convert U.S. output.

$$(5) \qquad Q^{\text{USA}} = \left[(1 - S)\frac{M^{\text{USA}}}{M^{\text{MX}}} + S\frac{T^{\text{USA}}}{T^{\text{MX}}}\right] \times 100, \quad Q^{\text{MX}} = 100,$$

$$(6a) \qquad S = \left(1 - \frac{H^{\text{MX}}}{H^{\text{USA}}}\right) \text{ if } H^{\text{MX}} < H^{\text{USA}}$$

or

$$(6b) \qquad S = \left(1 - \frac{H^{\text{USA}}}{H^{\text{MX}}}\right) \text{ if } H^{\text{MX}} > H^{\text{USA}}.$$

The share S was derived by calculating the difference between the Mexican and the U.S. average freight haul or passenger trip, according to equation (6a) or (6b). H^{USA} and H^{MX} represent the average distance over which freight or passengers were transported in 1975 in the United States and Mexico, respectively (see table 11.3). The greater the difference between H^{USA} and H^{MX}, the higher S will be (i.e., the greater the weight of terminal services in the composite index). Below, two examples are presented of the derivation of U.S. relative output: rail freight (longer U.S. haul compared to Mexico) and rail passenger transport (Mexican average trip length is longer than U.S. length).

Example 1: Rail Freight Transport. The Mexican average freight haul was shorter than the average U.S. haul: 532 compared to 870 kilometers. Mexican railways therefore produced relatively more terminal services than their U.S. counterparts. This can be seen by the higher relative U.S. output of ton kilometers of freight moved ($M^{\text{USA}}/M^{\text{MX}} = 1,100,727/33,393 = 33.0$) compared to the relative U.S. output of freight loaded and unloaded ($T^{\text{USA}}/T^{\text{MX}} = 1,265/63 = 20.2$). Mexican output would be underestimated if only the movement of freight were considered (the ratio M). Total transport output was therefore measured by the weighted average of the M and T ratios. The weight of the terminal services is determined by equation (6a) because $H^{\text{USA}} > H^{\text{MX}}$: $S = 1 - 532/870 = 0.39$. The weight of the movement services S is $(1 - 0.39) = 0.61$. U.S. relative output (Mexico is 100.0) is subsequently derived by equation (5): $Q^{\text{USA}} = (0.61 \times 33.0 + 0.39 \times 20.2) \times 100 = 2,799$.

Example 2: Rail Passenger Transport. The Mexican average rail passenger trip was longer than the U.S. trip: 168 compared to 59 kilometers. The proportionate amount of terminal services was therefore higher in the United States compared to Mexico. This can be seen by the higher relative U.S. output of passengers loaded and unloaded ($T^{\text{USA}}/T^{\text{MX}} = 269/25 = 10.9$) compared to the U.S. relative output of passengers moved ($M^{\text{USA}}/M^{\text{MX}} = 15,985/4,143 = 3.9$). The weight of the terminal services S is determined by equation (6b) because $H^{\text{USA}} < H^{\text{MX}}$: $S = 1 - 59/168 = 0.65$. The weight of the movement services is $(1 - 0.65) = 0.35$. U.S. relative output (Mexico is 100.0) is subsequently derived by equation (5): $Q^{USA} = (0.35 \times 3.9 + 0.65 \times 10.9) \times 100 = 840$.

If there is a large difference in the transport haul between countries, the proportionate importance of terminal services will vary. It will be higher in the country with the shorter average haul. This will result in an S closer to one, and U.S. relative output will tend to reflect the relative amount of U.S. terminal services (i.e., T^{USA}/T^{MX}). If a small difference in average freight haul or passenger trip length exists, the proportionate amount of terminal services will be almost equal in each country. This will result in a value of S close to zero, and U.S. relative output will reflect the relative amount of U.S. movement services (i.e., M^{USA}/M^{MX}).

This method was used to adjust railway output of each country, allowing for variations in distance over which passengers and freight were transported (see table 11.3).

Studies reveal the inferior quality of Mexican rail passenger transport: trains were more crowded than U.S. trains, were less comfortable, experienced more delays and more accidents, and traveled at lower speeds. The number of passengers per train kilometer demonstrates how crowded trains were (see table 11.4). U.S. trains carried on average less than half the number of passengers transported by Mexican trains, supposing that the size of Mexican and U.S. trains was similar. As this was the only indicator of quality available, I assumed it to be a general proxy for the quality of the service and adjusted Mexican output accordingly. A similar type of adjustment was made for the Brazil/ United States comparison of rail passenger transport.

Road Passenger Transport

This branch consists of passenger transport by bus (urban and suburban and long distance), tramway, and subway services, excluding school and sightseeing buses. Brazilians and Mexicans relied more heavily on bus transport than Americans and French (52 and 35 percent of transport GDP, respectively, compared with only 6 and 5 percent).

The number of passenger journeys is a first approximation to measuring output if average distances traveled are similar in different countries. While the average trip in urban and suburban areas is probably very similar, it can differ greatly for intercity travel (see Smith, Hitchens, and Davies 1982). Therefore, my output measure is biased only in the case of intercity bus passenger transport.

Important quality differences exist. Mexican buses had fewer seats available than their American counterparts because they were smaller and on average more crowded. Data on the number of passengers per vehicle kilometer (Meyer and Gómez-Ibáñez 1980, 315) in table 11.4 illustrate this. Mexican buses carried on average almost twice as many passengers per vehicle mile as their U.S. counterparts. Speed, adherence to posted schedules, number of accidents, and

Table 11.4   Quality Indicators in Transport and Communications: Brazil/United States and Mexico/United States, 1975

	Brazil	Mexico	United States	Brazil/ United States	Mexico/ United States
A. Rail passenger transport					
Number of passengers transported per train kilometer in 1975	60.3	77.5	36.5	1.7	2.1
B. Road passenger transport					
Number of passengers transported per vehicle kilometer in 1975:					
Urban and suburban buses		4.1	2.1		2.0
Intercity buses		.3	.2		1.7
Tramway and trolley services		7.3	3.6		2.0
Total		2.3	1.3		1.7
Number of passengers transported per bus in 1975	146,259	56,275	100,057	1.5	
C. Road freight transport					
Number of vehicle kilometers (millions) in 1975 of:					
Automobiles and motorcycles		39,674	1,673,360		
Trucks		16,245	453,738		
Buses		356	9,815		
Total		56,275	2,136,913		

(continued)

Table 11.4 (continued)

	Brazil	Mexico	United States	Brazil/United States	Mexico/United States
Length of paved and unpaved roads in kilometers[a]	1,428,707	124,745	6,175,664		
Congestion (vehicle kilometers per kilometer of road)		451,120	346,022		1.3
D. Telecommunications and postal services					
Local calls completed, 1989 (%)	39	92	99	.4	.9
Lines functioning, 1989 (%)	95	90	99	1.0	.9
Repair time, 1989 (days)	2	4	1	.5	.3
Degree of digitization, 1992 (%)	65	48	95	.7	.5
Geometric average				.6	.6
Post offices per 100,000 population, 1975	8	6	14	.5	.4

Source: Passengers per train kilometer: Brazil and Mexico from transport censuses as described in table 11.2; United States from Association of American Railroads (1978). Quality of road passenger and road freight transport: Brazil from Ministerio dos Transportes (1982); Mexico from transport census as described in table 11.2; United States from Department of Transportation (1981, 1992). Air transport: it was assumed that the quality of Brazilian and Mexican airlines was 70 percent of the U.S. level in 1975. Telecommunication quality indicators: ECLAC/UNIDO (1994). Number of post offices: Brazil from IBGE (1990); Mexico from INEGI (1994a); United States from Department of Commerce (1977).

[a]I assumed that the width of roads was similar across countries.

frequency of service are other indicators of quality. Our measure should reflect these quality differences. For lack of detailed information, I assumed that differences in passenger density is a proxy for all quality differentials. The average number of passengers transported by bus also provided the quality indicator for the Brazil/United States comparison.

Road Freight Transport

Road freight transport was the most important transport branch in all countries (see appendix table 11A.8). However, the Mexican census covered only vehicles that operate with special licenses, transport goods over a fixed route, and special kinds of product without a fixed route (see Islas Rivera 1992). Transporters without these licenses accounted for 80 percent of traffic. Owing to the very low coverage, other sources[12] were used to compare Mexican road freight transport with that of the United States.

According to table 11.4, congestion on U.S. roads was only three-quarters that on Mexican roads. Congestion decreases the quality of road freight transport, leading to a lower average vehicle speed, more traffic jams, and more accidents. Mexican output was adjusted by this ratio, taking it as a proxy measure for all quality differences. No data were available to make a similar quality adjustment for Brazilian road transport.

Air Transport

Passenger transport is the main element in air activity. The average passenger flight was 1,385 kilometers in Brazil, 999 kilometers in Mexico, and 1,334 kilometers in the United States in 1975. The proportionate importance of terminal services was higher in Mexico than in Brazil and the United States. A composite output index was constructed using passenger kilometers as an output indicator for flying activity and passengers as a measure of terminal services (see eq. [5]).

The quality of Mexican air passenger transport was inferior to that in the United States because of more frequent delays, poorer service, lesser frequency, and more accidents and because Mexican airlines served relatively fewer cities than American airlines did. I assumed that the quality of the service was 70 percent that in the United States and adjusted output correspondingly. The same terminal services and quality adjustment was made in the Brazil/United States comparison. Output of air freight transport was estimated by ton kilometers.

---

12. Islas Rivera (1992, 66) gives an estimate of the total movement services of Mexican trucking. The gross value of output was derived from the Mexican national accounts. The average freight haul for Mexico and the United States was derived from Department of Transportation (1994, 48–50). These estimates were for 1987, but I supposed that they also were valid for 1975. The number of tons transported was estimated using the data and ton kilometers and average freight hauls for both countries.

Water Transport

Two matches for water freight were made in the Brazil/United States and Mexico/United States comparisons: one for sea transport, coastal transport, and port activities and another for freight on lakes and rivers. I measured water freight transport output in tons because data on ton kilometers were lacking and assumed average freight hauls to be similar in Brazil and Mexico, on the one hand, and the United States, on the other. This assumption was not necessary in the France/United States comparison as data were available on the average freight haul of domestic water transport: 146 kilometers in France and 614 kilometers in the United States. A terminal services adjustment was made accordingly.

General Transport Services

These consist of a variety of services (including warehousing) to all modes of transport. No data were available on physical output produced in any of the countries included in the comparisons.

Telephone and Telegraph Services

A breakdown of communications GDP was available only for Mexico and the United States and showed that telephone and telegraph services accounted for 90 percent of the total. Appendix table 11A.4 presents several aspects of telecommunications. Americans used 130 million telephones in 1975, which is thirty-eight times the Brazilian and forty-five times the Mexican figure. This represents eighteen and twelve times as many telephones per capita in the United States as in Brazil and Mexico, respectively. Each American made seventeen/thirty-one times as many phone calls as a Brazilian/Mexican. In 1987, the United States had 30 percent more telephones per capita than France, and each American made 2.6 times as many phone calls as a French citizen.

I relied on national accounts for data on physical output quantities, gross value of output, value added, and employment. Telecom service output was estimated by a weighted average of two indicators: the number of telephones in use and the number of phone calls. The same weights were used as those from the allocation of employment in telecommunications, as estimated by the McKinsey Global Institute (1992) for five countries in 1989: 85 percent of the employees were engaged in installing and maintaining the network and maintaining the customer relationship; the other 15 percent worked in traffic-related areas (i.e., providing directory services and operating switches). Paige and Bombach (1959) used the same procedure to estimate output of telephone services. Physical output in telegraph services was approximated by the number of messages transmitted.

Brazil, Mexico, and the United States showed a large variation in the quality of telecom services, as table 11.4 demonstrates. While Brazil outperformed Mexico on repair time and the share of lines out of function, its percentage of local calls completed was much lower than that of Mexico. It was assumed that relative quality differences among Brazil, Mexico, and the United States were similar in 1975. A geometric average of the four indicators was used to adjust physical output.

Postal Services

Postal services include mail handling, banking, and miscellaneous services. Terminal work is predominant, comprising sorting, delivery, counter, and other handling services of mail. Smith, Hitchens, and Davies (1982) estimated that carriage costs are less than 10 percent of the total cost in the United Kingdom and the United States. I measured output in terms of pieces of mail handled and assumed a similar commodity mix, that is, the composition of mail handled, in all countries. The number of post offices per 100,000 population (see table 11.4) served as an indicator of access to postal services and was assumed to represent overall quality differences. No information was available on the speed of mail delivery in these countries.

11.2.2   Purchasing Power Parities

Dividing revenue by physical output allows one to derive an estimate of the value per unit of production. The PPP equals the ratio of the own country's unit value to the U.S. unit value.[13] To derive a PPP for a combination of activities, the specific PPPs were weighted by the own-country or U.S. quantities produced (eqq. [1] and [2]). The own country's weights generate a Paasche PPP; U.S. weights generate a Laspeyres PPP. The geometric average is the Fisher PPP. As the second step of aggregation from branch to sector level, the PPPs for each branch were weighted by the value added of each branch in the own country or the United States (eqq. [3] and [4]). Value-added weights of the national accounts as listed in appendix table 11A.8 were used as they give a better indication of the relative importance of each branch in total transport than the census does.

Table 11.5 shows the Fisher PPPs for the three binary comparisons. PPPs obtained by the "traditional approach" of passenger kilometer or freight kilometer measures for output are presented. In addition, table 11.5 demonstrates the results of output adjusted for terminal services and, finally, the price ratios obtained after the terminal services and quality adjustment of output. As the quality of French and U.S. transport and communications is similar, no quality adjustment was introduced. In most cases, the terminal services adjustment increased the output of Brazil, Mexico, and France relative to that of the United States, causing a lower price per unit of output and a lower PPP. The effect of the terminal services adjustment was fairly small, as shown in table 11.5, except for French railways and water transport.

The quality adjustment reduced the volume of services produced and raised

13. The United States was the "numeraire" country.

Table 11.5   Purchasing Power Parities in Transport and Communications, Fisher Results: Brazil/United States, 1975; Mexico/United States, 1975; and France/United States, 1987

	Brazil/United States, 1975 (Cr$ per US$)			Mexico/United States, 1975 ($ per U.S.$)			France/United States, 1987 (Fr per U.S.$)	
	With Traditional Measure	With Terminal Services Adjustment	With Terminal Services and Quality Adjustment	With Traditional Measure	With Terminal Services Adjustment	With Terminal Services and Quality Adjustment	With Traditional Measure	With Terminal Services Adjustment
Transport								
Railways	3.84	3.05	3.22	9.32	8.33	8.56	13.67	5.93
Road passenger transport	2.10	2.10	3.07	3.45	3.45	6.80	5.98	5.99
Road freight transport	4.47	3.94	3.94	8.91	7.74	10.09	5.76	5.76
Water transport	11.14	11.14	11.14	18.49	18.49	18.49	10.65	7.08
Air transport	9.87	9.55	12.79	10.90	10.36	14.29	7.58	7.63
Transportation services	4.60	4.26	5.06	7.39	6.85	9.67	7.63	6.10
Total (all branches)	4.0	4.26	5.06	7.39	6.85	9.67	7.63	6.10
Communications	10.32	10.32	18.45	10.64	10.64	18.86	5.96	5.96
Transport & communications	5.54	5.27	7.23	7.83	7.44	11.50	6.88	6.05
Exchange rate	8.13	8.13	8.13	12.50	12.50	12.50	6.01	6.01

Sources: Volume indicators and value of output from appendix tables 11A.1–11A.3. Terminal services adjustment made using shares of table 11.3 above, and quality adjustment was based on table 11.4 above. *Traditional* refers to the use of passenger kilometer and freight kilometer output measures or passengers and freight tonnage if passenger kilometer or ton kilometer measures were not available (see appendix tables 11A.1–11A.3). *Terminal services adjustment* was made as indicated in the text for railways (Brazil/United States, Mexico/United States, and France/United States), road passenger transport (France/United States), road freight transport (Brazil/United States and Mexico/United States), water transport (France/United States), and air passenger transport (Brazil/United States, Mexico/United States, and France/United States). *Quality adjustment* was based on table 11.4 above and applied to rail and road passenger transport (Brazil/United States and Mexico/United States), road freight transport (Mexico/United States), and air transport and communications (Brazil/United States, Mexico/United States).

the price per unit of output in Brazil and Mexico relative to the United States. This increased the PPPs in the Brazil/United States and Mexico/United States comparisons. The effect of the quality adjustment was substantial as the Fisher PPP of railways rose 46 percent, that of air transport 34 percent, and that of communications 79 percent in the Brazil/United States comparison. The largest increments of Mexico/United States Fisher PPPs were in air transport and communications.

The PPPs of table 11.5 were used to convert value added from table 11.2 to a common currency. Dividing value added in common prices by labour input from table 11.2 yields relative productivity levels, as presented in table 11.6. Using the "traditional" measure of output, Brazilian productivity was 48 percent of the U.S. level in transport and 16 percent in communications. Relative levels varied widely among branches: 18 percent in water to 110 percent in road passenger transport. Brazil's relative performance improved almost 4 percentage points after adjusting for terminal services and subsequently dropped by 8 percentage points after incorporating quality differences. Relative productivity in communications dropped by 7 percent after allowing for quality differences.

Mexico's relative productivity performance improved to the same extent as that of Brazil after the terminal services adjustment but dropped by more than 15 percentage points after allowing for quality differences. The quality adjustment in communications decreased relative productivity by almost half. This seems reasonable because, otherwise, Mexican relative productivity would have been the same as that of France in 1987, which is unlikely.

The effect of the terminal services adjustment was very substantial in the France/United States comparison, causing relative productivity levels to increase by 17 percentage points. French relative productivity improved 10 percentage points in transport and 7 percentage points in communications when we moved from a per person engaged basis to an hours-worked basis.

11.2.3   Wholesale and Retail Trade[14]

The main novelty of this study is that it experiments with a measure of value added in comparable prices by double deflation, using ICP expenditure PPPs as converters for sales and ICOP industry-of-origin PPPs as converters for purchases of goods produced in other industries that are destined for resale and for other inputs such as transport, energy, and so forth. The Kravis, Heston, and Summers (1982) ICP PPPs were used for sales and ICOP studies (van Ark and Maddison 1994; Maddison and van Ooststroom 1993; Houben 1990; and Mulder 1991) for the "input" PPPs. Other analysts (e.g., Hall, Knapp, and Winsten 1961; and Smith and Hitchens 1985) used a simpler approach, adjusting both sales and purchases by ICP expenditure PPPs.

---

14. I am indebted to Angus Maddison, with whom I wrote the paper that served as the basis for this section (Mulder and Maddison 1993), comparing Mexican and U.S. distribution. In the text, I use both *I* and *we,* referring in both cases to Mulder and Maddison.

Table 11.6   **Labor Productivity in Transport and Communications, Fisher Results: Brazil/United States, 1975; Mexico/United States, 1975; and France/United States, 1987**

	Brazil/United States, 1975 (United States = 100)			Mexico/United States, 1975 (United States = 100)			France/United States, 1987 (United States = 100)	
	With Traditional Measure	With Terminal Services Adjustment	With Terminal Services and Quality Adjustment	With Traditional Measure	With Terminal Services Adjustment	With Terminal Services and Quality Adjustment	With Traditional Measure	With Terminal Services Adjustment
Transport								
Railways	23.5	29.6	28.0	17.5	19.6	19.1	25.9	59.6
Road passenger transport	109.9	109.9	75.2	179.3	179.3	91.0	96.2	96.0
Road freight transport	52.6	57.3	51.1	36.3	41.8	32.1	72.3	72.3
Water transport	17.8	17.8	17.8	43.1	43.1	43.1	69.2	104.2
Air transport	37.6	38.9	29.1	72.6	76.4	55.4	108.7	108.0
Transportation services	102.8	111.0	93.6	82.7	89.2	63.2	75.8	94.8
Total (all branches)	48.0	51.8	43.7	48.6	52.4	37.1	67.3	84.2
Communications	16.0	16.0	9.0	44.7	44.7	25.2	43.4	43.4

Sources: Value added and employment are from table 11.2 above. Fisher PPPs are from table 11.5 above.

A wide array of studies exists on international comparisons of distributive output and productivity. Some of these touched on retailing (Jefferys and Knee 1962; McKinsey Global Institute 1992), while others also included wholesaling. Important differences exist among the studies. They applied different measures of output: Paige and Bombach (1959) used quantities of goods produced weighted by gross margins; Hall, Knapp, and Winsten (1961) and Jefferys and Knee (1962) used sales; Smith and Hitchens (1985) used gross margins; and Pilat (1991) and the McKinsey Global Institute (1992) used value added.

All the studies reviewed measure output in a common set of prices, using exchange rates or PPPs for total consumer expenditure for specific product groups. These PPPs were also used to convert gross margins (Smith and Hitchens 1985) or value added (Pilat 1991; McKinsey Global Institute 1992). Hall, Knapp, and Winsten (1961) and Smith and Hitchens (1985) used expenditure PPPs for different groups of consumer expenditure as the converters for sales and/or gross margins.

For this study, I relied on information contained in censuses. Brazilian, Mexican, French, and U.S. wholesale and retail trades were matched at a detailed, four-digit level of the standard industrial classification (SIC). In the detailed calculations, twenty-eight product groups were distinguished, which were subsequently consolidated into durable and nondurable products, with food products as a subcategory of nondurables. From these sources, we derived comparable estimates of the value of sales and gross value added as well as employment (which we had to adjust in the case of the United States to include family workers and working proprietors). In order to get the same coverage for the four countries, we had to exclude a number of items from the U.S. censuses of wholesale and retail trade as they could not be matched with items in the Brazilian, Mexican, or French censuses of distribution. Sales of the excluded U.S. trades were 4.0 percent of those in our sample, 9.5 percent of value added, and 18.1 percent of persons engaged in 1977. For Brazil and Mexico, we also had to exclude a number of trades that could not be matched with U.S. statistics. Sales of excluded Brazilian trades made up 1.4 percent of our sample, 1.9 percent of value added, and 1.8 percent of persons engaged. Sales of excluded Mexican trades were 5.4 percent of our sample, 6.7 percent of value added, and 3.9 percent of persons engaged (for a list of the excluded trades, see Mulder and Maddison [1993] and Mulder [1994a, 1994c]).

The censuses of wholesale and retail trade contained most of the required statistics but do not provide information on the quantities of goods distributed, only money values of total sales. The U.S. census does not give detailed information on inventory changes and input costs, but the relevant information can be derived from other sources (e.g., Department of Commerce, Bureau of the Census 1981a, 1981d)[15] on a somewhat more aggregate level than appears in

---

15. These sources show sales, purchases of goods, inventory changes, and other input costs on a two-digit level for wholesaling and resaling.

the census. Information on input costs is available only for merchant wholesalers in wholesale trade. They accounted for 53.7 percent of sales and 79.5 percent of establishments in wholesale trade in 1977. Nonmerchant wholesalers are essentially branches of manufacturing firms who sell goods directly to consumers or retailers. Ratios of input costs to sales of merchant wholesalers were assumed to be representative for other types of wholesale trade. Our census data for sales for the United States are for 1977 in 1977 prices. In order to compare with Brazil and Mexico in 1975, U.S. sales data were adjusted to a 1975 basis.[16] Subsequently, we applied ratios of purchased goods and other inputs to sales derived from Department of Commerce, Bureau of the Census (1981a, 1981d), to estimate gross margins and value added for individual trades (three or four digits). Value added data in the censuses were adjusted so that they correspond with the national accounts concept presently in use.[17]

The same procedures were followed to derive measures of gross margin, inputs, and value added for the United States in 1987. In contrast to 1977, nonmerchant wholesalers were excluded. Wholesale establishments without a payroll, not covered in the 1975/77 comparisons, were included in the 1987 comparison using unpublished government sources.

Table 11.7 provides the first element of the comparative representation. It shows the number of establishments per 100,000 inhabitants and the average size of establishment measured by the number of persons employed. Brazil and Mexico had fewer establishments per head of population than France and the United States, especially in wholesale trade. Brazil had more wholesalers but fewer retailers per head of population than Mexico. The U.S. figures excluded wholesale establishments that did not have a payroll, mainly agents and brokers. When these would be included, the number of wholesalers per 100,000 would increase to 318 and surpass the French figure. France had more than 75 percent more retailers than the United States in 1987.

Mexican wholesalers employed more people than Brazilian ones did, although Brazilian retailers were on average smaller than their Mexican counterparts in 1975. It is surprising that the size of French wholesalers was smaller than that of those in Brazil and Mexico and that French retailers employed the same number of people as Brazilian retailers. U.S. wholesalers were about the same size as Mexican wholesalers, although American retailers were larger than those in the other three countries.

Appendix tables 11A.5–11A.7 present sales, the gross margin, and value

16. This was done using consumer price indexes in the case of retailing and wholesale (producer) price indexes in the case of wholesaling. Price indexes were taken from Department of Labor, Bureau of Labor Statistics (1978a, 1978b). Price indexes are given for individual products at a very detailed level. Annual averages were used to calculate price changes.
17. From the Mexican *valor agregado censal bruto* (gross value added), I deducted *gastos por uso de patentas y marcas, asistencia tecnica y otros pagos por tecnologia* (cost of patents, licenses, technical assistance, and technology) and *gastos por rentas y alquileres* (cost of renting). From U.S. census value added, the following items were deducted: purchased advertising services, purchased communications services, lease and rental payments, and purchased repair services.

Table 11.7   Number of Establishments in Wholesale and Retail Trade per Capita and Average Size: Brazil, Mexico, France, and the United States, 1975, 1977, 1987

	Number of Establishments per 100,000 Population					Average Size (persons per establishment)				
				United States					United States	
	Brazil, 1975	Mexico, 1975	France, 1987	1977	1987	Brazil, 1975	Mexico, 1975	France, 1987	1977	1987
Wholesale trade										
Durables	13	5	144	94	112	9.6	15.1	6.4	12.1	11.6
Nondurables	34	13	127	66	71	7.0	10.2	6.1	13.0	13.3
Food	13	7	44	16	17	7.2	7.0	7.1	17.2	18.3
Total (all branches)	47	18	271	160	183	7.7	11.6	6.2	12.5	12.3
Retail trade										
Durables	83	77	476	209	336	6.0	5.3	2.6	10.5	4.9
Nondurables	516	660	774	335	381	2.6	1.8	3.2	6.4	9.1
Food	382	494	406	101	119	2.1	1.6	3.6	9.2	10.5
Total (all branches)	599	737	1,250	544	717	3.1	2.1	3.0	8.0	7.1
Distribution	646	755	1,521	704	900	3.4	2.4	3.6	9.0	8.2

Sources: Number of establishments, except France, and employment from distribution censuses as described in table 11.2. French number of establishments from INSEE (1988). Population from Maddison (1995).

added in distribution in our three binary comparisons. Table 11.8 summarizes the results. The lowest margins were found in the trade of food products in all countries. High margins were observed in durable goods trade. The censuses also reveal that Brazil had the lowest ratio of intermediate inputs (such as electricity, stationary, etc.) to sales whereas the French ratios were the highest. The ratio of input costs (other than purchases destined for resale) to sales, often used as a proxy of overall efficiency, was higher in France and Mexico than in the United States. The cost/sales ratio was surprisingly lower in Brazil, for which I have no explanation.

11.2.4   Derivation of PPPs for Gross Value Added

To convert value added in national currency in table 11.2 I used PPPs. For this purpose, both the double deflation technique and the more traditional single deflation technique are used. The traditional single deflation uses expenditure (ICP) PPPs to convert sales, the gross margin, and value added. However, ICP PPPs are not suitable converters for the gross margin and value added because they apply only to sales of retailers. ICP PPPs do not represent relative prices of goods purchased by distributors destined for resale, nor do they represent relative prices of other inputs such as communication costs, fuels, and office supplies. Therefore, I developed a method of double deflation in which two sets of converters are used, that is, one set that applies to sales and another that applies to purchases of goods for resale of establishments and other input costs.

Double Deflation

PPPs for Sales. The first step was the detailed conversion of Brazilian, Mexican, and U.S. sales of fifty-six types of wholesale and fifty types of retail trade by ICP Paasche and Laspeyres PPPs. Table 11.9 lists the PPPs for broad product categories (derived by weighting the detailed PPPs by the sales of the detailed wholesale and retail categories).

PPPs for Goods Purchased. We used Paasche and Laspeyres PPPs derived from the Groningen ICOP studies for purchases of goods by distributors from other sectors of the economy for resale. The main difference between the ICP and the ICOP approach is that the ICP (or expenditure) approach estimates PPPs comparing final expenditures (i.e., private consumer expenditure, investment, and government) across countries, whereas the ICOP (or industry-of-origin) estimates are based on ex-factory prices of goods from the commodity-producing sectors. The latter PPPs are therefore more suitable to convert purchases than ICP PPPs. This provided the second step in the process of double deflation. Table 11.9 includes ICOP binary PPPs for broad categories. Subtracting the cost of goods purchased by distributive establishments (i.e., the value of inventories at the beginning of the year plus purchases of goods during the year and less the value of inventories at the end of the year) from sales

Table 11.8   Ratio of Gross Margin to Sales and Ratio of Other Inputs to Sales in Brazilian, Mexican, French, and U.S. Distribution, 1975, 1977, 1987

	Ratio of Gross Margin to Sales					Ratio of Other Inputs to Sales				
	Brazil, 1975	Mexico, 1975	France, 1987	United States 1977	United States 1987	Brazil, 1975	Mexico, 1975	France, 1987	United States 1977	United States 1987
Wholesale trade										
Durables	22.1	35.5	32.0	25.4	24.1	3.5	7.6	12.2	4.1	4.4
Nondurables	17.9	26.9	17.7	16.8	16.4	2.5	6.8	8.5	3.4	2.9
Food	13.8	23.9	16.9	16.4	15.2	3.1	4.5	8.0	3.2	2.5
Total (all branches)	19.1	29.7	23.0	20.5	20.1	2.8	7.1	9.9	3.7	3.6
Retail trade										
Durables	26.1	37.6	30.5	28.0	27.1	4.7	7.9	11.2	4.7	5.5
Nondurables	19.2	29.3	30.6	26.9	29.9	3.8	6.6	10.7	5.2	6.5
Food	17.9	28.1	27.1	23.2	25.7	3.3	4.7	9.9	4.8	5.9
Total (all branches)	22.2	33.2	30.6	27.5	28.7	4.2	7.2	10.8	4.9	6.1
Distribution	20.5	32.2	26.6	22.9	24.3	3.5	7.2	10.3	4.1	4.8

Sources: See appendix tables 11A.5–11A.7.

Table 11.9   ICP Fisher PPPs for Sales, ICOP Fisher PPPs for Purchases and Other Inputs, and Implicit Fisher PPPs for Value Added and Wholesale and Retail Trade: Brazil (1975)/United States (1977) and Mexico (1975)/United States (1977), 1975 Prices

	Brazil (1975)/United States (1977), Fisher Results (Cr$ per U.S.$)				Mexico (1975)/United States (1977), Fisher Results ($ per U.S.$)			
	ICP PPP for Sales	ICOP PPP for Purchases	ICOP PPP for Other Inputs	Implicit PPP for Value Added	ICP PPP for Sales	ICOP PPP for Purchases	ICOP PPP for Other Inputs	Implicit PPP for Value Added
Wholesale trade								
Durables	9.39	6.08	6.12	a	11.80	14.02	13.66	9.68
Nondurables	8.36	8.97	6.43	5.46	11.33	13.03	14.00	7.16
Food	5.56	6.59	6.50	4.82	8.70	11.48	14.31	a
Total (all branches)	8.72	7.86	6.29	14.17	11.65	13.34	13.88	8.74
Retail trade								
Durables	8.90	6.93	6.42	16.31	11.90	15.10	13.12	6.94
Nondurables	7.71	7.79	6.57	7.61	9.96	11.11	14.10	5.48
Food	5.42	5.70	6.65	4.57	8.29	9.97	14.88	a
Total (all branches)	8.16	7.46	6.49	10.05	10.80	12.50	13.60	6.35
Distribution	8.46	7.70	6.40	11.88	11.37	12.71	13.74	8.33
Exchange rate	8.13	8.13	8.13	8.13	12.50	12.50	12.50	12.50

Sources: ICP augmented binary PPPs for sales are from worksheets from Kravis, Heston, and Summers (1982). ICOP binary PPPs for purchases and other inputs are from Houben (1990), van Ark and Maddison (1994), and Maddison and van Ooststroom (1993).

aFisher PPP cannot be calculated because either the Paasche or the Laspeyres PPP was less than zero.

furnishes a first approximation to gross value added (i.e., the gross margin). In national accounts terminology, the gross margin corresponds to the gross value of output of wholesale and retail trade.

PPPs for Other Inputs. Next, "other inputs" were deducted. The ICOP PPPs for communications, electricity, and transport were taken from Mulder (1991, 1994c, 1995). Similar data for fuels and packaging materials were derived from van Ark and Maddison (1994). The Brazilian, Mexican, and U.S. censuses give cost data for these inputs.[18] The inputs included in the double deflation exercise represented 1.4 percent of total inputs (including purchases of goods for resale) in Brazil, 1.5 percent in Mexico, and 1.7 percent in the United States. No ICOP PPPs were available to convert the remaining input costs listed in the Brazilian, Mexican, and U.S. sources, such as advertising, technical services, rental costs, etc. These conversion-resistant inputs represented 2.8 percent of total inputs (including purchases of goods for resale) in Brazil, 6.0 percent in Mexico, and 3.4 percent in the United States. We used a weighted average of the ICOP Paasche PPPs for electricity, packaging materials, and transport costs to convert the residual input costs in cruzeiros (pesos) to U.S. dollars in the Brazilian (Mexican) case and a weighted average of the Laspeyres PPPs in the U.S. case to convert the U.S. residual from U.S. dollars into cruzeiros (pesos).

Implicit PPPs for Value Added. We derived implicit Paasche and Laspeyres PPPs for gross value added by dividing for Brazil (Mexico) the cruzeiro (peso) value of gross value added by our double deflated Paasche estimate in U.S. dollars (see table 11.9). For the United States, the implicit Laspeyres PPP for value added is found by dividing the double deflated Laspeyres value-added estimate in cruzeiros (pesos) by value added in U.S. dollars. The implicit Paasche PPP for total distribution was 8.55; the Laspeyres PPP equals 16.52 cruzeiros per U.S. dollar in the Brazil/United States comparison. For the Mexico/United States comparison, we estimated the Paasche PPP for distribution as a whole to equal 5.75 and the Laspeyres PPP to be 12.05 pesos per U.S. dollar for gross value added.

Double deflation yielded erratic results at the branch level, even negative readings in some cases (see table 11.9). These results arise from the many types of errors in the execution of the double deflation procedure: ICP and ICOP PPPs had often limited availability without specific commodity types

18. ICOP Paasche PPPs were available for the following inputs listed in the Brazilian census: communication, electricity, fuels and lubricants, and freight and carriage (i.e., transport). The Mexican census gives data on electricity and packaging materials. The input-output table (SPP 1981b) is another source from which information can be obtained on input costs: it appears that transport costs were a significant input (i.e., 10.5 percent of total "other" input costs). We applied this percentage to each trade. Neither of the U.S. censuses contained data from which we could derive input costs. Two other sources were used instead—Department of Commerce, Bureau of the Census (1981a, 1981d). The following inputs were included in the double deflation exercise: communications and electricity, fuels, office supplies, and packing and wrapping materials.

and often did not match exactly the type of wholesale or retail trade. Because value added accounts for a small share of sales, a tiny measurement error in the ICP or ICOP PPPs is magnified in the implicity derived value-added PPPs. It should be noted that the erratic character of our double deflation results is not unusual. Szirmai and Pilat (1990) had the same experience in their experiments with double deflation for manufacturing comparisons of Japan and the United States.

Traditional Single Deflation Technique

As a cross-check on our double deflation technique, we used the traditional single deflation approach. Single deflation represents the conversion of value added with one set of PPP converters, that is, expenditure PPPs derived from the International Comparison Project (ICP). This method was also used in previous studies (see Hall, Knapp, and Winsten 1961; and Smith and Hitchens 1985). We applied ICP binary PPPs for detailed commodity categories to convert sales and value added of wholesalers or retailers selling those types of commodities. In cases where PPPs of specific commodity categories are combined in order to estimate a PPP for a group of trades, we employed consumer expenditures as weights. Two sets of weights can be used: Brazilian (Mexican) expenditure weights (i.e., derivation of a Paasche PPP) and U.S. expenditure weights (derivation of a Laspeyres PPP). The geometric average of the Paasche and Laspeyres estimates represents the Fisher PPP.

Table 11.10 shows the ICP reweighted Paasche and Laspeyres PPPs, which we used to convert value added into the other currency. The Fisher PPPs of the Brazil/United States and France/United States comparisons were above the prevailing exchange rates. Wholesale price ratios were above the retail price ratios in all comparisons. PPPs of durables were higher than those of nondurables, which in turn were larger than those of groceries. The same patterns were found in the implicit PPPs of value added derived by double deflation.

A comparison of tables 11.9 and 11.10 indicates the erratic results of the double deflation technique: the ratio of the highest to the lowest Fisher PPP for the Brazil/United States comparison was 3.6 for the double deflation and 1.7 for the single deflation. The Mexico/United States ratios are 1.8 for the double and 1.4 for the single deflation exercise. In the case of single deflation, the results are more plausible by branch because there are no negative readings. For this reason, we prefer the single deflation results. Nevertheless, we think that the double deflation exercise was useful and cannot be dismissed on the aggregate level as errors may be compensating, that is, for wholesale and retail trade as a whole.

11.2.5   Labor Productivity

The PPPs of tables 11.9 and 11.10 were used to convert value added to a set of common prices. Value added was divided by employment to derive productivity levels (see table 11.11). With our double deflation approach, labor pro-

Table 11.10	ICP Reweighted Fisher PPPs for Gross Value Added and Wholesale and Retail Trade: Brazil (1975)/United States (1977), Mexico (1975)/ United States (1977), and France/United States (1987), 1975 Prices

	Brazil, 1975/ United States, 1977 (Cr$ per U.S.$)	Mexico, 1975/ United States, 1977 ($ per U.S.$)	France/ United States, 1987 (Fr per U.S.$)
Wholesale trade			
Durables	9.42	12.08	8.90
Nondurables	8.68	11.08	7.61
Food	5.56	8.59	6.79
Total (all branches)	9.11	11.80	8.23
Retail trade			
Durables	9.25	11.70	9.15
Nondurables	7.79	9.91	6.88
Food	5.44	8.31	6.87
Total (all branches)	8.45	10.68	7.52
Distribution	8.78	11.36	7.80
Exchange rate	8.13	12.50	6.01

Sources: ICP augmented binary PPPs for sales are from worksheets from Kravis, Heston, and Summers (1982). French/U.S. expenditure PPPs have been kindly provided by Eurostat.
Note: These PPPs deviate from those for sales in table 11.9 above because value added was used as a weight instead of sales.

Table 11.11	Labor Productivity in Wholesale and Retail Trade, Double and Single Deflation Results: Brazil (1975)/United States (1977), Mexico (1975)/ United States (1977), and France/United States (1987)

	Brazil (1975)/ United States[a] (1977) (United States = 100)		Mexico (1975)/ United States[a] (1977) (United States = 100)		France/ United States (1987)
	Single Deflation	Double Deflation	Single Deflation	Double Deflation	Single Deflation (United States = 100)
Wholesale trade					
Durables	55.3	[b]	33.6	42.0	51.8
Nondurables	58.8	93.4	28.8	44.5	54.2
Food	53.7	61.9	39.5	[b]	62.1
Total (all branches)	57.3	36.9	30.1	40.6	53.3
Retail trade					
Durables	59.9	34.0	78.7	132.7	54.9
Nondurables	26.4	27.0	31.8	57.5	92.3
Food	30.0	35.8	30.0	[b]	98.9
Total (all branches)	35.4	29.7	44.3	74.5	77.6
Distribution	35.2	26.0	29.0	39.5	68.6

Sources: Value and employment are from table 11.2 above. Fisher PPPs are from table 11.10 above.
[a]For the United States only, merchant wholesalers were included.
[b]Productivity ratio cannot be derived owing to negative double deflated value added.

ductivities (value added per person engaged) in the Brazilian and Mexican distributions in 1975 were 26 and 40 percent of those in the United States, respectively. Using the traditional single deflation technique, labor productivity remained substantially different, at 35 and 29 percent of the U.S. level, respectively. The disaggregated results for the different parts of distribution using double deflation showed an erratic pattern reflecting possible error. At the aggregate level, double deflation results have greater validity as these errors may be compensating. We conclude that Brazilian and Mexican labor productivity in distribution in 1975 lay in a range between 26 and 35 percent for Brazil and between 29 and 40 percent for Mexico of the U.S. level, but the single deflation results probably deserve greater credence.

The single deflation results of the France/United States comparison show that French productivity in wholesale trade was 53 percent of the U.S. level and that the relative retail trade performance was 78 percent. French productivity in wholesale and retail trade combined was 69 percent of that in the United States. French performance rose 1.5 percentage points after adjusting for hours worked.

11.3   Conclusion

This paper introduces two new elements in the international comparisons of output and productivity in transport: the inclusion of loading and unloading services in the overall measure of output and the adjustment of output for differences in service quality. The productivity results for transport presented in table 11.1 accounted for this. Table 11.6 demonstrates that the traditional method of output measurement, which does not cover loading and unloading services, yields lower productivity ratios for Brazil, Mexico, and France relative to the United States. If output had not been adjusted for quality differences, Brazilian and Mexican relative productivity would have been 8 percentage points and 15 percentage points higher, respectively (see table 11.6). The results adjusted for terminal services and quality differences provide an upper boundary, whereas those adjusted for quality and terminal services provide a lower boundary, of relative productivity performance. It should be stressed that the measures of quality introduced here were very crude and need refinement.

The productivity results for wholesale and retail trade in table 11.1 were obtained by single deflation. The new procedure for deriving PPPs, by double deflation, yielded lower relative productivity in the Brazil/United States comparison and higher productivity in the Mexico/United States comparison (see table 11.11). Although double deflation produced erratic results at the detailed level, it is clearly preferred to single deflation on theoretical grounds. The robustness of double deflation will increase when expenditure and producer price relatives are available at the more detailed level, reducing the margin of error.

Appendix A

Table 11A.1   Movement and Terminal Transport Services: Brazil and the United States, 1975

	Quantities Produced (million)						Value of Output	
	Movement Services (number of passenger km or freight [ton] km)			Terminal Services (number of passengers or tons of freight)				
	United States	Brazil	United States/ Brazil	United States	Brazil	United States/ Brazil	United States (million U.S.$)	Brazil (million Cr$)
Passenger transport								
Rail	15,985	10,621	1.5	269	292	.9	297	395
Bus	N.A.	N.A.		5,435	11,455	.5	2,564	11,340
Subway	N.A.	N.A.		1,673	22	77.0	517	N.A.
Air								
Domestic	211,905	5,106	41.5	189	6	30.8	10,290	3,724
International	50,040	5,276	9.5	16	1	11.9	2,435	1,178
Freight transport								
Rail	1,100,727	58,933	18.7	1,265	126	10.1	15,390	3,345
Road	662,551	42,618	15.5	1,267	124	10.2	47,400	13,641
Rivers and lakes	365,042	N.A.		645	3	241.7	2,157	146
Ocean and coastwise	N.A.	31,740		890	17	53.1	6,064	1,154
Air								
Domestic	5,006	521	9.6	N.A.	N.A.		949	419
International	3,612	847	4.3	N.A.	N.A.		478	429

Sources: Brazil Ministério dos Transportes (1982); IBGE (1982). United States: Department of Transportation (1981, 1994); Department of Commerce (1977, 1978).

Note: N.A. = not available.

Table 11A.2   Movement and Terminal Transport Services: Mexico and the United States, 1975

	Quantities Produced (million)						Value of Output	
	Movement Services (number of passenger km or freight [ton] km)			Terminal Services (number of passengers or tons of freight)				
	United States	Mexico	United States/ Mexico	United States	Mexico	United States/ Mexico	United States (million U.S.$)	Mexico (million $)
Passenger transport								
Rail	15,985	4,143	3.9	269	25	10.9	297	311
Urban transport	N.A.	N.A.		5,084	6,146	.8	1,438	6,227
City bus	N.A.	N.A.		1,673	551	3.0	517	601
Subway	N.A.	N.A.		231	243	.9	32	144
Long-distance bus	40,869	N.A.		351	512	.7	1,126	5,353
Air	261,945	7,239	36.2	205	7	28.3	12,725	4,092
Freight transport								
Rail	1,100,727	33,393	33.0	1,265	63	20.2	15,390	4,570
Road	662,551	53,158	12.5	1,267	155	8.2	47,400	33,878
Rivers and lakes	365,042	N.A.		645	3	171.5	2,157	60
Ocean and coastwise	N.A.	N.A.		890	10	100.9	6,064	1,420
Air	8,618	330	26.1	N.A.	92		1,427	294

Sources: Mexico: SPP (1977, 1979, 1980, 1981a). United States: See table 11A.1.
Note: N.A. = not available.

Table 11A.3   Movement and Terminal Transport Services: France and the United States, 1987

	Quantities Produced (million)						Value of Output	
	Movement Services (number of passenger km or freight [ton] km)			Terminal Services (number of passengers or tons of freight)				
	United States	France	United States/ France	United States	France	United States/ France	United States (million U.S.$)	France (million Fr)
Passenger transport								
Rail	8,637	59,700	.1	21	781	.0	681	35,820
Urban transport	N.A.	N.A.		8,806	3,681	2.4	14,172	33,400
Long-distance bus	35,237	33,700	1.0	333	280	1.2	1,717	12,677
Air	650,680	44,314	14.7	448	28	16.1	45,866	28,804
Freight transport								
Rail	1,377,504	49,700	27.7	1,244	142	8.8	25,797	18,389
Road	1,039,066	99,900	10.4	N.A.	N.A.		136,300	75,449
Inland water	599,798	4,656	128.8	977	32	30.6	19,100	1,462
Sea	N.A.	N.A.		88	49	1.8	2,614	16,555
Air	14,617	4,098	3.6	N.A.	N.A.		7,621	7,212

Sources: France: Ministère de Transport (1989, 1990); INSEE and Ministère de Transport (1990); INSEE (1990a, 1991). United States: Department of Transportation (1992, 1994); Department of Commerce (1989, 1990).

Table 11A.4   Communications Output in Brazil, France, Mexico, and the United States, 1975/87

	Brazil, 1975	Mexico, 1975	France, 1987	United States, 1975	United States, 1987
Domestic mail sent (million pieces)	1,246	1,026	15,342	88,334	153,931
Telegraph (million messages)	17	29		68	
Number of telephones (thousands)	458	2,915	24,800	130,000	
Number of access lines (thousands)	N.A.				126,700
Number of calls (millions)	6,428	2,086		228,917	449,785

Sources: See tables 11A.1–11A.3.

Table 11A.5 Sales, Purchases of Goods for Resale, Other Inputs, and Value Added in Brazilian and U.S. Distribution, 1975/77 (million national currency)

	Sales		Purchased Goods Destined for Resale		Other Inputs		Value Added	
	United States, 1977 (1975 U.S.$)	Brazil, 1975 (Cr$)	United States, 1977 (1975 U.S.$)	Brazil, 1975 (Cr$)	United States, 1977 (1975 U.S.$)	Brazil, 1975 (Cr$)	United States, 1977 (1975 U.S.$)	Brazil, 1975 (Cr$)
Wholesale trade								
Durables	465,245	144,736	346,183	112,798	19,370	5,038	99,693	26,901
Nondurables	603,126	358,651	503,392	294,450	20,361	9,078	79,373	55,123
Food	178,964	109,583	149,569	94,476	5,765	3,406	23,630	11,701
Total (all branches)	1,068,372	503,387	849,575	407,247	39,731	14,116	179,065	82,024
Retail trade								
Durables	285,621	188,139	204,812	139,051	13,818	8,849	66,991	40,239
Nondurables	272,684	240,468	199,725	194,360	13,804	9,218	58,556	36,890
Food	142,349	121,916	109,316	100,054	6,768	3,976	26,265	17,886
Total (all branches)	557,705	428,608	404,536	333,412	27,622	18,068	125,547	77,128
Distribution	1,626,077	931,995	1,254,111	740,659	67,353	32,184	304,612	159,152

Sources: See table 11.2.

Table 11A.6 Sales, Purchases of Goods for Resale, Other Inputs, and Value Added in Mexican and U.S. Distribution, 1975/77 (million national currency)

	Sales		Purchased Goods Destined for Resale		Other Inputs		Value Added	
	United States, 1977 (1975 U.S.$)	Mexico, 1975 ($)	United States, 1977 (1975 U.S.$)	Mexico, 1975 ($)	United States, 1977 (1975 U.S.$)	Mexico, 1975 ($)	United States, 1977 (1975 U.S.$)	Mexico, 1975 ($)
Wholesale trade								
Durables	465,245	25,577	346,183	17,776	19,370	2,104	99,693	7,696
Nondurables	603,126	55,673	503,392	40,709	20,361	3,775	79,373	11,188
Food	178,964	19,415	149,569	14,773	5,765	874	23,630	3,769
Total (all branches)	1,068,372	83,249	849,575	58,485	39,731	5,880	179,065	18,885
Retail trade								
Durables	285,621	105,897	204,812	66,102	13,818	8,338	66,991	31,457
Nondurables	272,084	121,893	199,725	86,152	13,804	8,095	58,556	27,646
Food	142,349	65,213	109,316	46,863	6,768	3,086	26,265	15,264
Total (all branches)	557,705	227,790	404,536	152,254	27,622	16,433	125,547	59,103
Distribution	1,626,077	311,039	1,254,111	210,739	67,353	22,313	304,612	77,988

Sources: See table 11.2.

Table 11A.7   Sales, Purchases of Goods for Resale, Other Inputs, and Value Added in French and U.S. Distribution, 1987 (million national currency)

	Sales		Purchased Goods Destined for Resale		Other Inputs		Value Added	
	United States (U.S.$)[a]	France (Fr)	United States (U.S.$)[b]	France (Fr)	United States (U.S.$)	France (Fr)	United States (U.S.$)[b]	France (Fr)
Wholesale trade								
Durables	1,218,628	630,440	925,507	428,959	53,020	77,019	136,092	124,461
Nondurables	1,245,926	1,066,164	1,041,200	877,662	36,127	90,566	99,353	97,936
Food	380,945	407,321	323,205	338,659	9,687	32,423	28,132	36,240
Total, unadjusted	2,464,554		1,968,532		88,799		235,445	
Total, adjusted	2,512,756	1,696,603	2,006,567	1,306,621	90,515	167,585	235,776	222,397
Retail trade								
Durables	561,816	547,884	409,531	380,667	30,768	61,140	121,517	106,077
Nondurables	797,050	981,897	559,071	681,570	51,918	104,716	186,061	195,610
Food	309,460	648,403	229,946	472,638	18,247	64,206	61,268	111,559
Total (all branches)	1,358,866	1,529,780	968,602	1,062,238	82,686	165,856	307,578	301,686
Distribution, *unadjusted*	3,823,419		2,893,525		184,080		543,023	
Distribution, *adjusted*[c]	3,871,621	3,226,384	3,871,621	2,368,859		333,442		524,084

Sources: See table 11.2.

[a]Includes all types of wholesalers.

[b]Excluded nonmerchant wholesalers.

[c]Unadjusted total excludes nonemployer wholesalers, whereas they were included in the adjusted total.

Table 11A.8 **Reconciliation between Census Estimates and National Accounts: Brazil (1975), Mexico (1975), France (1987), and the United States (1977, 1987)**

	Value Added (million national currency units)			Employment (thousands)		
Branch	Census (1)	National Accounts (2)	(1)/(2) (3)	Census (4)	National Accounts (5)	(4)/(5) (6)
Brazil						
Railways	595	2,332	.26	28	136	.21
Road transport	10,889	26,405	.41	329	1,019	.32
Water transport	530	4,574	.12	13	40	.33
Air transport	2,133	3,448	.62	24	28	.84
Transport services	5,777			62		
Total (all branches)	19,923	36,759	.54	456	1,224	.37
Wholesale & retail trade	162,109	148,855	1.09	2,361	2,313	1.02
Mexico						
Railways	3,752	3,395	1.11	99	89	1.11
Road passenger transport	11,734	19,455	.60	167	278	.60
Road freight transport	3,817	23,951	.16	62	389	.16
Water transport	896	1,466	.61	6	9	.61
Air transport	3,489	2,571	1.36	18	13	1.36
Transport services	3,218	4,320	.75	27	36	.74
Total (all branches)	26,906	55,158	.49	379	815	.46
Wholesale & retail trade	85,448	23,407	.36	1,118	1,886	.59
France						
Railways	33,008	29,141	1.13	141	128	1.10
Road passenger transport	30,120	35,797	.84	154	188	.82
Road freight transport	30,395	50,184	.61	208	227	.92
Water transport	4,412	980	.89	16	20	.77
Air transport	20,050	19,340	1.04	49	55	.88
Transport services	18,970	61,739	.31	92	190	.48
Total (all branches)	136,957	201,181	.68	659	808	.82
Wholesale & retail trade	506,846	663,151	.76	2,918	3,034	.96
United States						
Wholesale & retail trade, 1977	392,908	275,955	1.42	19,206	20,761	.93
Wholesale trade, 1987	246,988	255,935	.97	5,609	5,984	.94
Retail trade, 1987	373,411	354,999	1.05	17,780	19,144	.93

Sources: Census estimates of GDP and employment are as described in table 11.2. For national accounts, see app. B.

Appendix B
Sources for Time Series of GDP and Employment

Brazil. GDP: 1970–80 in constant prices taken from Gumão Veloso (1987), linked to 1980–93 figures from IBGE (1992, 1995). Employment: 1970 from IBGE (1990, 75 [population census]); 1975 and 1980 benchmarks from IBGE (1987, 1994); other years from IBGE, *Pesquisa mensual de amostra por domicilios* (various issues).

Mexico. GDP and employment trends from INEGI (1994b).

United States. GDP: 1970–77 from Department of Commerce, Bureau of Economic Analysis (1986); linked to new series from Department of Commerce, Bureau of Economic Analysis, *Survey of Current Business* (May 1993; April 1995). Employment: 1970–88 from Department of Commerce, Bureau of Economic Analysis (1992); 1989–93 from Department of Commerce, Bureau of Economic Analysis, *Survey of Current Business* (January 1992; July 1994).

References

Association of American Railroads. 1978. *Railroad facts.* Washington, D.C.

Barger, H. 1951. *The transportation industries, 1889–1946: A study of output, employment and productivity.* New York: National Bureau of Economic Research.

Deakin, B. M., and T. Seward. 1969. Productivity in transport: A study of employment, capital, output productivity and technical change. Occasional Paper no. 17. Department of Applied Economics, Cambridge University.

Department of Commerce. 1977, 1978, 1989, 1990. *Statistical abstract of the United States.* Washington, D.C.

Department of Commerce. Bureau of the Census. 1981a. Characteristics of retail trade. In *1977 Census of Retail Trade.* Washington, D.C.: U.S. Government Printing Office.

———. 1981b. *1977 Census of Retail Trade.* Washington, D.C.: U.S. Government Printing Office.

———. 1981c. *1977 Census of Wholesale Trade.* Washington, D.C.: U.S. Government Printing Office.

———. 1981d. 1977 merchant wholesalers. In *1977 Census of Wholesale Trade.* Washington, D.C.: U.S. Government Printing Office.

———. 1990a. *1987 Census of Retail Trade.* Washington, D.C.: U.S. Government Printing Office.

———. 1990b. *1987 Census of Wholesale Trade.* Washington, D.C.: U.S. Government Printing Office.

———. 1991a. Measures of value produced, capital expenditures, depreciable assets, and operating expenses (Subject Series RC87-S-2). *1987 Census of Retail Trade.* Washington, D.C.: U.S. Government Printing Office.

———. 1991b. Measures of value produced, capital expenditures, depreciable assets, and operating expenses (Subject Series WC87-S-2). In *1987 Census of Wholesale Trade*. Washington, D.C.: U.S. Government Printing Office.

Department of Commerce. Bureau of Economic Analysis. 1986. *The national income and product accounts of the United States, 1929–1982*. Washington, D.C.: U.S. Government Printing Office.

———. 1992. *The national income and product accounts of the United States, 1929–1988*. Washington, D.C.: U.S. Government Printing Office.

———. Various issues. *Survey of Current Business.*

Department of Labor. Bureau of Labor Statistics. 1978a. *Consumer prices and price indexes*. Suppl. 1976, Data for 1975. Washington, D.C.: U.S. Government Printing Office.

———. 1978b. *Producer prices and price indexes*. Suppl. 1978, Data for 1977. Washington, D.C.: U.S. Government Printing Office.

———. 1982. *Labor force statistics derived from the population survey: A databook*. Washington, D.C.: U.S. Government Printing Office.

Department of Transportation. 1981, 1992. *National transportation statistics*. Washington, D.C.: U.S. Government Printing Office.

———. 1994. *North American transportation: Statistics on Canadian, Mexican and US transportation*. Washington, D.C.: U.S. Government Printing Office.

Economic Commission for Latin America and the Caribbean (ECLAC)/UN Industrial Development Organization (UNIDO). 1994. Telecommunications in Latin America. Santiago de Chile: ECLAC. Mimeo.

Gadrey, J., T. Noyelle, and T. M. Stanback Jr. 1990. Productivity in air transportation: A comparison of France and the United States. Working Paper no. 90–4. New York: University of Lille and Eishenhower Center for Conservation of Human Resources.

Girard, J. M. 1958. *La productivité du travail dans les chemins de fer*. Paris: Centre d'Etudes et de Mesures de Productivité.

Gumão Veloso, M. A. 1987. Brazilian national accounts. Paper presented at twentieth conference of the International Association for the Research in Income and Wealth, Roca di Papa, Italy.

Hall, M., J. Knapp, and C. Winsten. 1961. *Distribution in Great Britain and North America*. Oxford: Oxford University Press.

Hariton, G., and R. Roy. 1979. Productivity changes in Canadian air and rail transport in the last two decades. *Logistics and Transportation Review* 15, no. 4:507–16.

Houben, A. 1990. An international comparison of real output, labour productivity and purchasing power in the mineral industries of the United States, Brazil and Mexico for 1975. Research Memorandum no. 368. Institute of Economic Research, University of Groningen.

Institut National de Statistiques et Etudes Economiques (INSEE). 1988. *Système informatique pour le répertoire des entreprises et des établissements* (SIRENE). Paris.

———. 1989. *Enquête annuelle d'entreprise dans le commerce*. Paris.

———. 1990a. *Annuaire rétrospective de la France, 1948–88*. Paris.

———. 1990b. *Vingts ans de comptes nationaux, 1970–89*. Paris.

———. 1991. *Annuaire statistique de la France*. Paris.

———. Various issues. *Rapport sur les comptes de la nation*. Paris.

INSEE and Ministère de Transport, Observatoire Economique et Statistique de Transports (OEST). 1990. *Enquête annuelle d'entreprise: Les entreprises de transport, année 1988*. Paris: INSEE.

Instituto Brasileiro de Estatísticas e Geografia (IBGE). 1981a. *Censo comercial*. Rio de Janeiro.

———. 1981b. Inquérito especial transporte. In *Censos econômicos de 1975*. Rio de Janeiro.

———. 1982. *Anuário estatístico do Brasil*. Rio de Janeiro.

————. 1987. *Matriz de relações intersetoriais—Brasil, 1975.* Rio de Janeiro.

————. 1990. *Estatísticas históricas do Brasil.* Rio de Janeiro.

————. 1992, 1995. Contas consolidadas para a nação. Rio de Janeiro. Mimeo.

————. 1994. *Matriz de insumo produto do Brasil—1980.* Rio de Janeiro.

————. Various issues. *Pesquisa nacional por amostra de domicilios.* Rio de Janeiro.

Instituto Nacional de Estadísticas, Geografía e Informática (INEGI). 1994a. *Estadísticas históricas de México.* Mexico City.

————. 1994b. *Sistema de cuentas nacionales de México* (CD-ROM). Mexico City.

Islas Rivera, V. 1992. *Estructura y desarrollo del sector transporte en México.* El Colegio de México, Mexico City.

Jefferys, J. B., and D. Knee. 1962. *Retailing in Europe.* London: Macmillan.

Kendrick, J. W. 1973. *Post-war productivity trends in the United States, 1948–1969.* New York: Columbia University Press.

Kravis, I. B., A. Heston, and R. Summers. 1982. *World product and income: International comparisons of real gross product.* Baltimore: Johns Hopkins University Press.

Maddison, A. 1995. *Monitoring the world economy, 1820–1992.* Paris: OECD Development Centre.

Maddison, A., and H. van Ooststroom. 1993. The international comparison of value added, productivity and purchasing power parities in agriculture. Research Memorandum no. 536 (GD-1). Groningen Growth and Development Centre, University of Groningen.

McKinsey Global Institute. 1992. *Service sector productivity.* Washington, D.C.

Meyer, J. R., and J. A. Gómez-Ibáñez. 1980. Measurement and analysis of productivity in transportation industries. In *New developments in productivity measurement and analysis* (Studies in Income and Wealth, no. 44), ed. J. W. Kendrick and B. N. Vaccara. Chicago: University of Chicago Press.

Meyer, J. R., and A. L. Morton. 1975. The US railroad industry in the post–World War II period: A profile. *Explorations in Economic Research* 2:449–501.

Ministère de Transport. Observatoire Economique et Statistique de Transports (OEST). 1989, 1990. *Mémento de statistiques des transports.* Paris: OEST.

Ministério dos Transportes. 1982. *Anuário estatístico do transportes.* Brasilia: Ministério dos Transportes.

Mulder, N. 1991. An assessment of Mexican productivity performance in services: A comparative view. University of Groningen, Economics Department. Mimeo.

————. 1994a. Output and productivity in Brazilian distribution: A comparative view. Research Memorandum no. 578 (GD-17). Groningen Growth and Development Centre, University of Groningen.

————. 1994b. La productivité dans les services en France et aux Etats-Unis. *Economie Internationale* 60, no. 4:89–118.

————. 1994c. Transport and communications in Mexico and the United States: Value added, purchasing power parities and labour productivity, 1950–87. Research Memorandum no. 579 (GD-18). Groningen Growth and Development Centre, University of Groningen.

————. 1995. Transport and communications output and productivity in Brazil and the USA, 1950–1990. Research Memorandum no. 580 (GD-19). Groningen Growth and Development Centre, University of Groningen.

————. 1999. The economic performance of the service sector in Brazil, Mexico and the USA: A comparative historical perspective. Monograph Series no. 4. Groningen Growth and Development Centre, University of Groningen.

Mulder, N., and A. Maddison. 1993. The international comparison of performance in distribution: Value added, labour productivity and purchasing power parities in Mexican and US wholesale and retail trade 1975/77. Research Memorandum no. 537 (GD-2). Groningen Growth and Development Centre, University of Groningen.

Observatoire Economique et Statistique de Transports (OEST). Various issues. *Mémento de statistiques des transports.* Paris.

Paige, D., and G. Bombach. 1959. *A comparison of national output and productivity of the United Kingdom and the United States.* Paris: OEEC/Cambridge University.

Pilat, D. 1991. Levels of real output and labour productivity by industry of origin: A comparison of Japan and the United States. Research Memorandum no. 408. Institute of Economic Research, University of Groningen.

———. 1994. *The economics of rapid growth: The experience of Japan and Korea.* Aldershot: Edward Elgar.

Rostas, L. 1948. *Comparative productivity in British and American industries.* National Institute of Economic and Social Research Occasional Paper no. 13. Cambridge: Cambridge University Press.

Sandoval, V. 1987. Productivité dans les transports de marchandises. *Transports,* no. 321:20–27.

Scheppach, R. C., and L. C. Woehlcke. 1975. *Transportation productivity: Measurement and policy applications.* Lexington: D. C. Heath.

Secretaría de Programación y Presupuesto (SPP). 1977, 1980. *Anuario estadístico de los Estados Unidos Mexicanos.* Mexico City.

———. 1979. *VII censo de transportes y de comunicaciones.* Mexico City.

———. 1981a. *Manual de estadísticas del sector comunicaciones y transportes.* Mexico City.

———. 1981b. *Matriz de insumo-producto.* Mexico City.

———. 1981c. *VII censo comercial 1976, datos de 1975.* Mexico City.

Smith, A. D., and D. M. W. N. Hitchens. 1985. *Productivity in the distributive trades: A comparison of Britain, America and Germany.* National Institute of Economic and Social Research. London: Cambridge University Press.

Smith, A. D., D. M. W. N. Hitchens, and D. W. Davies. 1982. *International industrial productivity: A comparison of Britain, America and Germany.* Cambridge: Cambridge University Press.

Szirmai, A., and D. Pilat. 1990. The international comparison of real output and labour productivity in manufacturing: A study for Japan, South Korea and the USA for 1975. Research Memorandum no. 354. Institute of Economic Research, University of Groningen.

van Ark, B., and A. Maddison. 1994. An international comparison of real output, purchasing power and labour productivity in manufacturing industries: Brazil, Mexico and the USA in 1975. Research Memorandum no. 567 (GD-6). Groningen Growth and Development Centre, University of Groningen.

Comment   Peter Hooper

In making international comparisons, there are several areas that researchers have tended to shy away from, perhaps because they are particularly challenging. One is *services:* goods are easier to measure and have tended to get more

Peter Hooper is deputy director of the Division of International Finance, Board of Governors of the Federal Reserve System.

attention. Another is *developing countries:* data tend to be easier to come by in industrial countries. A third is comparisons of output or productivity *levels,* especially at the sector level—the BLS has been warning us about the pitfalls in making level comparisons of productivity in manufacturing for many years. And a fourth is measuring *quality*—quantity concepts being far easier to deal with. Mulder's paper takes on not one but all four of these challenges.

The international comparison of output and productivity in services is a relatively new area of endeavor, and let me say first and foremost that I think that we will benefit from the fact that the ICOP has devoted some of its considerable energies and talents to this effort. Actually, a good deal of work has already been accomplished by Nanno Mulder, Angus Maddison, and their colleagues in this area, and this paper draws together much of that effort.

In looking through the literature and wondering why more had not been done in this area, I came across Zvi Griliches's invocation of Simon Kuznets at the 1990 CRIW conference on measuring service output. Kuznets had observed in his 1941 treatise that "the main point is that ingenuity cannot fully or effectively compensate for lack of basic information" (Griliches 1992, 1).

Mulder's paper exhibits considerable ingenuity, largely out of necessity, and for that I applaud the author. However, Kuznets's observation is also an admonition that we must be cautious in interpreting and using the results of such efforts. To support this point, my comments will touch on three specific areas: (1) judgments made about quality adjustment in transportation services; (2) the issue of double deflation; and (3) the substance of some of the results and how they compare to the estimates of other researchers.

Adjustment for quality in the Brazil/United States and Mexico/United States comparisons makes a large difference to the relative productivity estimates. In the case of passenger transportation, for example, output is measured in terms of passenger miles traveled. This output measure could be adjusted for quality in several dimensions, including speed, reliability, safety, and comfort. Mulder basically adjusts for comfort, using the degree of crowding or number of passengers per bus or plane. On this basis, Mexico's productivity in road passenger transportation compared to that of the United States is cut by half and that in air transportation by nearly one-third. This quality indicator for crowding makes some sense, but it could well overstate productivity differences on this dimension. The measured productivity of Mexican firms is effectively penalized for their being more efficient at filling their vehicles to capacity. And U.S. firms may have "benefited" from the fact that the United States was in a recession in the base year, 1975, a factor that may have kept vehicle occupancy rates down, at least in the airline industry.

In the case of road freight transportation, a somewhat broader concept of quality is considered: speed and reliability. Here quality is measured in terms of road traffic congestion, computed as the total number of vehicle kilometers traveled divided by the total length of paved and unpaved roads in the country.

A more accurate indicator of congestion would factor in the type of road surface and the average width or number of lanes per road.

In brief, a great deal of basic information about quality is missing, and one needs to be careful in interpreting the results.

My second comment has to do with the issue of double deflation in the measurement of value added in the distribution sectors. When computing real output or value added at the sectoral level, one needs to account for shifts in the relative prices of gross outputs and intermediate inputs, that is, to engage in double deflation. This technique has now been widely adopted in GDP accounting. It also applies to the comparison across countries of value added at the sectoral level. Mulder uses ICP PPPs for total consumer expenditures to translate outputs from one currency to another. In order to transform those final expenditure PPPs to be appropriate for value added in the retail sector, he needs to adjust them for PPPs specific to the inputs into the retail sector, including the goods that are purchased for resale by the retail distributors. To make this adjustment, he uses the ICOP PPPs or unit value ratios for goods. A priori, this seemed to be a reasonable course of action. The problem is that the results produced are implausible in some cases and cast doubt on either the ICP PPPs or the ICOP unit value ratios or both.

Mulder reverts to single deflation, which basically assumes that the ICP PPP for total consumer expenditures is relevant for both the gross output and the inputs of the retail sector.[1]

Even in single deflation, Mulder will want to consider adjusting his ICP PPPs for indirect taxes. If his value-added data are measured at factor cost, as is the case in most national accounts, the difference between U.S. and French indirect taxes could be biasing his results by as much as 15 percent.

My third comment concerns the substance of some of the results and how they compare with other available estimates. The paper, by the way, does a nice job of *presenting* the results but offers relatively little commentary on or analysis of their substance. A study that covers similar territory is the McKinsey Global Institute's (1992) analysis of service sector productivity in the major industrial countries. The overlap between that study and the current one is on the France/United States comparisons of labor productivity in retail trade, in airline transportation, and in telecommunications.

With respect to retail trade, there seems to be a fair amount of agreement between the two studies. Whereas Mulder reported results for retailing of durables and of total merchandise, including food and other nondurables, McKinsey considered establishments dealing in durables and semidurables. The results seem broadly consistent and suggest that French productivity is

---

1. In a separate line of research, I have addressed a somewhat related problem from a different angle—i.e., I have tried to transform ICP PPPs to be suitable for translation of goods at factory gate prices. This was done by adjusting the expenditure PPPs for cross-country differences in indirect taxes and wholesale and retail distribution margins. There may be some useful overlap in this approach with what Mulder is trying to do. See, e.g., Hooper (1996).

much closer to the U.S. level in food and other nondurable retailing than in durables.

Turning to air transportation, I found it somewhat counterintuitive to think that productivity in France was above that in the United States, as Mulder's results suggested. Throughout the 1980s, the airline industry in France and the rest of Europe was dominated by government ownership and heavy regulation of traffic rights. The U.S. industry, however, was largely deregulated in the late 1970s, opening it up much more to market discipline and competitive pressures. McKinsey's finding that labor productivity in the airline industry for Europe as a whole was below that in the United States seems more consistent with this view.

Finally, on communications, there is a wide gap between the Mulder and the McKinsey estimates, with Mulder showing French productivity below U.S. productivity by a much greater amount than the McKinsey estimates imply. Mulder seems to include the post office with telecommunications, whereas McKinsey does not, but it is difficult to believe that the French post office is *that* much less productive than its U.S. counterpart. On telecommunications, Mulder professes to use a methodology similar to McKinsey's, although I suspect that there may be a problem in his case with comparing the number of telephones (the measure used for France) with the number of telephone access lines (the measure used for the United States). In any event, this wide a discrepancy seems quite puzzling.

In sum, this paper is an important step forward, but there are enough puzzles and a sufficient lack of basic information about prices, quantities, and qualities in this area to suggest that the results should be used with considerable caution.

References

Griliches, Zvi, ed. 1992. *Output measurement in the service sectors.* Studies in Income and Wealth, vol. 56. Chicago: University of Chicago Press.

Hooper, Peter. 1996. Comparing manufacturing output levels among the major industrial countries. In *Industry productivity: International comparison and measurement issues.* Paris: Organization for Economic Cooperation and Development.

McKinsey Global Institute. 1992. *Service sector productivity.* Washington, D.C., October.

12 Prices, Quantities, and Productivity in Industry: A Study of Transition Economies in a Comparative Perspective

Bart van Ark, Erik Monnikhof, and Marcel Timmer

The recent breakup of socialist regimes in Eastern Europe and the troublesome process of transformation of former centrally planned economies into market economies has added a new aspect of interest to the debate on catch-up and convergence. It raises such questions as, What were the main bottlenecks characterizing the slowdown in growth performance in the centrally planned economies (CPEs) relative to the advanced market economies during the 1980s, and how have the basic parameters changed since transition began?[1]

In earlier papers, the present authors and others dealt with the comparative productivity performance of manufacturing in a wide range of countries, including centrally planned economies. Table 12.1 summarizes estimates of levels of manufacturing productivity for twenty-three countries relative to the United States for the period 1970–94 derived from the International Comparisons of Output and Productivity (ICOP) project. These estimates are based on the industry-of-origin method, which is briefly explained in section 12.1.

Bart van Ark and Erik Monnikhof are affiliated with the Groningen Growth and Development Centre, University of Groningen, The Netherlands. When this paper was written, Marcel Timmer was affiliated with the Department of Technology and Development Studies at the University of Eindhoven, The Netherlands.

The authors are grateful to Remco Kouwenhoven, Adam Szirmai, and Ren Ruoen for making available their detailed product match information for the Soviet Union/United States (Kouwenhoven 1996) and China/United States (Szirmai and Ruoen 1995). The authors thank Irwin Collier, Steve Dowrick, Robert Lipsey, Nick van der Lijn, and D. S. Prasada Rao for their comments on an earlier version. They also thank Elsbeth Hardon for statistical assistance. They acknowledge Labour Cost Research Associates (LCRA) for their financial support in developing some of the recent binary comparisons for 1992 and 1993. The latter estimates have not been published but are available from the authors on request.

1. In this paper, we will use the terms *transition economies* and *centrally planned economies* interchangeably. Both terms, as well as the term *historically planned economies* used by Marer (1991), do not adequately characterize the present or even the historical situation of the countries in this group for the purpose of this paper. For the sake of simplicity, we mostly stick to the terminology *centrally planned economies.*

Table 12.1 ICOP Estimates of Comparative Levels of Labor Productivity in Manufacturing, 1970–94, United States = 100

	1970		1980		1987		1994	
	Value Added per Person Employed	Value Added per Hour	Value Added per Person Employed	Value Added per Hour	Value Added per Person Employed	Value Added per Hour	Value Added per Person Employed	Value Added per Hour
China	4.5[a]		4.9		4.5			
India	7.0	5.8	5.6	5.0	7.2	5.7		
Indonesia	7.2		10.6		10.0	8.8		
Taiwan	10.4		14.1	10.1	19.1	14.6	27.5[b]	
Hungary	18.9		22.0		20.1		20.0	
Poland	27.1		26.8		21.2		17.0	
East Germany	27.3		27.6		22.5	23.5	46.5	
Czechoslovakia	26.5		28.8		24.0	18.8		
Portugal	22.2		27.4		24.5			
Soviet Union[c]	25.3	28.1	28.2	29.9	24.8	26.3		
Korea	14.8	10.2	22.1	15.0	26.3	18.2		
Brazil	41.4	38.6	42.7	38.5	30.7	28.4		
Mexico	37.2	34.9	39.7	35.4	30.5			
Spain	27.1	33.8	44.0	64.6	46.5		60.7	67.6
Australia	56.6	55.5	57.4	57.1	48.4	49.9		
United Kingdom	51.8	51.3	48.6	52.3	53.6	58.0	59.3	70.2
Finland	58.8	59.1	63.0	67.7	65.9	74.3		

Sweden	73.8	72.8	94.4	68.4	87.4	77.9	96.1
West Germany	79.7	87.1	95.1	70.2	82.2	66.1	85.3
France	73.0	83.0	89.8	71.2	84.0	72.9	89.3
Japan	53.5	77.0	66.2	76.4	67.5	73.4	72.4
Canada	86.3	86.8	89.0	77.3	80.8	71.6	75.2
Netherlands	75.4	90.3	107.5	83.3	105.4	78.7	103.2
United States	100.0	100.0	100.0	100.0	100.0	100.0	100.0

Sources: Benchmark estimates: China/United States (1987) from Szirmai and Ruoen (1995); India/United States (1975) from van Ark (1991); Indonesia/United States (1987) from Szirmai (1994); Taiwan/United States from Timmer (1996); Hungary/West Germany (1987) from Monnikhof (1996); Poland/West Germany (1989) from Liberda, Monnikhof, and van Ark (1996); East Germany/West Germany (1987) from Beintema and van Ark (1994) with revisions (see van Ark 1995a); Poland/West Germany (1993) are unpublished ICOP/LCRA estimates (January 1996); East Germany/West Germany (1992) are unpublished ICOP/LCRA estimates (January 1996); Czechoslovakia/West Germany from van Ark and Beintema (1993) with revisions (see van Ark 1996); Soviet Union/United States (1987) from Kouwenhoven (1996); Portugal/United Kingdom (1984) from Peres Lopes (1994) linked to United Kingdom/United States (1987) from van Ark (1992); Korea/United States (1987) and Japan/United States (1987) from Pilat (1994); Brazil/United States (1975) and Mexico/United States (1975) from van Ark and Maddison (1994); Spain/United Kingdom (1984) from van Ark (1995b) linked to United Kingdom/United States (1987) from van Ark (1992); Australia/United States (1987) from Pilat, Rao, and Shepherd (1993); United Kingdom/United States (1987) from van Ark (1992); Finland/United States (1987) and Sweden/United States (1987) from Maliranta (1994); West Germany/United States (1987) from van Ark and Pilat (1993); France/United States (1987) from van Ark and Kouwenhoven (1994); Canada/United States (1987) from de Jong (1996); Netherlands/United States from Kouwenhoven (1993). Extrapolations from benchmark years are mostly from (modified) national accounts series on real GDP and employment in manufacturing; see original publications above with extensions according to the ICOP industry database (University of Groningen).

Note: Countries are ranked according to their level of value added per person employed in 1987. All estimates have been converted to the United States as the base country.

[a]1975.

[b]1993.

[c]Extrapolated by series for all industry (including mining, construction, and public utilities).

Table 12.1 shows that, in 1987, the level of manufacturing labor productivity was lowest in China, whereas other CPEs show productivity levels in a range between those of typical low-productivity economies such as India and Indonesia and higher-productivity economies such as Korea, Brazil, and Mexico.[2] Compared to studies of Eastern Europe and the Soviet Union for earlier years, our estimates for the CPEs are relatively low.[3] This is related partly to a genuine decline in comparative productivity performance of the CPEs since the 1970s and partly to differences in methodology between this study and the earlier ones. Our estimates are based on value added rather than gross output, and we use industry purchasing power parities (PPPs), which are a geometric average of PPPs at market economy and CPE weights (see sec. 12.1).

The explanation of productivity differences between countries has been addressed from various angles. In earlier papers, we applied a "level accounting" approach, which accounted for the role of typical supply-side factors, such as differences in physical and human capital intensity, industry composition, and firm size (van Ark and Pilat 1993; van Ark 1993; Pilat 1994). Van Ark (1996) suggests that the emphasis on "extensive growth" strategies, based on rapid accumulation of factor inputs without substantive total factor productivity (TFP) growth, explains much of the relative decline in the productivity performance of the CPEs, in particular during the 1970s and 1980s.

Another plausible explanation for the relatively low productivity levels in CPEs is the misallocation of resources and final output because of a distorted relation between prices and quantities. The CPEs were characterized by a system of administrative prices that do not reflect scarcities in the market but are primarily based on cost plus net indirect taxes and a markup. This explanation for the bad performance of centrally planned economies has been put forward in many studies by key scholars in this field, including Bergson (1961, 1978, 1987) and Kornai (1980, 1992).

In this paper, our aim is not to explain the productivity performance of the CPEs in the first place. In relation to the latter type of explanation, we will investigate to what extent our estimates of price relatives and quantity relatives suggest a greater distortion in CPEs than in other countries. Second, we investigate regularities and irregularities in terms of price and quantity structures for groups of countries given their relative productivity levels.

In section 12.1, we present our estimates of manufacturing output and productivity for four East European countries. Binary comparisons were made for East Germany and Hungary compared to West Germany for 1987 and Czechoslovakia and Poland compared to West Germany for 1989. For two of these countries (i.e., the East German *Länder* and Poland), more recent benchmark comparisons for 1992/1993 were made as well. We also briefly outline the major

---

2. Taiwan's labor productivity in manufacturing was still somewhat below that of the CPE countries in 1987, but, as table 12.1 shows, it increased very substantially between 1987 and 1993.
3. For details on earlier studies, see n. 13 below.

characteristics of the industry-of-origin approach as compared to the expenditure approach in international comparisons, and we deal extensively with the specific methodological problems that arise from the inclusion of centrally planned economies in those studies.

In the second half of the paper, we focus on the relative price and quantity structures between CPEs and non-CPEs and on the relation between price and quantity relatives. As our comparisons are all of a binary nature, we begin in section 12.2 by analyzing the difference in purchasing power parities (in our terminology, *unit value ratios* [UVRs]) at quantity weights of the "own" country (the Paasche UVR) with those at quantity weights of the "numeraire" (or base) country (the Laspeyres UVR). We find that the Paasche-Laspeyres (PL) ratio, which provides an indication of the "Gerschenkron effect," is much higher for the CPEs than might be expected given their relative level of labor productivity. Subsequently, we analyze the issue from a mathematical perspective, by making use of the "Bortkiewicz formula" (Bortkiewicz 1922, 1924). According to this formula, the PL ratio is decomposed into three components: (1) the variance of price relatives; (2) the variance of quantity relatives; and (3) the correlation between price and quantity relatives. The relation between price and quantity relatives, which can be interpreted as a measure of distortion, is analyzed, and various measures of the (dis)similarity of price and quantity structures between the countries are discussed. Subsequently, each of these three components will be looked at in more detail and will be related to the relative labor productivity level in manufacturing.

12.1   Manufacturing Productivity Levels in Centrally Planned Economies

12.1.1   The Industry-of-Origin Method Compared to the Expenditure Method

International comparisons of GDP and per capita income are mostly made by converting national income into a common currency on the basis of expenditure-based purchasing power parities (PPPs). These PPPs are obtained by expenditure category (private consumption, investment, and government expenditure).[4] There is a long tradition of such comparisons, also for centrally planned economies, including several studies by the UN Economic Commission for Europe (see, e.g., ECE 1988, 1994).[5]

Comparisons of productivity should preferably be based on the industry-of-

4. For early postwar comparisons, see, e.g., Gilbert and Kravis (1954) and Gilbert et al. (1958). Since the late 1960s, surveys were conducted at regular intervals by the International Comparisons Project (ICP); see, e.g., Kravis, Heston, and Summers (1982) and the subsequent Penn World Tables (e.g., Summers and Heston 1988, 1991), which were derived from the ICP estimates.

5. For a review of ICP studies including CPEs, see Marer (1985). For a review of historical comparisons of the Soviet Union and the United States, see Kudrov (1995).

origin approach. It involves comparisons of real output by sector of the economy (agriculture, industry, and services) and branches and industries within these sectors. The earliest industry-of-origin studies were mainly based on direct comparisons of physical quantities produced (tons, liters, units) (see, e.g., Rostas 1948).[6] Later on, industry comparisons switched to using "industry" purchasing power parities to convert the output value by industry, branch, or sector to a common currency.[7]

Since 1983, a substantial research effort has been made at the University of Groningen to develop the industry-of-origin approach as part of the International Comparisons of Output and Productivity (ICOP) project. So far, most ICOP studies dealt with comparisons of manufacturing productivity, which now include almost thirty countries, most of which are reported in table 12.1.[8]

The most solid basis for industry-of-origin studies is provided when, for each country, all information can be derived from a single primary source, which, in the case of manufacturing, is the census of production or industrial survey. It contains considerable detail on the output and input structure by industry and information on the sales values and quantities of most products. The "industry" PPPs are based on ratios of unit values (derived from the sales values and quantities reported) for matched products between two countries. This method is fundamentally different from the pricing technique in the ICP expenditure approach, which makes use of prices for specified products. The industry-of-origin technique provides unit values with a quantity counterpart, as quantities times "prices" equals the value equivalent.

As the production censuses and industry surveys are harmonized across countries only to a limited extent, the most practical approach is to make the industry-of-origin comparisons on a two-country basis. For ICOP comparisons, the United States or West Germany is mostly taken as the "numeraire" (or base) country.[9]

Unit value ratios cannot be obtained for all output produced, mainly because of differences in product mix and product quality across countries, the lack of information for reasons of confidentiality, and the existence of unique products in one of two countries compared. In practice, between 67 (in the case of the China/United States comparison for 1987) and 414 (in the case of the Germany/United States comparison for 1992) unit value ratios are obtained, which cover between 10 and 50 percent of the total value of manufacturing sales (see table 12.5 below). Coverage percentages are usually somewhat below the average for typical investment goods (such as machinery and transport equip-

6. For a Soviet Union/United States comparison of this nature, see Galenson (1955).
7. For an early comparison of this nature for the United Kingdom and the United States in 1950, see, e.g., Paige and Bombach (1959). For comparisons including Austria, Czechoslovakia, France, and Hungary for the 1960s, see Conference of European Statisticians (1971, 1972).
8. For an overall review of ICOP studies, see Maddison and van Ark (1994). For manufacturing, see van Ark (1993).
9. For an application of multilateral indexes to original binary ICOP comparisons at aggregate levels of industries and branches, see Pilat and Prasada Rao (1996).

ment) and above average in nondurable consumer goods (such as food and kindred products). By reweighting UVRs at various stages from the product level up to the industry, branch, and sector level, using either quantities (at the product level) or value added (at higher levels) as weights, it is assured that the UVRs of products in bigger industries affect the UVR for total manufacturing more strongly than those of smaller industries. At the same time, the sensitivity of the aggregate UVR to outlier UVRs is reduced in this way.

Despite their shortcomings (which can be reduced by using more detailed product information or by adjusting existing UVRs for observed quality differences),[10] ICOP UVRs are preferred over ICP PPPs as a conversion factor for sectoral studies. First, expenditure-based PPPs include prices of imports but not of exports. Second, the expenditure prices include trade and transport margins, which may differ between countries. Finally, expenditure PPPs exclude price ratios for intermediate products, which form a substantial part of manufacturing output.[11]

12.1.2 Comparisons of Prices and Productivity for East European Countries[12]

Studies of comparative output and productivity levels for centrally planned economies raise specific problems that are less important for comparisons among market economies.

1. Centrally planned economies have less meaningful prices on the basis of which output is compared to that of market economies. Official price quotations are mostly administered prices, which are determined differently from the price-formation process in a market economy. Comparisons between CPEs and market economies have therefore often been made on the basis of pricing the products at Western prices only, for example, at U.S. dollars or West German marks.[13] Such comparisons usually imply that the output of the country

---

10. See, e.g., Gersbach and van Ark (1994) for a detailed description of adjustments to ICOP PPPs used in a comparative study of manufacturing productivity between Germany, Japan, and the United States, by the McKinsey Global Institute (1993).

11. For recent applications of expenditure PPPs to industry-of-origin comparisons, see Hooper and Vrankovich (1995) and Pilat (1996).

12. This section concentrates on the main problems of comparisons including former CPEs. For a more detailed account of methods and procedures for each binary comparison and more detailed estimates, see van Ark and Beintema (1993). For the comparison of Czechoslovakia and West Germany, see van Ark (1996). For East Germany vis-à-vis West Germany in 1987, see Beintema and van Ark (1994) and van Ark (1995a). For Poland and West Germany in 1989, see Liberda, Monnikhof, and van Ark (1996). For Hungary vs. West Germany, see Monnikhof (1996). Details of comparisons for East and West Germany in 1992 and Poland and West Germany in 1993 have not yet been published. The Soviet Union/United States and China/United States comparisons are not dealt with in this section. For this, the reader is referred to Kouwenhoven (1996) and Szirmai and Ruoen (1995).

13. Van Ark (1995a) extensively describes earlier comparisons of East and West German output, which include Sturm (1974), Wilkens (1970), and Görzig and Gornig (1991). There has also been one study comparing Czechoslovakia and France in the framework of a four-country comparison (Austria, Czechoslovakia, France, and Hungary) at the end of the 1960s (Conference of European Statisticians 1971, 1972). All these studies make use, to a considerable extent at least, of the

for which the prices are substituted by the prices of the other country gets overstated. This stylized fact, which may be referred to as the *Gerschenkron effect,* will be discussed in more detail in section 12.2.

Although the unit values of the CPEs represent administered prices, these remain the most practical for calculating unit value ratios because of the identity of quantities times prices and values in our data set: the CPE output value that needs to be converted to West German marks is expressed in the same administered prices as the unit values in the unit value ratios.[14] Table 12.2 shows the average unit value ratio for manufacturing for the benchmark years of our comparisons for four East European countries. The table shows that, in all cases, the UVRs are substantially below the commercial exchange rate. The commercial exchange rates reflect the relatively high price of exported goods, when expressed in domestic currencies, compared to the amount of West German marks these goods earn on the world market. The exchange rate deviation index is therefore substantially above one in all cases.

2. There are significant differences between the quality of products produced in CPEs and that of those produced in market economies. Although one can safely assume that, on the whole, average product quality was lower in CPEs than in market economies, it is not clearly documented whether such differences were equally large across the whole range of manufacturing products. Furthermore, given the administrative nature of the pricing system in the CPEs, one cannot be sure to what extent quality differences were or were not reflected in the actual prices.

The present comparisons for Czechoslovakia (1989), East Germany (1987), and Poland (1989) include a rough quality adjustment for passenger cars. This adjustment was derived from a price valuation of a Czech-made car (a Skoda) in West Germany compared to the average price of a car of West German make in 1989. The overall effect of the quality adjustment for cars on the unit value ratio for manufacturing as a whole was 16 percent for the Czechoslovakia/West Germany comparison, 11 percent for the East Germany/West Germany comparison in 1987, and 8 percent for the Poland/West Germany comparison in 1989.[15]

3. A third problem that affects output and productivity comparisons between

method by which quantities were valued at Western prices only. Most comparisons between former CPEs were carried out by the CMEA (Council for Mutual Economic Assistance) Standing Statistical Commission. These estimates were based on detailed repricing of individual commodities mostly with the former Soviet Union as the numeraire country. Until the dissolution of the CMEA, these estimates were not disclosed, although recently estimates for 1988 were published by Comecon (1990). For a detailed description of earlier estimates for these countries, see Drechsler and Kux (1972). Kouwenhoven (1996) and Kudrov (1995) provide a review of former Soviet Union/United States estimates.

14. Here, we ignore the distorting effect that administrative prices may have on the weighting system, which may affect the interpretation of the aggregate results (see, e.g., Marer 1985).

15. For further details, see van Ark (1995a, 1996) and Liberda, Monnikhof, and van Ark (1996). These sources also show the results without the quality adjustment. For the Hungary/West Germany comparison, no adjustment for quality was made as there were no cars produced in Hungary.

Table 12.2   Unit Value Ratios for Total Manufacturing and Commercial Exchange Rates for (former) CPEs, 1987–93

	Unit Value Ratio (own currency/DM)			Commercial Exchange Rate (own currency/DM) (4)	Exchange Rate Deviation Index (4)/(3) (5)
	At Own Country Quantity Weights (1)	At West German Quantity Weights (2)	Geometric Average (3)		
Czechoslovakia/West Germany (1989)	3.72	4.03	3.87	8.01	2.07
East Germany/West Germany (1987)	1.81	1.98	1.89	4.52	2.39
Hungary/West Germany (1987)	12.5	15.3	13.8	25.8	1.87
Poland/West Germany (1989)	343.1	342.8	343.0	1,439.2	4.20
East Germany/West Germany (1992)	.77	.73	.75	1.00	1.33
Poland/All Germany (1993)	5,313.4	5,221.9	5,267.5	10,957.0	2.08

Source: See table 12.1 and appendix table 12A.1. Exchange rates from World Bank (1993).

Note: For details on the matching procedure, see appendix table 12A.1.

CPEs and market economies concerns differences in industry classification schemes. For the CPEs, there are difficulties in separating activities in mining and utilities from those in manufacturing. More important is that employment estimates for manufacturing in CPEs often include employees from a wide range of secondary activities, such as repair and maintenance and social services provided by firms on a much wider scale than in market economies. Where possible, adjustments to Western classification schemes were made. Similarly, as far as possible, labor input in social services etc. was excluded from the employment data.

4. Finally, differences in the concept of output between CPEs and market economies have been a matter of major concern in comparative economics. Comparisons across countries can be made either on the basis of gross output or on the basis of value added. The difference between these two output measures is the intermediate inputs. According to the traditional material product system (MPS) accounting system used by the CPEs, output concerns only material production, and intermediate inputs concern only material inputs (raw materials, energy, packaging) and some industrial services (e.g., contract labor). Nonindustrial service inputs were not measured.

As we did not have detailed information on nonindustrial services for the CPE countries, our output comparisons are in terms of gross output and value added, where, in the latter case, we only deducted material cost from gross output (see appendix table 12A.2).[16] Table 12.3 shows the comparative levels of gross output, value added, and gross output and value added per employee that were obtained with the help of the unit value ratios from table 12.2.[17] The estimates show that the output gap between the CPEs and West Germany was smaller in terms of gross output than in terms of value added, which suggests a greater use of intermediate inputs in the CPE countries. This can also be derived from the final column of table 12.3, which shows the ratio of material inputs to gross output in domestic prices. In all cases but one, this ratio was substantially larger in the CPEs (between 60 and 65 percent of gross output) than in West Germany (between 48 and 53 percent).[18]

16. For the 1992/1993 comparisons, we stayed as much as possible with the same concepts as for the late 1980s, partly to retain comparability and partly because, in the case of Poland, the statistics of the early 1990s have not yet been fully adjusted to Western concepts of output and employment.

17. With the exception of Poland (1989), the same unit value ratios were used for the comparisons of value added and gross output, assuming that the price ratios for gross output were also representative for the intermediate inputs. Although this assumption (which can be contrasted with double deflation when intermediate inputs are converted with an independent UVR for intermediate inputs) could not be cross-checked with other evidence, there is no immediate reason to expect a systematic difference between UVRs at the gross output level and UVRs for intermediate inputs. Only in the case of Poland (1989) did we develop separate UVRs for intermediate inputs, which were obtained by backdating the gross output UVRs with six months (assuming that this was the average time during which intermediate inputs were kept in stock), using the producer price index for Poland. (See Liberda, Monnikhof, and van Ark 1996.)

18. The Polish case for 1989 was exceptional. Because of the high inflation during the benchmark year, intermediate inputs were valued at much lower prices than gross output, so the ratio of the value of intermediate inputs to gross output was lower than usual.

Table 12.3 **Gross Value of Output, Value Added, and Labor Productivity in Manufacturing in (former) CPEs as a Percentage of West Germany,[a] 1987–93**

	Gross Value of Output (1)	Value Added (2)	Gross Value of Output per Employee (3)	Value Added per Employee (4)	Material Inputs as a % of Gross Output[b] (5)
Czechoslovakia (1989)	14.7	10.6	44.7	32.3	65.1
East Germany (1987)	19.6	12.9	48.6	32.0	65.8
Hungary (1987)	6.3	5.3	33.4	28.6	59.5
Poland (1989)	16.5	13.5[c]	35.2	29.3[c]	41.9
West Germany (1987–89)	100.0	100.0	100.0	100.0	48.0–51.9
East Germany (1992)	5.9	4.8	56.0	46.9	61.1
Poland (1993)[a]	9.1	7.9	27.0	23.5	59.1
West Germany (1992)	100.0	100.0	100.0	100.0	52.9

Source: Appendix tables 12A.1 and 12A.2.

Note: The conversion to common currency was done at the geometric average of the unit value ratios at own country weights and (West) German weights.

[a]Poland as a percentage of all Germany.

[b]Calculated on the basis of domestic prices.

[c]After adjustment of gross output UVR to a value-added UVR by using a UVR for intermediate inputs that was derived by backdating the gross output UVR by six months using the producer price index. This adjustment was necessary because of an inflation rate of over 700 percent in Poland in 1989.

There are various explanations for the larger share of material inputs in gross output in CPEs compared to market economies. First, there has been a greater wastage of intermediate inputs. Although in recent decades value added rather than gross output was the major performance criterion in CPEs, there was no budget constraint on inputs. This led to an inefficient use of raw materials, energy, and other intermediate inputs. Production prices were raised to allow for greater wastage, and product-oriented subsidies were accorded when prices became too high. Related to this, a second reason for the larger use of intermediate inputs is the misallocation of inputs across industries owing to the distortion of prices. Third, firms tended to hold large stocks of materials and semifinished products, which they used to exchange with other firms in order to compensate for general shortages. Fourth, there may have been a trade-off between the low technology content and high material input content for many products from CPE countries. For example, CPEs often invested in heavy and solid machine tools that performed relatively simple functions with large margins of tolerance. The latter were typical "low-value-added" products, characterized by relatively low ratios of value added to gross output.[19]

In our comparisons, we use value added rather than gross output because, at the aggregate level of total manufacturing, the use of value added prevents double-counting. Moreover, by using value added, we take account of at least part of the quality problem outlined above, namely, as far as it is related to the typical low-value-added content of CPE products. To the extent that the use of excessive intermediate inputs per unit of output was meant to compensate for the low technology content of the products, an implicit correction is made for the low quality content of the products in the CPE country. Admittedly, this method is crude and does not provide an exact adjustment for quality. However, as the latter type of adjustment is very difficult to come by directly, our value-added comparisons are a better proxy for "quality-adjusted" productivity than the gross output comparisons.

Table 12.3 shows that gross output per employee in manufacturing varied from 33 percent of the West German level in Hungary to 49 percent in East Germany during the late 1980s. The value added per person employed as a percentage of West Germany varied from 29 percent in Hungary and Poland to 32 percent in Czechoslovakia and East Germany. The two comparisons for the early 1990s suggest a significant improvement in manufacturing productivity in East Germany relative to West Germany but a worsening of the productivity performance in Poland versus all Germany.

The ICOP papers cited in the source notes to table 12.1 and appendix tables 12A.1 and 12A.2 document the binary comparisons in more detail and provide disaggregated productivity results by industry and branch. Table 12.4 summa-

19. This difference in the nature of products produced in former CPEs compared to high-productivity market economies comes out clearly in a study comparing manufacturing plants in East and West European countries producing similar products (see Hitchens, Wagner, and Birnie 1993, chap. 5).

Table 12.4 Comparative Levels of Value Added per Employee in Manufacturing, Czechoslovakia, East Germany, Hungary, and Poland as a Percentage of West Germany,[a] 1987–93

	Czechoslovakia, 1989 (1)	East Germany, 1987 (2)	Hungary, 1987 (3)	Poland, 1989 (4)	East Germany, 1992 (5)	Poland, 1993[a] (6)
Food products, beverages, and tobacco	23.7	46.3	29.3	30.4	44.5	29.6
Textile products, wearing apparel, leather products, and footwear	31.0	41.1	32.9	24.2	43.4	19.2
Chemicals, rubber and plastic products, and oil refining	73.9	44.4	29.6	39.1	33.7	27.5
Basic and fabricated metal products	35.7	40.1	30.0	21.9	63.7	19.7
Electrical and nonelectrical machinery and transport equipment	28.0	22.4	29.8	34.4	48.1	25.9
Other manufacturing[b]	34.2	27.7	26.3	25.6	47.5	17.8
Total manufacturing	32.3	32.0	28.6	29.3	46.9	23.5

Source: See table 12.1. For statistical sources, see appendix tables 12A.1 and 12A.2.

[a]Poland as a percentage of all Germany.

[b]Includes wood products and furniture; paper and paper products and printing; nonmetallic minerals and "other manufacturing."

rizes these results at the level of six major branches in manufacturing. The estimates suggest a varied pattern across the (former) CPEs. In Czechoslovakia and East Germany, the machinery and equipment branch experienced relatively low productivity levels compared to West Germany, whereas chemicals scored relatively well. In East Germany, basic metals and metal products also showed high productivity levels compared to the other CPE countries. In Poland, chemicals and machinery and equipment showed a relatively good productivity performance, whereas basic metals and metal products had by far the lowest productivity level compared to West Germany. Finally, Hungary showed relatively little variation in productivity levels by major branch around the mean for total manufacturing.

12.2   The Gerschenkron Effect and the Role of Distortion

The literature on the comparative performance of (former) centrally planned economies has put much emphasis on distortion of the price formation process in these countries. If prices do not fulfill their role to secure an optimal resource allocation, this may lead to a distorted relation between prices and produced quantities.

A first indication of distortion may be derived from the nonexistence of the Gerschenkron effect. In a two-country framework, the Gerschenkron effect implies that, the more the quantity structures of the two countries differ, the more the use of price weights of one country will lead to an overstatement of the other country's output (Gerschenkron 1951). This effect occurs because goods with a high (low) price in one country relative to the other country are associated with relatively small (large) quantities. Similarly, the more the price structures of the two countries differ, the more the use of quantity weights of one country will lead to an overstatement of the other country's prices. In terms of unit value ratios, this implies that the Laspeyres UVR (using quantity weights of the base country, i.e., the United States or Germany) is higher than the Paasche UVR (using quantity weights of the own country).

Table 12.5 shows that the Paasche-Laspeyres (PL) ratio is below one in twenty-five of the twenty-six cases. We grouped our countries into "high-productivity market economies" (HMEs), "low-productivity market economies" (LMEs), and "(former) centrally planned economies" (CPEs).[20] Within each group, the countries are ordered according to their level of labor productivity relative to the United States. On average, the PL ratio is 0.81 for all countries together, 0.87 for the HMEs, 0.65 for the LMEs, and 0.93 for the CPEs.

From a theoretical point of view, the results in table 12.5 are somewhat un-

20. China was included with the LMEs even though, from a political-economic point of view, it would have been correct to include China with the CPEs. As we will show below, the price and quantity characteristics of Chinese manufacturing are much more like those of LMEs than those of CPEs.

Table 12.5 Paasche and Laspeyres Unit Value Ratios (at product quantity weights) for 26 Binary Comparisons of Ex-Factory Product Unit Values in Manufacturing

	Number of Products in Sample (1)	Paasche UVR (own country currency/numeraire country currency at own country quantity weights) (2)	Laspeyres UVR (own country currency/numeraire country currency at numeraire country quantity weights) (3)	Paasche-Laspeyres Ratio (2)/(3) (4)
High-productivity market economies (HMEs)				
West Germany/United States (1992)	412	1.95	2.12	.92
Canada/United States (1987)	198	1.36	1.41	.97
Japan/United States (1987)	190	156	225	.69
France/United States (1987)	63[a]	5.04	5.88	.86
West Germany/United States (1987)	273	2.08	2.18	.95
Japan/United States (1975)	163	214	289	.74
Spain/United States (1992)	240	120	156	.77
United Kingdom/United States (1987)	171	.66	.71	.93
Australia/United States (1987)	175	1.28	1.39	.92
United Kingdom/United States (1975)	120	.42	.44	.96
Arithmetic average HMEs	201			.87
(Former) centrally planned economies (CPEs)[b]				
East Germany/West Germany (1992)	263	.75	.74	1.02
Czechoslovakia/West Germany (1989)	70	3.71	4.29	.86
East Germany/West Germany (1987)	335	1.85	1.99	.93
Soviet Union/United States (1987)	132	.48	.51	.93
Poland/West Germany (1989)	236	347	389	.89
Hungary/West Germany (1987)	386	12.4	14.8	.84
Poland/Germany (1993)	216	4,961	4,993	.99
Arithmetic average CPEs	234			.93

(continued)

Table 12.5 (continued)

	Number of Products in Sample (1)	Paasche UVR (own country currency/ numeraire country currency at own country quantity weights) (2)	Laspeyres UVR (own country currency/ numeraire country currency at numeraire country quantity weights) (3)	Paasche-Laspeyres Ratio (2)/(3) (4)
Low-productivity market economies (LMEs)				
Brazil/United States (1975)	129	6.42	8.31	.77
Mexico/United States (1975)	131	11.5	12.9	.89
South Korea/United States (1987)	184	639	951	.67
South Korea/United States (1975)	159	326	607	.54
Taiwan/United States (1976)	104	25.7	48.3	.53
Indonesia/United States (1987)	198	1,093	1,574	.69
South Korea/United States (1967)	114	220	350	.63
India/United States (1975)	111	4.29	8.25	.52
China/United States (1987)	58	1.26	1.98	.64
Arithmetic average LMEs	132			.65
Arithmetic average all countries	186			.81

Sources: See references to benchmark comparisons in table 12.1 and appendix table 12A.1. West Germany/United States (1992) are unpublished estimates from ICOP/LCRA (January 1996); East Germany/West Germany (1992) from ICOP/LCRA (January 1996); Japan/United States (1975) from Pilat (1994); South Korea/United States (1967, 1975) from Pilat (1995); the United Kingdom/United States (1975) from van Ark (1990); Taiwan/United States from Timmer (1996).

Note: The (number of) UVRs reported in this table are slightly different from those used to convert output by manufacturing branch to a common currency (such as, e.g., in sec. 12.2) as the latter have been reweighted by the output share of sample industries. However, in only two cases, we found very big differences: the PL ratio for Korea/United States (1975) was 0.75 after reweighting, and the PL ratio for the Soviet Union/United States was 0.58 after reweighting.

[a] Excluding UVRs for food products that are available only at U.S. quantity weights.

[b] The exchange rates for the CPEs are mostly "commercial" exchange rates. These are expressed as national currencies to the West German mark.

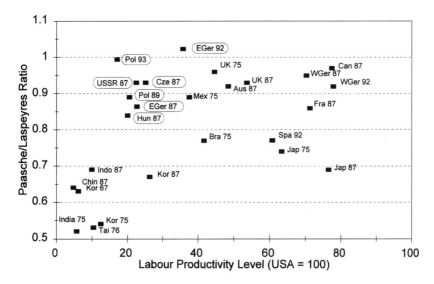

Fig. 12.1   Relation between Paasche-Laspeyres ratios and comparative levels of value added per person employed in manufacturing for 26 binary comparisons
Source: Table 12.5.

expected, as there is a priori less reason to expect the Gerschenkron effect to exist with producer prices than with expenditure prices, which were used in earlier studies (see Kravis, Heston, and Summers 1982; Nuxoll 1994). When prices rise, producers are expected to substitute for more expensive rather than cheaper products.[21] On an ad hoc basis, one may hypothesize that consumer substitution effects are stronger than the producer substitution effects and that therefore the Gerschenkron effect continues to exist even for the ICOP UVRs. This hypothesis is reinforced by the results for the CPEs, for which the PL ratio is even closer to one (and, in one case, exceeds one) than for the HMEs. The nonexistence of a Gerschenkron effect for these countries could perhaps imply that producer effects dominate the PL ratio and that consumer preferences are not reflected in the price setting.[22]

The special position of the CPEs is confirmed in figure 12.1, which relates the Paasche-Laspeyres ratio to the comparative level of labor productivity of each country relative to the United States. Figure 12.1 shows that (former) CPEs have a higher PL ratio than their comparative level of productivity would suggest.

We also analyzed the results statistically by regressing the PL ratios on the

21. For a theoretical exposition of these contrasting effects in neoclassical consumer and producer theories, see, e.g., Usher (1980).

22. We emphasize, however, that this explanation remains unsatisfactory as both producer and consumer theories are essentially static, whereas dynamic theories about substitution are called for. We have therefore not pursued this line of investigation further in this paper.

comparative productivity performance of each country relative to the United States (see regression 1 in appendix table 12A.4). The regression shows a highly significant coefficient for the productivity ratio. When a separate dummy variable is introduced for the CPE countries, the results become even more significant.

To analyze the atypical pattern of the Paasche-Laspeyres ratio for the CPE countries in more detail, we used the Bortkiewicz formula, which decomposes the PL ratio into three independent elements: (1) the weighted coefficient of variation of the price relatives between two countries (σ_p); (2) the weighted coefficient of variation of the quantity relatives between two countries (σ_q); and (3) the weighted coefficient of correlation (r_{pq}) between the price and the quantity relatives.[23] In a formula:

$$(1) \qquad \frac{P^{XU(X)}}{P^{XU(U)}} = \frac{Q^{XU(X)}}{Q^{XU(U)}} = 1 + r_{pq} \frac{\sigma_p}{P^{XU(U)}} \frac{\sigma_q}{Q^{XU(U)}},$$

where $P^{XU(U)}$ and $Q^{XU(U)}$ are the Laspeyres price and quantity indexes between countries X and U of all manufacturing goods, respectively, and $P^{XU(X)}$ and $Q^{XU(X)}$ are the Paasche price and quantity indexes between countries X and U of all manufacturing goods, respectively. The weighted coefficients of variation, σ_p and σ_q, are defined as

$$(2) \quad \sigma_p = \sqrt{\frac{\sum_{i=1}^{m} w_i^U (P_i^{XU} - P^{XU(U)})^2}{\sum_{i=1}^{m} w_i^U}}, \quad \sigma_q = \sqrt{\frac{\sum_{i=1}^{m} w_i^U (Q_i^{XU} - Q^{XU(U)})^2}{\sum_{i=1}^{m} w_i^U}},$$

and the weighted coefficient of correlation (r_{pq}) as

$$(3) \qquad r_{pq} = \frac{\sum_{i=1}^{m} w_i^U (P_i^{XU} - P^{XU(U)})(Q_i^{XU} - Q^{XU(U)})}{\sum_{i=1}^{m} w_i^U},$$

where P_i^{XU} is the ratio of the price of good i in country X and country U, Q_i^{XU} is the ratio of the quantity of good i in country X and country U, and w_i^U is the value of good i in country U.

Table 12.6 shows the values of these three components. In the next section, we will deal with the variation in price and quantity relatives (cols. 1 and 2). Here, we focus on the correlation coefficient (col. 3), which may be used as a proxy of the degree of distortion. When the price relatives between country X and country U do not show a clear negative relation to the quantity relatives, a greater distortion in country X is suggested on the assumption that the numeraire country U (which is either the United States or West Germany) has rela-

---

23. For an extensive description and derivation, see Allen (1975, 62–65). For an application of the Bortkiewicz formula to a time series of U.S. machinery output from 1899 to 1939, see Jonas and Sardy (1970). See also Dikhanov (1994).

Table 12.6   Coefficients of Variation of Price and Quantity Relatives and the Correlation between Prices and Quantities for 26 Binary Comparisons in Manufacturing (all at numeraire country weights)

	Coefficient of Variation		Coefficient of Correlation (between price and quantity relatives) (3)
	Price Ratios (between own country and numeraire country) (1)	Quantity Ratios (between own country and numeraire country) (2)	
High-productivity market economies (HMEs)			
West Germany/United States (1992)	.53	1.69	−.09
Canada/United States (1987)	.29	1.61	−.07
Japan/United States (1987)	.64	2.95	−.17
France/United States (1987)	.41	.77	−.45
West Germany/United States (1987)	.34	1.16	−.12
Japan/United States (1975)	.55	3.01	−.16
Spain/United States (1992)	.49	4.61	−.10
United Kingdom/United States (1987)	.37	.85	−.22
Australia/United States (1987)	.36	1.81	−.12
United Kingdom/United States (1975)	.38	1.11	−.09
Arithmetic average HMEs	.43	1.96	−.16
(Former) centrally planned economies (CPEs)			
East Germany/West Germany (1992)	.36	1.28	.05
Czechoslovakia/West Germany (1989)	.30	1.40	−.33
East Germany/West Germany (1987)	.47	1.36	−.11

(continued)

Table 12.6 (continued)

	Coefficient of Variation		Coefficient of Correlation (between price and quantity relatives) (3)
	Price Ratios (between own country and numeraire country) (1)	Quantity Ratios (between own country and numeraire country) (2)	
Soviet Union/United States (1987)	.80	2.58	−.03
Poland/West Germany (1989)	.49	2.18	−.10
Hungary/West Germany (1987)	.40	2.23	−.18
Poland/Germany (1993)	.52	2.52	−.00
Arithmetic average CPEs	.48	1.94	−.10
Low-productivity market economies (LMEs)			
Brazil/United States (1975)	.47	2.72	−.18
Mexico/United States (1975)	.40	2.42	−.12
South Korea/United States (1987)	.56	7.52	−.08
South Korea/United States (1975)	.72	5.48	−.12
Taiwan/United States (1976)	.63	18.68	−.04
Indonesia/United States (1987)	.55	3.57	−.16
South Korea/United States (1967)	.56	3.34	−.20
India/United States (1975)	.76	4.94	−.13
China/United States (1987)	.59	6.28	−.10
Arithmetic average LMEs	.58	6.08	−.13
Arithmetic average all countries	.50	3.38	−.13

Sources: See tables 12.1 and 12.5 and appendix table 12A.1.

tively little or no distortion. Column 3 of table 12.6 shows that the sign of the correlation coefficient between price and quantity relatives is negative in twenty-five of the twenty-six cases. However, as the (absolute) mean is lower for the CPE countries (-0.10) than for the HMEs (-0.16) and the LMEs (-0.13), this may be interpreted as a sign of greater distortion in CPEs.[24]

The relation between price and quantity relatives can also be analyzed by looking at the unweighted coefficient of correlation instead of a value-weighted one, as in equation (3). For this purpose, we carried out a simple OLS (ordinary least squares) regression over all products in each comparison:[25]

$$(4) \qquad \log P_i^{XU} = \alpha + \beta \times \log Q_i^{XU}.$$

Column 1 in table 12.7 shows that a negative relation is found for all countries, and column 2 indicates that this relation is significantly different from zero for all but two binary comparisons.[26] Column 3 shows the sample correlation coefficient, r. A low (absolute) r indicates that, even when a significant relation is found as indicated by the t-statistic, the variability is high; that is, the observations are relatively far from their "predicted" value. A low r can therefore be interpreted as a measure of distortion as it suggests a weak relation between relative quantities and prices. Table 12.7 therefore confirms the conclusion that we drew from table 12.6, namely, that CPEs clearly show a greater distortion of prices ($r = 0.21$) than either HMEs ($r = 0.34$) or LMEs ($r = 0.41$). Again, for all but two countries, r is significantly different from zero. A two-tailed test rejects the hypothesis of equal price distortion of the CPEs vis-à-vis the HMEs and LMEs at the 99 percent significance level (with a t-value of 2.99).

As our ultimate interest is in the relative productivity performance of these countries, we can compare the correlation coefficient, r, to the comparative productivity performance of each country relative to the United States. The results are plotted in figure 12.2, which shows that no relation can be found between the degree of distortion, as measured here, and the manufacturing value added per person employed relative to the United States.

Finally, it is noted alongside that, for all three groups of countries, the sample coefficient of correlation, r, is rather low, which suggests that, apart from the negative effect of quantity relatives on price relatives, other factors determine the value of the UVRs as well.

---

24. Czechoslovakia is a strong outlier in the opposite direction, which is caused by the relatively small number of matched items in the sample (see table 12.5).

25. Several functional forms were experimented with, of which the present double log form gave the best fit.

26. Lack of significance was found for the Poland/Germany comparison for 1993 and for the Canada/United States comparison for 1987. The latter effect is caused by the fact that the range of values for the UVRs and quality indexes hardly differs from the mean. When using OLS regression, the influence of measurement errors is greatly magnified when the values of the variables are within very small ranges.

Table 12.7   Results of Unweighted Regression of Log Price Ratios on Log
Quantity Ratios for 26 Binary Comparisons in Manufacturing

	Coefficient of Log of Quantity Relatives (log QI) (1)	t-Statistic (2)	Coefficient of Correlation (3)
High-productivity market economies (HMEs)			
West Germany/United States (1992)	−.11	−6.5	−.31
Canada/United States (1987)	−.01	−.7	−.05
Japan/United States (1987)	−.15	−6.9	−.45
France/United States (1987)	−.20	−5.0	−.54
West Germany/United States (1987)	−.07	−4.4	−.26
Japan/United States (1975)	−.16	−7.1	−.49
Spain/United States (1992)	−.15	−7.1	−.42
United Kingdom/United States (1987)	−.13	−4.5	−.33
Australia/United States (1987)	−.14	−5.9	−.41
United Kingdom/United States (1975)	−.08	−2.2	−.20
Arithmetic average HMEs	−.12	−5.0	−.34
(Former) centrally planned economies (CPEs)			
East Germany/West Germany (1992)	−.09	−3.8	−.23
Czechoslovakia/West Germany (1989)	−.09	−2.3	−.26
East Germany/West Germany (1987)	−.09	−3.4	−.18
Soviet Union/United States (1987)	−.16	−1.6	−.38
Poland/West Germany (1989)	−.06	−2.0	−.13
Hungary/West Germany (1987)	−.07	−5.0	−.25
Poland/Germany (1993)	−.01	−.7	−.06
Arithmetic average CPEs	−.08	−3.1	−.21
Low-productivity market economies (LMEs)			
Brazil/United States (1975)	−.16	−5.9	−.46
Mexico/United States (1975)	−.05	−2.2	−.19
South Korea/United States (1987)	−.18	−10.0	−.60
South Korea/United States (1975)	−.14	−6.0	−.43
Taiwan/United States (1976)	−.13	−5.1	−.45
Indonesia/United States (1987)	−.10	−4.4	−.30
South Korea/United States (1967)	−.18	−7.4	−.57
India/United States (1975)	−.11	−3.9	−.35
China/United States (1987)	−.14	−2.5	−.31
Arithmetic average LMEs	−.13	−5.3	−.41
Arithmetic average all countries	−.11	−4.6	−.33

Sources: See tables 12.1 and 12.5 and appendix table 12A.1.

12.3   The Role of Relative Quantity and Price Structures

The existence of a distortion between price and quantity relatives does not tell us anything about differences between countries in terms of their structure of prices and/or their structure of quantities. In the previous section, the Bortkiewicz formula showed that these factors also affect the Paasche-Laspeyres ratio of our price and quantity relatives. For this, we need to look in more detail

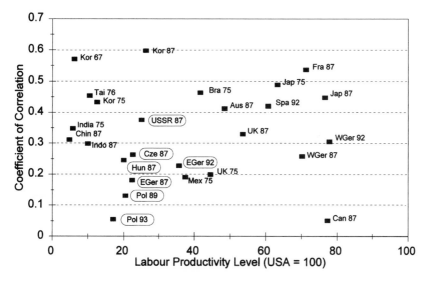

Fig. 12.2   Relation between coefficients of correlation of price and quantity relatives and comparative levels of value added per person employed in manufacturing for 26 binary comparisons
Source: Table 12.7.

at the other two terms on the right-hand side of equation (1), the weighted coefficients of variation of the price and quantity relatives, which are given in equation (2). Column 1 in table 12.6 shows that the coefficient of variation of the price index (σ_p) is 0.50 for all countries together, 0.43 for HMEs, 0.58 for the LMEs, and 0.48 for the CPE countries. The coefficient of variation of the quantity index (σ_q) is 3.38 for all countries, 1.96 for the HMEs, and 6.08 for the LMEs (table 12.6, col. 2).[27] For the CPEs, the average coefficient of variation for the quantity index is virtually equal to that of the HMEs, namely, 1.94.

The results suggest that price structures are more similar across countries than quantity structures. The LMEs have a higher price and quantity dispersion compared to their numeraire country than do the HMEs. The price dispersion of the CPEs fits nicely between that of the HMEs and LMEs. However, the quantity dispersion of CPEs is clearly closer to that of the HMEs than to that of the LMEs.

A second way of measuring the spread of price relatives and of quantity relatives is to calculate the standard deviations of the price indexes, $P_i^{XU(U)}$, and the quantity indexes, $Q_i^{XU(U)}$. This method was also suggested by Allen and Diewert (1981). In contrast to the variables in the Bortkiewicz formula, price and quantity relatives are not weighted by their relative value shares (see eq.

---

27. Taiwan is a strong outlier, which increases σ_q for the LMEs. This is caused by the fact that the sample is dominated by the product entry for rubber and plastic shoes. However, even after excluding Taiwan, the coefficient of variation for the LMEs is still as high as 4.5.

[2]). In fact, for the purpose of studying dispersion, we see no a priori reason to give a bigger weight to goods with higher value shares than to goods that are less important.[28]

The results on the dispersion of price and quantity relatives in table 12.8 largely correspond with those presented in table 12.6. There is a much lower dispersion of the UVRs (col. 1) than of the quantity relatives (col. 2), and the dispersion of the quantity relatives for the CPEs is very close to that for the HMEs.

Figures 12.3 and 12.4 suggest a significant relation between both price and quantity dispersion and the comparative level of labor productivity, respectively. However, figure 12.4 shows that the CPEs are clear outliers: given their relative productivity level, the CPEs' quantity dispersion is much closer to that of the HMEs than to that of the LMEs. The latter observation is confirmed by the results of regression 2 (appendix table 12A.4), which shows that the coefficient on the CPE dummy is highly significant.

A third way of comparing price and quantity structures is by calculating so-called similarity indexes. The basic idea behind similarity indexes is to construct for each country a price (or quantity) vector constituted of the prices (or quantities) of all m items in the sample. For each country, the prices (or quantities) of all items are related and represented by one single vector. For the case of two countries, A and B, and two goods, 1 and 2, figure 12.5 may be illustrative.

In case of a price comparison, the x- and y-axes show the prices of good 1 and good 2, respectively. The angle α between the two price vectors can be seen as a measure of the similarity between the two vectors. The similarity index, which is defined as the cosine of the angle, varies between zero and one and is lower in case of greater dissimilarity. Using the definition of the cosine of an angle of two vectors in an m-dimensional space, and introducing quantity weights for each observation in the sample in order to make the indexes "unit invariant," the following price similarity indexes can be derived:

(5)
$$SP^{XU(U)} = \frac{\sum_{i=1}^{m}(p_i^X q_i^U)(p_i^U q_i^U)}{\sqrt{\sum_{i=1}^{m}(p_i^X q_i^U)^2 \sum_{i=1}^{m}(p_i^U q_i^U)^2}},$$

$$SP^{XU(X)} = \frac{\sum_{i=1}^{m}(p_i^X q_i^X)(p_i^U q_i^X)}{\sqrt{\sum_{i=1}^{m}(p_i^X q_i^X)^2 \sum_{i=1}^{m}(p_i^U q_i^X)^2}},$$

28. We use the logarithm of the relatives as only in the log form do ratios smaller than one have a symmetrical influence on the total as ratios bigger than one. This makes the measures more suitable for constructing similarity indexes than the untransformed relatives used in the Bortkiewicz formula. Note that the logs of the price and quantity relatives have been normalized by their unweighted mean.

Table 12.8   **Dispersion of Normalized Log Unit Value Ratios and Log Quantity Ratios for 26 Binary Comparisons in Manufacturing**

	Standard Deviations	
	Log of Unit Value Ratio (log UVR) (1)	Log of Quantity Relative (log QI) (2)
High-productivity market economies (HMEs)		
West Germany/United States (1992)	.25	.64
Canada/United States (1987)	.13	.53
Japan/United States (1987)	.22	.64
France/United States (1987)	.19	.52
West Germany/United States (1987)	.17	.59
Japan/United States (1975)	.20	.61
Spain/United States (1992)	.25	.69
United Kingdom/United States (1987)	.17	.43
Australia/United States (1987)	.18	.53
United Kingdom/United States (1975)	.18	.44
Arithmetic average HMEs	.19	.56
(Former) centrally planned economies (CPEs)		
East Germany/West Germany (1992)	.19	.50
Czechoslovakia/West Germany (1989)	.16	.48
East Germany/West Germany (1987)	.24	.51
Soviet Union/United States (1987)	.29	.70
Poland/West Germany (1989)	.29	.65
Hungary/West Germany (1987)	.24	.79
Poland/Germany (1993)	.28	.72
Arithmetic average CPEs	.24	.62
Low-productivity market economies (LMEs)		
Brazil/United States (1975)	.24	.67
Mexico/United States (1975)	.20	.73
South Korea/United States (1987)	.26	.88
South Korea/United States (1975)	.33	1.02
Taiwan/United States (1976)	.26	.90
Indonesia/United States (1987)	.37	1.14
South Korea/United States (1967)	.29	.92
India/United States (1975)	.28	.87
China/United States (1987)	.44	1.00
Arithmetic average LMEs	.30	.90
Arithmetic average all countries	.24	.70

Sources: See tables 12.1 and 12.5 and appendix table 12A.1.

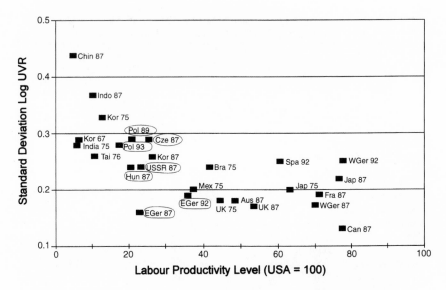

Fig. 12.3 Relation between relative price dispersion and comparative levels of value added per person employed in manufacturing for 26 binary comparisons
Source: Table 12.8.

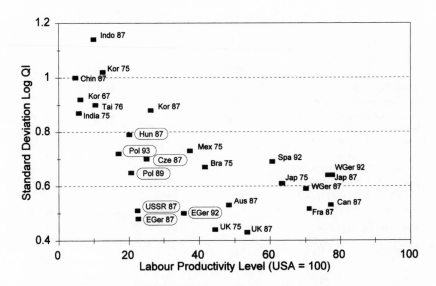

Fig. 12.4 Relation between relative quantity dispersion and comparative levels of value added per person employed in manufacturing for 26 binary comparisons
Source: Table 12.8.

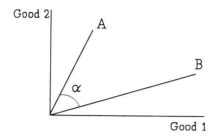

Fig. 12.5   Illustration of a comparison of two price (or quantity) vectors

where $SP^{XU(U)}$ is the price similarity index between countries X and U, using quantities of country U as weights, and $SP^{XU(X)}$ is the price similarity index between countries X and U, using quantities of country X as weights. In the same way, price weights are applied in the quantity similarity indexes:

$$
SQ^{XU(U)} = \frac{\sum_{i=1}^{m}(p_i^U q_i^X)(p_i^U q_i^U)}{\sqrt{\sum_{i=1}^{m}(p_i^U q_i^X)^2 \sum_{i=1}^{m}(p_i^U q_i^U)^2}},
$$

(6)

$$
SQ^{XU(X)} = \frac{\sum_{i=1}^{m}(p_i^X q_i^X)(p_i^X q_i^U)}{\sqrt{\sum_{i=1}^{m}(p_i^X q_i^X)^2 \sum_{i=1}^{m}(p_i^X q_i^U)^2}},
$$

where $SQ^{XU(U)}$ is the quantity similarity index between countries X and U, using prices of country U as weights, and $SP^{XU(X)}$ is the quantity similarity index between countries X and U, using prices of country X as weights. These similarity measures are also used in ICP reports—although in a different form—including Kravis, Heston, and Summers (1982) and Heston and Summers (1993). An important feature of our indexes is that these have natural weights attached to them, that is, quantity weights for the price similarity index and price weights for the quantity similarity index.

Table 12.9 shows the Fisher quantity and price similarity indexes for our sample of twenty-six binary comparisons.[29] As was observed above, it is clear that the price similarity indexes are much closer to each other than are the quantity indexes, again suggesting that price structures are more similar across countries than are quantity structures. However, in contrast to the results presented earlier, the HMEs show much greater quantity similarity relative to their base country than the CPEs (col. 2, table 12.9). The quantity structure of the LMEs is most dissimilar from that of the HMEs. This outcome is more in line with the natural dichotomy between low- and high-productivity economies.

29. The Fisher index is the geometric average of the Paasche and Laspeyres indexes presented in eqq. (4) and (5). For the Paasche and Laspeyres similarity indexes, see appendix table 12A.3.

Table 12.9   **Price and Quantity Similarity Indexes for 26 Binary Comparisons in Manufacturing**

	Price Similarity Index (1)	Quantity Similarity Index (2)	Quantity Similarity Index (excluding cars) (3)
High-productivity market economies (HMEs)			
West Germany/United States (1992)	95	59	59
Canada/United States (1987)	99	80	65
Japan/United States (1987)	87	66	59
France/United States (1987)	99	98	73
West Germany/United States (1987)	99	80	63
Japan/United States (1975)	87	68	58
Spain/United States (1992)	88	54	54
United Kingdom/United States (1987)	94	92	83
Australia/United States (1987)	97	82	79
United Kingdom/United States (1975)	92	84	77
Arithmetic average HMEs	94	76	67
(Former) centrally planned economies (CPEs)			
East Germany/West Germany (1992)	96	45	84
Czechoslovakia/West Germany (1989)	98	40	73
East Germany/West Germany (1987)	94	41	71
Soviet Union/United States (1987)	85	62	66
Poland/West Germany (1989)	93	45	65
Hungary/West Germany (1987)	89	64	64
Poland/Germany (1993)	89	73	59
Arithmetic average CPEs	92	53	69
Low-productivity market economies (LMEs)			
Brazil/United States (1975)	91	59	50
Mexico/United States (1975)	96	85	77
South Korea/United States (1987)	88	50	33
South Korea/United States (1975)	74	22	24
Taiwan/United States (1976)	89	38	38
Indonesia/United States (1987)	96	39	51
South Korea/United States (1967)	89	32	35
India/United States (1975)	90	26	26
China/United States (1987)	85	27	39
Arithmetic average LMEs	89	42	41
Arithmetic average all countries	91	58	59

Source: See tables 12.1 and 12.5 and appendix table 12A.1.

Note: The similarity indexes are geometric (Fisher) averages of the indexes at own country weights and numeraire country weights (see appendix table 12A.3). Column 3 is as col. 2, but the product matches for cars have been taken out of the product sample.

Regression 5 in appendix table 12A.4 shows a fairly strong positive relation between the quantity similarity indexes and the comparative productivity ratios but no significant coefficient for the CPE dummy.

One possible explanation for the difference in results between the quantity similarity indexes from table 12.9 and the dispersion of the quantity relatives in table 12.8 might be related to the effect of the product match for cars. In our product sample for the centrally planned economies, cars accounted for more than 15 percent of the product sample, with the exception of Hungary. As discussed in section 12.1, the product match for cars in CPEs is relatively sensitive to the problem of quality differences. It appears that, after deleting cars from the product sample, the average quantity similarity index for the CPEs goes up very substantially and is again very close to that for the HMEs (table 12.9, col. 3).

12.4   Conclusions

Manufacturing productivity levels in (former) centrally planned economies back to 1950 have been substantially lower than in high-productivity market economies and were on average in between labor productivity levels of Asian (except Korea) and Latin American low-productivity economies. After their recent transition to a market economy, most Eastern European countries experienced a collapse in productivity which has been followed by a recovery in which they have attained or even surpassed pretransition levels.

This paper showed that the difference between the Paasche and the Laspeyres measures of industry purchasing power parities was relatively small for the CPEs given their relative level of labor productivity, suggesting the absence of a typical Gerschenkron effect. One possible explanation for this small gap might be that producer substitution effects in CPEs dominated consumer substitution effects. The Gerschenkron effect theoretically exists only in the latter case. Alternatively, the high Paasche-Laspeyres (PL) ratio may be the result of a distortion between relative price and quantity indexes. The pricing system in CPEs was traditionally based on a cost-plus-taxes-plus-markup system, with net indirect taxes being used to reallocate resources according to socially desirable goals.

We decomposed the PL ratio into the effects of dispersion (or dissimilarity) of price and quantity relatives and the effect of the relation between price and quantity relatives. We found that CPEs were characterized by (1) a relatively weak (negative) relation between price and quantity indexes, indicating distortion, and (2) a relatively similar structure of quantities compared to high-productivity market economies. Even though we did not find a relation between our measure of distortion and the comparative level of labor productivity, it is not unlikely that the greater price distortion in CPEs led to a misallocation of resources, which in turn might explain the atypical quantity structure that was observed.

Table 12.10   Average Shares by Major Branch in Total Employment in High-Productivity Market Economies, Low-Productivity Market Economies and (former) Centrally Planned Economies

	Share of Employment		
	HMEs[a]	CPEs[b]	LMEs[c]
Food products, beverages, and tobacco	9.8	12.3	22.9
Textile products, wearing apparel, leather products, and footwear	10.4	15.0	19.6
Chemicals, rubber and plastic products, and oil refining	11.7	10.0	12.6
Basic and fabricated metal products	12.1	11.5	10.2
Electrical and nonelectrical machinery and transport equipment	35.7	34.5	15.4
Other manufacturing[d]	20.3	16.8	19.2
Total manufacturing	100.0	100.0	100.0

Sources: See table 12.1.

[a]High-productivity market economies: arithmetic average for France (1987), Germany (1987), Japan (1987), the United Kingdom (1987), and the United States (1987).

[b](Former) centrally planned economies: arithmetic average for Czechoslovakia (1989), East Germany (1987, 1992), Hungary (1987), and Poland (1989, 1993).

[c]Low-productivity market economies: arithmetic average for Brazil (1975), India (1975), Indonesia (1987), and Mexico (1975).

[d]Includes wood products and furniture, paper and paper products and printing, nonmetallic mineral and "other manufacturing."

Given the lower productivity performance of CPEs, how should the quantity similarity between CPEs and high-productivity market economies be interpreted? One possible explanation is that the industrialization strategies of the CPEs were successful insofar as they stimulated the production of capital intensive production of, in particular, investment goods. This led to a convergence of their quantity structures to that of high-productivity market economies. Production plans and pricing policies of CPEs were geared toward boosting the production of capital intensive goods.

A first indication for that explanation can be obtained from table 12.10, which compares the average employment structure of the manufacturing sector between CPEs with that of some low-productivity market economies (Brazil, India, Indonesia, and Mexico) and some high-productivity market economies (France, Germany, Japan, the United Kingdom, and the United States). The table clearly shows that the employment structure (which serves here as a proxy for resource allocation) of the CPEs was much closer to that of the HMEs than to that of the LMEs. It is particularly striking that the share of employment in electrical and nonelectrical machinery and transport equipment was almost as high in CPEs as in HMEs. As was noted above, the comparative levels of productivity in this major branch were relatively low in CPEs, in particular, in Czechoslovakia and East Germany. It suggests that the CPEs failed in transforming their atypical pattern of industrialization into a successful long-term growth strategy. It led to a typical pattern of "extensive" growth in CPEs, which ground to a halt once no more potential resources remained idle (van Ark 1996).

Finally, although the CPEs show a price structure that is not too dissimilar from that of the non-CPEs, CPEs lacked incentives for a systematic improvement of product quality. In fact, pricing policies stimulated price increases of so-called new products without observable improvements in product quality. A more full-scale adjustment of the ICOP estimates for lower product quality in the CPEs might imply lower "real" quantities of, in particular, investment goods and durable consumer goods. This might therefore increase the quantity dissimilarity between (former) centrally planned economies and high-productivity market economies beyond what has been observed in this paper.

Appendix

Table 12A.1   **Number of Unit Value Ratios and Coverage Percentages of Matched Output in Manufacturing**

	Number of Unit Value Ratios	Matched Output as a % of Gross Output	
		Own Country	West Germany
Czechoslovakia/West Germany (1989)	69	32.0	23.2
East Germany/West Germany (1987)	335	41.1	33.7
Hungary/West Germany (1987)	383	33.1	19.3
Poland/West Germany (1989)	236	33.6	19.4
East Germany/West Germany (1992)	255	28.0	20.4
Poland/All Germany (1993)	305	57.8	32.3

Sources: Czechoslovakia/West Germany (1989) from van Ark and Beintema (1993), adjusted in van Ark (1996); data on product detail for Czechoslovakia (1989) derived from Federal Statistical Office, *Monthly Inquiry on Production and Sales of Selected Industrial Products,* and *Annual Survey of Industrial Enterprises.* East Germany/West Germany (1987) from Beintema and van Ark (1994), adjusted in van Ark (1995a); original information on product detail for East Germany (1987) from Staatliche Zentralverwaltung fuer Statistik, *Abrechnung der Erzeugnispositionen der Erzeugnis- und Leistungsnomenklatur: Jahreserhebung 1987* (Berlin). Hungary/West Germany (1987) from Monnikhof (1996); original information on product detail for Hungary from Kozponti Statisztikai Hivatal, *Statisztikai Evkonyv, 1987* (Budapest, 1989), supplemented with unpublished data provided by the Hungarian Central Statistical Office. Poland/West Germany (1989) from Liberia, Monnikhof, and van Ark (1996); original information on product detail for Poland from Glowny Urzad Statystyczny, *Produkcja wyrobow Przemyslowych w 1989 R* (Warsaw, 1991). East Germany/West Germany (1992) are unpublished ICOP/LCRA estimates (January 1996); original information on product detail for both parts of Germany from Statistisches Bundesamt, *Produktion im Produzierenden Gewerbe* (Wiesbaden, 1992). Poland/all Germany (1993) are unpublished ICOP/LCRA estimates (January 1996); original information on product detail for Poland from Glowny Urzad Statystyczny, *Produkcja wyrobow przemyslowych w 1993 R* (Warsaw, 1995). Original information on product detail for West Germany from Statistisches Bundesamt, *Produktion im Produzierenden Gewerbe* (Wiesbaden, 1987, 1989, 1992, and 1993).

Table 12A.2   Gross Value of Industrial Output, Value Added, Number of Employees: Centrally Planned Economies and Germany, 1987–93

	Own Country				(West) Germany			
	Gross Value of Output (million national currency)	Value Added (million national currency)	Intermediate Inputs as % of Gross Output	Number of Employees (thousands)	Gross Value of Output (million DM)	Value Added (million DM)	Intermediate Inputs as % of Gross Output	Number of Employees (thousands)
Czechoslovakia/West Germany (1989)	833,285	290,940	65.1	2,326.6	1,469,432	710,484	51.6	7,105.9
East Germany/West Germany (1987)	467,418	160,017	65.8	2,763.6	1,260,359	655,041	48.0	6,855.5
Hungary/West Germany (1987)	1,230,699	498,909	59.5	1,284.4	1,421,796	683,593	51.9	6,772.7
Poland/West Germany (1989)	91,850	53,329	41.9	3,170.1	1,625,474	798,334	50.9	6,856.7
East Germany/West Germany (1992)	82,140	31,930	61.1	741.2	1,870,273	881,006	52.9	7,224.7
Poland/All Germany (1993)[a]	878,168	359,140	59.1	2,340.3	1,841,698	864,740	53.0	7,202.4

Sources: Czechoslovakia/West Germany (1989) from van Ark and Beintema (1993), adjusted in van Ark (1996); data on output and employment for Czechoslovakia derived from Federal Statistical Office, *Annual Survey of Industrial Enterprises for 1989.* East Germany/West Germany (1987) from Beintema and van Ark (1994), adjusted in van Ark (1995a); original information on output and employment for East Germany from Gemeinsames Statistisches Amt, *Ergebnisse der Erfassung der Arbeitsstaeten der Betriebe des Wirtschaftbereiches Industrie* (Berlin, 1990). Ratio of value added to output from Staatliches Zentralverwaltung fuer Statistik, *Verflechtungsbilanz des Gesellschaftlichen Gesamtproduktes, 1987* (Berlin, 1988). Hungary/West Germany (1987) from Monnikhof (1996); original information on output and employment for Hungary from Kozponti Statisztikai Hivatal, *Statisztikai Evkonyv, 1987* (Budapest, 1989), and *Iparstatistikai Evkonyv, 1987* (Budapest, 1989). East Germany/West Germany are unpublished ICOP/LCRA estimates (January 1996); original information on output and employment for both parts of Germany from Statistisches Bundesamt, *Kostenstruktur der Unternehmen, 1992* (Wiesbaden, 1994). Poland/all Germany (1993) are unpublished ICOP/LCRA estimates (January 1996); original information on output and employment for Poland from Glowny Urzad Statystyczny, *Rocznik Statystyczny Przemyslu, 1993* (Warsaw, 1995). Original information on output and employment for West Germany from Statistisches Bundesamt, *Kostenstruktur der Unternehmen* (Wiesbaden, 1987, 1989, 1992, and 1993).

[a]Polish values in billion zlotys.

Table 12A.3   Price and Quantity Similarity Indexes for 26 Binary Comparisons in Manufacturing

| | Price Similarity Index | | Quantity Similarity Index | |
	At Quantity Weights of Numeraire Country (1)	At Quantity Weights of Own Country (2)	At Price Weights of Numeraire Country (3)	At Price Weights of Own Country (4)
High-productivity market economies (HMEs)				
West Germany/United States (1992)	96	94	60	58
Canada/United States (1987)	99	99	81	79
Japan/United States (1987)	80	95	80	54
France/United States (1987)	99	100	99	97
West Germany/United States (1987)	99	100	81	80
Japan/United States (1975)	83	90	79	58
Spain/United States (1992)	92	83	50	58
United Kingdom/United States (1987)	95	93	93	91
Australia/United States (1987)	98	96	82	82
United Kingdom/United States (1975)	92	91	89	79
Arithmetic average HMEs	93	94	79	74
(Former) centrally planned economies (CPEs)				
East Germany/West Germany (1992)	99	93	46	45
Czechoslovakia/West Germany (1989)	99	97	40	39
East Germany/West Germany (1987)	98	89	40	41
Soviet Union/United States (1987)	88	83	61	63
Poland/West Germany (1989)	96	90	43	47
Hungary/West Germany (1987)	95	84	61	68
Poland/Germany (1993)	88	90	80	66
Arithmetic average CPEs	95	89	53	53
Low-productivity market economies (LMEs)				
Brazil/United States (1975)	89	93	59	58
Mexico/United States (1975)	96	95	84	87
South Korea/United States (1987)	85	92	61	40
South Korea/United States (1975)	83	67	18	27
Taiwan/United States (1976)	89	90	36	41
Indonesia/United States (1987)	96	95	36	43
South Korea/United States (1967)	95	83	26	38
India/United States (1975)	87	94	28	23
China/United States (1987)	93	78	34	21
Arithmetic average LMEs	90	87	43	42
Arithmetic average all countries	93	90	60	57

Source: See tables 12.1 and 12.5 and appendix table 12A.1.

Note: The geometric (Fisher) averages of the similarity indexes at own country weights and numeraire country weights are presented in table 12.9.

Table 12A.4   Results of OLS Regressions on Level of Value Added per Person Employed with and without Dummy for Centrally Planned Economies

	Constant	PROD	CPE Dummy	R^2
1. Paasche-Laspeyres ratio				
1a	.71	.0028		.21
		2.49		
1b	.59	.0042	.2355	.63
		5.13	5.18	
2. Standard deviation of QIs				
2a	.88	−.0049	.40	
		−4.03		
2b	.99	−.0063	−.2193	.64
		−6.06	−3.85	
3. Standard deviation of UVRs				
3a	.31	−.0019		.44
		−4.34		
3b	.33	−.0021	−.0404	.50
		−4.81	−1.68	
4. Price similarity index				
4a	88.05	.09		.16
		2.18		
4b	86.70	.11	2.73	.21
		2.43	1.11	
5. Quantity similarity index (all products)				
5a	34.90	.63		.51
		4.97		
5b	32.38	.66	5.06	.52
		4.86	.68	
6. Quantity similarity index (excluding cars)				
6a	46.39	.33		.23
		2.64		
6b	35.05	.47	22.78	.53
		4.45	3.90	

Note: The first line for each regression gives parameter estimates, the second line the corresponding t-values. The number of observations for all regressions was 26. PROD = comparative level of value added per person employed (United States = 100). CPE dummy = dummy variable: one if centrally planned economy, zero otherwise.

References

Allen, R. C., and W. E. Diewert. 1981. Direct versus implicit superlative index number formulae. *Review of Economics and Statistics* 63:430–35.

Allen, R. G. D. 1975. *Index numbers in theory and practice.* Chicago: Macmillan.

Beintema, N. M., and B. van Ark. 1994. Comparative productivity in East and West German manufacturing before reunification. Discussion Paper Series no. 895. London: Centre for Economic Policy Research.

Bergson, A. 1961. *The real national income of Soviet Russia since 1928.* Cambridge, Mass.: Harvard University Press.

———. 1978. *Productivity and the social system: The USSR and the West.* Cambridge, Mass.: Harvard University Press.

———. 1987. Comparative productivity: The USSR, Eastern Europe and the West. *American Economic Review* 77, no. 3 (June): 342–57.

Bortkiewicz, L. von. 1922, 1924. Zweck und Struktur einer Preisindexzahl (The purpose and structure of a price index number). *Nordisk Statistik Tidskrift,* vol. 1 and 3.

Comecon. 1990. Results of international comparisons of the most important cost indices of economic growth of the CMEA member countries and the Socialist Federated Republic of Yugoslavia for 1988. Moscow. Mimeo.

Conference of European Statisticians. 1971. Methodological problems of international comparison of levels of labour productivity in industry. Statistical Standards and Studies no. 21. New York: United Nations.

———. 1972. Comparison of labour productivity in industry in Austria, Czechoslovakia, France and Hungary. Statistical Standards and Studies no. 24. New York: United Nations.

de Jong, G. J. 1996. Canada's postwar manufacturing performance. A comparison with the United States. University of Groningen, Groningen Growth and Development Centre. Mimeo.

Dikhanov, Y. 1994. Sensitivity of PPP-based income estimates to choice of aggregation procedures. Washington, D.C.: World Bank. Mimeo.

Drechsler, L., and J. Kux. 1972. *International comparisons of labour productivity* (in Czech). Prague: SEVT.

Economic Commission for Europe (ECE). 1988. International comparison of gross domestic product in Europe in 1985. Statistical Standards and Studies no. 41. New York and Geneva.

———. 1994. *International comparison of gross domestic product in Europe 1990.* Geneva: United Nations.

Galenson, W. 1955. *Labour productivity in Soviet and American industry.* New York: Cambridge University Press.

Gersbach, H., and B. van Ark. 1994. Micro foundations for international productivity comparisons. Research Memorandum no. 572 (GD-11). University of Groningen, Groningen Growth and Development Centre.

Gerschenkron, A. 1951. A dollar index of Soviet machinery output, 1927–28 to 1937. Report R-197. Santa Monica: Rand.

Gilbert, M., and I. B. Kravis. 1954. *An international comparison of national products and the purchasing power of currencies.* Paris: Organization for European Economic Cooperation.

Gilbert, M., et al. 1958. *Comparative national products and price levels.* Paris: Organization for Economic Cooperation and Development.

Görzig, B., and M. Gornig. 1991. *Produktivität und Wettbewerbsfähigkeit der Wirtschaft der DDR.* Beiträge zur Strukturforschung, Heft 121. Berlin.

Heston, A., and R. Summers. 1993. What can be learned from successive ICP benchmark estimates? In *Explaining economic growth: Essays in honour of Angus Maddison,* ed. A. Szirmai, B. van Ark, and D. Pilat. Amsterdam: North-Holland.

Hitchens, D. M. W. N., K. Wagner, and J. E. Birnie. 1993. *East German productivity and the transition to the market economy.* Aldershot: Avebury.

Hooper, P., and E. Vrankovich. 1995. International comparisons of the levels of unit labor costs in manufacturing. International Finance Discussion Papers no. 527. Washington, D.C.: Board of the Governors of the Federal Reserve System, October.

Jonas, P., and H. Sardy. 1970. The Gerschenkron effect: A re-examination. *Review of Economics and Statistics* 52, no. 1 (February): 82–86.

Kornai, J. 1980. *Economics of shortage.* Amsterdam: North-Holland.

———. 1992. *The socialist system: The political economy of communism.* Princeton, N.J.: Princeton University Press.

Kouwenhoven, R. D. J. 1993. Analysing Dutch manufacturing productivity. University of Groningen, Groningen Growth and Development Centre. Mimeo.

———. 1996. A comparison of Soviet and US industrial performance. Research Memorandum GD-29. University of Groningen, Groningen Growth and Development Centre.

Kravis, I. B., A. Heston, and R. Summers. 1982. *World product and income.* Baltimore: Johns Hopkins University Press.

Kudrov, V. 1995. National accounts and international comparisons for the former Soviet Union. *Scandinavian Economic History Review* 43, no. 1:147–66.

Liberda, B., E. J. Monnikhof, and B. van Ark. 1996. Manufacturing productivity performance in Poland and West Germany in 1989. Economic Discussion Papers no. 25. University of Warsaw.

Maddison, A., and B. van Ark. 1994. The international comparison of real product and productivity. Research Memorandum no. 567 (GD-6). University of Groningen, Groningen Growth and Development Centre.

Maliranta, M. 1994. Comparative levels of labour productivity in Swedish, Finnish and American manufacturing. Helsinki School of Economics. Mimeo.

Marer, P. 1985. *Dollar GNPs of the USSR and Eastern Europe.* Baltimore: Johns Hopkins University Press.

———. 1991. Conceptual and practical problems of comparative measurement of economic performance: The East European economies in transition. In *Economic statistics for economies in transition: Eastern Europe in the 1990s.* Washington, D.C.: U.S. Bureau of Labor Statistics/Eurostat.

McKinsey Global Institute. 1993. *Manufacturing productivity.* Washington, D.C.

Monnikhof, E. J. 1996. Productivity performance in manufacturing in Hungary and West Germany, 1987–1994. University of Groningen, Groningen Growth and Development Centre. Mimeo.

Nuxoll, D. A. 1994. Difference in relative prices and international differences in growth rates. *American Economic Review* 84, no. 5:1423–36.

Paige, D., and G. Bombach. 1959. *A comparison of national output and productivity.* Paris: Organization for European Economic Cooperation.

Peres Lopes, L. M. 1994. Manufacturing productivity in Portugal in a comparative perspective. Notas Economicas no. 4. Universidade de Coimbra.

Pilat, D. 1994. *The economics of rapid growth: The experience of Japan and Korea.* Aldershot: Edward Elgar.

———. 1995. Comparative productivity of Korean manufacturing, 1967–1987. *Journal of Development Economics* 46:123–44.

———. 1996. Labour productivity levels in OECD countries: Estimates for manufacturing and selected service sectors. Economics Department Working Papers no. 169. Paris: Organization for Economic Cooperation and Development.

Pilat, D., and D. S. Prasada Rao. 1996. Multilateral comparisons of output, productivity, and purchasing power parities in manufacturing. *Review of Income and Wealth,* ser. 42, no. 2 (June): 113–30.

Pilat, D., D. S. Prasada Rao, and W. F. Shepherd. 1993. Australia and United States manufacturing: A comparison of real output, productivity levels and purchasing power, 1970–1989. Comparison of Output, Productivity and Purchasing Power in Australia and Asia Series no. 1. Centre for the Study of Australia-Asia Relations, Griffith University, Brisbane.

Rostas, L. 1948. *Comparative productivity in British and American industry.* London: Cambridge University Press.

Sturm, P. 1974. A comparison of aggregate production relationships in East and West Germany. Ph.D. diss., Yale University.

Summers, R., and A. Heston. 1988. A new set of international comparisons of real product and price levels: Estimates for 130 countries, 1950–1985. *Review of Income and Wealth,* ser. 34, no. 1 (March): 1–43.

———. 1991. The Penn world table (March 5): An expanded set of international comparisons, 1950–1988. *Quarterly Journal of Economics* 56 (May): 327–68.

Szirmai, A. 1994. Real output and labour productivity in Indonesian manufacturing, 1975–90. *Bulletin of Indonesian Economic Studies* 30, no. 2:49–90.

Szirmai, A., and R. Ruoen. 1995. China's manufacturing performance in comparative perspective. Research Memorandum no. 581 (GD-20). University of Groningen, Groningen Growth and Development Centre.

Timmer, M. P. 1996. Taiwan's manufacturing performance: An international comparison, 1960–1994. Research Memorandum GD-40. Groningen Growth and Development Center, University of Groningen.

Usher, D. 1980. *The measurement of economic growth.* Oxford: Blackwell.

van Ark, B. 1990. Comparative levels of manufacturing productivity in postwar Europe: Measurement and comparisons. *Oxford Bulletin of Economics and Statistics* 52, no. 4 (November): 343–73.

———. 1991. Manufacturing productivity in India: A level comparison in an international perspective. Occasional Papers and Reprints no. 1991-5, New Delhi and The Hague: Indo-Dutch Programme on Alternatives in Development.

———. 1992. Comparative productivity in British and American manufacturing. *National Institute Economic Review,* no. 142 (November): 63–74.

———. 1993. International comparisons of output and productivity. Monograph Series no. 1. University of Groningen, Groningen Growth and Development Centre.

———. 1995a. The manufacturing sector in East Germany: A reassessment of comparative productivity performance. *Jahrbuch für Wirtschaftsgeschichte,* no. 2:75–100.

———. 1995b. Producción y productividad en el sector manufacturera español: Un análisis comparativo, 1950–1992. *Informacio Comercial Española: Revista de economia,* no. 746 (October): 67–78.

———. 1996. Convergence and divergence in the European periphery: Productivity in Eastern and Southern Europe in retrospect. In *Quantitative aspects of postwar European Economic growth,* ed. B. van Ark and N. F. R. Crafts. Cambridge: Cambridge University Press.

van Ark, B., and N. M. Beintema. 1993. Output and productivity levels in Czechoslovak and German (FR) manufacturing. University of Groningen, Department of Economics. Mimeo.

van Ark, B., and R. D. J. Kouwenhoven. 1994. Productivity in French manufacturing: An international comparative perspective. Research Memorandum no. 571 (GD-10). University of Groningen, Groningen Growth and Development Centre.

van Ark, B., and A. Maddison. 1994. An international comparison of real output, purchasing power and labour productivity in manufacturing industries: Brazil, Mexico and the USA in 1975. Research Memorandum no. 569 (GD-8). 2d. ed. University of Groningen, Groningen Growth and Development Centre.

van Ark, B., and D. Pilat. 1993. Productivity levels in Germany, Japan and the United States. *Brookings Papers on Economic Activity: Microeconomics,* no. 2 (December): 1–68.

Wilkens, H. 1970. Arbeitsproduktivität in der Industrie der DDR und der Bundesrepublik—ein Vergleich. *Deutsche Institut für Wirtschaftsforschung Wochenbericht* (Berlin), 14 May.

World Bank. 1993. *Historically planned economies: A guide to the data.* Washington, D.C.

Comment   Irwin L. Collier Jr.

The gap between a Laspeyres and a Paasche index is something like the Chinese character for *crisis* with its double meaning of "danger" and "opportunity." The original "index number problem" came from the discovery that the choice of weights mattered for the numerical value of a price index, that is, that going from here to there typically results in a different answer than coming from there to here. The positive sign of the difference between the Laspeyres and the Paasche price indexes was soon recognized as an empirical regularity, and it was a Berlin professor of economics and statistics, the great Ladislaus von Bortkiewicz, who provided an elegant proof that the inverse correlation of price and quantity relatives lies at the heart of the matter. Van Ark, Monnikhof, and Timmer attempt to exploit the Paasche-Laspeyres ratio in their paper as an indicator of price distortion in the former centrally planned economies, and to this end they harness Bortkiewicz's formula. Thus, what began as an empirical puzzle appears to have evolved into an opportunity for analysis. With great respect for both the careful and the extensive empirical work that stands behind this paper, I nevertheless sense that a certain danger may still be lurking within the Paasche-Laspeyres ratios calculated by van Ark, Monnikhof, and Timmer for the former centrally planned economies. I use my opportunity to comment in order to add a note of caution to the empirical tale told by the authors.

Their tale is fairly straightforward. An important reason they see for the relatively poor productivity performance of the former centrally planned economies was a distorted relation between prices and quantities. For a summary measure of this distortion, the authors point to the peculiarly high Paasche-Laspeyres ratios that they have calculated for the unit value ratios (UVRs) in binary comparisons of the centrally planned economies with a market economy.[1] Controlling for differences in productivity levels, the centrally planned economies can be seen to differ from market economies, where the benchmark is taken to be the average Paasche-Laspeyres ratio in binary comparisons between market economies. The Bortkiewicz decomposition of such ratios leads the authors to consider the correlation between the price and the quantity relatives along with the relative dispersion of quantity relatives and the relative dispersion of price relatives.[2] The moral of this tale is found in the relatively

Irwin L. Collier Jr. is professor of economics at the Freie Universität Berlin.

1. For all but one comparison between the Soviet Union and the United States, the binary comparisons of centrally planned economies were exclusively with West Germany.
2. The intuition behind the last two terms is that "the index number problem" goes away (more precisely, the Paasche-Laspeyres ratio is unity) when either all prices or all quantities differ by a single factor of proportionality.

low correlation found between price and quantity relatives in the binary comparisons of centrally planned economies with market economies. Another empirical abnormality reported by van Ark, Monnikhof, and Timmer is that the centrally planned economies had quantity structures that resembled the "high-productivity market economies" rather than the "low-productivity market economies." A pretty good story all told, but can the Paasche-Laspeyres ratios calculated from UVRs in bilateral comparisons involving a centrally planned economy carry this interpretive load safely?

Earlier generations of comparative economists, in particular those who cut their teeth on Abram Bergson's *The Real National Income of Soviet Russia since 1928* (1961), were raised to shun the official valuations coming from the centrally planned economies. It was regarded unwholesome to rely on relative prices that could be presumed to approximate neither the slopes of production possibilities frontiers nor the slopes of private or social indifference curves.[3] Recognizing the problem of using a market economy's prices to value a centrally planned economy's quantities,[4] the solution was sought in estimating weights thought to better approximate relative factor costs rather than in a symmetrical treatment of prices across economic systems. For the goal of comparing outputs and inputs, this was a reasonable strategy.

This is not to say that van Ark, Monnikhof, and Timmer can be accused of simply rushing in where Bergson feared to tread. There is a genuine innovation in the use of the Paasche-Laspeyres ratio to serve as a summary indicator of overall price distortion, quite a different question from that of relative economic performance. But pointing us in this direction does not really get us very far in terms of economic content. What does it ultimately mean if the gap between the Paasche-Laspeyres indexes is half or double what it would be between two market economies? To make matters murkier, we have the problem common to all summary indicators—many other things are confounded in the final number, such as measurement error (e.g., the relative quality issue) and specification error (e.g., the different function of prices under different economic systems). The signal heard by van Ark, Monnikhof, and Timmer may be loud; it is hardly clear.

There is also a fundamental inconsistency with interpreting the Paasche-Laspeyres ratios as an indicator of price distortion and then turning around to use estimates of relative productivity, apparently based at least in part on these problematic UVRs, to analyze the Paasche-Laspeyres (PL) ratios. One can expect that there would be an errors-in-variables bias for any simple regression analysis of the PL ratio using International Comparisons of Output and Produc-

3. The late Evsey Domar compared using published economic statistics of the Soviet Union with ordering from the menu in a restaurant he did not trust. Domar would always order steak rather than goulash, fearing the aggregation that took place in the kitchen. Thus, whenever possible, Domar preferred to work with quantity data from the Soviet Union rather than with expenditure totals.
4. For example, an easy way to make the Soviet military threat look particularly menacing was to use the wages of the U.S. volunteer army to value the Soviet conscript army.

tivity (ICOP) estimates of CPE (centrally planned economy) relative productivity as an explanatory variable (see their appendix table 12A.4).[5] To add to the statistical confusion, the binary comparisons for all the market countries involve the United States, whereas the former centrally planned economies have been compared with the old Federal Republic of Germany.[6] This last problem need not necessarily affect the substantive conclusions of the paper; it is the sort of detail that does not help tighten confidence intervals either.

For comparisons in which we are completely free to determine a sampling strategy, it should make no difference whether we sample price comparisons or quantity comparisons for deflating expenditure totals. However, the ICOP quantity relatives had to be painstakingly culled from side-by-side comparisons of national industrial statistics and hardly constitute a random sample of quantity relatives. I presume that what ICOP got is what we see. One would feel just as uncomfortable were International Comparison Program (ICP) price relatives limited to comparisons of mail-order catalogs across countries. While the problem of nonrandom sampling of quantity relatives is common to all ICOP comparisons, I fear that the results are especially vulnerable for comparisons between the high-productivity market economies and the former centrally planned economies. The sensitivity of the quantity similarity indexes calculated in this paper to the single quality adjustment for automobiles should serve as a clear warning against building too high on such a weak foundation.

My final reservation has to do with the premise of the paper that there was a significant causal link running from the price structure of the former centrally planned economies to economic performance. Given that fundamental decisions in the centrally planned economies involving resource allocation were coordinated through a system of material balances, it is not obvious why price distortion in such economies should have played a very important role for productive efficiency.[7] Could this be an instance where the symmetrical treatment of different economic institutions is worse than leaving an unwanted Gerschenkron effect from valuing CPE quantities at market prices uncorrected?

With these few words of caution now added to the record, the authors surely deserve a final salute for their innovative use of the Laspeyres-Paasche ratio and its Bortkiewicz decomposition. This particular expedition by members of the ICOP team reflects the sort of daring that is sadly missing in so much of empirical economics. The glory of discovery goes only to those who accept the rigors of the voyage of discovery. Anyone who has attempted such an em-

5. The authors explicitly acknowledge that they are ignoring the distorting effect that administrative prices may have on the weighting system, which may affect the interpretation of the aggregate results. The authors then refer to the 1985 Marer World Bank project report on dollar estimates of GNPs in the Soviet Union and Eastern Europe. If anything, Marer and his team of country specialists warned that one should not ignore such distortions. Ignorance may be bliss, but not many of the older hands in the comparative business would have ignored the aggregation distortion.
6. With the single United States/Soviet Union exception noted in n. 1 above.
7. In contrast, in a market system where the information and incentive functions of the price system are critical for the workings of the system, the link is fairly clear and obvious.

pirical voyage will join in wishing van Ark, Monnikhof, and Timmer godspeed in future explorations.

Reference

Bergson, Abram. 1961. *The real national income of Soviet Russia since 1928.* Cambridge, Mass.: Harvard University Press.

V   Applications of International Comparison Data

13   The Effects of Price
Regulation on Productivity
in Pharmaceuticals

Patricia M. Danzon and Allison Percy

The purpose of this paper is to measure productivity growth over time and to compare productivity levels cross-nationally for the pharmaceutical industry in four major European markets and the United States. The pharmaceutical industry raises interesting issues for productivity measurement. The product mix includes thousands of different compounds, and the range available differs significantly across countries and over time. Research and development (R&D) is a very important input and determinant of productivity; however, the stock of R&D capital cannot be measured accurately because of inadequate data, long and variable lags between investments and product launch, and international spillovers. The high rate of technological change leads to potential bias in measuring price change. For example, Berndt, Griliches, and Rosett (1993) and Berndt and Greenberg (1996) show that the U.S. PPI for drugs has been seriously upwardly biased owing to delay in incorporating new drugs; Griliches and Cockburn (1996) illustrate the bias from treating generics as new drugs rather than as new forms of old drugs.

Measurement of price change and real productivity growth is complicated in many European countries by the fact that drug prices are regulated, either directly (France and Italy) or indirectly (the United Kingdom). Consequently, trends in drug prices over time deviate significantly from economywide price inflation, and these trends differ across countries (Danzon and Kim 1996).

Patricia M. Danzon is the Celia Moh Professor of Health Care Systems, Insurance, and Risk Management at the Wharton School of the University of Pennsylvania. She is associate editor of the *Journal of Health Economics* and the *Journal of Risk and Insurance*. Allison Percy is a Ph.D. candidate in the Health Care Systems Department of the Wharton School of the University of Pennsylvania. Her research interests include health insurance community rating laws, international health policy comparisons, and social insurance issues.

This research was supported by a grant from the Chair in Health Economics at the Institut d'Etudes Politiques de Paris. The authors thank Ernst Berndt, Robert Lipsey, Jean Jacques Rosa, and participants at two NBER workshops for very helpful comments.

371

Regulation, nontariff barriers to trade, and other factors induce significant prices differences for the same drugs across countries, after conversion at either exchange rates or GDP purchasing power parities (PPPs). This paper demonstrates the sensitivity of estimates of country-specific productivity growth to the price indexes used to deflate nominal expenditure data. Similarly, the adjustment for cross-national price differences affects the estimates of cross-national productivity differences.

A second purpose of this paper is to show the effects of price regulation on input use and productivity and the implications of such regulation-induced distortions on the estimation of productivity growth. The price regulatory schemes in several European countries are designed to promote domestic employment and investment in addition to their primary purpose of controlling drug expenditures.[1] For example, France and Italy grant higher prices for products that are produced locally. The United Kingdom regulates the rate of return on capital invested in the United Kingdom, and the allowed rate of return for a firm depends on its contribution to the U.K. economy. Regulation that grants higher prices for use of certain inputs tends to distort resource allocation (Averch and Johnson 1962), leading to excessive costs and suboptimal productivity. We show that, with input-distorting regulation, factor shares are biased proxies for output elasticities in measuring growth in multifactor productivity.

Our empirical analysis uses data for the pharmaceutical industry from the OECD Structural Analysis (STAN) database, for France, Germany, the United Kingdom, Italy, and the United States for the period 1970–90.[2] In order to distinguish the effects of regulation from other factors that may contribute to cross-national productivity differences, we compare pharmaceuticals to other industries (chemicals and total manufacturing) that are not subject to the same regulatory constraints. We report country-specific estimates of productivity growth using three country-specific price indexes: the GDP deflator, the official pharmaceutical PPI, and a Divisia price index constructed from IMS data (Danzon and Kim 1996).[3] For cross-national comparison of productivity levels, we report results both with GDP PPPs and with a drugs-specific Fisher price index (Danzon and Kim 1998) that is based on prices for all matching drugs in the countries under comparison.

The findings demonstrate that estimates of country-specific productivity growth and cross-national comparisons are very sensitive to the price indexes used and that none is perfect. At minimum, these findings confirm the importance of using industry-specific price indexes for productivity measurement in an industry that is subject to heavy price regulation, such as pharmaceuticals.

---

1. The transparency rules of the European Union in principle constrain regulatory bias toward local firms, but, in practice, price setting for medical services has remained an area of national discretion.

2. *Germany* in this paper refers to the former Federal Republic of Germany.

3. IMS International is a market research firm that collects data on pharmaceutical sales.

With these caveats, the empirical results are generally consistent with the hypothesized effect, that biased price regulation has increased input use and reduced productivity in France. For the United Kingdom, pharmaceutical productivity is high, relative to other U.K. manufacturing and relative to other European pharmaceutical industries, despite the United Kingdom's biased regulatory system.

Note that the productivity measures analyzed here are GDP-based measures of value added for all firms operating in each country, including local subsidiaries of multinational firms, since this corresponds to the scope of regulation. These GDP-based measures do not reflect productivity in the discovery of innovative new drugs. Innovation in R&D is a critical component of the overall productivity of a particular country's pharmaceutical industry but is beyond the scope of this paper.[4] However, our results suggest that both the level and the returns to unobserved R&D capital are lower in France than in the United States and the United Kingdom. This is generally consistent with other evidence, that France has lagged the United States and the United Kingdom in pharmaceutical innovation (Barral 1995).

In this paper, section 13.1 briefly describes the regulatory regimes and their expected effects. Section 13.2 discusses measurement issues in cross-national comparisons of productivity for pharmaceuticals. Section 13.3 describes the data and methods used in this study. Section 13.4 compares within-country growth rates and cross-national levels of productivity for pharmaceuticals, compared to other manufacturing. Section 13.5 reports estimates of total factor productivity growth. Section 13.6 concludes.

13.1 Forms of Price Regulation and Previous Literature

We selected France, Italy, and the United Kingdom as examples of countries with biased regulation. Germany and the United States provide a benchmark of productivity in countries where price constraints are neutral with respect to location of production. The four European countries have similar populations and similar opportunities for export within the European Union (EU). Although the U.S. market is much larger than the domestic market of any single European country, the total EU market represents larger total sales volume than the U.S. market. Thus, opportunities to exploit economies of scale should be similar, absent regulatory inducements for domestic production and/or barriers to exports.

---

4. Comanor (1965) and Cocks (1973, 1981) analyze productivity in R&D, focusing on effects of safety and efficacy regulation (see also Peltzman 1973; and Thomas 1990, 1992, 1996). Hancher (1990) describes the regulatory systems in France and the United Kingdom.

13.1.1   Forms of Price Regulation

Biased Price Regulation: France and Italy

France and Italy regulate the manufacturer's price as a condition of reimbursement by the social insurance program. The criteria used for setting prices have included costs, therapeutic merit, and international comparisons. Contribution to the local economy is widely acknowledged to be a bargaining strategy for a higher price, notwithstanding the Treaty of Rome and other non-discrimination provisions of the European Union (see, e.g., Burstall 1991; Burstall and Reuben 1988).

Price regulation that favors domestic production is more likely to be a binding constraint on multinational firms than on domestic firms that would voluntarily locate a larger fraction of their operations in the home country. Domestic firms are therefore predicted to command a larger market share in countries with biased price regulation, other things equal.

Rate-of-Return Regulation: The United Kingdom

The U.K. pharmaceutical price regulation system (PPRS) regulates the rate of return on capital by comparing net revenues generated from sales to the National Health Service (NHS) to capital that contributes to sales to the NHS. Within this constraint, manufacturers can set prices freely for individual new products. Prices of generics are regulated. Simple rate-of-return regulation is predicted to induce substitution of capital for labor (Averch and Johnson 1962). However, this tendency is mitigated because the permitted return that each firm negotiates with the PPRS depends, within the range of 17–21 percent, on such factors as number of jobs created, innovation, and other contributions to the U.K. economy.

In general, the U.K. system favors domestic firms that would in any case locate corporate headquarters, R&D, and other overhead capital in the United Kingdom. The PPRS may also create incentives for multinationals to shift facilities to the United Kingdom from other countries if the permitted return is increasing in exports or if joint costs can be allocated to the U.K. rate base.

Reference Price Reimbursement: Germany

Prior to 1989, Germany permitted free pricing of drugs. Political concern over the level and growth of drug expenditures led manufacturers to adopt a voluntary price freeze from 1984 to 1989. In 1989, the government introduced a reference price system of reimbursement, focused initially on off-patent drugs.[5] Although this system constrains prices for relatively high-priced (usually originator) drugs, it is formally neutral with respect to input mix and loca-

---

5. Products are grouped on the basis of similarity of therapeutic effect, and all products in a group are reimbursed at a common reference price. The patient must pay any excess of the manufacturer's price over the reference price. In practice, most manufacturers have dropped their prices to the reference price level (Remit 1991; Danzon and Liu 1996).

tion of production, except that it indirectly favors low-priced drugs, which are typically generics produced by local firms. Since this system was phased in gradually starting in September 1989, our data are too early to show full effects. Our data also do not show the effects of the much more stringent controls adopted in 1993.[6]

"Free" Pricing: The United States

Pharmaceutical firms may set prices freely in the United States, subject to market constraints. Since the late 1980s, managed care has expanded rapidly to pharmacy benefits, through health maintenance organizations (HMOs) and pharmacy benefit management companies (PBMs) that manage drug benefits for indemnity plans. Pharmacy benefit management has accelerated the growth in generic market share and led brand manufacturers to discount their drugs to managed care purchasers. Since 1990, Medicaid and other public programs demand similar discounts. These initiatives are neutral with respect to manufacturer or country of origin, except to the extent that they favor generics, which are usually locally produced.

One potential distortion in the United States is the possessions tax credit, which reduces corporate tax rates based on employment and income generated in Puerto Rico.[7] To show the effects of this tax incentive, we report results with and without Puerto Rico for the years with available data.

13.1.2 Previous Literature

Most previous cross-national comparisons of productivity are at the one- or two-digit SIC level (e.g., van Ark and Pilat 1993). The Bureau of Labor Statistics (BLS) publishes international comparisons of growth rates for two-digit industries but does not compare productivity levels. Since pharmaceuticals are a small fraction of chemicals and allied products (SIC 28), these analyses shed little light on pharmaceuticals. Cocks (1974, 1981) provides detailed estimates of total factor productivity growth for a single firm in the United States.

The only existing international comparison of productivity in pharmaceuticals is Burstall and Reuben's (1988) study of potential savings from plant consolidation in the European Community. Using industry interviews and OECD data for 1985, Burstall and Reuben conclude that scale economies in primary production (active ingredients) had already been realized since most multinational firms operate primary plants in only one or two locations. However, secondary production (processing and packaging) was extremely decentral-

---

6. The 1993 controls included a price cut and a global limit on drug expenditures, with physicians at risk for exceeding the drug budget. This led to significant volume reduction and substitution toward cheaper drugs (Danzon and Liu 1996).

7. Section 936 of the Internal Revenue Code, enacted in 1976, provides a tax credit equal to the federal tax liability on certain income earned in Puerto Rico. This was modified in 1982. The tax credit affects incentives to locate primary production of active ingredients in Puerto Rico since the value of R&D is realized as the value added to the raw ingredients. The mix of labor and capital within the production process should be unaffected.

ized, with many plants operating below capacity. Industry interviews attributed this in part to government pressure. Burstall and Reuben estimated that half to two-thirds of these plants could be closed.[8] Their cross-national productivity comparisons are based on GDP PPPs. Thus, the question remains how much of any apparent cross-national differences in productivity in fact simply reflect price differences. Their study also did not attempt to model or estimate the effects of regulation on country-specific productivity growth.

13.2   Theory and Measurement Issues with Biased Regulation

13.2.1   Incentive Effects of Biased Regulation

Biased regulation that grants higher output prices as a reward for local production creates incentives for the pharmaceutical firm to deviate from cost-minimizing input levels. Consider a firm that produces output Q with two variable inputs, labor L and capital K, and a technology-related fixed input M, subject to the production function $Q(L, K; M)$ and constant factor prices, w_L and w_K. With biased regulation, output price $P(L, K; M)$ is increasing in domestic employment of L and K with $P_{X_i} > 0$, $P_{X_i X_i} \leq 0$, $X_i = L, K$. For simplicity, assume that Q is independent of P.[9] The firm selects L and K to maximize profits R:

$$(1) \qquad R = P(L, K; M)Q(L, K; M) - w_L - w_K.$$

Taking first-order conditions for an interior maximum, and rearranging,

$$(2) \qquad PdQ/dX_i = w_i - dP/dX_i Q, \quad X_i = L, K.$$

Equation (2) differs from the standard first-order condition owing to the last term, which reflects the distorting effect of biased regulation. Thus, employment is expanded beyond the cost-minimizing level; this increase is greater the more responsive is the regulated price to increases in local employment or investment.

In a global context with trade, the net effect of regulatory bias depends on the costs to multinational corporations of shifting operations between countries. If multinationals can costlessly shift production from countries with neutral or no regulation to countries with biased regulation that favors domestic production, the location of production is affected, but productivity and costs

8. Burstall and Reuben estimated the potential savings at only 3.5–4.5 percent of the total labor force. They concluded that value added per employee was relatively high in pharmaceuticals compared to manufacturing as a whole in France, contrary to the conclusions reached here.

9. This may be a reasonable assumption for the countries with price regulation for the period under study. Patient cost sharing was minimal in France and Italy owing to exemptions and supplementary insurance. In the United Kingdom, roughly 80 percent of scripts are exempt from cost sharing; for the remaining patients, cost sharing is a fixed amount per script, independent of the price of the drug.

would be unaffected. Capital investment, employment, and exports would increase in countries with biased price regulation, with an offsetting decrease in neutral countries.[10]

However, if shifting production between countries is costly, for example, owing to nontariff barriers to trade[11] or regulatory demands in multiple countries, then the profit-maximizing strategy subject to regulation may be to operate an excessive number of plants at suboptimal scale or suboptimal capacity utilization. The effect on capital/labor ratios depends on the costs and political returns to increasing capital and labor, respectively. Even if capital/labor ratios are unaffected, both labor productivity and multifactor productivity are predicted to be lower if biased regulation induces the firm to forgo economies of scale or scope.

13.2.2 Productivity Measurement

Consider the simple production relation

$$(3) \qquad Q_t = A_t f[X_t],$$

where Q is real output, X is a vector of real input flows, including labor, capital, energy, etc., t indicates time period, and A is an index of multifactor productivity that reflects technology, unmeasured management skill, organization, and other factors. Productivity growth can be estimated from the dynamic version of equation (3). Under assumptions of perfect competition in output and input markets, Hicks neutral technical change, and constant returns to scale, the growth in multifactor productivity (MFP) is equal to the difference between the growth in output and the growth in the weighted sum of inputs:

$$(4) \qquad \dot{A} = \dot{Q} - \Sigma g_i \dot{X}_i,$$

where $g_i = d \ln Q/d \ln X_i$ is the output elasticity of input i, and $\cdot$ denotes the percentage time derivative of a variable. To obtain empirical estimates of output elasticities g_i, a common assumption is that firms are in competitive, long-run equilibrium. The first-order conditions for profit maximization imply

$$(5) \qquad dQ/dX_i = w_i/P,$$

where w_i is the price of the ith input, and P is the final output price. Substituting in (4), MFP is estimated as the residual:

10. In practice, until recently most trade has been in active ingredients, whereas each country's processing and packaging was done locally. This suggests greater economies of scale in primary production of active ingredients, which partly reflects the costs of compliance with environmental and safety requirements.

11. During the period analyzed here, each country retained a separate system of market approval for prescription drugs. Although the European Union has explicitly authorized so-called parallel importing of approved drugs and this does increasingly constrain price differences within the European Union, nontariff barriers to imports have been significant until recently.

(4')
$$\dot{A} = \dot{Q} - \Sigma s_i \dot{X}_i,$$

where the observable factor revenue share $s_i = w_i X_i / PQ$ is used as a proxy for the unobserved output elasticity g_i for factor i. In long-run equilibrium with perfect competition and constant returns to scale, $\Sigma s_i = 1$. This implies that unobservable service flows from quasi-fixed inputs are proportional to—and hence can be measured by—observable stocks, and one unobservable factor share can be estimated as a residual.

The measure of MFP obtained using factor share approximations for output elasticities is inaccurate if firms are not in long-run, cost-minimizing equilibrium (Berndt and Fuss 1986)[12] or if firms have market power such that prices exceed marginal cost (Hall 1988, 1990). For pharmaceutical firms, the latter condition almost certainly applies: pricing at short-run marginal cost would not pay a normal return on sunk investments in R&D and so cannot be a sustainable equilibrium.

Biased regulation is an additional reason why observed factor shares provide a potentially biased measure of output elasticities in the pharmaceutical industry. To illustrate, write equation (2) in elasticity form:

(2')
$$E_{Q, X_i} = w X_i / PQ - E_{P, X_i}$$

or

(2'')
$$s_i = E_{Q_i X_i} + E_{P, X_i}.$$

From equation (2''), the measured factor share is equal to the output elasticity *plus* the elasticity of the regulated price with respect to input levels. Thus, the assumption commonly used in productivity measurement, that factor shares serve as a proxy for output elasticities, does not hold under biased regulation.

In addition, the existence of unobserved sunk investments in R&D capital, M, leads to bias in the standard procedure of estimating the share of physical capital as the residual, after subtracting the share of measured inputs. Assume that investments in M are committed before the regulatory regime is known and that variable inputs are adjusted to the regulatory regime, as in equation (2). Define the ex ante expected shadow user cost of M as

(6)
$$Z_M^* = P^* Q_M (L^*, K^*),$$

where * denotes expected, optimized values in the absence of regulation. The ex post realized shadow user cost of M depends on politically constrained prices and variable factor inputs:

(7)
$$Z_M = P(L, K; M) Q_M (L, K; M).$$

---

12. Under nonconstant returns to scale, long-run equilibrium is defined as output at the point of tangency between the SRAC and the LRAC curves.

By definition, the ex post factor shares, including the ex post return to the quasi-fixed factor, sum to one:

(8) $$s_L + s_K + s_M = 1$$

or

(8') $$1 - s_L = s_K + s_M.$$

Thus, if the unobserved share of physical capital is estimated as the complement of the labor share $1 - s_L$, the resulting estimate $\hat{s}_K$ is upwardly biased for the true value s_K; the upward bias is greater the greater the unobserved investment in M and the greater its ex post return, Z_M. However, this upward bias in $\hat{s}_K$ is partially offset if the elasticity of regulated price with respect to labor is positive:

(9) $$\hat{s}_K = s_K + s_M = 1 - \hat{s}_L = 1 - E_{QL} - E_{PL}.$$

From equations (8) and (2''):

(10) $$s_M = 1 - (s_L + s_K),$$

(10') $$s_M = 1 - \Sigma[E_{Q_iX_i} + E_{P_iX_i}].$$

Thus, the more elastic is the regulated price with respect to variable inputs, $E_{P_iX_i}$, the lower will be the observed ex post return to the quasi-fixed factor. Of course, investments in fixed factors will not be made in the long run if realized returns are systematically below expected returns. But products that are developed by innovative pharmaceutical R&D are diffused worldwide; hence, the incentives for R&D depend on global revenues. The returns to unobserved intangible capital can thus differ significantly across countries. In particular, a country that is small relative to the global market can pay a less than competitive or even zero return Z_M on the global R&D of multinational companies without affecting the supply of drugs, as long as it pays prices sufficient to cover its country-specific marginal costs.

13.3   Data and Methodology

13.3.1   Data

The data on outputs and input levels used here are from the OECD Structural Analysis (STAN) database (1994), described in appendix A, which also lists other sources. The STAN data are generally national accounts compatible. Where national accounts data were not available, STAN substitutes survey-based data. Since definitions for these survey data are not necessarily national accounts compatible, consistency across countries is not assured; however, within-country trends should be consistent.[13] We report within-country trends over time and cross-national comparisons of input levels and productivity. The cross-national comparisons should provide the best tests of the hypothesized effects of regulation. In addition, under the plausible assumption that regulation has become more stringent over the period studied, particularly in France and the United Kingdom, the differences in trends across countries may also provide evidence on the effects of regulation, assuming other factors unchanged.

The measure of productivity in this database is value added, defined as gross output minus the cost of materials, energy, supplies, and some contract work. Labor is reported as number of employees, unadjusted for hours worked, skill, age distribution, etc. The measure of capital is gross fixed capital formation. We apply a perpetual inventory calculation to estimate the stock of capital and assume that the flow of capital services is proportional to the stock.[14] Other inputs, such as contracted business services, advertising, licensing and royalty fees, etc., are reflected in value added. These data thus do not permit a gross production approach to productivity measurement. The potential bias from not netting out these intermediate inputs should not be great if they are competitively supplied. Data sources and definitions are described in more detail in appendixes A and B.

13.3.2 Data Limitations

Ideally, productivity measurement and comparison across countries would be based on a homogeneous set of products, with product-specific price indexes and quality-adjusted measures of all inputs. In that case, cross-national productivity differences for pharmaceuticals, relative to other manufacturing, would provide a pure measure of the effects of pharmaceutical regulation, after controlling for other country-specific factors that affect all industries in a country, such as management skills.

The available data on outputs, prices, and inputs deviate from these ideal conditions in ways that may influence the productivity estimates. This section outlines the main data limitations that should be borne in mind in interpreting the empirical findings.

---

13. For the United States, STAN reports the aggregate of SICs 2833–2836. Of these, pharmaceutical preparations account for 82 percent of total value of shipments. The remainder includes medicinals and botanicals, diagnostic substances, and biological products (1987 Census of Manufacturing, ind. ser. table 1a-1).

14. The capital stock in year t is estimated as $K_t = (1 - d)K_{t-1} + I_t$ and $K_1 = (1/d)I_{1-3}$, where I_{1-3} is the mean of gross investment in the first three years with reported data. The results reported here assume a uniform ten-year life of capital. We also made estimates based on the country-specific depreciation rates for equipment and structures reported in Berndt and Hesse (1986), assuming a weight of 0.66 for equipment and 0.37 for structures. For SIC 2383, depreciation charges were 7.8 percent of gross book value of depreciable assets in 1987 (Census of Manufacturing, table 3b), which implies a 12.8-year life of capital in steady state. Cocks (1974) assumes a fifteen-year life for equipment.

Heterogeneous Product Mix

Pharmaceutical markets in all countries comprise thousands of compounds, ranging from some truly global products, which are marketed in all major markets of the world, to purely local products that are marketed in only one country. Each product is available in a range of dosage forms, strengths, and pack sizes that change over time and differ across countries. The extent of global diffusion of a drug is a commonly used measure of its therapeutic value (e.g., Barral 1995) because manufacturers have incentives to launch a drug in any country where it could pass regulatory requirements for safety and efficacy and generate revenues sufficient to cover the country-specific marginal costs.

In 1992, products that were marketed in seven major markets of the world accounted for over two-thirds of sales in the United States, the United Kingdom, and Canada but less than 50 percent of sales in France, Germany, Italy, and Japan.[15] The diffusion of global products, either through outlicensing to local firms or direct marketing through multinational subsidiaries, implies common technologies across markets at least for those products. However, because the key technologies of pharmaceuticals are product specific and are protected by patents, technology does not diffuse throughout the industry until patent expiration. Thus, cross-country differences in product mix in pharmaceuticals are likely to imply cross-national differences in available technology. These differences are likely to be greater the greater the share of local products.

Local products include herbal, homeopathic, and other medicines that typically have less research content than global products. These local products complicate productivity measurement in part because differences in research content and production technologies may imply differences in true productivity and in price-marginal cost margins. In addition, regulation-induced inefficiencies may be different for local products that are produced by domestic firms than for global products produced by multinationals. Estimates of the effects of regulation may therefore be influenced by the market share of local products. Third, since local products are necessarily omitted from cross-national price indexes, these indexes yield a biased measure of overall relative price levels if regulation is more stringently applied to global than to local products.[16]

Countries also differ in the market share of generic versions of originator products and in the share of over-the-counter (OTC) versus prescription-bound (Rx) sales. The available data include all pharmaceutical products, including originator, generics, Rx, and OTC products; thus, separate estimates based solely on global products cannot be made. The markup of price over short-run

15. The market share of local products reflects insurance coverage and medical norms as well as regulatory requirements for proof of efficacy.
16. Systematic bias is plausible, even aside from regulatory favoring of local companies, if regulation focuses on high-priced products and global products have relatively high prices.

marginal cost is generally higher for research-based originator drugs than for generics, which incur minimal research or promotional expense. The marketwide average measure of value added should therefore be higher in countries with low generic market shares, ceteris paribus. Of the countries studied here, the United States, the United Kingdom, and Germany all have large generic market shares (over 30 percent of prescriptions), whereas generics are a negligible share in France and Italy. However, the low generic presence in these markets partly reflects lack of incentive for generic entry because of low price-cost margins on originator drugs by the time of patent expiration. Thus, on net, the expected sign of the correlation between generic market share and average value added marketwide is theoretically indeterminate.

Operations Mix

The functions undertaken by a pharmaceutical firm—R&D, primary production of the active ingredients, secondary processing and packaging, promotion and distribution—have very different input requirements. Functional mix may differ across countries, reflecting product mix and other real factors, in addition to possible reporting differences with respect to administrative personnel.[17] Such differences cannot be identified in the data and may contribute to the observed productivity differences.[18] Countries with relatively numerous primary production plants are expected to have relatively high value added because these primary production plants have low costs of bulk chemical inputs but the output is valued at transfer prices that reflect the intangible value of the embodied R&D.[19] Value added is expected to be much lower in the more numerous plants for processing and packaging, for which the transfer price of the active ingredient is an input cost.

Drug promotion has traditionally been predominantly through highly labor intensive detailing of individual physicians. Differences in optimal detailing effort therefore could affect observed levels of labor inputs and labor/capital ratios.[20] However, in a simple model of optimal promotion effort, sales force is increasing in the operating margin per unit sold and in the demand elasticity

17. We thank Ernie Berndt for noting this possibility of inconsistent reporting of central administrative and office personnel.

18. For the United States in 1987, production workers accounted for 46 percent of total employees and 35 percent of payroll. As a percentage of value of shipments, cost of materials, payroll, and new capital expenditures were 26 percent, 13 percent, and 4.7 percent, respectively (U.S. Census of Manufacturers, data for SIC 2833).

19. Multinational companies generally locate primary production of each compound in only one or two plants worldwide, with location generally determined by tax considerations. The output (transfer) price may be constrained by rules governing transfer pricing, including the price realized in the country of first launch. More generally, the value-added data used here may be contaminated by tax-induced transfers of profits across countries. This applies to all industries. Hence, comparisons between pharmaceuticals and other industries should be unbiased if the extent of such transfers is similar across industries.

20. Detailing entails frequent visits to individual physicians by sales personnel, to provide information and product samples.

with respect to detailing effort. Thus, if regulation depresses operating margins, it should decrease labor inputs to promotion, other things equal. The U.K. regulatory system specifically limits the expenditure on promotion that can be included in the rate base.

Unobserved R&D

Investment in R&D as a percentage of sales is higher for pharmaceuticals than for any other industry (U.S. Congressional Budget Office 1994). However, R&D stocks cannot be accurately estimated from the available data. The OECD-STAN data for labor and capital presumably include R&D inputs employed in in-house research facilities. However, R&D inputs are not identified separately and would in any case provide an incomplete measure of R&D investments. Omitted are payments to contractors engaged in clinical trials, license fees and royalties for compounds licensed from abroad, and public investments in R&D, which are a substitute for in-house research.

Estimates of R&D spending obtained from pharmaceutical trade associations' surveys of their members are reported here. These data should include payments to outside contractors but omit expenditures by nonmember firms, nonrespondents to the surveys, and public R&D expenditures. Expenditures on labor and capital are not reported separately. Thus, neither these trade-association data nor the OECD-STAN data provide a comprehensive, country-specific measure of R&D investment flows.

Even if country-specific investments in R&D could be accurately measured, conversion to a stock of knowledge available in each country, by year, would be problematic because of lags and international spillovers. The lag between initial investment in a target compound and final regulatory approval of a new drug averages about twelve years in the United States (DiMasi, Bryant, and Lasagna 1991). This cannot be extrapolated to other countries because of differences in product mix and regulatory systems. More generally, the international diffusion of knowledge through global products, sold under license or through multinational subsidiaries, severs any close link between a country's domestic R&D expenditure, the cumulative stock of knowledge in that country, and the technology underlying the production process. For these reasons, we do not attempt to construct a country-specific measure of R&D stock.[21] We discuss the effects of unobserved R&D stocks below.

13.3.3   Price Indexes

Country-Specific Inflation

Accurate measurement of real productivity growth requires accurate price indexes to convert the value-added data from current to constant local currency units. Price indexes for pharmaceuticals can diverge significantly from those

---

21. Cocks (1974) develops methods to estimate R&D stocks for a single firm in a single country.

for other goods and services because of regulation, insurance (which insulates consumers from price levels), and nontariff trade barriers. The country-specific GDP deflator reflects economywide inflation and hence can be interpreted as a measure of the opportunity cost of drug expenditures. We use the GDP deflators to deflate all inputs—labor, capital, and R&D expenditures—under the assumption that inputs are purchased in economywide markets. The GDP deflators are also used to adjust output measures for the nonpharmaceutical manufacturing industry.

For pharmaceutical output, we report results using the GDP deflator and two pharmaceutical price indexes. The ideal index would measure the rate of change of a quality-constant, representative basket of drugs sold through all relevant outlets since the expenditure data include both prescription and nonprescription drugs sold through retail pharmacies, hospitals, and other outlets. Given the rapid rate of technical change, the ideal index should use continually updated weights. The official PPIs for drugs may be imperfect because of lags in incorporating new products, inappropriate methods of incorporating new forms of old compounds, use of list rather than transactions prices, and nonrepresentative sampling. The U.S. PPI-drugs was upwardly biased by as much as 50 percent during the late 1980s (Berndt, Griliches, and Rosett 1993), primarily because of delay in incorporating new products. Similar or other biases may be present in the PPIs for other countries (Danzon and Kim 1996). For France, a national accounts price index for drugs is available only from 1988. For the prior years, we use a weighted average of manufacturer price indexes for reimbursable and nonreimbursable drugs reported in SNIP (1993).[22]

Our Divisia pharmaceutical price indexes are based on IMS data for prescription and nonprescription products sold through retail pharmacies. They incorporate new compounds in their second year on the market through chained weights. These indexes nevertheless provide an imperfect deflator for total pharmaceutical output because the indexes exclude sales through hospitals, mail order, supermarkets, and other outlets, they exclude multimolecule drugs, and they exclude discounts; hence, they may overstate the growth in net manufacturer prices in the United States.

Defining a unit of pharmaceutical output is problematic because of the large and continually changing range of compounds, forms, strengths, and pack sizes. For the Divisia indexes used here, the unit of observation is the average price per standard unit for a specific molecule. A standard unit is defined by IMS as one tablet, one capsule, five milliliters of a liquid, etc. It is a rough proxy for a dose and has the advantage that it is defined for all dosage forms, packs, etc. such that the indexes can be based on the universe of data. This measure implicitly assumes that all forms of a given molecule are perfect substitutes. To the extent that generics are in fact imperfect substitutes for origina-

---

22. These indexes presumably pertain only to outpatient drug sales. Hospital prices are not regulated in France and so may differ from outpatient prices. For the other countries, it is unclear whether the indexes include both prescription drugs and OTC sales and whether hospital sales are included.

tor drugs, these indexes understate price growth and overstate productivity growth; but, to the extent that line extensions and other new forms of old compounds offer real quality improvements, price growth is overstated and productivity growth downwardly biased.[23]

These three indexes are reported in table 13.1 for the years for which all three are available. For all countries except the United States, pharmaceutical prices declined in real terms. The PPI and Divisia indexes are more similar to each other than to the GDP deflator and, on theoretical grounds, are likely to be more accurate. The subsequent discussion focuses on the drugs-specific indexes.

Cross-National Comparisons

For currency conversion for cross-national comparisons, we use GDP PPPs for all input prices and for nonpharmaceutical output. Since GDP PPPs reflect consumer prices rather than producer prices, they are not ideal for comparing productivity at manufacturer prices but are probably the best available measure for the nonpharmaceutical manufacturing sector. However, for pharmaceuticals, conversion at GDP PPPs can lead to systematic bias owing to regulation of manufacturer prices and other factors.

For the cross-national comparisons of pharmaceutical productivity, we therefore also report results using a drugs-specific Fisher price index for the years 1981–91 based on IMS data at manufacturer price levels. For each country compared to the United States, these indexes include all compounds that are available in both countries (see app. B below; and Danzon and Kim 1998). Because these indexes necessarily omit nonmatching (local) drugs, they may be biased if prices for matching drugs, which include the global products produced by multinational corporations, differ systematically from prices for nonmatching local products.[24]

We do not use the medical care PPPs or the pharmaceuticals PPPs reported by the OECD because both have severe limitations for productivity comparisons. The medical PPPs, like the GDP PPPs, are intended to measure consumer price levels, whereas our output data are at manufacturer prices. Because government expenditures are excluded from the medical PPPs, they may be seriously biased as a measure of average price levels in countries where governments account for the majority of medical expenditures and may pay different prices from retail consumer prices.

Moreover, because many medical services are not reimbursed on a fee-for-service basis, the reported prices may not correspond even to list prices—for example, hospitals were paid global budgets in France, Germany, and the

---

23. These indexes are described in more detail in app. B and in Danzon and Kim (1996), which reports molecule and product indexes, using fixed weights and chained (Divisia) weights. Comparisons between these indexes, the official PPI-drugs, and the OECD price indexes for pharmaceuticals are also discussed.

24. Danzon and Kim (1998) compare price indexes constructed using IMS data to the OECD medical PPPs and GDP PPPs.

Table 13.1   Measures of Pharmaceutical Price Inflation (1980 = 100)

	1980	1981	1982	1983	1984	1985	1986	1987	1988	1989	1990	1991
France[a]												
GDP price index[b]	100.0	111.3	124.7	136.8	146.7	155.3	163.5	168.5	173.8	179.8	185.2	191.0
Divisia price index[c]	100.0	105.5	112.8	117.4	124.1	128.8	133.6	138.2	142.8	146.9	149.0	149.7
PPI-drugs[d]	100.0	110.1	116.6	121.9	126.6	129.4	131.7	134.1	135.1	135.1	136.7	137.9
Germany[e]												
GDP price index[b]	100.0	104.1	108.8	112.4	114.8	117.4	121.2	123.6	125.6	128.8	133.2	138.7
Divisia price index[c]	100.0	104.0	107.0	112.4	116.6	117.6	118.7	118.4	118.1	118.0	115.3	116.0
PPI-drugs[d]	100.0	104.1	107.2	112.3	116.1	119.6	121.4	122.4	123.8	125.9	126.2	128.0
Italy[f]												
GDP price index[b]	100.0	118.9	139.4	160.4	179.1	194.9	210.3	222.8	237.6	252.4	271.3	291.0
Divisia price index[c]	100.0	113.3	128.4	145.4	157.5	170.3	184.0	191.4	199.0	202.5	205.7	216.7
PPI-drugs[d]	100.0	118.9	137.5	156.6	166.6	189.5	190.2	210.5	219.3	223.0	227.3	238.0
United Kingdom[g]												
GDP price index[b]	100.0	111.4	119.8	126.2	131.9	139.5	144.4	151.6	161.5	172.9	183.8	196.2
Divisia price index[c]	100.0	106.3	112.9	120.1	121.2	123.3	125.5	130.6	135.9	141.0	142.9	143.5
PPI-drugs[d]	100.0	107.0	115.5	121.0	124.8	131.4	128.5	134.2	135.9	136.8	141.4	144.7
United States[h]												
GDP price index[b]	100.0	110.0	116.8	121.6	127.0	131.6	135.1	139.5	144.9	151.3	157.9	164.2
Divisia price index[c]	100.0	111.3	123.7	137.8	151.5	161.8	172.8	182.1	191.8	206.7	227.9	247.0
PPI-drugs[d]	100.0	109.0	117.0	128.0	137.9	149.1	160.9	172.9	185.2	200.6	214.7	229.2

[a]SNIP (1993).

[b]From OECD HEALTH DATA (CREDES).

[c]1980 base imputed from average growth rates from 1981–82 and 1982–83. From Danzon and Kim (1996) using IMS data. See app. B.

[d]For Germany, Italy, and the United Kingdom, the 1980 base imputed from the average for 1981–82 and 1982–83. 1981 index imputed from growth rate for June–December 1981. 1980 index imputed from the growth rate for June 1981–December 1982.

[e]*Preise und Preisindizes fur gewerbliche Produkte*, Statistisches Bundesamt.

[f]*Bolletino mensile di statistica*, Istituto Nazionale di Statistica.

[g]*Annual Abstract of Statistics*, Central Statistical Office, H.M. Stationery Office, London.

[h]Bureau of Labor Statistics, Producer Price Index, http://www.bls.gov/ppihome.htm.

United Kingdom during much of this period, physicians in the United Kingdom are paid either a salary or a capitation per enrolled patient, etc. Even where physicians are paid fee for service, as in Germany, the duration and content of a "visit" tends to be reduced as the prices are reduced and may also change owing to technological change. Estimating an accurate, quality-constant price index is particularly difficult in medical care because of the rapid rate of technical change and hence in the real content of services that do not change in name. For example, the real content of a hospital day is very different today than twenty years ago, but this quality change is typically embedded in the reported measure of price change.[25]

In the case of the pharmaceutical PPPs, the sample is very small; retail prices may differ significantly from manufacturer prices;[26] the index is unweighted; it includes medical devices; and it includes imputed values where prices are unavailable, which is inappropriate if unavailability reflects systematic differences between the unavailable products and the available products, owing to preferences and regulation. The differences between the OECD PPPs and our pharmaceutical indexes based on IMS data are discussed further in Danzon and Kim (1998).

The Fisher indexes for the United States relative to each comparison country are reported in table 13.2. They show the differences that remain in pharmaceutical prices after converting at exchange rates. Prices are lowest in France and decline steadily for most of the period, consistent with the hypothesis of increasing regulatory stringency. Italy has the second lowest prices, with considerable variation over the period that reflects exchange rate fluctuations as well changing regulatory stringency. The United Kingdom is third lowest and also shows declining prices over time, relative to the United States, which again suggests increasing regulatory stringency in the United Kingdom. Germany's prices decline, relative to the United States, following the introduction of reference pricing in 1989.

These data indicate that regulation has constrained the level and growth of drug prices at the manufacturer level relative to the unregulated U.S. prices. This confirms the importance of using sector-specific prices indexes for cross-national comparisons of a heavily regulated industry such as pharmaceuticals. Note that the estimates of U.S. price levels and growth are upwardly biased owing to the omission of discounts to managed care and public purchasers, which increased during the late 1980s and 1990s.[27]

---

25. Cutler et al. (1996) discuss the upward bias in the U.S. CPI for medical care, relative to a true cost-of-living index.

26. Distribution margins account for up to half of purchaser price levels for pharmaceuticals in some European countries (Healy 1995).

27. The Fisher indexes conceal significant differences between the U.S.-weighted Laspeyres indexes and the foreign-weighted Paasche indexes. The Laspeyres indexes show Germany, Canada, and Japan with higher prices than the United States. The Paasche indexes show foreign prices uniformly lower than U.S. prices, by as much as 50 percentage points (see Danzon and Kim 1998; Danzon and Chao 1999).

Table 13.2   **U.S. Relative to Foreign Prices for Pharmaceuticals, Fisher Price Indexes,[a] Single Molecule Products, Retail Pharmacy: Matching by Molecule/Therapeutic Category**

	1981	1982	1983	1984	1985[b]	1986	1987[b]	1988	1989	1990	1991	1992
France	1.66	1.84	2.13	2.52	2.38	2.24	2.35	2.46	2.81	2.68	2.65	2.06
Germany	.87	.99	1.09	1.26	1.24	1.23	1.18	1.13	1.42	1.39	1.35	1.44
Italy	1.84	2.11	2.06	2.39	2.21	2.04	2.00	1.95	2.25	2.13	1.93	1.79
United Kingdom	1.04	1.20	1.41	1.67	1.68	1.68	1.54	1.39	1.56	1.66	1.66	1.71

[a]IMS data. See Danzon and Kim (1998).
[b]1985 and 1987 values were estimated by taking the average of 1984 + 1986 and 1986 + 1988, respectively.

13.4   Empirical Results

13.4.1   Pharmaceutical Production

In all countries, growth in production of pharmaceuticals has far outpaced total manufacturing in the 1980s, regardless of the price index used (table 13.3). Using the Divisia indexes, pharmaceutical production increased 170 percent in Italy, 90 percent in France, 96 percent in the United Kingdom, 55 percent in Germany, and 18 percent in the United States. Relative to this benchmark, the estimates based on the GDP deflator are downwardly biased by 40–50 percentage points for France, Italy, and the United Kingdom, but the U.S. estimate is upwardly biased by 52 percentage points. The slow growth in Germany, relative to the other European countries, supports the hypothesis that production has been diverted from Germany to countries whose regulatory environments specifically reward local production, such as France, Italy, and the United Kingdom.

13.4.2   Employment

Between 1980 and 1990, employment in pharmaceuticals grew almost three times as rapidly in France (15.8 percent) as in the United States (5.8 percent) and the United Kingdom (3.5 percent) (table 13.4). By 1990, pharmaceutical employment was 2.0 percent of total manufacturing employment in France, compared to 1.4 percent in the United Kingdom, 1.2 percent in Germany, 1.3 percent in Italy, and 0.95 percent in the United States excluding Puerto Rico. Although this evidence is consistent with the hypothesis that regulation has stimulated employment in France and the United Kingdom since production has also grown rapidly in France, the alternative hypothesis of demand-driven expansion of production and sales force cannot be dismissed without evidence on productivity. Whether the growth in pharmaceutical employment is a net gain, as intended by industrial policy, or simply a diversion from other sectors remains an open question.

13.4.3   Value Added

Trends in value added are similar to trends in total production, with much more rapid growth in pharmaceuticals than in other manufacturing industries (table 13.5). Again, results are very sensitive to the price index.

To provide a measure that is independent of the price index, we calculated the cumulative growth in value added relative to the cumulative growth in production between 1980 and 1990. This ratio is 0.58 in Italy and 0.87 in France; by contrast, the ratio is 1.06 in the United States, 1.12 in the United Kingdom, and 1.13 in Germany. Thus, the ratio of value added to output declined in countries with strict price regulation but increased in the other three countries. This is consistent with the hypothesis that biased price regulation reduced the rate of growth of productivity.

Table 13.3 Growth in Production, 1970–90ᵃ (GDP deflator adjusted values unless noted; 1980 = 100)

	1970	1975	1980	1981	1982	1983	1984	1985	1986	1987	1988	1989	1990
France													
Total manufacturing	70.6	81.8	100.0	99.2	98.6	96.9	98.7	98.6	93.4	93.2	97.7	103.1	103.8
Chemical products	56.3	72.8	100.0	101.3	97.2	95.4	99.6	99.2	82.5	80.7	83.8	88.1	88.3
Drugs & medicines	71.5	87.4	100.0	107.2	108.6	113.7	116.2	121.6	125.2	126.6	138.2	145.3	152.6
Divisia price index	...	...	100.0	113.1	120.1	132.5	137.4	146.6	153.2	154.4	168.1	177.8	189.8
PPI-drugs	...	...	100.0	108.4	116.2	127.6	134.7	145.9	155.4	159.0	177.8	193.3	206.8
Germany													
Total manufacturing	81.1	85.1	100.0	100.1	97.2	96.7	101.0	104.8	101.2	99.5	103.5	109.2	113.1
Chemical products	61.8	73.9	100.0	104.6	99.5	99.9	106.4	109.0	93.1	89.7	93.5	98.9	99.8
Drugs & medicines	71.1	108.0	100.0	102.9	99.8	107.0	112.0	113.1	116.2	116.7	124.7	126.0	134.0
Divisia price index	...	...	100.0	103.0	101.5	107.0	110.3	112.9	118.7	121.8	132.6	137.5	154.8
PPI-drugs	...	...	100.0	102.9	101.3	107.1	110.7	111.1	116.0	117.8	126.5	128.9	141.4
Italy													
Total manufacturing	58.3	82.9	100.0	98.3	96.3	92.7	97.8	100.0	95.8	97.8	105.0	111.0	106.9
Chemical products	40.2	81.0	100.0	101.0	100.8	100.3	111.9	118.0	109.2	117.4	126.9	134.1	129.1
Drugs & medicinesᵇ	64.4	76.4	100.0	107.7	111.0	118.6	131.6	149.5	152.2	164.9	177.1ᶜ	207.5ᶜ	204.6ᶜ
Divisia price index	...	...	100.0	113.0	120.5	130.8	149.7	171.1	173.9	191.9	211.5	258.6	269.9
PPI-drugs	...	...	100.0	107.7	112.5	121.5	141.5	153.8	168.3	174.5	191.9	234.9	244.2

United Kingdom													
Total manufacturing[b]	96.2	105.2	100.0	90.7	89.6	91.4	97.1	98.5	94.8	101.3	104.8	106.7	104.3
Chemical products[b]	65.9	94.5	100.0	91.8	90.4	94.0	102.6	100.9	84.8	101.7	99.8	102.6	102.1
Drugs & medicines[b]	88.5	85.8	100.0	97.1	104.3	106.2	113.8	118.3	125.6	135.3	144.8	150.3	152.3
Divisia price index	...	...	100.0	101.8	110.7	111.6	123.9	133.8	144.6	157.1	172.1	184.3	196.0
PPI-drugs	...	...	100.0	101.1	108.2	110.8	120.3	125.6	141.2	152.9	172.1	190.0	198.0
United States													
Total manufacturing	71.1	80.6	100.0	99.3	90.1	92.0	98.2	95.9	93.4	96.0	100.2	102.1	100.6
Chemical products	49.8	67.5	100.0	102.2	91.0	88.8	90.1	85.3	74.2	79.0	82.5	84.8	87.7
Drugs & medicines[b]	69.5	81.9	100.0	101.6	105.5	113.0	114.6	119.1	127.2	140.2	151.3	161.7	169.5
Divisia price index	...	...	100.0	100.4	99.6	99.8	96.0	96.9	99.4	107.4	114.3	118.4	117.5
PPI-drugs	...	...	100.0	102.5	105.3	107.4	105.5	105.1	106.8	113.1	118.3	122.0	124.7

[a]Production is national accounts compatible (gross output).
[b]Survey-based data may not be national accounts compatible.
[c]Figures are estimated using the ratio of Drugs and Medicines to Other Chemicals for the closest year for which data are available.

Table 13.4   Growth in Number of Employees, 1975–90 (1980 = 100)

	1975	1980	1981	1982	1983	1984	1985	1986	1987	1988	1989	1990
France												
Total manufacturing	106.2	100.0	96.8	95.5	93.6	90.7	88.1	86.4	84.2	82.8	83.1	83.5
Chemical products	105.2	100.0	97.2	95.4	93.0	92.1	90.8	90.6	89.7	89.5	91.0	92.0
Drugs & medicines[a]	101.9[b]	100.0	102.4	102.9	104.2	105.6	106.8	107.8	107.2	108.6	112.2	115.8
Germany												
Total manufacturing	100.0	100.0	98.2	95.3	92.1	91.7	92.9	94.3	94.4	94.2	95.6	98.3
Chemical products	97.7	100.0	99.3	98.6	96.7	97.7	99.7	101.7	103.3	105.4	106.0	109.2
Drugs & medicines	105.1[b]	100.0	101.4	102.7	102.9	104.6	104.5	107.1	107.7	109.2	108.4	113.4
Italy												
Total manufacturing	94.7	100.0	96.4	93.9	90.2	86.1	85.0	84.5	83.7	84.8	85.2	85.2
Chemical products	99.0	100.0	93.4	90.2	88.1	86.4	86.2	88.3	91.0	92.9	94.7	94.5
Drugs & medicines[a]	101.4[b]	100.0	99.8	99.2	96.7	98.8	97.0	97.9	99.4	103.2	104.2[b]	104.2[b]
United Kingdom												
Total manufacturing	108.1	100.0	89.9	84.8	80.0	78.8	78.5	76.7	76.2	77.3	77.8	77.6
Chemical products	104.8	100.0	90.6	86.4	82.0	82.6	82.4	81.2	81.7	84.1	85.5	85.7
Drugs & medicines[a]	90.0	100.0	95.2	93.5	92.6	92.7	91.4	92.7	96.8	98.7	104.1	103.5
United States												
Total manufacturing	89.5	100.0	99.7	92.3	90.9	95.6	94.7	93.6	94.0	96.0	96.3	95.0
Chemical products	88.3	100.0	101.3	96.5	95.3	98.7	98.2	96.9	100.0	102.2	103.5	104.4
Drugs & medicines[a]	86.7	100.0	98.3	96.0	97.1	96.5	94.8	96.0	99.4	101.2	106.4	105.8

[a]Survey-based data may not be national accounts compatible.

[b]Figures are estimated using the ratio of Drugs and Medicines to Other Chemicals for the closest year for which data are available.

Table 13.5 Growth of Value Added, 1970–90[a] (GDP deflator adjusted values unless noted; 1980 = 100)

	1970	1975	1980	1981	1982	1983	1984	1985	1986	1987	1988	1989	1990
France													
Total manufacturing	85.3	95.5	100.0	97.0	97.0	96.9	95.9	97.9	100.8	99.8	105.2	108.8	110.6
Chemical products	84.4	89.1	100.0	94.9	93.3	100.4	98.5	105.2	115.7	109.9	117.3	117.2	117.7
Drugs & medicines	64.7	79.2	100.0	103.7	101.9	113.1	105.6	106.1	117.0	122.6	126.4	123.7	132.8
Divisia price index	...	...	100.0	109.4	112.6	131.8	124.8	128.0	143.1	149.6	153.7	151.4	165.1
PPI-drugs	...	...	100.0	104.8	109.0	127.0	122.4	127.4	145.2	154.1	162.5	164.7	179.9
Germany													
Total manufacturing	90.8	90.4	100.0	98.0	95.7	97.0	99.2	103.5	107.5	106.1	109.1	111.8	116.4
Chemical products	84.0	89.6	100.0	99.9	95.6	102.5	106.6	109.2	117.5	106.7	114.8	116.7	117.0
Drugs & medicines	81.4	90.5	100.0	105.8	107.2	116.6	117.1	120.3	130.6	125.6	135.1	148.9	150.8
Divisia price index	...	...	100.0	105.9	109.1	116.6	115.4	120.0	133.4	131.0	143.6	162.6	174.3
PPI-drugs	...	...	100.0	105.8	108.8	116.7	115.8	118.1	130.4	126.8	137.0	152.4	159.2
Italy													
Total manufacturing	67.2	79.2	100.0	96.6	93.8	90.3	91.7	93.5	94.0	95.4	100.1	102.8	100.3
Chemical products	72.9	88.7	100.0	93.2	90.9	91.4	98.5	110.6	107.6	112.9	119.5	123.7	118.0
Drugs & medicines[b]	92.3	92.8	100.0	100.4	101.9	105.8	110.6	116.5	109.9	115.2	118.1[c]	127.2[c]	118.3[c]
Divisia price index	...	...	100.0	105.4	110.6	116.8	125.8	133.4	125.6	134.1	141.0	158.5	156.1
PPP-drugs	...	...	100.0	100.4	103.3	108.4	118.9	119.8	121.5	121.9	128.0	143.9	141.2

(continued)

Table 13.5 (continued)

	1970	1975	1980	1981	1982	1983	1984	1985	1986	1987	1988	1989	1990
United Kingdom													
Total manufacturing	100.8	101.1	100.0	91.3	91.7	91.7	92.1	97.3	101.1	101.9	106.6	108.9	106.2
Chemical products	81.4	96.7	100.0	89.4	90.6	95.2	100.7	106.8	114.4	118.7	124.1	127.6	124.6
Drugs & medicines[b]	75.2	75.3	100.0	96.4	106.8	106.7	115.7	121.2	129.6	146.1	159.4	164.9	170.0
Divisia price index	...	...	100.0	101.0	113.4	112.2	125.9	137.1	149.2	169.6	189.4	202.2	218.7
PPI-drugs	...	...	100.0	100.4	110.8	111.3	122.3	128.6	145.7	165.0	189.4	208.5	221.0
United States													
Total manufacturing	88.3	89.4	100.0	100.7	93.6	96.7	104.5	103.3	104.6	105.4	109.0	109.1	106.0
Chemical products	84.9	91.8	100.0	105.8	106.3	113.3	118.7	116.6	125.8	126.9	139.0	139.7	140.2
Drugs & medicines[b]	77.5	86.6	100.0	100.3	107.8	118.1	120.1	128.0	133.9	149.6	158.7	168.3	179.5
Divisia price index	...	...	100.0	99.1	101.8	104.2	100.6	104.0	104.7	114.6	119.9	123.2	124.4
PPI-drugs	...	...	100.0	101.2	107.6	112.2	110.6	112.9	112.4	120.7	124.2	127.0	132.0

[a]Value added is national accounts compatible value added.

[b]Survey-based data may not be national accounts compatible.

[c]Figures are estimated using the ratio of Drugs and Medicines to Other Chemicals for the closest year for which data are available.

13.4.4   Value Added per Employee

The results for value-added per employee (table 13.6) again depend critically on the price index. The estimates based on the GDP deflator imply that labor productivity growth in France has been 50 percent lower in pharmaceuticals than in total manufacturing, despite (or because of) the more rapid growth in employment in pharmaceuticals than in total manufacturing. A similar pattern holds for Italy. By contrast, for the United Kingdom, Germany, and the United States, labor productivity growth in pharmaceuticals appears to have outpaced total manufacturing.

However, using either the PPI-drugs or the Divisia indexes increases the estimates of labor productivity growth for all countries except the United States, reflecting the decline in real drug price over time in all countries except the United States. With these indexes, labor productivity growth is roughly twice as high in the United Kingdom as in France, Germany, and Italy, which are similar. The United States lags the other four countries for pharmaceuticals, as it does for total manufacturing. These results seem inconsistent with the hypothesis that increasingly stringent price regulation in France and Italy has generated increased distortions of productivity over time. A possible confounding factor—and a plausible explanation for the apparently inconsistent results—is that the market share of global drugs has increased over time, relative to local drugs. Assuming that productivity is absolutely higher for global drugs, an increasing market share of global drugs in France and Italy could bias upward the estimates of productivity growth for each sector separately.[28]

Tables 13.7 and 13.8, which compare labor productivity levels relative to the United States, illustrate the sensitivity of international comparisons to the conversion index. Converting at GDP PPPs (table 13.7), value added per employee in pharmaceuticals is more than twice as high in the United States as in all European countries. Adding Puerto Rico to the United States widens the gap by 3–4 percentage points. Of the European countries, the United Kingdom leads with value added per employee of 47 percent of the United States, followed by Germany 33.2 percent, Italy 28.7 percent, and France 19.8 percent. This shortfall of labor productivity in Europe relative to the United States is much greater in pharmaceuticals than for total manufacturing, for which the 1990 figures are 92.7 percent for France, 79.4 percent for Italy, 77.2 percent for Germany, and 62.6 percent for the United Kingdom.

However, because the low estimates of labor productivity for pharmaceuticals in Europe relative to the United States partly reflect the lower prices in Europe (see table 13.2), table 13.8 reports labor productivity, relative to the United States, with all countries adjusted to U.S. price levels using the pharma-

28. Market shares of global and local drugs over time are not available. However, the decline in the number of pharmaceutical companies operating in France, from 507 in 1970 to 353 in 1991, is consistent with a declining market share of local products. In 1989, French companies accounted for 48 percent of sales (SNIP 1993).

Table 13.6   Growth of Value Added per Employee, 1970–90[a] (GDP deflator adjusted values unless noted; 1980 = 100)

	1970	1975	1980	1981	1982	1983	1984	1985	1986	1987	1988	1989	1990
France													
Total manufacturing	83.3	90.0	100.0	100.2	101.5	103.6	105.7	111.1	116.7	118.6	127.0	131.0	132.4
Chemical products	87.4	84.6	100.0	97.6	97.7	107.9	106.9	115.9	127.7	122.4	131.1	128.8	127.9
Drugs & medicines[b]	...	77.8	100.0	101.3	99.0	108.5	100.0	99.4	108.6	114.4	116.3	110.3	114.6
Divisia price deflator	...	...	100.0	106.1	109.2	126.9	119.8	122.3	136.5	144.5	147.6	141.5	150.4
Germany													
Total manufacturing	81.6	90.4	100.0	99.8	100.4	105.3	108.2	111.5	113.9	112.4	115.8	117.0	118.4
Chemical products	82.7	91.7	100.0	100.6	97.0	106.0	109.1	109.5	115.6	103.3	108.9	110.1	107.2
Drugs & medicines	...	86.1[c]	100.0	104.4	104.4	113.4	112.0	115.1	121.9	116.6	123.7	137.4	133.0
Divisia price deflator	...	...	100.0	106.2	108.4	116.4	114.7	120.5	131.8	129.1	139.9	159.7	163.5
Italy													
Total manufacturing	74.2	83.6	100.0	100.3	99.9	100.1	106.4	110.0	111.3	114.0	118.0	120.6	117.7
Chemical products	81.3	89.6	100.0	99.9	100.8	103.7	114.1	128.4	121.9	124.0	128.6	130.7	124.8
Drugs & medicines[b,d]	...	91.5[c]	100.0	100.6	102.8	109.4	112.0	120.1	112.2	115.9	114.5	122.1	113.6
Divisia price deflator	...	...	100.0	107.5	115.7	128.0	138.1	151.8	144.0	152.9	156.3	175.4	174.2
United Kingdom													
Total manufacturing	84.3	93.6	100.0	101.6	108.1	114.6	116.9	123.9	131.9	133.8	137.9	139.9	136.8
Chemical products	75.8	92.2	100.0	98.7	104.9	116.1	122.0	129.6	140.9	145.4	147.5	149.2	145.4
Drugs & medicines[b,d]	76.7	83.7	100.0	101.3	114.2	115.2	124.8	132.6	139.8	150.9	161.5	158.5	164.2
Divisia price deflator	...	...	100.0	106.1	121.0	121.3	136.8	152.1	164.1	179.8	198.4	203.0	221.4
United States													
Total manufacturing	92.9	99.9	100.0	101.0	101.4	106.4	109.3	109.1	111.7	112.2	113.6	113.2	111.5
Chemical products	95.3	104.0	100.0	104.4	110.1	118.8	120.3	118.7	129.8	126.8	136.0	135.0	134.3
Drugs & medicines[b,d]	102.4	99.9	100.0	102.0	112.3	121.6	124.4	135.0	139.6	150.5	156.9	158.3	169.7
Divisia price deflator	...	...	100.0	101.6	107.4	109.9	107.4	113.5	113.1	120.2	124.2	122.1	125.4

[a]Value Added is national accounts compatible value added.

[b]Employment figures are survey-based data and may not be national accounts compatible.

[c]Figures are estimated using the ratio of Drugs and Medicines to Other Chemicals for the closest year for which data are available.

[d]Value added for Drugs and Medicines are survey-based data and may not be national accounts compatible.

Table 13.7   Value Added per Employee relative to United States, GDP PPP Conversion[a] (United States = 100)

	1970	1975	1980	1981	1982	1983	1984	1985	1986	1987	1988	1989	1990
France													
Total manufacturing	70.5	...	79.4	78.5	79.3	76.9	76.1	79.9	81.9	82.7	87.5	90.5	92.7
Other chemicals	46.6	45.7	63.2	62.5	53.5	53.4	48.1	48.6	47.8	49.0	49.8	51.5	53.4
Drugs & medicines[b]	...	23.2[c]	29.8	29.5	26.2	26.5	23.7	21.7	22.9	22.3	21.8	20.4	19.8
Drugs & medicines (including Puerto Rico)	...	...	...	...	23.7	...	...	...	...	20.5	...	...	...
Germany													
Total manufacturing	63.9	66.3	73.3	72.3	72.3	72.3	72.0	74.3	74.3	72.7	74.1	75.1	77.2
Other chemicals	43.7	48.1	45.7	59.4	49.8	51.4	49.1	48.8	49.0	45.2	46.9	48.2	46.2
Drugs & medicines	...	36.8[c]	42.7	43.6	39.5	39.7	38.2	36.2	37.1	32.8	33.4	36.8	33.2
Drugs & medicines (including Puerto Rico)	...	...	...	...	35.8	...	...	...	...	30.1	...	...	...

(*continued*)

Table 13.7 (continued)

	1970	1975	1980	1981	1982	1983	1984	1985	1986	1987	1988	1989	1990
Italy													
Total manufacturing	60.8	64.0	76.6	75.8	75.2	71.7	73.8	76.3	75.3	76.7	78.4	80.3	79.4
Other chemicals	56.7	48.5	65.9	56.2	50.1	46.3	50.2	54.1	46.1	47.5	48.7	52.6	46.9
Drugs & medicines[b,d]	...	39.9[c]	43.7	42.9	39.8	39.1	39.0	38.4	34.7	33.1	31.4[c]	33.2[c]	28.7[c]
Drugs & medicines (including Puerto Rico)	...	...	...	...	36.0	...	...	...	...	30.5	...	...	...
United Kingdom													
Total manufacturing	47.1	48.6	51.6	51.5	54.3	55.5	54.1	57.5	60.4	60.9	62.5	63.0	62.6
Other chemicals	27.7	29.4	37.1	34.4	32.5	31.5	32.5	34.7	34.9	35.0	36.3	36.4	35.2
Drugs & medicines[b,d]	37.0	41.3	49.1	48.4	49.3	46.5	48.3	47.4	48.7	48.7	50.4	48.6	47.0
Drugs & medicines (including Puerto Rico)	...	...	...	...	44.6	...	...	...	...	44.8	...	...	...

[a]Calculated using GDP PPPs.
[b]Survey-based employment data may not be national accounts compatible.
[c]Figures are estimated using the ratio of drugs and medicines to chemicals for the closest year for which data are available.
[d]Survey-based value-added data may not be national accounts compatible.

Table 13.8   Value Added per Employee relative to United States, Fisher Price Indexes[a] (United States = 100)

	1981	1982	1982[b]	1983	1984	1985	1986	1987	1987[b]	1988	1989	1990
Drugs & Medicines												
France[c]	50.7	43.5	39.3	46.3	44.2	38.0	50.2	59.2	54.4	60.5	60.1	64.2
Germany	39.2	37.1	33.5	38.7	37.8	34.0	46.7	47.3	43.5	46.1	58.6	59.6
Italy[c,d]	61.2	60.4	54.7	57.1	61.3	54.4	60.8	67.3	61.9	63.6[e]	74.8[e]	72.5[e]
United Kingdom[c,d]	52.3	55.0	49.7	52.6	58.1	56.2	66.2	68.9	63.3	71.3	73.3	83.6
United States[c,d]	100.0	100.0	100.0	100.0	100.0	100.0	100.0	100.0	100.0	100.0	100.0	100.0

[a]For Fisher price indexes, see table 13.2, app. B below, and Danzon and Kim (1998).

[b]Figures in these columns use the United States and Puerto Rico as base.

[c]Survey-based employment data may not be national accounts compatible.

[d]Survey-based value added may not be national accounts compatible.

[e]Figures are estimated using the ratio of drugs and medicines to chemicals for the closest year for which data are available.

ceuticals-specific Fisher indexes. Although this dramatically improves the European productivity measures, Germany is still only 60 percent of the United States, France 64 percent, Italy 73 percent, and the United Kingdom 84 percent. All countries except the United Kingdom still show lower productivity for pharmaceuticals than for total manufacturing. This may understate the productivity shortfall in pharmaceuticals because of the exclusion of local products from these Fisher indexes. If local products, which are produced by local firms and have relatively low prices, are less stringently regulated than global products that are produced by multinational corporations and are generally higher priced, then the Fisher indexes understate foreign prices and overstate foreign productivity, relative to the United States.

For the United States, the OECD data exclude Puerto Rico, which accounted for roughly 14 percent of U.S. production and 9 percent of employment in the 1980s. Adding Puerto Rico (where available) raises U.S. value added by about 3 percentage points (1987 data), as expected given the tax incentives to locate high-value-added operations in Puerto Rico.

Note that, for purposes of comparing productivity cross-nationally, pricing the output of different countries at a common price level is appropriate. The table 13.8 estimates, with all countries compared at U.S. prices using the Fisher indexes, therefore provide a more accurate comparison of labor productivity in pharmaceuticals than the table 13.7 estimates that use GDP PPPs.[29] However, for purposes of evaluating the efficiency of resource allocation to drugs relative to other sectors within each country, each country's output should be valued at local prices; thus, for this purpose, the table 13.7 comparisons that use local prices and GDP PPP conversion are more appropriate. These show significantly lower labor productivity in pharmaceuticals than in other manufacturing in France and Italy, yet employment has grown more rapidly in pharmaceuticals than in other manufacturing in these countries. We return to this below.

13.4.5   Capital Investment

Between 1980 and 1990, fixed capital investment in pharmaceuticals increased 150 percent[30] in France, compared to roughly 60 percent in the United States and the United Kingdom and compared to 33 percent for total manufacturing in France (table 13.9). Investment per employee increased 116 percent in pharmaceuticals in France, compared to 59 percent in total manufacturing (table 13.10), consistent with the hypothesis of biased regulation. The more

---

29. The use of the United States as the benchmark price level does not affect the results because the Fisher indexes are the geometric mean of the Laspeyres and Paasche indexes, which, respectively, use consumption patterns in the United States and the foreign country as weights. Ideally, inputs should also be measured at common price levels. This adjustment cannot be made with the available data.

30. The 1990 figure of 250 appears to be above trend; the three-year average for 1989–91 is 237. Using this lower figure would not affect the conclusions.

Table 13.9   Growth in Gross Fixed Capital Formation, 1975–90[a] (GDP deflator adjusted values; 1980 = 100)

	1975	1980	1981	1982	1983	1984	1985	1986	1987	1988	1989	1990
France												
Total manufacturing	83.3	100.0	93.3	88.4	85.3	86.2	94.4	97.9	102.6	113.3	120.7	132.6
Chemical products	79.3	100.0	91.3	82.0	76.9	72.7	85.1	85.7	91.8	96.6	105.7	117.9
Drugs & medicines[b]	…	100.0	114.1	141.5	131.3	135.4	156.7	183.7	204.9	205.6	232.5	250.1
Germany												
Total manufacturing	76.2	100.0	94.2	85.4	86.1	84.8	96.4	103.0	107.7	109.7	120.1	132.6
Chemical products	97.2	100.0	97.6	89.9	88.7	85.9	95.7	105.3	117.1	116.9	127.7	137.9
Drugs & medicines	…	100.0	105.6	100.4	112.0	115.5	119.5	134.4	132.3	111.1	125.3	136.2
Italy												
Total manufacturing	82.2	100.0	89.2	80.9	71.9	75.6	69.6	70.3	77.7	85.2	92.7	…
Chemical products	199.1	100.0	86.1	80.1	73.0	77.1	78.0	74.8	89.4	102.0	88.0	…
Drugs & medicines	…	…	…	…	…	…	…	…	…	…	…	…
United Kingdom												
Total manufacturing	95.9	100.0	76.8	74.4	73.9	87.7	100.8	93.7	99.1	105.7	114.8	108.3
Chemical products	89.8	100.0	75.0	69.2	72.8	80.6	100.2	94.3	103.3	99.6	104.2	102.0
Drugs & medicines[b]	76.2	100.0	113.5	93.0	94.6	97.8	131.5	135.1	136.0	153.6	158.1	161.9
United States												
Total manufacturing	75.3	100.0	106.2	96.0	73.9	85.3	93.4	80.2	86.1	85.2	100.6	101.7
Chemical products	93.0	100.0	110.7	113.5	80.0	80.5	84.2	68.2	76.7	86.5	107.3	106.2
Drugs & medicines[b]	76.8	100.0	106.1	118.9	108.7	125.1	123.9	109.5	139.3	157.8	175.7	160.4

[a]Gross fixed capital formation is national accounts–compatible gross fixed capital formation (land, buildings, machinery, and equipment).
[b]Survey-based data may not be national accounts compatible.

Table 13.10 Growth in Gross Fixed Capital Formation per Employee (GDP deflator adjusted values; 1980 = 100)

	1975	1980	1981	1982	1983	1984	1985	1986	1987	1988	1989	1990
France												
Total manufacturing	78.5	100.0	96.4	92.6	91.1	94.9	107.2	113.3	121.9	136.8	145.3	158.8
Chemical products	75.4	100.0	93.9	85.9	82.7	78.9	93.8	94.6	102.3	108.0	116.1	128.2
Drugs & medicines[a,b]	…	100.0	111.5	137.5	126.0	128.3	146.8	170.4	191.2	189.3	207.2	215.9
Germany												
Total manufacturing	76.1	100.0	95.9	89.6	93.4	92.4	103.8	109.2	114.1	116.4	125.6	134.9
Chemical products	99.5	100.0	98.3	91.1	91.7	87.9	96.0	103.6	113.4	110.9	120.5	126.3
Drugs & medicines	…	100.0	104.2	97.7	108.8	110.4	114.3	125.5	122.9	101.7	115.5	120.1
Italy												
Total manufacturing	86.8	100.0	92.5	86.1	79.7	87.7	81.9	83.1	92.9	100.4	108.7	…
Chemical products	201.1	100.0	92.2	88.8	82.9	89.3	90.5	84.8	98.2	109.7	93.0	…
Drugs & medicines[b]	…	…	…	…	…	…	…	…	…	…	…	…
United Kingdom												
Total manufacturing	88.8	100.0	85.4	87.8	92.4	111.3	128.3	122.1	130.1	136.7	147.4	139.7
Chemical products	85.7	100.0	82.8	80.1	88.7	97.7	121.7	116.0	126.4	118.5	121.9	119.0
Drugs & medicines[a,b]	84.4	100.0	119.2	99.5	102.1	105.4	143.9	145.7	140.4	155.6	151.9	156.3
United States												
Total manufacturing	84.1	100.0	106.5	104.0	81.3	89.2	98.7	85.7	91.6	88.7	104.4	107.1
Chemical products	105.3	100.0	109.2	117.5	83.9	81.6	85.8	70.3	76.7	84.7	103.7	101.8
Drugs & medicines[a,b]	88.6	100	107.9	123.9	112	129.6	130.7	114.1	140.1	156	165.2	151.7

[a]Survey-based data may not be national accounts compatible.
[b]Employment figures are survey-based data and may not be national accounts compatible.

rapid growth in labor productivity in the French pharmaceutical industry relative to other French manufacturing (measured using the Divisia indexes) may thus in part reflect the increasing capital/labor ratio.

Between 1980 and 1990, the United Kingdom also experienced more rapid growth in capital investment, both absolutely and per employee, in pharmaceuticals than in total manufacturing, consistent with the predicted effects of rate-of-return regulation. The growth in capital/labor ratios may have contributed to the growth in value added per employee in pharmaceuticals relative to total manufacturing (64 vs. 37 percent) in the United Kingdom.

Lower capital/labor ratios in France and Germany may contribute to their lower labor productivity relative to the United States in pharmaceuticals.[31] Capital formation per employee in pharmaceuticals, relative to the United States, is 57 percent for France, 49 percent for Germany, and 99 percent for the United Kingdom (table 13.11). By contrast, capital formation per employee for total manufacturing relative to the United States is 125 percent in France, 84 percent in Germany, and only 65 percent in the United Kingdom. For Germany, whereas capital formation per employee in total manufacturing has increased relative to the United States (from 61 percent in 1975 to 84 percent in 1990), for pharmaceuticals the trend is reversed, dropping from 79 percent of the U.S. level in 1975 to 40 percent in 1988 and 49 percent in 1989. These results are consistent with the hypothesis that pharmaceutical investments have been diverted from Germany to other European Union countries.

13.4.6 R&D

Table 13.12 reports estimates of R&D expenditures, using survey data from pharmaceutical trade associations (Centre for Medicines Research 1993). R&D expenditures in constant local currency units have grown most rapidly in the United States, both absolutely and relative to labor, and most slowly in Germany since the mid-1980s. R&D investment per employee is roughly twice as high in the United States as in other countries (table 13.12, panel C). As noted earlier, country-specific R&D stocks cannot be directly calculated from R&D investment flows because of lags in launch and international diffusion. However, assuming that R&D stocks are positively correlated with investment flows, these data suggest that stocks of unobserved R&D capital are significant and are probably larger in the United States than in other countries.

13.5 Multifactor Productivity Growth

Estimates of multifactor productivity growth require measures of output elasticities. As discussed earlier, the conventional use of factor shares as prox-

---

31. We compare capital formation rather than the estimated capital stock per employee because the capital stock estimates depend on the assumed life of capital for which we have no accurate data. With our base-case assumption of a ten-year life of capital in all countries, the capital formation and capital stock estimates are highly correlated.

Table 13.11   Gross Fixed Capital Formation per Employee, 1975–90, Relative to the United States[a] (GDP PPP conversion; United States = 100)

	1975	1980	1981	1982	1983	1984	1985	1986	1987	1988	1989	1990
France												
Total manufacturing	79.9	85.4	77.1	75.8	95.3	90.1	91.8	111.5	112.0	129.8	117.1	124.5
Other chemicals	68.4	59.3	60.7	54.7	66.0	57.8	63.7	77.6	59.3	71.6	66.8	78.6
Drugs & medicines[b,c]	...	40.8	42.0	45.1	45.6	40.0	45.3	60.1	54.8	48.8	50.4	57.0
Drugs & medicines (including Puerto Rico)[b,c]	...	...	...	43.2	...	...	...	...	51.8	...	...	...
Germany												
Total manufacturing	61.1	67.4	60.6	57.8	77.2	69.3	70.4	85.4	83.1	87.7	80.4	84.3
Other chemicals[b]	66.0	67.1	57.4	47.6	57.5	54.8	62.7	78.3	62.8	57.9	61.9	64.0
Drugs & medicines[c]	...	62.1	59.9	48.8	60.2	52.5	53.9	67.9	53.9	40.1	43.1	48.8
Drugs & medicines (including Puerto Rico)[c]	...	...	...	46.8	...	...	...	...	51.0	...	...	...
Italy												
Total manufacturing	118.3	114.9	99.4	94.7	111.9	111.9	94.3	110.0	114.7	128.1	117.8	...
Other chemicals[c]	...	...	...	...	...	...	...	...	...	...	...	...
Drugs & medicines[c]	...	...	...	...	...	...	...	...	...	...	...	...
Drugs & medicines (including Puerto Rico)[c]	...	...	...	...	...	...	...	...	...	...	...	...
United Kingdom												
Total manufacturing	53.6	50.6	40.3	42.1	57.4	61.9	64.7	71.5	71.1	77.7	70.5	65.3
Other chemicals	57.4	57.4	48.4	44.5	52.9	51.3	65.5	70.0	57.4	52.7	52.5	52.6
Drugs & medicines[b,c]	93.1	97.2	106.7	77.0	88.5	77.6	105.3	123.1	96.5	96.7	88.4	99.2
Drugs & medicines (including Puerto Rico)[b,c]	...	...	...	73.9	...	...	...	...	91.2	...	...	...

[a]Gross fixed capital formation is national accounts–compatible gross fixed capital formation (land, buildings, machinery, and equipment).

[b]Figures are survey-based data and may not be national accounts compatible.

[b]Employment figures are survey-based data and may not be national accounts compatible.

Table 13.12   Growth in Drugs and Medicines R&D

	1981	1982	1983	1984	1985	1986	1987	1988	1989	1990	1991
Total R&D expenditures[a,b]											
France	100.0	111.2	120.9	133.9	149.8	154.2	176.0	184.0	203.5	218.3	201.6
Germany	100.0	102.5	119.0	139.9	165.1	168.8	159.6	150.9	158.1	174.5	188.2
Italy	100.0	106.0	108.3	107.1	124.5	130.6	149.7	169.2	194.8	208.6	217.6
United Kingdom	100.0	105.6	119.9	131.2	143.6	156.9	155.5	184.2	200.8	210.1	220.6
United States	100.0	114.8	129.8	139.5	153.2	171.6	194.0	217.3	239.9	254.4	276.2
R&D per Employee[b,c]											
France	100.0	110.6	118.7	129.8	143.6	146.5	168.1	173.4	185.6	192.9	181.0
Germany	100.0	101.1	117.3	135.5	160.1	159.7	150.2	140.0	147.8	155.9	161.7
Italy	100.0	106.7	111.8	108.3	128.2	133.1	150.4	163.7	186.7	199.8	...
United Kingdom	100.0	107.5	123.2	134.7	149.6	161.0	152.9	177.7	183.6	193.2	...
United States	100.0	117.6	131.3	142.1	158.8	175.7	191.8	211.1	221.6	236.4	...
R&D per employee, relative to the United States[c,d]											
France	63.2	59.4	57.0	57.3	56.6	52.1	54.7	51.3	52.2	50.8	...
Germany	77.4	66.3	69.0	73.3	77.5	69.9	60.1	50.9	51.2	50.7	...
Italy	49.3	44.7	41.9	37.4	39.5	37.0	38.2	37.8	41.1	41.1	...
United Kingdom	66.6	60.5	62.8	62.4	62.1	60.8	52.9	56.3	54.9	54.2	...
United States	100.0	100.0	100.0	100.0	100.0	100.0	100.0	100.0	100.0	100.0	...

[a]R&D data from national trade associations (Center for Research in Medicines 1993).

[b]GDP deflator adjusted values; 1981 = 100.

[c]Number of employees for France, Italy, the United Kingdom, and the United States are survey-based data and may not be national accounts compatible.

[d]GDP PPP conversion; United States = 100.

ies for output elasticities for pharmaceuticals is potentially biased for several reasons. First, patent protection could lead to prices that exceed long-run marginal cost (including a competitive return to R&D), in which case factor shares of revenue or value added would be downwardly biased estimates of output elasticities (Hall 1988, 1990). On the other hand, if regulation constrains prices below long-run marginal cost, revenue-based factor shares will exceed output elasticities. Second, factor shares are upwardly biased measures of output elasticities for labor or physical capital if price regulation induces excessive factor inputs (see eq. [2″]). Third, if the output elasticity for physical capital is estimated as the complement of the labor share, this estimate will be upward biased since it includes the unmeasured returns to the stock of intangible R&D capital, and MFP growth will be downward biased. Assume that there is no bias in prices, that both the stock of intangible capital M and its return s_M are unobserved, and that s_K is estimated as $1 - s_L$. In that case, the Solow residual reflects conventional TFP plus the contribution of this unobserved input:

$$(11) \qquad \dot{Q} - s_L \dot{L} - s_K \dot{K} = \dot{A} + s_M \dot{M}.$$

Since R&D investments are the main source of technical change in this industry, distinguishing between production function shifts due to A and M is conceptually problematic as well as infeasible given the data.

To illustrate the severity of potential measurement bias, table 13.13 reports revenue-based and cost-based estimates of factor shares for labor and physical capital. Labor share s_L is labor compensation divided by either value added (revenue based) or estimated total variable cost (cost based). The first estimate of the share of capital s_K is a residual income measure $(1 - s_L)$. The second estimate of s_K is a cost-based estimate of the rental cost of capital, $(\rho + \delta)K$. The real cost of funds ρ is assumed to be 10 percent, and the depreciation rate δ is also assumed to be 10 percent, assuming a ten-year life of capital.[32]

The revenue-based factor shares imply a much larger share of labor in France (71–92 percent, depending on the price deflator for value added), compared to 23–29 percent for the labor share in the United States, 30–36 percent in the United Kingdom, and 43 percent in Germany. The cost-based estimates are much closer, ranging from 82 percent in the United States to 86 percent in France. The two alternative estimates of s_K are fairly similar for France. However, for other countries, the residual income measure of s_K exceeds the rental cost measure; for the United States, this difference is greatest (77 vs. 5 percent). The difference presumably reflects the ex post return to unobserved R&D capital and other unmeasured services, including contractual payments for R&D services and license fees that are appropriately subsumed into

---

32. Strictly, the rental price of capital reflects tax offsets as well as the real cost of funds and the depreciation rate (Hall 1990). Since we lack country-specific data on tax offsets, these are ignored here. Myers and Shyam-Sunder (1996) estimate beta of roughly one and a real cost of capital of 9.9–10.7 percent for the period 1980–90. This is consistent with previous estimates (Grabowski and Vernon 1990).

Table 13.13   **Share of Labor and Capital**

| | Value-Added-Based Shares | | | | | | | | | Cost-Based Shares[d] | | | | | |
| | Labor Share (s_L)[a] | | | Capital Share (s_{K1})[b] | | | Capital Share (s_{K2})[c] | | | Share of Labor (s_L)[e] | | | Share of Capital (s_K)[f] | | |
	1976–80	1981–85	1986–90	1976–80	1981–85	1986–90	1976–80	1981–85	1986–90	1976–80	1981–85	1986–90	1976–80	1981–85	1986–90
France															
Total manufacturing	.66	.69	.62	.34	.31	.38	.26	.27	.26	.72	.72	.70	.28	.28	.30
Chemical products	.46	.51	.44	.54	.49	.56	.29	.31	.27	.62	.62	.62	.38	.38	.38
Drugs & medicines	.94	.94	.92	.06	.06	.08	.12	.19	.20	.88	.83	.82	.12	.17	.18
PPI-drugs	...	.84	.71	...	.16	.29	...	.17	.16	...	.83	.82	...	.17	.18
Germany															
Total manufacturing	.66	.69	.67	.34	.31	.33	.21	.22	.21	.76	.76	.76	.24	.24	.24
Chemical products	.50	.54	.55	.50	.46	.45	.24	.23	.22	.68	.70	.71	.32	.30	.29
Drugs & medicines	.48	.46	.43	.52	.54	.57	.20	.18	.16	.70	.72	.73	.30	.28	.27
PPI-drugs	...	.46	.43	...	.54	.57	...	.18	.16	...	.72	.73	...	.28	.27
Italy															
Total manufacturing	.60	.57	.54	.40	.43	.46	.37	.37	.34	.62	.61	.62	.38	.39	.38
Chemical products	.64	.58	.55	.36	.42	.45	.93	.75	.52	.41	.43	.52	.59	.57	.48
Drugs & medicines	...	...	...	...	...	...	...	...	...	...	...	...	...	...	...
PPI-drugs	...	...	...	...	...	...	...	...	...	...	...	...	...	...	...

(continued)

Table 13.13 (continued)

| | Value-Added-Based Shares | | | | | | | | | Cost-Based Shares[d] | | | | | |
| | Labor Share (s_L)[a] | | | Capital Share (s_{K1})[b] | | | Capital Share (s_{K2})[c] | | | Share of Labor (s_L)[e] | | | Share of Capital (s_K)[f] | | |
	1976–80	1981–85	1986–90	1976–80	1981–85	1986–90	1976–80	1981–85	1986–90	1976–80	1981–85	1986–90	1976–80	1981–85	1986–90
United Kingdom															
Total manufacturing	.78	.77	.72	.22	.23	.28	.25	.27	.24	.76	.74	.75	.24	.26	.25
Chemical products	.72	.71	.66	.28	.29	.34	.44	.46	.37	.62	.61	.64	.38	.39	.36
Drugs & medicines	.36	.38	.36	.64	.62	.64	.19	.20	.18	.65	.66	.67	.35	.34	.33
PPI-drugs	...	.36	.30	...	.64	.70	...	.19	.15	...	.66	.67	...	.34	.33
United States															
Total manufacturing	.71	.72	.68	.29	.28	.32	.21	.23	.22	.77	.75	.76	.23	.25	.24
Chemical products	.59	.57	.50	.41	.43	.50	.40	.37	.29	.60	.61	.63	.40	.39	.37
Drugs & medicines	.30	.27	.23	.70	.73	.77	.11	.11	.09	.73	.72	.71	.27	.28	.29
PPI-drugs	...	.29	.29	...	.71	.71	...	.11	.12	...	.72	.71	...	.28	.29

[a] $s_L = L/Q$ where L = labor compensation (real), Q = value added (real).

[b] $s_{K1} = 1 - s_L$.

[c] $s_{K2} = K(r + d)/Q$ where K = capital stock (real), r = real cost of funds 10 percent, and d = depreciation rate 10 percent.

[d] Total cost = $L + K(r + d)$.

[e] $s_L = L/[L + K(r + d)]$.

[f] $s_K = K(r + d)/[L + K(r + d)]$.

R&D.[33] Note that, using the more appropriate rental cost of capital, the shares of labor and physical capital sum to more than one in France, implying a negative return to intangible capital, whereas the sum of these shares is 52 percent or lower in all the other countries.

Table 13.14 reports estimates of total factor productivity growth for 1975–90, with alternative factor share proxies for output elasticities. The results are very sensitive to the price deflator and, to a lesser extent, to the estimates of output elasticity. Using the GDP deflator for value added, TFP growth in France is lower than in total manufacturing in France and much lower than pharmaceuticals in the United States or the United Kingdom. In other countries, TFP growth is higher in pharmaceuticals than in total manufacturing.[34] Using the PPI-drugs estimates of value added reverses the conclusions for France and the United States.

13.6 Conclusions

This paper has demonstrated some of the problems in estimating productivity growth and cross-national comparisons for an industry such as pharmaceuticals, which has a high rate of investment in R&D that is subject to cross-national diffusion, hence large stocks of unmeasured, intangible capital and a high rate of technological change. In addition, the pharmaceutical industry is subject to price regulation and safety and efficacy regulation; as a result, prices and product mix differ significantly across countries. Country-specific rates of price change, as measured by either the official PPI-drugs or our Divisia indexes, diverge significantly from economywide inflation. These two drugs-specific price indexes are more similar to each other than either is to the GDP deflator; however, they differ by enough to make estimates of productivity growth extremely tentative. The divergence of pharmaceutical prices cross-nationally means that the GDP PPPs do not provide an accurate basis for cross-national productivity comparisons. The drugs-specific Fisher price indexes used here are more accurate but are also imperfect.

Because of these measurement problems, conclusions on the cross-national comparisons are tentative. The evidence is generally consistent with the hypothesis that labor productivity is lower in the French pharmaceutical industry than in the French manufacturing sector generally, as predicted by the theory that biased regulation leads to excessive input use and suboptimal productivity. The relatively large market share of local drugs, which may have lower productivity than global drugs, may be a contributing factor. For the United Kingdom, although capital investment has been very rapid, TFP growth in pharmaceuti-

33. Cocks (1974) estimates that $s_L = 0.6$ and $s_K = 0.4$ for a single U.S. firm for the period 1967–71, before adjusting for R&D; these are both revised to 0.5 after netting out labor that is devoted to R&D.

34. Unfortunately, TFP estimates are not available for Italy because data on labor compensation and capital are unavailable.

Table 13.14   Growth in Value Added, Number Employed, Capital Stock, and Total Factor Productivity (percentage changes)

	Value Added		Number Employed		Capital Stock		% Change in Total Factor Productivity					
							Value-Added-Based Shares				Cost-Based Shares	
							With s_{K1}[a]		With s_{K2}[b]			
	1976–85	1981–90	1976–85	1981–90	1976–85	1981–90	1976–85	1981–90	1976–85	1981–90	1976–85	1981–90
France												
Total manufacturing	−4.0	8.4	−9.7	−9.6	1.4	5.5	2.1	12.8	2.2	13.2	2.6	13.6
Chemical products	−4.6	17.4	−8.0	−3.4	3.0	3.2	−2.3	17.3	−1.6	18.0	−.8	18.3
Drugs & medicines	18.9	17.3	3.9	5.7	80.1	28.3	10.4	10.1	2.6	6.5	4.1	7.7
PPI-drugs	…	36.6	3.9	5.7	…	28.3	…	25.6	…	27.6	…	26.9
Germany												
Total manufacturing	−.6	11.6	−4.6	1.4	4.4	8.5	1.0	8.0	1.6	8.9	1.9	8.5
Chemical products	2.5	11.5	1.3	6.8	−.9	5.6	2.3	5.2	2.1	6.5	1.9	5.0
Drugs & medicines	12.7	21.9	2.9	5.8	1.3	6.6	10.7	15.6	11.1	18.2	10.3	15.9
PPI-drugs	…	24.9	2.9	5.8	…	6.6	…	18.6	…	21.2	…	18.9
Italy												
Total manufacturing	−.8	5.7	−7.7	−6.2	−.5	−4.1	3.9	11.0	3.9	10.6	4.1	11.1
Chemical products	−1.6	20.0	−11.8	3.9	−20.6	−17.9	13.6	25.6	23.0	29.0	15.3	27.5
Drugs & medicines	17.2	10.0	−1.5	3.5	…	…	…	…	…	…	…	…
PPI-drugs	…	19.2	−1.5	3.5	…	…	…	…	…	…	…	…

United Kingdom

Total manufacturing	-12.5	13.1	-20.7	-6.4	-3.8	1.1	4.4	17.6	4.5	17.6	4.0	17.6
Chemical products	-8.7	26.2	-17.9	-1.4	-4.6	.2	5.5	27.1	6.2	27.1	4.1	27.0
Drugs & medicines	15.3	40.8	-1.3	6.5	18.2	25.3	4.3	22.4	12.2	33.8	9.8	28.0
PPI-drugs	...	62.1	-1.3	6.5	...	25.3	...	42.8	...	55.9	...	49.3

United States

Total manufacturing	-2.3	7.1	-4.5	.4	7.0	.6	-1.1	6.6	-.7	6.7	-.6	6.7
Chemical products	7.6	19.8	-.9	3.5	1.7	-5.8	7.4	20.6	7.4	19.8	7.4	19.9
Drugs & medicines	19.4	37.6	2.8	5.4	15.1	19.3	7.8	21.7	16.9	34.4	13.2	28.3
PPI-drugs	...	13.2	2.8	5.4	...	19.3	...	2.1	...	9.4	...	3.9

Note: Percentage changes for 1976–85 are between the mean values for the two five-year periods 1976–80 and 1981–85. Percentage changes for 1976–90 are between the mean values for the two five-year periods 1981–85 and 1985–90.

[a] $s_{K1} = 1 - s_L$, where $s_L = L/Q$, where L = labor compensation (real), Q = value added (real).

[b] $s_{K2} = K(r + d)/Q$, where K = capital stock (real), r = real cost of funds 10 percent, and d = depreciation rate 10 percent.

cals is as high as in the United States and higher than in other manufacturing in the United Kingdom. Value added per employee, relative to the United States, is higher for pharmaceuticals in the United Kingdom than for other manufacturing. One plausible explanation is that rate-of-return regulation in the United Kingdom has permitted high returns to R&D investments and that any tendency for excessive investment has therefore been in more productive forms of capital.

Appendix A
Data Sources and Definitions

The primary source for this analysis is the OECD's 1994 Structural Analysis (STAN) industrial database. STAN draws on the OECD's Industrial Structure Statistics (ISIS) and four other databases, using national accounts–compatible data where available, supplemented by other industrial surveys. For the four-digit drugs and medicines category, the data for most countries are from industrial surveys, so strict comparability across countries is not assured. The R&D data from national trade associations may also not be strictly comparable.

Variable Definitions

Production. National accounts–compatible production (gross output), at producer prices, excluding VAT.

Value added. Gross output, less the cost of materials, fuels, electricity, and other supplies, contract and commission repair, and maintenance work done by others.

Exports. From the OECD's Compatible Trade and Production database, which contains flows by ISIC revision 2 category. It has been converted from the Standard International Trade Classification (SITC) using a converter developed by the OECD. These trade data are compatible across countries but may not be strictly comparable to trade flows published in other sources. Values f.o.b.

Imports. See *exports.* Values c.i.f.

Employees (number engaged). Annual average number of workers, full-time and part-time, including employees, self-employed, owner-proprietors, and unpaid family members. For France, data are from SNIP. The SNIP definition of the industry probably leads to downwardly biased counts of employees, compared to the STAN measures of production.

Gross fixed capital formation. National accounts–compatible gross fixed capital formation (land, buildings, machinery, and equipment). No data are reported for Italy for drugs and medicines.

Labor compensation. National accounts–compatible labor costs, including wages and employers' compulsory contributions to pension, medical care, etc. This presumably omits voluntary employer contributions to pensions and health insurance in the United States and tax-financed medical care in the United Kingdom.

Research and development expenditures. National trade associations, as reported by Centre for Medicines Research (1993).

Appendix B
Pharmaceutical Price Indexes

Fisher Index of Cross-National Price Differences

The methodology used to construct the Fisher indexes is described in Danzon and Kim (1998). Although that study pertains to cardiovascular drugs only, the same methods are applied to all therapeutic categories for the indexes used here. The indexes include all single-molecule drugs that are available in pharmacies in both the United States and the other country under comparison. Products are designated as matching across countries if they have the same active ingredient (molecule) and are in the same therapeutic category.

For each pair of countries, we computed four indexes: using U.S. quantity weights and foreign quantity weights and using price per gram of active ingredient and price per standard unit (a tablet or capsule etc.) as the unit of measurement. For each pricing measure—per gram or per standard unit—the Fisher indexes are the geometric mean of the indexes based on U.S. and foreign weights. Here, we use the arithmetic average of these two Fisher indexes. The Fisher index is transitive and has other desirable theoretical properties (Diewert 1981).

Although these indexes provide a more accurate measure of relative prices than GDP PPPs, they are not perfect measures of pharmaceutical prices for several reasons. First, the price data for the United States overstate true transactions prices to manufacturers owing to omission of discounts and rebates, particularly in the most recent years. Second, because the cross-national indexes necessarily include only products that are available in both of the two countries, this may introduce bias if prices for these matching, global drugs are not representative of all drug prices. To the extent that regulation is biased against the global products that are included, either because they are produced disproportionately by foreign firms or because they have high potential prices or volumes, these indexes based only on matching products may understate overall price levels in countries with price regulation. If so, use of these indexes will lead to upwardly biased estimates of the U.S. dollar value of production in price-regulated countries.[35]

---

35. We use weights based on the sample included in the indexes rather than reweighting to reflect shares in overall drug consumption (van Ark and Pilat 1993). Such reweighting implicitly assumes that included products are representative of all products, which may not be true for

Divisia Price Indexes

The methodology used to construct the country-specific Divisia indexes is described in Danzon and Kim (1996). The sample includes all single-molecule drugs sold through retail pharmacies. The unit of observation is the standard unit for the molecule. Chained weights permit the incorporation of new compounds in their second year on the market. Line extensions and generic forms of existing molecules are incorporated in their first year on the market. The indexes for the United States are upwardly biased to the extent that discounts and rebates, which are omitted, have become more prevalent over time.

References

Averch, H., and L. L. Johnson. 1962. Behavior of the firm under regulatory constraint. *American Economic Review* 52, no. 5:1052–69.

Barral, P. E. 1995. *Twenty years of pharmaceutical research results throughout the world.* Antony: Rhône-Poulenc Rorer.

Berndt, E. R., and M. A. Fuss. 1986. Productivity measurement with adjustments for variation in capacity utilization and other forms of temporary equilibrium. *Journal of Econometrics* 33:7–29.

Berndt, E. R., and P. Greenberg. 1996. An updated and extended study of the price growth of prescription pharmaceutical preparations. In *Competitive strategies in the pharmaceutical industry,* ed. R. B. Helms. Washington, D.C.: American Enterprise Institute Press.

Berndt, E. R., Z. Griliches, and J. G. Rosett. 1993. Auditing the producer price index: Micro evidence from prescription pharmaceutical preparations. *Journal of Business and Economic Statistics* 11, no. 3:251–64.

Berndt, E. R., and D. M. Hesse. 1986. Measuring and assessing capacity utilization in the manufacturing sectors of nine OECD countries. *European Economic Review* 30:961–89.

Burstall, M. A. 1991. Europe after 1992: Implications for pharmaceuticals. *Health Affairs* 10, no. 3:157–71.

Burstall, M. A., and B. G. Reuben. 1988. The cost of non-Europe in the pharmaceutical industry. Economists Advisory Group. Luxembourg: Commission of the European Communities, Office of Publications.

Centre for Medicines Research. 1993. Trends in worldwide pharmaceutical R&D expenditure for the 1990s. Carshalton.

Cocks, D. L. 1973. The impact of the 1962 drug amendments on R&D productivity in the ethical pharmaceutical industry. PhD diss., Oklahoma State University.

———. 1974. The measurement of total factor productivity for a large U.S. manufacturing corporation. *Business Economics* 9, no. 4 (September): 7–20.

———. 1981. Company total factor productivity: Refinements, production functions and certain effects of regulation. *Business Economics* 16, no. 3 (May): 5–14.

---

drugs. Moreover, since the indexes reflect over 50 percent of sales in all countries (and over 80 percent in the United States and the United Kingdom), the case for reweighting is weaker here than in the van Ark and Pilat study, where the unit value ratios reflected less than 25 percent of sales in all countries.

Comanor, W. S. 1965. Research and technical change in the pharmaceutical industry. *Review of Economics and Statistics* 47:182–90.

Cutler, D. M., M. McClellan, J. P. Newhouse, and D. Remler. 1996. Are medical prices declining? Working Paper no. 5750. Cambridge, Mass.: National Bureau of Economic Research.

Danzon, P. M., and L. W. Chao. 1999. Cross national differences in pharmaceutical prices: How large, and why? Working paper. University of Pennsylvania, Wharton School.

Danzon, P. M., and J. Kim. 1996. Price indexes for pharmaceuticals: How accurate are international comparisons? Working paper. University of Pennsylvania, Wharton School, Health Care Systems Department.

———. 1998. International price comparisons for pharmaceuticals: Measurement and policy issues. *Pharmacoeconomics* 14, suppl. 1:115–28.

Danzon, P. M., and H. Liu. 1996. Reference pricing and physician drug budgets: The German experience in controlling pharmaceutical expenditures. Working paper. University of Pennsylvania, Wharton School, Health Care Systems Department.

Diewert, W. E. 1981. The economic theory of index numbers: A survey. In *Essays in the theory and measurement of consumer behavior in honor of Sir Richard Stone,* ed. A. Deaton. London: Cambridge University Press.

DiMasi, J. A., N. R. Bryant, and L. Lasagna. 1991. The cost of innovation in the pharmaceutical industry. *Journal of Health Economics* 10:107–42.

Grabowski, H. G., and J. M. Vernon. 1990. A new look at the returns and risks to pharmaceutical R&D. *Management Science* 36:804–21.

Griliches, Z., and I. Cockburn. 1996. Generics and new good in pharmaceutical price indexes. In *Competitive strategies in the pharmaceutical industry,* ed. R. B. Helms. Washington, D.C.: American Enterprise Institute Press.

Hall, R. E. 1988. The relation between price and marginal cost in U.S. industry. *Journal of Political Economy* 96:921–47.

———. 1990. Invariance properties of Solow's productivity residual. In *Growth, productivity and employment: Essays to celebrate Bob Solow's birthday,* ed. Peter Diamond. Cambridge, Mass.: MIT Press.

Hancher, L. 1990. *Regulating for competition: Government, law, and the pharmaceutical industry in the United Kingdom and France.* Oxford: Clarendon.

Healy, B. 1995. Competition and regulation in health system reform: The experience with pharmaceuticals. Paper presented at OECD Business and Industry Advisory Committee conference, Paris, May.

Myers, S. C., and L. Shyam-Sunder. 1996. Measuring pharmaceutical industry risk and the cost of capital. In *Competitive strategies in the pharmaceutical industry,* ed. Robert B. Helms. Washington, D.C.: American Enterprise Institute Press.

Peltzman, S. 1973. An evaluation of consumer protection legislation: The 1962 drug amendments. *Journal of Political Economy* 81, no. 5: 1049–91.

Remit Consultants. 1991. Cost containment in the European pharmaceutical market: New approaches. Final report prepared for the Pharmaceutical Manufacturers Association, London.

Syndical National de l'Industrie Pharmaceutique (SNIP). 1993. *The realities of the pharmaceutical industry in France.* Paris.

Thomas, L. G. 1990. Regulation and firm size: FDA impacts on innovation. *RAND Journal of Economics* 21, no. 4:497–517.

———. 1992. Price regulation industry structure and innovation: An international comparison of pharmaceutical industries. *PharmacoEconomics* 1, suppl. 1:9–12.

———. 1996. Industrial policy and international competitiveness in the pharmaceutical industry. In *Competitive strategies in the pharmaceutical industry,* ed. R. B. Helms. Washington, D.C.: American Enterprise Institute Press.

U.S. Bureau of Labor Statistics. 1994. International comparison of manufacturing pro-

ductivity and unit labor cost trends, 1993. News Release USDL:94-403. Washington, D.C., 17 August.
U.S. Congressional Budget Office. 1994. *How health care reform affects pharmaceutical R&D.* Washington, D.C.
van Ark, B., and D. Pilat. 1993. Productivity levels in Germany, Japan and the United States: Differences and causes. *Brookings Papers on Economic Activity: Microeconomics,* no. 2:1–69.

Comment   Ernst R. Berndt

Over the last few years, Patricia Danzon has contributed significantly to our empirical understanding of intercountry price comparisons for prescription pharmaceuticals and of the difficulties in interpreting differentials. In this paper, Danzon and Percy extend this price research in a different direction— analyzing the effects of differential price regulation among countries on the productivity of domestic pharmaceutical operations.

There are a great deal, indeed, almost an overabundance, of empirical findings in this paper; the paper includes, for example, fourteen tables summarizing detailed calculations. This is also an ambitious paper for it falls in between two traditional genres of international comparison studies—one very aggregated at perhaps the national or sectoral level and the other much more detailed, almost at the case-study level of specificity. Danzon and Percy pursue a middle ground, conducting an international comparison of the pharmaceutical industry among five countries: France, Germany, Italy, the United Kingdom, and the United States.

Drawing on the theory of regulation, Danzon and Percy structure their paper by outlining hypotheses that are then examined empirically. Specifically, Danzon and Percy hypothesize that price regulation biases upward levels of labor intensity (reduces average labor productivity), that price regulation also biases upward levels of capital intensity (reduces average capital productivity), and therefore that price regulation reduces levels of multifactor (capital and labor) productivity (MFP). Whether price regulation has a differential effect on capital than on labor is also considered; to the extent that the United Kingdom has price regulation that is more like traditional rate-of-return regulation, Danzon and Percy conjecture and find some evidence tending to suggest that the U.K. productivity is more capital biased than labor biased. Finally, although Danzon and Percy are somewhat silent on this, their hypotheses and expectations appear to refer more to levels of productivity than to their growth rates.

The data used in this paper come from several sources. Aggregate employment, capital formation, and revenue data are taken from OECD-STAN (which

Ernst R. Berndt is professor of applied economics at the Sloan School of Management, Massachusetts Institute of Technology, and a research associate of the National Bureau of Economic Research.

may not be consistent with national income and product account data), as are aggregate GDP PPP data series; country-specific aggregate producer price indexes for pharmaceuticals are also drawn from OECD sources. However, Danzon and Percy have also undertaken a painstaking set of calculations to compute bilateral price comparisons for literally thousands of drugs (chemical compounds, not just brands) that are sold in both countries, for each pair of bilateral comparisons. This research has been reported on elsewhere. Finally, Danzon and Percy also address a difficult problem with U.S. data concerning offshore manufacturing in Puerto Rico.

Danzon and Percy find reasonable support for their hypotheses involving productivity levels for labor and capital, but the multifactor productivity (MFP) results, both in level and in growth-rate form, are much more ambiguous and in particular are found to depend critically on the choice of deflator.

In attempting to interpret Danzon and Percy's findings, I would have found it useful had the paper contained a bit more discussion on three questions; these questions may have been addressed in other papers by Danzon.

First, what types of drug medications are produced in the five countries, and how does this composition vary among countries? What it is that constitutes a prescription drug, and what an over-the-counter product, can vary considerably across countries, except perhaps for psychotropic drugs. Do the countries differ in the relative proportions of patent protected and generic drugs, or what variations are there in "world" and primarily local drugs? Is there a systematic difference in the proportion of herbal and homeopathic medications (more prevalent in Germany and the United Kingdom)? Finally, do pharmaceutical operations differ considerably among the five countries in terms of manufacturing and (re)packaging? Although some of these issues are briefly noted, I would have found it helpful to have found a greater discussion of these issues as background to interpreting the observed productivity differentials.

Second, concerning the aggregate employment, capital formation, and revenue data by country, it is my impression that such data derive ultimately from establishment data and that what constitutes an establishment may differ across countries. In particular, in the United States, the establishment data taken from annual surveys of manufacturing refer only to production and manufacturing activities, not to central administrative and office (CAO) personnel. For the U.S. pharmaceutical industry, which is both research and development (R&D) and marketing intensive, the possible exclusion of CAO employees may have a critical effect on labor productivity findings. For example, how one interprets Danzon and Percy's finding that the average number of employees per establishment is about half as large in the United States as in France depends on what constitutes an establishment.

Third, some information on the size distribution of firms or establishments would also have been useful. Is the size distribution much more skewed in the United Kingdom and Italy than in the United States and France? How different are means from medians?

Let me now turn to some more specific comments. As always, MFP calculations depend on estimates of capital and labor shares. Danzon and Percy find substantial differences in MFP growth depending on whether one calculates the capital cost share using a residual property income notion or a measure of capital expenditures dependent on a rental price of capital.

Given that the MFP results are somewhat ambiguous and fragile, we might ask what else we know about manufacturing efficiency in the pharmaceutical industry. An MIT colleague in chemical engineering, Charles Cooney, has recently published results of a benchmarking study comparing manufacturing operations of pharmaceutical and biotech firms in several countries (see Cooney and Raju 1996). Cooney and Raju find significant variations among firms and countries, with one of the most significant sources of differences being practices involving inventories of chemical materials—while some firms follow "just-in-time" protocols, a surprising number instead appeared to follow the less efficient "just-in-case" practice. Unfortunately, Cooney and Raju cannot reveal the identities of the establishments and the countries in which they operate owing to confidentiality restrictions.

How else might one think of interpreting the productivity of pharmaceutical firms in various countries? One possible way is to compare them on the basis of the extent to which their products have worldwide markets or, related, on the basis of successful patent applications. While such comparisons could be informative, one should remember that, even within the United States, there are some very successful (in terms of stock price growth) pharmaceutical firms who have had few innovative new products. There are a variety of ways in which one might want to envisage productivity, and they could well be quite inconsistent with one another.

In summary, this paper brings into sharp focus the notions that international comparisons are quite difficult and are likely to render somewhat inconclusive findings when not all major differences can be properly taken into account. In the present context, Danzon and Percy are surely correct in noting that differences in R&D among countries could have a significant effect on the interpretation of their results. It would be interesting to see if related problems emerge when other industries are compared across countries, such as the telecommunications industry, which also has very high sunk costs and relatively small marginal costs.

Reference

Cooney, Charles L., and G. K. Raju. 1996. "Benchmarking" pharmaceutical manufacturing performance. Working paper. Massachusetts Institute of Technology, Program on the Pharmaceutical Industry, February.

14   Specialization and Productivity Performance in Low-, Medium-, and High-Tech Manufacturing Industries

Edward N. Wolff

This paper investigates patterns of industry specialization as measured by a country's share of total industry production for fourteen OECD countries over the period 1970–93. It also employs regression analysis to examine the relation between specialization and relative productivity performance. The study makes use of the 1994 version of the OECD Structural Analysis (STAN) industrial database, which subdivides manufacturing into thirty-three individual industries. Of particular interest are differences in performance between low-, medium-, and high-tech industries, which are classified into groups on the basis of their research and development (R&D) intensity.

There are three principal questions of interest. First, given the continued convergence of overall productivity and capital intensity in these countries, how similar are the industries of specialization among these countries, and have they become more or less similar over this period? Second, do countries have different strengths in terms of labor productivity, and do they maintain their relative productivity positions over time? Third, what factors help explain rising or falling market shares in individual industries?

I find that, despite the continued convergence of aggregate productivity and factor abundance, these countries tended to specialize manufacturing production in different industries and to maintain specialization in the same industries in 1993 as in 1970. They also tended to be strong in different industries in terms of labor productivity performance, but correlations over time in relative industry labor productivity performance within country are considerably weaker than those for market shares.

Edward N. Wolff is professor of economics at New York University.

The author thanks William Baumol, Robert Lipsey, and Dale Jorgenson for their very helpful comments and the Alfred P. Sloan Foundation and the C. V. Starr Center for Applied Economics at New York University for their support of the research reported herein.

419

Despite the apparent differences in stability of market shares and relative productivity performance over time, the results show that improvement in relative labor productivity is a powerful predictor of a rising market share. This result holds across all industry groups. The rate of capital formation also plays an important role in the determination of market share for low-tech industries but is less significant for medium-tech industries and not significant for high-tech ones. The results also show that relatively higher labor costs generally reduce competitiveness in a particular industry and hence market share but, somewhat surprisingly, that this effect is statistically significant only among low-tech industries and only in the 1970s.

The remainder of the paper is organized as follows. Section 14.1 considers some general guidance from trade theory and reviews some related research on this issue. Section 14.2 presents descriptive statistics on specialization and section 14.3 on the productivity performance of OECD countries over the time period. In section 14.4, I present regression results on the relation between production shares and technology indicators. Concluding remarks are made in section 14.5.

14.1 Theoretical Background

There are two principal approaches found in trade theory that are employed to explain why different countries will specialize production in different industries. The first is the Heckscher-Ohlin (HO) model with factor-price equalization. It makes very sharp predictions about cross-country patterns in labor and total factor productivity at the industry level: namely, that industry productivity levels should be the same in all countries. As a consequence, industries of specialization depend only on relative factor abundance—a country will specialize in those industries that use more intensively the factor that is relatively abundant in that country.

Leamer's (1984) empirical study of trade patterns for over one hundred economies found that general patterns could be explained fairly well by an endowment-based model with ten factors, including capital, several types of natural resources and land, and three skill classes of labor. However, it should be noted that, in that study, manufacturing was disaggregated into only four industry classifications and the model was considerably more successful at explaining trade in primary products than trade in manufactures. Those results are consistent with the argument that the broad pattern of exports—primary versus secondary goods, heavy versus light manufactures—can be explained by general factor endowments but that the specific pattern of exports of manufactures at a more disaggregated level depends on industry-specific factors that do not depend largely on resource endowments.

The second approach emphasizes the role of increasing internal returns to scale (IIRS) and learning by doing in the formation of comparative advantage. The underlying theory was developed by Krugman (1979, 1980), Helpman

(1984), and Helpman and Krugman (1985) and later expanded in Gomory (1992) and Gomory and Baumol (1992). This line of analysis suggests that it is the presence of economies of scale and/or high startup costs that allows different countries to achieve specialization in different products. The country that enters a new product line first may be able to dominate that line by increasing production to the point at which its costs are so low that potential new competitors are unable to enter the field successfully (at least, without dramatic innovations or sufficient subsidies from the government). Even more important is the accumulation of specialized knowledge that is acquired only by being in the industry. This may include knowledge of the details of production steps as well as specialized skills that are mainly acquired on the job, knowledge of marketing channels, and a knowledgeable sales force that is known to customers. This process is also referred to as *learning by doing* since the firm or country that first establishes an industry may be able to descend the cost curve by acquiring the expertise that comes through experience in making the product (see Arrow 1962).

Which industries a country may specialize in may depend on history and a variety of influences, some of them perhaps fortuitous (for an illuminating discussion of the process, see Krugman [1991]). Moreover, an important role can be played by the availability or unavailability of ancillary industries that can substantially facilitate a country's success in the production of some particular product or type of products. Geographic externalities may also play an important role since, once an industry is established in a country or place, there is greater likelihood of suppliers and customers also specializing there. This approach suggests that leadership positions may persist for long periods of time, thus ensuring relatively stable industry specialization over time.

Earlier work (Dollar and Wolff 1993) found strong evidence of convergence on the economywide level in GDP per worker, the capital/labor ratio, aggregate labor productivity, total factor productivity (TFP), and average real wages for a sample of nine OECD countries covering the period 1970–86. Dollar and Wolff also examined the same variables for nine manufacturing sectors and found that, except for real wages, convergence at the industry level was generally not as strong as that for the economy as a whole. In fact, aggregate convergence in labor productivity could to some extent be attributed to the modest labor productivity leads that different countries enjoyed in different industries. The results are similar for TFP and capital intensity.

A further result of this development is that the export patterns of the industrial countries were not converging or becoming more similar. This result is consistent with Dollar and Wolff's conclusion that specialization has continued at the industry level in the advanced industrial countries. Moreover, in a bilateral comparison of Japan and the United States, a clear relation is evident between TFP growth at the industry level and changing comparative advantage. The industries in Japan with growing comparative advantage over this period tended to be those in which its TFP relative to the United States increased rapidly. Dollar and Wolff argued that TFP captures some influence that contributes to comparative advantage and that this factor is likely to be technology as disembodied knowledge, as embodied in machinery, or as reflected in skilled labor.

These earlier results seem less in accord with an HO type of model than with one based on the IIRS approach. HO theory suggests that convergence in aggregate performance, particularly aggregate capital/labor ratios, should be accompanied by a convergence in the trade patterns of these countries. The IIRS approach, in contrast, emphasizes technology differences between countries as the basis of specialization and suggests that trade patterns may shift in accordance with movements in productivity levels.

In this paper, I examine whether these results hold up for a larger sample of countries, a more detailed industry classification, and a longer time period. Moreover, using econometric techniques, I analyze more formally the relation between comparative advantage as reflected in a country's market shares in individual industries and relative productivity performance.

It should also be noted that the convergence of real wages at the industry level, found in Dollar and Wolff (1993), greatly strengthens the notion that productivity growth should be an important determinant of changing comparative advantage. Those results imply that, among OECD countries, differences in the cost of labor (and, to some extent, capital) were not important determinants of differences in unit costs by the 1980s.[1] Given the similarity in factor prices, trends in relative productivity then may become more crucial determinants of cost competitiveness and production share.

14.2   Convergence of Production Patterns?

In this section, I investigate whether industrial production patterns of developed countries have tended toward convergence over the last two decades. I use the 1994 OECD STAN database, available on diskettes. The time period covered is 1970–93. This source provides statistics on value added, which is measured in both current and 1985 local prices;[2] gross capital formation in current prices (although this version unfortunately lacks capital stock data); total employment; employee compensation;[3] and purchasing power parity (PPP) conversion factors for each country and year (although not available on the industry level). Data on each of these variables are provided on the industry level—a total of thirty-three manufacturing industries—although they are not

---

1. Nakamura's (1989) study of Japan, Germany, and the United States also found that, by the late 1970s, input prices were quite similar among these three countries, with the result that the "relative TFP level has become the principal determinant of sectoral cost advantage and disadvantage among the three countries" (p. 713).

2. The value added is exclusive of value-added taxes and other indirect business taxes.

3. This is defined as the sum of wages and salaries, social insurance taxes, and other employee fringe benefits paid by the employer.

available for nonmanufacturing sectors. The STAN database has relatively complete data on fourteen OECD countries—Australia, Belgium, Canada, Denmark, Finland, France, Germany, Italy, Japan, the Netherlands, Norway, Sweden, the United Kingdom, and the United States.[4]

Comparisons of output among the countries is made on the basis of value added by industry in 1985 local currency converted to 1985 U.S. dollars on the basis of the 1985 PPP rate for that country. This is problematic for two reasons. First, gross output (sales) is the preferable measure to use when computing market share. Second, ideally, conversion to a common currency should be made on the basis of industry-specific PPPs for each country, as is the practice in the International Comparison of Output and Productivity (ICOP) project (see, e.g., Maddison and van Ark 1989).

Despite these limitations, calculations of production shares based on value added are very highly correlated with those calculated from gross output among the industries and countries for which the data exist (correlation coefficients are on the order of 0.95–0.98). Second, since manufactures are generally tradables, there is some presumption that local prices will tend toward equilibrium international prices of individual industries. Third, in most of the analysis—particularly the econometric applications—I am interested in changes over time in production shares and related variables. Thus, insofar as biases tend to remain stable over time (e.g., percentage differences between industry-specific and overall PPPs for a given country), the biases will "wash out" in equations that use first differences.

I begin (in table 14.1) with measures of production shares (PRODSHR) for thirty-three manufacturing industries in the three largest economies, Germany, Japan, and the United States. The production share for country h in industry i is defined as

(1) $$\text{PRODSHR}_i^h = Y_i^h / \Sigma_h Y_i^h,$$

where Y_i^h is country h's production of good i valued in 1985 U.S. dollars, and output is based on value added by industry. The aggregation over h covers the fourteen countries in the STAN database with the requisite data, and the index therefore shows country h's share of the total production of product i among the fourteen countries.

The thirty-three industries selected are the most detailed ones available with the requisite data. They are all three-digit ISIC industries, with the exception of transport equipment, which is available on the four-digit level. These industries are divided into three technology groups on the basis of the average R&D intensity of production of these industries in OECD countries in 1985, as follows: *low tech*, less than 0.5 times the mean R&D intensity; *medium tech*, from

---

4. Data are also provided for Austria, Korea, Mexico, New Zealand, Portugal, and Spain, which are unfortunately incomplete for many series. As a result, these countries will not be included in the data analysis reported here.

Table 14.1   Production Shares (PRODSHR) of Germany, Japan, and the United States and the OECD Leader, 1970 and 1993[a]

ISIC Code[b] and Industry	1970				1993			
	GER	JPN	USA	Leader	GER	JPN	USA	Leader
3000 Total manufacturing	.14	.13	.40	USA	.11	.23	.37	USA
Low-tech industries[c]								
311.2 Food	.09	.20	.30	USA	.07	.21	.33	USA
313 Beverages	.20	.19	.20	GER	.14	.15	.26	USA
314 Tobacco	.24	.02	.50	USA	.35	.04	.29	GER
321 Textiles	.11	.16	.28	USA	.08	.12	.36	USA
322 Wearing apparel	.12	.14	.36	USA	.05	.19	.41	USA
323 Leather & products	.14	.15	.21	USA	.08	.20	.20	ITA
324 Footwear	.12	.03	.33	USA	.06	.05	.16	ITA
331 Wood products	.09	.10	.48	USA	.08	.11	.51	USA
332 Furniture & fixtures	.17	.16	.32	USA	.12	.15	.34	USA
341 Paper & products	.09	.10	.48	USA	.09	.16	.45	USA
342 Printing & publishing	.06	.19	.45	USA	.05	.20	.41	USA
353 Petroleum refineries	.28	.06	.30	USA	.21	.12	.25	USA
354 Petroleum & coal products	.22	.05	.49	USA	.15	.12	.53	USA
355 Rubber products	.16	.09	.42	USA	.08	.09	.40	USA
356 Plastic products nec	.12	.22	.33	USA	.12	.20	.38	USA
361 Pottery, china, etc.	.11	.15	.12	ITA	.08	.23	.12	ITA
362 Glass & products	.10	.21	.41	USA	.14	.18	.31	USA
369 Nonmetal products nec	.15	.16	.29	USA	.13	.18	.29	USA
371 Iron & steel	.16	.16	.45	USA	.15	.22	.30	USA
372 Nonferrous metals	.12	.16	.45	USA	.15	.29	.29	USA
381 Metal products	.15	.10	.38	USA	.15	.25	.37	USA
3841 Shipbuilding & repair[d]	.05	.16	.34	USA	.06	.31	.30	JPN
39 Other manufactures nes	.06	.20	.39	USA	.04	.44	.30	JPN

Medium-tech industries[c]

351 Industrial chemicals	.19	.11	.37	USA	.13	.17	.37	USA
3842 Railroad equipment[d]	.04	.06	.20	USA	.05	.13	.20	USA
3843 Motor vehicles[d]	.17	.18	.38	USA	.16	.29	.32	USA
3844 Motorcycles & bicycles[d]	.06	.19	.16	ITA	.06	.30	.12	ITA
3849 Other transport equipment[d]	.11	.27	.00	JPN	.09	.39	.00	JPN

High-tech industries[c]

352 Other chemical products[e]	.15	.11	.48	USA	.11	.20	.43	USA
382 Nonelectrical machinery[f]	.16	.12	.38	USA	.10	.21	.45	USA
383 Electrical machinery[g]	.17	.02	.49	USA	.10	.40	.31	JPN
3845 Aircraft[d]	.03	.01	.74	USA	.04	.03	.73	USA
385 Professional goods[h]	.21	.05	.54	USA	.12	.12	.56	USA

GDP Share	.09	.13	.45		.09	.18	.42
Correlation with United States	.07	−.57			−.06	−.42	
Correlation with Germany		−.33				−.23	
Rank correlation with United States	.17	−.49				−.28	
Rank correlation with Germany		−.34				−.09	

[a]The production share of country h in industry i is defined as

$$\text{PRODHSR}_i^h = Y_i^h / \sum_h Y_i^h ,$$

where the aggregation over h is based on 14 OECD countries with pertinent data: Australia (AUS), Belgium (BEL), Canada (CAN), Denmark (DNK), Finland (FIN), France (FRA), Germany (GER), Italy (ITA), Japan (JPN), the Netherlands (NET), Norway (NOR), Sweden (SWE), the United Kingdom (UK), and the United States (USA).

[b]Revision 2 ISIC codes.

[c]Division of industries into technology groups is based on the average R&D intensity of production of OECD countries in 1985 as follows: low tech, less than 0.5 times the mean R&D intensity; medium tech, from 0.5 to 1.5 times the mean R&D intensity; and high tech, over 1.5 times the mean R&D intensity.

[d]Calculations exclude Belgium.

[e]Includes drugs and medicines and other chemicals nec.

[f]Includes office and computing machinery and machinery & equipment nec.

[g]Includes radio, TV & communication equipment, and electrical apparatus nec.

[h]Includes scientific instruments.

0.5 to 1.5 times the mean R&D intensity; and *high tech,* over 1.5 times the mean R&D intensity.

In 1970, Germany accounted for 14 percent of total manufactures of this group of fourteen countries, Japan 13 percent, the United States 40 percent, and the three together two-thirds. Germany's share of total manufacturing was considerably greater than its share of the fourteen-country GDP (14 vs. 9 percent), Japan's share was almost identical to its GDP share (13 percent), whereas the U.S. manufacturing share was smaller (40 vs. 45 percent).

In 1970, Germany's manufacturing was particularly strong in petroleum refineries (28 percent), petroleum and coal products (22 percent), industrial chemicals (19 percent), motor vehicles (17 percent), electrical machinery (17 percent), and professional goods and scientific instruments (21 percent). Japan's strengths were in food products (20 percent), plastics (22 percent), glass and glass products (21 percent), motor vehicles (18 percent), and other transport equipment (27 percent). The United States accounted for about half the total fourteen-country output of tobacco products, wood products, paper and paper products, petroleum and coal products, other chemical products (including pharmaceuticals), electrical machinery, and professional goods and scientific instruments and three-fourths of the production of aircraft. Generally speaking, in 1970, the United States dominated the high-tech industries, particularly aircraft; both Germany and Japan were strong in the medium-tech transport equipment industries, such as motor vehicles; and the three countries each specialized in different industries within the low-tech group.

The fourth column of table 14.1 shows the leading producer in each industry in 1970. It is, perhaps, not surprising that the United States dominated almost all industries (twenty-nine of thirty-three) in 1970 since it was by far the largest economy. However, Germany was the leading producer of beverages, Italy of pottery and china and motorcycles and bicycles, and Japan of other transport equipment.

Between 1970 and 1993, both the German and the U.S. share of total manufacturing production declined by 3 percentage points, whereas the Japanese share increased sharply, by 10 percentage points. By 1993, Japan's manufacturing output was more than double Germany's and over 60 percent that of the United States. Germany's share of output remained the same or fell in almost every manufacturing industry. The U.S. share likewise remained unchanged or declined in almost all industries, with the major exception of textiles (rising from 28 to 36 percent), wearing apparel (from 36 to 41 percent), plastics (from 33 to 38 percent), and nonelectrical machinery (including office and computing machinery; from 38 to 45 percent).

Japan's share, on the other hand, increased in most of the industries—notably, electrical machinery, including radios, televisions, and communications equipment (rising from 2 to 40 percent), rubber products (from 9 to 20 percent), iron and steel (from 16 to 29 percent), shipbuilding (from 16 to 31 percent), motor vehicles (from 18 to 29 percent), motorcycles and bicycles (from

19 to 30 percent), and other transport equipment (from 27 to 39 percent). Japan's inroads were particularly marked in the medium- and high-tech industries. In contrast, Germany basically held its production shares in the medium-tech industries but declined in the high- and low-tech industries. The United States made its major gains in low-tech industries, such as food, apparel, and wood products; lost share in the medium-tech industries; but retained its share in the high-tech industries.

Despite the major gains of Japanese manufacturing, the United States still lead all producers in 1993 in twenty-four of the thirty-three industries. Japan was dominant in four industries (particularly, shipbuilding, transport equipment, and electrical machinery), Italy in four (leather products, footwear, pottery and china, and motorcycles and bicycles), and Germany in only one.

The bottom four rows of table 14.1 show the correlation and rank correlation between the distribution of production shares between the countries. There are, of course, statistical problems with using a correlation coefficient between two distributions since the individual elements in each distribution are not independent. In particular, if one share is high, one or more others must be low since the sum of productions shares within an industry and across countries must equal 1.0. The same is true for the ranking of industries. However, the correlation coefficient and the rank correlation do provide rough measures of the similarity between two distributions. What is, perhaps, most striking is the low correlation coefficients among the three countries—in 1970, 0.07 between Germany and the United States, -0.57 between Japan and the United States, and -0.33 between Germany and Japan and, in 1993, -0.06, -0.42, and -0.23, respectively. The rank correlations are similar. The three countries have specialized production in distinctly different industries, and there has been very little change over time in the degree of dissimilarity in their patterns of specialization.

While production shares reveal which countries are the major producers in each product line, they are not a good indicator of specialization since they also reflect the overall size of the economy. A better indicator of specialization is the share of the total production of a given commodity made in an individual country relative to its share of GDP:

$$(2) \qquad \text{RELPSHR}_i^h = [Y_i^h / \Sigma_h Y_i^h] / (\text{GDP}^h / \Sigma_h \text{GDP}^h),$$

where the GDP figures, obtained from the OECD International Sectoral Database (ISDB), are in 1985 U.S. dollars. This index is analogous to Balassa's revealed comparative advantage (RCA) measure (Balassa 1965), which is used to measure trade specialization. The numerator of RELPSHR indicates country h's share of the total production of industry i, while the denominator measures country h's share of total GDP for these fourteen countries. A value above (below) one indicates that country h's share of the group's total production of product i is higher (lower) than its share of the total GDP of this group. This index indicates in which product lines a country's production is concentrated, which is taken as a measure of specialization. In general, some values of RELPSHR for a country will be greater than one, while others will be less than one.[5]

Calculations of RELPSHR for Germany, Japan, and the United States are shown in table 14.2. The rank order of industries within each country is the same as for PRODSHR, but the relative magnitudes across countries are quite different. The specialization of Germany in beverages, petroleum refineries, petroleum and coal products, industrial chemicals, and professional goods and scientific instruments (all values of RELPSHR exceed 2.0), as well as in motor vehicles and electrical machinery (both values exceed 1.8), in 1970 is now apparent. Japan in 1970 was particularly strong in plastics, glass and glass products, and other transport equipment (all values above 1.6). The major specialization of the United States was aircraft (a value of 1.7).

The specialization patterns are quite different with this new measure. In 1970, Germany had the highest relative production shares among all fourteen countries in total manufacturing, all the high-tech industries except aircraft, motor vehicles, and seven low-tech industries. Italy had the highest value in five industries, including textiles, wearing apparel, footwear, and motorcycles and bicycles. Japan was the leader in only one industry (food products), the United States in only one (aircraft), Belgium in three (including industrial chemicals), Sweden in one (wood products), Finland in one (paper and paper products), Norway in two (including shipbuilding), Australia in two (including railroad equipment), and Denmark, the Netherlands, and the United Kingdom in one each.

By 1993, Germany remained extremely specialized in only three industries, including motor vehicles, and the United States in only aircraft, while Japan was now highly specialized in iron and steel, shipbuilding, motor vehicles, motorcycles and bicycles, other transport equipment, and, especially, electrical machinery (all values above 1.6). Japan now had the highest relative production share in total manufacturing and in two high-tech industries, nonelectrical machinery and electrical machinery, as well as other manufactures. Italy had the highest value in eight industries, the United Kingdom and Germany in three, the Netherlands, Finland, Belgium, and Australia in two, and Sweden, France, Denmark, Canada, Norway, and the United States in one.

I next investigated what has happened to the cross-country dispersion in relative production shares. The first three columns of table 14.3 show the coefficient of variation in country values of RELPSHR for each industry. If countries were becoming more alike in their patterns of production, then the coeffi-

---

5. I have defined RELPSHR as a country's share of the total output of a particular industry relative to its share of total GDP rather than relative to its share of total manufacturing output in order to reflect the fact that some countries, such as Germany and Japan, have specialized production in manufacturing relative to nonmanufacturing sectors. Countries with a large manufacturing sector will tend to have a large number of industries with values of RELPSHR exceeding one, and conversely. If I had used the share of total manufacturing output as the denominator in equation (2), then, by construction, if some values of RELPSHR for a country exceed one, others must be less than one (unless the country has exactly the same share of every product).

Table 14.2 Relative Production Shares (RELPSHR) of Germany, Japan, and the United States and the OECD Country with the Highest Value, 1970 and 1993[a]

Industry	1970				1993			
	GER	JPN	USA	Highest	GER	JPN	USA	Highest
Total manufacturing	1.48	1.01	.89	GER	1.22	1.27	.89	JPN
Low-tech industries								
Food	.93	1.56	.67	JPN	.84	1.16	.78	DNK
Beverages	2.15	1.51	.44	GER	1.62	.82	.61	UK
Tobacco	2.62	.18	1.12	GER	3.94	.24	.70	NET
Textiles	1.23	1.25	.63	ITA	.86	.68	.86	ITA
Wearing apparel	1.26	1.08	.81	ITA	.55	1.04	.97	ITA
Leather & products	1.47	1.15	.48	BEL	.86	1.12	.48	ITA
Footwear	1.30	.25	.74	ITA	.68	.27	.39	ITA
Wood products	.94	.81	1.08	SWE	.86	.59	1.23	SWE
Furniture & fixtures	1.84	1.21	.71	GER	1.31	.85	.82	ITA
Paper & products	.99	.80	1.06	FIN	.96	.88	1.09	FIN
Printing & publishing	.62	1.45	1.01	NOR	.53	1.15	.98	UK
Petroleum refineries	2.98	.47	.67	GER	2.30	.67	.60	FRA
Petroleum & coal products	2.37	.39	1.10	GER	1.66	.52	1.27	NET
Rubber products	1.68	.73	.94	GER	.94	1.12	.95	ITA
Plastic products nec	1.28	1.72	.74	AUS	1.31	1.31	.92	GER
Pottery, china, etc.	1.22	1.19	.26	ITA	.88	1.01	.28	ITA
Glass & products	1.11	1.65	.91	BEL	1.56	1.03	.75	BEL

(continued)

Table 14.2 (continued)

Industry	1970				1993			
	GER	JPN	USA	Highest	GER	JPN	USA	Highest
Nonmetal products nec	1.58	1.27	.65	DNK	1.50	1.22	.69	AUS
Iron & steel	1.67	1.28	1.00	GER	1.71	1.66	.72	GER
Nonferrous metals	1.25	1.28	1.01	NOR	1.65	1.41	.70	NOR
Metal products	1.63	.76	.85	ITA	1.69	1.02	.89	GER
Shipbuilding & repair	.54	1.26	.77	NOR	.72	1.73	.71	FIN
Other manufactures nes	.66	1.59	.87	UK	.40	2.46	.71	JPN
Medium-tech industries								
Industrial chemicals	2.07	.89	.84	BEL	1.49	.96	.88	BEL
Railroad equipment	.43	.48	.44	AUS	.54	.71	.49	AUS
Motor vehicles	1.83	1.38	.85	GER	1.82	1.64	.76	GER
Motorcycles & bicycles	.68	1.48	.35	ITA	.66	1.68	.30	ITA
Other transport equipment	1.15	2.07	.00	NET	1.03	2.20	.00	CAN
High-tech industries								
Other chemical products	1.57	.85	1.09	GER	1.19	1.13	1.03	GER
Nonelectrical machinery	1.74	.93	.86	GER	1.10	1.21	1.09	JPN
Electrical machinery	1.86	.19	1.11	GER	1.18	2.23	.74	JPN
Aircraft	.30	.11	1.66	USA	.40	.15	1.76	USA
Professional goods	2.29	.38	1.20	GER	1.35	.66	1.34	UK

[a]For additional details, see the notes to table 14.1. The relative production share of country h in industry i based on the 14 OECD countries is defined as
$$\text{RELPSHR}_i^h = [Y_i^h/\sum_h Y_i^h]/[(\text{GDP}^h/\sum_h \text{GDP}^h)].$$

Table 14.3   **Relative Dispersion of Indexes of Specialization across 14 OECD Countries for 33 Manufacturing Industries, 1970, 1979, and 1993[a]**

	Coefficient of Variation[b] of RELPSHR			Standard Deviation of LN(RELPSHR)[c]		
	1970	1979	1993	1970	1979	1993
Total manufacturing	.18	.18	.21	.16	.17	.22
Low-tech industries						
Food	.24	.24	.29	.26	.25	.29
Beverages	.37	.36	.39	.44	.43	.43
Tobacco	.81	.84	1.05	.76	.75	.86
Textiles	.55	.61	.93	.50	.48	.63
Wearing apparel	.31	.49	.65	.30	.56	.78
Leather & products	.74	.72	1.04	.64	.61	.70
Footwear	.77	1.16	1.50	.64	.77	.97
Wood products	.61	.59	.56	.68	.59	.54
Furniture & fixtures	.27	.34	.48	.27	.34	.43
Paper & products	.76	.77	.89	.61	.57	.64
Printing & publishing	.34	.28	.27	.34	.29	.28
Petroleum refineries	1.04	.99	.80	1.06	1.13	.81
Petroleum & coal products	.77	.78	.63	1.01	.95	.93
Rubber products	.44	.38	.41	.49	.48	.58
Plastic products nec	.67	.42	.31	.61	.39	.33
Pottery, china, etc.	.97	1.12	1.28	.79	.76	.85
Glass & products	.59	.59	.70	.48	.47	.56
Nonmetal products nec	.28	.25	.36	.29	.24	.38
Iron & steel	.51	.50	.44	.66	.63	.54
Nonferrous metals	.64	.62	.58	.76	.73	.69
Metal products	.42	.36	.36	.37	.32	.34
Shipbuilding & repair[d]	1.06	.90	.62	.95	.85	.62
Other manufactures nes	.67	.74	.83	.60	.68	.69
Medium-tech industries						
Industrial chemicals	.52	.62	.72	.50	.50	.49
Railroad equipment[d]	.86	.77	.67	1.15	1.10	.99
Motor vehicles[d]	.61	.69	.75	.86	.94	1.06
Motorcycles & bicycles[d]	.98	.98	1.22	1.30	1.28	1.23
Other transport equipment[d]	.90	.97	1.16	1.50	1.44	1.40
High-tech industries						
Other chemical products	.36	.33	.29	.35	.34	.34
Nonelectrical machinery	.41	.34	.31	.42	.35	.34
Electrical machinery	.41	.39	.70	.49	.35	.66
Aircraft[d]	.96	.86	.91	.98	.91	.89
Professional goods	1.01	.73	.68	.91	.79	.85

[a]For definitions of production shares (PRODSHR) and relative production shares (RELPSHR) and other technical details in the calculations, see the notes to tables 14.1 and 14.2.

[b]The coefficient of variation is defined as the ratio of the standard deviation to the (unweighted) mean.

[c]LN is the natural logarithm. If RELPSHR equals zero, LN(RELPSHR) is set to -3.75. For details, see the text.

[d]Calculations exclude Belgium.

cient of variation should decline over time. There is no noticeable trend in this direction. Between 1970 and 1993, dispersion in the low-tech group of industries increased in thirteen industries and decreased in ten; in the medium-tech group, it rose in four and fell in one; while, in the high-tech group, dispersion grew in only one and declined in four. By 1993, the industries with the highest dispersion (coefficients of variation exceeding 0.9) were tobacco products, textiles, leather products, footwear, pottery and china, motorcycles and bicycles, other transport equipment, and aircraft. Those with the smallest dispersion (coefficients of variation less than 0.4) were food, beverages, printing and publishing, plastics, nonmetal products, metal products, other chemical products, and nonelectrical machinery. Both sets of industries span the gamut between low- and high-tech enterprises.

It is also of interest that changes in the degree of specialization were more pronounced between 1979 and 1993 than between 1970 and 1979. In the earlier period, the coefficient of variation changed by more than 0.10 in only six industries, whereas, in the later period, this occurred in sixteen industries. This seems to accord with casual observation that much more industrial restructuring occurred during the 1980s than during the 1970s.

One unfortunate property of the RELPSHR measure is that it is both asymmetrical and highly skewed, with a range from zero to infinity. As a result, industry production shares greater than average receive greater weight in the computation of the coefficient of variation than those less than average (which range in value from 0.0 to 1.0). An alternative measure is the LN(RELPSHR), the natural logarithm of RELPSHR, which has a more normal distribution and gives equal weight to below- and above-average production shares. Moreover, since the mean of LN(RELPSHR) is close to zero, I have used the standard deviation of LN(RELPSHR) in table 14.3 rather than its coefficient of variation to measure cross-country dispersion.[6] Results are very similar for the two measures of dispersion. Over the period 1970–93, the standard deviation of LN(RELPSHR) increased in fifteen industries, declined in fifteen, and remained constant (a change of 0.01 or less) in three.

One reason why the degree of specialization among manufacturing industries may have changed relatively little is that countries are maintaining specializations in different industries. To examine this idea further, table 14.4 lists for each country in 1993 the industries with the highest and lowest RELPSHR indexes. Inspection of this table indicates that these countries' production is generally concentrated in different industries. In general, if the RELPSHR for industry i is high in one country, it is low somewhere else. But there is no algebraic constraint on two or three countries having similar RELPSHR values. In 1993, Australia's and Denmark's production relative to its GDP was most

---

6. One unfortunate property of the logarithmic measure is that production shares of zero are not defined. I have arbitrarily chosen a value of -3.75 for the LN(RELPSHR) measure in this case because the minimum value observed is -2.75. Experimentation with other values, from -4.0 to -6.0, yields very similar results on the standard deviation of LN(RELPSHR).

Table 14.4   **Specialization in Manufacturing Industries by Country, 1993**

	Highest RELPSHR	Lowest RELPSHR
Australia	Railroad equipment, 4.10	Motorcycles & bicycles, .0
	Nonmetal products nec, 1.88	Aircraft, .24
Belgium	Industrial chemicals, 3.98	Professional goods, .18
	Glass & glass products, 3.35	Petroleum & coal products, .20
Canada	Transport equipment nec, 6.97	Motorcycles & bicycles, .0
	Railroad equipment, 2.51	Professional goods, .0
Denmark	Railroad equipment, 3.02	Motor vehicles, .0
	Shipbuilding & repairing, 2.39	Aircraft, .0
		Transport equipment nec, .0
Finland	Paper & paper products, 4.81	Aircraft, .10
	Shipbuilding & repairing, 3.52	Motor vehicles, .16
France	Petroleum refineries, 3.15	Transport equipment nec, .0
	Motorcycles & bicycles, 1.78	Professional goods, .44
Germany	Tobacco products, 3.94	Aircraft, .40
	Petroleum refineries, 2.30	Printing & publishing, .53
Italy	Footwear, 6.84	Tobacco products, .41
	Pottery, china, etc., 6.07	Aircraft, .43
Japan	Electrical machinery, 2.23	Aircraft, .15
	Transport equipment nec, 2.20	Tobacco products, .24
Netherlands	Tobacco products, 4.09	Railroad equipment, .0
	Transport equipment nec, 3.51	Motor vehicles, .22
Norway	Shipbuilding & repairing, 2.96	Motorcycles & bicycles, .0
	Nonferrous metals, 2.65	Motor vehicles, .07
Sweden	Paper & paper products, 2.93	Wearing apparel, .14
	Transport equipment nec, 2.42	Footwear, .15
United Kingdom	Beverages, 1.98	Nonferrous metals, .46
	Tobacco products, 1.78	Motorcycles & bicycles, .47
United States	Aircraft, 1.76	Pottery, china, etc., .28
	Professional goods, 1.76	Motorcycles & bicycles, .30

heavily concentrated in railroad equipment, Belgium's in industrial chemicals, Canada's in transport equipment, Finland's and Sweden's in paper and paper products, France's in petroleum refineries, Germany's and the Netherlands's in tobacco products, Italy's in footwear, Japan's in electrical machinery, Norway's in shipbuilding, the United Kingdom's in beverages, and the United States's in aircraft.[7] The absolute size of the RELPSHR values is also of interest; small differences in production patterns would be indicated by RELPSHR values that deviate little from one. In table 14.4, however, there are quite a few in the two to eight range, indicating very substantial specialization, especially for the smaller economies. The high degree of specialization for the relatively small economies suggests that economies of scale may be important, either in direct

7. The other side of the ledger tends to be dominated by the various transport equipment products, such as motor vehicles and aircraft, which are produced in only a limited number of countries.

production or, more likely, in development of the specific capabilities such as knowledge and skilled labor needed to produce particular manufactures.

It is also striking that most countries retain their specialization over time. Table 14.5 shows correlation coefficients of both RELPSHR and LN(RELPSHR) values by industry between 1970 and 1979 and between 1970 and 1992. The correlations are generally stronger for the latter measures because, as noted above, the logarithmic form gives equal weight to industries in which production is very high and those in which production is very low. With only a few exceptions, these correlations remain very high over time. Between 1970 and 1979, the correlation coefficients of the logarithmic measure are 0.88 or greater for all fourteen countries, and, between 1970 and 1993, they are 0.79 or higher for ten of the fourteen countries. The exceptions are Belgium, Japan, Sweden, and the United Kingdom (although, even among them, the correlations exceed 0.60).

Rank correlations are also shown. They are almost as strong for the period 1970–79 as the correlations of LN(RELPSHR), exceeding 0.85 for all fourteen countries. However, they are weaker for the period 1970–93, exceeding 0.70 for ten countries, in the range of 0.58–0.69 for the other four countries (Finland, Japan, Sweden, and the United Kingdom). These results again suggest greater industrial restructuring in the 1980s than in the 1970s.

Although countries tend to retain their industries of specialization over time,

Table 14.5   Correlation over Time in Relative Production Share (RELPSHR) in Manufacturing Industries by Country, 1970–79 and 1970–93[a]

	Relative Production Share (RELPSHR)		Log of Relative Production Share (LN[RELPSHR])		Rank Correlation Relative Production Share (RELPSHR)	
	1970–79	1970–93	1970–79	1970–93	1970–79	1970–93
Australia	.97	.83	.97	.85	.94	.73
Belgium[b]	.80	.67	.88	.75	.86	.73
Canada	.98	.94	.98	.93	.95	.85
Denmark	.99	.92	.99	.94	.97	.85
Finland	.98	.88	.95	.79	.89	.67
France	.97	.90	.99	.98	.87	.84
Germany	.96	.76	.96	.82	.95	.77
Italy	.96	.91	.96	.89	.96	.86
Japan	.84	.58	.88	.71	.86	.64
Netherlands	.94	.75	.95	.88	.90	.78
Norway	.98	.78	.96	.79	.93	.77
Sweden	.98	.75	.95	.64	.92	.58
United Kingdom	.92	.59	.92	.61	.92	.60
United States	.96	.86	.98	.95	.93	.70

[a]Correlations are based on 33 industries unless otherwise indicated.
[b]All industries except shipbuilding & repair, railroad equipment, motor vehicles, motorcycles & bicycles, other transport equipment, and aircraft.

Table 14.6   Correlation of the Logarithm of Relative Production Shares (RELPSHR) between the United States and Other Countries and the Sum of Squared Values of RELPSHR, 1970, 1979, and 1993[a]

	Correlation of LN(RELPSHR) with the United States			Sum of Squared Values of LN(RELPSHR)		
	1970	1979	1993	1970	1979	1993
Australia	−.10	−.05	−.02	31.9	28.0	31.2
Belgium[b]	−.29	−.22	−.16	22.5	14.3	20.6
Canada	−.25	−.31	−.27	42.9	39.5	41.8
Denmark	.15	.19	.28	64.3	60.9	59.3
Finland	−.21	−.12	.05	20.4	18.5	19.3
France	.36	.36	.36	33.5	33.1	32.7
Germany	.05	.09	.03	10.9	8.8	8.4
Italy	−.41	−.39	−.37	18.5	18.8	20.4
Japan	−.42	−.38	−.33	18.3	12.3	12.1
Netherlands	−.33	−.22	−.25	31.1	32.8	33.2
Norway	−.15	−.01	.09	49.7	55.4	58.7
Sweden	−.40	−.34	−.08	13.1	13.4	18.6
United Kingdom	−.31	−.24	−.07	5.0	4.8	4.6
United States	1.00	1.00	1.00	20.4	20.9	21.2
All countries				382.5	361.5	382.2

[a]Correlations and sum of squared values are based on 33 industries unless otherwise indicated.
[b]All industries except shipbuilding & repair, railroad equipment, motor vehicles, motorcycles & bicycles, other transport equipment, and aircraft.

it is still possible that the production structures of countries have become more alike over time. This is a difficult issue to test formally. In table 14.6, I have presented two ways of looking at the question. The first three columns show the correlation in LN(RELPSHR) between the United States and other countries, calculated across industries. The correlations were positive for only three of the thirteen countries in 1970, and only in one case (France) did the correlation exceed 0.20. However, in 1993, the correlations were positive for five countries and exceeded 0.20 for two (France and Denmark). Moreover, between 1970 and 1993, the correlation coefficients increased for all but three countries. The results do suggest that other countries have been growing more similar in their industrial structure to the United States over the period, although, even by 1993, most countries still had very different industries of specialization than the United States.

This measure is, unfortunately, problematic for two reasons. First, the U.S. production structure may itself be unusual, and changes in the correlation coefficient may therefore reflect mainly changes in the U.S. production structure over time. Second, there is a bias toward showing negative correlations because, if the value of RELPSHR is high for the United States, it must, of necessity, be low for other countries. An alternative measure, the sum of squared values of LN(RELPSHR), where the summation is performed across industries within country, is also shown in table 14.6. This measure has the virtue, at least, of comparing each country's industry production with the cross-country average production of that industry. Since the cross-country average value of LN(RELPSHR) is generally zero (the average value of RELPSHR is close to one), the sum of squared values is similar to a variance measure, showing how different a country's industry production is from the average of the fourteen countries.[8] If countries are becoming less specialized over time, then their production structure should be converging on the overall average of the countries, and this index should decline.

In 1970, Denmark was the most specialized country, according to this index, followed by Norway and Canada, and the United Kingdom the least specialized. It is noteworthy that these indexes remain relatively stable over time, with the exception of Japan (for whom the index declines from 18.3 in 1970 to 12.1 in 1993), Norway (increases from 49.7 to 58.7), and Sweden (increases from 13.1 to 18.6). The total sum of squares (summed across all countries) is almost identical in 1970 and 1993 (about 382 in both years), although it does fall somewhat between 1970 and 1979 and then rise in the second period.

The general stability in industries of specialization over time would lend support to the IIRS approach and tend to contradict HO-type models. The IIRS model stresses the advantages of initial leadership in an industry and the consequent cost reduction emanating from increased production volume. In contrast, the HO model would predict that specialization among the advanced countries would become less marked over time as their relative factor abundance converged. The coefficient of variation in the overall capital/labor ratio (computed from the OECD ISDB) among these fourteen countries fell from 0.28 in 1970 to 0.17 in 1992. Despite the growing similarity in relative factor abundance, these countries tended to maintain specialization in the same industries in 1993 as in 1970.

14.3   Labor Productivity Differences

I next turn to a comparison of industry labor productivity levels among the same fourteen countries. Here, there are more problems with missing data, particularly for the transport equipment subsectors (ISIC codes 3841–3849). Let us first define the labor productivity level, LP, of industry i in country h as

$$(3) \qquad LP_i^h = Y_i^h / L_i^h,$$

where L_i^h is total employment in industry i in country h. The (weighted) average labor productivity of industry i in the fourteen countries is given by

$$\overline{LP}_i = \Sigma_h Y_i^h / \Sigma_h L_i^h.$$

8. This measure is also similar to a chi-square distribution. However, because the values of RELPSHR observed in different countries are not independent (if RELPSHR is high in one country, it must be low in others), the sum of squared values does not meet the formal requirements for a chi-square distribution.

In analogous fashion to RELPSHR, I also compute

(4) $RELLP_i^h = LP_i^h / \overline{LP}_i$,

which show productivity in industry i of country h relative to the average productivity in industry i of the fourteen countries.

In 1970, U.S. labor productivity in total manufacturing was about 50 percent greater than that in Germany and more than double that in Japan (see table 14.7). U.S. productivity was above average in every industry except beverages and particularly high in tobacco, wood products, paper products, rubber products, iron and steel, industrial chemicals, transport equipment, other chemical products, electrical machinery, and professional goods. Germany's labor productivity was above average in twelve of the twenty-eight industries and exceptionally high in petroleum refineries and petroleum and coal products. Japanese labor productivity exceeded the international average in seven industries and was particularly strong only in beverages, wearing apparel, leather products, and glass products—all low-tech industries. The U.S. led all countries in terms of labor productivity in twelve of the twenty-eight industries (including three of the four high-tech ones), Germany in two, and Japan in only one (wearing apparel). Canada lead in four, Australia and Belgium in three, Italy in two, and the United Kingdom in one.

By 1993, Japan had surpassed Germany in labor productivity in total manufacturing, but U.S. productivity was still a third greater than Japan's and 50 percent greater than Germany's. German labor productivity remained high in petroleum refineries and petroleum and coal products; Japanese labor productivity was unusually strong in iron and steel, nonferrous metals, shipbuilding, miscellaneous manufactures, and other transport equipment and U.S. labor productivity in textiles, wood products, rubber products, metal products, other chemical products, nonelectrical machinery, and professional goods. Although the United States remained the overall leader in labor productivity in total manufacturing, its lead was cut to only eight of the thirty-three industries (excluding 384, transport equipment); these eight, however, included four of the five high-tech industries. Belgium led in eight industries, Italy in six, France in five, and Germany, Japan, Australia, Norway, and Finland in one.

It is also of note that there was very little correlation in industry labor productivity between Germany, Japan, and the United States. The correlation coefficients in industry RELLP for both 1970 and 1993 are negative in every case (the rank correlations are negative in all but one case). These results indicate that the three countries were strong in different industries not only in terms of relative production shares but also in terms of productivity performance.[9]

---

9. As in comparing production shares, there are statistical problems with using a correlation coefficient between RELLP values in two countries since the individual elements in each are not independent. In particular, if $RELLP_i$ is above unity in one country for industry i, the value of $RELLP_i$ must be less than one in at least one other country since the weighted sum of $RELLP_i$ across countries must equal 1.0. However, there is no algebraic constraint on two countries having similar RELLP values across industries.

Table 14.7   Relative Labor Productivity (RELLP) of Germany, Japan, and the United States and the OECD Leader, 1970 and 1993[a]

Industry	1970				1993			
	GER	JPN	USA	Leader	GER	JPN	USA	Leader
Total manufacturing	.97	.63	1.47	USA	.84	.93	1.26	USA
Low-tech industries								
Food	.76	.93	1.15	CAN	.64	.74	1.33	ITA
Beverages	.77	1.42	.87	CAN	.64	.90	1.15	ITA
Tobacco	1.25	.28	2.00	USA	2.01	.45	1.06	NOR
Textiles	1.09	.53	1.46	USA	1.11	.39	1.44	ITA
Wearing apparel	.90	1.35	1.11	JPN	.81	.98	1.10	BEL
Leather & products	.83	1.26	1.00	BEL	.84	1.17	.99	BEL
Footwear	.86	.74	1.27	BEL	.89	.68	1.13	BEL
Wood products	.92	.34	1.86	USA	.85	.47	1.43	USA
Furniture & fixtures	1.22	1.10	1.04	AUS	.86	1.12	.98	BEL
Paper & products	.79	.61	1.54	USA	.76	.80	1.36	USA
Printing & publishing	.68	.94	1.32	USA	.80	.91	1.05	ITA
Petroleum refineries	2.18	.59	.76	GER	1.83	.86	.68	FRA
Petroleum & coal products	9.88	.25	1.28	GER	6.01	.47	1.09	GER
Rubber products	1.05	.52	1.56	CAN	.69	.73	1.46	BEL
Plastic products nec	.77	.76	1.34	AUS	.88	.82	1.18	FRA
Pottery, china, etc.	.59	.64	1.27	BEL	.62	.75	1.12	BEL
Glass & products	.58	1.46	1.47	USA	.87	1.06	1.21	BEL
Nonmetal products nec	1.18	.65	1.33	CAN	1.09	.74	1.16	FRA
Iron & steel	.71	1.11	1.69	USA	.73	1.23	1.35	USA
Nonferrous metals	.66	1.15	1.46	AUS	.73	1.25	.96	FRA
Metal products	.88	.49	1.48	ITA	.88	.78	1.45	USA
Shipbuilding & repair	: :	: :	: :	: :	.85	1.37	.92	FRA
Other manufactures nes	.78	.78	1.20	UK	.64	1.74	.83	UK

Medium-tech industries							
Industrial chemicals	1.10	.65	1.52	USA	.68	1.10	1.35	BEL
Transport equipment	1.07	.72	1.57	USA	.89	1.05	1.27	USA
Railroad equipment	…	…	…		.30	1.06	1.37	AUS
Motor vehicles	…	…	…		.98	1.15	1.00	ITA
Motorcycles & bicycles	…	…	…		.51	1.07	.94	ITA
Other transport equipment	…	…	…		1.14	2.67	NA	JPN
High-tech industries							
Other chemical products	.90	.75	1.53	USA	.64	1.14	1.43	USA
Nonelectrical machinery	1.04	.55	1.47	USA	.71	.92	1.52	USA
Electrical machinery	1.06	.10	1.84	USA	.73	1.16	1.13	FIN
Aircraft	…	…	…		.60	1.08	1.26	USA
Professional goods	1.10	.29	1.59	ITA	.74	.64	1.44	USA
Correlation with United States[b]	.10	-.54			-.22	-.36		
Correlation with Germany[b]		-.33			-.39			
Correlation with United States[c]					-.19	-.41		
Correlation with Germany[c]					-.40			
Rank correlation with United States[b]	.14	-.53			-.16	-.35		
Rank correlation with Germany[b]		-.62				-.46		

[a] Relative labor productivity of industry i in country h defined as

$$RELLP_i^h = LP_i^h / \overline{LP}_i,$$

where the calculation of $\overline{LP}_i$ is based on 14 OECD countries with pertinent data: Australia (AUS), Belgium (BEL), Canada (CAN), Denmark (DNK), Finland (FIN), France (FRA), Germany (GER), Italy (ITA), Japan (JPN), the Netherlands (NET), Norway (NOR), Sweden (SWE), the United Kingdom (UK), and the United States (USA). The exceptions are as follows: (1) DEN, NET: 1991 data used for 1992 in all industries except total manufacturing (1992 data used). (2) GER: 1991 data used for 1992 in chemicals (351–356). (3) SWE: 1991 data used for 1992 in industries 353 and 354. (4) Industries 3841–3849: (a) BEL: missing data for all years; (b) FRA, ITA: missing data for 1970, 1979; (c) AUS: 3842, 3845, 3849 missing data for 1970, 1979; (d) GER: 3842, 3843, 3844, 3849 missing data for 1970; (e) JPN: 3842, 3844, 3845, 3849 missing data for 1970, 1979; (f) UK: 3842, 3844, 3845, 3849 missing data for 1970 (g) USA: 3842, 3844, 3845 missing data for 1970; (h) DNK: 3841, 3842, 3844 missing data for 1990–92. (i) 1991 data used for 1992, except CAN, SWE, which use 1990 data. For other technical details on the sectoring, see the notes to tables 14.1 and 14.2.

[b] Includes 384; excludes 3841–49.

[c] Excludes 384, 3849; includes 3841–45.

Table 14.8   Dispersion of Relative Labor Productivity (RELLP) across 14 OECD Countries for 29 Manufacturing Industries, 1970, 1979, and 1993[a]

	Coefficient of Variation of RELLP			Standard Deviation of LN(RELLP)		
	1970	1979	1993	1970	1979	1993
Total manufacturing	.25	.21	.19	.24	.21	.20
Low-tech industries						
Food	.28	.26	.30	.30	.26	.31
Beverages	.29	.40	.41	.32	.42	.42
Tobacco	.74	.80	.74	.77	.83	.84
Textiles	.26	.23	.30	.27	.27	.35
Wearing apparel	.30	.24	.29	.31	.25	.31
Leather & products	.53	.38	.41	.47	.34	.42
Footwear	.39	.24	.20	.42	.23	.20
Wood products	.42	.31	.31	.51	.35	.33
Furniture & fixtures	.29	.21	.25	.31	.23	.25
Paper & products	.37	.27	.23	.33	.26	.23
Printing & publishing	.27	.24	.22	.27	.24	.23
Petroleum refineries	.73	.82	.62	.93	.98	.66
Petroleum & coal products	1.80	1.71	1.22	1.04	.94	.79
Rubber products	.42	.34	.43	.39	.32	.41
Plastic products nec	.67	.37	.17	.54	.33	.18
Pottery, china, etc.	.49	.36	.48	.44	.34	.40
Glass & products	.39	.32	.33	.40	.33	.33
Nonmetal products nec	.27	.29	.27	.27	.28	.28
Iron & steel	.48	.48	.25	.45	.45	.25
Nonferrous metals	.46	.46	.37	.45	.51	.38
Metal products	.38	.30	.26	.36	.29	.24
Other manufactures nes	.54	.54	.76	.51	.56	.75
Medium-tech industries						
Industrial chemicals	.27	.32	.35	.26	.31	.36
Motor vehicles	.31	.36	.37	.31	.35	.38
Transport equip excluding vehicles[b]	.42	.29	.36	.36	.26	.34
High-tech industries						
Other chemical products	.35	.39	.32	.34	.39	.30
Nonelectrical machinery	.28	.22	.31	.28	.21	.31
Electrical machinery	.40	.31	.33	.68	.31	.38
Professional goods	.49	.37	.32	.58	.41	.30

[a]For definition of RELLP and other technical details in the calculations, see the notes to table 14.7.
[b]Includes ISIC codes 3841, 3842, 3844, 3845, 3849.

Table 14.8 shows the cross-country coefficient of variation in industry RELLP by industry. Considerable convergence had already been achieved in the overall level of labor productivity in total manufacturing among the fourteen countries by 1970. The coefficient of variation for 1970 is 0.25, compared to 0.36 in 1963 (see Dollar and Wolff 1993, 52). There was still some additional convergence after that, with the coefficient of variation declining to 0.21 in 1979 and 0.19 in 1992.

On the individual industry level, the time patterns are quite different. Between 1970 and 1979, the coefficient of variation declined in nineteen of the twenty-nine industries, increased in seven, and remained constant in the other four, while, from 1979 to 1992, the index declined in thirteen industries, rose in fifteen, and stayed the same in one. Convergence in labor productivity on the industry level was thus much spottier than for total manufacturing over the period 1970–93.[10]

Another striking finding is that the actual value of the coefficient of variation is substantially higher in every industry (except one in each year) than the corresponding value for total manufacturing. For over half the industries, the index is more than 50 percent greater than that for total manufacturing. These results clearly support the argument that convergence in overall labor productivity in manufacturing has been achieved to a large extent through countries' specializing in different industries in terms of both production shares and productivity levels. This has been especially the case in the 1980s.

Correlations over time in industry relative labor productivity levels are shown by country in table 14.9. They are quite high for the period 1970–79, exceeding 0.70 in all fourteen countries, 0.79 on twelve countries, 0.88 in five. Rank correlations are quite similar. In contrast, the correlations are much weaker for the period 1979–92, exceeding 0.60 in only seven countries. In the case of Canada, Denmark, and the Netherlands, the coefficients fell below 0.30 and are not statistically significant. The rank correlations are even weaker for this period, exceeding 0.60 in only one case.

These results indicate that high performance in terms of productivity can erode over time and that poor performance can likewise improve. It is also of note that correlations are much weaker for relative industry productivity performance than for industry production shares, particularly for the period 1979–92. This suggests that there may be other factors, such as resource endowments and specialized skills, that contribute to competitive advantage and industry specialization but are not captured in standard productivity measures and that these factors may remain more stable over time than labor productivity.

Another important difference between relative productivity performance and production share is that, whereas countries have generally retained their industries of specialization in terms of production over the period 1970–93, they have become less differentiated in terms of labor productivity. Evidence for this is given in the last three columns of table 14.9, where I have computed the sum of squared values of industry values of LN(RELLP) for each country. If countries are becoming more similar to the overall (weighted) average in terms of labor productivity, then this index should decline. It is of note that all countries show a decline in the value of this measure between 1970 and 1992,

10. Results are very similar on the basis of the standard deviation of the natural logarithm of RELLP, also shown in table 14.8. This is partly due to the fact that the distribution of RELLP, unlike that of RELPSHR, is not highly skewed but quite symmetrical, with over 90 percent of the values in the range 0.5–1.5.

Table 14.9   Correlation over Time in Industry Relative Productivity Levels (RELLP) by Country and Sum of Squared Values, 1970–93[a]

	Correlation over Time in LN(RELLP)		Rank Correlation over Time in RELLP		Sum of Squared Values of LN(RELLP)		
	1970–79	1970–93	1970–79	1970–93	1970	1979	1993
Australia	.84	.45	.83	.33	6.0	3.9	5.4
Belgium	.87	.75	.78	.59	26.0	15.3	15.8
Canada[b]	.70	.12	.79	.19	3.7	1.9	1.9
Denmark	.79	.24	.64	.08	14.1	9.6	12.8
Finland	.79	.54	.73	.47	7.4	7.8	3.2
France[c]	.80	.77	.85	.79	1.9	2.2	2.5
Germany	.96	.88	.86	.51	7.5	7.4	6.2
Italy	.89	.67	.84	.54	7.8	7.1	5.1
Japan	.72	.44	.83	.60	15.3	7.2	4.0
Netherlands	.81	.04	.79	.12	3.1	2.4	2.2
Norway	.81	.39	.88	.23	6.7	12.4	8.6
Sweden	.90	.77	.84	.56	5.8	7.3	12.3
United Kingdom	.94	.68	.91	.59	7.9	9.0	4.6
United States	.88	.61	.87	.56	4.0	2.3	1.8
Total					117.3	95.8	86.4

[a]Correlations are based on the 28 3-digit ISIC industries (including 384, transport equipment), unless otherwise indicated.
[b]Excludes ISIC 385 (professional goods).
[c]Excludes ISIC 354 (petroleum & coal products).

with the exception of France, Norway, and Sweden. Declines are particularly marked for Belgium, Finland, and Japan (from 15.3 to 4.0). The total sum of squared values (summed across all countries) also shows a pronounced decrease, from 117.3 in 1970 to 95.8 in 1979 and 86.4 in 1992.

14.4   Changes in Relative Production Share and Productivity Growth

On the surface, at least, there appears to be very little correlation between RELPSHR and RELLP. The United States, for example, led in terms of labor productivity in a dozen or so industries but had the highest relative production share in only one, aircraft (see tables 14.2 and 14.7 above). The reason is that the larger economies tend to be more diversified than the smaller ones and that they are therefore not as likely to have as many high values of RELPSHR. As a result, the high labor productivity of the U.S. and Japanese manufacturing industries does not necessarily translate into large relative production shares. In fact, the simple correlation coefficient between RELPSHR and RELLP across all industries and countries is only 0.33 for 1970, 0.35 for 1979, and 0.40 for 1992. However, there may still be a close relation between changes in relative productivity levels and changes in relative production shares.

The linkage between changes in production share and productivity growth at the industry level is not an easy question to formalize. The reason is that the productivity growth of a particular industry in a particular country should be considered relative to the same industry in other countries and to other industries within the same country. In other words, rapid productivity growth may have no effect on relative production share if it is occurring in the same industry in every country. At the same time, rapid productivity growth in every industry of one country will also have little effect on relative production share since it would not enhance the competitiveness of any industry relative to other industries in the economy.

I now turn to regression analysis to provide a formal analysis of these relations. Two estimating forms are used. The first is

$$
\text{(5)} \quad \text{DRELPSHR}_i^h = b_0 + b_1 \cdot \text{DRELLP}_i^h + b_2 \cdot \text{DRELWAGE}_i^h
$$
$$
+ b_3 \cdot \text{RELKFL}_i^h + \varepsilon_i^h.
$$

DRELPSHR is the change in the natural logarithm of RELPSHR (relative production share) in industry i and country h, and DRELLP is the change in the natural logarithm of RELLP (relative labor productivity) in industry i and country h. $\text{DRELWAGE}_i^h = \Delta[\ln(w_i^h/\overline{w}_i)]$, where w_i^h is the average wage (in current U.S. dollars) in industry i and country h, and $\overline{w}_i$ is the (weighted) average wage in industry i among the fourteen countries. The conversion to U.S. dollars is based on the actual market exchange rate.

The variable $\text{RELKFL}_i^h = \ln(kfl_i^h/\overline{kfl}_i)$, where kfl_i^h is the ratio of average capital formation (kf) in 1985 U.S. dollars to average employment (l) over the period in industry i and country h, and $\overline{kfl}_i$ is the ratio of the (weighted) average capital formation in industry i among the fourteen countries to the (weighted) average employment in industry i among the fourteen countries.[11] The term ε_i^h is a stochastic error term, which is assumed to be independently but may not be identically distributed. The regressions reported in tables 14.10 and 14.11 below were estimated using the White procedure for a heteroskedasticity-consistent covariance matrix.

The logarithmic form is used for the dependent variable RELPSHR because, as noted above, the variable is highly skewed, with a range from zero to infinity, while the logarithm is more normally distributed. The rationale for using first differences for RELPSHR is that industry specialization may be highly dependent on historical developments in a country as well as its resource base. The levels equation can thus be interpreted as a fixed-effect model, and first differencing allows us to remove the unobservables from the equation.

Another rationale for using the first-difference form is that relative productivity growth is likely to be measured with greater accuracy than relative productivity levels. The reason is that comparing productivity levels across coun-

---

11. I used the capital formation deflator computed from the OECD ISDB to convert capital formation in local currency to 1985 U.S. dollars.

tries is sensitive to the choice of price deflators and PPP exchange rates. If there are biases in the productivity-level estimates, there is a good chance that these biases are relatively stable over time and that relative productivity growth rates may therefore be measured with less error than relative productivity levels.

The coefficient b_1 is predicted to have a positive sign. The coefficient b_2 is predicted to have a negative sign since relatively higher labor costs in a country, measured on the basis of the market exchange rate, should reduce that country's competitiveness in that industry and hence its production share. The coefficient of RELKFL is predicted to have a positive sign. The rationale is that new technology may be embodied in new capital investment and that greater capital formation relative to employment should therefore be associated with more modern technology in an industry and thus with lower costs and greater competitiveness.

The second form is

$$\text{DRELPSHR}_i^h = b_0 + b_1 \cdot \text{DRELLPC}_i^h + b_2 \cdot \text{DRELWAGC}_i^h$$
$$(6) \qquad + b_3 \cdot \text{RELKFLC}_i^h + \varepsilon_i^h.$$

$\text{DRELLPC}_i^h = \text{DRELLP}_i^h - \Delta[\ln(\overline{LP^h}/\overline{LP})]$, where $\overline{LP^h}$ is the average labor productivity in country h (the ratio of GDP to total employment), and $\overline{LP}$ is the weighted average labor productivity of the fourteen countries (the ratio of total GDP to total employment in the fourteen countries). DRELLPC_i^h thus shows how an industry's productivity performance in a given country relative to the average productivity performance of that industry compares to the country's overall productivity performance relative to the overall average productivity performance of the fourteen countries. The variables DRELWAGC_i^h and RELKFLC_i^h are defined in like fashion: $\text{DRELWAGC}_i^h = \text{DRELWAGE}_i^h - \Delta[\ln(\overline{w^h}/\overline{w})]$, and $\text{RELKFLC}_i^h = \text{RELKFL}_i^h - \ln(\overline{kfl^h}/\overline{kfl})$. The second form is the preferred specification since it accords more closely with the underlying theory. The predictions for the coefficients b_1, b_2, and b_3 are the same as for the first specification.

It should also be noted that there are econometric difficulties with the specifications in equations (5) and (6). By construction, there may be introduced a correlation between RELPSHR and RELLP since, in both cases, the numerator is the industry's production share. Therefore, any errors in measurement in industry output will bias the coefficient estimates. Moreover, the two variables are likely to be procyclic, which will cause the same problem to arise. As a result, it would be desirable to use instrumental variables to perform the actual estimation, although, at the moment, no suitable instrument appears to be available.

Regressions are run separately for the periods 1970–79 and 1979–93. Besides the full set of industries, regressions are run separately on low-, medium-, and high-tech industries. Moreover, equation (5) is run with one variation, which is to substitute KFL, the ratio of average capital formation to average employment over the period, for RELKFL. Results for equation (5) are shown in table 14.10 and those for equation (6) in table 14.11.

The results show a very strong relation between the log change in relative production share (DRELPSHR) and the log change in labor productivity relative to the industry average (DRELLP). The coefficients are all positive and significant at the 1 percent level except among medium-tech industries in the period 1970–79. Likewise, the results in table 14.11 show an equally strong relation between DRELPSHR and the log change in labor productivity relative to both the industry and the country average (DRELLPC). These coefficients are all positive and significant at the 1 percent level except among high-tech industries in the period 1970–79.

The coefficient values can be interpreted as elasticities. Among all industries, a 1 percent increase in an industry's labor productivity relative to the international industry average is associated with about a 0.65 percent gain in the industry's market share. A 1 percent increase in the industry's labor productivity relative to both the international industry average and the country average is associated with a 0.25 percent gain in the industry's market share in 1970–79 and a 0.41 percent gain in 1979–93.

Wage changes relative to the international industry average (DRELWAGE) had a negative coefficient in every case. For the period 1970–79, DRELWAGE is significant at the 1 percent level among all industries and among the low-tech group but not statistically significant among medium- and high-tech industries. For the period 1979–92, the coefficient is significant in only one case—at the 5 percent level among low-tech industries. In contrast, the coefficient estimates for DRELWAGC, wage growth relative to both the industry and the country averages, are significant in only one case—at the 5 percent level among medium-tech industries in the period 1979–93. These results suggest that relative labor costs played a strong role in determining a country's relative production share only among low-tech industries during the 1970s. The effect was very weak during the period 1979–93. Moreover, it also appears that industries in a given country tend to lose market share if their wages are growing faster relative to the international industry average, not the country average, than the same industry in other countries.

Average investment per worker has a uniformly positive effect on relative production share. The results are generally significant among all industries and among low-tech industries as a group but less significant among medium-tech industries and not significant at all among high-tech industries. RELKFL, average capital formation per worker, relative to the industry average, is statistically significant, at the 5 percent level, only for low-tech industries in the period 1970–79 and medium-tech industries in the period 1979–92. KFL, the ratio of capital formation to employment, is significant at the 1 percent level among low-tech industries in both periods and at the 5 percent level among medium-tech industries in the first of the two periods. RELKFLC, the ratio of

Table 14.10   Regressions of the Change in RELPSHR on the Growth in Labor Productivity, Wages, and Capital Formation Relative to the Industry Average[a]

Constant	DRELLP	DRELWAGE	RELKFL	KFL	R^2	Adj. R^2	Standard Error	Industry Sample	Sample Size
				A. 1970–79					
.003	.666**	−.177**	.049*		.425	.421	.209	All	377
(.27)	(9.73)	(4.13)	(2.24)						
−.031*	.678**	−.161**		5.43**	.439	.435	.207	All	377
(2.25)	(17.0)	(4.66)		(3.71)					
.003	.748**	−.255**	.055*		.475	.470	.189	Lo tech	293
(.25)	(12.6)	(6.75)	(2.43)						
−.035*	.774**	−.241**		6.25**	.502	.496	.185	Lo tech	293
(2.57)	(16.8)	(6.64)		(4.57)					
−.059	.193	−.144	.014		.111	.007	.278	Med. tech	28
(.93)	(1.06)	(.98)	(.15)						
−.198*	.224	−.194		17.61*	.257	.164	.254	Med. tech	28
(2.52)	(1.46)	(1.22)		(2.17)					
.086**	.745**	−.105	.035		.621	.599	.213	Hi tech	56
(2.91)	(7.34)	(1.26)	(.56)						
.092	.738**	−.008		56.73	.620	.598	.213	Hi tech	56
(1.28)	(8.84)	(.85)		(.21)					

B. 1979–93

−.021	.672**	−.033	.044		.454	.450	.254	All	404
(.45)	(11.5)	(.59)	(1.60)						
−.079**	.636**	−.027		9.24**	.501	.498	.243	All	404
(5.45)	(17.5)	(.59)		(6.49)					
−.045**	.773**	−.129	.037		.468	.463	.255	Lo tech	299
(3.12)	(10.2)	(1.90)	(1.90)						
−.101**	.726**	−.122*		9.10**	.527	.522	.240	Lo tech	299
(6.13)	(15.5)	(2.09)		(6.25)					
.038	.388**	−.052	.153*		.424	.384	.226	Med. tech	47
(1.19)	(4.10)	(.48)	(2.09)						
−.107	.329**	−.013		13.66	.385	.342	.233	Med. tech	47
(1.71)	(4.10)	(.12)		(1.91)					
.019	.945**	−.176	−.004		.687	.670	.203	Hi tech	58
(.66)	(10.7)	(1.36)	(.09)						
.009	.940**	−.179		27.55	.688	.671	.203	Hi tech	58
(.17)	(10.2)	(1.28)		(.25)					

[a]The dependent variable is DRELPSHR. The absolute values of t-ratios are shown in parentheses below the coefficient estimate. The estimation uses the White procedure for a heteroskedasticity-consistent covariance matrix. DRELPSHR$_i^h$: change in the logarithm of RELPSHR (relative production share) of industry i in country h. DRELLP$_i^h$: change in the logarithm of the ratio of LP (labor productivity) of industry i in country h to the 14-nation average LP in industry i. DRELWAGE$_i^h$: change in the logarithm of the ratio of wages of industry i in country h to the 14-nation average wages in industry i. KFL$_i^h$: the logarithm of the ratio of capital formation to employment of industry i in country h (index). RELKFL$_i$: KFL$_i^h$ minus the logarithm of the ratio of the 14-nation average of capital formation to employment in industry i.

*Significant at the 5 percent level (2-tailed test).

**Significant at the 1 percent level (2-tailed test).

Table 14.11   Regressions of the Change in RELPSHR on the Growth in Labor Productivity, Wages, and Capital Formation Relative to Industry and Country Averages[a]

Constant	DRELLPC	DRELWAGC	RELKFLC	R^2	Adj. R^2	Standard Error	Industry Sample	Sample Size
A. 1970–79								
-.458**	.247**	-.065	.102**	.180	.173	.250	All	377
(7.24)	(7.20)	(.67)	(3.78)					
-.482**	.252**	-.186	.111**	.191	.183	.235	Lo tech	293
(7.29)	(7.38)	(1.89)	(4.07)					
-.427**	.242**	.339	.076	.277	.187	.251	Med. tech	28
(2.91)	(3.17)	(1.06)	(1.11)					
-.420	.275	.249	.079	.198	.152	.310	Hi tech	56
(1.85)	(1.97)	(.76)	(.54)					
B. 1979–93								
.758**	.408**	.006	.108**	.301	.295	.288	All	404
(11.0)	(10.5)	(.08)	(3.56)					
-.845**	.453**	.073	.102**	.298	.291	.293	Lo tech	299
(8.78)	(8.41)	(.68)	(2.64)					
-.448**	.263**	-.182*	.170*	.517	.483	.207	Med. tech	47
(3.59)	(4.31)	(2.02)	(2.23)					
-.796**	.438**	-.225	.134	.291	.252	.306	Hi tech	58
(5.20)	(4.64)	(1.06)	(1.85)					

[a]The dependent variable is DRELPSHR. The absolute values of t-ratios are shown in parentheses below the coefficient estimate. The estimation uses the White procedure for a heteroskedasticity-consistent covariance matrix. DRELPSHR$_i^h$: change in the logarithm of RELPSHR (relative production share) of industry i in country h. DRELLPC$_i^h$: DRELLP$_i^h$ relative to the log change of overall labor productivity (LP) in country h minus the log change of the 14-nation average LP. DRELWAGC$_i^h$: DRELWAGE$_i^h$ relative to the log change of overall average wages in country h minus the log change of the 14-nation average wages. RELKFLC$_i^h$: RELKFL$_i^h$ relative to the logarithm of the ratio of total capital formation to total employment in country h minus the logarithm of the 14-nation ratio of total capital formation to total employment.

*Significant at the 5 percent level (2-tailed test).

**Significant at the 1 percent level (2-tailed test).

capital formation to employment, relative to both the industry and the country averages, is significant at the 1 percent level among low-tech industries in both periods and at the 5 percent level among medium-tech industries in the later period.

For both equations (5) and (6), the goodness of fit, as measured by the adjusted R^2 statistic and the standard error of the regression, is almost uniformly superior (with the exception of one case) for the period 1979–93 than for the period 1970–79. Moreover, the coefficient estimates for DRELLP and DRELLPC are also uniformly higher (again with the exception of one case) for the later period than for the earlier one. Differences in results between the two periods are particularly marked for the medium-tech industries. These results suggest that competitive advantage has become more dependent on relative productivity performance over time.

There are also important differences among the three industry groups. Capital formation clearly plays a much more important role in explaining market share for low-tech industries than the other two groups and a somewhat more significant role for medium- than high-tech industries. These results suggest that low-tech industries, which, by definition, engage in relatively little R&D, acquire much of their new technology through capital investment, whereas medium-tech industries acquire some new technology through this venue and high-tech industries, who invest intensively in R&D, acquire very little.

For equation (5), at least, the goodness of fit is markedly superior for high-tech industries than for the other two groups. Moreover, the coefficient estimate of DRELLP has the highest value for the high-tech group, suggesting that relative productivity performance plays the most important role in determining international competitiveness in this group of industries, which includes computers, televisions, and communication equipment. The estimated coefficient of DRELLP is also more than twice as great for the low-tech industries than the medium-tech ones. This suggests that, in the latter group, which includes automobiles and other transport equipment, "quality" differences, which are not captured in standard productivity measures, may matter a great deal in determining international competitiveness.

It is also of note that, in equation (5), changes in relative wages (DRELWAGE) are significant only among the low-tech industries for the period 1970–79. In these industries, which include apparel, textiles, metal products, and basic chemicals, relative labor costs and price competition played an important role in determining market share in this period, whereas, in the other two technology groups, superior productivity performance and technology played the crucial role. Moreover, in the 1980s, by which time the intercountry variation in wages had become quite small, relative labor costs were no longer a significant influence on relative production shares.

It is also notable that, although equation (6) is the theoretically preferred specification, the goodness of fit is greater for equation (5), with the exception of medium-tech industries. These results appear to indicate that competitiveness depends more on how an industry in a given country is performing relative to the same industry in other countries rather than to other industries in the same country. This result is consistent with the models developed by Gomory (1992) and Gomory and Baumol (1992), which show that industry output shares of a given country depend on absolute productivity and technology advantage rather than comparative productivity and technology performance (i.e., relative to other industries in the same country).

14.5 Summary and Concluding Remarks

Three principal findings emerge from this study. First, despite the continued convergence of overall productivity and capital intensity in manufacturing (the coefficient of variation fell from 0.25 in 1970 to 0.19 in 1992 for labor productivity and from 0.28 to 0.17 for the capital/labor ratio), the major industrialized countries in the world tended to specialize manufacturing production in very different industries, and most countries retained their specialization over the period 1970–93. This was particular so for the three largest economies—Germany, Japan, and the United States. On net, there was no tendency over this period toward greater similarity in industries of specialization, as measured by relative production shares, among the fourteen countries. These results appear to be more supportive of an IIRS type of model than one based on the HO theorem.

Second, these countries also tended to be strong in different industries in terms of labor productivity performance. However, whereas countries have generally retained their industries of specialization in terms of relative production share over the period 1970–93, correlations over time in relative industry labor productivity performance within country are considerably weaker than those for relative production shares. These results suggest that high performance in terms of labor productivity can erode over time and that poor performance can change for the better. They also suggest that there are other factors, such as resource endowments, specialized skills, and history, that contribute to industry specialization and remain more stable over time than labor productivity.

Third, despite the apparent differences in the stability of production shares and that of relative productivity performance over time, the regression results strongly support the central thesis of the paper that there is a positive and significant relation between changes in relative industry market shares and the industry's relative productivity growth. The results are generally stronger for the period 1979–93 than for the period 1970–79, suggesting that market share is becoming more dependent on relative productivity performance and technology levels over time. The estimated elasticity of relative market share with respect to relative labor productivity is somewhat higher for high-tech industries than for low-tech ones and markedly greater for these two groups than for medium-tech industries. The results suggest that unmeasured quality differences in this latter group, which includes automobiles and other transport equipment (except aircraft), may play a crucial role in determining international competitiveness.

The results on capital formation per worker are consistent with the embodiment hypothesis—namely, that new technology is embodied in new machinery and equipment. Gains in market share appear to depend directly on the new technology embodied in recent investment. Capital formation clearly plays a much more important role in explaining market share for low-tech industries than medium-tech industries and more for the latter than the high-tech group. This result is consistent with the argument that the latest vintage of technology embodied in new capital investment is a major vehicle for productivity gain in low-tech industries, whereas medium-tech industries also rely on their own R&D investments and high-tech ones rely almost exclusively on R&D for new technology.

The results also show that relatively higher labor costs in a country (measured relative to the international industry average) generally reduce that country's competitiveness in that industry and hence its production share but that this effect is very significant only among low-tech industries in the period 1970–79. In these industries, which include apparel, textiles, and basic metal products, it appears that relative labor costs and price competition played an important role along with relative productivity gains in determining market share in the 1970s, whereas, for medium- and high-tech industries and for low-tech industries in the later period, superior productivity performance and technology played the crucial role. These results are consistent with those reported in Dollar and Wolff (1993), who found that, among OECD countries, differences in labor costs were not important determinants of differences in unit costs by the 1980s.

The fact that changes in specialization are generally significantly related to productivity changes does support the view that productivity growth encapsulates the expansion of industry-specific productive factors that contribute, at least to some degree, to competitive advantage. Moreover, this analysis redirects attention to the determinants of high levels of productivity. To the extent that it reflects technology-related assets owned by the firm or embodied in technical labor, investment in research and development and the training of skilled labor is clearly an important ingredient in promoting rapid productivity growth.

References

Arrow, Kenneth. 1962. The economic implications of learning by doing. *Review of Economic Studies* 29, no. 2:155–73.
Balassa, Bela. 1965. Trade liberalization and "revealed" comparative advantage. *Manchester School* 33 (May): 99–123.

————. 1978. Exports and economic growth: Further evidence. *Journal of Development Economics* 5 (June): 181–89.

Dollar, David, and Edward N. Wolff. 1993. *Competitiveness, convergence, and international specialization.* Cambridge, Mass.: MIT Press.

Gomory, Ralph E. 1992. A Ricardo model with economies of scale. C. V. Starr Working Paper no. 92–29. New York University, June.

Gomory, Ralph E., and William J. Baumol. 1992. Scale economies, the regions of multiple equilibria, and gains from acquisition of industries. C. V. Starr Working Paper no. 92–10. New York University, June.

Helpman, Elhanan. 1984. Increasing returns, imperfect markets, and trade theory. In *Handbook of international economics,* vol. 1, ed. Ronald W. Jones and Peter B. Kenen. Amsterdam: North-Holland.

Helpman, Elhanan, and Paul R. Krugman. 1985. *Market structure and foreign trade: Increasing returns, imperfect competition, and the international economy.* Cambridge, Mass.: MIT Press.

Krugman, Paul R. 1979. Increasing returns, monopolistic competition, and international trade. *Journal of International Economics* 9:469–79.

————. 1980. Scale economies, product differentiation, and the patterns of trade. *American Economic Review* 70, no. 5 (December): 950–59.

————. 1991. History versus expectations. *Quarterly Journal of Economics* 106 (May): 651–67.

Leamer, Edward. 1984. *Sources of international comparative advantage.* Cambridge, Mass.: MIT Press.

Maddison, Angus, and Bart van Ark. 1989. International comparisons of purchasing power, real output and labour productivity: A case study of Brazilian, Mexican, and US manufacturing, 1975. *Review of Income and Wealth,* ser. 35, no. 1 (March): 31–56.

Nakamura, Shinichiro. 1989. Productivity and factor prices as sources of differences in production costs between Germany, Japan, and the U.S. *Economic Studies Quarterly* 40 (March): 701–15.

15   Wage Dispersion and Country Price Levels

Robert E. Lipsey and Birgitta Swedenborg

It has long been obvious that price levels, converted to a single currency via exchange rates, differ greatly from country to country. That fact has been demonstrated most conclusively in the reports on the UN International Comparison Program since the 1970s. The history of the finding and explanations for it have been reviewed in quite a number of papers (Kravis and Lipsey 1983, 1987; Bhagwati 1984; Clague 1985, 1986, 1993; Bergstrand 1991; Falvey and Gemmell 1991; and Kleiman 1993). Many of these focus on factors that affect the price of services, or the service component of prices of goods, on the ground that the sources of price differences must be concentrated in nontradable sectors of the economy.

In a recent paper, the present authors examined differences in the price levels for food products and found that, despite the presumed tradability of foods, price levels for them differed among countries even more than for the GDP as a whole, with its large service component (Lipsey and Swedenborg 1996). The main explanatory factors found for these price differences were levels of protection for farm products and levels of indirect taxation, mainly VAT on foods. Other factors, not specific to food prices, were real income per capita, presumably operating through its effect on the cost of services, and deviations of general price levels from those implied by per capita incomes, presumably as a consequence of temporary factors affecting exchange rates or of omitted characteristics of the countries' economies such as, possibly, inefficient or monopolistic service sectors.

Our explanation of the role of per capita income started from the idea that

Robert E. Lipsey is professor emeritus of economics at Queens College and the Graduate Center, City University of New York, and a research associate of the National Bureau of Economic Research. Birgitta Swedenborg is deputy director of the Center for Business and Policy Studies (SNS), Stockholm.

The authors are indebted to Ewa Wojas for research and computer assistance.

industries could be characterized as labor intensive or capital intensive. If we think of goods production as relatively capital intensive and service production as relatively labor intensive and of goods production as tradable and service production as nontradable (ignoring the oversimplification involved in these assumptions), services should be relatively cheap in poor countries, where labor is relatively cheap, as suggested in Kravis and Lipsey (1983) and Bhagwati (1984). Goods prices, at least at the producers' level, would tend to be more equal across countries because of the price-equalizing effects of trade. They could, however, differ at the purchasers' level because they may incorporate large elements of service input in, for example, wholesale and retail trade.

We speculated in that paper that another factor, missing in our analysis, might be the dispersion of wages among workers and industries. If we compare two countries in which labor prices are, on average, the same relative to capital input prices but one pursues a policy of equalizing wages among workers while the other allows large differences based on skill, the structure of service prices could differ. In the absence of major possibilities for substitution among types of labor, the country with large wage differences among workers should face relatively lower prices for services intensive in low-skill labor but relatively high prices for services intensive in high-skill labor. The country with a "solidaristic" wage policy, on the other hand, should face relatively high prices for low-skill services and low prices for high-skill services.

The effect of the wage structure will depend on the elasticity of substitution between skilled and unskilled labor. If the elasticity of substitution is high, the effect on service prices will be small. However, countries with wide wage dispersion will have higher proportions of unskilled workers in all industries than countries with a narrow range of wages, where it will be more profitable to employ skilled workers because the differential is small. Thus, we might observe the effects of wage dispersion in the price of services, the skill distribution of employment, or both.

15.1   Data

15.1.1   Measures of Wage Dispersion

The measure of wage dispersion that we use is based on data for individual workers and shows the differences between different deciles and median wage levels. Wage data by deciles were published in OECD (1996b), its *Employment Outlook*. We have experimented also with industry wage data, as published in Gittleman and Wolff (1993), with results similar to, but weaker than, those from individual wage dispersion data, perhaps because the industry data are available only for broad industries, especially outside the manufacturing sector. These equations are not shown here.

We use the individual wage dispersion data for fifteen countries reported in OECD (1996b), taking as our measure of the wage dispersion measure the ratio of wages at the fifth (median) decile to those in the first (lowest) decile. An alternative measure, the ratio of the ninth decile to the median, is highly correlated with this one.

Among the countries reporting these data, the United States showed one of the highest degrees of inequality and Sweden the lowest. The ratio of wages in the ninth decile to those in the first was 4.3 in the United States and 2.1 in Sweden in 1995 (OECD 1996b). Most of the other European countries were closer to Sweden than to the United States in this respect. Much of the wage compression is in the lower half of the distribution; those in the lowest decile of wage earners in the United States earn 37 percent of the median wage while those in the lowest decile in Sweden earn 76 percent of the median wage. As a result, workers in the lowest decile in Sweden earned 60 percent more than those in the lowest decile in the United States in a year in which average real income (per capita GDP adjusted for purchasing power) was more than 25 percent higher in the United States than in Sweden (Björklund and Freeman 1997).

The degree of wage dispersion appears to be a fairly permanent characteristic of a country, reflecting union policies and government regulations. The ranking of countries with respect to wage dispersion has been relatively constant. For example, the correlation between the 1970 and the 1993 wage dispersions for countries with data for both years is 0.85.

To the extent that we accept the idea of worldwide equality of traded goods prices at the producer level (despite the evidence against it in the case of food prices), the factor proportions in the production of tradables should be irrelevant in determining their prices in different countries. International price differences would arise only as goods passed through national distribution systems, from differences in distribution margins and in taxes. The smaller the margin between producer and consumer prices for a tradable product, the smaller the differences among countries in prices should be at the consumer level. The larger the distribution margin, the more prices of tradables should vary across countries positively with per capita incomes, as we know they do (see Kravis and Lipsey 1987, 1988), and negatively with wage dispersion.

If these differences in wage dispersion reflected differences in the dispersion of productivity in the labor force, there would be little or no effect on prices or employment. In an analysis of the Swedish case, Björklund and Freeman (1997) concluded that wage compression in Sweden did not reflect the productivity or education of the workforce. Edin and Topel (1997) reached the same conclusion and attributed wage compression in Sweden to the egalitarian goals of Swedish unions and central wage negotiations in a highly regulated labor market.

The OECD (1996b) study finds strong negative correlations across countries between the incidence of low pay and both the degree of collective-bargaining coverage and unemployment benefit replacement rates. These relations suggest that differences in wage structure probably reflect differences in wage policy.

Björklund and Freeman (1997, 67) suggest that, "if low-skill workers are paid more . . . than they would be paid in a more market-driven system of wage setting, someone must foot the bill for the higher wages of those workers." One of the questions asked here, in effect, is whether that someone is domestic consumers.

The limitation to fourteen or fifteen countries means that we are always somewhat short of degrees of freedom for comparisons across countries in any single year. We try to overcome this difficulty by pooling data across years and across industries, where that is possible.

15.1.2 Measures of Price Levels

Data on price levels originate in the benchmark-year surveys of the UN International Comparison Program (ICP), covering 1970, 1973, 1975, 1980, 1985, 1990, and 1993. The history of the program is summarized in Kravis and Lipsey (1991). GDP and other measures from the ICP for many countries are extrapolated to other years in a series of calculations called *Penn World Tables* by Robert Summers and Alan Heston (1991). The most recent of these, which is used here, is version 5.6. Annual price levels for foods for 1979–90 have been estimated by extrapolation from 1985 in Lipsey and Swedenborg (1996). The OECD publishes annual estimates of GDP price levels in its national accounts volumes. Detailed price data for 1970 and 1975 for over 150 categories and summary measures for 1973 appear in Kravis et al. (1975) and in Kravis, Heston, and Summers (1978, 1982). Price data for OECD countries, at various levels of detail, are from OECD (1987, 1992, 1995) and Ward (1985).

Unfortunately, the weighting systems and index number formulas differ from one data set to another. The three earlier data sets are based on worldwide final purchase weights, and the indexes are constructed using the Geary-Khamis method. The OECD data are based on the final purchase weights of the OECD countries, and those for 1990 and 1993 use the EKS formula. We have not yet learned how much these differences in method affect our results.

15.2 Explaining Price Levels

15.2.1 GDP Price Levels

If our hypothesis about the effect of wage dispersion is correct, and if service industries are typically intensive in the use of unskilled labor, we would expect that GDP price levels would be associated negatively, across countries, with wage dispersion. We test that proposition using the three-year averages of national price levels from Lipsey and Swedenborg (1996), with the results shown in table 15.1. The independent variables are the ones used in the earlier paper—real GDP per capita, the ratio of indirect taxes to GDP, and the net producer subsidy equivalent (NPSE), a measure of protection on foods—to which we have added here wage dispersion and a measure of the deviation of

Table 15.1   **Equations Relating GDP Price Levels to Wage Dispersion and Other Variables (PL = F[RGDPC, INDT, NPSE, XRR, DISP]; 15 OECD countries,[a] 1979–90)**

Period	Constant Term	RGDPC	INDT	NPSE	XRR	DISP	Adj. R^2	Prob F
1979–81	126.39	.57	2.52	.41	−1.18	−73.58	.812	.0007
	(2.66)	(2.28)	(2.92)	(2.00)	(2.11)	(3.67)		
1982–84	64.48	.65	1.36	.69	2.03	−45.01	.931	.0001
	(2.69)	(6.47)	(2.65)	(6.12)	(8.02)	(3.87)		
1985–87	66.43	.32	1.23	.40	1.53	−20.36	.733	.003
	(1.31)	(.72)	(1.23)	(1.48)	(1.38)	(1.74)		
1988–90	68.28	.56	.36	.45	2.21	−25.23	.709	.004
	(2.01)	(2.49)	(.38)	(2.94)	(1.67)	(1.63)		

Source: Lipsey and Swedenborg (1996), appendix table 15A.1 of this paper, and procedures described there for exchange rates.

Note: PL = GDP at exchange rates divided by GDP at PPP (OECD average = 100). RGDPC = real GDP per capita at international prices. INDT = indirect taxes as a percentage of GDP. NPSE = net producer subsidy equivalent on foods. DISP = wage dispersion, ratio of median wage to wage at lowest decile. XRR = deviation of the exchange rate from 1979–93 trend value. *t*-statistics are given in parentheses.

[a]Australia, Austria, Belgium, Canada, Denmark, France, Germany, Italy, Japan, the Netherlands, Norway, Portugal, Sweden, the United Kingdom, and the United States.

each country's exchange rate from its trend over the period 1979–93. We expect the coefficients of all these variables except wage dispersion to have positive signs.

The coefficient for wage dispersion was consistently negative, as we expected, and statistically significant in the first two periods. The higher the degree of wage dispersion, the lower the overall price level. As in our earlier study, higher per capita GDP, indirect taxes, and protection of agricultural products were all associated with higher GDP price levels. In addition, positive deviations of the value of a country's currency from its long-term trend also usually produced higher price levels, although the first period was an exception.

15.2.2   Price Levels for Broad Product Groups

The ICP groups its more than 150 detailed categories of consumption and fixed investment into eleven broad groups that are reasonably consistent since the first ICP report for 1970. We can use these groups by pooling results for six scattered years to test for effects of wage dispersion. At the highly tradable end of the range we cover foods, beverages, and tobacco, clothing and footwear, and producer durables. At the other end of the spectrum, among the least tradable, we have rent, fuel, and power, medical and health care, education, recreation, and culture, construction, and government consumption, mainly compensation of government employees. For each of these groups, we have observations for all the OECD countries in 1985, 1990, and 1993 and smaller

Table 15.2   **Results of Equations Explaining Price Levels for Broad Final Product Groups by Wage Dispersion and per Capita GDP, 1970, 1973, 1975, 1985, 1990, and 1993 Pooled (PL = F[DISP, CGDPX])**

	Intercept	CGDPX	DISP	Adj. R^2	Prob F
Clothing and footwear	1.13	17.49	−.72	.145	.0027
	(3.2)	(2.9)	(3.5)		
Collective consumption by government	.79	9.71	−.32	.088	.0207
	(3.6)	(2.6)	(2.5)		
Construction	.72	14.16	−.45	.122	.0061
	(2.7)	(3.1)	(2.9)		
Education, recreation, and culture	.71	12.95	−.39	.198	.0004
	(3.7)	(4.0)	(3.6)		
Food, beverages, and tobacco	1.12	12.92	−.55	.122	.0063
	(3.8)	(2.6)	(3.2)		
Gross rent, fuel and power	.72	7.57	−.18	.030	.1451
	(3.2)	(2.0)	(1.4)		
Household equipment and operation	1.01	8.76	−.33	.065	.0449
	(4.3)	(2.2)	(2.4)		
Machinery and equipment	1.47	7.22	−.47	.090	.0193
	(5.2)	(1.5)	(2.9)		
Medical and health care	−.33	16.73	−.16	.408	.0001
	(2.1)	(6.2)	(1.7)		
Miscellaneous goods and services	.75	22.09	−.77	.237	.0001
	(2.4)	(4.2)	(4.3)		
Transport and communication	1.85	8.78	−.71	.298	.0001
	(8.0)	(2.2)	(5.3)		

Source: OECD (1996a, 1996b).

Note: PL = PPP/XR (United States = 1). PPP = purchasing power parities for final expenditure on GDP per U.S. dollar (United States = 1). XR = period average exchange rates (foreign currency per U.S. dollar). DISP = wage dispersion, ratio of median wage to wage at lowest decile. CGDP = GDP per capita at current prices and current PPPs. CGDPX = index of GDP per capita at current prices and current PPPs where United States = 100 each year. *t*-statistics are given in parentheses.

numbers of countries in 1970, 1973, and 1975. The results of the analysis are shown in table 15.2.

For only one of the eleven groups, gross rent, fuel, and power, did our equation, using only per capita income and wage dispersion as independent variables, fail to provide a significant explanation of price levels. All the coefficients for per capita income were positive, and all but one were statistically significant at conventional levels. All the coefficients for wage dispersion were negative, and the only ones for which wage dispersion was not significant were gross rent, fuel, and power and medical and health care. In the former case, one reason may be that the real estate industry and the petroleum and power-generation industries are all highly capital intensive. The housing sector is also subject to rent controls and subsidies in some countries, and taxes on fuel vary widely. In the latter case, the high degree of subsidization of consumption and the variance in the extent of subsidization across countries may blur the effects of other variables.

One might have expected that the equations would explain prices of services better than those of goods because goods are more tradable. There are no obvious differences among these groups attributable to that distinction; goods prices seem as well explained as service prices. Furthermore, the size of the coefficients does not seem to differ consistently between goods and services. However, these groups are too broad and too mixed in content to permit a reliable judgment. That issue is investigated further below, using detailed categories that can be more clearly defined as mostly goods or mostly services. Adding the variable used above to represent deviations of exchange rates from their trend values has virtually no effect on these equations, as can be seen in table 15.3. All the coefficients for the exchange rate deviation are positive, as we expect, but the addition of the variable reduces the degree of explanation almost as often as it increases it.

The previous conclusion remains undisturbed. Price levels for broad groups of final products are related positively to per capita income and negatively to wage dispersion, and the relations hold for goods as well as services and for capital goods as well as consumption goods.

15.2.3   Individual Product and Service Price Levels

To analyze these relations at the detailed product level, we concentrate on the three years (1985, 1990, and 1993) for which the product classification is the same. The most detailed breakdown of goods and services in the OECD reports on the ICP consists of almost 200 items, of which 143 are goods and 46 are services.

One difficulty in explaining service industry price levels is that some services are delivered free to consumers or are heavily subsidized. Major examples are services provided by the government rather than by private firms, such as education and medical services in most countries. In the earlier rounds of the ICP, an attempt was made to calculate the full cost of these services rather than the subsidized price, but it is not clear how successful the effort was. In any case, the effort was abandoned after 1975.

We begin by summarizing the results in terms of the signs of the coefficients for wage dispersion, per capita income, and exchange rate deviations in two ways. One is for equations with a significant degree of explanation of price levels, which we define as prob $F < .05$. The other is for all equations, regardless of the significance of the equations as explanations of price levels. Equations for goods and for services, pooling data for 1985, 1990, and 1993, are the basis for table 15.4.

As might be expected, the proportion of statistically significant equations was higher for services than for goods. Half the equations for services were significant, as compared with about 40 percent for goods. Among these significant equations, the coefficients of wage dispersion, per capita GDP, and the

Table 15.3   Results of Equations Explaining Price Levels for Broad Final
Product Groups by Wage Dispersion, Exchange Rate Residuals,
and per Capita GDP, 1970, 1973, 1975, 1985, 1990, and 1993
Pooled (PL = F[DISP, CGDPX, XRR])

	Intercept	CGDPX	DISP	XRR	Adj. R^2	Prob F
Clothing and footwear	1.13	18.45	−.77	.71	.158	.0033
	(3.2)	(3.1)	(3.7)	(1.4)		
Collective consumption by government	.79	10.24	−.35	.39	.097	.0253
	(3.6)	(2.8)	(2.7)	(1.3)		
Construction	.72	14.48	−.47	.23	.113	.0149
	(2.7)	(3.1)	(2.9)	(.6)		
Education, recreation, and culture	.71	13.52	−.42	.42	.217	.0004
	(3.8)	(4.2)	(3.8)	(1.6)		
Food, beverages, and tobacco	1.12	13.69	−.58	.57	.134	.0076
	(3.9)	(2.8)	(3.4)	(1.4)		
Gross rent, fuel and power	.72	7.92	−.20	.27	.025	.2104
	(3.2)	(2.1)	(1.5)	(.8)		
Household equipment and operation	1.01	9.22	−.35	.35	.066	.0650
	(4.3)	(2.3)	(2.5)	(1.0)		
Machinery and equipment	1.47	8.00	−.51	.58	.106	.0188
	(5.3)	(1.7)	(3.1)	(1.5)		
Medical and health care	−.33	16.68	−.16	−.04	.399	.0001
	(2.1)	(6.1)	(1.7)	(.2)		
Miscellaneous goods and services	.75	22.36	−.78	.20	.227	.0003
	(2.4)	(4.2)	(4.3)	(.4)		
Transport and communication	1.85	8.92	−.71	.11	.287	.0001
	(7.9)	(2.2)	(5.2)	(.3)		

Source: OECD (1996a, 1996b), appendix table 15A.1 of this paper, and procedures described
there for exchange rates.

Note: PL = PPP/XR (United States = 1). PPP = purchasing power parities for final expenditure
on GDP per U.S. dollar (United States = 1). XR = period average exchange rates (foreign currency per U.S. dollar). DISP = wage dispersion, ratio of median wage to wage at lowest decile.
CGDP = GDP per capita. CGDPX = index of GDP per capita at current prices and current PPPs
where United States = 100 each year. XRR = deviation of exchange rate from 1970–93 trend
value. *t*-statistics are given in parentheses.

exchange rate deviation overwhelmingly had the expected signs. The coefficients with *t*-values of two or above were almost unanimous in showing positive effects for per capita GDP and negative coefficients for wage dispersion,
but the exchange rate deviation was significant in only one case among services. If we tally the results from all equations, regardless of the *F*-test indications, we again find that the signs of the coefficients were as hypothesized, to
a high degree, and again the statistically significant coefficients were almost
unanimous. Over half the coefficients for per capita GDP were significant in
service-price-level equations but less than a third in equations for goods price
levels. The exchange rate deviation was significant in only a few goods-price-
level equations and in only one service-price equation. For wage dispersion,
the variable of most interest to us, over half the coefficients in goods and in

Table 15.4   **Signs of Coefficients for Wage Dispersion, per Capita Income Index, and Exchange Rate Deviation in Equations Explaining Detailed Goods and Services Price Levels, 1985, 1990, and 1993, Pooled**

		Coefficients for:	
	Wage Dispersion	Per Capita GDP Index	Exchange Rate Residuals
		Equations with Prob $F < 0.05$	
Goods			
Negative	56	9	4
	(52)	(2)	(0)
Positive	2	49	54
	(1)	(34)	(16)
Total	58	58	58
	(53)	(36)	(16)
Services			
Negative	21	—	3
	(15)		(0)
Positive	1	22	19
	(0)	(20)	(1)
Total	22	22	22
	(15)	(20)	(1)
		All Equations	
Goods			
Negative	137	21	10
	(75)	(2)	(0)
Positive	7	123	134
	(1)	(42)	(20)
Total	144	144	144
	(76)	(44)	(20)
Services			
Negative	43	1	10
	(23)	(0)	(0)
Positive	1	43	34
	(0)	(25)	(1)
Total	44	44	44
	(23)	(25)	(1)

Source: Appendix table 15A.2.
Note: Figures in parentheses are number of coefficients with $t \geq 2$.

services were significant. Thus, among the three variables that we use to explain product price levels, wage dispersion accounts for the largest number of significant coefficients.

Another way of summarizing the results is by the size of the coefficients for the three variables. The averages of the coefficients for which t-statistics were above one and those for which they were above two are shown in table 15.5.

Table 15.5   Averages of Coefficients for Wage Dispersion, per Capita Income Index, and Exchange Rate Deviation in Equations Explaining Detailed Goods and Services Price Levels, 1985, 1990, and 1993, Pooled

	Average Coefficients for:		
	Wage Dispersion	Per Capita GDP Index	Exchange Rate Deviations
	Coefficients with t-Statistics ≥ 2		
Goods	−.86	13.34	1.36
Services	−1.03	15.59	.87
	Coefficients with t-Statistics ≥ 1		
Goods	−.73	12.08	1.04
Services	−.84	14.58	.77

Source: Appendix table 15A.2

The influence of wage dispersion on price levels is larger, on average, for services than for goods, as we expect, and the same is true for the effect of per capita income. More surprising, the exchange rate deviation has a larger effect on goods prices than on prices for services, despite the presumption that goods are more tradable and therefore more subject to international arbitrage that would prevent exchange rate fluctuations from affecting prices calculated in a common currency. Thus, we can explain price levels more frequently for services than for goods, presumably because price differences are not arbitraged away by trade, and, in those cases where these variables do explain price levels, the effects are larger for services than for goods, at least the effects of wage dispersion and per capita income.

One reason for failures to explain some price levels well is that we are attempting to explain all of them by the same limited set of variables when there must be particular factors that affect individual products, such as specific taxation or subsidy elements in their prices. It is therefore not surprising that, among the six items in alcoholic beverages and tobacco products, price levels for only one are explained to a significant degree (appendix table 15A.2). In medical and health care, another group where we would expect to find a variety of subsidy and payment arrangements, eight of sixteen equations were significant but only four coefficients for wage dispersion. Two other items for which we could not explain price levels were telephone and related services and education fees, neither of which is a surprise, but the equation for postal services and its coefficient for wage dispersion were significant, which is a surprise.

If we think of the wage dispersion as being a result of conscious policy, we can ask how much of a difference in prices of typical goods and services would be implied by a change in the degree of dispersion. The average wage dispersion in the fifteen countries in 1993 was 1.6 (appendix table 15A.1), meaning that the median wage was 60 percent above the lowest decile. The range was from 1.3 to 2.3. The detailed product equations imply that an increase of 0.3 in dispersion, which would raise the dispersion in the country with the lowest to the OECD average, would lower the price of the typical good or service by about a quarter. That would be roughly sufficient to lower the Swedish price level, for example, to the OECD average.

15.3   Conclusions

It seems safe to conclude that there is a pervasive relation between wage dispersion and country price levels and that it applies to both goods and services. It applies more frequently to services, and, where it does apply, the effect of wage dispersion is larger for services than for goods. The higher the degree of wage dispersion, at least at the low end of the wage scale, between the lowest-paid workers and the median, the lower is the country's price level. A compressed wage structure is associated with relatively high prices for both goods and services. This effect is in addition to the association between high per capita income and high price levels and to the effect of unusually high or low levels of the exchange value of a country's currency. The relation of prices to wage dispersion seems even a little more consistent than the relation to the other two variables.

Although it seems reasonable to attribute the differences in price levels at least partly to wage dispersion, along with per capita income and exchange rate fluctuations, there remains the possibility that there are some other common features of countries that follow policies to reduce wage dispersion that also produce high prices for goods and services.

We began our investigation on the assumption that the sources of international price differences would be found mainly in the service sector of the economy because arbitrage would tend to reduce international differences in goods prices. There is plenty of evidence that international differences in service prices are larger than differences in goods prices, as has been pointed out in many studies of international price level differences, such as Kravis, Heston, and Summers (1982), Kravis and Lipsey (1983, 1987, 1988), and Bhagwati (1984), among others. Given the similarity in coefficients between goods and services equations here, despite the more frequent indications of significant effects in services equations, it would reinforce our explanation of price levels if we found that the relation was stronger for products that are relatively labor intensive and particularly for those intensive in the use of unskilled labor in production. The same would be true if we found the relation particularly strong for products requiring heavy distribution costs between the original producers and consumers. Both of these are issues that we intend to explore further.

To investigate the role of factor intensities, particularly the role of the labor intensity of production, it would be necessary to match these price levels for individual goods and services to data available only by industry on labor input per unit of output, from input-output accounts or industrial census data, a difficult problem even for one country. If we do not wish to assume identical factor intensities across countries for individual industries, it would be desirable to collect data from several countries. Observed factor intensities are likely to differ among countries. If there is any possibility of substitution in response to factor price differences, factor intensities measured in physical terms will differ. Factor intensities measured in value terms will also differ unless all elasticities of substitution are unitary. If no factor substitution is possible, factor intensities in an industry, measured in physical terms, will be identical in all countries, but factor intensities in value terms will vary with factor prices.

If we derive factor intensities from census data rather than from input-output data, it would be important to take account of the wedges between the producer prices in industry data and prices paid by final purchasers, represented in our country-price-level data. There are some data from the United States, such as those published by the U.S. Department of Commerce (1994a, table C), that show inputs of wholesale and retail trade and transportation that are incorporated into final demand at purchasers' prices.

The effect of wage dispersion on prices presumably depends not only on labor intensity but particularly on intensity in the use of unskilled labor. Data would be available only by industry, at best, and even these are probably available for very detailed industries only for the United States. Average wage levels across industries give some indication of average skill levels, but a more appropriate unskilled labor intensity would be the input of labor in the low-skill occupation classes or the input of labor with low education levels, as reported in U.S. decennial census data or the *Current Population Reports.*

Another variable possibly worth exploring is the tradability of different products. To some extent that may be encompassed by the transportation margin already referred to, but there may be other factors that determine the extent of trade. With few exceptions, consumer services are rarely traded across international borders, but, for goods, tradability may determine how much arbitrage takes place to reduce international price differences. Tradability might be measured by ratios of world trade to world production (if they could be assembled) or by similar ratios from U.S. input-output tables.

An extension of the analysis of the effects of egalitarian wage policy would be to think of it as the equivalent of a tax levied on consumers of the goods and services for which prices are raised by the policy. Then it would be of interest to calculate the incidence of the tax as related to the income levels and family characteristics of consumers of the various goods and services.

Appendix

Table 15A.1   Data for Independent Variables Used in the Regressions

	Wage Dispersion	Exchange Rate Residuals	GDP per Capita (United States = 100 each year)
1, 1970, Belgium	1.39	−6.350	65.13
2, 1970, France	1.61	−5.103	71.25
3, 1970, Germany	1.47	−.530	72.84
4, 1970, Italy	1.49	11.690	58.34
5, 1970, Japan	1.59	16.857	57.47
6, 1970, Netherlands	1.33	−.360	71.68
7, 1970, United Kingdom	1.47	11.860	64.54
8, 1970, United States	2.44	7.487	100.00
1, 1973, Belgium	1.39	−3.280	67.74
2, 1973, France	1.61	2.358	72.89
3, 1973, Germany	1.47	−1.837	72.93
4, 1973, Italy	1.49	11.043	56.66
5, 1973, Japan	1.59	6.525	61.04
6, 1973, Netherlands	1.33	−3.049	71.36
7, 1973, United Kingdom	1.47	−.201	64.69
8, 1973, United States	2.44	−8.890	100.00
1, 1975, Belgium	1.39	−.567	71.37
2, 1975, Denmark	1.41	3.643	75.81
3, 1975, France	1.64	7.666	75.72
4, 1975, Germany	1.47	−2.376	75.41
5, 1975, Italy	1.49	3.944	59.59
6, 1975, Japan	1.59	−9.030	62.14
7, 1975, Netherlands	1.33	−.508	76.32
8, 1975, United Kingdom	1.43	−7.242	65.64
9, 1975, United States	2.44	−11.142	100.00
1, 1985, Austria	1.57	−3.489	72.89
2, 1985, Australia	1.61	10.334	73.04
3, 1985, Belgium	1.40	−9.002	70.84
4, 1985, Canada	2.40	24.032	84.67
5, 1985, Denmark	1.42	−7.244	70.47
6, 1985, France	1.41	−7.795	77.16
7, 1985, Germany	1.61	−5.067	76.42
8, 1985, Italy	1.44	−10.547	69.79
9, 1985, Japan	1.61	.196	71.91
10, 1985, Netherlands	1.55	−5.804	70.29
11, 1985, Norway	1.45	6.397	82.51
12, 1985, Portugal	1.56	−24.560	35.83
13, 1985, Sweden	1.35	−1.619	77.52
14, 1985, United Kingdom	1.64	4.554	67.97
15, 1985, United States	2.03	42.602	100.00

(continued)

Table 15A.1   (continued)

	Wage Dispersion	Exchange Rate Residuals	GDP per Capita (United States = 100 each year)
1, 1990, Austria	1.67	.242	75.68
2, 1990, Australia	1.68	−4.093	72.57
3, 1990, Belgium	1.40	.780	74.29
4, 1990, Canada	2.28	−3.744	83.33
5, 1990, Denmark	1.38	2.313	75.33
6, 1990, France	1.62	1.975	78.97
7, 1990, Germany	1.40	.087	72.80
8, 1990, Italy	1.43	10.707	74.09
9, 1990, Japan	1.65	−16.691	80.11
10, 1990, Netherlands	1.57	1.049	72.65
11, 1990, Norway	1.32	−4.357	79.65
12, 1990, Portugal	1.72	−.42	42.66
13, 1990, Sweden	1.33	.568	77.41
14, 1990, United Kingdom	1.72	1.451	72.27
15, 1990, United States	2.02	−13.026	100.00
1, 1993, Austria	1.67	−4.320	79.03
2, 1993, Australia	1.64	−6.243	71.47
3, 1993, Belgium	1.40	−.150	79.68
4, 1993, Canada	2.26	−5.610	79.64
5, 1993, Denmark	1.38	3.247	78.98
6, 1993, France	1.61	5.437	77.07
7, 1993, Germany	1.37	−1.220	76.20
8, 1993, Italy	1.60	7.060	73.02
9, 1993, Japan	1.64	20.977	83.62
10, 1993, Netherlands	1.54	−1.640	73.16
11, 1993, Norway	1.32	−10.410	87.94
12, 1993, Portugal	1.75	23.870	48.64
13, 1993, Sweden	1.36	−13.320	69.37
14, 1993, United Kingdom	1.74	−4.610	69.86
15, 1993, United States	2.06	−9.403	100.00

Source: GDP per capita with United States = 100 for each year from OECD (1996a, pt. 7, table 2). Wage dispersion is ratio of median to lowest decile, from OECD (1996b). Exchange rate residuals are residuals from trends in exchange rates. Exchange rates in dollars per unit of currency were taken from OECD (1996a) by dividing GDP in own currency by GDP in U.S. dollars. They were put in terms of relatives (1970–93 = 100) and converted to indexes with OECD averages for each year set to 100. Simple linear trends were then fitted to each country's index.

Table 15A.2   Results for Individual Goods (G) and Services (S)

	DISP	t-Stat.	CGDPX	t-Stat.	XRR	t-Stat.	Adj. R^2	Prob > F
Food, beverages, and tobacco								
G Food and beverages	−.69	2.7	13.88	2.1	.77	.9	.210	.0345
G Rice	−.73	2.9	13.26	2.5	.70	1.3	.196	.0101
G Flour and other cereals	−.37	.8	16.31	1.7	1.47	1.5	.065	.1382
G Bread	−.62	2.4	17.06	3.1	.59	1.0	.203	.0087
G Other bakery products	−.64	2.0	13.96	2.0	1.40	2.0	.150	.0270
G Pasta products	−.76	2.6	14.26	2.2	.68	1.0	.149	.0274
G Other cereal products	−.60	2.2	8.29	1.4	.83	1.4	.090	.0880
G Fresh, frozen, and chilled beef	−1.32	2.5	13.66	1.2	1.17	1.0	.083	.0999
G Fresh, frozen, and chilled veal	−.27	.7	14.22	1.7	.51	.6	.013	.3328
G Fresh, frozen, and chilled pork	−.82	3.1	15.60	2.8	.67	1.1	.227	.0050
G Fresh etc. lamb, mutton, and goat	−.74	3.4	13.59	2.9	.08	.2	.249	.0030
G Fresh, frozen, and chilled poultry	−1.99	5.0	23.87	2.8	.39	.4	.379	.0001
G Delicatessen	−1.35	3.6	17.81	2.2	1.07	1.2	.227	.0050
G Other meat preparations, extracts	−.57	1.4	9.85	1.1	.50	.5	−.009	.4596
G Other fresh, frozen, chilled meat	−1.39	3.2	4.50	.4	1.63	1.6	.172	.0186
G Fresh, frozen, or deep-frozen fish	−.38	2.6	9.84	3.1	.32	1.0	.211	.0072
G Dried, smoked, or salted fish	−.24	1.5	3.68	1.0	.45	1.2	.021	.2928
G Fresh, frozen, deep-frozen seafood	−.43	1.2	9.72	1.3	.55	.7	.001	.3983
G Preserved or processed fish & seafood	−.35	1.8	9.39	2.2	.69	1.6	.126	.0438
G Fresh, pasteurized, sterilized milk	−.05	.2	9.42	1.9	.42	.8	.046	.1927
G Condensed, evaporated, powdered milk	−.46	1.5	.55	.1	.79	1.2	.001	.3984
G Other milk products excluding cheese	.10	.4	7.27	1.1	.74	1.2	.026	.2711
G Processed and unprocessed cheese	−.56	1.4	5.42	.6	1.60	1.8	.041	.2090
G Eggs and egg products	−1.37	4.2	14.82	2.1	.31	.4	.283	.0013
G Butter	−.07	.3	.54	.1	.75	1.2	−.036	.6676
G Margarine	−.34	1.4	6.95	1.3	.70	1.2	.028	.2580
G Edible oils	−.98	2.4	24.80	2.9	−.79	.9	.189	.0117
G Other animal and vegetable fats	−.98	3.2	12.01	1.8	.33	.5	.171	.0173
G Fresh fruit	−.50	2.4	12.57	2.7	.65	1.4	.186	.0125
G Dried fruit and nuts	−.16	.8	5.97	1.4	.13	.3	−.014	.4926
G Frozen and preserved fruit and juices	−.53	2.1	−1.48	.3	1.65	2.8	.148	.0281
G Fresh vegetables	−.93	3.7	15.99	2.9	.91	1.6	.283	.0013

(continued)

	DISP	t-Stat.	CGDPX	t-Stat.	XRR	t-Stat.	Adj. R^2	Prob > F
G Dried vegetables	−2.25	2.1	35.20	1.5	1.87	.8	.065	.1369
G Frozen vegetables	−.95	3.4	13.68	2.3	1.23	2.0	.245	.0033
G Preserved vegetables, juices, soups	−1.08	3.3	−.25	.0	1.90	2.6	.221	.0057
G Potatoes and other tuber vegetables	−.03	.1	13.55	2.5	.35	.6	.099	.0742
G Potato products	−.71	2.2	8.91	1.3	.33	.5	.057	.1588
G Raw and refined sugar	−.39	2.3	5.70	1.5	.50	1.3	.094	.0810
G Coffee and instant coffee	−.47	1.8	3.67	.7	1.02	1.8	.057	.1597
G Tea and other infusions	−1.31	2.6	3.31	.3	1.87	1.6	.107	.0642
G Cocoa excluding cocoa preparations	−.18	.4	6.85	.7	1.38	1.3	−.010	.4641
G Jams, jellies, honey, and syrups	−.70	2.2	7.54	1.1	1.58	2.2	.123	.0467
G Chocolate and cocoa preparations	−.13	.6	1.64	.3	.52	1.0	−.044	.7329
G Confectionery	−.60	2.0	11.13	1.7	.20	.3	.058	.1576
G Edible ice and ice cream	−.91	2.0	2.86	.3	.09	.1	.029	.2545
G Salt, spices, sauces, condiments	−.46	1.2	13.55	1.6	.43	.5	.010	.3456
G Mineral water	−.30	.6	20.69	2.1	.20	.2	.035	.2332
G Other soft drinks nec	−.73	2.0	8.66	1.1	.99	1.2	.049	.1831
G Spirits and liqueurs	−1.44	2.9	23.86	2.2	.05	.0	.163	.0207
G Wine (not fortified or sparkling)	−.05	.2	16.50	3.7	−.08	.2	.220	.0059
G Beer	−.17	.5	17.84	2.7	.07	.1	.099	.0734
G Other wines and alcoholic beverages	−1.26	1.7	23.47	1.5	−.04	.0	.026	.2676
G Cigarettes	−.57	1.8	16.11	2.3	−.25	.3	.094	.0811
G Other tobacco products	.07	.2	9.48	1.2	−.66	.8	−.030	.6179
Clothing and footwear								
G Men's clothing	−.60	3.0	4.82	1.1	.97	2.2	.179	.0145
G Ladies' clothing	−.60	2.6	8.89	1.8	.90	1.7	.147	.0287
G Children's clothing	−.66	2.3	−3.04	.5	1.65	2.6	.149	.0279
G Infant's clothing	−1.36	1.7	−3.31	.2	2.01	1.1	.018	.3064
G Materials, yarns, accessories, etc.	−1.13	4.1	9.11	1.5	1.38	2.2	.284	.0013
S Repair and maintenance of clothing	−1.45	3.4	15.26	1.7	1.05	1.1	.191	.0114
G Men's footwear	−.53	2.8	10.23	2.5	.77	1.8	.209	.0075
G Ladies' footwear	−.47	1.4	12.03	1.6	1.25	1.6	.078	.1098
G Children's and infant's footwear	−.65	1.5	8.44	.9	2.63	2.7	.135	.0370
S Repairs to footwear	−.42	2.7	16.16	4.9	.38	1.1	.383	.0001
Gross rent, fuel and power								
S Rents of tenants	−.14	.8	19.84	5.1	−.08	.2	.370	.0001
S Imputed rents of owner-occupiers	−.34	1.8	20.53	5.0	.06	.1	.357	.0002

Table 15A.2 (continued)

	DISP	t-Stat.	CGDPX	t-Stat.	XRR	t-Stat.	Adj. R^2	Prob > F
S Repair and maintenance of housing	−.74	3.0	16.51	3.1	.82	1.5	.250	.0029
S Sanitary services and water charges	−.84	1.8	4.05	.4	.21	.2	.010	.3461
S Electricity	−.53	2.1	−4.31	.8	.82	1.4	.081	.1035
S Town gas and natural gas	−1.50	3.2	7.39	.7	.79	.8	.158	.0249
G Liquefied petroleum gas	−1.94	2.2	32.40	1.7	1.05	.5	.081	.1027
G Liquid fuels for heating and lighting	−.60	1.9	2.19	.3	.91	1.3	.032	.2435
G Coal, coke, and other solid fuels	−1.92	2.0	31.87	1.5	1.68	.8	.056	.1615
G Water, electricity, gas, and fuel	−.70	3.1	7.09	1.6	1.84	3.2	.410	.0010
Household equipment and operation								
G Furniture and fixtures	−.32	1.1	3.59	.6	1.03	1.5	.004	.3809
G Carpets and other floor coverings	−.17	.7	3.80	.8	.77	1.5	.003	.3856
S Repair of furniture, floor coverings	−.69	2.0	14.06	1.9	.34	.4	.073	.1232
G Household textiles, other furnishings	−.23	.9	7.81	1.4	.66	1.1	.017	.3110
S Repair of houshold textiles etc.	−.89	3.2	14.33	2.3	.76	1.2	.214	.0085
G Refrigerators and freezers	−.36	1.2	6.05	.9	.83	1.2	−.002	.4146
G Washing machines, dryers, dishwashers	−.67	2.0	2.00	.3	1.32	1.7	.059	.1542
G Cookers, hobs, and ovens	−.57	1.9	−10.95	1.7	.86	1.3	.126	.0438
G Heaters and air-conditioners	−.30	.8	3.72	.4	−.22	.2	−.056	.8445
G Vacuum cleaners, polishers, etc.	.36	2.2	6.54	1.8	.50	1.3	.245	.0033
G Other major household appliances	−1.08	2.9	2.74	.3	1.40	1.7	.141	.0328
S Repair of major household appliances	−.32	1.0	12.98	1.8	−.07	.1	.013	.3308
G Glassware and tableware	−.21	.6	10.75	1.5	.57	.7	.001	.3952
G Cutlery and silverware	−1.40	2.9	28.10	2.7	.24	.2	.189	.0119
G Motorless kitchen and domestic utensils	−.40	1.4	12.37	2.0	.12	.2	.045	.1955
G Motorless garden appliances	−.36	.9	5.70	.7	.83	.9	−.032	.6360
G Electric bulbs, wires, plugs, etc.	−.24	1.2	9.21	2.0	.64	1.3	.086	.0941
S Repair of glassware, tableware, etc.	−1.31	3.3	25.21	3.0	−.11	.1	.256	.0033
G Cleaning and maintenance products	−.86	3.1	13.46	2.2	.71	1.1	.189	.0118
G Other nondurable household goods	−.69	2.0	9.98	1.3	.97	1.2	.058	.1563
S Laundry and dry cleaning	−1.13	3.6	7.97	1.2	.41	.6	.203	.0086

(continued)

Table 15A.2   (continued)

	DISP	t-Stat.	CGDPX	t-Stat.	XRR	t-Stat.	Adj. R^2	Prob > F
S Other household services	−.29	1.2	13.15	2.5	.16	.3	.087	.1012
S Domestic services	−.53	1.7	19.69	3.0	−.19	.3	.146	.0293
Medical and health care								
S Medical and health care	−.07	.7	9.65	4.6	.06	.3	.324	.0005
G Drugs and medical preparations	.19	1.0	7.38	1.4	−.41	.6	.095	.1496
G Other medical supplies	−.54	1.9	15.09	2.4	.50	.8	.115	.0549
G Spectacle lenses and contact lenses	−.49	2.0	10.45	1.9	.54	1.0	.086	.0952
G Orthopedic and therapeutic appliances	.00	.0	.16	.0	.03	.1	−.081	.9997
S Services of general practitioners	−.09	.7	11.12	3.4	.17	.6	.178	.0165
S Services of specialists	−.24	1.6	8.62	2.5	.21	.6	.111	.0626
S Services of dentists	−.04	.3	5.90	1.6	.08	.2	−.004	.4274
S Services of nurses	−.14	.6	4.60	.9	−.14	.3	−.053	.8082
S Services of other practitioners	−.94	2.5	21.96	2.7	.15	.2	.158	.0227
S Medical analyses	−.22	.8	9.59	1.7	.04	.1	.001	.3975
S Medical staff	.10	1.4	11.82	7.4	.08	.5	.625	.0001
S Nonmedical staff	−.07	.7	12.54	5.9	.14	.6	.461	.0001
G Pharmaceutical products	.22	1.3	9.32	2.7	−.05	.1	.177	.0152
G Therapeutical equipment	−.35	2.0	10.26	3.0	1.13	2.5	.344	.0035
G Other equipment	−1.36	4.6	11.55	1.5	−.51	.5	.415	.0011
Transport, communication								
G Passenger vehicles	−.50	2.0	−1.80	.3	.58	1.1	.047	.1891
G Motorcycles and bicycles	−.80	4.0	3.20	.7	.13	.3	.250	.0029
G Tyres, tubes, parts, accessories	−.28	1.1	1.28	.2	1.07	1.9	.027	.2654
S Maintenance and repair services	−2.37	2.1	20.88	.9	−.46	.2	.049	.1836
G Motor fuels, oils, and greases	−1.52	4.6	−4.47	.6	1.59	2.1	.339	.0003
G Car hire, driving schools, tolls, etc.	−.98	1.8	15.24	1.1	.98	.8	.013	.3330
S Local by bus, train, tube, tram, taxi	−.51	2.3	16.86	3.4	.12	.2	.215	.0066
S Long distance by coach and rail	−.10	.4	13.41	2.7	.01	.0	.099	.0744
S Long distance by air and sea	−.19	1.4	5.80	2.0	.30	1.0	.070	.1271
S Other purchased transport services	−2.09	2.5	14.33	.8	1.08	.06	.074	.1172
S Postal services	−.71	4.2	10.44	2.9	.87	2.3	.349	.0002
S Telephone, telegraph, telex services	−.04	.2	6.26	1.3	−.20	.4	−.032	.6332
Education, recreation, and culture								
S Recreation, cultural, religious affairs	−.25	2.5	13.28	6.9	.02	.1	.548	.0001
G Radio sets	−.91	3.6	−.09	.0	.44	.8	.212	.0071
G Television sets, video recorders, etc.	−.77	3.3	3.67	.7	.66	1.3	.170	.0178

Table 15A.2 (continued)

	DISP	t-Stat.	CGDPX	t-Stat.	XRR	t-Stat.	Adj. R^2	Prob > F
G Record players, cassette recorders, etc.	−.71	1.1	8.61	.6	1.48	1.0	−.023	.5582
G Cameras and photographic equipment	−.02	.1	−12.42	4.6	.15	.5	.324	.0004
G Other durable recreational goods	−.70	5.8	−5.32	2.0	.79	2.9	.509	.0001
G Records, tapes, cassettes, etc.	−.52	2.0	1.50	.3	.95	1.6	.052	.1721
G Sports goods and camping equipment	−1.08	2.5	.63	.1	1.65	1.7	.106	.0644
G Games, toys, and hobbies	−1.43	2.6	.64	.1	1.72	1.4	.103	.0690
G Films and photographic supplies	−.32	2.0	2.24	.7	−.02	.1	.036	.2278
S Parts and repairs for recreational goods	−.29	1.0	18.08	2.8	−.10	.1	.108	.0622
S Cinemas, stadiums, museums, zoos, etc.	−.17	.9	6.20	1.5	.60	1.4	.050	.1791
G Radio & TV license, rental, subscription	−1.49	4.9	20.89	3.2	.97	1.4	.391	.0001
S Photographic services, services for pets	−1.08	2.1	13.13	1.2	1.61	1.4	.066	.1348
G Books	−.41	1.5	7.35	1.2	1.15	1.9	.073	.1190
G Newspapers and other printed matter	−1.22	4.9	15.77	2.9	.77	1.4	.380	.0001
S Education fees	−.38	.4	13.54	.7	.03	.0	−.063	.9035
Miscellaneous goods and services								
S Hairdressers, beauty parlors, etc.	−.47	2.1	12.95	2.7	.51	1.0	.162	.0210
G Durable toilet articles and repairs	−.79	2.6	10.00	1.5	.42	.6	.100	.0732
G Nondurable toilet articles	−.77	2.9	12.73	2.2	.36	.6	.160	.0219
G Jewelry, watches, and their repair	−.47	1.8	6.67	1.2	.27	.5	.019	.3025
G Travel goods and baggage items	−.71	4.0	−3.36	.9	.64	1.6	.283	.0013
G Goods for babies, personal accessories	−.39	1.4	−.05	.0	1.33	2.1	.052	.1782
G Writing & drawing equipment & supplies	−1.31	4.4	15.90	2.5	.26	.4	.318	.0005
G Flowers, plants, pets, and pet food	−.76	1.3	12.36	1.0	2.50	1.9	.053	.1696
S Restaurants and takeaways	−.83	4.3	8.71	2.1	.30	.7	.288	.0011
S Pubs, cafés, bars, and tearooms	−1.56	4.4	29.25	3.8	.29	.4	.375	.0001
S Staff canteens	−1.24	2.2	26.04	2.1	−.61	.5	.108	.0656
S Hotels and other lodging places	−1.09	2.7	13.47	1.5	.53	.6	.108	.0623
S Charges for financial services nec	−.81	2.1	16.71	1.6	.69	.7	.060	.1600
S Fees for other services nec	−1.86	2.1	28.08	1.5	−.20	.1	.065	.1372

(continued)

Table 15A.2 (continued)

	DISP	*t*-Stat.	CGDPX	*t*-Stat.	XRR	*t*-Stat.	Adj. R^2	Prob > F
Machinery and equipment								
G Structural metal products	−.42	1.1	1.86	.2	1.29	1.6	.002	.3912
G Products of boilermaking	−.53	1.9	8.67	1.4	.12	.2	.041	.2090
G Tools and finished metal goods	−.78	2.5	.75	.1	1.85	2.6	.154	.0249
G Agricultural machinery and tractors	−.12	.7	2.96	.8	.96	2.5	.101	.0707
G Machine tools for metalworking	.09	.5	2.47	.6	.22	.5	−.041	.7144
G Equipment for mining, metallurgy, building, and civil engineering	−.31	2.8	5.13	2.1	.51	2.0	.199	.0094
G Textile machinery	−.56	1.9	2.03	.3	.69	1.0	.021	.2905
G Machinery for food, chemical, and packaging industries	−.21	1.1	.57	.1	1.00	2.4	.072	.1215
G Machinery for working wood, paper; laundry equipment	−.30	.5	−4.98	.4	.71	.5	−.062	.8897
G Other machinery & mechanical equipment	−.21	.7	1.43	.2	.94	1.4	−.023	.5645
G Office and data-processing machines	−1.58	1.0	−14.89	.4	1.59	.4	−.040	.7026
G Precision and optical instruments, photographic equipment	−.16	.8	−2.44	.5	.28	.6	−.045	.7455
G Optical instruments, photographic equipment	−.12	.6	−3.27	.7	.32	.7	−.044	.7279
G Electrical equipment including lamps	−.64	2.0	5.53	.8	1.21	1.7	.072	.1228
G Telecommunication & electrical equipment nec	−.20	1.1	−2.90	.7	1.02	2.5	.082	.1017
G Electronic equipment etc.	−.26	.7	7.35	.9	1.14	1.4	.006	.3670
G Motor vehicles and engines	−.46	1.7	−.92	.2	.98	1.6	.030	.2508
G Boats, steamers, tugs, platforms, rigs	−.53	2.5	−.57	.1	.70	1.5	.098	.0752
G Locomotives, vans, wagons	−.44	1.6	2.42	.4	.79	1.2	.008	.3557
G Aircraft and other aeronautical equipment	−.55	2.6	−.70	.2	.60	1.3	.102	.0705
G Other transport equipment	−.55	2.6	−1.81	.4	.58	1.2	.120	.0589
Construction								
G One-family dwellings	−1.01	4.4	13.40	2.7	.48	.9	.319	.0005
G Multifamily dwellings	−.44	3.6	12.57	4.8	.20	.7	.404	.0001
G Agricultural buildings	−.58	3.0	4.24	1.0	.72	1.7	.153	.0256
G Industrial buildings	−.52	2.8	10.12	2.5	.23	.6	.175	.0159
G Buildings for market services	−.42	2.2	9.80	2.3	.54	1.2	.139	.0340
G Buildings for nonmarket services	−.44	2.2	11.43	2.6	.68	1.5	.169	.0183

Table 15A.2   (continued)

	DISP	t-Stat.	CGDPX	t-Stat.	XRR	t-Stat.	Adj. R^2	Prob > F
G Roads, streets, and highways	−.29	1.7	8.10	2.2	.33	.9	.092	.0847
G Other transport routes and utility lines	−.47	1.5	11.16	1.6	.73	1.0	.045	.1947
G Other civil engineering works	−.12	.4	5.56	.8	.92	1.3	−.002	.4138
G Other products	−.58	3.9	7.95	2.7	.84	2.1	.439	.0005
Collective consumption by government								
S Social security and welfare services	−.22	2.0	13.74	6.4	.13	.6	.501	.0001

References

Bergstrand, Jeffrey H. 1991. Structural determinants of real exchange rates and national price levels: Some empirical evidence. *American Economic Review* 81, no. 1 (March): 325–34.

Bhagwati, Jagdish N. 1984. Why are services cheaper in the poor countries? *Economic Journal* 94, no. 374 (June): 279–86.

Björklund, Anders, and Richard B. Freeman. 1997. Generating equality and eliminating poverty, the Swedish way. In *The welfare state in transition: Reforming the Swedish model,* ed. Richard B. Freeman, Robert Topel, and Birgitta Swedenborg. Chicago: University of Chicago Press.

Clague, Christopher. 1985. A model of real national price levels. *Southern Economic Journal* 51:998–1017.

———. 1986. Determinants of the national price level: Some empirical results. *Review of Economics and Statistics.* 68, no. 2 (May): 320–23.

———. 1993. Why are prices so low in America? *World Economy* 16, no. 5 (September): 601–10.

Edin, Per-Anders, and Robert Topel. 1997. Wage policy and restructuring: The Swedish labor market since 1960. In *The welfare state in transition: Reforming the Swedish model,* ed. Richard B. Freeman, Robert Topel, and Birgitta Swedenborg. Chicago: University of Chicago Press.

Falvey, Rodney E., and Norman Gemmell. 1991. Explaining service-price differences in international comparisons. *American Economic Review* 80, no. 5 (December): 1295–1309.

Gittleman, Maury, and Edward N. Wolff. 1993. International comparisons of interindustry wage differentials. *Review of Income and Wealth* 39, no. 3 (September): 295–312.

Kleiman, Ephraim. 1993. Taxes and the price level: A further examination of the PPP hypothesis. Working paper. Washington, D.C.: International Monetary Fund, Fiscal Affairs Department, February.

Kravis, Irving B., Alan Heston, and Robert Summers. 1978. *International comparisons of real product and purchasing power.* Baltimore: Johns Hopkins University Press.

———. 1982. *World product and income.* UN International Comparison Project, Phase III. Baltimore: Johns Hopkins University Press.

Kravis, Irving B., Zoltan Kenessey, Alan Heston, and Robert Summers. 1975. *A system of international comparisons of gross product and purchasing power.* UN International Comparison Project, Phase I. Baltimore: Johns Hopkins University Press.

Kravis, Irving B., and Robert E. Lipsey. 1983. Toward an explanation of national price levels. Princeton Studies in International Finance no. 52. Princeton University, International Finance Section.

———. 1987. The assessment of national price levels. In *Real-financial linkages among open economies,* ed. Sven W. Arndt and J. David Richardson. Cambridge, Mass.: MIT Press.

———. 1988. National price levels and the prices of tradables and nontradables. *American Economic Review* 78, no. 2 (May): 474–78.

———. 1991. The international comparison program: Current status and problems. In *International economic transactions: Issues in measurement and empirical research* (Studies in Income and Wealth, vol. 55), ed. Peter Hooper and J. David Richardson. Chicago: University of Chicago Press.

Lipsey, Robert E., and Birgitta Swedenborg. 1996. The high cost of eating: Causes of international differences in food prices. *Review of Income and Wealth* 42, no. 2 (June): 181–94.

Organization for Economic Cooperation and Development (OECD). 1987. *Purchasing power parities and real expenditures, 1985.* Paris.

———. 1992. *Purchasing power parities and real expenditures, EKS results, vol. 1, 1990.* Paris.

———. 1995. *Purchasing power parities and real expenditures, EKS results, 1993.* Paris. On diskette.

———. 1996a. *National accounts, 1960–1994, volume 1, main aggregates.* Paris.

———. 1996b. *OECD employment outlook.* Paris.

Summers, Robert, and Alan W. Heston. 1991. The Penn world table (Mark V): An expanded set of international comparisons, 1950–88. *Quarterly Journal of Economics* 106, no. 2 (May): 327–68.

U.S. Department of Commerce. 1994a. Benchmark input-output accounts for the U.S. economy, 1987. *Survey of Current Business* 74, no. 4 (April): 73–115.

———. 1994b. Benchmark input-output accounts for the U.S. economy, 1987: Requirements tables. *Survey of Current Business* 74, no. 5 (May): 62–86.

Ward, Michael. 1985. *Purchasing power parities and real expenditures in the OECD.* Paris: Organization for Economic Cooperation and Development.

Comment   Andrew Levin

Since the advent of the UN International Comparison Project, a large literature has developed concerning international differences in purchasing power. Much of the cross-country variation in relative prices can be explained by differences in per capita income (cf. Kravis and Lipsey 1988), but a surprising degree of variation occurs even among industrial countries with similar income levels. This paper provides persuasive evidence that relative price variation within the OECD is systematically related to differences in wage dispersion, which are closely tied to unionization rates and unemployment benefits. The paper also

Andrew Levin is a senior economist in the Division of International Finance at the Board of Governors of the Federal Reserve System.

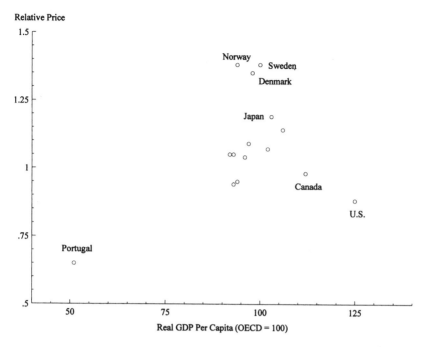

Fig. 15C.1   Influence of real GDP per capita

reinforces the earlier findings of Lipsey and Swedenborg (1996) concerning the relative price effects of food subsidies and tax rates. These results indicate that egalitarian wage policies and distortionary agricultural policies can have a significant effect on the general price level and thereby generate a substantial tax on consumers.

To analyze the relative price effects of wage dispersion, the authors perform a large number of cross-sectional and panel regressions for various time periods and levels of industry disaggregation. However, the basic results can be illustrated by considering cross-country differences in purchasing power for a single year. In particular, figure 15C.1 provides a cross-plot between relative prices and real GDP per capita for fifteen OECD countries in 1990.[1] The country with the lowest price level, Portugal, has about half the per capita income of the other fourteen countries, consistent with the general pattern obtained by comparing the relative prices of industrial and developing economies.

Nevertheless, if Portugal is excluded, figure 15C.1 appears to indicate a

1. As defined by the authors, the relative price variable (PL) is the ratio of real GDP (in international purchasing power parity–based prices) to the nominal value of GDP (converted using market exchange rates). The index of real GDP per capita (RGDPC) is also computed using international purchasing power parity–based prices, with the OECD average equal to one hundred. Wage dispersion (DISP) is defined as the ratio of median earnings to the level of earnings at the lowest decile.

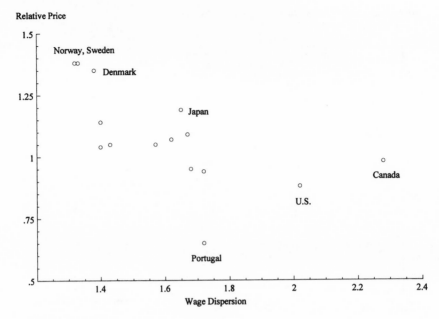

Fig. 15C.2   **Influence of wage dispersion**

negative relation between income and relative prices: the United States and Canada have high income levels and relatively low prices, while the three Scandinavian countries and Japan exhibit moderate per capita income combined with exceptionally high price levels. The results of Lipsey and Swedenborg (1996) shed some light on this anomaly since the latter four countries have the highest food tax and subsidy rates in the OECD, but this factor does not explain why the United States and Canada are such outliers in comparison with the other eight countries (Australia, Austria, Belgium, France, Germany, Italy, the Netherlands, and the United Kingdom.

Figure 15C.2 provides a cross-plot between relative prices and wage dispersion in 1990 for the same fifteen OECD countries. Within this group, the United States and Canada have dramatically higher levels of wage dispersion, while the three Scandinavian countries have the lowest wage dispersion. Portugal appears to be an outlier in figure 15C.2, but we have already seen that its low relative price can be attributed to a much lower income level than the other countries. Thus, figures 15C.1 and 15C.2 indicate the presence of a systematic negative relation between wage dispersion and relative prices. Although these figures represent data for only a single year, both wage dispersion and relative prices exhibit a very high degree of persistence (see table 15C.1), and essentially the same negative relation will therefore tend to be evident in other time periods as well. Furthermore, the policy implications are fairly dramatic: these

Table 15C.1   **Trends in Wage Dispersion, 1975–93**

	1975	1993
Belgium	1.39	1.40
Denmark	1.41	1.38
France	1.64	1.61
Germany	1.47	1.37
Italy	1.49	1.60
Japan	1.59	1.65
Netherlands	1.33	1.54
United Kingdom	1.43	1.72
United States	2.33	2.40

results suggest that the three Scandinavian countries (Denmark, Norway, and Sweden) could achieve a 20 percent reduction in consumer prices by moving toward wage structures and agricultural policies comparable to those of the continental European countries, which in turn could achieve a 15–20 percent price reduction by moving toward wage structures and agricultural policies like those of the United States and Canada.

References

Kravis, Irving B., and Robert E. Lipsey. 1988. National price levels and the prices of tradables and nontradables. *American Economic Review* 78, no. 2 (May): 474–78.

Lipsey, Robert E., and Birgitta Swedenborg. 1996. The high cost of eating: Causes of international differences in food prices. *Review of Income and Wealth,* ser. 42, no. 2 (June): 181–94.

16   The World Distribution of Well-being Dissected

Robert Summers and Alan Heston

This paper will attempt to illuminate the condition of well-being of the 5.5 billion people on earth. More *what* questions will be addressed here than *why* questions, but, until we know more than we do, there is plenty of room for a division of labor in dispelling darkness. The arithmetic that follows, in the form of tables and graphs, means and Gini coefficients, frequency distributions and Lorenz curves, etc., is the easy part. Determining which numbers are the relevant ones for the arithmetic is the hard part. Illumination is our modest objective.[1]

The primary data available for what follows, of greater or less quality, are time series of *real* gross domestic product (GDP) and its major components for nearly all the countries of the world.[2] These come from an update of the Penn World Table (PWT), last described in Summers and Heston (1991),

Robert Summers is professor of economics at the University of Pennsylvania. Alan Heston is professor of economics and South Asia studies at the University of Pennsylvania.

The research reported here was supported by the National Science Foundation under grant SBR93-21471. Discussions with Klaus Deininger, Maurine Cropper, Alan Kelley, Sam Preston, and Kip Viscusi were all very helpful. Mark McMullen and Taisir Anbar Colas provided invaluable research assistance.

1. The world income distribution has been the subject of too many investigations to provide all the relevant citations here. Suffice it to say, the earliest study consulted here that attempted systematically to estimate the parameters of the world distribution in the spirit of the present work was Andic and Peacock (1961), where country GDPs were made comparable using exchange rates. Another study using an economic indicators approach was Beckerman and Bacon (1970). Earlier efforts by the present authors were Summers, Kravis, and Heston (1981, 1984).

2. The objections of some distinguished, knowledgeable economists to the use of national accounts data to measure welfare should at least be noted before the objections are ignored (see, e.g., Okun 1971). The well-known disparities between the utility-generating effects of a country's activities and the imperfect valuation of them using market data and relatively few imputations are indeed problems. With one exception, in the work described below we do not follow another trend among some economists to "correct" the deficiencies in the national accounts (see, e.g., Nordhaus and Tobin 1972; and Eisner 1988).

which in turn is based on the work of the International Comparison Program (ICP).[3] Unlike the values of the GDPs and components of the system of national accounts (SNA), all the country numbers are expressed in a common currency unit, based on a set of average world prices of a particular year, so they are directly comparable across countries and time. Since time series of country populations are also available, describing world well-being would appear to be a very simple matter, at least at a very primitive level. The introductory economics way of handling these numbers for any particular year would be to divide each country's GDP by its population to get the country's GDP per capita (GDP_{pc}). (Never mind yet exactly what the meaning of this number is.) Then the mean and, say, the standard deviation of the collection of GDP_{pc}'s would be calculated and somehow interpreted. (For example, is the mean increasing fast enough? Is the standard deviation too big—or too small—and how is it changing over time?) Of course, when the persons engaged in this exercise get to intermediate economics, they will learn more sophisticated ways of getting at inequality than the standard deviation, and they will be reminded that they have not taken account of differences in income of people *within* countries. And, it may be hoped, there will be a clarification of what exactly GDP_{pc} is a measure of. This paper will go through these introductory and intermediate economics exercises on data covering almost a half century, clarifying what is being measured and what might be better measured. In an effort to improve on the usual GDP approach, some additional country variables involving age composition, particular subaggregates of national output, and quintile expenditures will be introduced.

Section 16.1 sharpens the concept *well-being*. First, the distinctions between *material* well-being and other kinds are considered. For concreteness, some thoughts are advanced about a broadened measure of well-being that encompasses both material well-being and longevity. (Please note: this does not augur an imminent entry into the still small cottage industry of researchers developing social welfare indexes that embrace material and sociological-cum-political-cum-demographic-cum-etc. well-being.) An effort is made then to illuminate—there is that word again—the overused concept *per capita* and suggest an alternative. Finally, two versions of the concept *current material well-being* are discussed that are designed to get at comparisons of present standards of living.

Sections 16.2–16.4 contain the empirical findings derived from the PWT international data set for the concepts in section 16.1. The concluding section, section 16.5, summarizes the empirical findings.

---

3. References to the voluminous ICP work can be found in Summers and Heston (1991). The data underlying the present work come from the Penn World Table (Mark 5.6), a large space-time system of national accounts that has been under development since 1980, when the Mark 1 version appeared in Summers, Kravis, and Heston (1980). (Mark 5.6 is an update of the Mark 5 version described in Summers and Heston [1991].)

16.1   The Concept of *Well-being*

16.1.1   What Should Enter an Empirical Social Welfare Function?

How many arguments should one consider in thinking about a social welfare function (SWF) for a country? Although there are at least a couple of dozen candidates in the data volumes of the World Bank and other international organizations, most economists are glad to restrict their attention to their own bread and butter, namely, *material* well-being. They may use various social indicators to help explain differences in countries' material well-being, or they may investigate how the social indicators are affected by material well-being. It is only the venturesome who attempt, so far with extremely limited success, to incorporate nonmaterial and material dimensions of well-being in a single empirical indicator.

If there is agreement that a particular social indicator does measure something that contributes to countries' well-being, why should it not be included in the social welfare function? It should be if one can figure out how it should be fitted in. The problem is that rarely (if ever) can one find an acceptable "scientific" basis for combining the social indicator with the material well-being measure that economists are ready to embrace. Economists have no trouble coping with a multiple-argument social welfare function when they have a basis for weighting the utilities generated by each of the entries. Shoelaces and Chevrolets are easy to combine if a price of each is available that reflects the relative utilities flowing from a unit of each. But where does one find the appropriate "prices" for such social indicators as, say, political freedom or literacy or an extra year of life? In section 16.4, a pricing notion for the value of an extra year of life will be explored with a view to taking a baby step toward a broader social welfare function than one involving only material goods and services.

16.1.2   Material Well-being: Numerators Looking for Denominators

Denominators

The directly preceding discussion raises the question—without answering it!—of including more than just material well-being in assessing the overall welfare of countries. Here, and immediately below, however, the focus is on the simpler problem of judging material well-being alone. The conventional measure is GDP_{pc}.[4] Obviously, GDP by itself cannot be the measure. India's GDP is far greater than Ireland's, but no one would for a moment think that

---

4. Strictly speaking, gross national product (GNP) is more appropriate than GDP. In some individual cases, Luxembourg particularly, the distinction may be important, but estimated distributions are not likely to be sensitive to the difference. Only GDP is considered in this paper.

was conclusive. GDP measures the quantity of goods and services available to meet a country's needs but is silent on the magnitude of those needs. Dividing GDP by the number of mouths to be fed adjusts for need; this is a way of rationalizing the use of the per capita concept. But what if some mouths are bigger than others (perhaps stomach size would be a more apt metaphor) and the proportion of little mouths is greater in some countries and less in others? (Remember these stylized facts: in developed countries, 20 percent of the population is under fifteen years of age, while, in developing countries—China apart at 25 percent—the percentage is more like 40.) Should one worry about taking account of these demographic differences across countries?[5] The view here is, "Let's try." The reader will be able to judge from the presentation in section 16.2 whether the present attempt is helpful and, more specifically, whether it makes a difference.

Numerators

GDP is a very useful multipurpose measure of the quantity of goods and services available to a country, but it is not an *all*-purpose measure. Its breadth is attractive to development economists concerned with the level and change of a country's "stage of development." However, some questions call for a measure of a country's *standard of living,* which in the end is what motivates productive activity. To put it in a suggestive way, consider an alternative concept, SL, that is concerned with *current* material well-being. This *now* emphasis still allows the use of the real national accounts database, but one must be selective in extracting elements from the ICP national accounts tableau. One should leave out the goods relating to the future and omit any part of GDP that does not directly contribute to material well-being. The first part is easy: simply leave out investment (including net foreign investment) and include only total consumption, private and public. The second part is more problematic: exclude any regrettable necessities that are measurable and that most people will agree on.[6]

The presentation in section 16.3 will focus primarily on SL. (Unfortunately, in the latest PWT, SL is available only for the years 1970–89.) Following this, a supplemental standard-of-living measure will be presented for a distinctly limited number of countries and years. This alternative, SL_q, melds some income distribution information with (private) consumption to show the per capita consumption of the middle quintile of the population for each available data point. Very loosely speaking, this may be thought of as an estimate of an expanded version of a country's median private spending.

---

5. Beware of stepping off onto slippery slopes! Are the material needs of people in a cold climate not greater than the needs of those in a temperate climate? How about taking account of rugged vs. gentle terrains? And so on.

6. Another *very* slippery slope!

16.2   The GDP Facts

16.2.1   Levels

GDP and GDP per Capita

Graphs of both world income, the sum of the GDPs of all the countries of the world, and world income per capita are presented for the years 1960–90 in figures 16.1 and 16.2. (A log scale is used on the vertical axes to facilitate growth rate comparisons at different times.) Also, the world is subdivided into groups of countries at three income stages: forty-five low-income countries; sixty-five middle-income countries, further subdivided into fifty-one nonoil countries and fourteen oil; and twenty-four industrialized countries.[7] Graphs depicting the income experiences of the four groups of countries also appear in figures 16.1 and 16.2.

The assignments are based on the World Bank's current classification system rather than an equivalent first-period 1960 classification system. This was to make the findings consistent with other research findings of the Bank. Of course, this grouping by late-period status presents problems for convergence analysis because the fastest-growing countries among the low- and middle-income countries in 1960 will have graduated to higher status by 1990, with the effect of understating the growth rate of the group of low-income countries and overstating the growth rate of the group of high-income countries. (If an Asian Tiger in the bottom category in 1960 reached the top category by 1990, its high rate of growth would have been credited to the top category under the Bank's system, even though it should have been credited to the bottom category.) Note, however, that using the late-period assignments means that, if we conclude on the basis of our empirical observation that low-income countries have improved their condition between 1960 and 1990, we can be really sure of it because we have not counted the growth of the star performers of the group.

The simplest questions answered by the graphs are, Is the world going uphill or downhill with respect to increasing its output and increasing its output faster than its needs have increased? The positive slopes of the world time series in both figure 16.1 and figure 16.2 indicate that the answers are uphill and uphill. Do the rich get richer and the poor get poorer? No, the positive slopes of both the GDP and the GDP_{pc} graphs of the industrialized and low indicate that the rich and the poor are both getting richer. Do the rich get richer faster than the poor get richer? The naked eye is not good at comparing the slopes of the industrialized and low graphs over a long period, but the latter slope appears smaller in the early years and greater in the later years. Table 16.3 below, to be discussed shortly, contains the growth rates that will make the comparisons

---

7. For the specific country assignments, see the appendix. The *World Bank Atlas* (1995) lists an additional 75 countries and territories, all very small, beyond the 134 covered here that account for all but 3 percent of the world's 1990 population. The Penn World Table (Mark 5.6) contains data on 151 countries, but the time series for 17 of them were too short to be useful in this paper.

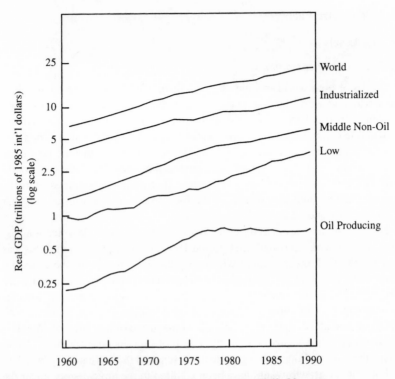

Fig. 16.1   Real GDP: world and by income group, 1960–90

clear. (Another dynamic question, apparently frivolous but not at all without content, is, Do the rich get richer and the poor get children? Rather than compare income-group slopes between fig. 16.1 and fig. 16.2, this question will also be reserved for the discussion of table 16.3.) First, however, How much richer are the rich than the poor? The entries in table 16.1 show this striking stylized fact in 1990: the poor (the lows) had just over half the population of the world but received only a sixth of the world's output, while the rich (the industrialized) had about a sixth of the population and got about half the output. Leading up to 1990, the rich share of world output went down between 1960 and 1990; the poor share stayed virtually the same; and the middles got what the rich lost. (More of that comes out in examining the growth rates of table 16.3.)

Table 16.2 is provided to show whether the message of table 16.1 is really dominated by the facts[8] about the most populous country in the world, China. It turns out that excluding China from the calculations in table 16.1 does not

8. *Facts* is not an apt word for describing the real national accounts of China. The hard facts that go behind the soft estimates so far available, which it is hoped will become available soon, will probably not change the differences between table 16.1 and table 16.2 much.

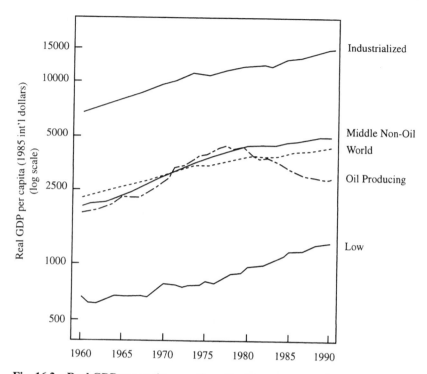

Fig. 16.2   Real GDP per capita: world and by income group, 1960–90

alter the pattern of change much. The low population is much smaller, of
course, and the populations of the other groups are now a larger proportion of
the world total. This affects the magnitude of change of the aggregate outputs
of the groups, but it does not change the basic conclusion. The shares of the
rich and middle are greater, and the poor's share is lower, but the changes in
the shares between 1960 and 1990 are roughly the same as when China is included.

GDP and GDP per Equivalent Adult

Table 16.1 has been used so far to comment on countries' capacities to meet
their *per capita* needs. Are the poor really as bad off relative to the rich if need
is defined in a way that better takes account of countries' demographics? To
say the least, it is hard to find proper equivalent-adult scales across 134 countries that value the relative consumption needs of persons in different demographic categories, but the equivalent adult (EA) entries of table 16.1 are meant
to help put the big mouth/little mouth consideration in perspective.[9] How dif-

9. In the light of the well-known significant increasing returns from consumption of families of
different sizes, demographic considerations are better taken into account by working with house-

Table 16.1   **Real Shares of World Output: GDP 1960, 1970, 1980, 1990**

	Low	Oil	Nonoil	Total	Industrial
			Middle		
No. of countries	45	14	51	65	24
1960					
% of population	51.5	3.8	24.2	28.0	20.5
% of equivalent adults	50.5	3.7	24.3	27.9	21.6
% of GDP	15.1	3.3	21.5	24.8	60.2
1970					
% of population	52.9	4.2	24.1	28.3	18.7
% of equivalent adults	51.7	4.0	24.3	28.3	20.0
% of GDP	13.3	3.9	23.6	27.5	59.2
1980					
% of population	54.8	4.4	23.8	28.2	16.9
% of equivalent adults	53.6	4.1	24.1	28.2	18.2
% of GDP	13.8	4.5	27.5	32.0	54.2
1990					
% of population	56.3	5.1	23.5	28.6	15.2
% of equivalent adults	55.7	4.7	23.4	28.1	16.2
% of GDP	16.6	3.4	27.2	30.6	52.8

ferent are the needs of the income groups when they are defined in terms of equivalent adults, albeit very crudely scaled? The proportion of the world's total number of equivalent adults located in each income group is given for the not-implausible case of the EA value for children under fifteen years being set at 0.5 and that for everyone else at 1.0. Table 16.1's slightly surprising story is that judgments about the difference in well-being between the rich and the poor are only slightly affected by equivalent adult considerations.[10]

16.2.2   Growth

Table 16.3 lays out the growth patterns of GDP, GDP_{pc}, and GDP per equivalent adult over the three decades 1960–90.[11] (Table 16.4, analogous to table

---

hold size data for different countries as well as age composition. Data limitations across 124 countries make it impossible to follow the *much* more satisfactory equivalent adult procedures described in Burckhauser, Smeeding, and Merz (1996). Our early minor effort in this direction foundered because sufficiently detailed data on household size was available for only a small number of developed countries.

10. Furthermore, the equivalent adult story remains essentially the same when EA is set at either 0.4 or 0.6. Unless one wants to make the case that EA is smaller than 0.4 or that it is smaller for the poor than for the rich, the only defensible conclusion remains that per capita and per equivalent adult considerations tell essentially the same story.

11. The reader is reminded of a point made earlier. The country assignments are based on 1990 GDP per capita. This means that fast-growing Japan, Hong Kong, and Singapore are included in the industrialized group, although in 1960 they would not have been. If the classification had been based on 1960 incomes, the average industrialized growth rate would have been lower.

Table 16.2		Real Shares of World Output: GDP, Excluding China, 1960, 1970, 1980, 1990			
			Middle		
	Low	Oil	Nonoil	Total	Industrial
No. of countries	44	14	51	65	24
1960					
% of population	37.3	5.0	31.3	36.3	26.5
% of equivalent adults	36.2	4.7	31.3	36.0	27.8
% of GDP	9.9	3.5	22.8	26.3	63.8
1970					
% of population	39.0	5.4	31.3	36.7	24.3
% of equivalent adults	37.7	5.1	31.4	36.5	25.9
% of GDP	8.5	4.1	24.9	29.0	62.5
1980					
% of population	41.4	5.7	30.9	36.6	22.0
% of equivalent adults	39.9	5.3	31.2	36.5	23.6
% of GDP	8.4	4.8	29.2	34.0	57.5
1990					
% of population	43.7	6.5	30.2	36.7	19.5
% of equivalent adults	42.4	6.1	30.4	36.5	21.1
% of GDP	10.5	3.6	29.2	32.8	56.7

16.2 in its exclusion of China, is provided without comment, just for completeness.) Now the focus is on the growth differences among the three income
groups. Note that world growth in GDP slowed down over the decades, from
5.2 to 4.0 to 3.1 percent. Both the industrialized and the middle growth rates
went down (from 5.1 to 3.1 to 2.8 percent in the first case and from 6.4 to 5.6
to 2.6 percent in the other). However, the growth rate of low went the other
way, from 3.9 to 4.4 to 5.0 percent. Over the thirty years, not only was the
poor's output increasing, but it was increasing at a faster rate than the rich's—
4.4 versus 3.6 percent! (The middle growth rate went down more sharply than
the rich, but its average was still higher.) So much for output, but what about
need? Over the thirty years, the low's GDP went up *faster* than the industrialized's—but its population growth was *much* greater. Its GDP_{pc} growth fell
short of that of the industrialized group, 2.1 against 2.6 percent.

The overall conclusions about the condition of countries around the world
over the last thirty-odd years, in question-and-answer form, are as follows:
(i) Has the output of the rich gone up while the output of the poor gone down?
Not at all. (ii) Have the rich gotten rich faster than the poor? Not in terms
of output, but, if need is adequately measured by population size, then yes.
(iii) Have the rich gotten richer and the poor gotten children? Yes, but the
output of the poor has gone up more than enough to still make them better off.
(iv) Is the estimated gap between the rich and the poor greater if one takes

Table 16.3 **Average Annual Rates of Growth (%): GDP, GDP per Capita, GDP per Equivalent Adult, 1960–70, 1970–80, 1980–90, 1960–90**

| | | Middle | | | | |
	Low	Oil	Nonoil	Total	Industrial	World
1960–70						
GDP	3.9	7.2	6.2	6.4	5.1	5.2
GDP per capita	1.6	4.2	4.2	4.2	3.9	3.2
GDP per equivalent adult	1.7	4.3	4.2	4.2	3.8	3.2
1970–80						
GDP	4.4	5.6	5.6	5.6	3.1	4.0
GDP per capita	2.2	3.2	3.8	3.7	2.3	2.1
GDP per equivalent adult	2.0	3.1	3.7	3.6	2.0	2.0
1980–90						
GDP	5.0	.1	2.9	2.6	2.8	3.1
GDP per capita	2.9	−3.0	1.3	.7	2.2	1.3
GDP per equivalent adult	2.6	−3.0	1.3	.7	2.0	1.1
1960–90						
GDP	4.4	4.2	4.9	4.8	3.6	4.1
GDP per capita	2.2	1.4	3.1	2.9	2.8	2.2
GDP per equivalent adult	2.1	1.4	3.0	2.8	2.6	2.1

Table 16.4 **Average Annual Rates of Growth, Excluding China (%): GDP, GDP per Capita, GDP per Equivalent Adult, 1960–70, 1970–80, 1980–90, 1960–90**

| | | Middle | | | | |
	Low	Oil	Nonoil	Total	Industrial	World
1960–70						
GDP	3.7	7.2	6.2	6.4	5.1	5.3
GDP per capita	1.3	4.2	4.2	4.2	3.9	3.3
GDP per equivalent adult	1.4	4.3	4.2	4.2	3.8	3.3
1970–80						
GDP	3.8	5.6	5.6	5.6	3.1	3.9
GDP per capita	1.3	3.2	3.8	3.7	2.3	2.1
GDP per equivalent adult	1.3	3.1	3.7	3.6	2.0	2.0
1980–90						
GDP	5.2	.1	2.9	2.6	2.8	3.0
GDP per capita	2.8	−3.0	1.3	.7	2.2	1.1
GDP per equivalent adult	2.6	−3.0	1.3	.7	2.0	1.0
1960–90						
GDP	4.3	4.2	4.9	4.8	3.6	4.1
GDP per capita	1.8	1.4	3.1	2.9	2.8	2.2
GDP per equivalent adult	1.7	1.4	3.0	2.8	2.6	2.1

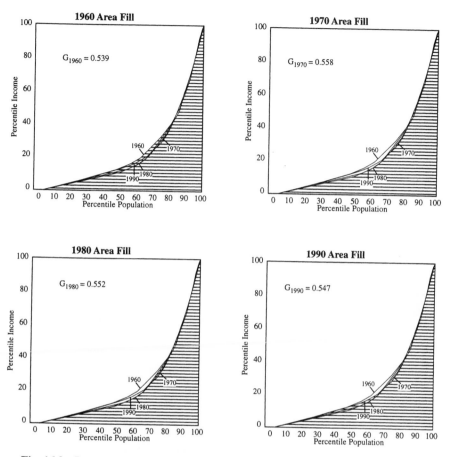

Fig. 16.3   Intercountry inequality: GDP per capita, Lorenz curves, and Gini coefficients, 1960, 1970, 1980, and 1990

account of the differences in age composition of the two groups? Allowing for the smaller consumption needs of children does not have much effect on the size of the gap.

16.2.3   Inequality

Tables 16.1–16.4 show how groups of countries at different points of the income spectrum fared over the last thirty years. In a last examination of the world distribution of material well-being as measured in GDP terms, figure 16.3 displays world Lorenz curves for each of the decennial years under study. The great similarity of the curves[12] is consistent with table 16.5's report of very

---

12. The Lorenz curves are so similar that a single diagram depicting all four of them is difficult to digest. The device of displaying the diagram four times, each with the area under just one of the curves shaded in, helps clarify which curve is lowest where.

Table 16.5   Intercountry Income Inequality: GDP (Gini coefficients: 1960, 1970, 1980, 1990)

	Low	Middle Oil	Middle Nonoil	Middle Total	Industrial	World
1960	.117	.452	.207	.252	.222	.539
1970	.108	.467	.218	.268	.141	.558
1980	.097	.442	.216	.261	.113	.552
1990	.117	.385	.258	.295	.090	.547

small differences between the Gini coefficients for the four years (0.539, 0.558, 0.552, and 0.547). This suggests that the four world income distributions are equivalent as far as inequality is concerned. However, the Lorenz curves cross. Close study of the curves shows what could have been gleaned from table 16.1. The great similarity of the Ginis means that the average difference between all pairs of observations—country pairs in the present case—did not change much. The fact that the low grew more slowly than the industrialized (see table 16.3) would make one think that the average difference went up. How, then, could the Gini have remained practically the same? Observe in table 16.3 that the middle grew faster than the industrialized. This narrowed the difference between those groups enough to leave the overall difference more or less the same. The Gini did not change, so one should expect that the low was not left behind by the other two groups in 1990. Indeed, it ended up with a slightly reduced share of total world output, relative to its greater share of the world's population. A detailed examination of the Lorenz curves shows that the bottom quintile of the world got 4.74 percent of world output in 1960 but slightly less, 4.58 percent, in 1990. This is a 3.4 percent difference, hardly negligible for the most hungry part of the world's population. A comparison of the Ginis for the two years does not highlight this.

Incidentally, table 16.5 provides information about changes in inequality *within* as well as across the low, middle, and industrialized groups.[13] The only observed changes worth remarking on probably are a result of the way countries were assigned to income groups: they were assigned on the basis of their last-period rather than first-period incomes.

16.2.4   Some Miscellaneous Facts about the World Distribution of Income

Inequality in the World Distribution of Utility

The existence of diminishing marginal utility of income is widely recognized by economists, and its implications underlie many parts of political debate. The conceptual and operational problems associated with any kind of

13. Note that the absolute degree of inequality in each group is of no significance because that is dictated by the (somewhat arbitrary) choice of cutoff points defining the groups.

measurements associated with the notion of utility are so formidable that it is very difficult to make any kind of policy decisions that depend on "scientific" judgments flowing from interpersonal comparisons of utility. (The progressivity of most income tax schedules is testimony to the widespread belief in the declining marginal utility, but the degree of progressivity legislated never flows from any *scientific* evaluations of the rate of decline, particularly relative to its effect on incentives.) Nonetheless, one does see studies that either implicitly or explicitly value utilities of incomes rather than income.[14] Interpersonal comparisons apart, *diminishing* marginal utility implies that people are less than twice as well off if their incomes are twice as great. If even just for speculative purposes one is willing to consider the possibility that people have equivalent "utilometers" all over the world,[15] then the obvious implications for how the inequality of world utility compares with inequality of world income should be considered. (This line of discussion may be skipped by readers who cannot abide such out-of-fashion, unscientific notions as these. However, the temptation is overwhelming to ask such skeptics if they think that Bill Gates enjoys a utility level compared with his subordinates anything like proportional to their relative incomes!)

Diminishing marginal utility of income requires that the relation between the utility of income (U) and income (y) have a negative second derivative. Many different functional forms can be used for the relation—Atkinson has a whole one-parameter family of them—but a common one because it is so simple is of the form $U = \log y$. If the Gini for the world distribution of income in the years between 1960 and 1990 is just over 0.50, what would the Gini for the world distribution of utility be if utility is taken to be the log of income? (Of course, this functional form is entirely arbitrary—at one end of Atkinson's family—so the answer to the question has no operational significance.) How much less than 0.50? The computed values for 1960, 1970, 1980, and 1990 were 0.073, 0.076, 0.074, and 0.069, respectively. Apart from the absolute size of these Ginis, they increased and decreased across the decades essentially like the GDP ones.[16]

14. This is done, e.g., in the UN Development Program's construction of its Human Development Index (see UNDP 1994).

15. A point heretofore ignored is whether tastes are the same all over the world. If not, a variety of objections can be raised to the ways in which the ICP makes country real incomes comparable. Certainly, nothing in this section makes sense in the absence of similar tastes. It is reassuring, therefore, to find that, to the limited extent that the ICP data throw light on the issue, they have been found to be consistent at least roughly with the similar-tastes hypothesis (see, e.g., chap. 9 of Kravis, Heston, and Summers [1982] and a number of studies by Henri Theil).

16. The authors were surprised at how easy it is to reduce *apparently* the great disparities in income so ubiquitously displayed around the world! However, there is a problem with base-country invariance when dealing with utility functions. PWT estimates of country GDPs are denominated in international dollars, but all GDP relations, across countries and time, would be the same if the algorithm underlying PWT was set to generate estimates denominated in some other country's international currency unit. A similar base-country invariance does *not* carry over for utility expressed as a function of income.

Intercountry Inequality and Intracountry Inequality

Intercountry Inequality Compared with Intracountry Inequality. All discussion so far has treated each country as though its citizens received the same average (per capita or per equivalent adult) income, thus ignoring all intracountry inequality. This leads naturally to an interesting question: Is the inequality of average income across countries greater or less than the inequality of income within countries?[17] For example, is the worldwide inequality greater or less than that of the United States and the United Kingdom, India and Indonesia, Bolivia and Brazil, etc.?[18] Light, if not positive resolution, on the general *inter* versus *intra* question is shed by the following simple, informal exercise. We arrayed the Gini coefficients of the ninety-four countries included in the admirable data set of Deininger and Squire (1996). (Where more than one Gini is provided for a country—for different years—the largest of them was used.) Then the world Ginis (0.539, 0.558, 0.552, and 0.547) were compared with the array to see where world inequality ranks in the country list. Only eighteen of the ninety-four country maximum Ginis exceeded the world's 0.539.[19] The implication of this is better understood if the spread in the country Ginis is displayed (see table 16.6).

No obvious viable stochastic model presents itself in table 16.6. The Deininger and Squire data set also contains detailed quintile data for the countries. Examination of the quintile patterns reveals no single functional form to which one can resort in carrying out a decomposition.[20] Fortunately, the fact that the World Ginis—for both GDP and consumption—are so deep in the tail of the country distribution makes plausible without a formal statistical test the judgment that the intercountry inequality exceeds the intracountry inequality.[21]

Total Inequality: Intercountry Plus Intracountry. Nothing new can be said here about world total inequality, but, for completeness, a brief review is presented

---

17. An analytic economist would ask the question more elegantly, in decomposition terms. Unfortunately, an empirical investigation in such terms requires detailed country data that are not available.

18. For the curious, the country Ginis referred to above are United States, 0.38; United Kingdom, 0.32; India, 0.37; Indonesia, 0.39; Bolivia, 0.42; and Brazil, 0.62.

19. Here, the intracountry Ginis have been compared with the intercountry Gini for *GDP.* Logically, perhaps, they should be compared with the intercountry Gini for consumption. Since the latter differed only very slightly from the GDP Ginis (0.529, 0.549, 0.551, and 0.558 for 1960, 1970, 1980, and 1990, respectively), this shifting of concepts only reinforces the conclusion.

20. The availability of quintile data in the Deininger and Squire data set makes possible the use of a more transparent inequality index (II) for making the same kind of inter- vs. intracountry comparisons. Consider II, the ratio of the total income received by persons in the top quintile to the total income received by persons in the bottom quintile. (The larger a country's II, the greater its inequality.) As in the case of the world Ginis, the world II falls in the upper tail of the frequency distribution of country II's.

21. Incidentally, it may be remarked that, as expected, the countries represented in the frequency distribution with high Ginis all have low incomes. The eighteen countries with Ginis greater than 0.539 all had low incomes: eight of them had GDP_{pc} less than a tenth of that of the United States in 1990, and all were below a third.

Table 16.6   **The Spread in the Country Ginis**

Gini	Frequency	Gini	Frequency
.25 < G ≤ .30	5	.50 < G ≤ .55	13
.30 < G ≤ .35	12	.55 < G ≤ .60	10
.35 < G ≤ .40	20	.60 < G ≤ .65	3
.40 < G ≤ .45	17	Total	94
.45 < G ≤ .50	14		

of the work done on this subject in a previous investigation (Summers, Kravis, and Heston 1984). Complete world distributions were synthesized under various conditions to see how the overall Gini (G_w) based on the incomes received by all the individuals in each of the countries of the world exceeded the Gini (G_{Mean}) calculated on the assumption that all individuals received the mean incomes of their own countries. An artificial world was defined that consisted of each of the countries included in the Penn World Table of that time (Mark 3), and all the country income distributions were assumed to be lognormal. For each year considered, each country was assigned as its mean income (μ_j) the GDP per capita estimate in PWT 3 for that year. The procedure for each trial then was as follows: (i) a Gini coefficient (G_j) was assigned to each country; (ii) each country's income distribution was synthesized on the basis of its μ_j and assigned G_j; (iii) on the basis of the synthesized country income distributions, the incomes of all the individuals in all the countries were combined into a single world distribution, for which G_w was computed; (iv) finally, G_w was compared with G_{Mean}. By repeating trials involving different assumptions about the {Gini: country income} relation, it was possible to flesh out in rough terms how much greater G_w would be than G_{Mean} for plausible G_j's.

Various {G_j: μ} relations were considered: (i) $G_j = 0.3$ and 0.5; (ii) G_j equals a rising function of μ; (iii) G_j equals a falling function of μ; and (iv) G_j equals a Kuznetzian up-and-down function of μ. The resulting G_w's based on G_{Mean}'s of about 0.5 were between 0.57 and 0.66.[22]

Where Are the Rich Countries and Where Are the Poor Ones?

To make this question interesting, one must have a basis for judging what kinds of *where* are interesting. The possibilities are endless, starting with a usual breakdown, continents, to breakdowns from big/small or mountainous/flat to cold/hot or dry/wet. (This sort of list can go on and on. How about old countries/young, or short peopled/tall peopled?) If economic or political categories are the focus, the question becomes the mainspring of the endogenous growth community.

Here, a very brief reference will be made to the geographic classification of countries by Theil and Seale (1994). They distinguish between countries in

22. The point of the original exercise was to start with the actual μ_j's of particular years and estimate just how much the G_w's had changed.

the northern temperate zone, in the southern temperate zone, and in various groupings within the world's tropical zone. Contrary to expectation, distance from the equator without adjustment is not a very effective explanatory variable for affluence in simple regressions. However, when the tropical countries are appropriately grouped, the influences for which one thinks distance stands seem to play a critical role. (It would be interesting to know if a mechanical numerical taxonomy algorithm would have led to the same Theil-Seale clusters.)

16.3   The Standard-of-Living Facts

16.3.1   Current Material Well-being: SL

The goods and services that contribute directly to the *current* material well-being of the members of a society are those identified in the national accounts as total consumption, which consists of consumption (C: private consumption) and government (G: public consumption). GDP allows for C and G[23] but also takes into account the production of goods meant to help in the production of goods in the future. Investment (I), without doubt a praiseworthy activity, has its payoffs—in fact, material well-being payoffs—but they are realized in the future rather than in the present.[24] For many purposes, their potential contribution to material well-being should be noted, but not in valuing *current* material well-being. Therefore, the numerator of the standard-of-living variable, SL, excludes I (and also net foreign investment) from GDP.[25]

A not very subtle criticism of GDP is that some of the goods valued in GDP do not really generate intrinsic utility. The mildly protesting term *regrettable necessities* is usually used in this situation. The regrettable necessity that plays an important role in SL is *military expenditures*. We accept as a given that, if a society uses a portion of its resources to produce military goods and services, it is because, at the appropriate margin, such goods and services have a greater value to the society than alternative uses of the resources that went into their production. No judgment is made here, explicit or implicit, about the true value to the society of military goods and services. Subtracting military expenditures

23. Participants in the Hicks-Kuznets debate of the late 1930s would want note taken of the Kuznets view that in fact what government buys with its government expenditures are really intermediate goods and services. By accepting the notion of public consumption, we are simply taking the side of the winner of that debate.

24. *Gross* domestic product is not really the right measure of material well-being, even apart from current well-being considerations. The well-known difficulties associated with estimating depreciation make the more appropriate measure, net domestic product, unpopular. In a future version of the Penn World Table, estimates (of uncertain quality!) will be provided, based on new depreciation rates, for something perhaps called *maintainable* domestic product.

25. Some readers may find it helpful to be reminded of an important difference between the treatment of government expenditures on final goods and services in the system of national accounts and in the national accounts of the United States. In the latter, all public investment is retained in the government category, but in the former it is transferred from government to investment.

from GDP is not motivated by pacifist notions of any kind. The point of the exclusion is very simple: whatever the yeas or nays about military expenditures, the military goods and services that they buy are not part of the goods and services that SL is meant to quantify. Cannons, bombers, and submarines do not make a direct contribution to *current material well-being*.[26] To summarize, our definition of SL is

$$SL = \{C + [G - \text{military expenditures}]\}/\text{population.}[27]$$

The first, most obvious question to ask is whether shifting from GDP per capita to the SL concept makes a difference in one's judgment about countries' relative conditions.[28] Figure 16.4 and table 16.7, directly analogous with the GDP materials already discussed, provide the answer to the question: Yes, a little. In general, the gap between the living standards of very poor developing countries and developed ones is a little smaller when measured by SL than by GDP_{pc}. A broad generalization is that the bottom 50 percent of the world has about 10 percent more of the world's SL output than GDP output. To avoid repeating the prolonged GDP discussion but with SL centerstage, the SL discussion will concentrate on the relation between SL/GDP_{pc} (denoted STLIV for short) and GDP_{pc}. If STLIV is negatively associated with GDP_{pc}, then the world distribution of the goods and services constituting SL will be less unequal than the world distribution of all goods and services; and the opposite will be the case if the association is positive. Without doubt, it is basically negative. In regressions run on a variety of $\{SL: GDP_{pc}\}$ data sets (different years and different collections of countries), the first derivatives were always negative and significantly so. One sample scatter diagram is provided in figure 16.5 to illustrate this. No sophisticated econometric analysis is required to see that the points are higher for very poor countries than for rich ones but that the points for middle countries tend to be lower than those of the rich. In fact, regressions containing quadratic terms on the right confirm that there is a little (significant) curvature in the best fit to the scatter.

26. Nothing in the social sciences is ever entirely free of ambiguity:
1. Suppose that a very poor, homeless, starving person is recruited into the army. The food and quarters supplied by the army surely should be regarded as a contribution to the person's current material well-being and therefore subtracted from the military expenditure total. Unfortunately, the data needed for such an adjustment are not available.
2. Perhaps, for some people in a country, military expenditures buy peace of mind. Is this part of *current material well-being?* A visit to a psychiatrist's couch in quest of peace of mind surely merits inclusion in SL. We think that, for better and not for worse, the more general peace of mind purchased by military expenditures should not be included in SL.
The saving grace in all this is that military expenditures are generally only a very small proportion of GDP, and the awkward parts of military expenditures are in most cases not a significant proportion of total military expenditure. This places these considerations in that most familiar of scientific economic categories, a problem acknowledged and then ignored!
27. The consumption and government components of SL have been taken from the Penn World Table (Mark 5.6). The military expenditure component is from Heston and Aten (1993), which supplies references to the original sources of the underlying data.
28. The difference-cubed principle provides the basis for the ultimate, minimum judgment about whether the SL innovation is of any value: A difference that makes no difference is no difference.

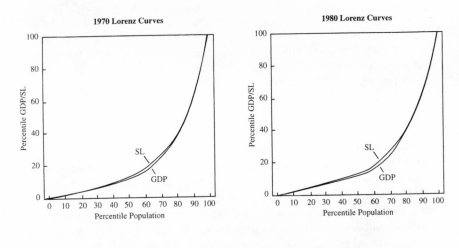

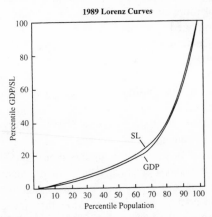

Fig. 16.4   Intercountry income inequality: GDP and current material well-being, 1970, 1980, and 1989

What is going on here? It is convenient to look in detail at the most recent year available, 1989. In that year, STLIV for the United States was 74.9. Then the SL of any country with an STLIV greater than 74.9 would be closer to the U.S. SL_{US} than its GDP_{pc} would be to the U.S. GDP_{pc}. Using GDP_{pc} as the criterion, classify countries into two groups, *richer* (the twenty richest) and *poorer* (the rest). About four-fifths of these latter developing countries had STLIVs that exceeded 74.9; only a fifth had STLIVs below 74.9. (Could an unusually low U.S. STLIV account for this four-to-one split? No. The simple unweighted average of the STLIVs of all twenty richest countries is even lower than 74.9!) The explanation for this pattern lies in the way the investment and military expenditure shares of GDP vary with GDP_{pc}. The investment share significantly exceeds the military expenditure share, and, on average, richer

Table 16.7   **Real Shares of World Current Material Well-being: Standard of Living (SL), 1970, 1980, 1989**

| | Low | Middle | | | Industrial |
		Oil	Nonoil	Total	
No. of countries	45	14	51	65	24
1970					
% of population	52.9	4.2	24.1	28.3	18.7
% of SL	15.1	2.9	22.5	25.4	59.5
1980					
% of population	54.8	4.4	23.8	28.2	16.9
% of SL	15.4	4.0	26.0	30.0	54.7
1989					
% of population	56.1	5.0	23.5	28.6	15.3
% of SL	18.1	3.3	25.9	29.2	52.7

	1970	1980	1989
World Gini coefficients for standard of living	.5483	.5385	.5293

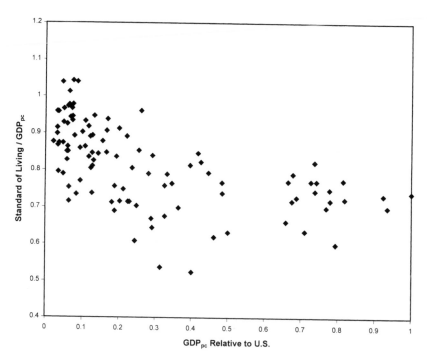

Fig. 16.5   A scatter diagram of the relation between SL/GDP$_{pc}$ and GDP$_{pc}$ relative to the United States, 1980

countries devote a larger proportion of their output to investment than poorer ones. The gap-narrowing tendency is present in all the years covered by tables 16.1 and 16.7.

The logic here is entirely straightforward. Unfortunately, the facts are somewhat less so. Everything said about the rich and the poor has been correct. The middles are not simply halfway between the two, however. This is not enough to make the speculative judgments wrong, but it keeps them from showing up strongly. Figure 16.4 shows how the SL Lorenz curves compare with the GDP Lorenz curves. They look more alike than might be expected because the middle does not toe the same mark as the low. Still, the increment of about 10 percent in the low's share of the world's current material well-being output (compared with the low's share of world GDP) is not at all trivial.

16.3.2   Current Material Well-being: SL_Q

Consider another variable designed to measure current material well-being, SL_Q. This is an estimate of the average spending on consumption (private only) of the people of a country in the middle spending quintile of the country. (An intuitive way of thinking of this measure is that it is an "expanded median" of the consumption spending distribution. It is meant to reflect the same standard of living idea, but it concentrates on the spending by people in the middle of the spending distribution.)

The data requirement for estimating SL_Q is availability of quintile data. These are available for ninety-six countries but in each case only for a quite limited number of years. Trying to construct an intercountry world distribution of SL_Q would be hopeless under the circumstances, but perhaps one could get an idea of the inequality of that distribution by examining the relation between SL_Q and SL. Regressions of the form $SL_Q = \alpha SL + \beta$ generated inconclusive results. The estimates of α for 1970 and 1989 data sets were slightly greater than one; the estimate for 1980 was very slightly greater than one. There is no reason for thinking that the world distribution of SL_Q would exhibit either more or less inequality than that of SL.

16.4   Material Well-being and Longevity

We return to the question of how one might combine a social indicator like longevity (L) with GDP_{pc} to get a social welfare index that satisfactorily takes account of both dimensions of well-being. This topic is raised here, even though no numbers will appear in this section, because, if a good social welfare index can be computed for each country in the world, it would be illuminating to examine the world distribution of the combined welfare that the index represents.[29]

---

29. In effect, one is looking here for an indifference map that shows the relative preferences for units of material goods and services and years of longevity. In a careful study of the structural

Any simple version of averaging L and GDP_{pc} clearly cannot be satisfactory. The problem is not that the unit of L, years, and the currency unit of GDP_{pc} are incommensurate. A variety of scaling devices can be found to get around that. In constructing its Human Development Index, the UN Development Program (UNDP) in effect computes a country's GDP_{pc} position relative to the richest and poorest countries in the world in percentage terms, does the same for L, and then computes half the sum of the two. (Actually, the UNDP works with more than one social indicator.) This would probably be all right if, instead of an unweighted average, a properly weighted one was used that takes into account the importance—value, that is—of extra international dollars of GDP_{pc} relative to extra years of life. But the UNDP's approach stops far short of that. The trick is to find the right relative values. As indicated above, economists do not find this a formidable problem when the two well-being elements are goods traded in anything resembling free markets. The relative prices provide a basis for the weighting. (Again, why should a Chevrolet be given more weight than a pair of shoelaces in the averaging process? It is not that Chevrolets are big and shoelaces are small but that marginal utility ratios can be assumed to equal price ratios.)

What can be done about valuing more years of life relative to more GDP_{pc}? The economist's natural way to go about this is to look for a market where in effect one can get a dollar reading on the market valuation of an extra year of life. There are no malls or mail-order houses that sell extra years of life—although some advertisements seem to offer such a product! However, there is a great deal of activity in which agents make economic decisions (not necessarily spending decisions) that reflect their valuation of an extra year of life. One common thread is to observe what workers do when faced with a choice between a more risky job with greater pay and a less risky one with lesser pay. Perhaps the very substantial "value-of-a-life" literature now published in both mainline and specialized journals can be mined to get, in effect, the needed prices for rich countries. With more difficulty, the same might be done for developing countries.

The various pitfalls here are formidable. (i) Clearly, one must not rely on values arising from just courtroom damage judgments because these are likely to reflect lost earnings; one must stick to the value of living, not capacity to earn while living. (ii) One must avoid the double-counting implicit in greater longevity being bought with the goods and services of the medical or public components of GDP: count the value of extra years but not the cost of the components; count the cost of the components but not the value of the extra years bought with them (essentially what is down now when longevity is ig-

relation between health and goods and services, Pritchett and Summers (1997) use (among other variables) life expectancy as a health indicator. They provide a country cross-sectional scatter diagram that shows just how correlated longevity and GDP per capita are. Their title, "Wealthier is Healthier," indicates the character of the relation. If the relation was monotonic with no scatter around the fitted curve, there would be no need for sec. 16.4 of this paper.

nored); but do not count both. (iii) One should at least try to take account of the shape of the mortality table and not simply its mean value. The extra value to the Japanese of having a longevity of seventy-nine, three years more than that of Americans, would depend on whether the extra three years carry with them the certain quality of life enjoyed by people aged seventy-six, seventy-seven, and seventy-eight or the quality associated with other years but with different probabilities.[30]

The approach suggested here has already been exploited by Williamson (1984). The notion in the present discussion is primarily a cross-sectional one, but the Williamson valuation of the increase in longevity in Britain in the eighteenth and nineteenth centuries is a strict time-series counterpart. He supplements the standard estimates of annual growth of real output with an estimate of the corresponding growth rate of the value, expressed in output-growth terms, of increased longevity over the period. His approach is equivalent to what is being suggested here. However, it is to be expected that all the differences between cross-sectional and time-series analyses come into play to make the working out of the details quite different. (For example, Britain was poor in a different epoch from the subsequent ones when it was rich; the feedback from poor to rich in medical knowledge and technology was a reality but not the reverse. In the cross-sectional case, however, the poor countries live in the same epochs as the rich with much more interaction likely to be the rule.)

If one had the necessary data for developing longevity prices in developing countries, one could begin to develop estimates of the world distribution of a welfare that includes longevity as well as material well-being. In the absence of such estimates, one can only speculate on whether the distribution would be more or less unequal than the distribution of material well-being. Would the Lorenz curve of the broader measure of welfare lie above or below the Lorenz curve of GDP alone? The fact that longevity is positively correlated with GDP_{pc}, and significantly so, does not resolve the question. The degree of tilt of L/GDP_{pc} with respect to GDP_{pc} plays a critical role.

16.5 Conclusion

The concept *well-being* for people all over the globe has a number of dimensions, some of which have been examined empirically in this paper. *Material* well-being flowing from the availability of goods and services, expressed in either current or long-run terms, has been spelled out in some detail in the form of the world distribution of income and the distributions for different tiers of countries. *Nonmaterial* well-being, for example, longevity, defined for kinds of welfare conditions that do not necessarily flow simply from the availability of goods and services, has been discussed from an empirical point of view, but with only highly speculative conclusions. The problem of quantifying *need* has

---

30. Account should be taken of the fact that values of different years of life are not all the same.

been examined as well to get a basis for determining how far a quantity of goods and services goes in enhancing the material well-being of any particular population. Most of the empirical conclusions have a time dimension because they cover the forty-year period 1960–90.

Appendix
Country Assignments to Income Groups

Low Income (45)

Benin	Liberia	Zambia
Burkina Faso	Madagascar	Zimbabwe
Burundi	Malawi	Haiti
Cape Verde Islands	Mali	Honduras
Central African Republic	Mauritania	Nicaragua
Chad	Mozambique	Guyana
Comoros	Niger	Bangladesh
Egypt	Rwanda	China
Ethiopia	Sierra Leone	India
Gambia	Somalia	Indonesia
Ghana	Sudan	Myanmar
Guinea	Tanzania	Nepal
Guinea-Bissau	Togo	Pakistan
Kenya	Uganda	Sri Lanka
Lesotho	Zaire	Yemen

Oil Exporting (14)

Algeria	Trinidad and Tobago	Kuwait
Angola	Ecuador	Oman
Congo	Venezuela	Saudi Arabia
Gabon	Iran	United Arab Emirates
Nigeria	Iraq	

Middle Income (51)

Botswana	Seychelles	Guatemala
Cameroon	South Africa	Jamaica
Ivory Coast	Swaziland	Mexico
Mauritius	Tunisia	Panama
Morocco	Barbados	Puerto Rico
Namibia	Costa Rica	Argentina
Réunion	Dominican Republic	Bolivia
Senegal	El Salvador	Brazil

Chile	Philippines	Malta
Colombia	Syria	Poland
Paraguay	Taiwan	Portugal
Peru	Thailand	Romania
Suriname	Bulgaria	Turkey
Uruguay	Cyprus	Soviet Union
Jordan	Czechoslovakia	Yugoslavia
Korea, Republic of	Germany, East	Fiji
Malaysia	Hungary	Papua New Guinea

Industrialized (24)

Canada	Denmark	Netherlands
United States	Finland	Norway
Hong Kong	France	Spain
Israel	Germany, West	Sweden
Japan	Iceland	Switzerland
Singapore	Ireland	United Kingdom
Austria	Italy	Australia
Belgium	Luxembourg	New Zealand

References

Andic, S., and A. T. Peacock. 1961. The international distribution of income. *Journal of the Royal Statistical Society* ser. A, vol. 124.

Beckerman, Wilfred, and Robert Bacon. 1970. The international distribution of incomes. In *Unfashionable economics: Essays in honor of Lord Balogh,* ed. Paul Streeten. London: Weidenfeld & Nicolson.

Burckhauser, Richard V., Timothy M. Smeeding, and Joachim Merz. 1996. Relative inequality and poverty in Germany and the United States using alternative equivalence scales. *Review of Income and Wealth,* ser. 42, no. 4 (December): 381–400.

Deininger, Klaus, and Lyn Squire. 1996. A new data set measuring income inequality. *World Bank Economic Review* 10, no. 3:565–91.

Eisner, Robert. 1988. Extended accounts for national income and product. *Journal of Economic Literature* 26, no. 4 (December): 1611–84.

Heston, Alan, and Bettina Aten. 1993. Real military expenditures: 134 countries, 1980 and 1985. In *Economic issues of disarmament,* ed. Jurgen Brauer and Manas Chatterji. New York: New York University Press.

Kravis, Irving B., Alan Heston, and Robert Summers. 1982. *World product and income.* Baltimore: Johns Hopkins University Press.

Nordhaus, William D., and James Tobin. 1972. Is growth obsolete? In *Economic growth,* Fiftieth Anniversary Colloquium, vol. 5. New York: National Bureau of Economic Research and Cambridge University Press.

Okun, Arthur M. 1971. Social welfare has no price tag. *Survey of Current Business* 51, no. 7 (pt. 2): 129–33.

Pritchett, Lant, and Lawrence H. Summers. 1997. Wealthier is healthier. *Journal of Human Resources* 31, no. 4:841–68.

Summers, Robert, and Alan Heston. 1991. The Penn World Table (Mark 5): An expanded set of international comparisons, 1950–1988. *Quarterly Journal of Economics* 106, no. 2 (May): 327–68.

Summers, Robert, Irving B. Kravis, and Alan Heston. 1980. International comparisons of real product and its composition: 1950–77. *Review of Income and Wealth,* ser. 26, no. 1:19–66.

———. 1981. Inequality among nations: 1950 and 1975. In *Disparities in economic development since the Industrial Revolution,* ed. P. Bairoch and M. Levy-Leboyer. London: Macmillan.

———. 1984. Changes in the world income distribution. *Journal of Policy Modeling* 6, no. 2 (May): 237–69.

Theil, Henri, and James L. Seale Jr. 1994. The geographic distribution of world income, 1950–1990. *De Economist* 142, no. 4:387–419.

UN Development Program (UNDP). 1994. *Human development report, 1994.* New York: Oxford University Press.

Williamson, Jeffrey G. 1984. British mortality and the value of life, 1781–1931. *Population Studies* 38:157–72.

World Bank. 1995. *World Bank atlas.* Washington, D.C.: World Bank.

Comment   Timothy M. Smeeding

In this provocative paper, Robert Summers and Alan Heston turn from data producers to data users, using their own Penn World Tables (Summers and Heston 1991) to generate "the world distribution of well-being dissected." The authors are careful to note that theirs is essentially a measurement exercise in the level and trend of intercountry inequality, summarized by various measures of inequality as applied to GDP per capita and other related measures of economic well-being. They leave us with few suggestions for further research in this arena, although their concluding sections offer some ideas on concocting broader measures of well-being, for instance, those that include longevity as well as economic well-being.

My comments on this work fall into two areas: first, critical comments on what has been learned here and how it might be improved and, second, a few brief ideas on how to move forward with the issues that are raised in this paper.

Main Findings and Critique

Summers and Heston begin by constructing a set of shares of world output (in constant purchasing power parity–adjusted dollars) generated by the world's various nations and trends in shares of output accruing to various groups of nations. The authors adjust for both number of persons (per capita) and number of equivalent adult units (counting those over age fifteen at 1.0 and those under age fifteen at 0.5). They then show (tables 16.1 and 16.3)

Timothy M. Smeeding is professor of economics and public administration and director for the Center of Policy Research at the Maxwell School, Syracuse University.

trends in both world income shares and world growth rates in income per capita (and per adult equivalent) from 1960 to 1990.

There are three primary results of this exercise. First, income per capita (or per equivalent adult) has risen more rapidly in rich (high-income) nations than in poor (low-income) nations over this period, although income per capita in poor nations has grown as well. Second, the lesser share of output found in the rich nations in 1990 (as compared to 1960) was gained mainly by the middle-income nations, whose income share increased: low-income nations gained little over this period taken as a whole. Third, the per capita and per equivalent adult calculations show much the same results, indicating that differences in household size and composition as they are deployed in this paper make little difference to the results of their analyses.

The authors are careful to tell us where they have classified the rapidly growing nations of the Asian Pacific region, for example, Singapore, Taiwan, Korea, and Japan. They are classified by their 1990 status (as rich industrial nations), not by their 1960 status (as low- or middle-income nations). While we cannot tell how much difference this classification makes to their results, we clearly know that the income shares and economic growth rates of the low-income (and also the middle-income) nations are biased downward by this treatment.

What strikes this reader, however, is how different are the period 1980–90 results shown in tables 16.1 and 16.3 from the 1960–90 results. Over this most recent decade, the major gain in share of world output and most rapid growth rates are found in the low-income countries. Their share of world output rises from 13.8 to 16.6 percent, while the middle- and high-income nations both lose output share from 1980 to 1990. The growth rates of GDP per capita (per equivalent adult) are 2.9 (2.6) percent in low-income nations over this period, as compared to 2.2 (2.0) percent in high-income countries, and an anemic 1.8 (1.3) percent in the middle-income nations. Moreover, these findings persist over and above the biases introduced by classifying the "Asian Tigers" in the high-income group. Hence, the 1980–90 pattern is quite different from the 1960–90 pattern. In fact, it is completely different.

When these changes are combined with UN projections of low and falling fertility rates in the 1990s across a wide spectrum of nations, including the developing world, one would expect to find even more rapid growth rates in income per capita (and income per equivalent adult) in the developing world for two reasons: fewer children to feed in the developing world and both fewer children and more retirees to be supported by fewer workers in the developed world (UN Population Division 1996; Wattenberg 1997). Indeed, this is the case. Bloom and Brenner (1993) have shown that, over the next two decades, the share of the world's labor force (ages fifteen to sixty-four) in the low-income countries will rise from 75 percent (1990) to 90 percent or higher (2015). If world financial markets (or Chilean-style mandatory national defined contribution pension plans) continue to provide the financial capital that these nations need to complement their labor power, their growth rates will continue to climb.

The implication is that, with the opening of free trade, the increases in life expectancy in most nations, and growing world literacy as evidenced in UN Development Program (1997), the low-income countries have begun to expand more rapidly than in previous decades. One eagerly awaits the 1995 and subsequent versions of these tables to see if these predictions will be upheld.

My second comment refers to the per capita versus the per equivalent adult comparisons offered by Summers and Heston. The reason why we use adult equivalence scales and not income per capita alone in micro-data-based studies of income inequality is to capture the economies of scale *within* households. A "per capita" adjustment is just an equivalence scale adjustment that says that there are no scale economies *within* households; that is, four persons need four times as much income as do two persons to be as well off. In contrast, a common equivalence scale that says that "needs grow only half as fast as incomes" when family size expands from one to four would say that the four-person unit needs only twice the income of the single person to be as well off (Gottschalk and Smeeding 1997). This is, indeed, the type of adjustment that Summers and Heston hope to achieve.

However, their adjustments do not control for this factor! All they have at their disposal is the number of children and the number of adults (including elders) for each nation, and they do crudely control for this difference. However, they cannot adjust for the number of children per family, the number of elders who live with their children (as opposed to living apart from them), and other factors that differ systematically across rich and poor nations. Indeed, their adjustments relatively understate true income per equivalent adult in poor nations (where family size is much larger) and overstate it in rich nations (where families are smaller and most elders have their own households). Given what they have, I am not at all surprised by what they find. A better adjustor would be average household size for each nation (or an equivalence adjustment pegged to average household size). If these adjustments were made, the results would again show greater shares of income and greater rates of growth in developing nations as compared to rich nations.

Intracountry versus Intercountry Inequality

The authors go on to construct intercountry Gini coefficients (table 16.5). These are based on Lorenz curves that treat each nation and its income per capita as a single unit. The results are that world inequality has modestly increased over the period 1960–90 but that rich-nation inequality has fallen by more than half (low-income-country inequality is constant; middle-income-nation inequality rises but by less than rich-country inequality falls). The authors also compare the level of inequality they find in 1990 to the level of inequality found in the recent Western nation inequality estimates provided by

Deininger and Squire (1996) of the World Bank, whose database now contains summary estimates of inequality within countries for almost a hundred nations. Summers and Heston find that their measures of inequality *across* nations are generally greater than is the inequality they find *within* these nations using the Deininger and Squire data.

First, regarding the comparative level of inequality, I applaud Deininger and Squire's work. That said, their data need to be scrutinized carefully before they are used. Many of their estimates are based on expenditures, not incomes. In many cases, incomes are measured quite differently: some nations present after-tax distributions; others do not. Income produced by households for own consumption, a very large fraction of real income in very-low-income nations (e.g., in Sub-Saharan Africa and in Latin America), is not measured at all in most nations. This adjustment may make a great deal of difference in a nation such as China, for instance. While these data are undoubtedly a great improvement over previous series, one should not ignore the warning signs and guideposts declared by the data set creators themselves (Deininger and Squire 1996).

Second, Summers and Heston find a trend toward greater equality among the rich nations of the world. Of course, these comparisons are hazardous, and Summers and Heston tend to understate the hazards on several grounds. Most important (and well recognized by the authors) is that their estimates ignore intracountry inequality. In fact, the degree of income inequality within twenty of their twenty-four rich countries can be studied directly using both national data and the Luxembourg Income Study (LIS) micro data for each nation. When we look into the LIS data set, we find (1) that income inequality has increased, not declined, over the past twenty to thirty years within most nations (Gottschalk and Smeeding 1997, 1998) and (2) that the level of inequality (as measured by the Gini around 1990) for these nations ranges from roughly 0.225 to 0.360, with none below 0.225. Summers and Heston find an industrial or rich-nation intercountry Gini of 0.090 in 1990 and a drop in the rich-country Gini from 0.141 in 1970 to 0.090 in 1990. What these comparisons indicate is that intercountry measures of the level and trend in overall world inequality based on some single indicator of average well-being for each nation cannot be compared to intracountry levels and trends in inequality.

Moreover, if we compare real incomes at various percentiles of the distribution (not just at the average or median), we find that country rankings can shift tremendously. For instance, in a sample of sixteen of these twenty-four nations, the United States has the highest real disposable income per equivalent adult (and also the highest real income per capita) at the median of the distribution. Yet, at the bottom of the distribution, the person at the tenth percentile in the United States "enjoys" a lower real income than do fourteen of the sixteen other countries' residents at these income levels. The real living standards of the "average" person in each nation may, therefore, be quite different from the real living standards of persons at the top and bottom of each income distribution. In fact, what one would ideally like to have is the distribution of income that counts real household income per equivalent adult (in purchasing power–adjusted dollars) for each *person* in each nation, all in the same distribution. While such a comparison is possible for the twenty richest nations on earth using the LIS data, so far no one has made the calculation.

Finally, I join Summers and Heston in recognizing that better micro data estimates of the size distribution of real income for the remaining hundred-odd nations of the world are sorely needed. Deininger and Squire have made a beginning at collecting comparable household income micro data sets. What is needed is for the world's household income data collectors to pay greater attention to the work of the Canberra Group, a collection of twenty or more national central statistical offices and international organizations (e.g., LIS, OECD) that are working to develop practical guidelines for producing comparable income distribution estimates from high-quality surveys (Australian Bureau of Statistics 1997). The work of the Canberra Group is to provide the raw data that Summers and Heston (and Deininger and Squire) need as input to their work.

Future Work

Every study of world inequality such as this must be taken in the context of what has gone before and what will come after. In this light, this paper is a step forward, albeit a modest one. Greater use of micro data is within our grasp for the rich nations of the world and for many of the developing ones as well. We should use these data to their fullest extent and also support such bodies as the Canberra Group, which continues to produce better, more comparable national and international income distribution data.

Studies of the Summers and Heston variety still have real value in understanding how various nations' economic well-being and rates of growth are related to their shares of world output. Hence, Summers and Heston's tables 16.1 and 16.3 should be updated regularly to allow us to investigate newly emerging trends such as the growth of real income and living standards in poor nations.

Moving to broader measures of well-being, the United Nations has begun to construct a human poverty index to go with its human development index so that we can push beyond overall average income per capita, overall literacy, and mortality to look at how each of these components of well-being is changing *within* developed and developing countries. Such work demands greater attention and scrutiny.

In order to go further with international comparisons of real income distributions, one also needs to pay greater attention to intercountry differences in purchasing power parities that have emerged from different estimates made by the World Bank, the OECD, and other bodies. The Penn World Tables are no longer the only source of purchasing power parities extant, producing confusion as to which set is appropriate. Finally, the use of GDP-based purchasing power parities to adjust individual and household-based disposable after-tax-

and-transfer incomes is in its infancy. Prices and market baskets vary within nations between rich and poor and across nations as well. Many nations tax finance goods and services such as education and health care more heavily than their consumer finance in other nations. Hence, applying micro data–based purchasing power parities to micro data–based measures of disposal incomes may be misleading. Research on this topic should be near the top of the list of important contributions to world real income distribution measurement.

References

Australian Bureau of Statistics. 1997. *Canberra Group on Household Income Statistics: Papers and trial report of the first meeting.* Canberra: Australian Bureau of Statistics, February.

Bloom, David, and Adi Brenner. 1993. *Labor and the emerging world economy.* Washington, D.C.: Population Reference Bureau.

Deininger, Klaus, and Lyn Squire. 1996. A new data set measuring income inequality. *World Bank Economic Review* 10, no. 3:565–91. (The data set is accessible at http://www.worldbank.org/html/prdng/grthweb/dddeisqu.htm.)

Gottschalk, Peter, and Timothy M. Smeeding. 1997. Cross-national comparisons of earnings and income inequality. *Journal of Economic Literature* 35 (June): 633–87.

———. 1998. Empirical evidence on income inequality in industrialized countries. In *The handbook of income distribution,* ed. A. B. Atkinson and F. Bourgignon. London: North-Holland.

Summers, Robert, and Alan Heston. 1991. The Penn World Tables (Mark 5): An expanded set of international comparisons, 1950–1988. *Quarterly Journal of Economics* 105, no. 2 (May): 327–68.

UN Development Program. 1997. *Human development report, 1997.* New York: Oxford University Press.

UN Population Division. 1996. *World population prospects: The 1996 revision.* New York: UN Printing Office.

Wattenberg, Ben. 1997. The population explosion is over. *New York Times Magazine,* 23 November, 60–63.

Glossary

A modification of the glossary from the Handbook of the International Comparison Programme, United Nations, ser. F, no. 62 ST/ESA./Stat/Ser.F/62 (New York, 1992)

Base-country invariance   The index number property that involves the symmetrical treatment of all countries, with the result that the relative index number standings of the countries are not affected by the choice of the reference (numeraire) country.

Basic headings   The subdivisions of final expenditure that correspond to the first aggregation of price (or quantity) ratios for individual specifications or items. Basic headings are also referred to as *detailed categories.*

Bills-of-quantity approach   The method used to build up the costs of construction projects from the individual modules of activity involved.

Binary comparison   A price or quantity comparison between two countries that draws on data only for those two countries. Also called *bilateral comparisons.*

Bridge-country binary comparison   A price or quantity comparison between a pair of countries derived from the comparison of each country with a third country. For example, given $I_{j/k}$ and $I_{k/l}$, the bridge-country method of obtaining $I_{j/l}$ is to divide $I_{j/k}$ by $I_{l/k}$, where I is a price or quantity index, and j, k, and l are countries. This is a common way of linking through a *star* country, as in the case of the Group 2 countries in Europe, where Austria has served as the bridge country.

CEP (consumption expenditures of the population)   The ICP concept of *consumption* that includes both household expenditures and expenditures of government on such categories as *health* and *education.*

Characteristicity   The property whereby the sample of prices or quantities and the weights used in an international comparison conform closely to a representative sample of items and to the weights of each of the countries included in the comparison.

Circularity or transitivity   The property of indexes when the price or quantity relation among any two of three countries is the same, whether derived from an original country comparison between them or from the comparison of each country with any third country. In the case of three countries, where I is a price or quantity index and j, k, and l are countries, the circularity test is satisfied if $I_{j/k} = I_{j/l}/I_{k/l}$. When this test is satisfied, there is a unique cardinal scaling of countries with respect to relative quantities and prices.

Comparative price level   A comparative price level is defined as the purchasing power parity divided by the exchange rate (see *purchasing power parity*). Expressed another way, the comparative price level for a bundle of goods is its cost in one country as a percentage of the cost of the same bundle in another country when prices in both countries are expressed in a common currency, with the official exchange rate being used for currency conversions.

Country-product-dummy (CPD) method   A generalized bridge-country method in which regression analysis is used to obtain transitive price comparisons for each basic heading. The basic data for a given category consist of all the prices available for the various specifications for the entire collection of countries. The basic assumption is that, within a given basic heading for a given country, the price of an item depends in a multiplicative way on a country factor and a price factor to be estimated from the sample of item-country prices in each heading. It follows from this that the logarithms of the prices are regressed against two sets of dummy variables; one set contains a dummy for each specification, the second set a dummy for each country other than the numeraire country. The transitive price comparisons are derived from the coefficients of the country dummies.

Country-reversal test   This test is satisfied if, when country i is taken as the base country, the price or quantity index for countries i and j is the reciprocal of the index when country j is the base country. For example, $I_{i/j} \cdot I_{j/i} = 1$, where I is a price or quantity index.

Direct price or quantity comparison   Made by comparing for two or more countries the prices or quantities for a representative sample of equivalent commodities (*see also* indirect price or quantity comparison).

ECP   European Comparison Programme, the set of ICP comparisons for Europe carried out under the auspices of the Economic Commission for Europe. In the 1980 and 1985 comparisons, the ECP was composed of two parts, the EC countries and a second group, for which Austria served as the center for a set of binary comparisons.

EKS method   A multilateral method developed by Elternö, Köves, and Szulc that computes the nth root of the product of all possible Fisher indexes between n countries. It has been used at the detailed heading level to obtain heading parities and also at the GDP level. EKS has the properties of base-country invariance and transitivity.

Factor-reversal test   The condition that, for any given item, category, or aggregate and for any given pair of countries, the product of the price ratio (or index) and the quantity ratio (or index) be equal to the expenditure ratio.

Final products   Products purchased for own use and not for resale or for embodiment in a product for resale; those purchased by households, by government, or by business on capital account.

Fisher, or "ideal," index   In ICP work, the Fisher index is the geometric mean of two indexes: one, the harmonic mean of price (or quantity) relatives weighted by the numerator country's expenditures; the other, the arithmetic mean weighted by the denominator country's expenditures. (The more usual definition is the geometric mean of the own-weighted and base-country-weighted indexes or Paasche and Laspeyres indexes as defined below under index numbers).

Fixity   The practice of fixing the results of an ICP aggregation for a country group when the country group is compared with a larger group. For example, the relation of France and Italy as given by Geary-Khamis or EKS for the twelve European Community countries would be fixed so that, within the OECD, the France-Italy relation would be preserved.

GCF (gross capital formation)   The ICP concept of *gross capital formation* includes fixed capital formation, change in stocks, and net exports. Definitions of these three components correspond to SNA concepts, although the SNA does not include net exports in its definition of GCF.

GDP   Gross domestic product.

Geary-Khamis (GK) method   An aggregation method in which category "international prices" (reflecting relative category values) and country PPPs (depicting relative country price levels) are estimated simultaneously from a system of linear equations. Has the property of base-country invariance, matrix consistency, and transitivity.

GFCE (government final consumption expenditure)   The SNA concept of *government* that includes public expenditures on education, health, and similar categories.

Group I and Group II countries   In the development of the ICP European Comparison Program of the Economic Commission for Europe, the participating countries were divided into two groups. Group I involved the countries that were members of the European Communities, an expanding group. Group II centered on Austria and included various Eastern European countries and Finland, with usually these two countries providing the link with the Group I countries so that a full European comparison could be made.

Hedonic methods   Use of regression equations to estimate price as a function of various characteristics of products. The resulting equation can be used to then estimate prices in different countries for the identical values of the characteristics and to thereby permit price comparisons.

ICP   International Comparison Project or International Comparison Program of the United Nations.

"Ideal" index   *See* Fisher, or "ideal," index.

Identity   Specifications where the items compared in different countries are as close to identical as possible, as for the same brand name and model.

Imputed parities   The use of parities for one or several basic headings as estimates of the parities for other basic headings where similar items are purchased, for example, parities for books purchased by educational institutions imputed from book purchases by consumers.

Index number formula   The following are common index formulas that are often used in a time series but that also have their spatial context. The subscript k is over the items for which there are quantities or weights. The subscripts i and j in a time-series context would be earlier and later year. In a spatial context, i is the base country, and j is the other country. The Laspeyres and Paasche price and quantity index number formulas are given in equations (1)–(4) below. The PLS or Paasche-Laspeyres spread is the ratio between either equation (1) and equation (2) or equation (3) and equation (4) below. The Törnqvist price index is also provided as equation (5), where the w's are expenditure weights that sum to one hundred for each country. Finally, the Fisher quantity index is given in equation (6), where the ideal or Fisher price index would be the same substituting (1) and (2) for (3) and (4).

$$(1) \qquad L^p_{j/i} = \sum_{k=1}^{m} p_{jk} q_{ik} \Big/ \sum_{k=1}^{m} p_{ik} q_{ik},$$

$$(2) \qquad P^p_{j/i} = \sum_{k=1}^{m} p_{jk} q_{jk} \Big/ \sum_{k=1}^{m} p_{ik} q_{jk},$$

$$(3) \qquad L^q_{j/i} = \sum_{k=1}^{m} p_{ik} q_{jk} \Big/ \sum_{k=1}^{m} p_{ik} q_{ik},$$

$$(4) \qquad P^q_{j/i} = \sum_{k=1}^{m} p_{jk} q_{jk} \Big/ \sum_{k=1}^{m} p_{jk} q_{ik},$$

$$(5) \qquad \ln T_{j/i} = \sum_{k=1}^{m} [(w_{ik} + w_{jk})/2] \times (\ln p_{jk} - \ln p_{ik}),$$

$$(6) \qquad F^Q_{j/i} = \sqrt{L^q_{j/i} P^q_{j/i}}.$$

Indirect price or quantity comparison A comparison made by dividing the price or quantity ratio into the expenditure ratio. That is, the indirect quantity comparison between country i and country j for commodity k, q_{ik}/q_{jk}, is obtained from $(p_{ik}q_{ik}/p_{jk}q_{jk})/(p_{ik}/p_{jk}) = q_{ik}/q_{jk}$, where the p's are the commodity prices (*see also* Direct price or quantity comparison).

International dollars Dollars with the same purchasing power over total U.S. GDP as the U.S. dollar in a given year but with a purchasing power over subaggregates and over detailed categories determined by average international prices rather than by U.S. relative prices. Regional comparisons often use other *numeraire* currencies, as the Hong Kong dollar in ESCAP, or a composite, like the ECU in the Common Market.

International price In the Geary-Khamis system, the international price of basic heading i is defined as a quantity-weighted average of the purchasing power–adjusted parities at the basic heading level across the n countries.

Matrix consistency The property that makes it possible to have correct country-to-country quantity relations for each detailed category and, at the same time, to obtain the correct country-to-country quantity relations for any desired aggregation of categories simply by summing the quantities for the included categories. This requires that the quantities be stated in value terms so that (1) the values for any category are directly comparable between countries and (2) the values for any country are directly comparable between categories.

Multilateral comparison   A price or quantity comparison of more than two countries simultaneously that produces consistent relations among all pairs; that is, one that satisfies the circular test or the transitivity requirement.

Net foreign balance   Difference between exports and imports of goods and services. Also referred to as *net exports*.

Nominal expenditures   Expenditures in national currencies converted to a common currency at exchange rates.

Numeraire   Usually the currency unit of one country is chosen as numeraire for expressing real expenditures and PPPs. The CPD, EKS, and Geary-Khamis procedures are all invariant as to which country is the numeraire or base. The numeraire may also be the average of a group, as has been the case in the European Community and the African comparisons.

Own weights   The weights of the numerator country; that is, the weights of country j in the index I_{jlk}. The term is used, for example, to refer to the weights of the country other than the United States in a binary comparison in which the United States is the base country, k.

PFC (public final consumption expenditure)   The ICP concept of *government* that excludes public expenditures for education, health, and similar categories.

PFCE (private final consumption expenditure)   The SNA concept of *consumption* that excludes public expenditures on education, health, and similar categories.

PLS (Paasche-Laspeyres spread)   The ratio of an index using own-country weights in a binary comparison to an index using base-country weights (*see also* index numbers).

PPP   *See* purchasing power parity.

Purchasing power parity (PPP)   The number of currency units required to buy goods equivalent to what can be bought with one unit of the currency of the base country or with one unit of the common currency of a group of countries. Also referred to as a *purchasing power standard*. The PPP may be calculated over all of GDP but also at levels of aggregation, such as capital formation.

Quality adjustment   Term used to refer to adjustment of prices of items so that they represent a common quality.

Quantity index   The quantity per capita of a category or aggregate of goods in one country expressed as a percentage of the quantity per capita in another country.

Quantity ratio   The quantity of a particular commodity in one country as a proportion of the quantity of the same commodity in another country.

Real product or real quantity   The final product or quantity in two or more countries that is valued at common prices and, therefore, valued in comparable terms internationally.

Regionalization   The practice of building up world ICP comparisons on the basis of comparisons carried out in various country groupings like the European Community or the Economic and Social Commission for Asia and the Pacific.

Representativeness   A term used to describe how characteristic a particular item is of the types of goods and services included in a basic heading. Also *representativity.*

SNA   The UN system of national accounts.

Specification   A description of an item for which a price comparison is to be made. The description is designed to ensure that goods of equivalent quality are compared. The terms *item* and *specification* are used interchangeably.

Starred (*) items   The practice of assigning or not assigning an asterisk to items according whether the particular good or service is important or not in the country in that basic heading. Starred items are considered important in the basic heading and may be considered an extreme form of weighting. They are used in the following way in European Community and OECD comparisons. In each possible binary comparison within a basic heading, items are included in the Laspeyres comparison only if starred for the base country and in the Paasche comparison only if starred for the other country. Thus, prices of items that are not considered important or representative in either country are not included in that binary comparison.

Transitivity requirements   *See* circularity or transitivity.

Unit value   When the expenditures or value of production of an item is divided by the quantity, the result is termed a *unit value.* The more narrowly defined the quantity, the closer is a unit value to the price of a specification.

Contributors

Giuliano Amerini
Eurostat
Batiment Jean Monnet
rue Alcide De Gasperi
L-2920 Luxembourg

Bettina H. Aten
Department of Earth Sciences and Geography
Bridgewater State College
Bridgewater, MA 02325

Ernst R. Berndt
Sloan School of Management, E52-452
Massachusetts Institute of Technology
50 Memorial Drive
Cambridge, MA 02142

Maria Chişinevschi
National Commission for Statistics–
Romania
16, Libertăţii Avenue, sector 5
70542 Bucharest, Romania

Irwin L. Collier Jr.
Free University of Berlin
Department of Economics
Institute for Public Finance and Social
Policy
Boltzmannstr. 20
14195 Berlin, Germany

Patricia M. Danzon
Health Care Department
University of Pennsylvania
3641 Locust Walk
Philadelphia, PA 19104

W. Erwin Diewert
Department of Economics
University of British Columbia
#997-1873 East Mall
Vancouver, BC V6T 1Z1 Canada

Yuri Dikhanov
The World Bank
Room MC3373
1818 H Street, NW
Washington, DC 20433

Alfred Franz
Austrian Central Statistical Office
Hintere Zollamtsstrasse 2 b
P.O.B. 5000
A-1033 Vienna, Austria

Alan Heston
Department of Economics
362 McNeil Building
University of Pennsylvania
Philadelphia, PA 19104

Robert J. Hill
School of Economics
University of New South Wales
Sydney, NSW 2052 Australia

Peter Hooper
Stop 23
Federal Reserve Board
Washington, DC 20551

Mary F. Kokoski
Bureau of Labor Statistics
2 Massachusetts Avenue NE
Washington, DC 20212

Andrew Levin
Federal Reserve Board
20th and Constitution Ave., NW
Washington, DC 20551

Robert E. Lipsey
NBER
50 East 42nd Street, 17th Floor
New York, NY 10017

Erik Monnikhof
Faculty of Economics
University of Groningen
P.O. Box 800
9700 AV Groningen, The Netherlands

Brent R. Moulton
Bureau of Economic Analysis
U.S. Department of Commerce
Washington, DC 20230

Nanno Mulder
CEPII
9, rue Georges-Pitard
75740 Paris CEDEX 5 France

Allison Percy
Health Care Department
University of Pennsylvania
3641 Locust Walk
Philadelphia, PA 19104

Paul Pieper
Department of Economics (MC 144)
College of Business Administration
University of Illinois at Chicago
601 South Morgan Street, Rm. 2103
Chicago, IL 60607

Brooks Pierce
Bureau of Labor Statistics
2 Massachusetts Avenue NE
Washington, DC 20212

Joel Popkin
Joel Popkin and Co.
1101 Vermont Avenue NW
Suite 201
Washington, DC 20005

John Ruser
Bureau of Labor Statistics
2 Massachusetts Avenue NE
Room 4130
Washington, DC 20212

Jorge Salazar-Carrillo
Department of Economics
Florida International University
University Park
Miami, FL 33199

Timothy M. Smeeding
Center for Policy Research
426 Eggers Hall
Maxwell School
Syracuse University
Syracuse, NY 13244

Daniela Elena Ştefănescu
National Commission for Statistics
16, Libertăţii Avenue, Sector 5
70542 Bucharest, Romania

Robert Summers
Department of Economics
University of Pennsylvania
3718 Locust Walk
Philadelphia, PA 19104

Birgitta Swedenborg
Studieförbundet Näringsliv och Samhälle
Center for Business & Policy Studies
Sköldungagatan 1-2
Box 5629
114 86 Stockholm, Sweden

Marcel Timmer
Faculteit WMW
Dommelgebouw, Room 1.10
University of Eindhoven
POB 513
5600 MB Eindhoven, The Netherlands

Bart van Ark
Economics Faculty
University of Groningen
P.O. Box 800
9700 AV Groningen, The Netherlands

Seppo Varjonen
OECD
2, rue Andre Pascal
75775 Paris CEDEX 16 France

Edward N. Wolff
Department of Economics
New York University
7th Floor
269 Mercer Street
New York, NY 10003

Kimberly Zieschang
Senior Economist
International Monetary Fund
700 19th Street, NW
Washington, DC 20431

Author Index

521

Subject Index

Base-country invariance, 17
Bortkiewicz formula, 331, 344, 348, 349
Brazil: alternative price-level calculations, 220–25; Broad National Consumer Price Index (IPCA), 212–13; estimating interarea price levels, 214–20; interarea income differences, 219–20; interarea price levels, 214–20, 223–29; price data collection, 212–14, 227; price statistics, 211–12

Centrally planned economies (CPEs): comparative manufacturing sector labor productivity (1970–94), 327–30; labor productivity levels in manufacturing sector (1987–93), 331–40; Paasche-Laspeyres unit value ratios, 340–44
Chaining: across countries, 109; chronological, 109; linking bilateral comparisons as, 109; using spanning trees for, 109–10
Circularity: across several aggregation levels, 131–32; regression methodology for imposing, 124. *See also* Transitivity
Circularity test (Fisher), 32–33
Communication: comparisons of Brazilian, Mexican, French, and American, 287–310, 314t
Comparative advantage: factors in formation of, 420–21, 420–22; influence of total factor productivity on, 421–22; revealed comparative advantage, 427
Comparisons, bilateral: bilateral index number, 13; chaining across countries, 109–12; items used in ECP Group II

(1980–93), 241, 247–48t; Romania and Moldova (1993), 261–70
Comparisons, international: economic approach, 89; history of, 2–3; matrix of binary, 89–90; multilateral chaining, 109–12; shortest path method, 113–16; spanning trees to link vertices, 110–11
Comparisons, intracountry: history of, 3–4
Comparisons, multilateral: axioms or tests for, 14–20; of Baltic countries and Austria (1993), 251–59; choice of index number formula for, 89; comparing all countries simultaneously, 109; comparing by linking bilateral comparisons, 109; exchange rate method, 23; Geary-Khamis average price method, 26–28, 98–105; generalizations of Van Yzeren's unweighted and weighted balanced methods, 39–46, 94–97, 106–7; Gini-EKS system, 31–37, 94–98; own share system, 37–39, 97–98; symmetric mean average price and quantity methods, 23–26; Van Yzeren's unweighted average price and basket methods, 28–31, 93–94. *See also* Chaining
Compensation costs: indexes comparing employee, 171; place-to-place comparisons, 171, 172
Compensation indexes: comparison of interarea, 206–7; data to construct interarea, 180–84; interarea, 186–96; multilateral, 179–80; regressions in construction of interarea, 184–86; U.S. interarea, 186–95. *See also* Wage indexes